MARYLAND GENEALOGIES

A Consolidation of Articles from the Maryland Historical Magazine

MARYLAND GENEALOGIES

A Consolidation of Articles from
the Maryland Historical Magazine

IN TWO VOLUMES

*With an Introduction
by Robert Barnes*

Volume I

Indexed by Thomas L. Hollowak

CLEARFIELD

Reprinted for
Clearfield Company by
Genealogical Publishing Co.
Baltimore, Maryland
1997, 2008

Set ISBN-13: 978-0-8063-0887-6
Set ISBN-10: 0-8063-0887-7
Volume I ISBN-13: 978-0-8063-0885-2
Volume I ISBN-10: 0-8063-0885-0

Excerpted and reprinted from the
Maryland Historical Magazine
With added Introduction, Contents, and Indexes
Genealogical Publishing Co., Inc.
Baltimore, 1980

ι *the United States of America*

CONTENTS

INTRODUCTION

B EFORE the *Maryland Historical Magazine* began publication
in 1906 there were very few printed accounts of Maryland
families. Emily Emerson Lantz and others ran a weekly series
entitled "Maryland Heraldry" in the Baltimore *Sun* from 1905 to
1908; J. D. Warfield published his *Founders of Anne Arundel and
Howard Counties* in 1905; and of course there were the ubiquitous
mug books containing accounts of "leading families" of the
various counties of Maryland. Whatever the degree of accuracy
of these various compendia, they contain little or no documenta-
tion. Moreover, the accounts of the various families do not follow
any systematic format, and tracing a given individual's ancestry
back to the immigrant ancestor may require a close reading of the
entire article.

With the very first issue of the *Magazine*, however, the Maryland Historical Society began publication of articles pertaining to
old families. Volume I of the *Magazine* contained accounts of the
Brooke and Tilghman families, the articles spanning several
issues. Since 1906 the *Magazine* has included articles on families
from all parts of the state—from the Goldsboroughs, Lloyds and
Tilghmans of the Eastern Shore, to the Lowndes, Spriggs, and
Taskers of southern Maryland; from the Todds, Merrymans and
Gists of central Maryland, to the Brengles and Fritchies of western
Maryland.

While the families included in this consolidation of articles from
the *Magazine* arrived, for the most part, in the early colonial
period, the articles are by no means limited to families of British
extraction. The Fritchies and Brengles were of German descent,
and the Cohens were a noted Jewish family in nineteenth-century
Baltimore. The LeComptes were of French origin.

Most of the articles begin with the first member of the family
in Maryland and trace descendants in the male line down to the
early eighteenth century. The format is the so-called "New
England Register" plan, with the immigrant ancestor described,
then his children, then his grandchildren, etc., generation by gen-

eration. The work of the various authors is based, by and large, on primary sources rather than on pretty stories and family traditions. Perhaps because the first articles established such a high standard of scholarship most of the subsequent articles maintained that standard.

The most prolific contributor of genealogical articles was Christopher Johnston. When he died the newspapers devoted much time, space, and attention to his career as one of the world's eminent authorities on cuneiform writing, but mentioned his genealogical work only briefly. Nevertheless, his genealogical work has benefited many, not only in his capacity as verifying genealogist for the Colonial Dames of America and as editor of a volume of genealogies of the members of the Society of Colonial Wars in the State of Maryland, but as the author of over twenty articles on Maryland families which appeared in the *Magazine* from 1906 to 1923.

Another genealogist whose numerous articles appeared in the *Magazine* was Francis B. Culver, born in Baltimore in 1868. In his *vita*, filed in the Dielman-Hayward file at the Maryland Historical Society, he discusses many aspects of his life, education, and career, and in one laconic phrase adds: "am interested in historical and genealogical research." His articles appeared in the *Magazine* from 1915 to 1945. Like Johnston he was also editor of a volume of lineages of members of the Society of Colonial Wars in the State of Maryland. In format and style his articles closely resemble those of Johnston's.

Other authors who contributed several articles were Emerson B. Roberts and John Bailey Calvert Nicklin. Roberts' special area of interest was the Eastern Shore of Maryland, while Nicklin published articles between 1921 and 1934 on the various branches of the Calvert family. Contemporary genealogists are represented by Edwin W. Beitzell and Dr. John Walton, both of whom contributed articles on the Gerard family.

While most of the articles reprinted here are family lineages, tracing all lines of descent in the male line from a common ancestor, there are other types of articles as well. For example, there are Bible records, such as those of the Winchester, Owings, Price, and related families, contributed by Ferdinand B. Focke.

A few articles discuss in great detail the various theories concerning the origin of the immigrant ancestor. Examples of this type of article are those dealing with the Cromwell family, and Edward Dorsey. A third type of article deals with families from the same locality who are closely related through a series of marriages. Several of Emerson B. Roberts' articles fall into this category.

It would be wrong to suppose that none of the articles contain errors; indeed some corrections to the articles were published in the *Magazine* itself. Nevertheless, most of the errors in the articles are errors of omission rather than commission. Newer sources of genealogical material, better means of preservation, and easier means of travel to record repositories have all contributed to greater research possibilities; still, the articles that first appeared in the *Magazine* set a standard that has often been met but seldom surpassed.

Robert Barnes

NOTE

PAGE citations in the text and in the footnotes to articles as they previously appeared in the *Maryland Historical Magazine* may be worked out by referring to the descriptive table of contents in this volume, which contains the inclusive page numbers of the original articles.

THE ABINGTONS OF ST. MARY'S AND CALVERT COUNTIES.

ABINGTON OF DOUDESWELL, GLOUCESTERSHIRE, ENGLAND.

By HENRY J. BERKLEY.

Arms. " He beareth, argent, on a band gules, three eaglets dis-
played, or, an annulet of the second." (Shield of Anthony
Abington of Doudeswell.)

About the year 1650 there came into the Province of Maryland an English gentleman, a merchant of London, who was
destined to play a somewhat important part in its infant affairs,
but whose name, with that of his family, long extinct in this
State, has been entirely forgotten.

John Abington was the eldest son of Anthony Abington, of
Doudeswell, in the County of Gloucester. Shortly after his
majority in 1628, he married Lady Muriel (the Meriel of the
Maryland Archives), a daughter of Sir Richard Berkley of

1

Stoke-Gifford, of the same county, who, at that date, was greatly interested in the colonization of the New Continent.

In 1650, husband and wife arrived in the St. Mary's River, and soon thereafter patented, in East St. Maries Hundred, the Manor of Abington, 1000 Acres, "granted to him in special manner by his Lordship's special grant and on his Lordships hand and great seal at St. Clement, dated September 5th. 1655, surveyed for him, that is today, 650 acres of it the 23rd. September, 1653. Quit rent, £1/0/0, to be paid on Ladies Day at St. Maries." Other tracts were patented to him in 1658, another Abington on the South side of the Patuxent River, and Doudeswell, 1000 Acres in 1663, with Abington Cliffs, Calvert County, 200 acres additional.

In 1661, John Abington was appointed by Cecilius, Lord Baltimore, a Justice of the Peace of St. Mary's, with especial instructions "against felonies, witchcrafts, enchantments, sorceries, magick arts, trespasses, forestallings, whatsoever. He was reappointed Justice at a Council held at St. Mary's in 1667, Charles Calvert, Philip Calvert and Jerome White, attending. Again his Commission was reissued in 1669, his terms of service as Justice lasting about twelve years.

Besides being Justice, patenting and cultivating land, we find him commissioned to trade with the Indians, the privilege being granted in 1663. It was during this year that a violent dispute occurred between him and Josias Fendall, who even threatened his life, and the matter had to be taken to Court for a settlement.

In the early part of the year 1659, Thomas Cornwaleys left the Colony for England, deputising Mr. Richard Hotchkeys to act as his agent and attorney. Hotchkeys, unfortunately, died a few months later, and Captain Cornwaleys appointed John Abington, by letter, in his place, to collect his rents and see that his affairs were not allowed to fall asunder to his detriment. The tenants of Cornwaleys refused to pay to Abington their tobacco and other rentals.

On the 12th December, 1659, Abington petitioned the Governor and Council on behalf of the absent Captain Cornwaleys, with the result " that the Board doe allow the said John Abington to be sufficiently empowered by the said Captain Cornwaleys for the receiving and recovering of any tobacco or other debts owing, etc." Thereafter Abington was involved in endless litigation, summons and replevins following one another with the tobacco owners, the long, wearisome trials being the probable cause of his return to London.

Further, after his return home, the Archives of Maryland give little of value to be here recorded. We learn therefrom that a certain James Crawford was appointed his attorney to administer his estates, and that by the year 1696 this estate was wasted, Crawford disbarred for mismanagement, and finally, that the lands were sold by his widow in 1711.

After the so-called Protestant Rebellion headed by John Coode in 1668-9 was over, John Abington with eight other gentlemen who had lived in the Colony, or had done shipping business there for upwards of twenty-five years, were summoned by Charles Lord Baltimore on January 7th, 1689, in London, to testify on his behalf before the Committee of Trade and Plantations. Among the summoned were the venerable Mr. Tillingston, a clergyman of the Church of England who spent long years at St. Mary's, and Col. Tailler, also a lifelong resident of the County.

Abington's will was probated in 1694, as of the Parish of St. Farth, the Virgin, of London. Seemingly, he left no children; his wife Muriel becoming the sole heir to the Maryland Manors. His godson, John Abington, a son of his brother William, was appointed administrator of his affairs.

A family record of the Abington family of Doudeswell is not available to determine the exact relationship between John, Lord of Abington Manor, and the others of his name in St. Mary's and Calvert Counties.[1]

---

[1] By recent letters of Mrs. Rowland Berkeley of Worcester City, I am informed that the wills of both John Abington and his mother are still extant and fill many written pages.

In 1687, or about the time of the departure of John and Muriel from the Colony, an Andrew Abington was seated near Abington Cliffs on the Calvert side of the Patuxent River. In this same year he received the appointment of "Deputy Controller and Surveyor of the Port of Patuxent." About this date a meeting of the Council was held at his house, attended by Col. Henry Darnell, Mr. Nicholas Sewall and Mr. Clement Hill. In February 1689 he became High Sheriff of Calvert County. In the following year he was assessed 5500 lbs. of tobacco, for the "Public Charge of the Province" indicating a very active individual and a great land owner. Andrew seems to have returned to England during the Coode Rebellion, as letters addressed to him were to be forwarded to Plymouth. By 1691, however, he was back in Calvert Co., and High Sheriff there. His later fate is unknown, as there is no further mention of him in the Archives.

In St. Maries City, in 1691, there was a Charles Abington of whom there is only the record that he received the (new) Great Seal of Maryland "to be, by him, conveyed to Gov. Copley."

Also, at this date (1691), there was another John Abington, who resided near Mattawoman Creek, Potomac River, where he had married Mary Hutchinson, and resided on land inherited from her father.

On the opposite side of the Potomac River, on what afterwards became Wakefield, the Washington Home Plantation, lived Lawrence Abington (will proved 1670, Westmoreland Co.), who married Lydia Brooks, a daughter of Henry Brooks of Bridges Creek, who was one of the earlier settlers there before the Washingtons came into this neighborhood. Their children were William, Lawrence, Mary and Elizabeth Abington.

John Abington's several residences in St. Mary's present a degree of uncertainty in so far that his first Manor was in East St. Mary's Hundred, the bounds of which are uncertain. Apparently he moved from his earliest Manor to the Patuxent Region and yet on the list of county manors it is accredited to the East Hundred. On the Patuxent extensive tracts are quit rented to him. After Cornwaleys' departure from the province he returned to St. Mary's City to live at "the Cross," Cornwaleys Manor, and resided there for several years, possibly until his return to England.

The destiny of the several manors owned by John Abington is interesting. Abington Cliffs was sold to Cornelius and William Pake in 1658. Abington Manor, the one on the Patuxent River, was in 1753 in possession of David Arnold, William Holland and Thomas Reynolds, probably having been acquired at a considerably earlier date by parties unknown, probably through Crawford, the agent; while Doudeswell, the only one of which we find a direct record, was acquired in the year 1711, by Samuel Chew and W. H. R. Harrison, by purchase directly from Lady Muriel, the widow of John.

So ends the little that is known of the Abingtons of St. Mary's and Calvert Counties. In the later centuries the family name became unknown in this State, and there remains but little more than the imprint in ancient records, and Abington Creek, Patuxent River, to remind one of a once honoured name among the earlier colonists.

———————————

BALL OF BAYSIDE, TALBOT COUNTY, MARYLAND

By FRANCIS B. CULVER

Mr. Emerson B. Roberts, of Pittsburgh, contributed to the December, 1944, number of the *Maryland Historical Magazine* (vol. XXXIX, pp. 335-344) an interesting sketch of his Talbot County ancestors who were residents of the locality known as Bayside, an early Quaker settlement in that Eastern Shore county. Mr. Roberts, incidentally, alludes to a collateral line, represented through the marriage in 1706 of John Kemp (I) to Mary Ball, daughter of Lieutenant Thomas Ball of Bayside. It is of the latter family the following pages will treat.

The Ball family of Bayside is evidently of armigerous origin. On the back of a scrap of paper, time worn and yellow with age, containing data copied from the family Bible of Captain Athanasius Martin (*q. v. infra*), brother of the Hon. Luther Martin, and preserved in my mother's family, there is a reference to the armorial bearings of the Balls of " Long Point," in Bayside, which are described as " three fire balls." The description, of course, is not strictly heraldic, for at that early period books of heraldry were generally inaccessible; but it is enough to identify this family with the Balls of Mamhead in Devonshire, whose arms are as follows: *Argent, a chevron between three fire balls fusées gules.*[1] Burke mentions a branch of this family bearing similar arms, but with the tinctures reversed.

The connection, if any, between the Ball family of Bayside and the Ball family of Virginia is, apparently, remote. It may be added, however, that representatives of the Virginia family purchased or acquired parcels of land in Maryland at a very early date; namely, Major William Ball and Richard Ball. These tracts were situated on the western side of Chesapeake Bay.

---

[1] Polwhele's *History of Devonshire* (1797), II, 155.

JOHN BALL (I), a scion of the Anglo-Irish branch of the Balls of County Devon, England, came with his family to Talbot County, Maryland, from the vicinity of Dungannon, Tyrone, northern Ireland, in April, 1686. On 2 June 1686, he purchased from Colonel Vincent Lowe a tract of land containing 300 acres, located in Talbot county, on the west side of Tuckahoe, which was surveyed for the said John Ball by Thomas Smithson, Deputy Surveyor of the county, 15 June 1686. Ball died, intestate, before the patent was issued and title to the land passed to his heir-at-law, Thomas Ball of Talbot County.

The name of this survey was variously written, in the land records, "Coallen" or "Cowallyn"; a name for which I have failed to find any explanation in the onomasticons. Inasmuch as our early settlers, not infrequently, named their estates by way of reference to their Old World provenance, I am tempted to believe that it may have been a corrupted phonetic spelling, on the part of a Surveyor's deputy, of a place name. There was and is a place about four miles northeast of Dungannon, in County Tyrone, known as "Coal Island," the commercial history of which can certainly be traced from the time of the formation of the Tyrone Canal in 1744; but "mining" operations were conducted in that district quite early. The charcoal of the Greeks is translated "coal" in King James' Version of the New Testament in 1611, a word derived from the Anglo-Saxon *col* (*i. e.*, "charcoal") which, as a placename, refers to the production of charcoal on or near the site.

John Ball (I) died sometime between 1686 and 1693, survived by his wife Mary and three children. The widow Ball married (2) in 1694 Ralph Elston, Sr., of Talbot County, a Quaker, who came to Maryland in 1662 bringing his first wife Eleanor and a son Ralph Elston, Jr. John Ball and Mary his wife had issue as follows:

1. *Thomas Ball* (I), the heir-at-law, of whom presently.

2. *Benjamin Ball*, the younger son, acquired considerable real estate in Talbot County and elsewhere. In 1698, Ralph Elston, Sr., gives "my son-in-law (*i.e.*, stepson) Benjamin Ball" power of attorney in a conveyance of several tracts of land in Bayside. On 10 May 1703, Thomas Ball, "for a natural affection I bear unto my brother

Benjamin Ball " and for other good causes and considerations, conveyed all his right, title, interest, etc., in and to the tract called " Coallen " to the said Benjamin Ball who, on 10 Nov. 1703, patented the tract,[2] which he sold in 1717 to William Dudley.

Benjamin Ball owned also several tracts of land on the north side of " the Second Creek " (now Broad Creek), on the north side of Choptank River in Talbot County, including " Benjamin's Lot " (100 acres), " Long Point " (50 acres), " Long Neck " (200 acres). These several tracts, excepting twenty acres of " Long Neck," he sold in 1721 to his brother Thomas Ball and departed for Kent Island, in " Queen Anne's County," where in 1722 he purchased a tract of 770 acres called " Clover Field " (patented 10 July 1725).

He married in 1714 Elizabeth (b. 1692), daughter of William and Margaret (Smith) Richardson, of a well known Maryland Quaker family. Benjamin Ball died in 1728, without issue. In his will, he made bequests to his four nephews: John Ball (son of Thomas); John Leeds and Daniel and Benjamin Richardson, sons of his sister Ruth Ball by her two marriages. Benjamin Ball's widow married (2) Augustine Thompson.

3. *Ruth Ball*, sister of Thomas and Benjamin Ball, " came to Talbot with her family at about ten years of age, born of English parentage at Dungannon, County Tyrone, 25th day of 12th month 1677." [3] Ruth Ball married (1) in 1704 Edward Leeds (d. 1708), son of Captain William Leeds (d. 1688) who was a Burgess for Kent County, Md., in 1661, 1669. Edward Leeds (d. 1708), in his will, made his wife Ruth Leeds joint executrix with her brothers Thomas and Benjamin Ball. By her first husband, Ruth Ball had a son John Leeds (1705-1740), a noted mathematician, who married in 1726 Rachel, daughter of William and Elizabeth (Dickinson) Harrison. They were the parents of Lucretia Leeds (1728-1789), who married (in 1754) John Bozman (d. 1767).

[2] Md. Patents, Annapolis, Liber C. D., f. 109, 110.
[3] Dr. Samuel Harrison MSS., at Md. Historical Society.

Ruth Ball married (2) in 1712 Daniel Richardson (1670-1722), son of William and Elizabeth (Ewen) Richardson of Anne Arundel County, Md. In connection with this marriage, the Third Haven Meeting reports that Mary Elston, mother of Ruth, gave her consent to the union. By this marriage Ruth had two sons: Benjamin Richardson who married (in 1746) Mary Ringgold and Daniel Richardson who died early. Mrs. Ruth (Ball) Leeds-Richardson, widow, died in 1728 and, in her will, dated 26 Oct. 1727, she appointed her brother Benjamin Ball to aid the executor.

THOMAS BALL (I), son of John Ball (I), came with his parents to Talbot County, Maryland, and settled in " Bayside." On 7 Feb. 1694, Thomas Ball, Samuel Martin, Daniel Sherwood, Francis Harrison, Nicholas Goldsborough, Robert Grundy and other prominent gentlemen of Talbot County were constituted a Committee " to purchase land for the erecting of the Town of Oxford." [4] In 1694, Thomas Ball was a Lieutenant in the Provincial Militia of his county and one of the Maryland signers of an " address of felicitation " to King William of England, upon the arrival here of news of the failure of a " horrible intended conspiracy against his Royal person." [5]

In 1694, Thomas Ball purchased from John and Wealthy Ann Miller, for 7800 pounds of tobacco, a tract of land in Talbot County called " Miller's Purchase " (100 acres), lying on the north side of Great Choptank River and on the east side of Bolingbrooke Creek; which tract was sold in 1700 to William Carr by the said Thomas Ball. The land records of the County mention several real estate transactions between Thomas Ball and his brother, Benjamin Ball.

In 1702, the name of Thomas Ball appears for the first time in the Minutes of the Third Haven Meeting of Friends in Talbot County, as a witness to the marriage of one Thomas Tyler. From that time on, for a period of twenty years, his name appears prominently in the Friends' records until, on the 26th day of the 2d month 1723, it is recorded that Daniel Richardson and Thomas Ball " have been removed by death."

[4] Tilghman's *History of Talbot County*, II, 345.
[5] *Archives of Maryland*, XX, 538.

Thomas Ball (I) died in 1722 and his will, proved August 9th of that year, mentions his son John Ball, who was to live upon and enjoy the upper part of the tract called " Benjamin's Lot," and the upper part of the land called " Long Neck," on the lower side of Perch Cove Point and running across the Neck toward Choptank River to an oak standing near the river-side. A grandson Thomas Kemp, son of John and Mary (Ball Kemp, was devised all the remaining portions of the two aforementioned tracts and also a tract called " Long Point," on the north side of the Second Creek (now Broad Creek) on the north side of Choptank River. He mentions another grandson, Thomas Ball, " son of my son John Ball "; and a daughter Mary, wife of John Kemp. He mentions his wife Susanna Ball and also a servant, Elizabeth Waterworth.

The children of Thomas (I) and Susanna Ball were as follows:

1. *Mary Ball*, who married on 1 Jan. 1705/6 John Kemp (1681-1751), son of Robert and Elizabeth (Webb) Kemp. Among the several witnesses to the marriage were Edward and John Leeds, Thomas and Susannah Ball, John and Benjamin Ball, Elizabeth and Mary Elston. The writer of the article on the Kemp family, in the *Maryland Historical Magazine* (XXXIX, 336), gave the date of this marriage as 15 Nov. 1705. This was, in fact, the date of a " declaration of intention " to marry. According to the Third Haven Meeting records, the actual marriage date is there given as the 1st day of the 11th month (*i. e.*, January) 1705/6.[6]

2. *John Ball* (II), of whom presently.

JOHN BALL (II), son of Thomas (I), inherited by the will of his father. He lived in Bayside and was taxed on several parcels of land: " Long Point " (part), 25 acres; " Long Neck " (part), 90 acres; and " Benjamin's Lot " (part), 50 acres ('Talbot County Debt Books, " to Michaelmas, 1761 "). He married twice: first, in 1716, Mary (surname unknown), at which time he was reported to the Third Haven Meeting, on the 30th day of the 6th month (*i. e.*, August) 1716, for having been married, contrary to

---

[6] For continuation of this line, see *Maryland Historical Magazine*, XXXIX, 337-340.

Quaker discipline, by a "priest." His name is not mentioned in
this report, but it is evident that the allusion to "one of our
number" refers to John Ball, for a later report on 31st day of the
8th month (*i. e.*, October) 1716, states that John Ball, "the person spoken of in the last two monthly Meetings for taking a wife
by a priest," seems sorry and he was reported "sick" also, which
must have been a mitigating circumstance. Daniel Richardson,
the second husband of Mrs. Ruth (Ball) Leeds-Richardson (aunt
of John Ball (II)), was appointed to "visit him."

John Ball (II) married a second time, in June 1747, Mary
(———) Rainey; the marriage license, dated 1 June 1747, being
directed to the Rev. Henry Nicols, Rector of Christ Church, St.
Michael's, Md. It would appear as though Quaker ladies possessed little enchantment for John Ball (II), or *vice versa?* Mary
Rainey was probably a widow and is, possibly, to be identified as
the Mary Fairbanks who was married to Peter Rainey in June,
1742.[7]

John Ball (II) died in 1761 and his will, dated 30 Nov. 1760,
refers to two sets of children: the older children, by the first wife,
being designated "my children"; and the younger set, by the
second wife, being styled "her children." Mary Ball, acting
executrix and widow of John Ball, planter (deceased), with
Joseph Dawson and James Fairbanks her sureties, refers, in her
account of settlement, to money due from Thomas Ball, son of
the deceased, it being "a part of the estate of his grandfather
Thomas Ball." The accountant, widow of John Ball (II), mentions as residuary legatees in 1768: Jonathan Ball, aged 18 years;
Samuel Ball, aged 16 years; Mary Ball, aged 15 years; Ruth Ball,
aged 13 years; and William Ball, "of age."[8]

The children of John Ball (II), by his first wife Mary, were as
follows:

1. *Thomas Ball*, mentioned in the will of his grandfather
   Thomas Ball (I). In 1768, he patented "Ball's Resurvey," consisting of 260 acres, embracing "Piney
   Point" (41 acres) and parts of "Benjamin's Lot" (39
   acres) and "Long Neck" (180 acres). In 1798, it is
   recorded that he owned and occupied part of "Ben-

---

[7] Talbot County Marriage Licenses.
[8] Annapolis, "Accounts," Liber 60, f. 66, 17 Oct. 1768.

jamin's Lot," in Bay Hundred District of Talbot County.
He married on 6 April 1741 Mabel Dawson, the Rev.
Henry Nicols, of Christ Church, officiating.

2. *Benjamin Ball.*
3. *John Ball*, in 1798 owned and occupied part of " Benjamin's Lot," in Bay Hundred.
4. *Susannah Ball*, married ———— Haddaway.
5. *James Ball* (I), of whom presently.
6. *William Ball*, " of age " in 1768 and head of a family of four persons in 1790.

The children of John Ball (II), by his second wife Mary (Fairbanks?), were as follows:

7. *Jonathan Ball*, born 1750.
8. *Samuel Ball*, born 1752.
9. *Mary Ball*, born 1753.
10. *Ruth Ball*, born 1755.

JAMES BALL (I), son of John Ball (II) by Mary his first wife, was born on 23 Feb. 1731 in Bayside, Talbot County, Maryland. In 1762, he purchased from Richard Mansfield forty-three acres of land, being the remaining part of a fifty acres tract originally surveyed in 1667 and variously styled " Upper Holland," or " Up. Holland," on the north side of Choptank River, on the western side of Broad Creek. (There was an " Upholland," in the parish of Wigan, Lancashire, England.)

James Ball built staunch ships, before and during the American Revolution and subsequently, with the labor of slaves and the services of apprentices. In the Baltimore *Maryland Journal* of 21 March, 1780, John Ball advertises at his yard in Broad Creek, Great Choptank River in Talbot County, " on the stocks and ready to launch, a vessel about 40 hogsheads burthen." He was building ships as early as the year 1762.

In the records of the Third Haven Meeting, 30th day of the 12th month, 1762, it is stated that a request was presented to James Ball for the release of an apprentice named Harwood. We are informed, a little later, that " James Ball refuses to deliver up the indentures of Samuel Harwood 3d, but Friends think he [Harwood] should be removed owing to ill health," and Isaac

Dixon and James Kemp were appointed " to apply to his master, James Ball, for Harwood's release."

A well preserved letter, written in September, 1787, to James Ball by his son-in-law William Sheild of Kent County, concerns a controversy between Ball and a Captain John DeCorse over a vessel which the latter refused to accept upon its completion. This Captain DeCorse commanded a packet-boat which plied between Chestertown in Kent County and Baltimore, Md.

In a deed dated 16 January 1791, James Ball of Talbot County, shipwright, conveyed to Thomas Kemp of said county, boat-wright, three lots of land distinguished in the plat of St. Michael's as numbers 44, 45 and 46. Elizabeth Ball joined with her husband in the deed.[9]

The name of James Ball, the Quaker, appears on the list of those who, " on or before 1 March 1778," *affirmed* the Oath of Allegiance and Fidelity in Talbot County and submitted their names as being loyal to the State of Maryland. James Ball died on the 9 January 1808. He married in August, 1756, his cousin, Elizabeth Kemp (1732-1814), daughter of John and Mary (Ball) Kemp, and had issue as follows:

1. *John Ball*, born 16 Oct. 1757; died 21 Dec. 1787.

2. *Susannah Ball*, born 15 Dec. 1759; died 22 Feb. 1842, and was buried in the old Friends' Burying-ground, formerly at the s. e. corner of Aisquith and Fayette Streets, Baltimore. She married on 6 Feb. 1788, Captain Athanasius Martin, a brother of the Hon. Luther Martin, and had issue as follows:

   a. Capt. Thomas H. Martin (1788-1821) married in 1820 Louise Caroline Wood.

   b. Mary Martin, born 3 April 1792; died 10 March 1871.

   c. John Martin, born 3 Sept. 1795; died 4 July 1796.

   d. Thomas Martin, born 16 Aug. 1798; died 20 Oct. 1848.

3. *James Ball*, born 19 Oct. 1763. He inherited from his father, James Ball, Sr., the property called " Up. Hol-

---

[9] Talbot County Deed Book, XXIV, 229.

land" which he sold in 1812 to Samuel Harrison of
Talbot County.[10]

4. *Rachel Ball*, born 22 July 1766; died 21 July 1857, and was
buried in the old Friends' Burying-ground on the " Harford Road," Baltimore. She was married 8 April 1786,
by the Rev. John Gordon, Rector of Christ Church, St.
Michael's, Maryland, to William Sheild (1760-1816) of
Kent County, who sold his inherited estate " Pentridge,"
near Lankford Bay, Kent County and removed in 1789
to " Long Point " in Talbot County. Before removing
from Talbot County, William Shield disposed of his
realty by placing it on the market in 1799. The following advertisement is taken from the *Maryland Herald and
Eastern Shore Intelligencer*, published at Easton, and
otherwise called the " Easton Herald," dated February
19, 1799:

> A valuable Farm in Talbot County, commonly known by
> name of LONG POINT, beautifully situated & lying between
> Broad & Harrison's Creeks; has a full prospect of Choptank
> River & as far down the Bay as can be seen with the naked
> eye: well adapted to grow wheat, corn or tobacco: remarkable
> for fishing, fowling & oystering, & what still renders it more
> agreeable is the healthy situation of the place. . . . Apply to
> subscriber on the premises.
>
> WILLIAM SHEILD.

He served under Captain Edward Veazey at the Battle
of Long Island in August, 1776 and, later, in the Kent
County militia. He died in Baltimore on 2 Sept. 1816.
William and Rachel Sheild had issue:

    a. John Ball Sheild, born 1787. With " Lake Cham-
       plain Flotilla " in 1812-1814.

    b. Elizabeth Sheild, b. 1789; d. 1865; m. 1814 John
       Appleby (1789-1834), in War of 1812.

    c. Mary Sheild,[11] b. 1791; d. 1831; m. 1810 William
       Coppuck (1783-1857), in War of 1812.

---

[10] Deed Book, No. 1, f. 5.

[11] William and Mary (Sheild) Coppuck were the parents of Mrs. Amelia Ball
Welby, the noted poet of Maryland and Kentucky (see *The Sun*, Baltimore, Sunday,
Oct. 22, 1922, Part 10, Page 3). Likewise, descended from John Ball (I) and

    d. Ann Sheild, b. 1794; d. 1843; m. post 1826 Rev. Lenox Martin (1764-1846), of Old Town, Md.

    e. Susan M. Sheild, b. 1796; d. 1880, unmarried; buried in Friends' cemetery, Harford Ave.

    f. William Ball Sheild, b. 1798; d. 1834 in Baltimore, Md.

    g. Martha Sheild, b. 1803; d. 1830, unmarried.

    h. Sarah Ball Sheild, b. 1806; d. 1863, unmarried; buried in Friends' cemetery, Harford Ave.

5. *Thomas Ball*, born 9 March 1769; married Sarah Edgar and had Elizabeth Ball (m. Thomas Auld).

Mary his wife are representatives of several prominent Maryland families, including the Tilghmans, Shreves, Barrolls, Bozmans, Kerrs, Kemps and others. This Maryland family was unfortunate in having so few males to carry on the surname. The name survived, however, in " Ball's Creek "; but " Elston's Point " has become " Nelson's Point " on the modern maps of Talbot County.

BALL FAMILY

By Emerson B. Roberts and Francis B. Culver

John Ball married Mary ——— she m. (2) 1694 Ralph Elston
John Ball d. cir 1693 ——— of Long Point

- Lieut. Thomas Ball m. Susannah Kemp
  in Talbot 1686
  d. 1722
  she survived her husband

- Ruth m. (1) Wm. Leeds
  (2) Dan'l. Richardson
  son John by (1)
  Two sons by (2)

  m. (2) Mary Rainey (widow)
  m. 1747
  ——Jonathan, b. 1750
  ——Samuel, b. 1752 m. Lydia Kemp
  ——Mary, b. 1753 m. James Kemp
  ——Ruth, b. 1755

- Benjamin Ball
  d. 1728
  m. Eliz. Richardson
  no issue

- Mary m. 1706 John Kemp

John Ball m. (1) Mary ———
d. 1760/1   m. cir 1716

——William Ball

——Thomas Ball m. 1741 Mabel Dawson

——Benjamin Ball

——John Ball

——Susannah m. ——— Haddaway

——James Ball m. Eliz. Kemp
  b. 1731
  d. 1808
  m. 1756
  dau. John and Mary Kemp

  Susannah
  b. 1759 d. 1842
  m. 1788 Capt. Athanasius Martin

  James
  b. 1763

  Rachel
  b. 1766 d. 1857
  m. 1786 Wm. Sheild
  b. 1760
  d. 1816

  Thomas m. Sarah Edgar
  b. 1769
  ——Elizabeth m. Thomas Auld

  John Ball
  b. 1757
  d. 1787

A VISITATION OF WESTERN TALBOT

By EMERSON B. ROBERTS

In the introduction to his monumental work, *Pedigrees of the County Families of Yorkshire*,[1] Dr. Joseph Foster says that his recompense has been the contact that the work afforded him with " many a genial Yorkshireman." " I further hope " he adds, " that those who affect to dispise Pedigrees will, for the sake of their descendants, record, if only in their Family Bibles, what they do know of their forefathers and contemporary kinfolk, and so save much trouble to future genealogists and their own posterity."

The present writing is inspired by the old doctor in a double sense—not only the practical saving of time and the serving of essential accuracy, but more by the fact that as one turns the pages of the first volume of *County Families*, the sub-title of which is " West Riding," he is struck by the many names common to western Yorkshire and to the western part of Talbot.[2] Indeed, the village that grew up around the first Court House, on the headwaters of the Wye, was named by Act of Assembly, 1686, Yorke, in honor of the ancient city in Yorkshire. And there are records of Court holden in the town of York.[3]

As one might have set out from the present location of Easton a few miles south of Talbot Court House, or indeed if he makes the trip today, with someone beside him who knows the old roads,

---

[1] London, 1874.

[2] The word *riding* perhaps needs explanation, particularly as it is not used in America at all, and but little in England. It is a distinct noun, differently derived from " riding " of " riding and walking " connotation. Derived by corruption from *trithing*, perhaps a Danish word, it means a portion of a county, generally a third. Thus Yorkshire contained three trithings or ridings—north, west, and east. Each, in old days, had its reeve or principal officer, just as the shire. There was the shire-reeve or sheriff for the shire; the trithing-reeve for the trithing or the riding. The usage of the word has largely disappeared in England just as Hundred has disappeared in America—*Author*

[3] Tilghman, *History of Talbot County* (Baltimore, 1915), II, 217; Skirvin, *First Parishes in the Province of Maryland* (Baltimore, 1923), p. 144.

the inlets and branches of the creeks, and the names on the land, and rides in a generally westerly direction toward Claiborne, and then in a generally south-westerly direction down the " Bay Hundred " until he comes to Tilghman's Island, once Great Choptank Island, and yet earlier Foster's Island, he passes near at hand the home locations here recorded. On the trip he has crossed the old Hundred of St. Michael's and covered the full mainland of the Bay Hundred. In modern days counties are divided into Districts, but by many of the older county folk the term hundred is still employed. The area described was included in St. Michael's Parish, one of three in Talbot. The road remains virtually unchanged in location, and the homes are in close proximity, though here and there obscured from the road by the pine woods that skirt the creeks and headwaters of Third Haven, or Tred-Avon, Broad Creek, and Harris Creek, on the Choptank side, and the Miles or St. Michael's, and the Wye, on the north toward Eastern Bay. Most of the homes are near navigable waters which were the first highways of the tidewater country.

Stories of some the first settlers of these points and necks have been told in recent numbers of the Magazine.[4] Others are recorded here. Not all, but many were of Yorkshire origin.

BARTLETT OF " RATCLIFFE MANOR " AND " OLD BLOOMFIELD "

Scarcely two miles from the Court House is " Old Bloomfield," ancient home of the Bartletts. Yet standing on Third Haven, on the part called the " Great Neck," with its roof projection of four and a half feet, with its simple paneling, with its interesting odd windows, it is in good repair, though unoccupied.[5] " Old Bloomfield " was the property of the late James Dixon of " North Bend," a descendant of the Bartletts. Never has the property been out of the possession of this family.

Thomas Bartlett, Yorkshireman, immigrant to Maryland 1691, was by trade a blacksmith and evidently he prospered at his trade.

[4] Other families of the West Riding of Talbot have been treated in the *Maryland Historical Magazine* by the author: Dixon, Gary, Harwood, Christison, Sharp, in " Some Friends of ' Ye Friends of Ye Ministry '," XXXVII, p. 311-326; Kemp, Webb, Stevens, Gary, Ball in " Among the Meeters at the Bayside," XXXIX, pp. 335-344; and, with Francis B. Culver, " Ball of Bayside," XXXX, pp. 154-163.
[5] Architectural description and floor plans are to be found in Forman, *Early Manor and Plantation Houses of Maryland* (Easton, 1934), p. 184.

On September 21, 1698, he bought from Clement La Salle the tract of 960 acres, " Ratcliffe Manor," and it was either he or his son who built the manor house on the Great Neck. There is earlier record of " Ratcliffe Manor " in a deed, 1667, by which the property was conveyed by Robert Morris to James Wasse, but the original manor house is " Old Bloomfield." It adjoins that portion of " Ratcliffe " that was conveyed to the Hollydays, and on which they built, about 1754, the present charming " Ratcliffe Manor " house on Tred-Avon, nearly opposite Easton Point, then " Cow's Landing."

The Bartletts were Friends, and through the years their descendants have continued to be " followers of the inner light." On the first page of the records of Third Haven Meetings are Bartlett records and their steadfast influence has continued through the long history of the Meeting. Thomas Bartlett died in 1711, and his will was probated in Talbot, November 23, 1711.[6] The original of the will is among the few such in the Court House at Easton. The eldest son, Thomas, received a 200-acre portion of " Ratcliffe Manor " in addition to his father's working tools, the iron and the iron work in the shop. The second son, John, received " The Great Neck " portion, 300 acres of the manor, as well as some other land. The youngest son, James, received a 300 acre portion of the manor. The elder daughter, Mary, who had married, " the second day of the twelfth month, 1700, John Lowe, Sr., of " Grafton Manor," received 150 acres of " Ratcliffe Manor," while Esther or Hester, the wife of Howell Powell, received money. The widow, Mary Bartlett, received personal estate and plantation in life interest.[7]

An incomplete chart reveals some of the inter-marriages with other families and provides some of the threads later to be mentioned, but by no means does it record all of the descendants of the practical old Yorkshire Quaker immigrant.

[6] Wills, Liber 13, f. 451, Annapolis; Baldwin, *Calendar of Maryland Wills*, III, 231.

[7] An account of the Bartlett origins in America is given in *Tercentenary History of Maryland* (Chicago, 1925), IV, 635-637.

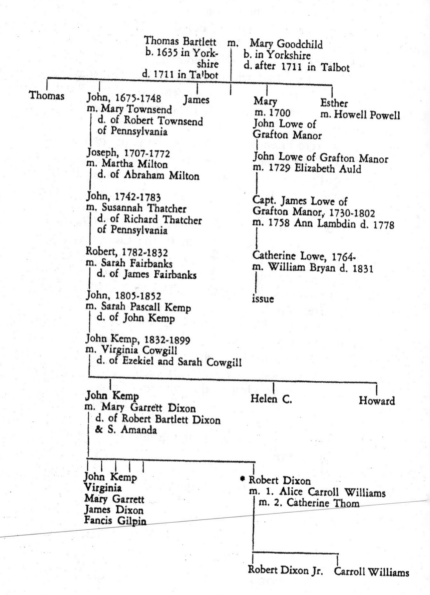

Thomas Bartlett m. Mary Goodchild
b. 1635 in York- b. in Yorkshire
shire d. after 1711 in Talbot
d. 1711 in Talbot

Thomas   John, 1675-1748   James   Mary   Esther
         m. Mary Townsend   m. 1700   m. Howell Powell
         d. of Robert Townsend   John Lowe of
         of Pennsylvania   Grafton Manor

         Joseph, 1707-1772   John Lowe of Grafton Manor
         m. Martha Milton   m. 1729 Elizabeth Auld
         d. of Abraham Milton

         John, 1742-1783   Capt. James Lowe of
         m. Susannah Thatcher   Grafton Manor, 1730-1802
         d. of Richard Thatcher   m. 1758 Ann Lambdin d. 1778
         of Pennsylvania

         Robert, 1782-1832   Catherine Lowe, 1764-
         m. Sarah Fairbanks   m. William Bryan d. 1831
         d. of James Fairbanks

         John, 1805-1852   issue
         m. Sarah Pascall Kemp
         d. of John Kemp

         John Kemp, 1832-1899
         m. Virginia Cowgill
         d. of Ezekiel and Sarah Cowgill

         John Kemp   Helen C.   Howard
         m. Mary Garrett Dixon
         d. of Robert Bartlett Dixon
         & S. Amanda

         John Kemp   * Robert Dixon
         Virginia   m. 1. Alice Carroll Williams
         Mary Garrett   m. 2. Catherine Thom
         James Dixon
         Fancis Gilpin

                                   Robert Dixon Jr.   Carroll Williams

                        * Present owner of "Old Bloomfield"

FRITH OF "FRITHLAND"

Along the road, to the right, we come to the west branch of the Miles. Here settled Henry Frith when he came to Maryland in 1664. He had married in England, and his wife, Elizabeth, in 1666, came to join him.[8] His age we do not know, but his wife was born in 1641.[9] On the Talbot Rent Rolls Henry Frith is charged with two tracts: "Frithland," 200 acres, April 30, 1664, at the head of the west branch of the St. Michael's River, and "Frith's Neck," 50 acres, surveyed May 7, 1667.

On May 7, 1666, Henry and Elizabeth Frith acknowledged a covenant of sale to Robert Fuller for "Frithland," 200 acres. Later this land was possessed by James Dawson to whom it had come from his brother, John, who devised it in this phrase: "To James Dawson interest in land I ought to have on St. Michael's Creek called 'Frithland.'"[10] The land became escheat and in 1735 was resurveyed for Edward Tottrell. It appears to be the area yet known as the Dawson farm at the left of the road, just as one crosses Oak Creek. By 1716 "Frith's Neck," at the head of the northeast branch of Harris Creek, was in the possession of John Valliant "in right of his wife." The tract adjoins "Clay's Neck" and is near the old Bayside Meeting House.

Henry Frith's will was probated, July 23, 1674. The widow, Elizabeth, was the sole legatee, but in the event of her remarriage the estate was to be divided among a son, Henry, under 16 when the will was made, and three daughters, unnamed, and under 14.[11] As administrators on the estate, the bond of Edward Elliott and Elizabeth, relict of Henry Frith, was filed July 23, 1674.

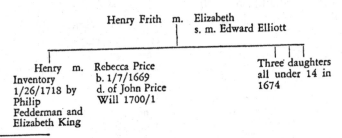

Henry Frith m. Elizabeth
s. m. Edward Elliott

Henry m. Rebecca Price
Inventory
1/26/1718 by
Philip
Fedderman and
Elizabeth King
b. 1/7/1669
d. of John Price
Will 1700/1

Three daughters
all under 14 in
1674

---

[8] Liber 6, f. 294 and Liber 10, f. 466, Annapolis.
[9] Chancery Court, P. L. 35, Annapolis.
[10] Talbot Rent Roll, Liber 1, f. 36.
[11] Wills, Liber 1, f. 638, Annapolis, and Baldwin, *Calendar of Maryland Wills,* I, 83.

ELLIOTT OF "DAVENPORT" AND "FRITHLAND"

On the south side of the Miles River lived Edward Elliott who had come to Maryland in 1667.[12] He was born about 1640.[13] Elizabeth, the widow Frith, was his second wife.[14] By 1698 Edward Elliott was Deputy High Sheriff of Talbot County.[15] On January 16, 1724/5 he is recorded as High Sheriff. But as well as through high county office he served his community as a carpenter. Not least, he gave the land and built the parish church of St. Michael's.

The following land patents reveal the ties of family relationship among the Friths, the Elliotts and the Aulds to whom we shall presently come: On January 15, 1677, Humphrey Davenport, County of Talbot, " Dokter of Physick," sold Edward Elliott of same county, house carpenter, for 8000 lbs. of Tobacco in Casque, two parcels of land, " Beach," lying on the south side of the St. Michael's River, 50 acres, and " Davenport," 200 acres.[16]

" Davenport," 200 acres, resurveyed, September 16, 1675, was owned by Edward Elliott, Sr. and James Auld.[17] " Davenport" extends from Deepwater Creek to Shipping Creek, now the harbor of St. Michael's.[18] " The Beach," surveyed for John Hollingsworth, was bought by Edward Elliott in 1667. It skirts St. Michael's harbor.

" Elliott's Folly," 100 acres, surveyed for Edward Elliott, November 26, 1685, lying south of a west line drawn from the head of Deepwater Creek, a tributary of the St. Michael's River, beginning at a black small walnut tree, consisted of 50 acres possessed by Edward Elliott and 50 acres by James Auld.[19]

" Elliott's Addition," 200 acres. By a certificate of survey, dated April 18, 1687, made by virtue of a warrant granted unto Edward Elliott, October 24, 1685, Thomas Smithson, surveyor, does certify that he has resurveyed the ancient tract therein ordered and has taken up for Edward Elliott, 200 acres by the name of " Elliott's

[12] Early Settler, Liber 15, f. 396, Annapolis.
[13] Chancery, P. L., f. 35 and P. C., f. 571 and Liber 1736-1745, f. 96.
[14] Bonds, 1662-1709, Easton and Test. Proc. Liber 6, f. 270, Annapolis.
[15] Liber 8, f. 516, Easton.
[16] Liber 3, f. 98, Eastin.
[17] Talbot Rent Roll.
[18] Plot in Land Office, Annapolis.
[19] Talbot Rent Roll.

Addition," lying on the south side of the Miles River and adjoining unto "Williston," "Martingham" and "Davenport." Possessed by James Auld, who married Elliott's daughter.[20] "Elliott's Addition" is the inland part of Edward Elliott's land. It adjoins "Crooked Intention," "Rolle's Range" and "Oak Level," as well as "Martingham" and "New Port Glasgow."

"Elliott's Lott," 476 acres, surveyed for Edward Elliott, April 4, 1695, lying on the south side of St. Michael's River, near the head of Shipping Creek. Possessed by Edward Elliott.[21] This evidently is a resurvey into which was brought most, if not all, of the land of Edward Elliott acquired by patent or purchase. It includes "Elliott's Folly," "Davenport," "Elliott's Addition," "Beach," and "Harley." "Harley" had come to Edward Elliott in 1691 by purchase from George Blades.

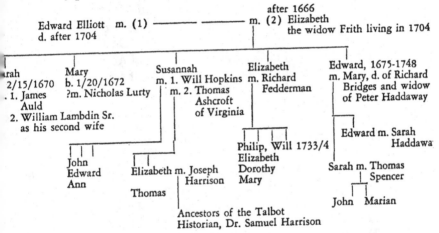

Ancestors of the Talbot
Historian, Dr. Samuel Harrison

The birth dates of the daughters are recorded on the leaves at the back of the volume in Easton marked BBL 2. The basis of some surmise of the marriage of Mary to Nicholas Lurty, second of the name in Talbot, is the testimony of Edward Elliott, Jr., April 9, 1740, that "forty years ago he was in conversation with his brother-in-law, Nicholas Lurty . . ."[22] However, the tie may have been through the family of Bridges.

[20] Talbot Rent Roll.
[21] Talbot Rent Roll.
[22] Liber 1736-1745, Easton.

Edward Elliott gave his daughter, Susannah, the wife of Will Hopkins, in 1704 the 476 acres embraced in the resurvey as "Elliott's Lott." Afterwards she married Thomas Ashcroft of Virginia and the land passed to her Hopkins sons, Edward and John. A part of this land is the site of the town of St. Michael's. John Johning Hopkins, grandson or great-grandson of Susannah Elliott, sold it to James Braddock, Liverpool merchant in 1777/8, and it was he who laid out the village.

In his will 1733/4, Philip Fedderman, the son of Richard Fedderman (Wedeman) and Elizabeth Elliott, Queen Anne's County, refers to 100 acres bought of Henry Frith (Jr.).

AULD OF DOVER POINT

The original home of the Aulds was "Dover Point" at the mouth of Deepwater Creek, a tributary of the St. Michael's River. On one side was William Hambleton's "Cambridge" and on the other, "Elliott's Folly." On modern maps Deepwater Creek is Long Haul Cove. On October 10, 1719, John Auld had a resurvey on a warrant of cultivation of parts of Elliott's Addition, Elliott's Folly, and Dover Point. The patent was issued to him as "New Port Glasgow." In later years, the tract came to Philemon Hambleton.

Wade's Point, over on the Bayside several miles distant from Deepwater Point, came to the Aulds probably from the Haddaways. Zachery Waid of Charles County had 300 acres due him, 1658, called Waid's Point. This he conveyed in 1663 to William Leeds, Quaker, son of Timothy Leeds, of the Isle of Kent. Sale was confirmed to John Leeds, 1712.[23] Edward Leeds, another son of Timothy, married Ruth Ball in the Bayside Meeting and their only son was John Leeds, and to him he devised Hatton and Wade's Point. John Leeds died 1789. From John "Wade's Point" passed to Lucretia, Rachel and Mary, then to John Leeds Bozman, son of Lucretia, and then was purchased in 1799 by Hugh Auld for £2,425.8.1-1/2. Hugh and Zipporah Auld sold "Wade's Point" and "Haddon" to Thomas Kemp in 1813 for $7,000.

In the family burial ground lie members of the Auld family illustrious in the military and civil annals of the state. James

---

[23] Land Record, Liber 12, f. 82, Easton.

Auld, the first of the name in Maryland, was a scion of the Clan McGregor, born in Ayr in 1665.[24] He died in 1721 and his will, the original of which is in the vaults at Easton, was proven July 28th of that year.[25] On April 10, 1722, Sarah Auld, the widow, and John Auld, the son, as executrix and executor, filed their bond " in common forme," with Philip Fedderman and Francis Rolle, their sureties.[26] The inventory of personal property amounted to £101.1.3, and final accounting was passed August 8, 1723[27] There were children as shown on the chart.

There is at Wade's Point a stone recording the military record and public service of Colonel Hugh Auld, but his remains, as well as those of his uncle, Lieutenant Hugh Auld, have been transferred to the National Cemetery at Arlington through the interest of Mrs. Laura Auld Flynn, great-great-granddaughter of Colonel Hugh Auld. The late Dr. Thomas E. Sears, was the son of John Lurty Sears and Ariana Amanda Auld, and a grandson of Colonel Auld.[28]

Among the manuscripts in the Maryland Historical Society (Sears Papers), is a volume, *The Practical Believer—The Knowledge of God*, London, MDCCIII, the flyleaves of which contain a genealogical record which begins with Edward Auld and Sarah, his wife; then follow the names and birth records of the children. The record is signed by Deborah Dawson, September 1, 1815, with this note, " wishing to preserve the memory of her worthy ancestors has set their names to these papers—the few she has knowledge of either by information or by personal acquaintance." Then this little prayer, " Oh Lord, Thou art my choice: uphold me with Thy mighty power—Deborah Dawson, St. Michael's, June 11, 1812, a pleasant day." Further the volume holds this, interesting to all Maryland Historical Society Members, " Presented July 13, 1893, by Mrs. Mary Elizabeth Thompson Mott,

[24] Chancery Liber P. L. f. 34, Annapolis.
[25] Wills, Liber 17, f. 105, Annapolis and Baldwin, *Calendar of Maryland Wills*, V, 86.
[26] Test. Proc. Liber 25, f. 95, Annapolis.
[27] Liber 25, f. 135 and Accounts Liber 5, f. 298, Annapolis.
[28] Mrs. Anna Ellis Harper, née Crouse, of St. Michael's, is the widow of Crittenden Harper, a great-grandson of Colonel Auld. Mrs. Harper is an antiquarian, who has aided greatly in the preparation of this article through her intimate knowledge of the St. Michael's and Bayside Districts. Let it also be recorded that she possesses the sword of Lt. Col. Auld, the weapon having been given her husband by his grandfather, Thomas Auld, of " Sharon," who had it from his father, Colinel Auld.

granddaughter of Mrs. Elizabeth Auld Dodson to Thomas Edward Sears, M. D., great-grandson of Lieutenant-Colonel Hugh Auld, Jr. of Talbot County." Dr. Sears was a prominent physician of Baltimore, a genealogist of merit, and for many years chairman of the genealogical committee of the Maryland Historical Society. Beneath the inscription in the hand of the late Dr. Sears is this:

> In this old book, if you choose to look
>   You will find a record kept,
> Of a family called by the name of Auld
>   Over whom a young girl wept
> And prayed that they should remembered be
> In the years when she too slept.

T. E. S., 1893

James Auld m. Sarah Elliott
b. Ayrshire ca. 1665 | b. February 15, 1670
d. Talbot Will 1721 | d. of Edward Elliott
s. m. 2. William Lambdin

James
b. 4/21/1669
not mentioned
in father's will

John
b. 1/9/1702
d. 7/22/1766

John m. Mary Sherwood
b. 1704 d. 1795
d. of Col. Daniel
Sherwood b. ca. 1688,
& Mary Hopkins,
b. 1672 d. 1746
d. of Thos. & Eliz. Hopkins
Col. Daniel Sherwood was
son of Col. Hugh Sherwood,
Gent., b. 1632 (P. C. f. 562,
Annapolis)

Edward
under 18 in
1721
Colonial
Militia 1740-8

Elizabeth under
16 in 1721
m. 1729/30 John
Lowe, Jr. of
Grafton Manor

Margaret under
16 in 1721
m. Nathaniel Cann

Sarah under 16
in 1721

James
Dorchester Co.
m. 1747 Rosannah
Piper (widow
Goldsborough)
removed to No.
Carolina

John
Rev. War
Daniel
Rev. War

Edward m. 1757 Sarah Haddaway
1734-1777 d. of Col. William
d. in Rev. Webb Haddaway and
Frances Harrison
d. of John Harrison
Col. Haddaway was son of
George Haddaway & gr. s.
of Roland Haddaway

Philemon
Rev. War

Hugh
1745-1813
Lieut. in Rev.
b. at Arling-
ton
m. Frances Harrison

Elizabeth m. John
Hambleton
Sarah m. Denton Carroll
Mary m. William Hambl-
b. of John
he m. 2. Rebecc
Raleig

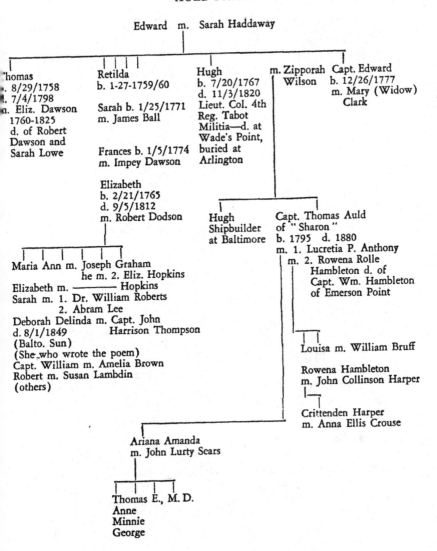

Edward m. Sarah Haddaway

Thomas
b. 8/29/1758
d. 7/4/1798
m. Eliz. Dawson
1760-1825
d. of Robert
Dawson and
Sarah Lowe

Retilda
b. 1-27-1759/60

Sarah b. 1/25/1771
m. James Ball

Frances b. 1/5/1774
m. Impey Dawson

Elizabeth
b. 2/21/1765
d. 9/5/1812
m. Robert Dodson

Hugh
b. 7/20/1767
d. 11/3/1820
Lieut. Col. 4th
Reg. Tabot
Militia—d. at
Wade's Point,
buried at
Arlington

m. Zipporah Capt. Edward
Wilson   b. 12/26/1777
              m. Mary (Widow)
              Clark

Maria Ann m. Joseph Graham
                  he m. 2. Eliz. Hopkins
Elizabeth m. ——— Hopkins
Sarah m. 1. Dr. William Roberts
          2. Abram Lee
Deborah Delinda m. Capt. John
d. 8/1/1849   Harrison Thompson
(Balto. Sun)
(She who wrote the poem)
Capt. William m. Amelia Brown
Robert m. Susan Lambdin
(others)

Hugh
Shipbuilder
at Baltimore

Capt. Thomas Auld
of "Sharon"
b. 1795   d. 1880
m. 1. Lucretia P. Anthony
m. 2. Rowena Rolle
      Hambleton d. of
      Capt. Wm. Hambleton
      of Emerson Point

Louisa m. William Bruff

Rowena Hambleton
m. John Collinson Harper

Crittenden Harper
m. Anna Ellis Crouse

Ariana Amanda
m. John Lurty Sears

Thomas E., M. D.
Anne
Minnie
George

Auld Family—In the Chart published on page 244 of the September, 1946, issue of this Magazine there was a typographical error which must be rectified. Hugh, Elizabeth, Sarah and Mary Auld (at bottom of page) were the children, not of Edward who married Sarah Haddaway, but of John and Mary (Sherwood) Auld, of the preceding generation. They were brother and sisters of Edward (1734-1777).—EDITOR.

BELT FAMILY.

CHRISTOPHER JOHNSTON.

HUMPHREY BELT entered his rights in the Maryland Land Office, 30 June, 1663, for himself, and for John, Ann, and Sarah Belt, demanding a warrant for 200 acres, which issued to him accordingly (Land Office, Lib. 5, fol. 373). In all probability John, Ann, and Sarah were the children of Humphrey, and it is probable that this John Belt was identical with John Belt of Anne Arundel County who died in 1698. The proved pedigree, however, begins with

1. JOHN BELT [1] of Anne Arundel County, who also owned land in Baltimore County. 29 April 1685, Thomas Lightfoot of Baltimore County, and Rebecca his wife, convey to John Belt of Anne Arundel County, a tract of 300 acres called Belt's Posterity, being part of two tracts, one of 1000 acres and one of 500 acres, both called Expectation, and lying in Baltimore County (Balto. Co., Lib. R. M. No. HS, fol. 123). This land was subsequently bequeathed by the grantee to his sons Joseph and Benjamin Belt. The will of John Belt, dated 13 May 1697, was proved 11 Nov. 1698 (Annapolis, Lib. 6, fol. 175). In it he mentions his wife, Elizabeth; his sons John, Joseph, and Benjamin; and his daughters Elizabeth, Charity and Sarah. He had, moreover, a son Jeremiah, not mentioned in the will, who

was doubtless born in 1698, after the will was made. The register of Allhallows Parish, Anne Arundel County, records the fact that Elizabeth, Charity, Sarah and Jeremy Belt, children of John and Elizabeth Belt, were baptized 14 December 1703. The same register records the marriage, 25 July, 1701, of Mr. John Lamb, merchant, and Elizabeth Belt widow of John Belt " late of this Parish deceased." By her second marriage Mrs. Elizabeth Belt had a daughter, Margaret Lamb, baptized 14 Dec. 1703 (Allhallows Parish). John Belt and Elizabeth his wife had issue:

2.   i.   JOHN BELT.[2]
3.   ii. COL. JOSEPH BELT of Prince George's Co., b. 1680; d. 26 June, 1761.
4.   iii. BENJAMIN BELT of Prince George's Co., b. 1682; d. 1773.
     iv. JEREMIAH BELT, b. 1698; bapt. 14 Dec., 1703; mar. Mary daughter of John Wight.
     v.   ELIZABETH BELT.
     vi. CHARITY BELT.
     vii. SARAH BELT, mar., 11 Sept., 1718, Thomas Harwood (Allhallows).

2.   JOHN BELT [2] (*John* [1]) received, by the terms of his father's will, a tract of 200 acres in Anne Arundel County called " Velmead." 20 October 1724, " John Belt of Anne Arundel County, merchant " and Lucy his wife convey to Gilbert Higginson of London, England, to whom the land had been previously mortgaged, 1 July 1710, all that piece of land whereon the said John Belt formerly dwelt, being that part of Velmead left the said John Belt by the will of his father John Belt deceased, containing 200 acres &c. (A. A. Co., Lib., S. Y. No. 1, fol. 79). Soon after this John Belt removed to Baltimore County. 6 May 1726, John Belt, Senr. of Baltimore County, conveys to his daughter Mary Belt, in consideration of a marriage shortly to be had and celebrated between said Mary Belt and Greenberry Dorsey, son of John Dorsey of said County, tract Belt's Point, 112 acres, on the south side of Patapsco River, according to certificate dated 2 Jan'y 1719/20 (Balto. Co., Lib. IS, No. H, fol. 236). There is also a deed of gift, dated 18 June 1726, from John Dorsey of Baltimore County to his son Greenberry Dorsey (*ibid.,* fol. 377) in consideration of his marriage with Mary Belt, and yet another deed, dated 1 May, 1727, from John Belt " to his son-in-law Greenberry Dorsey, son of Col. John Dorsey and Comfort

his wife " (*ibid.* fol. 441). John Belt left no will, and there is no record of the administration of his estate. He was, however, a member of the Society of Friends and it is probable that his estate was divided by private arrangement. He married, at West River and Cliff's Meeting, 10 February, 1701/2, Lucy daughter of Benjamin Lawrence. She had issue, with probably other children, as follows:—

5.   i. JOHN BELT,[3] b. 1703; d. 1 Dec., 1788.
      ii. MARY BELT, mar., 1726, Greenberry Dorsey.
     iii. MARGARET BELT, b. 10 June, 1719; d. about 1770; mar., 1 Dec., 1743, Basil Lucas.

3. COL. JOSEPH BELT [2] (*John* [1]) of Prince George's County, was born in 1680, and died 26 June, 1761. In a deposition, made in 1715, his age is given as 35 years (Chancery, Lib. P. C., fol. 277). By the terms of his father's will, he was left the reversion of the dwelling plantation, after his mother's death, and a part of Belt's Posterity in Baltimore County. Shortly before her second marriage, his mother assigned to him her life interest in the dwelling plantation. 12 April, 1701, Elizabeth Belt of Anne Arundel County, widow, conveys to her second son, Joseph Belt of Prince George's County, all her interest in a tract called " Friend's Choice," left by John Belt, late of Anne Arundel County, deceased, to his wife Elizabeth and, after her death, to his second son, Joseph Belt (P. G. Co., Lib. A., fo. 369). Belt's Posterity was later sold by Joseph Belt and his brother Benjamin. 21 Sept., 1745, Joseph Belt and Margery his wife and Benjamin Belt, all of Prince George's County, convey to Stephen Onion of Baltimore County, Belt's Posterity, 300 acres, at the head of Gunpowder River in Baltimore County, bequeathed by John Belt late of Anne Arundel County, deceased, in his will dated 13 May, 1697, to his sons the aforesaid Joseph and Benjamin (Balto. Co., Lib. T. B. No. D, fol. 334). Col. Joseph Belt was the Presiding Justice of Prince George's County Court from 1726 to 1728 (Com. Book), and represented the county in the Assembly from 1725 to 1737 (MS. House Journals). He is styled " Lieutenant-Colonel " in the House Journals from 1725 to 1727, while from 1728 to 1737 he is called " Colonel," implying that about 1727 or 1728 he attained the rank of Colonel commanding the County Militia. Col. Belt was twice married. His first wife was Esther daugh-

ter of Col. Ninian Beall, who appoints his "son-in-law Joseph Belt" one of the executors of his will; his second wife, who survived him and died in 1783, was Margery widow of Thomas Sprigg, Jr., and daughter of John Wight. 30 June, 1737, Joseph Belt and Margery his wife, administratrix of Mr. Thomas Sprigg, late of Prince George's County; Gent., rendered an additional account of the said deceased's estate (Accounts, Lib. 15, fol. 341). The *Maryland Gazette* of 2 July, 1761, has the following obituary: "Friday Night last [26 June] Died, at his Plantation in Prince George's County, aged 86 years, Colonel Joseph Belt, whose Death is supposed to be occasioned by Grief for the Death of his Son a few Weeks before." The age of Col. Belt is erroneously stated; it was 81 years not 86. Col. Joseph Belt and Esther (Beall) his first wife had issue, as recorded in the registers of Queen Anne Parish, Prince George's County:

   i.   JOHN BELT,[8] b. 13 March, 1707; mar., 4 March, 1727/8, Margaret Queen.
   ii.   ANNE BELT, b. 1708/9; d. 1762; mar. 1°, 1724, Thomas Clagett, 2°, Ignatius Perry.
   iii   RACHEL BELT, b. 13 Dec., 1711; mar., 11 July, 1727, Osborn Sprigg.
6.   iv.   JOSEPH BELT, b. 19 Dec., 1717; d. 6 May, 1761.
7.   v.   TOBIAS BELT, b. 20 Aug., 1720; d. 1785.
   vi.   MARY BELT, b. 24 Dec., 1722; mar. 1°. Edward Sprigg, 2°. Thomas Pindle.
8.   vii.   JEREMIAH BELT, b. 4 March, 17𝐿4; d. 1784.
   viii.   JAMES BELT, b. 23 July, 1726.

By his second wife, Margery, Col. Joseph Belt had:

   i.   HUMPHREY BELT.
   ii.   MARGERY BELT, mar. 1°. . . . Lyles, 2°. . . . Perry.

4.   BENJAMIN BELT [2] (*John* [1]) was born in 1682. Depositions made by him, and recorded in Prince George's County, give his age as 66 years in 1748 (Lib. E. E., fol. 713), and 73 years in 1755 (Lib. N. N., fol. 411), while, according to similar depositions, recorded in Anne Arundel County, he was 56 years old in 1738 (Lib. I. B. No. 1, fol. 116), and 83 in 1765 (*ibid.,* fol. 646). By his father's will he inherited 200 acres, part of Belt's Posterity in Baltimore County, the remaining 100 acres falling to his brother Joseph. In 1745 the two brothers sold their respective portions of this tract to Stephen Onion, and the deed whereby this land was conveyed has already been cited.

Benjamin Belt lived to an advanced age, dying in 1773. His will, dated 19 June, 1772, and proved 28 May, 1773, is recorded both in Prince George's County and at Annapolis. His wife, whose name was Elizabeth, was living in 1724, but who she was is unknown. She did not join her husband in his deed to Stephen Onion, in 1745, and was most probably dead at that time. From the fact that Benjamin Belt had a son named Middleton Belt, later a distinctive name in this branch of the family, it seems likely that Mrs. Elizabeth Belt may have been a Middleton, but a careful investigation of the records fails to elicit proof of the fact. Benjamin Belt and Elizabeth his wife had issue:—

9.	i.	COL. JOSEPH BELT,³ b. 1716; d. 16 June, 1793.
	ii.	MIDDLETON BELT, d. unmarried in 1745.
10.	iii.	BENJAMIN BELT, d. 1775.
	iv.	SOPHIA BELT, mar. ——— Beall.
	v.	ESTHER BELT, mar. John Watkins of Allhallows Parish, A. A. Co.
	vi.	ANNE BELT, mar. Basil Brashears.
	vii.	ELIZABETH BELT, mar. Basil Waring.

5. JOHN BELT ³ (*John,*² *John* ¹) of Baltimore County, was a member of the Society of Friends and an Elder in the Church. He was born in 1703 and died 1 December, 1788, aged 85 years, according to the Friends' Records. The births of three children of John and Lucy Belt are entered in the same records. The will of John Belt of Baltimore County, dated 24 Sept., 1788, was proved 17 Feb'y, 1789, and is recorded in Baltimore (Lib. 4, fol. 350). John Belt and Lucy his wife had issue:

i.	JOHN BELT.⁴
ii.	NATHAN BELT.
iii.	JOSEPH BELT, b. 10 June, 1750.
iv.	SARAH BELT, mar. . . . Randall.
v.	LUCY BELT, b. 25 November, 1744.
vi.	MARY BELT, b. 30 June, 1747.

6. JOSEPH BELT ³ (*Joseph,*² *John* ¹) of Prince George's County, was born 19 December, 1717, and died 6 June, 1761. The *Maryland Gazette* of 11 June, 1761, has the following obituary: " On Wednesday Evening last [6 June], Died, at his House near Upper Marlborough, aged a little above 40 Years, after a long Indisposition, Mr. Joseph Belt junior, a Gentleman who was deservedly esteemed by a numerous Acquaintance." The will of Joseph Belt Jr., dated 19 April, 1759, and proved 26 August, 1761, is re-

corded both in Prince George's County, and at Annapolis. He married Anne daughter of Thomas Sprigg and Margery (Wight) his wife, and had issue:

    i. THOMAS BELT [4]
    ii. JOSEPH BELT.
    iii. CHARLES BELT.
    iv. WILLIAM BELT.
    v. ELIZABETH BELT.
    vi. ANNE BELT.
    vii. MARY BELT.

7. TOBIAS BELT [3] (*Joseph,*[2] *John*[1]) was born 20 August, 1720, and died in 1785. His will, dated 13 November, 1774, was proved 17 May, 1785. He married Mary (d. 1795) daughter of George Gordon of Prince George's County. They had issue:

    i. HORATIO BELT.
    ii. JOSHUA BELT.
    iii. LEVIN BELT.
    iv. LLOYD BELT.
    v. FORBES BELT.
    vi. LUCY BELT, mar. . . . Addison.
    vii. DRYDEN BELT, mar. . . . Tyler.
    viii. ELIZABETH BELT, mar. John Macgill.
    ix. RACHEL BELT.

8. JEREMIAH BELT [3] (*Joseph,*[2] *John*[1]) of Prince George's County was born 4 March, 1724, and died in the latter part (probably December) of 1785. His will bears no date, but was proved 18 January, 1785 (Pr. Geo. Co., Lib. T. No. 1, fol. 202). He married, 21 June, 1746, Mary (b. 15 Dec., 1723) daughter of Thomas Sprigg, of Prince George's County, and Margery (Wight) his wife. Their issue:

    i. THOMAS SPRIGG BELT.
    ii. FIELDING BELT.
    iii. JOHN SPRIGG BELT.
    iv. TOBIAS BELT.
    v. MARY BELT.
    vi. MARGERY BELT.

9. COL. JOSEPH BELT,[3] (*Benjamin,*[2] *John*[1]) was born in Prince George's County in 1716, and died in Montgomery County 16 June, 1793, aged 77 years, according to family record. In agreement with this, there is of record in Prince George's County a deposition wherein "Joseph Belt son of Benjamin" states his age as 18 years in 1734 (Lib. T, fol. 364). He is mentioned in his father's will as "my son Joseph Belt," and receives a nominal bequest. He does not

appear as party to any deed in Prince George's County, and it is possible that he lived for some time abroad. His son Middleton certainly married in England. The Montgomery County records contain a deed, dated 25 April, 1780, whereby John Murdock of Montgomery County "out of love and affection" conveys to Joseph Belt of said County and Esther his wife, for the term of both their lives, 200 acres part of "Friendship," on the East Side of the main road from Georgetown to Frederick, and adjoining the land of Patrick Beall (Lib. A, fol. 538). According to the late Wiliam Murdock of Georgetown, D. C., a daughter of Col. Joseph Belt was the wife of his grandfather Col. John Murdock, and this statement would seem to be borne out by the above deed. The "inventory of the personal estate of Joseph Belt, late of Montgomery County deceased," was filed at Rockville 12 August, 1793, and amounted to £309. 12s. 03d. Middleton Belt (erroneously written "Beall" in the record) was his administrator (Montgomery Co., Wills, Lib. C, fol. 208). Col. Joseph Belt married, in or before 1739, Esther daughter of William Smith, Esq., of Prince George's County and Jane his first wife, daughter of Archibald Edmonston. She was born, according to family record, in 1722 and died 12 July, 1796, aged 74 years. Her father, William Smith, mentions his "son-in-law Joseph Belt son of Benjamin Belt" in his will. Col. Joseph Belt and Esther his wife had issue:

11. i. CAPT. MIDDLETON BELT, b. 1747; d. 5 January, 1807.
  ii. ESTHER BELT, b. 1744; d. 21 March, 1814; mar. Dr. Walter Smith
    (b. 1744; d. 1796) of Georgetown, D. C., and had issue:
  iii. ANN BELT, b. 1751: said to have married Col. John Murdock of
    Montgomery Co.

10. BENJAMIN BELT [3] (*Benjamin,*[2] *John* [1]) of Prince George's County died in 1775. His will, dated 11 April, 1775, was proved 28 June following (P. G. Co., T, No. 1, fol. 25). His wife's name was Ruth, and they had issue:

  i. BENJAMIN BELT. [4]
  ii. THOMAS BELT.
  iii. MIDDLETON BELT.
  iv. ELIZABETH BELT, mar. . . . Nixon.
  v. ESTHER BELT.
  vi. RACHEL BELT.

11. CAPT. MIDDLETON BELT [4] (*Joseph,*[3] *Benjamin,*[2] *John* [1]) was born in 1747, and died in Montgomery County, Md.,

15 January, 1807, aged 60 years according to family record.
He was married, 25 March, 1763, at St. John's Church,
Surrey, England, to Mary Ann Dyer. Middleton Belt was
but 16 years old at the time, and tradition says that the
youthful couple eloped and were married, but were afterwards obliged by their parents to return to school and finish
their education. The family record shows, by the way,
that they had no issue for eight years after their marriage.
Mary Ann (Dyer) Belt, widow of Capt. Middleton Belt,
died in Georgetown, D. C., 18 December, 1830, aged 85
years. Capt. Middleton Belt and Mary Ann (Dyer) his
wife had issue:

i.   ANNA MARIA BELT,[5] b. at Bristol England, 24 Nov., 1771; d.
     at Chilicothe, Ohio, April, 1808; mar. ——— McCormick.
ii. MIDDLETON BELT, b. in Fairfax County, Va., 24 April, 1777;
     mar. 29 Dec., 1796, William Smith of Prince George's
     County, Md.
iii. MARY ANN BELT, b. in Fairfax Co., Va., 29 March, 1779.
iv. CLARISSA BELT, b. in Montgomery Co., Md., 10 Nov., 1781.
v.   MIDDLETON BELT (son), b. in Georgetown, D. C., 13 Sept., 1785.
vi. WILLIAM DYER BELT, b. in Georgetown, D. C., 26 Feb'y, 1788.
vii. JAMES HANRICK BELT, b. in Georgetown, D. C., 31 January, 1792.

BERRY FAMILY OF CHARLES COUNTY.

Arthur L. Keith.

Probably all the Berrys of Charles County prior to 1800 are derived from and connected with Samuel Berry who first appears on the records of this county in 1690 and is called an old man in 1732 and died before 1753. There were other Berrys in Maryland as far back as 1652. The only Berry whose importation is shown prior to 1680 is that of William Berry, son of James Berry, whose importation is placed at 1652. He appears to have settled in Calvert County. Richard Preston of Calvert County in his will, Sept. 16, 1669, prob. Jan. 8, 1669/70, mentions his grandchildren William and James Berry. They probably belong to the William Berry of 1652. William Berry (grandson of Richard Preston) left issue who may be traced in Calvert, Prince George, and other counties. James Berry (grandson of Richard Preston) disappears from the records unless he is identical with the James Berry of St. Mary's County who in 1686 had recently married Anne, widow of Dr. John Wynne of Popular Hill St. Mary's County, whose will is dated Jan. 22, 1683/4, prob. March 10, 1684/5. I hope to prove in my forthcoming Cawood article that before she married Dr. John Wynne she had been the

wife of Stephen Cawood of Charles County, who died in 1676.
The significance of this point lies in the fact that the Berry
family of Charles County and the Cawood (also the Smallwood)
family were closely connected in the records.

The first Berry record found in Charles County is that of
Sam Berry who brought suit against John Wilder, 1690 (Lib.
R fol. 19). In 1697 William Hutchinson made deed to Humphrey Berry. So much we get from the index but Liber W
(for 1697) to which the index refers has been lost, so no further
information is to be had from that source. If he is identical
with the Humphrey Berry (son of Samuel) he must have been
very young at that time. No other Humphrey (unless this
is an exception) aside from the son of Samuel has been found.
On Oct. 2, 1704, Stephen Cawood (son of the Stephen Cawood
who died in 1676, and about 1695 he returned from St. Mary's
County) and wife Mary sold to Doctor Samuel Berry 100
acres, part of "Hull" (Lib. D No. 2, fol. 75). In March, 1713
Stephen Cawood and Samuel Berry sued James Maddox.
Cause and issue not shown. In 1732 Samuel Berry petitioned
to be levy-free. Petition was granted. He died before 1753
leaving no record of his death. In 1753 one Samuel Berry
was the possessor of the 100 acres of "Hull," bought in
1704 of Stephen Cawood, but he was not the Samuel Berry
who bought the land but the son of Humphrey Berry whose
will probated in 1772 (see below) confirmed his son Samuel
in the possession of this land. From this fact we may deduce
Humphrey Berry as a son of Dr. Samuel Berry. Another
Samuel Berry died in 1776 mentioning in his will his brother
Humphrey's son Samuel, and sisters Elizabeth Berry and Ann
Berry. These add other children to Dr. Samuel Berry. Also
Sarah Roby of Charles County is described in 1734 as the
daughter of Samuel Berry. I believe also that William Berry
who died in Charles County in 1733 was another son. I shall
speak of him later.

"Hull," patented for 600 acres by Stephen Cawood in 1675,
lies in the Mattawoman River about three miles northwest of
the village of Waldorf and about twenty miles south of Wash-

ington.   It was bounded by early Smallwood tracts, and other
Smallwood, Cawood, and Berry lands later were in the immediate vicinity.   The writer visited the place in July, 1926, and
"Hull' (it still goes by that name) is partly possessed today
by men of the name Berry.

Dr. Samuel Berry (no clue has been found as to his wife's
name) had the following children:

    1. Humphrey Berry.
    2. Samuel Berry.
    3. Sarah Berry.
    4. Elizabeth Berry (apparently died single).
    5. Ann Berry (apparently died single).

and probably also

    6. William Berry.

1. Humphrey Berry (son of Dr. Samuel) made will in
Charles County, Sept. 19, 1770, prob. Jan. 22, 1772.   Wife
Ann is named extx.   He leaves to son Samuel Berry " Mt.
Paradise," part of " Hull," and " Berry; " to son Humphrey
Berry he leaves " Smallwood's Plains; " to son Hezekiah Berry
he leaves " Nutwell " and " Discord; " to son Benjamin Berry
he leaves " Batchellor's Forest " and " Berry's Lott; " to son
Joseph Berry he leaves one negro.   Testator mentions daughter
Martha Smallwood, son-in-law Samuel Smallwood, and grand-
daughter Letitia Smallwood.   The will was witnessed by
Samuel Hanson, Geo. Lee, and Matthew Moore, Jr.   Humphrey
Smallwood married 1. Mary Smallwood, daughter of Thomas
Smallwood (see *Maryland Historical Magazine,* XXII, 151)
and had two children:

    7. Humphrey Berry (for his descendants see *Maryland Historical
       Magazine,* XXII, 171).
    8. Thomas Berry (died without issue before 1779, probably
       before 1770, since his father's will of that date does not
       mention him).

Humphrey Berry married 2. Ann Lovejoy, daughter of
Joseph Lovejoy of Prince George County.   They had the
following:

    9. Samuel Berry.
   10. Hezekiah Berry.

11. Benjamin Berry.
12. Joseph Berry.
13. Martha Berry (she married Samuel Smallwood. For her descendants see the *Maryland Historical Magazine*, XXII, 176).
14. John Berry, born about 1752 (not mentioned in his father's will).

2. Samuel Berry (son of Dr. Samuel) deposed on Aug. 2, 1774, in regard to " Berry's Hazzard " of Thomas Berry, that he was 56 years old. His birth may be set at about 1718. Before 1742 he had married Ann Thomas, daughter of Daniel Thomas. He made will in Charles County, Sept, 7. 1775, prob. March 18, 1776. He leaves to sister Elizabeth Berry 50 acres on Cool Spring Branch; mentions sister Ann Berry; cousin Samuel Berry, son of Humphrey Berry; Elizabeth Willett (relationship not shown); and son

15. Thomas Berry, "his only heir."

His will is witnessed by Ben Cawood, Jr., Thomas Smallwood, Jr., and Mary Cawood, wife of Benjamin Cawood.

3. Sarah Berry (daughter of Dr. Samuel) married before 1734 to ——— Roby. Their descendants have not been traced. Berry Robey appears in the 1790 census of Montgomery County. There was also a Berry Robey, Jr., who in the same county married Lucretia Barton, Aug. 19, 1801. These two Berry Robeys probably descend from the marriage of Sarah Berry and ——— Robey.

4. Elizabeth Berry (daughter of Dr. Samuel) made will in Charles County March 18, 1794, prob. April 7, 1794. She made bequest to nephew John Berry, his wife Elizabeth Berry, and their children William Berry and Mary Berry.

6. William Berry (probably son of Dr. Samuel) died about 1733. His account was presented in Charles County, Feb. 9, 1733 by his wife Esther Berry. No mention is made of children but here probably belongs one Esther Berry, born in Charles County in 1729, died in March, 1828 in Washington County, Virginia. She married Stephen Cawood, born Aug. 6, 1724 (son of John Cawood, son of Stephen, son of Stephen

who died in 1676). They reared a large family of whom I shall treat in my Cawood article. Because of the close relations between the family of Dr. Samuel Berry and the Cawood family it seems almost certain that Esther Berry, born in 1729, was of that family. Among the many children of Stephen Cawood by his wife Esther Berry was one Berry Cawood who served in the Revolution under Gen. George Rogers Clark, and who was the ancestor of the Hon. C. Bascom Slemp of Virginia.

9. Samuel Berry (son of Humphrey, Sr.) had the following children as shown by the Piscataway Parish records:

16. Joseph Berry, born Aug. 7, 1751.
17. Samuel Berry, born Jan. 2, 1753.
18. Benjamin Berry, born Feb. 21, 1756.
19. Mary Ann Berry, born May 7, 1758.

10. Hepekiah Berry (son of Humphrey, Sr.) married and had the following children:

20. Hepburn S. Berry.
21. George M. Berry.

11. Benjamin Berry (son of Humphrey, Sr.) is probably identical with the Benjamin Berry who made will in Charles County, July 2, 1802, prob. Nov. 6, 1804. He mentions wife Chloe Berry, daughter Linder (Verlinde?), "my single daughters," and "all my children." The will is witnessed by Jacob Roby, Hezekiah Berry, and Jerom Osburn. (It is possible that the Benjamin of this will was not the son of Humphrey, Sr., but of Humphrey, Jr., or of Samuel, son of Humphrey, Sr).

14. John Berry (son of Humphrey, Sr.) is not mentioned in his father's will but must belong here for the reason that Elizabeth Berry (sister of Humphrey, Sr.) calls him her nephew, and Thomas Berry (son of Samuel, 1718-1776) in his will, dated Oct. 24, 1778, calls him "cousin John Berry, son of Humphrey Berry." The Prince George County census of 1776 gives the age of John Berry as 24, and makes him a neighbor of William Smallwood. John Berry was born, there-

fore, about 1752, married Elizabeth ———— (see will of
Elizabeth Berry, above) and had:

22. William Berry.
23. Mary Berry.

15. Thomas Berry (son of Samuel who died in 1776) apparently died single. He made will in Charles County, Oct.
24, 1778, prob. Oct. 31, 1778. His will contains a wealth of
suggestions which if properly followed out would solve some of
the doubtful connections of the Berry, Smallwood, and Cawood
families. He makes bequest to aunt Elizabeth Berry, aunt
Ann Berry, to cousin John Berry, son of Humphrey Berry; to
Mary Eleanor Atchison (no relationship shown); to Anne
Conner, wife of Richard, during her life or until married
(sic!); to William Smallwood (of John) "the upper part of
my plantation in Prince George County * * * so long as he
conducts himself properly as a tenant;" to Charles Inness,
100 acres where he now lives, to remain as a tenant; to Samuel
Berry Atchison, son of Mary Eleanor Atchison, lands called
"Duck Pond," "Porkhall," and "Batchellor's Delight" (the
last two were once Smallwood holdings), lying in Charles
County, also certain negroes; to Benjamin Cawood, Jr., land
on east side of Duck Pond where the said Benjamin Cawood
now lives. Good friend Benj. Cawood, Jr., is appointed exor.
The will is signed "Tho Berry of Samuel." It is witnessed
by Notley Ford, John Ford, and John Acton, Jr. On Aug.
4, 1802, Samuel Atchison Berry sold part of "Porkhall." I
regard him as identical with Samuel Berry Atchison of Thomas
Berry's will. No record has been found showing that the
change of name had been made legally.

I next give records of Berrys who apparently belong to this
line but whose exact place has not yet been found.

Bassil Berry and wife Jemima Berry had daughter Elizabeth
Berry, bapt. April 10, 1768, in St. John's or Piscataway Parish,
Prince George County. In 1778 Bassil Berry was living in
Montgomery County.

Verlinda Berry owned part of "Hull" in 1782.

Ann Berry made will in Charles County in 1798, mentioning daughters Lyda Marlow and Verlinda Acton; grandchildren Hanson Marlow (son of John Marlow), William Marlow, John Marlow, and Barbary Acton.

Benjamin Berry is mentioned as son-in-law in will of William Brawner, 1802-03, Charles County. Lucy Berry is at same time mentioned as testator's daughter.

Samuel Berry was granted license to marry Ann Berry in Prince George County, Jan. 30, 1810.

A much earlier reference is found in the will of John Contee, gentleman, whose will was probated in Charles County, Aug. 21, 1708. (See *Baldwin* III, 111). In this will he mentions sister Agnes Berry of England. In the probate of the will depositions are taken from Col. James Smallwood, Eliza: Berry, spinster, aged 30, and others. The association of the names Berry and Smallwood is very suggestive. This may be a valuable clue to those who wish to trace the Berry family back to England, assuming of course that this Elizabeth Berry is of the family of Dr. Samuel Berry.

Other Berry references may be found in my article on the Smallwood family. See *Maryland Historical Magazine,* XXII, 139.

Vermillion, South Dakota.

BLADEN FAMILY.

CHRISTOPHER JOHNSTON.

According to Foster's *Visitations of Yorkshire* (p. 330) Robert Bladen of Hemsworth, Yorkshire, England, married Elizabeth, daughter of John Lacy of Cromwellbotham and Alice his wife, daughter of Martin Birkhead, Queen's Attorney in the North, and had a son John Bladen, living in 1632. The latter is evidently to be identified with John Bladen, son and heir of Robert Bladen of Hemsworth, Co. York, Gent., who was admitted to Gray's Inn, London, 6 March, 1624/5 (Foster's *Admissions to Gray's Inn*, p. 175). A thorough investigation of the English records would doubtless show the relationship of these Bladens to the Maryland family.

The following genealogy, where other evidences are not cited, is derived from the Bladen pedigree in Blore's *History of Rutland* (p. 180); from *Notes and Queries*, 3d series, vii, 326; and from the biography of the Right Hon. Martin Bladen in the *Dictionary of National Biography*.

1. THE REV. DOCTOR BLADEN,[1] who is perhaps to be identified with the Rev. Thomas Bladen A. M., Vicar of Rainham in Kent 1646, married Sarah daughter of Henry Blayney, 2d Baron Blayney of the Peerage of Ireland, and sister of Edward and Richard Barons Blayney. They had a son :—

   2. i. NATHANIEL BLADEN[2] of Hemsworth.

2. NATHANIEL BLADEN[2] Esq., of Hemsworth, Yorkshire, son of the Rev. Dr. Bladen[1] and Sarah Blayney his wife, was a barrister-at-Law, and was living in 1702. He was one of the witnesses to the will (dated 15 June 1702, proved 7 Dec. 1703) of Edward Randolph Esq., Surveyor General of Customs &c. in America, which, among other provisions, directed that testator's daughter Sarah should not marry without the consent of Mrs. Mary Fog and Nathaniel Bladen of Lincoln's Inn Esq. (*New Engd. H. and G. Register*, xlviii, 487). Nathaniel Bladen married Isabella Fairfax, daughter of Sir William Fairfax of Steeton and Frances his wife, daughter of

43

Sir Thomas Chaloner of Guisborough.   Nathaniel Bladen and Isabella (Fairfax), his wife, had issue :—

3.   i. WILLIAM BLADEN [3] of Maryland.
    ii. The Right Hon. MARTIN BLADEN of Albury Hatch, Co. Essex, Esq. ; b. 1680 ; d. 15 Feb'y 1745/6 ; mar. 1°. Mary, dau. of Col. Gibbs, 2°. Mrs. Frances Foche.
    iii. ISABELLA BLADEN.
    iv. CATHERINE BLADEN.
    v. FRANCIS BLADEN, mar. William Hammond, Esq.
    vi. ELIZABETH BLADEN, mar. Edward Hawke, Esq., of Lincoln's Inn, Barrister-at-Law, and was the mother of Lord Hawke, the celebrated Admiral.

Mrs. Isabella (Fairfax) Bladen was baptized at Steeton Chapel, 16 August 1637, and was buried, at Bolton Percy, 27 October 1691.   The pedigree in Blore's *Rutland* (p. 180) gives to Nathaniel Bladen a second wife, Jane daughter of Dudley Loftus, LL.D., younger son of Sir Adam Loftus of Rathfarnham, Bart., but appends a query expressing doubt as to whether she were not the second wife of Martin Bladen (son of Nathaniel).   It is evident that little reliance is to be placed upon this statement.   In all probability the Loftus connection came through the Blayney family.

3. WILLIAM BLADEN,[3] son of Nathaniel [2] and Isabella (Fairfax) Bladen, was born at Steeton 27 Feb'y 1673, and was buried at Annapolis, Md., 9 August 1718 (Register of St. Anne's, Annapolis).   He came to Maryland in or before 1695.   He was Clerk of Assembly from 1695 to 1697, and was Clerk of the Council from 1697 to 1714 (Journals of the Upper and Lower Houses).   A commission issued to him, 14 August 1699, to be Clerk of the Prerogative Court (Test. Proc. Lib. 18, fol. 3), and he was Commissary General of Maryland in 1714 (Charles Co. Rec.). In 1701 he was appointed Secretary of Maryland, and filed his bond, 16 April, for the due performance of the duties of the office (Prov. Court Rec., Lib. TL. no. 2, fol. 343).   In 1707 he was Attorney General of Maryland (Council Journal 1699–1714, p. 528).   He was the architect of the new State house in 1708 and in the same year was one of the Aldermen of Annapolis (Riley's *Ancient City*, pp. 80, 86, 88).   He married, in 1696, Anne daughter of Garrett Van Swearingen and Mary (Smith) his wife, of St. Mary's County.   The Register of St. Anne's, Annapolis, records his burial 9 August 1718. He died intestate.   8 September 1718, his widow, Mrs. Anne

Bladen, renounced her right to administer on the estate of William Bladen, Esq., deceased, in favor of Mrs. Anne Tasker, and administration was committed to Benjamin Tasker who married William Bladen's daughter Anne, said Mrs. Anne Tasker giving her consent thereto (Test. Proc., Lib. 23, fol. 251). Mrs. Anne Bladen was summoned to appear before the Prerogative in the matter of her deceased husband's estate, and, not appearing, was attached. At the August Court 1719 "Mrs. Anne Bladen, relict of William Bladen, deceased," was ordered to be proclaimed by the Sheriff of Anne Arundel County, for not appearing, although attached (Test. Proc., Lib. 24, fol. 33). William Bladen and Anne (Van Swearingen), his wife, had issue :—

4.   i. COL. THOMAS BLADEN,[4] b. 1698; d. 1780; Governor of Maryland.
     ii. ANNE BLADEN, mar. 31 August 1711, Hon. Benjamin Tasker of Annapolis.

4. COL. THOMAS BLADEN,[4] son of William [3] and Anne (Van Swearingen his wife) was born in 1698 and died in 1780. He disposed of his Maryland property and went to England to live. 11 Oct., 1720, Thomas Bladen of the Parish of St. Anne's, Westminster, son and heir of William Bladen, late of the City of Annapolis, Md., deceased, conveys to Benjamin Tasker of the said city and Province, Gent., a tract called " Woolchurch Rest," in Anne Arundel County (A. A. Co. Rec., Lib. CW. no. 1, fol. 403). The records of Maryland contain numerous other deeds executed by him. Col. Bladen was Governor of Maryland from 1742 to 1747, and was later member of Parliament for Old Sarum. He married Barbara, eldest daughter of Sir Theodore Janssen, Bart., and sister of Mary Lady Baltimore. They had issue :—

    i. HARRIOT BLADEN,[5] d. 1821; mar., March 1767, William Anne, 4th Earl of Essex; left issue.
    ii. BARBARA BLADEN, mar., 3 August 1773, General St. John.

BLADEN FAMILY.

In an account of the Bladen family, published in the *Magazine*, v, 297 ff., it is stated that Nathaniel Bladen of Hemsworth, Yorkshire, father of William Bladen of Maryland, was the son of Rev. Doctor Bladen and Sarah his wife, daughter of Henry Second Baron Blayney. This, however, though supported by the authority of Blore's *Rutland* (p. 180), is erroneous, as pointed out by Mr. Richard H. Spencer, who also presents some very convincing evidence in regard to the true pedigree. The license for the marriage of Rev. Thomas Bladen, Dean of Ardsere in Ireland, Bachelor, aged above 50 years, and Hon. Sarah Blayney of St. Martin's-in-the-Fields, Middlesex, Spinster (d. 1722) aged above 30, and at her own disposal, was issued 28 July 1691 (Harl. Soc., xxxi, 1888), and since William Bladen was born in 1673, it is evident that he could not have been the son of this marriage, much less the grand-son, and the pedigree must be sought in some other quarter. In my former paper on the Bladen family, cited above, I have stated that, according to Foster's *Visitations of Yorkshire* (p. 330), Robert Bladen, of Hemsworth, married Elizabeth daughter of John Lacy of Cromwellbotham, and Alice his wife, daughter of Martin Birkhead, Queen's Attorney in the North, 1585, and had a son John Bladen; living in 1632. The latter is clearly identical with John Bladen, son and heir of Robert Bladen of Hemsworth, Yorkshire, Gent., who was admitted to Gray's Inn, London, 6 March 1624/5 (Foster's *Admissions to Gray's Inn,* p. 175). In the Fairfax correspondence, edited by George W. Johnson, London, 1848, there are a member of letters written by John Bladen in 1631 to the "Right Honorable, My Very Good Lord, the Lord Fairfax, at Denton," and in one of these letters Bladen mentions his "uncle Birkhead." But John Bladen, also married a Birkhead, probably a more or less distant cousin. The will of Nathaniel Birkhead of East Heage, Parish of South Kirkby, Yorkshire, Esq., is dated 12 Feb'y 1649, and was proved 24 April 1650 (Yorkshire Arch. Assoc., ix, 10-11). In it, he bequeaths "to my grandchild Nathaniel Bladen son of John Bladen deceased, all those my manors of Harden and

Haworth, and lands in Wakefield." It may be well to note here that Nathaniel Bladen was evidently named for his maternal grandfather, Nathaniel Birkhead, and the name of Nathaniel's son, Martin Bladen, doubtless descended to him from his ancestor, Martin Birkhead. The pedigree must therefore run as follows (see Foster's *Visitations of Yorkshire*, p. 330):

1. JOHN LACY [1] mar. Ann daughter of Sir Richard Tempest and had a son:
2. RICHARD LACY [2] mar. Alice Townley. Their son was
3. JOHN LACY.[3] He married Alice, daughter to Martin Birkhead, the "Queen's Majestie's Attorney in the North, 1585," and had, with perhaps other issue, a daughter
4. ELIZABETH LACY,[4] wife of Robert Bladen of Hemsworth, Yorkshire, living in 1625. Their son
5. JOHN BLADEN [5] was admitted to Gray's Inn, London, 6 March 1624/5. He was living in 1632, and died before 1649. He married a daughter of Nathaniel Birkhead of East Heage and had, with perhaps other issue, a son:
6. NATHANIEL BLADEN,[6] named for his grandfather Nathaniel Birkhead. He married Isabella, daughter of Sir William Fairfax of Steeton, Yorkshire, son of Sir Philip Fairfax and Frances his wife, daughter of Edmund Sheffield, Earl of Mulgrave. They had issue:

   i. WILLIAM BLADEN, b. 27 Feb'y 1673; buried 9 August 1718 at Annapolis, Md.
   ii. MARTIN BLADEN, b. 1680; d. 15 Feb'y 1745/6.
   iii. ISABELLA BLADEN.
   iv. CATHERINE BLADEN.
   v. FRANCES BLADEN, mar. William Hammond, Esq.
   vi. ELIZABETH BLADEN, mar. Edward Hawke, Esq.

It is only fair to state that the credit for these interesting discoveries belongs altogether to Mr. Richard H. Spencer, who called my attention to the matter and furnished me with the memoranda some time since. This note is based, in large measure, on Mr. Spencer's memoranda.

CHRISTOPHER JOHNSTON.

BLAKISTONE FAMILY.

CHRISTOPHER JOHNSTON.

The Blakistone family of Maryland descends from the Blakistons of Newton Hall, a branch of the ancient family of Blakiston of Blakiston in the Palatinate of Durham. An elaborate pedigree, published in Surtees' *History of Durham* (iii, 162 ff., 402), carries the line back to the year 1341, and from this pedigree the earlier portion of the following genealogy is derived. The arms and crest, as given by the same authority, are as follows :—

Arms. Arg., two bars, and in chief three dunghill cocks, gu.
Crest. A dunghill cock or, crested, armed, wattled, and collared, gu.

The immediate ancestor of the Maryland family was

1. REV. MARMADUKE BLAKISTON [1] of Newton Hall, fifth son of John Blakiston of Blakiston by his first wife Elizabeth, daughter and coheir of Sir George Bowes of Dalden and Streatham, Knt. He was Vicar of Woodborne, Rector of Redmarshall in 1585, Rector of Sedgefield in 1599, and Prebendary of Durham, and was buried at St. Margaret's, Crossgate, 3 Sept. 1639. He married, at St. Mary-le-Bow, 30 June 1595, Margaret James, and she was buried at St. Margaret's, 10 March 1636. Rev. Marmaduke Blakiston and Margaret (James) his wife had issue as follows :—

    i. TOBYE BLAKISTON,[2] of Newton Hall, eldest son. His will, dated 24 April 1642, was proved by his brother John, 24 Dec. 1646. Mar. Frances younger dau. and coh. of Francis Briggs of Old Malton, Co. York.

2. ii. JOHN BLAKISTON, bapt. 21 Aug. 1603.

   iii. REV. THOMAS BLAKISTON, A. M., Vicar of North Allerton, 1628, Prebendary of Wistow; ejected during the Civil wars 1640/1; mar. and had issue.

   iv. REV. ROBERT BLAKISTON, bapt. 7 Jany. 1607; Rector of Sedgefield and Prebendary of Durham on the resignation of his father in 1631; mar. Elizabeth dau. of John Howson, Bishop of Durham; d. s. p. and was buried, 19 Jan. 1634/5, in Durham Abbey.

   v. REV. RALPH BLAKISTON, A. M., bapt. 24 June 1608; Rector of Ryton, Co. Pal.; d. unmar. and was buried at Ryton 30 Jan. 1676/7.

   vi. HENRY BLAKISTON of Old Malton, Co. York; d. 1666; mar. Mary dau. of Wm. Mauleverer of Arncliffe, Co. York: issue three daughters.

vii. PETER BLAKISTON, bapt. 23 Oct. 1614 ; sometime of Old Malton ;
    mar. Elizabeth dau. of George Mauleverer, Esq.
3. viii. GEORGE BLAKISTON.
   ix. FRANCES BLAKISTON, bapt. 2 Feb. 1605/6 ; mar., 13 Aug. 1626,
    John Cosin, Lord Bishop of Durham.
    x. MARY BLAKISTON, bapt. 30 June 1613 ; mar. at Brancepath, 9
    Sept. 1629, Ralph Allenson, merchant in Durham.
   xi. MARGARET BLAKISTON, mar. 28 Nov. 1631, Thomas Shadforth of
    Eppleton, Co. Pal., Esq.

2. JOHN BLAKISTON [2] (*Marmaduke* [1]) was baptized 21 Aug.
1603 and was married at All Saints, Newcastle, 9 Nov.
1626, to Susan Chambers. He was Member of Parliament
for Newcastle in 1641, was Mayor of Newcastle in 1645,
and was one of the judges who pronounced sentence of death
on King Charles I, in 1649. A sketch of his life is to be
found in the *Dictionary of National Biography*. He died in
1650. The following is an abstract of his will, dated 1 June
1649, and proved at London by his widow, 24 March 1650.
John Blakiston of Newton in the County Palatine of Durham ;
wife Susanna and son Mr. John Blakiston executors ; son
Neamiah Blakiston ; daughter Rebecca wife of Mr. James
Lance and her two children ; Mr. Lawson father-in-law of
my brother George Blakiston ; and whereas testator's said
brother George Blakiston has suffered greatly with him, the
testator, in public concerns, he gives to the six children of
the said George, viz : Robert, Sarah, John, Esther, Hannah,
and Justice, £50 each ; Cousin Mr. Robert Young's wife and
children❜ Cousin Margaret Lyons (Surtees' *Durham*, iii, 402),
Mrs. Susan Blakiston survived her husband, and in 1661
her effects were seized by the Sheriff of Durham as the widow
of a regicide.
    John Blakiston and Susan (Chambers) his wife had issue :—

   i. JOHN BLAKISTON,[3] bapt. 6 Jan. 1630 ; buried 13 April 1632.
4. ii. JOHN BLAKISTON, bapt. 18 April 1633.
  iii. JOSEPH BLAKISTON, bapt. 22 Oct. 1635 ; buried 28 Aug. 1637.
5. iv. NEHEMIAH BLAKISTON, named in his father's will, 1649.
   v. REBECCA BLAKISTON, bapt. 29 Aug. 1627 ; wife of James Lance in
    1649.
  vi. ELIZABETH BLAKISTON, bapt. 29 Sept. 1629 ; buried 30 Nov. 1629.

3. GEORGE BLAKISTON [2] (*Marmaduke* [1]) was Sheriff of Durham
in 1656 (Surtees' *Durham*, iii, 402-403). He is stated in
his brother's will to have " suffered much in public concerns,"
and it was probably for this reason, as well as on account of
his relationship to the Regicide, that he emigrated to Maryland with his family in 1668. He settled in St. Mary's

County and died the following year. 30 Sept. 1669, administration on the estate of George Blakiston, late of St. Mary's County deceased, was committed to "his son John Blakiston" who gave bond in 20,000 lb. Tobacco (Test. Proc., Lib. 3, fol. 272). The inventory of his estate, appraised by Luke Gardiner and Richard Foster, was filed 12 October following (*ibid.* fol. 273). George Blakiston married Barbara daughter of Henry Lawson of Newcastle (Surtees' *Durham*, iii, 163) and had issue :

i. ROBERT BLAKISTON,[3] bapt. 19 Sept. 1639 ; came to Md. 1668.
ii. JOSEPH BLAKISTON, buried 14 Oct. 1646.
iii. SAMUEL BLAKISTON, buried 8 Oct. 1647.
6. iv. JOHN BLAKISTON, died 1679.
v. SARAH BLAKISTON.
vi. ESTHER BLAKISTON.
vii. HANNAH BLAKISTON, came to Md. 1668.
viii. JUSTICE BLAKISTON, came to Md. 1668.
7. ix. EBENEZER BLAKISTON, b. 1650 ; d. 1709.

4. JOHN BLAKISTON[3] (*John,*[2] *Marmaduke*[1]), was baptised 18 April 1633. He was admitted to Gray's Inn 20 March 1649, and was a barrister-at-law. He lived at Newcastle-on-Tyne and was buried there, 12 March 1701/2. He left a will dated 16 Dec. 1701. John Blakiston married Phoebe daughter of William Johnston of Kiblesworth, Esq., sister of Sir Nathaniel Johnston, Bart., and had issue :—

i. WILLIAM BLAKISTON,[4] bapt. 14 Aug. 1665 ; buried 17 Sept. 1665.
8. ii. NATHANIEL BLAKISTON, Governor of Maryland.
iii. ROBERT BLAKISTON, bapt. 3 Aug. 1673 ; living 1681, but dead in 1701.
iv. JANE BLAKISTON, bapt. 4 Jan. 1668 ; buried 30 May 1671.
v. SARAH BLAKISTON, bapt. 12 April 1678 ; buried 26 Jan. 1680.
vi. MARGARET BLAKISTON, living 1701, wife of Maj. Edward Nott of Kingston in Surrey, Deputy Governor of Virginia (*Va. Mag.* XIV, 302).

5. COL. NEHEMIAH BLAKISTON[3] (*John,*[2] *Marmaduke*[1]), is named in his father's will, 1649. The exact date of his arrival in Maryland is not recorded, but he probably came with his uncle George Blakiston and his family in 1668, though he did not enter his rights for land until some years later. 17 Oct. 1674, "came Nehemiah Blakiston of St. Mary's County and proved his right to 300 acres of land for transporting himself, John Focbliss, John Snowden, John Slocer, Edward Smiley, and Mary Gibbons" (Land Office, Lib. 18, fol. 126). That this was not the date of his arrival is evident from the fact that his marriage took place in May

1669. At March Term 1678/9, he brought an action for false arrest against one Edward Husbands in the Provincial Court of Maryland. In his plea he sets forth the excellent reputation he had always enjoyed in the Province and mentions several particular circumstances. On the 6 of May 1669, he states, he married Elizabeth daughter of Thomas Gerard, Esq., with the consent of her said father who, in consideration thereof, settled upon him and his heirs lands and tenements in St. Mary's County of great value. The said Nehemiah Blakiston was moreover one of the attornies of the Provincial Court and of the Courts of St. Mary's and Charles Counties (Prov. Court, Lib. NN., fol. 784 ff). The father-in-law of Nehemiah Blakiston was Thomas Gerard of St. Clement's Manor, who was for a number of years a member of the Council of Maryland, but later removed to Westmoreland County, Virginia, and died there in 1673. The patent on the resurvey of St. Clement's Manor, 29 June 1678, gives a list of the lands conveyed by Thomas Gerard, Esq., in his lifetime. Among these lands were two tracts, one called Longworth's Point, the other called Dare's Neck, containing respectively 300 and 100 acres, which were conveyed to Nehemiah Blakiston and Elizabeth, his wife. (Land Office, Lib. 20, fol. 16.) The records show that Nehemiah Blakiston was sworn one of the attornies of the Provincial Court, 27 March 1676 (Prov. Court, Lib. NN., fol. 308). In addition to the active practice of the legal profession, he filled the office of Clerk of the King's Customs for Wiccocomico and Potomac Rivers, by commission dated 26 Sept. 1685 (Md. Arch. v, 526). It would appear, however, from his letter to the Commissioners of Customs, dated 20 April 1685, complaining of interference with himself and other officers of the Crown, that he must have held an earlier commission (Md. Arch. v, 436–439). In the revolution of 1689, Nehemiah Blakiston played an important part, and for his good services at this time he received a vote of thanks from the Assembly, 4 Sept. 1689 (Md. Arch., xiii, 247). On the same date he was commissioned Captain of a troop of horse in the St. Mary's County militia (*ibid.*, p. 241). In a letter dated " Longworth Point 7[ber] the 17, 1690," he writes that he has been appointed President of the Committee for the Present Government of this Province (Md. Arch., viii, 206–207). 21 April 1691 he was appointed Chief Justice of the Provincial Court of Maryland (*ibid.*, 241–242), and in the same year was Speaker of the Assembly (*ibid.*, 250). On the 26 of August 1691 he was commissioned a member of the Council of Maryland (*ibid.*, 271) and, 8 April 1692, was recommissioned a Justice of the Provincial Court, Governor Copley being Chief Justice (*ibid.*, 307). His commission as Colonel was probably dated 9 April 1692, since it is recorded that on the 8 of April "Capt. Nehemiah Blakiston" attended a Council meeting, while on the following day and always thereafter his name appears as "Col. Nehemiah Blakiston" (Md. Arch., viii, 306–310. He was present at a meeting of the Council 25 August 1693 (*ibid.*, p. 555), and died not long afterwards. For on the 11th of Dec. 1693, his widow, Madame Elizabeth Blakiston is cited to administer on the estate of her late husband Col. Nehemiah Blakiston (Test. Proc., Lib. 15ᶜ, fol. 14). Mrs. Blakiston married secondly, about 1696, Ralph Rymer, and thirdly Joshua Guibert of St. Mary's County, but appears to have had issue by her first husband only. Her will, dated 15 Dec. 1715, was proved 2 Oct. 1716. In it she bequeaths Longworth's Point to her son, John Blakiston, and names her daughters Susanna Attaway, Rebecca Walters, Mary Mason and Ann Blakiston —the latter being the wife of her son John—and her grandchildren, Nehemiah and Elizabeth Blakiston.

Col. Nehemiah Blackiston and Elizabeth (Gerard) his wife had issue :—

9. i. JOHN BLAKISTON,[4] d. 1724.
   ii. SUSANNA BLAKISTON, mar. 1° Thomas Hatton (d. Aug. 1701) grandson of Secretary Thomas Hatton slain at the battle of St. Mary's, 1665, 2° John Attaway.
  iii. REBECCA BLAKISTON, mar. . . . . . Walters.
  iv. MARY BLAKISTON, mar. Matthew Mason (b. 1689 ; d. 1729).

6. JOHN BLAKISTON [3] (*George* [2] *Marmaduke* [1]) came to Maryland in 1668 with his father and other members of his family. 27 December 1670, "John Blackstone" of St. Mary's County proved rights for the transportation of the following persons in 1668, viz: — himself, Sarah, George, Barbara, Robert, Hannah, and Justice Blackiston, and others (Land Office, Lib. 16, fol. 70). A comparison with the will, cited above, of John Blakiston the regicide judge leaves small doubt as to the identity of these persons. Sarah was doubtless John Blakiston's wife, and George and Barbara were his parents. It has been shown above that he administered in the estate of his father George Blakiston in 1669. Robert Blakiston does

not subsequently appear in the records, and probably died soon after his arrival. 18 March 1668/9, John Blakiston purchased from Richard Foster Sen., of St. Mary's County, 100 acres in St. Clement's Manor "now in the possession of John Tennison" (Prov. Court, Lib. FF., fol. 784). 9 April 1675, John Blakiston of St. Mary's County proved his right to 150 acres of land for the transportation of John Waterhouse, Richard Selby, and Charles Hayes (Land Office, Lib. 18, fol. 279). The records do not show that any warrant or patent issued to John Blakiston, and he doubtless assigned the rights entered by him. 18 January 1670/1, John and Ebenezer Blakiston witnessed the will of Robert Slye of Bushwood, St. Mary's County (Baldwin's *Calendar* i, 59), whose wife Susanna was a daughter of Thomas Gerard and sister of Elizabeth wife of Col. Nehemiah Blakiston. Between 1675 and 1678 John Blakiston removed to Kent County. 24 Sept. 1678, Ebenezer Blakiston of Cecil Co., Gent., and Elizabeth his wife, conveyed to "his brother" John Blakiston of Kent Co. and Sarah his wife, a tract of 300 acres called Boxley near Swan Creek in Kent County (Kent Co., Lib. A, fol. 441). This tract was purchased by Ebenezer Blakiston, 25 Aug. 1674, from Lawrence Symonds and William Davis of Kent County (*ibid.* fol. 318). John Blakiston died in 1679, and his wife Sarah in 1683 as is shown by the following extract from the Testamentary Proceedings. 3 April 1683 "Came Eben. Blakiston of Cecil Co. & showed that Jn°. Blakiston his brother late of Kent County dyed intestate in y° year 1679, that Sarah his widow did not adm. upon his estate & is since alsoe dec. giving by word & leaving when shee dyed what belonged to y° orphan of y° said dec. to other persons & therefore the s. Ebenezer prayed that hee may adm. on y° s. Sarah her estate that hee may secure y° estate to y° s. orphan to whom in R. it belongeth which was granted." (Test. Proc., Lib. 13, fol. 23).

John Blakiston and Sarah his wife had issue one son :—

10.   i. JOHN BLAKISTON,[4] b. 1669 ; d. Dec. 1733.

7. CAPT. EBENEZER BLAKISTON[3] (*George*[2] *Marmaduke*[1]) of Cecil, and later of Kent, County, appears to have been the youngest son of his parents. Both in the deed conveying Boxley and in his application for administration on Sarah Blakiston's estate he calls himself the brother of John Blakiston, and the fact that John and Ebenezer witnessed together

the will of Robert Slye is strong evidence of their identity.
Ebenezer is not named among the children of George and
Barbara Blakiston in the will of his uncle John the regicide
judge, dated 1 June 1649, but at that time he was not born.
In a deposition before the Maryland Council in 1697, "Capt.
Ebenezer Blakiston" of Cecil County gives his age as 47
years (Md. Arch. xxiii. 177), so that he was born in 1650,
the year following the date of his uncle's will.   Whether he
came to Maryland with his parents in 1668 or arrived somewhat later is uncertain.   In any case he was in St. Mary's
County in January 1670/1 when he witnessed the will of
Robert Slye, and soon after removed to the Eastern Shore.
17 October 1671, "Ebenezer Blakiston" of Baltimore
County proved his right to 50 acres of land for transporting
himself into the Province (Land Office, Lib. 16, fol. 341).
At this time Baltimore County extended around the head of
the Bay to the Eastern Shore, and included territory included
in Cecil County, erected in 1674.   17 October 1681, by
virtue of several assignments, Ebenezer Blakiston obtained a
certificate for a tract of 500 acres called St. Taunton's (Land
Office, Lib. 21, fol. 347).   4 Sept. 1689, he was commissioned Captain of a foot company in "Worten and South
Sassafras" Hundred, Cecil County (Md. Arch. xiii, 244),
and he was one of the Justices of the County in 1697-98,
and 1702 (Md. Arch. xxiii, 129, 401; xxv, 125).   According to the register of St. Paul's Parish, Kent County, he
was buried 25 October 1709.   He died intestate, but the
following extracts show that he had at least two sons.
8 Dec. 1709, Inventory of Mr. Ebenezer Blakiston, late
of Kent Co. deceased, appraised by Wm. Ringgold and
Edward Scott, and approved by Nathaniel Hynson (Annapolis, Inv. & Acc'ts, Lib. 31, fol. 193).   14 Dec. 1710,
additional inventory of Capt. Ebenezer Blakistone by Wm.
Blakistone his executor (sic !)—contains an item of "2588 lb.
Tobacco made on my father's plantation" (Kent Co. Invs.,
Lib. 1. fol. 71-72).   26 May 1711, additional account of
Wm. Blakiston administrator of Capt. Ebenezer Blakiston
late of Kent Co. deceased—contains an item of a silver cup
appraised to the estate but belonging to Ebenezer Blakiston
son of the deceased (Annapolis Inv. & Acc'ts, Lib. 32ᴮ, fol.
242).   The wife of Ebenezer Blakiston was Elizabeth sister
of John James, and they also had a daughter, Anna Blakiston,
named in the will of her maternal grandmother Mrs. Anna

Tolson (Baldwin's *Calendar*, i, 34, 188, 213 ; Test. Proc.,
Lib. 10, fol. 185).

    Capt. Ebenezer Blakiston and Elizabeth (James) his wife
had issue :—

11. i. EBENEZER BLAKISTON,[4] b. 1684/85 ; d. about 1746.
12. ii. WILLIAM BLAKISTON, d. 1737.
     iii. ANNA BLAKISTON.

8. NATHANIEL BLAKISTON,[4] (*John*,[3] *John*,[2] *Marmaduke*[1]) was
made free of the Merchant Adventurers' Company of London
in 1698 (Surtee's *Durham*, iii, 402). When Gov. Francis
Nicholson was transferred to Virginia, in October 1698,
Nathaniel Blakiston was appointed his successor and took the
oath of office as Governor of Maryland 2 January 1698/9
(Md. Arch., xxv, 51). His administration was highly acceptable to the Province, but some two years later, on
account of ill health, he tendered his resignation which
was accepted in June 1701 (Md. Arch., xxiv, 219), though
he remained in office until his departure for England in
July 1702 (Md. Arch., xxv., 121, 125). For some time
thereafter he acted as Agent for the Province in England
(Md. Arch., xxiv, 227, 364, 400). A number of his
letters, written between 1710 and 1714, are published in
the *Virginia Magazine of History and Biography* (iv, 15–23),
and show that he continued to interest himself in colonial
affairs. In one of them his daughter Rachel is mentioned
(*ibid.*, p. 17). A letter of James Blair, dated 6 Jan. 1704/5,
mentions Gov. Blakiston's brother-in-law, "Major Nott,
deputy Governor of Berwick, who married Blakiston's sister"
(*Va. Mag.*, v, 53). An abstract of Maj. Nott's will is given
in the *Virginia Magazine* for January, 1907 (xiv, 302–303).
The name of Gov. Blakiston's wife is unknown, but he had
at least two children (Surtees' *Durham*, iii, 402) :—

    i. NATHANIEL BLAKISTON.[5]
    ii. RACHEL BLAKISTON.

9. JOHN BLAKISTON[4] (*Nehemiah*,[3] *John*,[2] *Marmaduke*[1]) inherited
Longworth's Point, which, by the terms of his mother's will,
was entailed upon him and his heirs male "being Protestants." He also appears to have inherited land from his
father. In September, 1720, an action of ejectment was
brought by Thomas Bolt, lessee of Thomas Shanks, against
John Blakistone of St. Mary's County, Gent., for a parcel

of land in St. Clement's Manor, called Little Hackley, containing 300 acres. It was in evidence that John Shanks, grand-father of the plaintiff's lessor, devised said land by his will (dated 17 June 1683; proved 16 Feb. 1684) to his son John Shanks, who conveyed it, 2 March 1690, to Nehemiah Blakiston, father of the defendant, of which said Nehemiah the defendant is heir-at-law. The question at issue was as to whether the devise in the will of John Shanks constituted an estate tail, and a verdict was rendered for the plaintiff (Prov. Court, Lib. W. G., No. 1, fol. 299 ff.). John Blakiston married Anne Guibert, daughter of his step-father, Joshua Guibert who names in his will (dated 26 March, proved 16 May, 1713) his daughter Anne Blakistone and her husband John Blakistone. He died intestate in 1724, before the 4th of November on which date his widow Anne Blakistone gave bond for the administration of his estate in the sum of £600, her brothers Joshua and Thomas Guibert being her sureties (Test. Proc., Lib. 27, fol. 111).

John Blakistone and Anne (Guibert) his wife had issue :—

    i. NEHEMIAH BLAKISTONE,[5] mentioned in his grandmother's will; apparently died young.

13. ii. JOHN BLAKISTONE, d. 18 Jan. 1756; mar. Eleanor, dau. of Col. George Dent.

14. iii. THOMAS BLAKISTONE, d. s. p., Nov. 1742.

    iv. ELIZABETH BLAKISTONE, mentioned in her grandmother's will; mar. Roswell Neale (b. 1685; d. 1751) of St. Mary's Co.

    v. SUSANNA BLAKISTONE, mar. Robert Mason of St. Mary's Co.

10. JOHN BLAKISTON [4] (*John,*[3] *George,*[2] *Marmaduke*[1]) was born in 1669 and died in December 1733. In a deposition, made in 1726, he gives his age as 57 years and states that he has lived about 50 years "in these parts" (Kent Co., Lib. I. S., No. 10, fol. 44). He would therefore appear to have been born in St. Mary's County and to have been brought to Kent County by his father on the latter's removal thither about 1676. In 1699 he was one of a jury to value two acres of land adjoining the parish Church of St. Paul's, on the north side of Chester River and, in 1720, he and Ebenezer Blakiston occupied pew No. 25 in the parish church (*Old Kent,* pp. 347, 353). He inherited Boxley from his father, is recorded as possessing it in the Rent Roll of 1707, and devised it to his children in his will. John Blakiston died in December 1733. His will, dated 2 Dec. 1733, was proved 2 January following. In it he bequeaths his whole real and personal estate to his wife Hannah during widowhood; to his sons

Vincent and Ebenezer, "my now dwelling plantation," containing 100 acres, equally between them; to his son Prideaux Blakiston, the plantation whereon said son now dwells; to his three sons Thomas, William, and Michael, 150 acres part of Boxley; to his son John, with remainder to the testator's son Benjamin, 50 acres called Tolley's Chance; to his two daughters Mary Covington and Sarah Blakiston, two seats in St. Paul's Church, with 2000 lb. Tobacco to Sarah at her mother's decease. 2 January 1733/4, Hannah Blakiston, widow of the deceased, declares that she abides by the will.

John Blakiston and Hannah his wife had issue (order of birth uncertain):—

	i.	JOHN BLAKISTON,[5] died interstate, and without issue, about 1720.
14.	ii.	PRIDEAUX BLAKISTON, b. 1696.
15.	iii.	THOMAS BLAKISTON, bapt. 4 May 1701; d. 1753.
16.	iv.	VINCENT BLAKISTON, bapt. 6 Feb. 1703/4; d. 1769.
17.	v.	EBENEZER BLAKISTON, d. 1777.
18.	vi.	WILLIAM BLAKISTON, d. 1758.
19.	vii.	MICHAEL BLAKISTON, bapt. 2 Dec. 1711; d. 1758.
20.	viii.	BENJAMIN BLAKISTON, d. 1760. —
	ix.	MARY BLAKISTON, mar. . . . . . Covington.
	x.	SARAH BLAKISTON.

N. B. The above dates of baptism are from the register of St. Paul's Parish, Kent Co.

11. MAJ. EBENEZER BLAKISTON [4] (*Ebenezer,*[3] *George,*[2] *Marmaduke*[1]) was born in 1684 or 1685. His age is given in depositions as 41 in 1746 and 61 in 1745. He represented Kent County in the Maryland Assembly 1724, 1727-1734 (House Journals), and was a Justice of the County 1733-1744 (Commission Book). In the Journal of Assembly for 1724 he is styled "Captain," and in a deposition made in 1745 he is styled "Major" (Kent Co. Lib., IS. No. 25, fol. 327). He was undoubtedly the eldest son of his father. 28 Feb. 1721, Ebenezer Blakiston of Kent Co., with Sarah his wife, conveys to William Blakiston of said County, all his right, title, &c. to a tract of 100 acres called St. Taunton's (Kent Co., Lib. IS. No. 10, fol. 218). 20 Jan. 1714/5, Ebenezer Blakiston of Kent Co., with Sarah his wife, quit claims to Hans, George, and Frederick Hanson, a tract of 500 acres in Kent Co. called Tolchester and Tombe, formerly sold by Capt. Ebenezer Blakiston deceased, father of the grantor, to Col. Hans Hanson, father of the grantees (*ibid.* Lib. BC. No. 1, fol. 43). Maj. Blakiston married Sarah daughter of Thomas Joce of Kent County. Her father names

his "daughter Sarah Blakiston" in his will (proved 11 Feb. 1712), and the will of her brother Nicholas Joce (proved 3 May 1734), appoints his "brother Ebenezer Blakiston" his executor. Maj. Blakiston died intestate between 1745 and 1748, and his widow Sarah married John Garrett. The account of John Garrett and Sarah his wife, administratrix of Ebenezer Blakiston late of Kent Co. deceased, rendered 23 July 1748, states that Rosamond, wife of William Wilmer, is the daughter and sole representative of the deceased. (Annapolis, Accounts, Lib. 27, fol. 171).

Maj. Ebenezer Blakiston and Sarah (Joce) his wife had issue :—

    i. ROSAMOND BLAKISTON[5] b. 1722, sole dau. and heir, mar. William Wilmer of Kent Co. See *Old Kent*, p. 326.

12. WILLIAM BLAKISTON[4] (*Ebenezer,*[3] *George,*[2] *Marmaduke*[1]) administered on his father's estate in 1709. He represented Kent County in the Maryland Assembly 1722-1724 (House Journals), and died in 1737. His will, dated 16 March 1736/7, was proved 10 May 1737. In it he names his wife Ann ; his daughters Ann Miller, and Mary, Hannah, and Rose Blakiston ; his sons Ebenezer and William Blakiston ; the child whereof his wife is pregnant ; and his grandson Arthur Miller. Testator's four youngest children are minors. His wife Ann Blakiston is appointed executrix. 10 May 1737, Ann Blakiston, widow of the testator, elects to abide by the will.

William Blakiston and Ann his wife had issue :—

    i. EBENEZER BLAKISTON,[5] a minor in 1737.
    ii. WALTER BLAKISTON, a minor in 1737.
    iii. MARY BLAKISTON, b. 9 Marr 1711/2 (St. Paul's Register).
    iv. ANN BLAKISTON, mar. Arthur Miller (d. 1739) and had a son, Arthur Miller.[6]
    v. HANNAH BLAKISTON.
    vi. ROSE BLAKISTON, a minor in 1737.
    vii. . . . . . BLAKISTON, (?), unborn at date of will.

BLAKISTONE FAMILY.

CHRISTOPHER JOHNSTON.

---

13. JOHN BLAKISTONE [5] (*John,*[4] *Nehemiah,*[3] *John,*[2] *Marmaduke*[1]) inherited Longworth's Point and other property from his father. The Rent Roll for St. Mary's County records that, in 1754, he held two tracts of 450 acres and 100 acres respectively in St. Clement's Manor, and this land certainly included Longworth's Point which was subsequently devised by the will of his son Nehemiah Herbert Blakistone. John Blakistone died 18 Jan. 1756, having four days previously made a nuncupative will proved on the day of his death by the oaths of John Coode, John Mason, and Cyrus Simpson. In this will he names his sons Nehemiah Herbert (eldest), George, and John Blakistone; his wife Eleanor Blakistone; and his sister Susanna Mason (Annapolis, Lib. 30, fol. 45). He married Eleanor daughter of Col. George Dent of Charles County. She married, secondly, Alexander McFarlane of St. Mary's Co. (d. 1766), and thirdly, ... Bayard. John Blakistone and Eleanor (Dent) his wife had issue :—

21.   i. NEHEMIAH HERBERT BLAKISTONE,[6] d. 1816.
    ii. GEORGE BLAKISTONE, d. s. p., 1774. His will, dated 13 Jan., proved 30 April, 1774, mentions his mother and his two brothers.
    iii. JOHN BLAKISTONE, d. 1802, leaving by will (dated 21 April, 1791, proved 19 Feb. 1802) his whole estate to his wife Mary.

14ª. THOMAS BLAKISTONE [5] (*John,*[4] *Nehemiah,*[3] *John,*[2] *Marmaduke*[1]) died, apparently unmarried, in November, 1742. His will, dated 10 Nov., proved 8 Dec. 1742 (Annapolis, Lib. 23, fol. 15) mentions his sister Elizabeth Neale; Matthew Mason's three children, Matthew, Nehemiah Rodham, and Dorcas Mason; his sister Susanna Mason and "the child she is big with"; James, Bennett, and Raphael Neale, sons of Roswell Neale; and "my three brothers, John Blakistone, Roswell Neale, and Robert Mason." Testator's brother John Blakistone is constituted executor.

14. PRIDEAUX BLAKISTON [5] (*John,*[4] *John,*[3] *George,*[2] *Marmaduke*[1]) was born in 1696, and gives his age as 39 years in

a deposition made in 1735 (Kent Co. Records). 6 August 1720 he rendered an account as administrator of the estate of his brother John Blakiston, Jun. (Accounts, Lib. 3, fol. 62), his name being erroneously written in the record " Prederick " instead of Prideaux. He married, 27 July 1729 (St. Paul's, Kent Co.), Martha, widow of William Dunn and daughter of Michael Miller, and with his wife rendered an account of her former husband, William Dunn's estate in 1732 (Accounts, Lib. 11, fol. 596). Prideaux Blakiston had a son of the same name, as appears by a deed, dated 25 Jan. 1775, whereby Prideaux Blakiston of Kent County conveys to John Page of the same county, 44 acres, part of Boxley, " devised by my grandfather, John Blakiston to my father, Prideaux Blakiston " (Kent Co., Lib. DD., No. 5, fol. 17).

15. THOMAS BLAKISTON [5] (*John*,[4] *John*,[3] *George*,[2] *Marmaduke*[1]) was baptized 4 May 1701 (St. Paul's, Kent Co). In the entry of his baptism he is called the son of *Thomas* and Hannah—an obvious clerical error. He sold his share of Boxley to his brother Michael. 4 April 1741, Thomas Blakiston and Margaret, his wife, convey to Michael Blakiston, 50 acres, part of Boxley (Kent Co., Lib. IS., No. 23, fol. 240). Thomas Blakiston married Margaret, daughter of Col. Nathaniel Hynson. 26 August 1728, Joseph Young of Kent County and Mary, his wife, convey to Margaret Blakiston (formerly Margaret Hynson) wife of Thomas Blakiston of the same County, and daughter to the said Mary Young, the grantor, 100 acres, part of the tract Partnership, bequeathed to the said Mary by Col. Nathaniel Hynson, late of Kent County, deceased (Kent Co., Lib., IS., No. 10, fol. 277). In the will of Col. Nathaniel Hynson, dated 4 May 1721 and proved 16 Jan. 1721/2 (Kent Co., Lib. 1, fol. 213), this tract is devised to the testator's wife, Mary. The will of Thomas Blakiston, dated 17 April, proved 7 Sept., 1753 (Annapolis, Lib. 28, fol. 526), names the children given below. Thomas Blakiston and Margaret (Hynson), his wife, had issue :—

     i. ELIJAH BLAKISTON.[6]
     ii. THOMAS BLAKISTON.
     iii. JOHN BLAKISTON.
     iv. HANNAH BLAKISTON.
     v. MARY BLAKISTON.
     vi. REBECCA BLAKISTON.
     vii. LETTICE BLAKISTON.

16. VINCENT BLAKISTON [5] (*John*,[4] *John*,[3] *George*,[2] *Marmaduke*[1])
was baptized 6 Feb. 1703/4 (St. Paul's, Kent Co.) and died
in 1769. He was twice married. The register of St. Paul's
Parish records the births of three children of Vincent and
Mary Blakiston, while in his will he names his wife Susanna.
By his second marriage he seems to have had no issue. The
will of Vincent Blakiston of Kent County, dated 11 Nov.
1768, was proved 20 March 1769 (Annapolis, Lib. 37, fol.
561). He leaves his whole estate, real and personal, to his
wife, Susanna, during widowhood; negro boy Tom to my
wife's grand-daughter, Rebecca Miller; negro boy, Chester,
to James Blakiston, son of Ebenezer; bequest to my son-in-
law, Alexander Beck; the remainder of my land, being 50
acres, part of Boxley, to my said son-in-law, with remainder
to his children; if he has no child, then to the said James
Blakiston, son of Ebenezer; my wife executrix. Witnesses:
Thos. Ringgold, James Williamson, Richard Wickes. Vincent Blakiston and Mary, his first wife, had issue :—

   i. MARY BLAKISTON,[6] b. 10 Oct. 1731.
   ii. HANNAH BLAKISTON, b. April 17—.
   iii. PAGE BLAKISTON, b. 10 April 17—, d. s. p., 1762. His will (dated
      25 Jan., proved 1 Nov., 1762) leaves to Ralph Page all his right,
      title, etc., to tracts called Middle Branch and Hazard, and appoints
      him executor. Witnesses: Anne Blakistone, Sarah Blakistone,
      William Blakistone (Annapolis, Lib. 31, fol. 844).

17. EBENEZER BLAKISTON [5] (*John*,[4] *John*,[3] *George*,[2] *Marmaduke*[1]) sold his share of Boxley to his brother William.
29 July 1741, Ebenezer Blakiston, Jun. of Kent County,
with Mary, his wife, conveys to William Blakiston of same
County, 50 acres, part of Boxley, willed to the said Ebenezer
by his deceased father, John Blakiston, lying near Swan
Creek in Kent County (Kent Co., Lib. IS., No. 23, fol.
316). He died in 1777, intestate, 14 Nov. 1777, Mary
Blakiston of Kent Co., widow, gave bond in £1000 sterling,
as administratrix of Ebenezer Blakiston, late of said County,
deceased, her sureties being Thomas and Marmaduke Medford, both of Kent County (Kent Co. Admin. Bonds, Lib. 6,
fol. 32). Ebenezer Blakiston married, 14 April 1737, Mary
Maxwell (St. Paul's, Kent Co.), but as he left no will it is
difficult to trace his issue.

18. WILLIAM BLAKISTON [5] (*John*,[4] *John*,[3] *George*,[2] *Marmaduke*[1])
married 5 Feb. 1735/6 (St. Paul's register) Ann, daughter

of Jacob Glenn of Kent County, who mentions his daughter Ann Blakiston and her husband, William Blakiston in his will (dated 24 April, proved 1 Dec., 1746). She was born 4 Oct. 1714 (St. Paul's). William Blakiston held 50 acres of Boxley by the terms of his father's will, and he purchased 50 acres more from his brother, Ebenezer (see above). He held, therefore, 100 acres of this tract, and this he sold in 1742, to his brother Michael. 23 Nov. 1742, William Blakiston of Kent County and Ann, his wife, convey to Michael Blakiston of the same County, 100 acres, part of Boxley, near Swan Creek, in Kent County (Kent Co., Lib. IS., No. 24, fol. 71). Between this date and 1745 he removed to Kent County, Delaware. 12 Dec. 1745, John Hanmer of Kent Co., Md., conveys to William Blakiston of Kent Co., on Delaware, a tract of 200 acres on Longford's Bay, called New Key (Kent Co., Lib. IS., No. 25, fol. 352). He sold this land some two years later. 4 Sept. 1747, William Blakiston of Kent County, upon Delaware, and Ann, his wife, convey to John Ringgold of Kent County, Maryland, 200 acres, called New Key, purchased by the grantor from one John Hanmer, 12 Dec. 1745 (Kent Co., Lib. IS., No. 26, fol. 71). A closer approximation to the date of William Blakiston's removal to Delaware is given by a deed at Dover (Lib. N., fol. 2). 29 Aug. 1743, John Scott, late of Kent County, Delaware, but now of Orange County, Virginia, conveys to William Blakiston of Kent County, Delaware, part of a tract, called Chester, on Duck Creek. His wife Ann was living as late as 28 Feb. 1750, when she joined her husband in a deed (Dover, Lib. O., fol. 83). Between 26 Aug. 1755 and 12 May 1756 (Dover Records), William Blakiston married, as his second wife, Mary, widow of Thomas Williams and daughter of Thomas Courtney of Kent County, Delaware. He died in 1758, intestate and administration on his estate was committed to John Pleasanton, his widow, Mary having renounced her right to administer (Dover, Lib. K., fol. 180).

William Blakiston and Ann (Glenn) his wife had issue (with perhaps others):

    i. FRANCINA BLAKISTON,[6] b. 16 Jan. 1736/7 (St. Paul's, Kent Co.).
22. ii. PRESLEY BLAKISTON, b. 1 Jan. 1741 (Family Record).

19. MICHAEL BLAKISTON[5] (*John,*[4] *John,*[3] *George,*[2] *Marmaduke*[1]) was baptized at St. Paul's, 2 Dec. 1711; and he died in

1758. He married Ann Bradshaw, 8 Dec. 17—, the date being partly obliterated in St. Paul's register. His will dated 24 Oct. 1757 and proved 2 March 1758, names his wife, Ann, his sons, William, Michael, and John, and his daughter, Sarah, and provides that the residue of his personal estate is to be divided among "all my children" at majority, his sons to be of age at 21 and his daughters at 16 or marriage. The will of Ann Blakiston, widow of Michael, is dated 29 Sept. 1771 and was proved 7 Dec. following. She names her daughters, Sarah and Ann, her son, John, and her grand-children, Richard and Ann Blakiston, and leaves the residue of her estate "among all my children." The issue of Michael Blakiston and Ann (Bradshaw) his wife, as derived from their wills, and from the register of St. Paul's Parish, was as follows :—

    i. WILLIAM BLAKISTON,[6] d. s. p., 1763.
    ii. MICHAEL BLAKISTON, b. 24 Sept. 1738 ; mar. Rachel . . . . and had
        a) Richard,[7] b. 27 April 1768, b.) Ann,[7] b. 7 July 1769.
    iii. SARAH BLAKISTON, b. 22 July 1741.
    iv. JOHN BLAKISTON, b. 14 May 1743.
    v. JAMES BLAKISTON, b. 28 Nov. 1746.
    vi. GEORGE BLAKISTON, b. 2 Jan. 1748/9.
    vii. ANN BLAKISTON, b. 28 March 1750.
    viii. RICHARD BLAKISTON, b. 1 March 1757.

20. BENJAMIN BLAKISTON[5] (*John*,[4] *John*,[3] *George*,[2] *Marmaduke*[1]) died in 1760. His will, dated 3 May 1758 and proved 23 Dec. 1760, bequeaths a large landed estate lying in Kent and Queen Anne Counties, and mentions his wife, Sarah, his sons, John, William, and George (minor), his daughters, Sarah Comegys, Ann Spearman, and Priscilla Blakiston, and his grand-children, Benjamin, Richard, and Ebenezer Blakiston‘ sons of his son John. Testator's wife, Sarah and his son, William are appointed executors. The will of Mrs. Sarah Blakiston, widow of Benjamin (dated 8 Jan., proved 21 Jan. 1764) mentions her son, George Blakiston, her grand-daughter, Sarah Comegys, her grand-son, John Thormond, and her grand-daughter, Ann Worrell. The register of Shrewsbury Parish, Kent County, records the birth, 21 Sept. 1728, of Ebenezer, son of Benjamin and Sarah Blakiston ; he probably died before his parents. Benjamin Blakiston and Sarah, his wife, had issue :—

23.   i. JOHN BLAKISTON,[6] d. 1774.
    ii. EBENEZER BLAKISTON, b. 21 Sept. 1728.
24. iii. WILLIAM BLAKISTON, d. 1775.

25. iv. GEORGE BLAKISTON.
    v. SARAH BLAKISTON, mar. Bartus Comegys.
    vi. ANN BLAKISTON, mar. William Spearman.
    vii. PRISCILLA BLAKISTON, mar. Simon Worrell.

21. NEHEMIAH HERBERT BLAKISTONE[6] (*John,*[5] *John,*[4] *Nehemiah,*[3] *John,*[2] *Marmaduke*[1]) died in 1816. His will, dated 7 July 1814, was proved in St. Mary's County, 8 June 1816, and in it he devises to his children, Longworth's Point, which had descended to him from his great-grandfather, Col. Nehemiah Blakistone and Elizabeth Gerard, his wife. The records of King and Queen Parish, St. Mary's County, show that Nehemiah Herbert Blakistone was several times elected a vestryman of the parish. He married first, 30 Jan. 1772, Mary Cheseldine, daughter of Kenelm and Chloe Cheseldine (King and Queen register), and secondly, in August 1801, Eleanor Gardiner Hebb (St. Mary's Co. Mar. Lic.). By his first wife, Mary Cheseldine, he had issue (dates of birth from King and Queen register) :—

    i. THOMAS BLAKISTONE,[7] b. 10 April 1773.
    ii. ELEANOR BLAKISTONE, b. 14 Dec. 1774.
26. iii. KENELM BLAKISTONE, b. 24 Dec. 1776.
    iv. MARY BLAKISTONE, b. 6 Dec. 1778.
27. v. GEORGE BLAKISTONE, b. 28 Nov. 1780.
    vi. MARGARET BLAKISTONE, b. 1784; d. 20 Jan. 1846; mar. . . . . . Goldsmith.
    vii. DENT BLAKISTONE.

Nehemiah Herbert Blakistone and Eleanor Gardiner Hebb, his second wife, had issue :—

    i. HENRY HERBERT BLAKISTONE, mar. Dec. 1826, Ann E. Shanks.
    ii. JOHN BLAKISTONE, b. 1806; d. 14 Feb. 1863.
    iii. BERNARD BLAKISTONE, d. 1832; mar. Nov. 1831, Rebecca Jordan Allstone.
    iv. CAROLINE GARDINER BLAKISTONE, d. unmarried, 1817.
    v. JULIANA BLAKISTONE.
    vi. JANE MARIA BLAKISTONE, mar. Jan. 1831, Robert McK. Hammett.

22. PRESLEY BLAKISTON[6] (*William,*[5] *John,*[4] *John,*[3] *George,*[2] *Marmaduke*[1]) removed to Philadelphia as a young man and his descendants continue to reside in that city. He was married at Christ Church, Philadelphia, 12 Sept. 1765, to Sarah Warnock (b. 1746) and they had issue as follows :—

    i. ANN BLAKISTON,[7] b. 1 June 1766.
    ii. WILLIAM BLAKISTON, b. 21 July 1768.
    iii. ELIZABETH BLAKISTON, d. young.
    iv. JOHN BLAKISTON, b. 15 Nov. 1773; grandfather of Kenneth M. Blakiston, head of the publishing house, P. Blakiston's Son & Co.

v. SARAH BLAKISTON, b. 5 Aug. 1779.
vi. MARY BLAKISTON.
vii. REBECCA BLAKISTON, b. 1783.
viii. RACHEL OFFLEY BLAKISTON.
ix. ELIZABETH BLAKISTON.

23. JOHN BLAKISTON [6] (*Benjamin,*[5] *John,*[4] *John,*[3] *George,*[2] *Marmaduke*[1]) died in 1774. His will, dated 28 Nov. 1774, was proved 21 Dec. following. By Frances, his wife, he had issue :—

    i. BENJAMIN BLAKISTON,[7] d. 1785.
    ii. EBENEZER BLAKISTON.
    iii. JOHN BLAKISTON.
    iv. LEWIS BLAKISTON.
    v. RICHARD BLAKISTON, d. s. p. before 1774.

24. WILLIAM BLAKISTON [6] (*Benjamin,*[5] *John,*[4] *John,*[3] *George,*[2] *Marmaduke*[1]) died in 1775. His will, dated 3 April 1772, was proved 27 Jan. 1775. By Ann, his wife, he had issue :—

    i. BENJAMIN BLAKISTON,[7] d. 1801 ; married . . . . and had a) Ann Blakiston,[8] b) William Blakiston, c) James Blakiston.
    ii. SAMUEL BLAKISTON, d. 1796.
    iii. WILLIAM BLAKISTON.
    iv. ELIZABETH BLAKISTON.

25. GEORGE BLAKISTON [6] (*Benjamin,*[5] *John,*[4] *John,*[3] *George,*[2] *Marmaduke*[1]) died in 1778. His will, dated 9 Aug. 1778, and proved 1 Oct. following, is recorded at Dover, Delaware. By Martha, his wife, he had issue :—

    i. EBENEZER BLAKISTON.[7]
    ii. JOHN BLAKISTON.
    iii. FRANCES BLAKISTON.
    iv. SARAH BLAKISTON.
    v. PRISCILLA BLAKISTON.

26. KENELM BLAKISTONE [7] (*Nehemiah Herbert,*[6] *John,*[5] *John,*[4] *Nehemiah,*[3] *John,*[2] *Marmaduke*[1]) was born 24 Dec. 1776 and died in 1821. He married, 1°. Chloe Tarlton (license 6 Feb. 1800), 2°. Juliet Locke (license 22 April 1816). His will, dated, 12 Jan. (with codicil, 16 Jan.) 1821, was proved in St. Mary's County, 8 Feb. following.
Kenelm Blakistone had issue :—

    i. NATHANIEL BLAKISTONE,[8] mar., June 1822, Hopey Morgan.
    ii. STEPHEN BLAKISTONE.
    iii. FERDINAND BLAKISTONE.

27. GEORGE BLAKISTONE[7] (*Nehemiah Herbert*,[6] *John*,[5] *John*,[4] *Nehemiah*,[3] *John*,[2] *Marmaduke*[1]) was born 28 Nov. 1780, and his will, dated 7 Nov. 1842, was proved in St. Mary's County, 17 Jan. 1843. He married (license, 18 Jan. 1813) Rebecca Goldsmith and had issue :—

    i. JAMES THOMAS BLAKISTONE,[8] mar., Nov. 1840, Ann, daughter of Dr William Thomas of Cremona, St. Mary's Co., and Eliza, his wife, daughter of Henry and Mary (Sothoron) Tubman.
    ii. DR. RICHARD PINKNEY BLAKISTONE, mar. . . . .
    iii. GEORGE WELLINGTON BLAKISTONE, mar., 27 May 1845, Joanna Cheseldine.
    iv. LILIAS D. BLAKISTONE, mar., Jan. 1839, John F. Dent.
    v. ZACHARIAH DEMENEAU BLAKISTONE, mar., 10 Jan. 1860, Harriet Ann Shanks.
    vi. LUCINDA BLAKISTONE, mar., May 1854, J. R. W. Mankin.
    vii. ANN REBECCA BLAKISTONE, mar., Nov. 1856, Biscoe Cheseldine.
    viii. PRISCILLA HEBB BLAKISTONE, mar. . . . . Lancaster.

THE BLACKISTONE FAMILY OF MARYLAND:
EBENEZER BLAKISTON, 1705-1772

By FRANKLIN BLACKSTONE

An article on the Blackistone Family of Maryland appeared in the *Maryland Historical Magazine* for 1907 (Vol. II, pages 54-64 and 172-179). On page 174 is found the following:

" 17. EBENEZER BLAKISTON[5]: (John[4], John[3], George[2], Marmaduke[1].) sold his share of Boxley to his brother William 29 July, 1741 . . . 50 Acres, willed to said Ebenezer by his deceased father, John Blakiston . . . (Kent Co., Lib. IS., No. 23, fol. 316). He died in 1777, intestate, 14 Nov. 1777, Mary Blakiston, widow, gave bond in £1000 Sterling as Administratrix of Ebenezer Blakiston, late of said county, deceased, her sureties being Thomas and Marmaduke Medford (Kent Co. Admin. Bonds, Lib. 6, fol. 32). Ebenezer Blakiston married, 14 April, 1737, Mary Maxwell (St. Paul's, Kent Co.,) but as he left no will it is difficult to trace his issue."

Recent researches (1944-45) establish definitely that Ebenezer Blakiston died in April, 1772, as his will was probated 6 April, 1772 (Kent Co., Lib. Wills 5, f. 96). He appointed his wife "Hannahretta" as Executrix and named as his children, Stephen, Michael, James, Ebenezer and Joseph. Henrietta Blakiston filed her account on 22 December, 1772, and mentioned them. She was the *second* wife of said Ebenezer Blakiston, his first wife, as previously stated, having been Mary Maxwell, married 14 April, 1737, St. Paul's, Kent Co., Md. Date of her death is not known to the writer. Some years after the death of Ebenezer Blakiston, Hannahretta married Matthew Richardson, Sr., who joined with her in conveying 66 2/3 Acres of "Queen Charlton" to *her* son Joseph Blakiston (son of Ebenezer) born 16 February, 1760 (St. Paul's Parish records). The conveyance was recorded Kent Co., B. C. 4 folio 129, on 3d October, 1794. This property had been inherited by Hannahretta from her father Thomas Mahon (Mawhawn) (Will Book 2, folio 186, probated 24 January, 1742; also noted in Land Records, Kent Co., p. 163, on 25 March, 1749, and mentioned in Deed Book DD 2, 1765).

Joseph Blackiston, and wife Mary, sold the 66 2/3 Acres of "Queen Charlton" on 5 January, 1796, as recorded in B. C. 4 folio 566, to George Hanson. Joseph and Mary Blackiston also signed an agreement in 1797 to purchase land from Lewis Alfree in New Castle County, Del., but transferred it in 1799 to Jared Rothwell. The agreement was witnessed by James Blackston and Jacob Alfree and was proved in Common Pleas Court at New Castle, Del., May 24, 1808, by said James Blackston.

The wife of the Ebenezer Blackiston who died intestate in 1777 was *Mary Medford*, daughter of George Medford. The will of George Medford was proved 17 October, 1761, and mentions his "daughter, Mary, wife of Ebenezer Blakiston." Mary Medford Blackiston's will was proved 12 November, 1780. In it she mentions her "daughter Mary," her "sons George and Ebenezer" and her "*brother Marmaduke Medford*." Her sureties as administratrix of the estate of Ebenezer Blakiston, intestate 1777, were Thomas Medford and Marmaduke Medford. Her daughter, Mary, was born 29 April, 1763 (St. Paul's Parish records).

Hannahretta Mahon was the widow of Bartholemew Garnett when she married Ebenezer Blakiston, son of John and Hannah Blakiston. Ebenezer had brothers, John (no issue), Prideaux, Thomas, Vincent, William, Michael, Benjamin, and two sisters, Mary (married ——— Covington) and Sarah Blakiston (Register, St. Paul's Parish, Kent Co.; Kent Co., Deed Book D. D. 1765; Will Book 2, folio 186).

Hannahretta Blakiston was born 1 October, 1725, a daughter of Thomas Mahon and wife, née Mary Moore (St. Paul's Parish). Thomas Mahon and Mary Moore were married 12 April, 1716 (St. Paul's), and, in addition to Hannahretta, had son Thomas (no issue) and daughter Ann, born 13 March, 1726; Mary (married James Blake); Amelia Sophia Charlotta, born 3 October, 1737, married ——— Ricketts.

There were several Ebenezer Blakiston's in Kent County, Md.:

1. Captain Ebenezer Blakiston, b. 1650: d. 1709:
2. Major Ebenezer Blakiston, b. 1746: son of Captain Ebenezer:
3. Ebenezer Blakiston, b. 1705: d. 1772, son of John: subject of this article.
4. Ebenezer Blakiston, son of the Ebenezer who died 1772:
5. Ebenezer Blakiston, b. 1728 son of Benjamin:
6. Ebenezer Blakiston, son of William: a minor in 1737:
7. Ebenezer Blakiston, son of the John who died 1774, John being a brother of Ebenezer 1705-1772:
8. Ebenezer Blakiston, son of George: who died in Dover, Del., 1778, was son of Benjamin:

In his will (Annapolis, Lib. 37, f. 56) Vincent Blakiston, brother of Ebenezer Blakiston (sons of John), mentions James Blakiston, son of Ebenezer Blakiston.

In the many court house records of Maryland that relate to this line of the Blakiston family, descended from George son of Marmaduke, the name is spelled Blakiston, Blackiston, Blackstone, Blackistone, Blakistone and Blackston. The records duoted in the article prove that Ebenezer[5], son of John[4], John[3], George[2], Marmaduke[1], Blakiston left a will and had sons Stephen, Michael, James, Ebenezer and Joseph Blackiston.

The Reverend Marmaduke Blakiston, marked [1] in this article, was son of John Blakiston of Blakiston (England) whose wife was Elizabeth Bowes, a daughter of Sir George Bowes. Of the eight sons and three daughters of the Reverend Marmaduke Blakiston, Durham, England, George was the youngest son and came to Maryland in 1668. Another son of the Reverend Marmaduke Blakiston was John, one of the Judges who signed the death warrant of King Charles I. The widow of Judge John Blakiston and her sons were brought to Maryland by George Blakiston who had been Sheriff of Durham County, under Parliament, in 1656.

The name, as have many others, has undergone many changes in spelling from its original Norman: De Blaykestone, de Blakistone, de Blakiston, Blakiston, Blackiston, Blackistone, Blackstone, Blackston.

William Blackstone, a relative of George Blakiston the emigrant, served as a colonel in the army of King Charles I and is said to have been knighted during the Battle of Oxford. William Blackstone, one of the first three settlers of Boston, Mass., was also related to the Reverend Marmaduke Blakiston, the father of George Blakiston and the Judge. The Reverend Marmaduke Blakiston was the father of six other sons (four of whom were clergymen) and of three daughters. The old motto was " Fac bene non dubitans."

———

THE BRENGLE FAMILY OF FREDERICK

BERNARD C. STEINER.[1]

---

1. Jacob Brengle,[1] Brengel, Branckel, Brenckel, or Prengel, as the name is variously spelled, lived in Frederick County in the latter part of the Provincial period. He was a farmer, lived near Walkersville and married three times. The name of his first wife is unknown. The second wife, Gertrude Bell, married June 30, 1761, and the third wife, Margaret Bell, were probably the daughters of John Bell and sisters of John Bell, who sold land to Jacob Brengle in 1772. He died probably in January 1784, leaving a will and personal estate valued at £ 367.17. He also devised eight hundred acres of land in Kentucky. It is uncertain by which wife he was father of his children, except that Elizabeth was the daughter of Gertrude (Bell) Brengle. Mrs. Gertrude Brengle was confirmed in the Evangelical Reformed Church in Frederick in 1767. Jacob Brengle had issue:—

2.   i. GEORGE[2] BRENGLE, b. 1755, alive in 1823.
3.   ii. CHRISTIAN[2] BRENGLE.
4.   iii. LAWRENCE[2] BRENGLE, will probated Sept. 19, 1799.
     iv. ELIZABETH[2] BRENGLE, b. Dec. 19, 1767; mar. Henry Steiner, Oct. 13, 1787; d. Apr. 17, 1833. (See Steiner Genealogy, p. 32.)
     v. CATHERINE[2] BRENGLE, b. Apr. 13, 1775; mar. Sebastian Derr.
     vi. daughter[2] BRENGLE, b. —, mar. Dec. 3, 1797, John Scholl.

2. George[2] Brengle, mar. Catharine —— and went to Kentucky in 1783. His issue were:—

    i. ANNA MARIA[3] BRENGLE, b. Dec. 24, 1770.
    ii. ROSINA[3] BRENGLE, b. Nov. 21, 1772.
4.   iii. MARIA ELIZABETH[3] BRENGLE, b. Feb. 21, 1775.
5.   iv. son, d. June 25, 1829 of quick consumption.

---

[1] Valuable assistance in preparing this article has been received from Miss Fannie Schley Hewes and Mr. John Nicholas Brengle, of Frederick City.

3. Christian [2] Brengle of Fredericktown, mar. Elizabeth ——. He kept a tavern on Patrick St. and his son-in-law, Henry Brother succeeded to the business of tavern keeper in Nov. 1794. Christian Brengle removed to New Orleans and was alive there but palsied in 1823. Christian and Elizabeth Brengle had issue:—

  i. CATHERINE [3] BRENGLE, b. Feb. 22, 1768, mar. Joseph Adams.
  ii. ELIZABETH [3] BRENGLE, b. Oct. 31, 1771, mar. Henry Brother.
  iii. HARRIET [3] BRENGLE, deranged.

4. Lawrence or Lorenz Brengle,[2] mar. Eva Margaret, daughter of John and Rachel Gomber, and lived in Fredericktown; she died March 26, 1834, aged 81. They had issue:—

  i. CHRISTIAN [3] BRENGLE.
6. ii. JOHN [3] BRENGLE, b. Feb. 18, 1772; d. Aug. 24, 1835.
7. iii. JACOB [3] BRENGLE, b. Jan. 27, 1774; d. Dec. 27, 1836.
8. iv. JOHN NICHOLAS [3] BRENGLE, b. Oct. 4, 1776; d. Dec. 9, 1842.
  v. CATHARINE [3] BRENGLE, b. Nov. 23, 1778; mar. Michael Reel, May 22, 1802.
9. vi. PETER [3] BRENGLE, b. Aug. 1, 1780; d. Mar. 6, 1833.
  vii. ELIZABETH [3] BRENGLE, b. Mar. 30, 1784.
  viii. RACHEL [3] BRENGLE, b. Oct. 27, 1787; mar. Philip Pyfer, Jr., Aug. 15, 1812. They had issue:—
    i. MARGARET M.[4] PYFER, mar. Valentine S. Brunner.
    ii. ANN C.[4] PYFER, mar. Philip Baker Kunkel.
    iii. PHILIP H.[4] PYFER.
    iv. WILLIAM B.[4] PYFER.
  ix. LORENZ [3] BRENGLE, b. July 14, 1791.

5. —— [3] Brengle, lived near Fredericksburg, Washington Co., Ky. His wife survived him, but her name is not known. They had issue:—

  i. JOHN [4] BRENGLE, living in 1833.
  ii. CHARITY [4] BRENGLE, d. on her seventeenth birthday before 1823.
  iii. CHRISTIAN [4] BRENGLE, d. aged 24 before 1823.
  iv. NARCISSA [4] BRENGLE.
  v. HARRIET [4] BRENGLE.
  vi. MYRA [4] BRENGLE.
  vii. LAVINIA [4] BRENGLE, d. aet. 10 or 12 months before 1823.
  viii. AGNES [4] BRENGLE.
  ix. GEORGE [4] BRENGLE, d. aet. 4 years before 1823.

x. LAWRENCE⁴ BRENGLE.

xi. POLLY⁴ BRENGLE.

xii. SUSANNAH⁴ BRENGLE.

xiii. JACOB⁴ BRENGLE.

6. Capt. John³ Brengle of Frederick, married Elizabeth Ziehler, daughter of Henry Ziehler, on March 29, 1803 She was born Dec. 8, 1774, and died Oct. 18, 1850. For his service in the War of 1812 see Scharf's *Western Maryland,* Vol. I, p. 193. Their issue were:—

10. i. LAWRENCE JOHN⁴ BRENGLE, b. Dec. 4, 1805, d. Oct. 13, 1874.

ii. Elizabeth⁴ BRENGLE, b. May 24, 1807.

iii. EVA MARGARET⁴ BRENGLE, b. Mar. 19, 1809; mar. Capt. Edward Schley Dec. 4, 1827; d. Jul. 13, 1890. They had issue:—

    i. ANNIE E.⁵ SCHLEY.

    ii. MARY M.⁵ SCHLEY.

    iii. ELLA E.⁵ SCHLEY.

    iv. BENJAMIN HENRY⁵ SCHLEY.

    v. FRANKLIN⁵ SCHLEY.

    vi. ALICE⁵ SCHLEY.

    vii. LAURA⁵ SCHLEY.

    viii. EDWARD⁵ SCHLEY.

    ix. ROSA⁵ SCHLEY.

    x. FANNIE⁵ SCHLEY.

    xi. THOMAS⁵ SCHLEY.

    xii. GILMER⁵ SCHLEY.

iv. ANNA MARIA⁴ BRENGLE, b. Nov. 25, 1810, d. Feb. 27, 1886; mar. May 7, 1833, George Englebrecht or Englebright (b. Feb. 17, 1795, d. Feb. 22, 1874). They had issue:—

    i. ELIZABETH⁵ ENGLEBRECHT, b. Mar. 21, 1834.

    ii. ANN⁵ ENGLEBRECHT, b. June 14, 1835.

    iii. AGNES⁵ ENGLEBRECHT.

11. DANIEL⁴ BRENGLE, b. Nov. 10, 1812, d. May 10, 1842.

7. Jacob³ Brengle married Amelia. His issue were:—

12. i. WILLIAM⁴ BRENGLE, b. —— 1801, d. July 17, 1830.

ii. NICHOLAS⁴ BRENGLE.

13. iii. ALFRED FLEENER⁴ BRENGLE, b. Mar. 13, 1812; d. Apr. 23, 1865.

iv. JOHN⁴ BRENGLE, b. —— 1808, d. Sept. 23, 1823.

v. CAROLINE⁵ BRENGLE, mar. Daniel Kolb, Dec. 24, 1830 and had children:—

    i. ALFRED BRENGLE⁵ KOLB.

    ii. LEWIS A.⁵ KOLB.

    iii. SOPHIA M. A.⁵ KOLB.

    iv. NAOMI⁵ KOLB, who mar. —— Utermehle.

8. J. Nicholas [3] Brengle of Frederick, farmer, married Maria
or Mary Mantz, daughter of Major Peter and Catharine
(Hauer) Mantz. He was commissioned second lieutenant
in Capt. Hauer's company in the First Regimental Cavalry
District, June 16, 1812. Their children were:—

  i. MARGARET [4] BRENGLE, mar. Henry Semmes.
  ii. CATHARINE [4] BRENGLE, b. Apr. 16, 1803; d. Feb. 18, 1890; mar.
     Lewis Benedict Eader (b. Apr. 23, 1798; d. Jan. 2, 1873.)
     May 6, 1824. For their children see Steiner Genealogy, p. 45.
  iii. MARY [4] BRENGLE, b. —, mar. Daniel Root, Jr. Their children
     were:—
      i. MAY LOUISE [5] ROOT.
      ii. ANN MATILDA [5] ROOT.
  iv. LOUISA [4] BRENGLE, b. Mar. 9, 1809; mar. her cousin, Alfred F.
     Brengle and d. Mar. 19, 1888.
  v. EZRA MANTZ [4] BRENGLE, b. Sept. 15, 1811; d. May 23, 1899, mar.
     Rachel Blackburn (b. May 15, 1813; d. July 26, 1883.)
  vi. RACHEL E. [4] BRENGLE, b. Nov. 17, 1814; mar. Nov. 11, 1853, Le-
     onidas Johnson of Virginia.

9. Peter [3] Brengle of Frederick married, May 1, 1803, Catharine Mantz, daughter of David and Elizabeth (Miller)
Mantz. They had issue:—

  i. MATILDA [4] BRENGLE, b. Jan. 24, 1804; mar. Aug. 4, 1825 Noah
     A. Shafer. (He d. Mar. 8, 1835.) They had issue:—
      i. MARY E. M. [5] SHAFER, b. Jun. 26, 1826; d. Sept. 1, 1849.
  ii. DAVID [4] BRENGLE, b. Jan. 18, 1806; d. May 23, 1855.
14. iii. FRANCIS [4] BRENGLE, b. Nov. 26, 1807; d. Oct. 10, 1846.
15. iv. LEWIS AUGUSTUS [4] BRENGLE, b. Oct. 5, 1809.
16. v. GEORGE L. [4] BRENGLE, b. Aug. 13, 1813; d. Sept. 20, 1851.
  vi. MARIA CATHARINE [4] BRENGLE, b. Nov. 2, 1815; d. Feb. 13, 1888;
     mar. Jan. 19, 1837, Henry Houck. Their issue were:—
      i. VIRGINIA B. [5] HOUCK.
      ii. HENRY J. [5] HOUCK.
  vii. ANN REBECCA [4] BRENGLE, b. Sept. 16, 1817; d. Sept. 21, 1861;
     mar. J. William Gittinger, Aug. 7, 1839. Their issue were:—
      i. THOMAS GITTINGER.
      ii. FANNIE B. GITTINGER, b. Aug. 11, 1847.

10. Major Lawrence J. [4] Brengle of Frederick City married
twice; first on December 2, 1828, Catharine Clemm, fifth
daughter of Andrew and Elizabeth Shriver of Union

Mills, Carroll County. (She was born March 8, 1808, and died October 5, 1832), and second, on May 12, 1835, her elder sister, Eliza, third daughter of Andrew Shriver. (She was born March 14, 1799 and died March 3, 1879.) He lived for a time on a farm near the Monocacy River and, after his father's death, removed to the paternal homestead near Frederick and later into the town, of which he became one of the most prominent citizens. He accumulated a considerable estate and was the organizer and first president of the First National Bank. He served one session in the House of Delegates. A zealous Union man, he equipped the Brengle Home Guards in 1861, a local military organization which did much to check the progress of the movement for secession. After the Civil War, he affiliated with the Republican party and was its candidate for State Comptroller. He also served as Chief Judge of the Orphans' Court, Treasurer and afterwards President of the Chesapeake and Ohio Canal Company, President of the Board of Visitors of the Frederick Academy and Treasurer of the Board of Visitors of the State school for the Deaf and Dumb. He was a devoutly religious man and a communicant member of the Evangelical Reformed Church in Frederick.

Lawrence J. and Catharine (Shriver) Brengle had issue:—

   i. OLIVIA⁵ BRENGLE, b. Oct. 26, 1829; mar. Nov. 6, 1850 John Alexander Shriver of Baltimore and had issue:—

      i. ALICE⁶ SHRIVER, b. Nov. 26, 1851; d. Nov. 27, 1898; mar. Thomas R. Clendenin, Esq. Nov. 10, 1874.

      ii. FREDERICK⁶ SHRIVER, b. Apr. 26, 1853; mar. Martha A. Nicholson, Jan. 3, 1884; d. June 1, 1895.

      iii. LAWRENCE⁶ SHRIVER, b. Sept. 28, 1855; d. Jun. 24, 1856.

      iv. JOHN SHULZ⁶ SHRIVER, b. Jun. 17, 1857.

      v. ALEXANDER⁶ SHRIVER, b. Aug. 4, 1858; d. Feb. 8, 1864.

      vi. HENRY GAW⁶ SHRIVER, b. Jul. 17, 1860; d. Mar. 10, 1883.

      vii. CLARENCE⁶ SHRIVER, b. Dec. 22, 1864; mar. Caroline Totten of Pittsburgh, Penn., April 30, 1889.

      viii. JAMES ALEXIS⁶ SHRIVER, b. Apr. 3, 1872; mar. Harriet Van Bibber, of Bel Air, June 2, 1900.

ii. ELIZABETH [5] BRENGLE, b. May 14, 1832; d. Aug. 21, 1880; mar. Nov. 26, 1856 Charles L. Kemp of Baltimore, and had issue:—

  i. LAWRENCE BRENGLE [6] KEMP, b. Aug. 24, 1857; mar Nov. 27, 1883 Helen Richardson.

  ii. CHARLES LUTHER [6] KEMP, b. May 23, 1859; d. —.

  iii. ELIZABETH C.[6] KEMP, b. Feb. 16, 1873; d. —.

  iv. THOMAS WILLIAM [6] KEMP, b. Aug. 23, 1874.

  v. BERTHA BRENGLE [6] KEMP, b. Sept. 6, 1876; d. —.

Lawrence J. and Elizabeth (Shriver) Brengle had issue:—

iii. ELIZA JANE [5] BRENGLE, b. Mar. 23, 1836; d. Feb. 21, 1867; mar. Dr. R. Bradley Tyler of Frederick Nov. 15, 1865. They had no issue.

iv. JAMES SHRIVER [5] BRENGLE, b. Nov. 26, 1840; mar. Apr. 27, 1865 Millicent Anne Gaw and resided in Philadelphia. He d. in Philadelphia, Dec. 23, 1905. She d. in Baltimore, Apr. 15, 1906. They had issue:—

  i. HENRY GAW [6] BRENGLE, b. Feb. 26, 1866.

  ii. ELIZA [6] BRENGLE, b. May 17, 1869; mar. Henry R. Heard of Boston, Feb. 17, 1903.

  iii. ROSALIE LAWRENCE [6] BRENGLE, b. Oct. 22, 1874.

  iv. LAWRENCE JOHN [6] BRENGLE, b. Oct. 21, 1878; mar. Oct. 21, 1905, Katherine I. Curtin, daughter of Gov. Andrew G. Curtin of Pennsylvania.

11. Daniel [4] Brengle, a farmer of Frederick, married Dec. 3, 1833 Caroline E. Thomas, daughter of William and Catharine Hauer. (She was born Aug. 5, 1813 and died March 22, 1891.) They had issue:—

  i. JOHN W.[5] BRENGLE.

  ii. VIRGINIA [5] BRENGLE.

  iii. ROBERT [5] BRENGLE.

  iv. FANNIE C.[5] BRENGLE, b. Nov. 15, 1841; d. May 6, 1864.

12. William [4] Brengle, mar. May 8, 1821 Margaret Grove (b. July 11, 1800; d. Aug. 8, 1830). They had issue:—

  i. NICHOLAS [5] BRENGLE, b. Mch. 22. 1822.

  ii. AMELIA ANN [5] BRENGLE, b. Feb. 27, 1825; d. Oct. 13, 1838.

  iii. JACOB [5] BRENGLE, b. June 5, 1827.

13. Alfred F.[4] Brengle, mar. May 17, 1832 his cousin Louisa, daughter of Nicholas Brengle. They had issue:—

    i. SARAH REBECCA [5] BRENGLE, b. May 10, 1834.

   ii. HENRIETTA ELIZABETH [5] BRENGLE, b. Oct. 9, 1835.

  iii. LAURA [5] BRENGLE, b. —.

  iv. MARY AMELIA [5] BRENGLE, b. Jun. 26, 1838.

   v. ALICE LOUISA [5] BRENGLE, b. 1841; d. Nov. 4, 1853.

  vi. HENRY AUGUSTUS [5] BRENGLE, b. Aug. 4, 1844; d. Nov. 16, 1847.

 vii. ANNIE VIRGINIA [5] BRENGLE, b. Oct. 10, 1846; d. Nov. 17, 1847.

viii. CHARLES ALFRED [5] BRENGLE, b. Dec. 4, 1848; d. Nov. 23. 1875.

  ix. ANNIE [5] BRENGLE, b. Mch. 11, 1850; d. Dec. 9, 1862.

   x. HENRY EDWARD [5] BRENGLE, b. May 1854; d. July, 18, 1854.

14. Francis [4] Brengle of Frederick, an attorney, married Maria, daughter of Wm. D. (Sr.) and Cordelia H. Dorsey, He was elected as a Whig to the Twenty-Eighth Congress. (She was b. Apr. 19, 1816; d. Sept. 30, 1893). They had issue:—

   i. WILLIAM DOWNEY [5] BRENGLE, b. Sept. 2, 1836; physician; mar. Elizabeth Martin. He was assistant surgeon Third Georgia Battery, C. S. A. Their children were:—

     i. MARIA [6] BRENGLE.

    ii. ELIZABETH MARTIN [6] BRENGLE.

  ii. CORDELIA R. [5] BRENGLE, b. Aug. 9, 1841; d. Aug. 5, 1846.

 iii. FRANCIS [5] BRENGLE, b. Mch. 12, 1844; lawyer; d. —.

 iv. ANNIE [5] BRENGLE, b. Apr. 21, 1847; single; d. Mch. 14, 1886.

15. Lewis A. [4] Brengle of Frederick married Ann Rebecca Carlton. They had issue:—

   i. LEWIS AUGUSTUS [5] BRENGLE, b. Sept. 21, 1837.

  ii. THOMAS CARLTON [5] BRENGLE, b. Dec. 21, 1839; d. Nov. 19, 1859.

 iii. DAVID CARLTON [5] BRENGLE.

 iv. ALEXANDER [5] BRENGLE.

  v. DAVID M. [5] BRENGLE.

 vi. OLIVER [5] BRENGLE, d. aet. 3 weeks.

vii. ELIZA [5] BRENGLE, d. aet. 6 weeks.

16. George L. [4] Brengle mar. May 7, 1840 Susan D. Neill, daughter of John W. Neill. She was b. Feb. 20, 1819 and d. Jan. 21, 1842. They had issue:—

   i. MARY CATHARINE [5] BRENGLE, b. Mch. 10, 1841; d. Mch. 22, 1870.

Daniel [2] Brengle, a son of a brother of Jacob [1] Brengle, and his wife came to this country from a small town called

Beyer in Alsace, Germany, near the French border. They landed in New York in the year 1830. In the year 1832 they came to Frederick. Daniel Brengle was married twice,—his first wife was Catharine Brengle, daughter of Otto Brengle (not a relative). By this marriage there were six children:—

   i. John Nicholas[3] Brengle.
  ii. Daniel[3] Brengle.
 iii. Henry[3] Brengle.
  iv. Christian[3] Brengle.
   v. Elizabeth[3] Brengle.
  vi. Catharine[3] Brengle.

His second wife was Caroline Coleman. He had no children by his second marriage.

John Nicholas[3] Brengle was married twice. His first wife was Catharine Schwalm. By this marriage he had five children:—

   i. William H.[4] Brengle.
  ii. Charles[4] Brengle.
 iii. Lewis[4] Brengle.
  iv. Catharine[4] Brengle.
   v. Caroline[4] Brengle.

His second wife was Christina Miller, the widow of Adam Ross. By this marriage he had two children:—

  vi. George[4] Brengle.
 vii. Emma[4] Brengle.

William H.[4] Brengle married Margaret Jennie L. Hett, daughter of John Hett, on April 8, 1880. By this marriage, there were three children:—

   i. William H.[5] Brengle.
  ii. Nicholas John[5] Brengle. (Who died in infancy).
 iii. John Nicholas[5] Brengle, who on April 18, 1906, married Virgie Ijams Ways, daughter of William H. Ways.

SOME DESCENDANTS OF COLONEL PHILIP BRISCOE.

L. W. REID.

The ancestry of Dr. John Briscoe, who settled in Frederick (afterwards Berkeley) County, Virginia, about 1752, and his brother George Briscoe, who accompanied or more probably followed him, as given in *Colonial Families of the United States of America,* Vol. III, p. 84, is incorrect. They were, it seems, sons of Dr. Philip Briscoe, son of Philip,[1] usually called Colonel Philip, and Susanna (Swann) Briscoe. The proof is as follows:

In the Maryland Land Office, Accounts, Book 21, p. 446, we find "The Account of Elizabeth Briscoe, admx. of all and singular the Goods, Chattels, Rights and Credits of Philip Briscoe late of St. Mary's Co. Deceased." Net personal estate is £271, 1, 6¾. At the end of account is "Balance to be disposed of one third to the Deceased's widow, the residue to John Briscoe, Philip Briscoe, Edward Briscoe, James Briscoe, Walter Briscoe, George Cole Briscoe, Elizabeth Briscoe and Sarah Briscoe orphans of the Deceased." The date of this account is 17th July, 1745.

In the Land Office we find also, Inventories, Book 28, p. 518, Nov. 1743, "An Inventory of the Goods and chattels of Mr. Philip Briscoe late of St. Mary's Co. Deceased, appraised by Luke Gardiner and Wm. Bond the Day and Year above written."

Among the items in this inventory are "One young negro woman named Dinah £40, one young negro named Peter £41, one negro woman Susanna very old £10, one mulatto girl Priscilla £26." Among the items are also medicines and a "Doctor's Book."

In the will of Susanna (Swann) Briscoe, dated 5th Feb., 1739/40, prob. 24th July, 1740 (Land Office, Book 22, p. 212), she bequeaths to her son Philip Briscoe "a negro woman Susanna and her daughter Dinah my negro boy Peter and my mulatto girl Priscilla." It will be noted that these four negroes appear in the above inventory, proving that Dr. Philip Briscoe was the son of Col. Philip and Susanna (Swann) Briscoe.

Proof that Dr. John Briscoe and George Briscoe, who settled in Frederick Co., Va., were brothers is afforded by a chart made May 1838 by Maj. Thomas Briscoe (1791-1867), a grandson of Dr. John Briscoe. This chart is now in the possession of Miss Juliet Hite Gallaher of Waynesboro, Va., a granddaughter of Maj. Thomas Briscoe; she has kindly given me a copy of this chart and certain Bible records, to which I shall refer later, and allowed me to use them. I shall give this chart exactly as it is written by Major Briscoe, omitting all descendants after the third generation.

"Roots among the first settlers of Md. about 1633-35 A. D.
1st. Generation John Briscoe and Elizabeth, maiden name unknown.

    Issue: I. George Briscoe md. Frances McMillan of Pr. Wm. Co., Va.

    Issue: 1. James Briscoe, issue; 2. Cuthbert Briscoe, no issue.

        3. George Cole Briscoe, no issue; 4. Elizabeth md. Hedges, issue;

        5. Philip, no issue; 6. Samuel, issue; 7. Harrison, issue;

        8. Edward, issue.

2. Dr. John Briscoe 2nd., Berkeley Co., Va., md. 1st Elizabeth McMillan of Pr. Wm. Co., Va., gr. dau. of Thos. Harrison of Chappawamsick; md. 2nd. Ann Lamar of Queen Anne Co., Md., no issue. Issue by Elizabeth McMillan: 1. Israel; 2. Parmenas; 3. Dr. John Briscoe; 4. Elizabeth; 5. Sally; 6. Fanny; 7. Hezekiah.

3. ———— Briscoe, md. ————
Issue: 1. Miss Briscoe md. ———— Chapelier; 2. Cassandra, md. Purvis, no issue; 3. Philip Briscoe of St. Mary's Co., Md., and others not known."

A word of comment on this chart may not be out of place. Although Maj. Thomas Briscoe unfortunately gave the name of his greatgrandfather, the father of Dr. John and George Briscoe, incorrectly, as will be shown, a mistake which lead to the confusion in this line as published, he probably was well acquainted with his great uncle George Briscoe, who lived near him and did not die until 1805 (Bible records), and, of course, knew his closer relations descended from Dr. John Briscoe. The brother, 3, of Dr. John Brisioe and George Briscoe has not as yet been identified and it seems probable that "Philip Briscoe of St. Mary's Co., Md." given as his son was his brother, Philip [3] Briscoe (Philip,[2] Philip [1]). A Cassandra Briscoe married James Purvis (Mar. contract, dated 3d Mar., 1787, recorded Winchester, Deed Book 29), who was one of the executors of George Briscoe's will (see below). It is probable that Maj. Briscoe knew Mrs. Purvis as she lived near his home and did not die until 1819.

The chart deals no further with the children of George Briscoe, except as they intermarried with the descendants of Dr. John Briscoe; but it continues the lines of the children of Dr. John and Elizabeth (McMillan) Briscoe, especially that of their son Dr. John Briscoe, who married Eleanor Magruder, one child of this marriage being Maj. Thos. Briscoe.

The fact that George and Frances (McMillan) Briscoe

had a son George Cole Briscoe at once suggests a connexion with Dr. Philip [2] Briscoe (Philip [1]).

At Charles Town, Jefferson Co., West Va., is the will of a George Briscoe, dated 9th Feb., 1802, prob. 9th July, 1805 (Book 1, p. 207). It is in part as follows: " I give and bequeath to my seven sons the tract of land whereon I live supposed to contain between five and six hundred acres to be equally divided among them according to quality and quantity, to be enjoyed by them and their heirs forever, viz. John Briscoe, George C. Briscoe, Cuthbert Briscoe, Philip Briscoe, Samuel Briscoe, Harrison Briscoe and Edward Briscoe, nevertheless should any of my sons die under the legal age of 21 without heirs, then and in that case it is my will and desire that the property devised this son or sons shall be equally divided among the surviving or their heirs to be enjoyed by them forever."

To his daughter, Elizabeth Hedge, he leaves personalty.

Executors: Friends John Briscoe and James Purvis and son John Briscoe. (Signed) George Briscoe.

Witnesses: Richd. McSherry, George S. Washington, Andrew Rhonemies.

John Briscoe gives bond of $15,000.

That the George Briscoe of the above will is the George Briscoe of the chart, brother of Dr. John Briscoe, seems evident although Maj. Briscoe has called the eldest son " James " instead of " John."

That the full name of this George Briscoe was George Cole Briscoe will appear from the following records.

Although he signed his will as George Briscoe and in the appraisal of his personal estate, 8th April, 1806 (Charles Town Will Book 1, p. 277) which includes 20 slaves and 10 horses, the total being $6266.16, he is called George Briscoe, in the final account of his estate, 12th Sept., 1810 (Will Book, 1, p. 598), he is called Capt. George C. Briscoe.

At Martinsburgh, Berkeley Co., then Virginia now West Va., there is a deed dated 1st and 2nd Aug., 1777 (Book 4,

p. 221) by which Thos. Mason conveys to George Cole Briscoe two tracts of land adjoining, of 255 and 300 acres respectively.

At Charles Town, Jefferson Co., West Va., there is a deed, dated 20th March, 1807 (Book 4, p. 215) by which John M. Briscoe and Maria, his wife, Cuthbert Briscoe and Elizabeth, his wife, George Cole Briscoe by John Briscoe, his attorney in fact, Philip Briscoe, Samuel Briscoe, Harrison Briscoe and Edward Briscoe all of Jefferson Co., Va., convey to Wm. Cameron of Lancaster Co., Pa., two tracts of land devised by George C. Briscoe to the above, one tract having been bought by George C. Briscoe from Thomas Mason being next land of George Washington and Smith Slaughter, the other tract being bought by George C. Briscoe from Thos. Mason at the same time and being next to other land and to Richard McSherry's.

The land bequeathed by George Briscoe to his seven sons is the land conveyed by Thomas Mason to George Cole Briscoe.

We have also as further evidence that the full name of the George Briscoe of the will and chart was George Cole Briscoe three deeds recorded at Martinsburgh.

Book 4, p. 190, 16th and 17th June, 1777, George Cole Briscoe and Frankey Briscoe, his wife, convey to Richard Evans 378 acres of land on Middle Creek in Berkeley, formerly Frederick Co., Va.

Book 11, p. 622, 14th Aug., 1790, George Briscoe and Frances Briscoe, his wife, convey to Richard McSherry 55 acres, 70 roods of land; in body of deed grantor is designated as George Cole Briscoe, although he signed as George Briscoe. Book 11, p. 626, 21st Aug. 1792, George Cole Briscoe and Frances Briscoe, his wife, convey to Richard McSherry 233 acres of land.

Attention is called to the fact that in these three deeds the wife of George Cole Briscoe signs as Frances (or Frankey) Briscoe, which corresponds to the name of the wife of George Briscoe as given on chart.

To identify this George Cole Briscoe with George Cole [3] Briscoe (Philip,[2] Philip [1]), we have, so far as the writer knows, no direct evidence, but that there was a second George Cole Briscoe of suitable age will be seen to be highly improbable.

An examination of the descendants in the male lines of Col. Philip Briscoe for three generations shows that there are known only the two following George Briscoes in addition to George Cole [3] (Philip,[2] Philip [1]); that is, George [2] (Philip [1]), who predeceased his father, and George [3] (Edward,[2] Philip [1]) who died between 14th May, 1752 and 30th June, 1755.

Among the descendants of John Briscoe of Kent Co., (Will, 20th June 1709, 7th June, 1715) we find no George Briscoe of suitable age. We are lead therefore to the conclusion that the above George Cole Briscoe and his brother Dr. John Briscoe were sons of Philip [2] (Philip [1]) and they will be so designated hereafter in this article.

It is well to say that a careful search of the Maryland records reveals no persons who can be identified with the Dr. John II and Dr. John III of the article in Colonial Families in the United States of America, and it was this that lead the writer to an examination of the record at Martinsburgh and Charles Town with the above result.

At the end of this article will be found records taken from the Bible of Hezekiah [4] Briscoe (John,[3] Philip,[2] Philip [1]). They are published by the kind permission of Miss Gallaher, who owns the Bible in question.

The date of death of George Briscoe, "7th June, 1805," will be seen to accord with that of the will given above. The item "Elizabeth Briscoe (the mother of old Dr. John Briscoe, formerly of Frederick Co. then of Berkeley Co., who 2nd John was one of the early settlers of the valley of Virginia) was born in the year 1693 and died in the 74th year of her age in the year 1767" is especially interesting as the name of the widow and admx. of Philip [2] (Philip [1]) was Elizabeth and this is evidently the same person. Her maiden name has not been determined so far as the writer knows. She has been said to have been an Elizabeth De Courcy, but an examination of the early generations of the De Courcy (Coursey) family discloses no marriage to a Briscoe and indeed leads to the conclusion that she could not have been a De Courcy. The evidence is briefly as follows. Hezekiah Briscoe's Bible records state that Elizabeth Briscoe, mother of Dr. John Briscoe, whom we have seen to be John [3] (Philip,[2] Philip [1]), was born in 1693. It is impossible therefore that she could have been Elizabeth [4] Coursey, daughter of John [3] and Elizabeth (Macklin) Coursey, as stated in the above mentioned article in "Colonial Families of the United States of America," since this John Coursey was born 12th July, 1709. (Land Office Chan. Rec. Book 8A, p. 1053).

Elizabeth Macklin, moreover, is shown by the will of her father, Robert Macklin, (Land Office, Book 14, p. 450) to have been under 18 years of age 11th Nov., 1716.

An examination of the records shows that among the descendants of Col. Henry Coursey there are only two Elizabeth Courseys, who could have been born as early as 1693.

These are two granddaughters, the one, daughter of his son Henry by his first wife, Mary Harris; the other, daughter of his son John by his second wife, Elizabeth (Smith) Carpenter.

The former, Elizabeth [3] Coursey (Henry,[2] Henry [1]) was the wife of William Cummings, 7th Nov. 1727 (Will of her mother, Elizabeth (Desmyniers) Coursey (Land Office, Book 19, p. 644).

The latter, Elizabeth [3] Coursey (John [2] Henry [1]) was the wife of Thomas Wilkinson, 25th March, 1725 (Will of Elizabeth Coursey, widow of Col. William [2] Coursey (Land Office, Book 19, p. 28).

As John [3] Briscoe (Philip,[2] Philip [1]) was born in March 1717, according to Hezekiah Briscoe's Bible records, and his father was alive 5th Feb., 1740, (Will of Susanna Briscoe, see above), it is evidently impossible that his mother could have been either of the above Elizabeth Courseys.

It may be added, although it seems unnecessary, that there is evidence to show that it is improbable that either of the above Elizabeth Courseys could have been born as early as 1693.

The mother of John [3] Briscoe (Philip,[2] Philip [1]) could moreover not have been a descendant of either Maj. William Coursey or John Coursey brothers of Col. Henry Coursey, for John Coursey died unmarried and Maj. Wm. Coursey died prior to 12th Aug., 1685 (Land Office, Inv. and Acc. Book 8, p. 410), and had only one son, William, who left no issue. The name George Cole given one of the sons of Dr. Philip [2] and Elizabeth Briscoe suggests a possible connexion with the Cole family. A partial examination of the Cole records offers as a possibility for the wife of Dr. Philip [2] Briscoe Elizabeth Cole, youngest daughter of George Cole of Calvert Co. (Will; 2nd Oct., 1699, 3rd Oct., 1700. Land Office, Book 11, p. 5). According to this will, the daughter Elizabeth might have been born in 1693.

If any one has any data relating to this Elizabeth Cole or in any way to the wife of Dr. Philip [2] Briscoe, the writer would be grateful for it.

There is an item in the Rent Roll of the Manors of Frederick, Lord Baltimore (Scharf Papers, Md. Hist. Soc.) which seems to refer to George Cole Briscoe. In that for the manor of Chapticoe, entry no. 25 is the lease to Leonard Briscoe of 214 acres, 25th March, 1743, upon the lives of Leonard Briscoe and George Briscoe, whose ages at date of this rent roll, Jan. 1768, are given as 47 and 35 respectively. Entry 27 gives George Briscoe as "tenant in possession" of 310¼ acres, the only other information regarding this land being that lease was upon "One life as supposed about 45."

The George Briscoe mentioned in entry 25 was born in 1733 which accords with the probable date of birth of George Cole [3] (Philip,[2] Philip [1]).

There is also a deed at Winchester, Frederick Co. Va., dated 6th May, 1767, (Book 2, p. 399) by which Peter McKean conveys certain land to George Briscoe. In this deed, George Briscoe is described as of Frederick County, Colony of Virginia.

A good deal of data regarding the descendants of Dr. John [3] (Philip,[2] Philip [1]) has been published in the article in "Colonial Families of the United States of America," but nothing, regarding those of his brother George Cole Briscoe, has been published, except when there was an intermarriage between the two lines.

I shall give a few records which seem to relate to the children of George Cole Briscoe.

Cuthbert Briscoe and Elizabeth Thompson mar. 6th July, 1800, by the Rev. Alexander Balmain (Winchester, Va., Mar. Rec.).

Joseph Hedges and Elizabeth Briscoe mar. 24th Nov., 1798, by the Rev. John Hutt (Martinsburgh, West Va. mar. Rec.).

Samuel Briscoe and Eliza Creasan mar. 19th Oct., 1815 (Charles Town, West Va. Mar. Rec.).

John Briscoe and Margaret Williamson mar. 10th Jan., 1793, by the Rev. Moses Hoge (Martinsburgh, West Va., Mar. Rec.).

Harrison [4] Briscoe and Edward [4] Briscoe, sons of George Cole [3] Briscoe, married respectively Henny [5] Briscoe and Elizabeth [5] Briscoe, daughters of Parmenas [4] Briscoe (John,[3] Philip,[2] Philip [1]). The earliest unmistakable reference to Dr. Philip [2] Briscoe that the writer has found is in "The Account of John and Marmaduke Simms, joint exectrs. of the last will and testament of Fortune Simms late of Charles Co. deceased," one item being "To Dr. Philip Briscoe for physical means as by receipt appears, 778" (pounds of tobacco) (Land Office, Inv. and Acc., Book 23, p. 100). The date of the account is 19th Sept., 1702, and that of probate of will of Fortune Simms 10th Dec., 1701. This would seem to place date of birth of Dr. Philip Briscoe not later than 1680, and as his brother, Capt. John Briscoe was born in 1678 (Dep. Chas. Co. Rec., Lib. P. #2, fol. 2), he was probably born in 1679 or 1680. An earlier item which probably relates to Dr. Philip [2] Briscoe is found in "The Account of Joseph Walters, exectr. of Patience Burwell's will,' dated Feb. 14th, 1698/9 (Land Office, Inv. and Acc., Book 18, p. 137). It is "To pd. Mr. Briscoe for Physick and attendance of ye executrix 500 tobc."

If this is Dr. Philip [2] Briscoe, it would seem to indicate either that he and his elder brother, John, were born a little earlier that the above dates or that he practised medicine before he was of age. We notice also that as early as 5th March, 1705, his father distinguished himself as Philip Briscoe, Sr.

The writer has been able to gather very little information concerning the children of Dr. Philip and Elizabeth Briscoe other than John and George, but the following suggestions may be helpful. James may be the " James Briscoe of Berkeley Co. and Colony of Va.," who executed, 14 May, 1778, what seems to be merely a deed of gift conveying certain personal property to Elizabeth Davis for the support of her son Samuel, witnessed by John Briscoe and John Briscoe, Jr. This instrument is, however, recorded, 16 March, 1779, as the will of James Briscoe (Martinsburgh, West Va., Will Book 1, p. 160). Walter Baker, who married Elizabeth [4] Briscoe (John,[3] Philip,[2] Philip [1]) was appointed administrator, 16th March, 1779 (Order Book, 1777-79, p. 369), and John Briscoe Jr. was appointed guardian of Edward Briscoe orphan of James Briscoe, deceased (Order Book 4, p. 5). Walter is probably the Walter Briscoe who married Elizabeth Briscoe 13th May, 1762, (Trinity Parish, Charles Co. rec.). Edward may be the Edward Briscoe who married Rachel Chapelear, widow of Isaac Chapelear about 1741-42, although this Edward Briscoe is more probably Edward [3] (Edward,[2] Philip [1]).

It is tempting also to endeavour to identify the daughters, Elizabeth and Sarah, with the Elizabeth Garner and Sarah Parker (Barber?) mentioned by Susanna (Swann) Briscoe in her will as granddaughters, although the fact that they are referred to in the above given account of their father's estate by their maiden name seems to render this unlikely.

As to the son Philip, he may be the Philip Briscoe, who married Mary Parnham, widow of Dr. Francis Parnham, between 26th Jan. 1758, and 3rd July, 1758.

If the date of death of Chloe (Hanson) Briscoe, wife of

Philip[3] Briscoe (John[2] Philip[1]) was known, this might be decided. Chloe (Hanson) Briscoe was certainly alive 2nd Aug., 1755, when she joined her husband in a deed conveying certain land, but the writer has been unable to find any later reference to her. He would be grateful for any information regarding the date of her death.

RECORDS FROM THE BIBLE OF HEZEKIAH[4] BRISCOE
(JOHN,[3] PHILIP,[2] PHILIP[1]).

This Bible was printed in Edinburgh, 1762, by Alexander Kincaid. Miss Gallaher says: " It was given by Hezekiah Briscoe to his brother, John Briscoe, who, in turn, gave it to his son, Maj. Thomas Briscoe, who gave it to my Mother, Amelia Frances Briscoe, his youngest child, who gave it to me."

Briscoes were originally amongst the first settlers of Maryland. Elizabeth Briscoe (the mother of old Doctor John Briscoe, formerly of Frederick Co. then of Berkeley Co. who 2nd John was one of the early settlers of the Valley of Virginia) was born in the year 1693 and died in the 74th year of her age in the year 1767. The above named Doctor Jno. Briscoe (her son) was born in March 1717 and died the 7th Dec. 1788. Elizabeth Briscoe (who was Eliz. H. McMillian of Prince William Co., Va.), the wife of the above Dr. Briscoe, was born May 1730 and died 5th July 1774.

The above Dr. Briscoe married his second wife Ann (who was Ann Lamar of Prince George's Co., Maryland) on the 27th of March 1776 in the 46th year of her age, she died in year 1812, left no children.

John Briscoe, Esq., formerly of Berkeley Co., and afterwards of Jefferson, the son of the above Doctor Briscoe, was born 2nd July, 1752 and died May 12th 1818. He married

Eleanor Magruder, only daughter of Alexander and Susan Magruder of Frederick, Maryland, which Susan was Susan Lamar near Queen Anne Town, Pr. George's Co., Md., and sister to the above Ann Lamar and both daughters of old John Lamar.

Izreel Briscoe was born 11th April, 1747.

Parmenas Briscoe was born ye 1st day of May 1749 on Monday. Jno. Briscoe was born ye 2nd day of July 1752 on Thursday. Elizabeth Briscoe was born ye 10th day of August 1755 on Monday. Sarah Briscoe was born ye 13th day of October 1759 on Saturday. Frances Briscoe was born ye 28 of Oct. 1762 on Thursday.

Ruth McMillian was born ye 27th day of Feb. 1745.

John Briscoe Senr. was born in March 1717.

Elizabeth Briscoe Senr. was born in May 1730.

Old Elizabeth Briscoe died 22nd of February 1767 age 74.

Cuthbert McMillian died 28th of March 1771 age 25.

Hezekiah Briscoe was born ye 26 of June 1774.

Elizabeth Briscoe departed this Life ye 5th day of July 1774 at eleven at night.

John Briscoe Senr. was married to Ann his wife ye 27th day of March 1776, in ye 46 year of her Life, that is she was 46 on September ye 28th in ye aforesaid year.

Mrs. Frances Briscoe, now wife to W. Ignatius Davis Departed this Life 25 Day of June 1795, it Being on a Sunday, aged 32 years.

Mrs. Frances Briscoe, wife to George Briscoe, Departed this Life 24 June 1795 it being on a Wednesday.

George Briscoe died in ye year 1805 on June 7.

John Briscoe was born July 2nd, 1752 and lived to be 31 years of age and then married Eleanor Magruder, daughter of Alexander & Susanna Magruder, Feb. 19, 1784. Eleanor Magruder, my wife, was born January 6th, 1766, we both have lived to have ten children.

Frances Briscoe, daughter of John & Eleanor Briscoe was

born the 7th day of May 1799 about half past five in the morning it being on a Tuesday.

Warner Briscoe the second by that name son to John and Eleanor Briscoe was born the 28 June 1801 it being on a Sunday about nine in the evening.

Henry T. McMillian Briscoe the son of John and Eleanor was born the 22 March, 1805 on a Friday at eleven o'clock in the evening.

Departed this life Mrs. Susannah Magruder April 14, 1805 after living to the respectable age of 79 years, whose life and conduct can rarely be equaled.

My much beloved wife Eleanor Briscoe departed this life the 11th of March 1806, after a long illness of eighteen months at eight in the evening.

Thomas Briscoe, son of John & Eleanor Briscoe was born on the 20th of February 1791 on Sunday night at nine o'clock.

Magruder Briscoe, son of John & Eleanor Briscoe, was born on the 25 day of April 1785 at ten in the evening on Monday.

Elizabeth Briscoe, daughter of John & Eleanor Briscoe, was born on a Tuesday 24th day of October 1787.

John Briscoe, son of John & Eleanor Briscoe, was born 28th day of January 1789 on Wednesday at three o'clock in the evening.

Susannah Briscoe, daughter of John & Eleanor Briscoe was born on the 27th day of January 1793 on a Sunday evening about eight o'clock & departed this Life on the 3rd day of February 17— it being on a Sunday Evening about ten o'clock.

Maria Harrison Briscoe, daughter of John & Eleanor Briscoe, was born on the 13th of May 1794 ten minutes after one o'clock in the morning it being on a Tuesday. Maria Harrison Briscoe, daughter of John & Eleanor Briscoe, departed this Life 1 day of August it being on a Friday 1794.

Warner Briscoe, son to John & Eleanor, was born 16th day of April 1795, it being on a Thursday at sunrise.

Susan Lamar Briscoe, daughter of John & Eleanor, was

born 16th day of April 1795—it being on a Thursday morning at sunrise.

Susan Lamar Briscoe, daughter to John & Eleanor, departed this life the 28th day of April 1795.

Warner Briscoe, son to John & Eleanor. departed this life the 29th day of April 1795.

Courtney Ann Briscoe, daughter to John & Eleanor Briscoe, was born the 12th day of Oct. 1797 it being on a Wednesday morning about 4 o'clock.

Capt. John McMillian Departed this Life 31 day of October in the 77 year of his age. 1811.

Mr. Alexander Magruder died the 14th day of November in the year of our Lorde 1784 it being on a Sunday at Four o'clock in the Evening.

Susannah Magruder was Born the 23rd of November in the year 1726 and died in the year 1805 in the 79 year of her age, April 14th.

Eleanor Magruder was born the 26th January in the year 1766 and intermarried John Briscoe and died March the 11th, 1806.

Magruder Briscoe, son of John & Eleanor Briscoe, was born Monday the 25 of April 1785 at 10 o'clock at night.

Elizabeth Briscoe, Daughter to John & Eleanor Briscoe, was born the 24th day of October on Tuesday at 10 o'clock 1786.

John McMillian died ye year 1760 on the 22nd day of September.

John Briscoe, Senr died 7th day of December about 9 o'clock in the evening of Sunday 1788.

These records are given as nearly as possible in the exact form in which they appear in Hezekiah Briscoe's Bible. They occur on several pages in different handwritings and the order of their entry is uncertain. The first entries here given are thought to be in the handwriting of Maj. Thomas Briscoe. The words "2nd John" in the first entry are written on the margin at the end of a line in the same handwriting.

L. W. R.

THE BROOKE FAMILY.

A pedigree of this family, taken from the *Hampshire Visitation* of 1634, and including the Maryland emigrant Robert Brooke, is published in Berry's *Hampshire Genealogies*, p. 339. The arms of the family, as entered in the *Visitation*, are as follows:—

Arms.—Chequy or and az., on a bend gu. a lion passant of the first.
Crest.—A demi lion rampant or, erased gu.

1. RICHARD BROOKE[1] of Whitchurch, Hampshire, married in 1552 Elizabeth sister and heir of John Twyne. His will, dated 10 January 1588/9 and confirmed 16 February 1590/1, was proved 6 May 1594. The will of his widow Elizabeth, dated 16 May 1599, was proved 2 June 1599. Both wills are on record at Somerset House, London. A brass, erected in the Church at Whitchurch by their youngest son Robert Brooke, records that Richard Brooke died 16 January 1593/4, after forty-one years of wedded life, and that his widow Elizabeth died 20 May 1599.

Richard Brooke and Elizabeth (Twyne) his wife had issue:—

2.   i. THOMAS BROOKE.[2]
    ii. RICHARD BROOKE, d. s. p.
    iii. ROBERT BROOKE of London.
    iv. ELIZABETH BROOKE.
    v. BARBARA BROOKE.
    vi. DOROTHY BROOKE.

2. THOMAS BROOKE[2] (*Richard*[1]) was born in 1561. He matriculated 24 Nov. 1581 at New College, Oxford, his age being given as twenty years in the Matriculation Register, and received the degree of B. A. 4 May 1584. He was a barrister and was of the Inner Temple 1595, bencher 1607, and autumn reader 1611. He was Member of Parliament for Whitchurch 1604–1611 (Foster, *Alumni Oxonienses*). He married Susan daughter of Sir Thomas Foster, Knt., of Hunsdon, Herts, Judge of the Common Pleas, and Susan his wife, daughter of Thomas Foster, Esq., of St. John Street, London. Mrs. Susan Brooke was therefore a sister of Sir Robert Foster, Chief Justice of the King's Bench, who died in 1663. A pedigree of this family, tracing its descent from

the Forsters of Etherstone, in Northumberland, may be found in the Harleian Society's Publications, vol. xxii (*Visitation of Herts*), p. 43, and in Raine's *History of North Durham*, p. 306. The will of Thomas Brooke, dated 11 Sept. 1612, was proved 30 November following. He was buried at Whitchurch 17 Sept. 1612, and his wife Susan the following day (Whitchurch Register). A marble tomb, upon which their sculptured figures lie side by side, is still to be seen in the Church at Whitchurch.

Thomas Brooke and Susan (Foster) his wife had issue :—

    i. THOMAS BROOKE,[3] eldest son and heir, b. 1599. Matriculated, Oriel Coll., Oxford, 27 Oct. 1615, aged 16. A barrister-at-law. Buried at Whitchurch 25 Jan. 1665.
    ii. RICHARD BROOKE, d. s. p.
3. iii. ROBERT BROOKE, b. 3 June 1602.
    iv. JOHN BROOKE, b. 1605. Matriculated, Wadham Coll., Oxford, 11 May 1621, aged 16.
    v. WILLIAM BROOKE.
    vi. HUMPHREY BROOKE.
    vii. CHARLES BROOKE.
  viii. SUSAN BROOKE.
    ix. ELIZABETH BROOKE.
    x. FRANCES BROOKE.

3. ROBERT BROOKE[3] (*Thomas*[2], *Richard*[1]) was born, according to his family record "at London, 3rd June 1602, being Thursday, between 10 and 11 of the clock in the forenoon, being Corpus Christi day." He matriculated at Wadham College, Oxford, 28 April 1618, receiving the degree of B. A. 6 July 1620, and that of M. A. 20 April 1624 (Foster, *Alumni Oxonienses*). A manuscript copy of the *Visitation of Hampshire* (1634) in the British Museum has under his name the note "this Robert is a minister." He thus records his first marriage: "Mary Baker, born at Battel in Sussex. Robert Brooke and Mary Baker intermarried 1627, the 25th of February, being St. Matthias' Day and Shrove Monday." This lady was the daughter of Thomas Baker of Battle, Esq., Barrister-at-law, and Mary his wife, daughter of Sir Thomas Engham of Goodneston, Kent. A pedigree of the Baker family, as entered at the Visitation of 1634, is published in Berry's *Sussex Genealogies*. Mary Baker died in 1634, probably at the birth of her daughter Barbara, and her husband, Robert Brooke, re-married the following year. "May the 11th, 1635, Robert Brooke (aforementioned) was married to Mary, second daughter to Roger Mainwaring, Doctor of Divinity & Dean of Worcester, wh: Mary was born at St.

Giles-in-the-Fields, London." Roger Mainwaring, the father of Robert Brooke's second wife, subsequently became Bishop of St. David's, and came into collision with Parliament through his over zealous advocacy of the royal prerogative. Robert Brooke arrived in Maryland 30 June 1650, with his (second) wife Mary, his ten children, Baker, Thomas, Charles, Roger, Robert, John, William, Francis, Mary, and Anna Brooke, and twenty-eight servants, all transported at his own cost and charge (Md. Land Office, Lib. 1, fol. 165–166 ; Davis' *Day Star*, p. 74). With his two sons Baker and Thomas, he took the oath of fidelity to the Proprietary, 22 July 1650 (Md. Archives, iii, 256). A commission had been issued to him, dated at London, 20 Sept. 1649, as commander of a county to be newly erected, and he had also a separate commission of the same date as member of the Council of Maryland. He took the oath of office in the latter capacity 22 July 1650 (Md. Archives, iii, 237, 240, 256). A new county, called Charles County, was duly erected and Robert Brooke was constituted its commander, 30 October 1650 (Md. Archives, iii, 259). When Maryland was reduced, in 1652, by the Parliamentary Commissioners, he was placed at the head of the provisional council instituted by them, and served in this capacity from 29 March until 3 July 1652 (Md. Archives, iii, 271–276). He was a member of council and commander of Charles County until 3 July 1654, when an order was passed revoking his commissions and nullifying the act erecting the county, in place of which a new county was erected, called Calvert County (Md. Archives, iii, 308). According to the Brooke family record : "He was the first that did seat the Patuxent, about twenty miles up the river at De la Brooke, and had one son there, born in 1651, called Basil, who died the same day. In 1652 he removed to Brooke Place, being right against De la Brooke ; and on the 28th of November, 1655, between 3 & 4 o'clock in the afternoon, had two children, Eliza and Henry, twins. He departed this world the 20th day of July 1655, and lieth buried at Brooke Place Manor ; and his wife, Mary Brooke, departed this life the 29th November 1663." The careful family record kept by Robert Brooke names a number of relatives who served as god-parents to his children, and furnishes abundant evidence as to his connection with the English parent stock. This interesting family record is published in Tyler's *Memoir of Roger Brooke Taney* (pp. 22–25), where by an accidental omission the death of Robert Brooke is placed in 1663. The date is correctly given in manuscript copies preserved by the family.

Robert Brooke and Mary (Baker) his first wife had issue:—

- 4. i. BAKER BROOKE,[4] b. 16 Nov. 1628; d. 1679.
-    ii. MARY BROOKE, b. 19 Feb. 1630; d. in England.
- 5. iii. THOMAS BROOKE, b. 23 June 1632; d. 1676.
-    iv. BARBARA BROOKE, b. 1634; d. in England.

By his second wife, Mary Mainwaring, Robert Brooke had issue:—

-    i. CHARLES BROOKE, b. 3 April 1636; d. unmarried 1671.
- 6. ii. ROGER BROOKE, b. 20 Sept. 1637; d. 8 April 1700.
- 7. iii. ROBERT BROOKE, b. 21 April 1639; d. 1667.
-    iv. JOHN BROOKE, b. 20 Sept. 1640; d. 1677; mar. Rebecca Isaac but seems to have had no issue.
-    v. MARY BROOKE, b. 14 April 1642.
-    vi. WILLIAM BROOKE, b. 1 Dec. 1643.
-    vii. ANN BROOKE, b. 22 Jan. 1645; mar. Christopher Beans.
-    viii. FRANCIS BROOKE, b. 30 May 1648; d. unmarried 1671.
-    ix. BASIL BROOKE, b. 1651; d. an infant.
-    x. HENRY BROOKE (twin), b. 28 Nov. 1655; d. unmarried 1672.
-    xi. ELIZABETH BROOKE (twin), b. 28 Nov. 1655; mar., before 1679, Richard Smith, Jr., of Calvert County.

4. BAKER BROOKE[4] (*Robert*,[3] *Thomas*,[2] *Richard*[1]) was born at Battle, in Sussex, 16 Nov. 1628, and arrived in Maryland with his father 30 June 1650. He was commissioned a member of the council of Maryland 6 May 1658 (Md. Archives, iii, 342) and held the office until his death in 1679. He also filled the position of Surveyor General of the Province from 1 August 1671 (Md. Archives, v, 94) until his death. About 1664 he married Ann, daughter of Governor Leonard Calvert and niece of Cecilius Lord Baltimore. In 1661 William Calvert recovered land as the son and heir of Gov. Leonard Calvert in an action of ejectment brought against Thomas Stone (Lib. S., fol. 459), and in 1664 Gov. Charles Calvert writes to his father Cecilius that his cousin William Calvert's sister has arrived and that he is on the lookout for a good match for her (Calvert Papers I, 244, 247). Baker Brooke in his commission as Surveyor General is called by Lord Baltimore "our trusty and well beloved nephew" (Md. Archives, v, 94), and in his will designates Philip Calvert as the uncle of his wife Ann. Baker Brooke was in no way related to Lord Baltimore and could thus only have been his nephew by marriage, while Lord Baltimore and Philip Calvert had no other niece than the daughter of their brother Leonard.

The will of Baker Brooke is dated 19 March 1679 and was proved seven days later, on the 26th of the same month (Annapolis, Lib. 10, fol. 1). In it he mentions his wife Ann; his sons Charles, Leonard, and Baker; his daughter Mary Brooke; and his brother Col. Thomas Brooke, deceased. His wife is appointed executrix, and "her uncle Philip Calvert, Esq.," overseer. His wife, Ann, survived him and married 2ndly Henry Brent (d. 1693), and 3dly Richard Marsham (d. 1713).

Baker Brooke and Ann (Calvert, his wife) had issue :—

    i. CHARLES BROOKE, d. unmarried 1698.
8. ii. LEONARD BROOKE, d. 1718.
9. iii. BAKER BROOKE, d. 1698.
    iv. MARY BROOKE, mar. Raphael Neale (b. 1683 ; d. 1743) of Charles County. She d. 1763.

5. MAJ. THOMAS BROOKE[4] (*Robert,*[3] *Thomas,*[2] *Richard*[1]) was born at Battle, 23 June 1632, and arrived in Maryland with his father 30 June 1650. He was commissioned, 15 June 1658, Captain commanding the militia of Calvert County "from George Reade's on the south side and St. Leonard's Creek on the north side to the head of Patuxent River" (Md. Archives, iii, 256), and was commissioned Major, 11 Feb. 1660 (*ibid.* p. 402). In the will of his brother Baker he is styled "Colonel Thomas Brooke," but no commission to that effect appears upon record. He represented Calvert County in the Provincial Assembly 1663–1666 (Md. Archives, i, 460 ; ii, 8), and 1671–1676 (*ibid.* ii, 239, 311, 496, &c.) and was High Sheriff of the County 1666–1667 (Md. Archives, iii, 541 ; v, 3) and 1668–1669 (*ibid.* v, 27 ; Lib. C. D., fol. 403). He was Presiding Justice of the County Court in 1667 (Md. Archives, v, 14), and held the position until his death, except during his term of office as Sheriff. He married, about 1658, Eleanor daughter of Richard and Margaret Hatton and niece of Thomas Hatton, Secretary of the Province. She was born in 1642 (Md. Archives, x, 356) and came to Maryland with her widowed mother and her family in 1649 (Land Office, Lib. 1, fol. 440 ; Lib. 2, fol. 613).

The will of Maj. Thomas Brooke, dated 25 October 1676, was proved 29 December following (Annapolis, Lib. 5, fol. 123). In it he mentions his wife Eleanor ; his children as given below ; his brothers Baker and Roger Brooke, and Clement Hill ; and his god-sons Baker Brooke, Jr., and Thomas Gardiner. Two hogsheads of tobacco apiece are left to Mr. Michael Foster and Mr. Henry Carew, priests, "in token that I die a Roman Catholic & desire the good Prayers of the Church for my Soul." Mrs. Eleanor Brooke, widow of Maj. Thomas, married secondly Col. Henry Darnall (d. 17 June, 1711) and had issue by him also. In her will (dated 31 March 1724, proved 21 Feb. 1725) she mentions her sons Thomas Brooke, Clement Brooke, and Henry Darnall; her daughters Mary Witham, Eleanor Digges (wife of William Digges), Mary Carroll, and Ann Hill; and her grandsons Henry and Philip Darnall, sons of her daughter Eleanor Digges.

Maj. Thomas Brooke and Eleanor (Hatton) his wife had issue :—

10. i. COL. THOMAS BROOKE,[5] b. about 1659.
  ii. ROBERT BROOKE, 24 Oct. 1663; d. 18 July 1714; a Jesuit priest.
  iii. IGNATIUS BROOKE, b. 1670; entered the Society of Jesus 1697; d. 1751.
  iv. MATTHEW BROOKE, b. 1672; entered the Society of Jesus 1699; d. 1762.
11. v. CLEMENT BROOKE, b. 1676; d. 1737.
  vi. MARY BROOKE, mar. 1° Capt. James Bowling (d. 1693) of St. Mary's Co., 2° Benjamin Hall (d. 1721) of Prince George's Co., 3° Henry Witham.
  vii. ELEANOR BROOKE, mar. 1° Philip Darnall (d. 1705), son of her step-father Col. Henry Darnall by a former marriage, 2° William Digges.

6. ROGER BROOKE[4] (*Robert,*[3] *Thomas,*[2] *Richard*[1]) was born 20 Sept. 1637 at Brecknock College, in Wales, the episcopal residence of his maternal grandfather, the Bishop of St. David's, after whom he was named, and came to Maryland with his parents in his thirteenth year. He lived at Battle Creek, in Calvert County. He was one of the Justices of the County from 1674 to 1684, and was of the Quorum from 1679 to 1684 (Md. Archives, xv, 37, 68, 71, 268, 327, 395). He was commissioned High Sheriff 18 April 1684 (Lib. C. D., fol. 396) and served until 30 May 1685, when he was again commissioned one of the Quorum (Md. Archives, xvii, 379). Roger Brooke was twice married. His first wife was Dorothy, daughter of Capt. James Neale, who mentions, in his will, his three grandchildren, Roger, James, and Dorothy Brooke. His second wife was Mary, daughter of Walter Wolseley, Esq., and granddaughter of Sir Thomas Wolseley of Staffordshire. She was also the niece of Anne Wolseley, the first wife of Philip Calvert. Her cousin Mrs. Helen Spratt, widow of Thomas Spratt, D. D., Bishop of Rochester, thus speaks of her in a letter dated 18 August 1724: "My cousin Mary Wolseley went to our Aunt Calvert and was married from her house to one Mr. Brooks. I have letters I had from her too,

for I sent her a suit of laced child bed linen as a present,
such as was then in fashion. Her father's name was Walter
Wolseley, Esq. He was my grandfather Sir Thomas Wolseley's son, elder brother to my father, of Wolseley Bridge in
Staffordshire." Her aunt Mrs. Winifred Mullett mentions
her in her will (dated 20 April 1685, proved 9 Jan. 1693) as
"my niece Mary Brooke" and appoints her executrix.

The will of Roger Brooke, dated 5 April 1700, and proved
3 May following (Annapolis, Lib. 6, fol. 384), mentions his
sons Roger, James, John, and Basil, and his daughter "Ann
Daking." He died 8 April 1700, and his son Roger Brooke,
Jr., makes the following entry in his family record: "My
father Mr. Roger Brooke Sen.ʳ second Sone to Robert Brooke
Esq.ʳ By Mary his second Wife Departed this life yᵉ 8ᵗʰ of
April 1700 and Lyes Buried in yᵉ grave yard at his own
plantation at Battell Creeke Between his wives yᵉ first was
Mrs. Dorothy Neale and yᵉ second Mrs. Mary Wolseley:
whaire lyes Buried two Daughters by his second wife: Cassandra and Mary, and my eldest Sone Roger Brooke who
departed this life the 28ᵗʰ Day of May 1705 in yᵉ second yere
of his age."

Roger Brooke and Dorothy (Neale) his first wife had issue:—

12.   i. ROGER BROOKE,⁵ b. 12 April 1673 ; d. 1718.
     ii. JAMES BROOKE, d. s. p. before 1709.
    iii. DOROTHY BROOKE, b. 1678 ; d. 1730 ; mar. 1° Michael Taney (d.
         1702), 2° Richard Blundell (d. 1705), 3° Col. John Smith (d. 1717).

By his second wife, Mary Wolseley, Roger Brooke had issue:—

13.   i. JOHN BROOKE, b. 1687 ; d. 1735.
     ii. BASIL BROOKE, d. s. p. 1711.
    iii. ANN BROOKE, mar. 1° James Dawkins (d. 1701), 2° James Mackall
         (d. 1717). She d. 1733.
     iv. CASSANDRA BROOKE, d. young.
      v. MARY BROOKE, d. young.

7. ROBERT BROOKE⁴ (*Robert,*³ *Thomas,*² *Richard*¹) was born in
London, 21 April 1639, and died in Calvert County, Maryland, in the latter part of 1667. He married Elizabeth,
daughter of William Thompson of St. Mary's County, and,
10 Nov. 1667, "Elizabeth widow of Robert Brooke late of
Calvert County, Gent., deceased" gave bond for the administration of her husband's estate with James Thompson and
Thomas Edwards as her sureties (Test. Proc. Lib. 2, fol.
261, 437, &c.) The nuncupative will of her father William
Thompson, dated 21 Jan. 1660, commits the administration

of testator's estate to his wife and appoints his father-in-law, William Bretton, overseer on behalf of his children. The will was proved by his widow, Mary Thompson, 3 March 1660, on the attestation of Lieut. Col. John Jarboe, Walter Pakes, and Frances Pakes, wife of the latter (Annapolis, Lib. 1, fol. 123). The children of William Thompson are not named in his will, but the following extract from the Rent Roll of St. Mary's County affords evidence as to the parentage of Mrs. Elizabeth Brooke. "KOAXES, 200 acres, surv^d 28 June 1658 for Wm Thompson on the W. side of Bretton's Bay. This land is Res^d into Hopton Park, but Robert Brooke as son of the daughter of said Thompson claims it." Before 1671, Elizabeth, widow of Robert Brooke, married Thomas Cosden. Charles Brooke, of Brooke Place, Calvert County, brother of Robert, mentions in his will (dated 29 May, proved 15 Dec. 1671) his nephews and niece, Robert, William, and Mary Brooke, the children of his brother Robert, their mother, and their father-in-law, Thomas Cosden (Annapolis, Lib. 1, fol. 459).

Robert Brooke and Elizabeth (Thompson) his wife had issue:—

14.   i.   ROBERT BROOKE,[5] d. 1715/6.
      ii.   WILLIAM BROOKE.
     iii.   MARY BROOKE.

BROOKE FAMILY.

8.   LEONARD BROOKE[5] (*Baker*,[4] *Robert*,[3] *Thomas*,[2] *Richard*[1]) of St. Mary's County died in 1718. He married Ann, daughter of Maj. William Boarman of Charles County. She is mentioned in her father's will as "my daughter Ann Brooke," and the account of Maj. Boarman's estate, rendered 7 April 1711, contains an item of money paid to Leonard Brooke and Ann his wife. The will of Leonard Brooke is dated 1 November 1716, and was proved 2 April 1718. In it he mentions the children given below, his nephews Richard and Leonard Brooke, and his brother-in-law Raphael Neale.

Leonard Brooke and Ann (Boarman) his wife had issue:—

  i. CHARLES BROOKE,[6] d. unmar. before 1 July 1761, when his land was
       divided among his sisters.
 ii. ELEANOR BROOKE, d. 1760 ; mar. Clement Gardiner of St. Mary's
       Co., who d. 1747.
iii. JANE BROOKE, mar. John Smith of St. Mary's Co., who d. 1736.
 iv. ANN BROOKE, mar. William Neale.

9. BAKER BROOKE[5] (*Baker,*[4] *Robert,*[3] *Thomas,*[2] *Richard*[1]) of
St. Mary's County died in 1698. He married Katherine
Marsham, daughter of his step-father Richard Marsham, and
she married, secondly, Samuel Queen of St. Mary's County.
Her father, Richard Marsham, mentions in his will (proved
22 April 1723) his grandsons Richard and Leonard Brooke
and his daughter's five children by her second marriage.

   Baker Brooke and Katherine (Marsham) his wife had
   issue :—

       i. BAKER BROOKE,[6] d. s. p.
 15. ii. RICHARD BROOKE, d. 1719.
 16. iii. LEONARD BROOKE, d. 1736.
      iv. ANNE BROOKE, mar. Benedict Leonard Boarman (b. 1687 ; d. 1757)
           of Charles Co.

10. COL. THOMAS BROOKE[5] (*Thomas,*[4] *Robert,*[3] *Thomas,*[2] *Richard*[1]) of Brookfield, Prince George's County, was born about
1659 and died, according to family record, 7 January 1730/1.
He was frequently justice of Calvert County, and in November 1683 was appointed one of the Commissioners for laying
out towns and ports in the County. In 1695 his estate of
Brookfield was included in the newly formed county of Prince
George's. He was a member of the Council of Maryland
from 6 April 1692 (Md. Arch. viii, 306) until 1707 when
he was dismissed for non-attendance, but was reappointed in
1715 and served until 1724 (MS. U. H. Journals). He took
the oath of office as Justice of the Provincial Court 1 May
1694 (Md. Arch. xx, 53), was Deputy Secretary of Maryland
in 1695 (*ibid.* 291), and was commissioned, 26 June 1701,
Commissary General of the Province (Test. Proc., Lib. 19,
fol. 74). In 1720 he was President of the Council and Acting Governor of Maryland from the departure of Gov. John
Hart until the arrival of Gov. Charles Calvert (MS. U. H.
Journals ; Perry's *Church in Maryland,* p. 121). Col. Brooke
was twice married. His first wife, Anne, whose parentage is
unknown, was living in 1687 when she joined her husband
in a deed to Henry Lowe and Susanna his wife "late relict
of John Darnall Esq." and to Clement Hill, of part of De la
Brooke Manor (Prov. Court, Lib. E. I. no. 10, fol. 265).

His second wife was Barbara, daughter of Thomas Dent of St. Mary's County and Rebecca his wife, daughter of the Rev. William Wilkinson. Barbara Dent was born in 1676, after her father's death, and is therefore not named in his will, but her mother conveys land to trustees for her benefit, 20 November 1676, and this deed is confirmed, 6 June 1704, by Barbara's mother and the latter's second husband, Col. John Addison (Charles Co., Lib. 21, fol. 116, 121). In the deed of confirmation it is recited that Barbara " is now married to the Hon. Thomas Brooke Esq." The marriage took place before 4 January 1699, when Col. Thomas Brooke and Barbara his wife execute a deed together (Pr. Geo. Co., Lib. A., fol. 210). The will of Col. Thomas Brooke is dated 30 November 1730, and was proved 25 January 1730/1. His wife Barbara survived him, and died in 1754. Her will, dated 24 February 1748/9, was proved 26 June 1754. Several of Col. Brooke's children are not mentioned in his will, but were provided for by deeds executed in their father's life time.

Col. Thomas Brooke and Ann his first wife had issue:—

17. i. THOMAS BROOKE,[6] b. 1683; d. 1744.
     ii. ELEANOR BROOKE, mar. 1. John Tasker (d. 1711), 2. Charles Sewall (d. 1742).
     iii. SARAH BROOKE, d. 1724; mar. Philip Lee.
     iv. PRISCILLA BROOKE, mar. Thomas Gantt.

By his second wife, Barbara Dent, Col. Thomas Brooke had issue :—

i. NATHANIEL BROOKE.
ii. JOHN BROOKE.
iii. BENJAMIN BROOKE.
iv. BAKER BROOKE.
v. THOMAS BROOKE, b. 1717; d. 1768, unmarried.
vi. JANE BROOKE, d. 1779; mar. about 1720, Alexander Contee of Prince George's Co., who died 24 Dec. 1740.
vii. REBECCA BROOKE, d. 1763; mar. John Howard of Charles Co., who d. 1742.
viii. MARY BROOKE, d. 1758; mar. Dr. Patrick Sim of Prince George's Co., who d. 24 Oct. 1740. Her grandson, Thomas Sim Lee, was Governor of Maryland 1779–82, and 1792–94.
ix. ELIZABETH BROOKE, mar. Col. George Beall (b. 1695; d. 1780).
x. LUCY BROOKE, mar. Thomas Hodgkin.

The order of birth is uncertain. The fact that Col. Thomas Brooke had two sons named Thomas is attested by his will.

11. CLEMENT BROOKE[5] (*Thomas,[4] Robert,[3] Thomas,[2] Richard[1]*), of Prince George's County, was born in 1676, and died in 1737. He is mentioned in his father's will, dated 25 Octo-

ber 1676, as his youngest son, and gives his age as 59 years
in a deposition made in 1736 (Chancery, Lib. I. R. no. 2,
fol. 800). His will is dated 2 August 1734, and was proved
30 June 1737. He married Jane, daughter of Maj. Nicholas
Sewall of St. Mary's County and Susanna his wife, daughter
of Col. William Burgess of Anne Arundel County. Maj.
Sewall names his daughter Jane Brooke in his will, and the
fact of her marriage to Clement Brooke is stated in a deed,
dated 31 August 1704, in Anne Arundel County (Lib. WT.
no. 2, fol. 222). Mrs. Jane Brooke survived her husband and
died in 1761. Her will, dated 20 January 1761, was proved
20 February following.

Clement Brooke and Jane (Sewall) his wife had issue :—

18.   i. HENRY BROOKE,[6] b. 1704 ; d. 1751.
19.   ii. CLEMENT BROOKE, d. 1732.
      iii. JOSEPH BROOKE, d. unmar. 1767.
      iv. NICHOLAS BROOKE.
      v. CHARLES BROOKE, d. unmar. 1768.
      vi. WILLIAM BROOKE.
      vii. SUSANNA BROOKE, d. 1767 ; mar. 1. Walter Smith of Hall's Craft,
            Calvert Co. (d. 1734), 2. Hyde Hoxton (d. 1754).
      viii. ELIZABETH BROOKE, mar. Charles Carroll (b. 1702 ; d. 1781) of
            Annapolis. Their only son was Charles Carroll of Carrollton (b.
            1737 ; d. 1832), signer of the Declaration of Independence.
      ix. ELEANOR BROOKE, mar. . . . . Harrison.

12.   ROGER BROOKE[5] (Roger,[4] Robert,[3] Thomas,[2] Richard[1]), "Eldest sone to Mr. Roger Brooke Sen.: and Dorothy his wife
was borne ye 12th Day of Aprill 1673. And was marryed
to Eliza: Hutchings Jun.r second Daughter to Mr. Francis
Hutchings and Elza: his wife ye 23d Day of Feb'y 1702 "
(Family Record). Her Father, Francis Hutchins, who died
in 1698, represented Calvert County for a number of years in
the House of Burgesses. Roger Brooke removed to Prince
George's County and died there intestate in 1718. His widow
Elizabeth filed her bond 3 September 1718, in the sum of
£2000, as administratrix of Roger Brooke late of Prince
George's County deceased, her sureties being Nehemiah Birckhead, Jr., and Francis Hutchins (Test. Proc. Lib. 23, fol.
245). She married, secondly, Capt. Richard Smith.

Roger Brooke and Elizabeth (Hutchins) his wife had issue
as follows :—

      i. ROGER BROOKE,[6] b. 8 Dec. 1703 ; d. 28 May 1705.
20.   ii. JAMES BROOKE, b. 21 Feb. 1705 ; d. 11 March 1784.
      iii. ELIZABETH BROOKE, b. 23 Nov. 1707 ; mar. Nathaniel Beall.
      iv. DOROTHY BROOKE, b. 5 July 1709 ; mar. Archibald Edmondston of
            Frederick Co.

    v. MARY BROOKE, b. 29 Dec. 1710.
    vi. ANN BROOKE, b. 29 March 1712 ; mar. William Carmichael of Queen
        Anne Co.
21. vii. ROGER BROOKE, b. 10 June 1714 ; d. 1772.
    viii. CASSANDRA BROOKE b. 3 April 1716.
    ix. PRISCILLA BROOKE (twin), b. 16 Nov. 1717; d. 1783 ; mar. Charles
        Browne (d. 1766) of Queen Anne Co.
22. x. BASIL BROOKE (twin), b. 16 Nov. 1717; d. 1761.

13. JOHN BROOKE [5] (*Roger,[4] Robert,[3] Thomas,[2] Richard [1]*), of
Calvert County, was born in 1687 and died in 1735. According to a deposition he was 38 years old in 1725 (Test. Proc.,
Lib. 27, fol. 275), and his will, dated 21 December 1734,
was proved 21 March 1735. His wife Sarah gives her age
as 34 years in a deposition made in 1725 (Test. Proc., Lib.
27, fol. 276).

    John Brooke and Sarah his wife had issue :—

    i. JOHN BROOKE,[6] d. 1770 ; mar. Barbara . . . . and had a son, John
        Brooke.[7]
    ii. JAMES BROOKE.
23. iii. BASIL BROOKE, d. 1757.
    iv. ROGER BROOKE, d. 1770 ; mar. Ann . . . . , but had no issue.
    v. SARAH BROOKE, mar. 1. Michael Taney (d. 1743), 2. Edward Cole,
        Jr. (d. 1761), of St. Mary's Co.
    vi. MARY BROOKE.

14. ROBERT BROOKE [5] (*Robert,[4] Robert,[3] Thomas,[2] Richard [1]*), of
Calvert County, died in 1715/6. His will, dated 17 Janu-
ary 1715, was proved 10 April 1716. He married Grace,
widow of John Boone (d. 1689) of Calvert County. According to a deposition, she was aged 58 years in 1720 (Chancery,
Lib. P. L., fol. 519), and her will was proved 30 October
1725.

    Robert Brooke and Grace his wife had issue :—

24. i. ROBERT BROOKE,[6] b. 1692 ; d. 1753.
    ii. CHARLES BROOKE.
    iii. ELIZABETH BROOKE, mar. Cuthbert Fenwick (d. 1729) of St. Mary's
        County.

THE BROOKE FAMILY.

15. RICHARD BROOKE[6] (*Baker,*[5] *Baker,*[4] *Robert,*[3] *Thomas,*[2] *Richard*[1]) of St. Mary's Co., died in 1719. His will, dated 5 Dec. 1718 and proved 3 Aug. 1719, mentions his sons Richard and Baker, to whom he leaves "all my land being part of Delabrook Manor"; his uncle Leonard Brooke, deceased; and "my beloved wife." Testator's brother, Leonard Brooke, is appointed executor. Richard Brooke married Clare daughter of Maj. William Boarman of Charles Co. She married, secondly, Richard Sherburne of St. Mary's Co., and had by him a son Nicholas Sherburne. Her will, dated 21 Feb'y

1745 and proved 6 Aug. 1747, mentions her three sons Richard and Baker Brooke, and Nicholas Sherburne.

Richard Brooke and Clare (Boarman) his wife had issue:—

    i. RICHARD BROOKE,[7] d. 1755; mar. Monica, dau. of Clement Gardiner of St. Mary's Co., and had two daughters 1, Clare Brooke,[8] 2, Anna Brooke,[8] mar. . . . . Hill. Mrs. Monica Brooke, who d. 1772, mar. secondly Henry Queen (b. 1729; d. 1768).

    ii. BAKER BROOKE, d. 1756; mar. Mary, dau. of Wm. Simpson of Charles Co., but had no issue.

16. LEONARD BROOKE [6] (*Baker*,[5] *Baker*,[4] *Robert*,[3] *Thomas*,[2] *Richard*[1]) of Prince George's Co. died in 1736. His will, dated June 1735 and proved 4 May 1736, mentions his wife Ann and the children given below. Mrs. Ann Brooke survived her husband and died in 1779. Her will, dated 15 Dec. 1769, was proved in Prince George's Co. 2 July 1779.

Leonard Brooke and Ann his wife had issue:—

    i. BAKER BROOKE.[7]
    ii. OSWALD BROOKE.
25.   iii. LEONARD BROOKE, b. 1728; d. 1785.
26.   iv. RICHARD BROOKE, d. 1771.
    v. ANNA BROOKE.
    vi. KATHRINE BROOKE.
    vii. JANE BROOKE.
    viii. MARY BROOKE.
    ix. HENRIETTA BROOKE.

17. THOMAS BROOKE [6] (*Thomas*,[5] *Thomas*,[4] *Robert*,[3] *Thomas*,[2] *Richard*[1]) of Prince George's Co. was born in 1683, and died 28 Dec. 1744. His age is given in depositions as 47 in 1731, and 53 in 1736 (Pr. Geo. Co. Records). His will, dated 27 Dec. 1738 and proved 29 March 1745, mentions only his wife Lucy and his son Walter Brooke; the names of his other children are obtained from a family record. Thomas Brooke was representative for Prince George's Co. in the Maryland Assembly in 1713 (House Journal), and was High Sheriff of the County from 28 Aug. 1731 to 28 Aug. 1734 (Commission Book). He married, 9 May 1705, Lucy eldest daughter of Col. Walter Smith of Calvert Co. She was born in 1688, and died 15 April 1770. Her will, dated 25 Nov. 1769, was proved 30 Nov. 1770.

Thomas Brooke and Lucy (Smith) his wife had issue:—

27.   i. THOMAS BROOKE,[7] b. 30 April 1706; d. 1749.
28.   ii. WALTER BROOKE, b. 29 Dec. 1707; d. 9 March 1740/1.
    iii. MARY BROOKE, b. 8 Oct. 1709; mar. Peter Dent (b. 1694; d. 1757) of Pr. George's Co.

iv. ANNA BROOKE, b. 16 June 1711; mar. . . . . Harris.
v. NATHANIEL BROOKE, b. 1 March 1712.
vi. LUCY BROOKE, b. 10 Oct. 1714; d. 12 May 1718.
29.   vii. RICHARD BROOKE, b. 2 June 1716; d. 13 July 1783.
viii. ELEANOR BROOKE, b. 7 March 1718; mar. Col. Samuel Beall
        (d. 1778) of Frederick Co.
ix. RACHEL BROOKE, b. 12 Aug. 1719; d. unmarried 1789.
x. LUCY BROOKE, b. 10 April 1721; mar. John Estep (d. 1766) of
        Charles Co.
xi. ISAAC BROOKE (twin), b. 22 Jan. 1722; d. unmarried 1 Nov. 1756.
xii. REBECCA BROOKE (twin), b. 22 Jan. 1722.
xiii. ELIZABETH BROOKE, b. 22 Sept. 1724; d. unmarried 1794.
xiv. DANIEL BROOKE, b. 5 May 1726; d. 8 Nov. 1735.
xv. CHARLES BROOKE, b. 14 Sept. 1727; d. 21 Sept. 1727.
xvi. ROBERT BROOKE, b. 25 Nov. 1728; d. unmarried 1777.
30.   xvii. CLEMENT BROOKE, b. 1 Sept. 1730; d. 18 Nov. 1800.

18. HENRY BROOKE [6] (*Clement,*[5] *Thomas,*[4] *Robert,*[3] *Thomas,*[2]
Richard[1]) of Prince George's Co., was born in 1704, and
died in 1751. In a deposition his age is given as 37 years
in 1741 (Chancery, I. R. No. 4, 419), and his will, dated 25
Sept. 1751, was proved 26 October following. By Margaret
his wife he had issue :—

i. HENRY BROOKE.[7]
ii. CLEMENT BROOKE.
iii. JOHN BROOKE.
iv. NICHOLAS BROOKE.
v. JANE BROOKE.
vi. MARY BROOKE.
vii. ANN BROOKE, mar. . . . . Wade.
viii. RACHEL BROOKE, mar. . . . . Boarman.
ix. SUSANNA BROOKE.

19. CLEMENT BROOKE [6] (*Clement,*[5] *Thomas,*[4] *Robert,*[3] *Thomas,*[2]
Richard[1]) of Prince George's Co. died in 1732. In his will,
dated 31 Aug. 1731 proved 30 Aug. 1732, he states that he
is bound, with Mary his wife, on a voyage for London, and
mentions his daughter Rachel and his "honored father Mr.
Clement Brooke." Mrs. Mary Brooke, widow of Clement,
married secondly Dr. Charles Neale of Frederick Co. and
executed with him, in 1769, a deed of trust for the benefit of
her daughter Rachel.

Clement Brooke and Mary his wife had issue :—

i. RACHEL BROOKE,[7] mar. Henry Darnall of Prince George's Co. Their
    daughter Mary Darnall married, 5 June 1768, Charles Carroll of
    Carrollton.

20. JAMES BROOKE [6] (*Roger,*[5] *Roger,*[4] *Robert,*[3] *Thomas,*[2] *Richard*[1]) was born, according to family record, 21 Feb. 1705
and died 11 March 1784. He was married, 21 June 1725,

to Deborah, eldest daughter of Richard Snowden and Elizabeth (Coale) his wife. She died 29 April 1758. James Brooke and Deborah (Snowden) his wife had issue :—

    i. JAMES BROOKE,[7] b. 26 Feb. 1730/1 ; d. 21 Aug. 1767 ; mar. Hannah Janney of Virginia, and left issue,

    ii. ROGER BROOKE, b. 9 Aug. 1734; d. 7. Sept. 1790 ; mar. Mary Matthews, who d. 25 April 1808, and had issue.

    iii. RICHARD BROOKE, b. 8 July 1736; d. 2 May 1788 ; mar., 1758, Jane Lynn (d. 15 Sept. 1774) and had issue.

    iv. BASIL BROOKE, b. 13 Dec. 1738 ; d. 22 Aug. 1794 ; mar., 1 May 1764, Elizabeth Hopkins (d. 17 Aug. 1794) and had issue.

    v. ELIZABETH BROOKE, b. 22 March 1740/1 ; mar., 2 June 1761, Thomas Pleasants of Goochland Co., Va.

    vi. THOMAS BROOKE, b. 8 March 1743/4 ; d. 11 June 1789.

An account of the descendants of James and Deborah (Snowden) Brooke is given in *The Thomas Book* (New York, 1896), p. 219 ff.

21. ROGER BROOKE[6] (*Roger*,[5] *Roger*,[4] *Robert*,[3] *Thomas*,[2] *Richard*[1]) of Calvert Co. was born 10 June 1714, and died in 1772. His will, dated 8 Feb. 1772 and proved 9 April following, mentions his wife Elizabeth and his children Roger, Basil, John, Elizabeth, Sarah, Bowyer, and Dorothy Brooke, and Monica Taney. According to the statements of his descendants Roger Brooke was twice married, 1° to Sarah Bowyer of Philadelphia, who died about 1745-46, and 2° to Elizabeth Boarman.

By his first wife, Sarah Bowyer, he had issue :—

    i. ROGER BROOKE.[7] His will (dated 6 Jan., proved 16 Aug. 1776) names his wife Mary ; his daughter Sarah Brooke ; his brothers Basil and John Brooke ; and his kinsman Francis Brooke.

    ii. JOHN BROOKE (twin), b. 1737 ; d. young.

    iii. BOWYER BROOKE (twin), b. 1737 ; d. 1815 ; mar. 1° Mary Browne, 2° Hannah Reese, and left issue.

    iv. SARAH BROOKE.

    v. ANNA BROOKE.

By his second wife, Elizabeth Boarman, Roger Brooke had issue :—

    i. BASIL BROOKE, b. 1748 ; mar. Anne dau. of James and Mary (Brown) Duke, and had an only child, Elizabeth Brooke (b. 31 Dec. 1780 ; d. 6 Oct. 1805), who mar. Dr. John Dare.

    ii. MONICA BROOKE, b. 1752 ; mar. Michael Taney. Their son, Roger Brooke Taney (b. 1777 ; d. 1864) was Chief-Justice of the United States.

    iii. ELIZABETH BROOKE.

    iv. JOHN BROOKE, b. 1753 ; d. 1790 ; mar. Mary Wheeler and had two children, a) John James Brooke, b. 11 Aug. 1787 ; d. 16 March 1836 ; mar. 23 Oct. 1814 Juliet Duke and had issue, b) Harriet Brooke, b. Sept. 1789 ; mar. Dr. Ireland and d. s. p.

    v. DOROTHY BROOKE.

For this account of the children of Roger Brooke, by his two wives, I am indebted to Mrs. Samuel T. Brown of Baltimore, Md., a granddaughter of John James Brooke (*John,*[7] *Roger*[6]).

22. BASIL BROOKE [6] (*Roger,*[5] *Roger,*[4] *Robert,*[3] *Thomas,*[2] *Richard*[1]) of Charles Co. was born 16 Nov. 1717 and died in 1761. His will, dated 14 May 1761, was proved 13 July following. He married Henrietta daughter of Raphael Neale of Charles Co. and Mary his wife, daughter of Baker Brooke.[4] Her mother, Mrs. Mary Neale, mentions in her will (dated 29 Sept. 1760, proved 24 May 1763) her " daughter Henrietta Brooke " and her " son-in-law Basil Brooke." Mrs. Henrietta Brooke died in 1774, leaving a will dated 27 June 1773 and proved 16 June 1774.

Basil Brooke and Henrietta (Neale) his wife had issue :—

   i. RAPHAEL BROOKE.[7]
   ii. ROGER BROOKE.
   iii. JAMES BROOKE.
   iv. ANN BROOKE.

23. BASIL BROOKE [6] (*John,*[5] *Roger,*[4] *Robert,*[3] *Thomas,*[2] *Richard*[1]) of Charles Co. died in 1757. His will, dated 24 April 1755, was proved 8 March 1757. He married first Dorothy daughter of Michael Taney of Calvert Co., and secondly Sarah . . . . . Michael Taney, in his will dated 2 June 1743 and proved 24 March 1743/4, mentions his " daughter Dorothy Brooke " and his " son-in-law Basil Brooke," and the latter mentions his wife Sarah in his will.

Basil Brooke and Dorothy (Taney) his first wife had issue :—

   i. BASIL BROOKE.[7]
   ii. MICHAEL BROOKE.
   iii. MARY BROOKE.

24. ROBERT BROOKE [6] (*Robert,*[5] *Robert,*[4] *Robert,*[3] *Thomas,*[2] *Richard*[1]) of Calvert Co. was born in 1692 and died in 1753. According to a deposition he was aged 37 years in 1729, and his will, made in 1748, was proved 15 Sept. 1753. He married Jane daughter of Cuthbert Fenwick of St. Mary's Co., who names in his will (proved 23 March 1729) his grandchildren Robert and Mary Brooke. Mrs. Jane Brooke survived her husband and died in 1759. Her will, dated 19 May 1758, was proved 21 March 1759.

Robert Brooke and Jane (Fenwick) his wife had issue:—

 i. ROBERT BROOKE.[7]
 ii. WILLIAM BROOKE.
 iii. FRANCIS BROOKE.
 iv. HENRY BROOKE.
 v. CHARLES BROOKE.
 vi. MARY BROOKE, mar. Philip Fenwick.
 vii. SARAH BROOKE.
 viii. BARBARA BROOKE.
 ix. JANE BROOKE.

BROOKE FAMILY.

---

25. CAPT. LEONARD BROOKE[7] (*Leonard,*[6] *Baker,*[5] *Baker,*[4] *Robert*[3])
of Prince George's County was born in 1728 and died in
1785.　His age is given in a deposition as 29 years in 1757
(Pr. Geo. Co. Records), and his will, dated 27 Oct. 1783,
was proved in Prince George's County 10 Feb. 1785.　He
was a sea captain and, in 1755, was commander of a vessel
called the Horatio (Md. Gazette, 20 Feb. 1755).　He was
twice married.　His first wife was Anne daughter of Henry
Darnall of Portland Manor (Chancery, Lib. 1784–86, fol.
483), and his second wife Elizabeth is named in his will.
Capt. Leonard Brooke had issue by his two wives :—

 i. LEONARD BROOKE.[8]
 ii. BAKER BROOKE.
 iii. GEORGE BROOKE.
 iv. ANNE BROOKE.
 v. ESTHER BROOKE, mar. Henry Hill.
 vi. ELEANOR BROOKE.
 vii. CATHERINE BROOKE.

26. RICHARD BROOKE[7] (*Leonard*,[6] *Baker*,[5] *Baker*,[4] *Robert*[3]) of Charles County died in 1771. His will, dated 14 Jan. 1771, was proved in Charles County 9 April following. In it he appoints his "brother Leonard Brooke of Prince George's County" his executor and names the children given below. The name of his wife does not appear.

Richard Brooke had issue :—

   i. LEONARD BROOKE.[8]
   ii. BAKER BROOKE.
   iii. JAMES BROOKE.
   iv. RICHARD BROOKE.
   v. ANNE BROOKE.

27. THOMAS BROOKE[7] (*Thomas*,[6] *Thomas*,[5] *Thomas*,[4] *Robert*[3]) of Charles County was born 30 April 1706, and died in 1749. He married Sarah daughter of Col. George Mason of Gunston, Stafford Co., Va. According to the will of his brother, Dr. Richard Brooke (q. v.), she was his second wife. The name of the first wife does not appear, but she was probably the mother of the eldest son Thomas, while the two younger sons, Walter and Richard, were certainly the children of Sarah Mason. The will of Thomas Brooke, dated 2 Sept. 1748 and proved in Charles Co. 15 June 1749, mentions his wife Sarah, his sons Walter and Richard, his eldest son Thomas, and his brother Richard Brooke. To his wife and his two younger sons he leaves "the tract of land whereon I now dwell, near Chickamuxon in Charles County." Thomas Brooke had issue :—

   i. THOMAS BROOKE[8] (probably by first wife).
   ii. WALTER BROOKE, Commodore in the Virginia Navy 1775–78 (Va. Mag. i. 331). He married Ann Darrell and d. 1798 leaving issue.
   iii. RICHARD BROOKE.

28. WALTER BROOKE[7] (*Thomas*,[6] *Thomas*,[5] *Thomas*,[4] *Robert*[3]) of Prince George's County was born 29 Dec. 1707, and died 9 March 1740/1. He married Mary Ashcom Greenfield daughter of James Greenfield of Prince George's Co., who names his "daughter Mary Brooke" in his will (dated 21 Nov. 1733, proved 26 March 1734). She is also mentioned in the will of her aunt Winifred Ashcom (dated 20 Oct. 1717, proved 27 March 1718) as "my niece Mary Ashcom Greenfield." Walter Brooke in his will (dated 1 January 1740/1, proved 19 June 1741) mentions his wife Mary Ashcom Brooke, his son Thomas Brooke under 19 years of age, and his four daughters of whom only Sarah is named.

All five of his children are named in a deed dated 9 August 1738 (Pr. Geo. Co. Records) and in the final account of his estate. Walter Brooke and Mary Ashcom (Greenfield) his wife had issue :—

  i. THOMAS BROOKE,[8] under 19 in 1740 ; d. intestate 1768. He married 1°, 16 Sept. 1753, Frances, daughter of Thomas Jennings of Prince George's Co., 2° Elizabeth ———, and had an only son (by his first wife), Isaac Brooke[9] (b. 21 March 1759 ; d. 1785) who married, in August 1780, Sarah Ann daughter of Alex. Magruder of Prince George's Co., and had an only son, Thomas Alexander Brooke[10] (b. 3 Oct. 1782).
  ii. MARTHA BROOKE.
  iii. ANNE BROOKE.
  iv. LUCY BROOKE.
  v. SARAH BROOKE.

29. DR. RICHARD BROOKE[7] (*Thomas,[6] Thomas,[5] Thomas,[4] Robert[3]*) of Prince George's County was born 2 June 1716, and died 13 July 1783. His will, dated 26 April 1771, was proved in Pr. George's Co. 11 Aug. 1783. In it he names his wife Rachel ; his son Thomas ; his brother Rev. Clement Brooke ; Isaac Brooke "grandson of my dearly beloved brother Walter Brooke" ; and his nephew Richard Brandt. In case of failure of issue of these devisees he entails his estate of Brookfield, 1, on the issue of Peter Dent, deceased, and testator's sister Mary ; 2, on the issue of his sister Eleanor and her husband Col. Samuel Beall ; 3, on the heirs of "my brother Thomas and his second wife sister to Col. Mason of Virginia." Dr. Richard Brooke married, 1 Nov. 1767, Rachel daughter of Thomas Gantt of Pr. George's Co. and Rachel his wife daughter of Col. John Smith of Calvert Co. (Family Record). Mrs. Rachel Brooke died 28 June 1793 in the fiftieth year of her age.
Dr. Richard Brooke and Rachel (Gantt) his wife had issue :—

  i. FREDERICK THOMAS BROOKE,[8] b. 27 July 1770.
  ii. SARAH BROOKE, b. 15 March 1772 ; d. 27 August 1849 ; mar. 23 July 1789, Samuel Harper (d. 25 Dec. 1834, aged 69), and had issue.

30. REV. CLEMENT BROOKE[7] (*Thomas,[6] Thomas,[5] Thomas,[4] Robert[3]*) of Prince George's County was born 1 Sept. 1730, and died 18 Nov. 1800 (Family Record). He married, 19 May 1774, Anne Murdock of Pr. George's Co. and had issue:—

  i. KITTY MURDOCK BROOKE,[8] b. 11 March 1775.
  ii. THOMAS BROOKE, b. 29 August 1776.
  iii. ANNE ADDISON BROOKE, b. 28 July 1778.
  iv. WILLIAM MURDOCK BROOKE, b. 17 Nov. 1779.
  v. CLEMENT BROOKE, b. 2 April 1781 ; d. about 1827 ; mar. 2 April 1801, Ann Eleanor Whitaker and had issue.

A CHART OF THE BROOKE FAMILY OF MARYLAND.

Francis B. Culver.

At the Maryland Historical Society's rooms, Baltimore, Maryland, there is an elaborate, framed chart, embellished by numerous armorial bearings, which purports to be the " Pedigree Chart of Robert Brooke, who arrived in Maryland 30 June 1650, and Mary Baker his first wife who died in England, 1634." Mounted upon an easel and readily accessible to visitors, the display of this chart suggests the *quasi*-approval of the same on the part of the authorities of the Society.

It was compiled by the late Bennet Bernard Browne, M. D., and printed at London in 1912 by Alexander Moring, Ltd., for the late Douglas H. Thomas, of Baltimore, a descendant of the aforesaid Robert Brooke. The lineage is traced from Charlemagne (742-814), through succeeding royal and noble lines, from whom the descents of a number of American families can be established.

Those who are seeking genealogical information frequently have recourse to the chart as an authoritative work, and in several instances it has been copied in its entirety. Attention should be directed to the fact that it contains typographical errors such as the setting down of William the Conqueror and Matilda, his wife, as the parents of Gundred (1053-1085), who became the wife of William de Warren, first Earl of Surrey. Gundred was the daughter of Matilda, but William the Conqueror was not her father. In another place, the wife of Robert de Beaumont (1104-1168) is given as " Ancicia " instead of Amicia, and elsewhere Robert Brooke (1602-1655) is styled as of " White-marsh," instead of " Whitchurch," in county Southampton. Henry " the Fowler " was not the father of Louis IV. (d'Outremer), but of Gerberge, wife of the latter, etc., etc.

A more serious blunder, however, occurs with respect to the

mother of *Helen* the wife of Roger de Quincy (d. 1264), second
Earl of Saher and Winchester, son of Saher de Quincy (a Magna
Charta surety). Helen's father was Alan, Lord of Galloway,
but she was not by his wife *Margaret* who was daughter of
David, Earl of Huntington (grandson of David I, King of
Scotland). Margaret de Huntington was Alan's second wife,
by whom there were born but two daughters, Devorgilla and
Christiana. The latter married William de Fortibus, Earl of
Albemarle, and died without surviving issue. Devorgilla mar-
ried John de Baliol and had a son, John de Baliol, who was
declared King of Scotland in the time of King Edward I.

The aforesaid *Helen* (wife of Roger de Quincy), was the
daughter of Alan of Galloway by a first wife (name unknown)
who is said by some authorities to have been a daughter of
Reginald, Lord of the Isles. As heretofore stated, the descendants of Devorgilla and John de Baliol were claimants to the
throne of Scotland, but Helen's children, not being descendants
of Huntington, had no claim in their issue. Thus does genealogy in part explain the facts of history!

A proper revision of the chart in question will do away with
over one half of the lineages, *as published,* but the descent from
Charlemagne will stand, the same being established through
another line, that is to say: through Margaret de Beaumont,
wife Saher de Quincy, in the right of the House of Vermandois.

The writer of this article, in one or two instances during the
course of his own genealogical work, was led into the error described above, by following this chart too closely and so, in the
interest of truth and accuracy, he thus makes public announcement of the same, to the end that others may profit by his later
investigations.

THE BROOKE FAMILY.

By ELLON BROOKE CULVER BOWEN.
(Mrs. EDWIN LEROY BOWEN.)

Dr. Christopher Johnston's ably compiled "Brooke Family," as contained in the *Maryland Historical Magazine*, Vol. I, commencing on page 66, deals with the Brooke family of the older and lower counties of Maryland, including the seventh and touching lightly the eighth generation.

This present article will continue the numbering of the generations which it will record, as Dr. Johnston started them, commencing with the two parent generations of the Brooke line in Whitchurch, Co. Hampshire, England.

RICHARD BROOKE[1], THOMAS BROOKE[2], both of Whitchurch, to ROBERT BROOKE[3], who after long journeying in strange waters sailed into the beautiful Patuxent River, with its richly wooded shores, 30 June, 1650, and settled twenty miles from its mouth, having been in sight of his own lands after leaving the Chesapeake Bay. The Manor of De la Brooke was erected, a quaint brick building, with steep roof and dormer windows, with a wainscotted main floor and living room with massive cornice and floral designed frieze of rose and lily.

The second son of ROBERT BROOKE[3] was Major THOMAS BROOKE[4], whose eldest son was Col. THOMAS BROOKE[5], his eldest son was THOMAS BROOKE[6], Esq., of Prince George's Co., whose eldest son was THOMAS BROOKE[7]. With the seventh generation Dr. Johnston's Brooke Family stops, with a mention of the eighth generation. The line of Thomas Brooke[7] (*Maryland*

Hist. Mag., Vol. I, p. 377) had not been concluded, as only the name of the second wife, Sarah Mason, is given; the records of the first wife and other records had not been found by Dr. Johnston. The following is the additional record of Thomas Brooke[7], who was of Prince George's and Charles Counties, Maryland. He was the eldest son of Thomas Brooke[6], Esq., of Brookefield, Prince George's Co. (previous to 1695 Calvert Co., Md.), and his wife, Lucy Smith (dau. of Col. Walter Smith of Calvert Co., Md., and his wife, Rachael Hall), born to them at Brookefield, 30 April, 1706, died at his estate of "Nonesuch," near Chickamuxen, Charles Co., Md. His will was proved 15 June, 1749. Charles Co. Wills, Lib. A. C., No. 4, fol. 276.

THOMAS BROOKE[7] married first, Judith Briscoe (died ca. 1738), the widow of Charles Ashcom, of St. Mary's Co., Md. (see will of Charles Ashcom, Annapolis, Md., Lib. XIX, fol. 127, dated 20 Nov., 1725, Pro. 23 Mar. 1727), and the daughter of Philip Briscoe, Sr., of Charles Co., Md., and his wife, Susanna Swann. In the will of Philip Briscoe, Sr., Charles Co., Md., Lib. A. B., No. 3, fol. 176, under its date of 25 Apr., 1724, Pro. 29 Jan., 1724 [old style reckoning] mentions this daughter as "Judith Ashcom." Between the date of his will and the date of the will of his wife, Susanna Briscoe, Charles Co., Md., Lib. A. C., No. 4, fol. 116, dated 5 Feb., 1739, Pro. 24 July, 1740, Judith (Briscoe) Ashcom had remarried and died, and is mentioned in this will of her mother as "my daughter, Judith Brooke deceased." Under Testamentary Proceedings, Lib. No. 28, 1727-1730, Annapolis, Md., in the Will Codicil and Testamentary Bond on Estate of Charles Ashcom, late of St. Mary's Co., deceased, his widow, as executrix of his will, signs this bond for £5,000 sterling, as Judith Ashcom. Bond dated 23 March, 1727.

In Annapolis, Md., Inventory Book No. 12, 1727, fol. 261, the Inventory of Estate of Charles Ashcom, late of St. Mary's Co., Md., deceased, is appraised £939..8..9. Signed and proved by Judith Brooke, Extrix., dated 5 Sept., 1727. The dates and the change in her name, as given in the afore Test. Bond and the following one, on the Appraisement of Charles Ashcom's

Estate, show that Judith (Briscoe) Ashcom had become the wife of Thomas Brooke[7], between 23 March, 1727, and 5 Sept., 1727.

A record from Annapolis, Md., Account Book, No. 9, fol. 195, under Account of Estate of Charles Ashcom, late of St. Mary's Co., Md., deceased, dated 29 May, 1728, is signed by Thomas Brooke and Judith, his wife. Additional Account of Estate of Charles Ashcom, late of St. Mary's Co., Md., deceased, Annapolis, Md., Account Book No. 11, 1731-1733, fol. 525, is given " By Thomas Brooke, who intermarried with Judith, the Relict and Extrix. of said Charles Ashcom." Proved 21 Nov., 1732, by Thomas Brooke. The total of the estate being £1,056..19..1¾. A careful search of the records shows that the only Thomas Brooke of that generation who could have intermarried with Charles Ashcom's young widow, Judith Briscoe 1727, was Thomas Brooke of the seventh generation, being of Prince George's and Charles Co., as the only other unmarried Thomas Brooke in Maryland was not born until 1717 and died a bachelor 1768, he was the youngest son of Col. Thomas Brooke and his 2nd wife, Barbara Dent. See *Maryland Hist. Mag.*, Vol. I, page 186. The Marriage References, compiled by Mrs. George W. Hodges, on file at Annapolis, Md., Land Office, gives the date of 1732 for marriage of Thomas Brooke to Judith Briscoe, which date is the final account of the settlement of Charles Ashcom's estate, and is nearly five years later than the date of the marriage 1727, as shown in the preceding data of Court Proceedings quoted in this article.

Following are the Colonial Services of Thomas Brooke[7], known in Prince George's Co. as Thomas Brooke, Jr. (1706-1749):

Maryland Commission Record (1726-1786), Original MMS. Archives State of Maryland, No. 81. P. 77, Thomas Brooke Jun[r] appointed Justice for Prince George's Co., Md., Nov., 1746. Pp. 80, 83, Thomas Brooke Jun[r] appointed Justice of the Peace for Prince George's Co., Md., 6 Oct., 1747.

List of Civil Officers of Maryland (1637-1659), Goldsborough Bound MSS. (Md. Hist. Soc.). P. 607, Commission issued

Thomas Brooke Junr 12 June, 1746, as Associate Justice of Prince George's Co., Md. P. 613, Commission issued Thomas Brooke Junr 6 Oct., 1747, as Associate Justice of Prince George's Co., Md.

Thomas Brooke[7] died at his estate of "Nonesuch," near Chickamuxen, Charles Co., Md., at age of forty-three. "Nonesuch" is described according to the patent Eschoat, composed of the following tracts: 76 a. "Allison's Folly," 200 a. "Wicksall," 120 a. "Aspinall's Hope." Annapolis, Md., Rent Roll No. 2. Charles Co., Md., fol. 163. Previously "Nonesuch" had been surveyed 18 July, 1670, for Major Thomas Brooke. Rent Roll, Prince George's Co., Md., 1707, fol. 132. Thomas Brooke[7] in his will, dated 2 Sept., 1748, Proved 15 June, 1749, Lib. A. C., No. 4, fol. 276, Charles Co., Md., bequeaths Eschoat to his second "wife Sarah Mason, during her term of widowhood, afterwards to my two sons, Walter and Richard Brooke, should they die without issue, then the aforesaid Tract of Land and personal Estate to be equally divided between my wife Sarah and my eldest son Thomas Brooke." "Thomas Brooke, my eldest son" is again mentioned in his father's will and again in "the education of my three sons, Thomas, Walter and Richard Brooke to be under the direction of my loving brother Richard Brooke, but the expense of their education to be discharged by my Executrix."

Issue of THOMAS BROOKE[7] and his first wife, Judith Briscoe (widow of Charles Ashcom of St. Mary's Co., Md.).

   i. Thomas Brooke[8], b. 1734, d. 1789, Washington Co., Md. See further.

By his second wife, Sarah Mason of Fairfax Co., Va. (sister of Col. George Mason of Va.). *Maryland Hist. Mag.*, Vol. I, pp. 377-8.

   i. Walter Boroke, b. ca. 1740, d 1798, mar. 1774, Ann Darrell (b. 21 June, 1758, d. 10 Oct., 1823). Commodore Va. Navy 1775-78. Left surviving issue 3 sons and 2 daus. (Family Records.)
  ii. Richard Brooke.

Dr. Johnston in his "Brooke Family," Vol. I, p. 377, makes

it plain that Walter and Richard Brooke were the sons of Sarah Mason, while the first son was the child of the first wife.

In 1695 Prince George's Co., Md., was formed from Calvert Co., and included Brookefield, the estate of Col. Thomas Brooke[5]. Later when Brookefield came by inheritance to his eldest son, Thomas Brooke[6], by his first wife, Ann, there came to be three lineal generations of Thomas Brooke, of Prince George's Co., it then became necessary to designate them as Thomas Brooke[6], Esq. (1683-1744), his eldest son, Thomas Brooke[7], as Jun[r] (1706-1749), and his eldest son, Thomas Brooke[8], as the 3rd (1734-1789). After the death of the progenitors of Thomas Brooke the 3rd and his removing to Frederick Co., and Washington Co. being formed from Frederick, he was variously named as Thomas Brooke, Jr., of Washington Co., as Thomas Brooke of Washington Co., and as Thomas Brooke, son of Thomas. There are various ones in the Warrant Books in the Maryland Land Office in Annapolis between June 29, 1782, and Aug. 19, 1788. The clinching proof of the foregoing that Thomas Brooke[8] was identical with the Thomas Brooke of the Land Office records and Thomas Brooke who made his Washington Co. Will in 1789 is found in Annapolis Land Office Book of Patents, Lib. I. C. C., fol. 490.

The designation of these three lineal generations of Brooke in Prince George's Co., that perpetuated the beloved name of Thomas, each the eldest son of their line, appears frequently on the pages of the " Church Records of St. Paul's Parish, Prince George's Co. (1730-1819)," as well as in civil proceedings. P. 17. Thomas Brooke, Esq., late Sheriff, in balance of his account, etc. P. 16. The new Church, St. Paul's Parish, 2 Sept., 1735. Choice of Pews, Thomas Brooke, Esq., pew 18. Thomas Brooke, Jun[r], Walter Brooke, Baker Brooke and Gerard Truman Greenfield, Pew 3, in the gallery. P. 17. Thomas Brooke, Jun[r], as Vestryman of St. Paul's Parish, and like appointments recorded on pages 55, 61, 63, 65, 76, 77. Vestry Proceedings, St. Paul's Parish, p. 156, " Order given by the Register of the Parish to give Thomas Brooke, the 3rd, an order to have the church repaired."

THOMAS BROOKE[8] * (Thomas[7], Thomas[6], Thomas[5], Thomas[4], Robert[3], Thomas[2], Richard[1], the two latter of Whitchurch, Co. Hampshire, England), eldest son of Thomas Brooke[7], and his first wife, Judith Briscoe (widow of Charles Ashcom of St. Mary's Co., Md.). He was born 1734 (according to his sworn statement in a deposition before Justice John Stull, Hagerstown, Washington Co., Md., 8 Apr., 1786. Land Records, Lib. D, fol. 487). Died 1789, Washington Co., Md. Married Elizabeth ———, ante 1765, when she joins him in deed when living in Prince George's Co., Md. (Charles Co. Deeds, Lib. L, No. 3, fol. 612, 22 Feb., 1765.) Elizabeth Brooke died between 25 Aug., 1784 (at which time she stated under oath that she released her right voluntary in " Jonas Discovery." Wash. Co., Md., Deeds, Lib. D, fol. 120), and when on 1 Apr., 1785, her signature was not given, on an Indenture made by Thomas Brooke, her husband, a process of signature release being necessary if wife is living (Wash. Co., Md., Land Records, Lib. D, fol. 278). Thomas Brooke's will dated 6 March, 1786, shows her deceased, when in this will he tenderly states his desire " to be buried as near as may be to the body of my deceased wife, Elizabeth." Thomas Brooke[8] had been completely orphaned by the death of his father Thomas Brooke[7],

---

* The painstaking Dr. Christopher Johnston in his " Brooke Family," Vol. I, pp. 377-378, names four different eldest sons by the name of Thomas Brooke, all first cousins, belonging to the eighth generation. They were as follows:

1. Thomas Brooke[8], born 1734, as herein shown (date not given by Dr. Johnston), died 1789, Wash. Co., Md. Eldest son of Thomas Brooke[7] of Charles Co., Md.

2. Thomas Brooke[8], under 12 in 1740, died intestate 1768. Eldest son of Walter Brooke[7], of Prince George's Co., Md.

3. Frederick Thomas Brooke[8], born 27 July, 1770. Eldest son of Dr. Richard Brooke[7], of Prince George's Co., Md.

4. Thomas Brooke[8], born 29 Aug., 1776. Eldest son of Rev. Clement Brooke[7] of Prince George's Co., Md.

It is obvious that the death date, as well as the deducted birth year of the second of the four cousins and the dates of the birth of the third and fourth of the cousins, eliminate all of them from being Thomas Brooke[8], the first of the four cousins, born 1734, who became the Surveyor of Wash. Co., and whose will was proved 1789.

1749. Records show he was evidently reared by his grandmother, Lucy (Smith) Brooke, widow of Thomas Brooke⁶, Esq.,
and his maiden aunts Rachael and Rebecca, and bachelor uncle
Isaac Brooke, at Brookefield, Prince George's Co., Md. Learning the profession of surveying from his uncle, Isaac Brooke,
and following him to Upper Frederick Co., Md., he eventually
succeeded his uncle, as in the formation of Washington Co.,
from Frederick in 1776, Thomas Brooke⁸ became the First
Surveyor of Washington Co. (Scharf's *Hist. of Western Maryland*, Vol. 2, p. 989), which office he filled until his death in
1789. Thomas Brooke⁸ served his country faithfully in Colonial
service leading up to and including Revolutionary service.

American Archives, Documentary History, Prepared and
Published under authority of Act of Congress (1837-53) By
Peter Force. Fourth Series, 1774-1775. Vol. I, p. 986.
Thomas Brooke⁸, Frederick Co., Md., 18 Nov., 1774. Appointed
on a Committee to represent Frederick Co., Md., to carry into
execution the acts of the Association agreed upon by the
American Continental Congress and that any five of the
Committee have power to act.

P. 1173-4. Thomas Brooke⁸ of Frederick Co., Md., 24 Jan.,
1775, appointed on a Committee of Observation, with full
powers to act to prevent any infraction of and to carry into
execution the Resolves of American Congress and Provincial
Convention. In the larger districts any five of these gentlemen
to act for the good of the country.

The services of Thomas Brooke⁸ after 1776 are listed of
Washington Co., as this county at this date was formed from
Frederick Co.

The original MSS. of the Committee of Observation for the
State of Maryland. Printed in the *Maryland Hist. Mag.*, Vols.
12 and 13 (not published in the Maryland Archives).

Vol. 12, p. 152. Thomas Brooke⁸ on Committee of Observation for Elizabeth Town District (after 1814 Hagerstown),
Washington Co., and made Clerk of the Committee Feb., 1776.

Maryland Hist. Mag., Vol. 13, pp. 36, 42. Thomas Brooke⁸
on Committee of Observation for Elizabeth Town District,
Washington Co., Md., 11 Jan., 1777.

Thomas Brooke⁸ appointed Chairman on Committee of Observation, 18 Jan., 1777, and as Chairman at various meetings as recorded in *Maryland Hist. Mag.*, Vol. 13, pp. 42, 50, 52, 238.

Thomas Brooke⁸, the first surveyor of Washington Co., Md., was the fifth generation of this line perpetuating the name of Thomas in the direct line from Colonial Governor Robert Brooke. According to the will of Thomas Brooke⁸, of Washington Co., it evidences a divisible interest in the estate of DANN. This great tract of 4,000 acres was granted to his great-grandfather, Col. Thomas Brooke⁵, 28 July, 1694 (Annapolis, Md., Land " Certificates," Lib. B. 23, fol. 223-4). It is now embraced by the northwestern section of Washington, D. C., and includes some of the best residence and Rock Creek Park section of the National Capital. This tract of DANN is referred to in various other Brooke records, of some of those in lineal descent from Col. Thomas Brooke⁵. In addition the family land connections of Thomas Brooke⁶ of Washington Co., Md., may be cited further. The tracts of Gibeon, Ajalon and Brookefield, each of which had previously been owned or surveyed to Isaac, Rachael and Rebecca Brooke, of the seventh generation, of Prince George's Co., Md. (children of Thomas Brooke⁶ and his wife, Lucy Smith), and to Mary Ashcom Greenfield Brooke, widow of Walter Brooke⁷, were parts of the land holdings of Thomas Brooke⁸ of Washington Co., Md., and came by will to his eight children.

The issue of THOMAS BROOKE⁸ and his wife Elizabeth is listed in the *Maryland Hist. Mag.*, Vol. 10, pp. 283-344. All the names there given are verified by his will on file at the Court House, Hagerstown, Washington Co., Md. See " Wills," Lib. A, fol. 205.

i. Thomas Brooke⁹, died early in the Carolinas (probably following his father's profession of surveying). Mar., name of wife unknown. Living in 1786. Left issue.

ii. William Pitt Brooke, mar., deceased in 1816, left issue. Named for the Eng. statesman, the Earl of Chatham, who fearlessly upheld the cause of the American Colonies, before and during the Revolution.

iii. Clement Brooke, youngest son, b. 1770, Washington Co., Md., d. 1836 Zanesville, Ohio. Mar. Sept., 1794, Ann Dillon of whom further. Named for his father's uncle, Rev. Clement Brooke[7].

iv. Rachael Brooke, mar. 1° William Darrell (whose son Wm. Darrell, Jr., mar. Sarah Virginia Brooke, grand-daughter of Commodore Walter Brooke[8] of the Va. Navy (1775-78) and his wife Ann Darrell, thus uniting the blood of the 1° and 2° wives of Thomas Brooke[7], Judith Briscoe and Sarah Mason). Mar. 2° William Collard and had Eliza. of Retirement, near Alexandria, Va. Wm. Pitt Brooke and Elizabeth Brooke, being minors at the time of their father's death, their care and education was left to Wm. Darrell, Sr., their expenses to be paid by his estate. Rachael was named for her father's maiden aunt, Rachael Brooke[7] of Prince George's Co.

v. Susan Brooke, mar. William Lee ("whole executor" will of Thomas Brooke[8]) of Hagerstown, Md. In partnership at Baltimore 1801 with brother-in-law, Clement Brooke, later Trimble and Lee of Baltimore. Left among issue, Jeanette. Susan perpetuated the shortened form of her father's maternal grandmother, Susanna Briscoe, wife of Philip Briscoe, Sr., of Charles Co., Md.

vi. Judith Briscoe Brooke, mar. James Lindsay, a merchant of Uniontown, Pa. Left issue. She was named for her father's mother. 1° wife of Thomas Brooke[7].

vii. Ann Greenfield Brooke was living 1816. Mar. ———— Winder. Left issue.

viii. Elizabeth Brooke, youngest of five daughters, named for her mother. Mar. John Simonson. Both deceased in 1816. Left issue.

CLEMENT BROOKE[9] (Thomas[8], Thomas[7], Thomas[6], Thomas[5], Thomas[4], Robert[3], Thomas[2], Richard[1], the two latter of Whitchurch, Co. Hampshire, England). Youngest son of Thomas Brooke[8], of Washington Co., Md., and his wife, Elizabeth, he was born 1770, Washington Co, Md., died 1836, Zanesville, Ohio, married Ann Dillon, 26 day, 9 mo., 1794, at Redstone (now So. Brownsville), Fayette Co., Pa., Quaker Records, p. 75. Ann Dillon, born Long Green, Baltimore, Md., 27 day, 10 mo., 1774 [Record Gunpowder Monthly Meeting (Quaker), page 21 and Dillon Fam. Bible Records] died 1833, Zanesville, Ohio. Buried by her husband Clement Brooke, their graves being at the foot of those of her parents, Moses and Hannah (Griffith) Dillon in the Dillon, or Quaker, cemetery on the Dillon Falls road on the outskirts of Zanesville. The tombstone inscriptions attest the facts. Moses Dillon was born 10 March, 1746, Bucks

CLEMENT BROOKE"

ANN (DILLON) BROOKE

Co., Pa., grandson of Nicholas and Mary Dillon, who emigrated from northern Ireland in 1740, settling on a large farm adjoining the present village of Pipersville, Bucks Co., Pa., and were made members 7th Dec., 1741, of the Society of Friends at Buckingham Monthly Meeting. The will of Nicholas Dillon was proved 25 Sept., 1773, and mentions his only son, Thomas Dillon. Moses Dillon, was a member of the Society of Friends, Little Falls, Md., 1778, an architect and stone mason of Baltimore, 1795 (*Maryland Hist. Mag.*, Vol. 4, p. 20), married in 1772, Hannah Griffith[4], born 6 July, 1749, Bucks Co., Pa. (Record Richland Friends' Meeting, Bucks Co., Pa.), daughter of Isaac Griffith[3] (Abraham[2], Howell[1]), and his wife, Ann Burson. Howell Griffith, the emigrating ancestor, came from Wales in 1689 and purchased a lot on High street, now Market street, Philadelphia, where he died 17 Feb., 1710. Complete data of the Griffith, Burson, Lester and Potts families is given in " Early Friends' Families in Upper Bucks Co., Pa.", by C. V. Roberts and Warren Ely, Philadelphia, 1925.

Clement Brooke[9] was successfully engaged in the mercantile and shipping business in Baltimore during the closing years of 1700 and early 1800, and in active and extensive land speculations. During this time the portraits of the distinguished appearing Clement Brooke and his beautiful Quaker wife, Ann Dillon, were painted in Baltimore. Through the failing conditions of Jay's Treaty and the Jefferson Embargo, Clement Brooke suffered losses in his shipping ventures and was forced into virtual bankruptcy 1808/9. Putting his large real estate holdings of 40,000 acres in Virginia (now West Virginia) and lands in northern Maryland and southern Pennsylvania in the hands of trustees, for the benefit of his creditors, he removed with his wife Ann (" Nancy ") and four children to Zanesville, Ohio, and there became identified in business with Moses Dillon (*Maryland Hist. Mag.*, Vol. X, p. 361; Vol. XI, pp. 144-6), " who in 1805 had established near Zanesville, Ohio, the first successful blast furnace, iron foundries, and lumber mills in the state at Dillon Falls on the Licking River, and became Ohio's first real Captain of Industry, giving more employment than did any other manufacturer in the infant state. For over thirty years he was actively identified with the best interests, business, social and religious, in the state." After the War of 1812-15 the land holdings of Clement Brooke were placed in the hands of Uria Brown, a surveyor and conveyancer, of which he kept a unique " Journal " and which appears in six successive numbers of the *Maryland Hist. Mag.*, Vols. 10 and 11. (Afterwards this Uria Brown in 1821 became the first teacher of McKim's Free School in Baltimore.)

The issue of CLEMENT BROOKE[9] and his wife, Ann Dillon, were two sons and two daughters.

i. Dr. William Lee Brooke[10], b. 1796, mar. Elizabeth Goss, settled in Newark, Licking Co., Ohio, in practice of his profession. Died 1849, leaving numerous descendants, many of them in and around Newark. Named for his Aunt Susan Brooke's husband, William Lee, who had been made the "Whole Executor" by Thomas Brooke[8], in his will and the guardian, during minority, of his son Clement Brooke. William Lee became the business partner of the latter in Baltimore in early 1800.

ii. Moses Dillon Brooke, b. 16 Apr., 1798, named for his maternal grandfather, mar. Eliza McFadden, of whom further.

iii. Elizabeth Brooke, b. 17 March, 1800, Baltimore, Md., d. 29 Oct., 1873, Brownsville, Pa., leaving many descendants.

iv. Hannah Dillon Brooke, b. 29 May, 1804, Baltimore, Md., d. 15 Feb., 1862, Logan, Ohio; mar. 24 Dec., 1827, Dr. Reuben Culver, of whom further. Named for her maternal grandmother, Hannah (Griffith) Dillon.

MOSES DILLON BROOKE[10] (Clement[9], Thomas[8], Thomas[7], Thomas[6], Thomas[5], Thomas[4], Robert[3], Thomas[2], Richard[1], the two latter of Whitchurch, Co. Hampshire, England), b. 16 Apr., 1798, Baltimore Co., Md., d. 16 Apr., 1881, Madison, Ind. Second and youngest son of Clement Brooke[9] and his wife, Ann Dillon, mar. 9 July, 1822, Eliza McFadden, d. 1864, dau. Thomas and Ann Adams McFaddne, of Armagh, Ireland, later of Washington, Pa. Moses Dillon Brooke was a merchant at Thorndale and Somerset, Perry Co., Ohio, and continued the business when he removed to Madison, Ind., where he died. The names of their children who survived infancy, two sons and three daughters, were:

i. Robert Fulton Brooke[11], b. 19 July, 1829, Thornville, Ohio, d. 23 Nov., 1904; mar. 23 Jan., 1855, his cousin, Mary Wallace McFadden, b. 29 Feb., 1830. Issue:

  (A) Wallace Gibson Brooke[12], d. 29 July, 1923; mar. 21 Apr., 1885, Annie E. Evans, who had Clayton Evans Brooke[13], William Wallace Brooke[13].

  (B) Cora Fulton Brooke[12], d. 17 Feb., 1927; mar. 25 June, 1890, Anthony H. Creagh, who had Marie Elsie Creagh[13], Dorothea Brooke Creagh[13], William Brooke Creagh[13].

  (C) Charles Whitney Brooke[12]; mar. 29 June, 1886, Kate Van de Water, who had Marjorie Van de Water Brooke[13].

  (D) Jennie May Brooke[12]; unmarried.
      The four foregoing A, B, C, D issue were all residents of Greater New York.

ii. Mary Ellen Brooke[11], b. 4 March, 1831, Thornville, Ohio; mar. 23 Oct., 1849, John Lafayette Wilson, of Madison, Ind., later of a country estate, near Morrow, Warren Co., Ohio. Of nine children raised to maturity only one survives, Hon. Manly D. Wilson[12], of Madison, Ind., who mar. Margaret Johnson, 13 Oct., 1880, of Madison, Ind., and had Jeannette Wilson[13].

iii. Lucy Hazlette Brooke[11], of whom further, under Hannah Dillon Brooke[10], whose son she married.

iv. Gilbert McFadden Brooke[11], b. 17 July, 1834, Thornville, Ohio, d. 2 Aug., 1913, Knoxville, Tenn; mar. 18 May, 1858, Catherine Todd Smith and had

  (A) Charlton Perkins Brooke[12] of Miami, Fla., who mar. 14 Dec., 1893, 1° Margaret McTeer and had Charlton Perkins Brooke[13], Jr.; mar. 2°, 10 June, 1913, Charlotte M. Bell.

  (B) Bertha S. Brooke[12]; unmarried; lives at Knoxville, Tenn.

  (C) Florence Brooke; deceased.

v. Catherine F. Brooke[11], b. 6 Feb., 1837, Somerset, Ohio, d. Apr., 1914, St. Louis, Mo.; mar. Hiram H. Todd, 1857, of Madison, Ind., who died 1903. Issue, three sons and one daughter:

  (A) Charles Brooke Todd[12] of St. Louis, Mo.; mar. Oliva Hart 1 Sept., 1886, Logan, Ohio, and had the following seven children: Harold Hart Todd[13], mar. Elizabeth ————; Seymour S. Todd[13], mar. Gladys Taylor; Mary Oliva Todd[13]; Charles Brooke Todd[13], Jr., mar. Betty Graddon; Vernon Cary Todd[13]; Marshall Fulton Todd[13]; Katherine T. Todd[13].

  (B) Harry H. Todd[12] of St. Louis, Mo.; mar. Mabel Le Bosquet Brown of Kansas City, Mo., Nov., 1898, and had Marjorie Todd[13], Wylie Todd[13].

  (C) Vernon C. Todd[12] of Takoma, Wash.; mar. Mary Kroger and had Helen Todd[13]; Freda Todd[13], Stanley Todd[13], Doris Todd[13], Catherine Todd[13].

  (D) Mazie Brooke Todd[12], of whom further, under Hannah Dillon Brooke[10], whose grandson, Reuben Dillon Culvert, she married.

HANNAH DILLON BROOKE[10], (Clement[9], Thomas[8], Thomas[7], Thomas[6], Thomas[5], Thomas[4], Robert[3], Thomas[2], Richard[1], the two latter of Whitchurch, Co. Hampshire, England), b. 29 May, 1804, Baltimore, Md., d. 15 Feb., 1862, Logan, Ohio. Youngest of the four children of Clement Brooke and his wife, Ann Dillon, mar. 24 Dec., 1827, Zanesville, Ohio (where she was raised), Dr. Reuben Culver of Logan, Ohio, b. 4 Oct., 1798, Waterford, Ohio, d. 2 Apr., 1861, Logan, Ohio. Son of Reuben Culver and his wife, Olive Buell (both descendants of two of the original proprietors of Litchfield, Conn., Lieut. Edw. Culver and Capt. John Buell), who migrated from Litchfield, Conn., 1796, to Waterford, Ohio.

Dr. Reuben Culver, according to a biographical sketch of his life in "Eminent Americans," published prior to the Civil War, studied law, medicine and surgery in Charlestown, Va., now the capital of West Virginia, but by a coincidence settled in Logan, Ohio, where he became the first president of Logan Branch, of the State Bank of Ohio. In 1834 the Ohio Legislature appointed him Associate Judge of Hocking Co., which office he filled until it was abolished. Dr. Reuben Culver was the leading physician and surgeon of Hocking Co. until his death, 2 Apr., 1861.

The issue of Dr. Reuben Culver and his wife, Hannah Dillon Brooke, was three sons and one daughter.

i. Charles Vernon Culver, b. Sept., 1830, Logan, Ohio, d. 1910, Philadelphia, Pa.; mar. 1855, Mary Elizabeth Austin. Their only son died in infancy.

ii. Lucien Hambden Culver, of whom further.

iii. Lawrence Agustus Culver, of whom further.

iv. Mary Ellen Culver, b. 11 Nov., 1836, Logan, Ohio, d. Oct., 1885; mar. Gilruth Webb. Only child, Elizabeth, died in young womanhood.

LAWRENCE AGUSTUS CULVER, third and youngest son of Dr. Reuben Culver and his wife, Hannah Dillon Brooke, b. 9 Oct., 1834, Logan, Ohio, d. 12 Dec., 1918, Veedersburg, Ind. Spent his active life as a banker in Logan, Ohio. Mar. Madison, Ind., 27 July, 1859, his cousin, Lucy Hazlett Brooke, b. 6 Nov. 1831, Thornville, Ohio, d. 11 Apr., 1904, St. Louis, Mo., she was the daughter of Moses Dillon Brooke[10] and his wife, Eliza McFadden, daughter of Thomas McFadden, b. 1757, Armagh, Co. Armagh, Ireland, d. 8 Oct., 1812, and his wife, Ann Adams, b. 1766, Armagh, Co. Armagh, Ireland, d. 19 Aug., 1840. They were married 1786 in Armagh, migrated to America circa 1800, locating at Washington, Pa. They had ten children, all of whom married and had issue.

The issue of LAWRENCE AGUSTUS CULVER and his wife, Lucy Hazlett Brooke, two sons and two daughters, of whom the eldest

(A) Reuben Dillon Culvert, b. 10 May, 1860, Logan, Hocking Co., Ohio. Educated at Alleghany College, Meadville, Pa. Active business career at Veedersburg, Ind., with his younger brother, Lawrence Agustus Culver, Jr. In 1931 retired and living at Oakland, California. Married 30 Dec., 1883, Washington, D. C., his cousin, Mazie Brooke Todd, b. 13 July, 1862, Madison, Ind., only daughter of Hiram H. Todd and his wife, Catherine Brooke, of the eleventh Brooke generation. Hiram H. Todd was the grandson of Owen Todd and his wife, who was the daughter of Col. Thomas Paxton, of Bedford Co., Pa., who was Lieut. Col. in a Pennsylvania regiment in the Revolution. This Todd family descended from Robert Todd of Lanarkshire, Scotland, who was a progenitor of David Andrew Todd, b. Co. Down, Ireland, 8 Apr., 1725, later migrated to Montgomery Co., Pa. The issue of Reuben Dillon Culver and his wife, Mazie Brooke Todd, is an only son, Lawrence Frederick Culver, b. 25 July, 1885, Logan, Ohio; mar. 23 Mar., 1918, Cincinnati, Ohio, Helen Beverly Nichols, b. 23 Feb., 1894, St. Louis, Mo., eldest daughter of Walter Nichols, b. 3 Jan., 1862, near Covington, Ky., and his wife, Laura Bell McConahy, b. 25 Sept., 1867, Van Wert, Ohio; mar. 13 Dec., 1887, Philadelphia, Pa. Issue of Lawrence Frederick Culver and his wife, Helen Beverly Nicholas: Lwarence Frederick Culver, Jr., b. 2 Sept., 1920, Veedersburg, Ind., and Marjanne Culver, b. 8 Sept., 1923, Veedersburg, Ind.

(B) Lawrence Agustus Culver, Jr., b. Logan, Ohio, resides at Veedersburg, Ind. Mar. 26 Jan., 1899, Ivy Jane Todd (daughter of Elhannon Paxton Todd and his wife, Sarah Farmer, of Kansas City, Kansas) and had Dorothy Todd Culver, who mar. William Lee Todd Morton, of Danville, Va., and had Lawrence Culver Morton and William Lee Morton, Jr.

(C) Sophie Lee Culver, mar. 9 Oct., 1884, Sewell G. Bennett of Oklahoma City, Okla., and had three children: Brooke Culver Bennett, mar. Mildred Sparks who had Gwendolyn L. Bennett. Lives at Los Angeles, California. Paul Culver Bennett mar. Gertrude Grady. Lives at Oklahoma City, Okla. Virginia Bennett mar. Ralph W. Shank of Los Angeles, California.

(D) Florence E. Culver of Pasadena, California.

Lucien Hambden Culver, ninth in descent from Robert Brooke, Colonial Governor of Maryland, thirty-fourth in descent from King Alfred of England, and thirty-ninth in descent from Charlemagne, Emperor of the West, 800 A. D. He was the second son of Dr. Reuben Culver and his wife, Hannah Dillon Brooke, was born 25 Feb., 1833, Greene Township, Hocking Co., Ohio, died 22 Apr., 1881, Reno, Pa. Graduated from Wesleyan College, Delaware, Ohio. Studied law with Governor Dennison and General Carrington at their law office, Columbus, Ohio. Admitted to the Bar, 11 July, 1855. In 1863 engaged in private banking in New York City with his brother Charles Vernon Culver, as Culver, Penn and Company, establishing twelve branch banks in western Pennsylvania, and in production of oil at Reno, Pa., at which place he died at the early age of forty-eight years. Mar. 13 Apr., 1856, at Logan, Ohio, Cynthia Baker, b. 14 Sept., 1835, Lancaster, Ohio, d. 27 July, 1929, Paradise Valley, California; entombed Inglewood Park Mausoleum, Los Angeles, California. The above dates of birth, marriage and death are attested on the mausoleum and in the Culver and Baker family Bibles. Cynthia Baker was the daughter of Luman Baker[6], son of Timothy Baker[5], son of Aaron[4] (Cornwall, Vt., Town Records, Vol. I, p. 284), lineal descendants of Edward and Jane Baker of Baker's Hill, Lynn, Mass. (Lewis and Newhall's *History of Lynn*, Trumbull's *History of Northampton*, p. 110, Baker-Thompson *Lineage Book*, Baker family Bible), and his wife, Sarah Ann Hart, of Lancaster and Logan, Ohio (see " Stephen Hart and His Descendants," by Alfred Andrews, 1875, pp. 399, 451, 514). She was a daughter of Thomas Hart and his wife, Elizabeth McClelland, of Lancaster, Ohio, and a lineal descendant of Dr. Josiah Hart, who graduated at Yale, 1762. Dr Josiah Hart was made full surgeon in the Revolution, 1775, at a special session of the Connecticut Assembly (*Ancient Wethersfield,* Vol. I, p. 454).

From " Historical Register of Officers of Continental Army during the War of the Revolution (1775-1783)," by Francis B. Heitman, 1914 edition, p. 277:

Josiah Hart (Conn.). Surgeon's Mate 6th Conn. 6th July to Dec., 1775.

Surgeon 10th Continental Infantry 1st Jan. to 31st Dec., 1776.

Surgeon Conn. Militia 1777-1780. (Died Aug., 1812.)

The Public Records of the Colony of Connecticut, 1772-1775, edited by order of the Connecticut General Assembly, Vol. 14, p. 430, Vol. 15, p. 102. Josiah Hart service for Apr. 1775.

Connecticut Military Record, 1775-1848, under authority Adj. Gen. of Conn., pp. 72, 99. Josiah Hart (New Britain) Surgeon Col., S. H. Parson's Reg. 1776. 10th Continental Field and Staff, p. 562. Dr. Josiah Hart, Farmington, Conn., attached to 14th Reg. 6th Brigade. 1st March, 1780, to guard Sea Coast and Frontiers.

Sup. Index to Rev. MSS. Conn. Josiah Hart Surgeon indorsement sick bills 1775, pp. 6, 17. Also see D. A. R. Lineage Book 31, p. 258.

Cynthia (Baker) Culver was lineally descended from Colonial Governor Thomas Welles (1598-1660), who was also Treasurer and Secretary of the Colony of Conn.; Commissioner United Colonies; Deputy Governor and Governor of Conn. 1655-1658,

The issue of LUCIEN HAMBDEN CULVER and his wife, Cynthia Baker, are the following:

(A) Minnie Culver, of whom further.
(B) Anna Brooke Culver, b. 13 Nov., 1858, mar. 15 Jan., 1886, Charles Russell, d. 5 Dec., 1886.
(C) Mary Louise Culver, b. 5 March, 1860, d. in childhood.
(D) Ruth Austin Culver, b. 29 March, 1862; mar. 11 May, 1882, William Alexander Drake of Oil City, Pa.
(E) Elizabeth Brooke Culver, b. 9 Oct., 1864, Hudson City, N, J. Living in Los Angeles, Calif.
(F) Ellon Brooke Culver, b. 16 March, 1869, Reno, Pa., mar. Edwin Le Roy Bowen of Woodmere, Des Moines, Iowa, 16 Nov., 1892. Member Nat. Soc. Colonial Dames of America, Soc. Magna Charta Dames, Hereditary Order Descendants of Colonial Governors, Soc. Ark and Dove of Maryland, Club of Colonial Dames at Washington, D. C., Colonial Descendants Americans of Royal Descent, California Historical and Genealogical Soc., Maryland Historical Soc.

MINNIE CULVER, b. 8 June, 1857, Logan, Ohio, d. 26 Mar.,

1931, Redlands, California.   Interred with husband, San Antonio, Texas.   Eldest daughter Lucien Hambden Culver and his wife, Cynthia Baker.   Educated at Vassar College, mar. 27 Dec., 1882, Reno, Pa., Robert Emmet Hurley, b. 23 July, 1844, Herrick Township, Susquehanna Co., Pa., d. 25 Oct., 1913, San Antonio, Texas.   Grandson of John Hurley, of Lismore, Co. Waterford, Prov. of Munster, Ireland, and Margueretta La Haye, of Norman French ancestry, and son of Thomas Hurley, b. 4 July, 1805, Ireland, d. 11 Jan., 1880, Des Moines, Iowa, interred Woodland cemetery there.   He was the youngest son and had been highly educated for the priesthood, but instead came to America in 1824 and became a civil engineer; mar. by the Rev. John Powers, 4 July, 1827, New York City, to Elizabeth Watt, b. 20 Sept., 1810 in Scotland, d. 17 July, 1870, Scranton, Pa., interred there.   Daughter of Andrew Watt and his first wife, Sarah Browning, mar. in Scotland, 4 March, 1808, came to New York before 1819.   They settled at Bloomingdale, now part of Central Park of New York City, as a manufacturer of carriages and road coaches of the day.   (See " New York of Yesterday," p. 204, by Hopper Striker Mott. *Abridged Comp. Amer. Gen.,* Vol. III, p. 165).   Records from Thomas Hurley and Andrew Watt family Bibles, in possession of the present Hurley generation.

ROBERT EMMET HURLEY at age of twenty years served during the Civil War in the U. S. Navy, with rank of 2nd Lieut. S. S. Santiago de Cuba, attached in the Blockading Squadron, South Atlantic Coast, 1864, and was one of its three officers appointed to stand as body-guard over the body of President Lincoln at the Capitol at Washington on 18th Aug., 1865.   Later he was honorably discharged from the Navy.

The issue of ROBERT EMMET HURLEY and his wife, Minnie Culver, was three sons.

(A) Lucien Culver Hurley, b. 20 June, 1885, Des Moines, Iowa. Graduate of Scranton High School, 1903; graduate of Yale University, June, 1906. Entered 1918 the Great Lakes and Washington, D. C., U. S. N. training for World's War Service. Honorably discharged at Armistice. Resides in Denver, Colo., as president and treasurer of The Hurley Co. Through maternal grandmother descends from

Robert Fitzwalter, the successful leader of the barons who wrested Magna Charta from King John, 1215, upon which tenets our Declaration of Independence and Constitution are founded. Member of the Soc. of Barons of Runnemede. Mar. 15 May, 1915, Denver, Colo., Shirley Basey Watkins, b. 3 July, 1890, Denver Colo., daughter of Leonard Kendrick Watkins, b. 26 Aug., 1863, St. Louis, Mo., d. 13 Sept., 1913, Denver, Colo., and his wife, Annabel Basey, b. 3 July, 1862, Brunswick, Mo., whom he married 24 Feb., 1885. Shirley Basey Watkins is the grand-daughter of Leonard Alfred Watkins, b. 2 Oct., 1831, Birmingham, Eng., d. 18 Jan., 1895, Denver, Colo.; mar. in Birmingham, Eng., Emma Kendrick, b. 8 March, 1832, Birmingham, Eng., d. 2 June, 1915, Denver, Colo. They came to St. Louis, Mo., 1855. The issue of Lucien Culver Hurley and his wife, Shirley Basey Watkins are the following: Barbara Brooke Hurley, b. 12 May, 1917, Sheboygan, Wis.; Patricia Brooke Hurley, b. 1 Aug., 1920, Denver, Colo., died there 16 Oct., 1925; Leonard Watkins Hurley, b. 5 Feb., 1924, Denver, Colo.

(B) Robert Stanley Hurley, b. 25 Sept., 1888, Chicago, Ill. Graduate of Scranton, Pa., High School, 1906; Yale, 1906-1909. Entered marine training, World's War, Paris Island, South Carolina, 1917. Honorably discharged at Armistice, 21 Feb., 1919. Mar. 18 Aug., 1932, Velura Grayce McCain of Oak Park, Ill., the sister of the wife of his brother Howard.

(C) Howard Watt Hurley, b. 13 Sept., 1891, North Park, Scranton, Pa. Graduate of Scranton High School, 1910; graduated Yale University, 1914. Entered Reserve Officer's Corps, World's War. Commd. 2nd Lieut. Coast Artillery, 1917. Bat. "A," 65th C. A. C., France. After return from France officered train of soldiers to California, where at Camp Kearny was mustered out, 24 Feb., 1919. Mar. 29 Aug., 1922, at Oak Park, Ill., Leoda Delphine McCain, b. 12 Aug., 1888, Port Huron, Mich., daughter of Cyrus Alfred McCain, b. 13 Aug., 1865, Port Huron, Mich., and his wife, Georgiana Adele Zavitz, b. 25 Sept., 1860, Port Colburn, Ontario, Canada. She was the daughter of George Zavitz and his wife, Janet Haun, who was a lineal descendant of Oliver Cromwell, through his son Richard. Leoda Delphine McCain is the grand-daughter of William McCain, b. 1825, Ontario, Canada, d. 30 Oct., 1880, Port Colburn, Ontario, Canada, and his wife, Lavinah Nelson, b. 21 May, 1829, Ontario, Canada, d. 1885, Port Huron, Mich. The issue of Howard Watt Hurley and his wife, Leoda Delphine McCain: Two daughters, Nancy Cynthia Hurley, b. 11 July, 1923, Houston, Texas; Janet Brooke Hurley, b. 3 July, 1924, New Orleans, La.

THE CALVERT PEDIGREE.

[In Vol. I, p. 276 of the *Maryland Historical Magazine* mention is made of a pedigree drawn up by Benedict Leonard Calvert for the antiquary Thomas Hearne, and published in his Diary. As there have been many erroneous statements about the family, it is here reproduced.]

This Pedigree was drawn up and written (with his own Hand) by the Honble Benedict Leonard Calvert, Esqr, who gave it to me on Mond. Sept. I, MDCCXVIII. Tho. Hearne.

Leonard Calvert = Alicia, daughter and Heiresse of
John Crosland of Crosland.

Sr George Calvert, K^nt born at Kypling in Yorkshire = Ann, daughter to George
Secretary of State to James the 1st K. of England. By | Mynne of Hartingford-
him created Ld Baron of Baltemore in Ireland. First | bury in Com. Hartford
Ld Proprietor of Avalon in America. Granted him in | Died August, 1622
1623. Died 1632. Aged 53. And was buried att St.
Dunstan's in the west.

2 Leonard   1 Cecil Calvert Son and = Ann, his wife 2 daughter of   Ann   Dorothy   Elizabeth
3 George   Heire. Ld Baltemore to | the Ld Arundell of Wardour,
4 Francis   whom Maryland was grant- | and Count of the Sacred Roman
5 Henry   ed, June 20, 1632 | Empire, by wch all her des-
6 Philip | cendants, Male and Female
                                     are Counts and Countesses.

Charles, Lord Baltemore, Son and   = 1 . . . . Darnall, dyed in Childbed   Elizabeth   Ann
Heire. Married four wives. Died   = 2 Jane Seawell by whom he had . . . .
Feb. 20, 1715, buried at St. Pan-   = 3 Mary Banks, widow
cras, near London, aged 77   = 4 Margarett Charleton who survived him

Benedict Leonard, Lord Baltemore, born March 21   = Charlotte daughter to Edward Henry   Cecil, eldest, but   1 Jane
1679, died Apr. 16, 1715, aged 37. And was buried | Earl of Litchfield, etc., And Charlotte   died young   2 Ann
att Epsome in Surry. Married Jan. 2^d 169^8/9 to | his wife daughter of K. Charles II^d
                                                    | by Barbara, Dutchess of Cleveland.

Cecil, twin with his   Benedict Leonard, born   Charles, Eldest, now Lord   Charlott Mar-   Jane born   Barbara born
Eldest Sister, Char-   Sept. 20, 1700. Now of   Baltemore. Unmarried.   ried to Mr.   Nov. 1703   Oct. 1704
lott. Born Nov. 1702   X^t church, Oxon. Is married   Born Sept. 29, 1699.

THE CALVERT FAMILY

JOHN BAILEY CALVERT NICKLIN.

FOREWORD

The task confronting anyone who attempts to compile a genealogy of this distinguished family, whose history for a century and a half was that of Maryland, is almost forbidding, for doubt and mystery, tradition and myth have long concealed the facts and the truth of their lineage and history. And the legitimate male descendants of Governor the Honorable Leonard Calvert (1606-1647) have been ignored, while the descendants of Benedict Swingate (otherwise Calvert of "Mt. Airy") have received the attention of historians and genealogists, having produced many noted men and women.

Even the origin of this family is wrapped in obscurity and the etymology of the name is scarcely pleasing, if enlightening, for it is said to have been derived from the calve-herd, i. e., a keeper of a herd of calves: The name appears as early as 1366 when Margaretta Calverd (sic) is found on the Durham Manorial Rolls, and it is evidently an old Yorkshire name and there is little to support the "tradition" that they were of Flanders, although Calvaert was a not unknown Flemish name. What was the origin of the Calvert Arms (viz.: paley of six, or and sable, a bend counterchanged) does not appear, but Richard St. George, the Norroy King-at-Arms, is responsible for the addition of the crest of the Flemish Calverts when he issued an exemplification of arms in 1622 to Sir George Calvert (1579-1632), Knight (afterwards the first Lord Baltimore).

The monumental inscription on the tomb of the first Baron mentioned his father Leonard (and his grandfather, John Calvert), who was a country gentleman of means, who lived, near Danby Wiske,[1] at an estate called Kiplin, in the valley of the Swale, Yorkshire. This Leonard Calvert was born about 1550 and married, about 1575, Grace (more often called Alicia) Crossland, daughter of Thomas Crossland (who died Aug., 1587) and Joanna, his wife (who died July, 1575). The issue of this marriage is unknown save one son, George Calvert, the Founder of Maryland, but it is probably that Mary Calvert (who was born in 1586 and married, in 1606, Captain Isaac Chapline, R. N.) was a daughter of Leonard Calvert and Grace Crossland. (Two of their sons settled in America: John Chapline in Virginia and William Chapline in Maryland). In his will, the first Lord Baltimore refers to his "kindred" in the "North" (i. e., of England,—Yorkshire), but there is no record of any of them and he mentions none by name.

THE TITLED LINE

1. JOHN CALVERT,[1] of Kiplin, near Danby Wiske, Yorkshire, temp, Henry VIII., m.—

    ISSUE:

    2. i. LEONARD, b. c. 1550, of whom later.

2. LEONARD CALVERT [2] (John [1]), b. c. 1550; d. ——; M. c. 1575, Grace Crossland, dau. of Thomas Crossland and Joanna Hawksworth of "Crossland Hill," Yorkshire (see Foster's "Visitations of Yorkshire," p. 509), and descended from Roger de Crossland, temp. Henry III.

    ISSUE:

    3. i. GEORGE, b. 1578/9, of whom later.

---

[1] In 1659, Philip Calvert patented a manor of 900 acres, called Wiske *alias* Danby, in Baltimore county on Back River at the place now known as Porter's bar but formerly known as "Chancellor's Point," from the patentee. In the Rent Rolls and the original certificate it is erroneously described as lying on the North East river, but in reality lies on Back River, formerly known as North West river.—*Note by Wm. B. Marye.*

3. GEORGE CALVERT [3] (Leonard,[2] John [1]), b. 1578/9, near Bolton Castle, Yorkshire; d. in London, April 15, 1632, in his fifty-third year. He graduated from Oxford in 1597, receiving the degree of B. A. (eight years later he was created M. A.) and traveled extensively on the Continent, where he met Sir Robert Cecil (afterward Earl of Salisbury), whose private secretary he later became and through whose influence he began his career as a statesman. He was a Member of Parliament for Bosmay, Cornwall in 1603 and at Hampton Court he was knighted by King James I., on September 29, 1617, after having served as Clerk of the Crown and Assize in County Clare, Ireland. In 1613 he had become Clerk of the Privy Council and was later a member of the Commission for winding up the affairs of the Virginia Company in 1624. In 1619 he had been appointed by the King to the high office (resembling the present Prime Ministership) of Principal Secretary of State, succeeding Sir Thomas Lake and being associated with Sir Robert Naunton. This office he resigned on February 9, 1625, and one week later he was created by the King, in gratitude for his services, Baron Baltimore of Baltimore, in the County of Longford, Ireland, in which County the King had granted him February 18, 1621, a Manor of 2,300 acres (Baltimore). In 1624 he represented Oxfordshire in Parliament and retired to private life the year following. (Other offices he had held, such as one of the commissioners for the office of Treasurer and a member of Parliament for Yorkshire). As a young man he had been interested in the colonization of the New World and was a member of the Virginia Company in 1609. In 1622 the King had granted him the island of Avalon (Ferryland), a part of Newfoundland, where he had purchased an estate two years preceding. Here he attempted a settlement—which was unsuccessful—and spent a fortune in the attempt. About this time he became a Roman Catholic and offered his resignation (as Secretary of State) to the King, which His Majesty refused to accept on account of Cal-

vert's valuable services. He next turned his attention southward, sailed for Virginia (taking with him his second wife), and returned to England, where he besought the King (Charles I., who had succeeded his father, James I., in 1625) for a new grant of land. The King, who continued his father's friendship for Lord Baltimore, then granted him the territory which was later called Maryland (i. e., in Latin, Terra Mariae) in honor of the Queen of England (Henrietta Maria, an aunt of Louis XIV., of France). The settlement of Maryland needs no further mention. Lord Baltimore's life was cut short in his fifty-third year by his death, April 15, 1632—before the Charter of Maryland has passed the great Seal (so it was made out in the name of Cecil, the second Baron)—and was buried in the Chancel of St. Dunstan's in the West, London, which church was later destroyed by fire. His Lordship had been twice married: firstly, at St. Peter's, Cornhill, London, "Thursday, November 22, 1604, Mr. George Calvert of St. Martin's in the Fields, Gent., and Mrs. Anne Mynne, of Bexley in Hertfordshire." (So reads the Parish records!) His second wife—the first Lady Baltimore—was named Joan (mentioned as "Dame Joane Baltimore" by her husband in a deed under date of 1627), but of her parentage or history nothing is known. Lady Calvert (Anne Mynne), who was born November 20, 1579 and died August 12, 1622, was a daughter of George Mynne of Hertfordshire (who d. May 20, 1581) and Elizabeth Wroth, his wife (who d. August 14, 1614), dau. of Sir Thomas Wroth of Durance in Enfield, Middlesex, and his wife, the Lady Mary Rich, a dau. of Richard, Lord (Chancellor) Rich, of Henry VIII.'s reign. Sir Thomas Wroth (1519-1573) was at Court during the brief reign of King Edward VI., and that youthful monarch expired in his arms. His great-great-grandfather was Sir John Wroth, Lord Mayor of London in 1361. The Wroth Lineage is interesting: The mother of this Sir Thomas Wroth was Joane Haute, widow of Thomas Goodyere of Hadley and daughter of Sir Thomas and Lady Haute (Elizabeth Frowicke) of Hautesbourne, whose grandfather, William Haute, married Elizabeth Woodville, sister of Richard Woodville, Earl Rivers, and aunt of Elizabeth (Woodville) Grey, Queen of Edward IV., of England. William Haute was descended from Piers Fitz Haut, one of the soldiers of William the Conqueror.

To return to Lady Calvert (Anne Mynne): her father was buried in St. Mary's Church, Hertingfordbury, Hertfordshire. His tomb bore the following inscription (with the Mynne and Wroth coats-of-arms empaled): "Here lies buried the bodies of George Mynne, of Hertingfordbury, Esq., and Elizabeth, his wife, daughter of Sir Thomas Wroth, of Durance in Enfield, in the County of Middlesex, Knight; they had issue, three sons and three daughters. The said George Mynne departed this life the 20th day of May, in the year of our Lord 1581; his wife, Elizabeth taking afterward to her second husband Nicholas Butler, Esq., and she died the 14th of Aug., 1614." Through the Rich Family connection Lady Calvert was highly connected, as her grandmother (Lady Wroth, nee Rich) was aunt of Robert Rich, Earl of Warwick, and sister to Lady Peyton, Lady Dudley (afterwards the Baroness North), Lady Drewry and Lady D'Arcy.

By his first wife, Anne Mynne, Lord Baltimore had issue:

4.   i. CECIL, b. 1605 (of whom later), second Lord Baltimore.
9. ii. Leonard, b. 1606 (of whom afterward), first Governor of Maryland.
    iii. Anne, m. before 1632, William Peaseley, esq.
    iv. George, d. u. 1634, in Maryland.
    v. Dorothy, m. James Talbot and d. s. p.
    vi. Francis, d. s. p. v. p.
    vii. Henry, d. u. 1635.
    viii. Elizabeth, d. v. p. unmarried.
    ix. Grace, b. 1614; d. ———; m. 1631½, Sir Robert Talbot of Carton, a brother of the Duke of Tyrconnel.

ISSUE:

1. Frances Talbot, d. 1718; m. her cousin, Richard Talbot (d. 1703); ancestors of the present Lord Talbot de Malehide of London.

2.   William Talbot, d. s. p.

3.   George Talbot, of Maryland; d. s. p.

x. Helen, "said to have" m. Governor Thomas Green of Maryland (?).

xi. John, b. 1622; evidently d. y. (But who was the John Calvert who came to Maryland with Philip Calvert in 1660 and was a member of a Provincial Committee in 1669 with this same Philip Calvert, supposedly his half brother ?).

By his second wife, Joane ————, Lord Baltimore had issue:

i. Philip, b. 1626; d. 1682. He came to Maryland in 1660 and was long Chancellor; in 1669 he was Deputy Governor of the Province. Although twice married, he appears to have died issueless. He m. (1.) about 1658, Anne Wolseley (a first cousin of Jane Lowe Sewall, Lady Baltimore, q. v.), dau. of Sir Thomas Wolseley of Staffordshire, England; m. (2.) 1681, Jane Sewall, dau. of Jane (Lowe) Sewall, Lady Baltimore, by her first husband, Henry Sewall, M. D., of Maryland. Philip Calvert died shortly after his second marriage and his widow (Jane Sewall) married, secondly, John Paston.

4. CECIL CALVERT [4] (George,[3] Leonard,[2] John [1]) second Lord Baltimore, b. Aug. 8, 1605; baptised March 2, 1606, at Bexley, Kent; d. Nov. 30 (buried Dec. 7), 1675, at St. Giles-in-the-Fields, Middlesex. He entered Trinity College, Oxford, in 1621 and to him, on June 20, 1632, the grant of Maryland was issued. Although he was never able to visit his province, Lord Baltimore was the real founder of Maryland. He was a member of Parliament in 1634 and married, March 20, 1627/8, Anne Arundell, daughter of Sir Thomas Arundell, Lord Arundell of Wardour Castle (a Count of the Holy Roman Empire), by his second wife, Anne (the widow of one Thurgood), daughter of Miles Philipsin, of Crook in Westmoreland, by his wife, Barbara, sister of Francis Sandys of Conished in Lancashire. Lady Anne Arundell died July 23, 1649, aged 34 and was buried at Tisbury, in Wiltshire.

ISSUE:

i. Anne, evidently d. y.
ii. Mary, b. 1630; d. s. p. 1663; m. c. 1650, Sir William Blakiston of Gibside, Durham (d. 1692).
iii. George, b. Sept. 15, 1634; d. June 6, 1636.
iv. Elizabeth.
5. v. CHARLES, b. Aug. 27, 1637 (of whom later), third Lord Baltimore.

5. CHARLES CALVERT I.[5] (Cecil,[4] George,[3] Leonard,[2] John [1]). third Lord Baltimore, b. Aug. 27, 1637 (not 1630, as generally given!); d. Feb. 21. 1715, and was buried at St. Pancras, Middlesex. He came to Maryland in 1661 as Governor and brought his first wife with him (she died there in childbed). In 1684 he returned to England, where he died. Lord Baltimore, who was a Major-General in the British Army, was married four times:(1.) 1656, Mary Darnall, dau. of Ralph Darnall of Loughton in Herefordshire; (2.) 1666, Jane, widow of Henry Sewall, M. D., and dau. of Vincent Lowe of Denby in Derbyshire, by his wife, Anne Cavendish of London (Jane, Lady Baltimore, d. Jan. 19, 1700, and was buried at St. Giles-in-the-Fields, Middlesex); (3.) Dec. 6, 1701, Mary Thorpe (a widow), dau. of —————— Banks (she died March 13, 1710); (4.) 1712, Margaret Charleton, dau. of Thomas Charleton of Hexham in Northumberland (she died July 30, 1731, having married secondly, Nov. 9, 1718, Lawrence Eliot, of Yapton Place, Sussex).

ISSUE, by second marriage:

i. Cecil, b. 1667; d. 1681.
ii. Clare, b. 1670; d. before 1694; m. c. 1690, the Hon. Edward Maria Somersett.
iii. Anne, b. 1673; d. Feb. 10, 1731; m. (1.) 1694, the Hon. Edward Maria Somersett (q. v.); (2.) William Paston of Horton, in Gloucestershire, Esq.
6. iv. BENEDICT LEONARD, b. March 21, 1679; fourth Lord Baltimore (of whom later).
28. v. (?). Charles, b. c. 1680; d. 1733 (of whom afterward).

6. BENEDICT LEONARD CALVERT [6] (Charles,[5] Cecil,[4] George,[3] Leonard,[2] John [1]), fourth Lord Baltimore; b. March 21, 1679; d. April 16 (buried May 2), 1715, at Epson in Surrey. He was a Member of Parliament in 1714-5 and married, Jan. 2, 1698, Lady Charlotte Lee (who was divorced in 1705), dau. of Edward Henry Lee (1663-1716, Earl of Lichfield, by his wife, the Lady Charlotte FitzRoy, a daughter of King Charles II., by Barbara (Villiers) Palmer (1640-1709), Countess of Castlemain, Duchess of Cleveland, etc. After the death of Lord Baltimore she married secondly, Dec. 6, 1719, Christopher Crewe and, dying Jan. 21, 1721, was buried at Woodford in Essex.

ISSUE:

7.   i. CHARLES, b. Sept. 29, 1699 (of whom later), fifth Lord Baltimore.

  ii. Benedict Leonard, b. Sept. 20, 1700; d. u. June 1, 1732. In 1726 he was a member of Parliament for Harwich and later (1727) Governor of Maryland. While returning to England he died and was buried at sea.

  iii. Edward Henry, b. Aug. 31, 1701; d. 1730; m. Margaret Lee, who survived him and m. (2.), October 13, 1751, James Fitzgerald, Esq. Edward Henry Calvert was Commissary General of Maryland in 1728.

  iv. Cecelius, b. Nov. 6, 1702; d. u. 1765. He was Secretary of the Province and managed the affairs of His Lordship.

  v. Charlotte, b. Nov. 6, 1702; d. 1744; m. Thomas Brerewood, Esq.

ISSUE:

  1. Francis Brerewood.

  vi. Jane, b. Nov. 19, 1703; d. ———; m. May 4, 1720, John Hyde, of Kingston Lisle, in Berkshire, Esq. They had two sons, John and Henry Hyde.

  vii. Barbara, b. Oct. 3, 1704; d. i.

  viii. Anne.

7. CHARLES CALVERT II.[7] (Benedict Leonard,[6] Charles,[5] Cecil,[4] George,[3] Leonard,[2] John [1]), fifth Lord Baltimore, b. Sept. 29, 1699; d. April 24, 1751, and was buried at Erith in Kent. He was Cofferer to H. R. H. Frederick, Prince of Wales (after whom he named his son and succes-

sor) and represented Surrey in Parliament. He was also a Fellow of the Royal Society and a Lord of the Admiralty in 1741, but his high offices did not modify his "riotous living." He m., July 20, 1730, Mary Janssen (who died at Shaillot, near Paris, March 25, 1748), youngest daughter of Sir Theodore Janssen and sister of Stephen Theodore Janssen, Lord Mayor of London. Lady Baltimore was a granddaughter of Abraham Janssen, a son of the Baron de Heez in the Netherlands. Her mother (Lady Janssen) was a daughter of Sir Robert Henley of "the Grange," in Hampshire, by his wife, Barbara Hungerford, a daughter of Sir Edward Hungerford. Sir Robert Henley was a Member of Parliament.

ISSUE:

8.   i. FREDERICK, b. Feb. 6, 1732 (of whom later), sixth and last Lord Baltimore.

     ii. Frances Dorothy, b. 1734; d. March 5, 1736.

    iii. Louisa, m. John Browning, Esq.

    iv. Charles, b. Jan. 21, 1737; d. i.

     v. Caroline, m. Robert Eden (d. 1786), Governor of Maryland 1769-1776; ancestors of the present Sir Timothy Calvert Eden and of Lady Brooke of Warwick Castle. Before his marriage to Mary Janssen, Charles, fifth Lord Baltimore, was father of a son called Benedict Swingate. This boy was sent to Maryland about 1742, married, in 1748, Elizabeth Calvert, dau. of Gov. Charles Calvert, and assumed the name of Calvert, becoming head of the family who lived at "Mt Airy."

24. vi. Benedict, b. c. 1724 (of whom later).

8. FREDERICK CALVERT [8] (Charles,[7] Benedict Leonard,[6] Charles,[5] Cecil,[4] George,[3] Leonard,[2] John [1]), sixth and last Lord Baltimore, b. Feb. 6 1732; d. s. p. l., Sept. 4, 1771, at Naples, and was buried at Epson in Surrey. He m., March 9, 1753, the Lady Diana Egerton (1732-1758), dau. of Scrope Egerton, Duke of Bridgewater. (She died Aug. 18, 1758, s. p.). Lord Baltimore was a dissolute, but generous man; a traveler who never visited his Province; a writer and a rake. Although leaving no legitimate issue, he had several natural children, as follows:

By Hester Whelan of Ireland.

  i. Henry Harford, b. 1760, to whom he willed the Province of
Maryland, but the American Revolution soon swept
away his claims.

  ii. Frances Mary Harford, b. 1762; m. William Frederick Wyndham (1763-1828), son of Charles Wyndham (1710-
1763), second Earl of Egremont and grandson of
Charles Seymour, sixth Duke of Somerset.

ISSUE:

  i. George Francis Wyndham, fourth Earl of Egremont.

By Elizabeth Dawson of Lincolnshire:

  i. Sophia Hales, b. 1765.
  ii. Elizabeth Hales, b. 1765.

By Elizabeth Hope of Munster, Germany:

  i. Charlotte Hope, b. 1770, at Hamburg.

With the death of Frederick Calvert, sixth Lord Baltimore,
the title became "extinct" as there was no surviving (male)
member of his family in England and the descendants of Governor the Honorable Leonard Calvert in America were over-
looked or forgotten, although they were heirs male of the body
of the first Baron. (The chief authority for the above account
is from the records in the Office of the King-at-Arms, Dublin
Castle, Dublin, Ireland, which office informs the writer that the
title can be claimed by a descendant of Leonard Calvert in the
male line.

THE CALVERT FAMILY

PART II

JOHN BAILEY CALVERT NICKLIN

THE UNTITLED LINE

9. LEONARD CALVERT[4] (George,[3] Leonard,[2] John[1]), second son of the first Lord Baltimore, b. 1606, in England; d. June 9, 1647, in Maryland. He was Prothonotary and Keeper of the Writs in Connaught and Thomond (Ireland) in 1621. In 1633 he was appointed by his brother, Cecil, second Lord Baltimore, Governor of Maryland,

whither he sailed with his brother, George Calvert, Jr., and their fellow settlers on the "Ark" and the "Dove." He governed the Province wisely and returned to England in 1641/2 to consult with his brother, the Baron. After a lengthy visit (during which his marriage was solemnized) he returned to Maryland in 1643/4 (Giles Brent, his brother-in-law, having been left in charge of the Province during his absence) and continued to govern until his death four years later. While in England he had married (1642) Anne Brent (of whose life little or nothing has been found, but it would seem that she pre-deceased him), a sister of Mary, Giles, Fulke and "Mistress Margaret Brent," who came to Maryland in 1638. Anne Brent was a daughter of Richard and Elizabeth (Reed) Brent of Larke Stoke and Admington in Gloucestershire and a granddaughter of Giles and Katherine (Greville) Reed of Tusburie and Witten. Thru Katherine Greville the lineage runs back to John of Gaunt, Duke of Lancaster, and Thomas of Woodstock, Duke of Gloucester, sons of King Edward III, of England. Upon his death-bed Governor Leonard Calvert appointed Margaret Brent, his sister-in-law, executrix and attorney for his estate. He was Lord of St. Gabriel's, St. Michael's and Trinity Manors. ("Colonial Families of the United States," volume VII, page 289; Prov. Ct. Archives, 1683, page 366; "Chronicles of Colonial Maryland," page 53, note).

ISSUE:

10. i. WILLIAM, b. 1642/3, of whom later.

    ii. Anne, b. 1644; d. c. 1714; m. (1) 1664, Baker Brooke (1628-1679), Lord of De la Brooke Manor; m. (2), c. 1680, her cousin, Henry Brent (d. 1693); m. (3), c. 1694, Judge Thomas Tasker (d. 1699); m. (4), c. 1700, Richard Marsham (d. 1714). NOTE: The question of Anne Calvert's husbands is still perplexing, but the above account seems the most satisfactory and probable.

10. WILLIAM CALVERT[5] (Leonard,[4] George,[3] Leonard,[2] John[1]), b. in England 1642/3; d. in Maryland Jan. 10, 1682. He came to the Province in 1661, received a large grant of land

from his uncle (Cecil), Lord Baltimore, and inherited certain property of his father, including "Governor's Fields" and the mansion-house at St. Mary's City. He was Principal Secretary of Maryland and a man of high standing. His life was cut short by drowning when he was trying to ford the swollen Wicomico River in 1682. The grant of land from his uncle, the Lord Proprietory, was called "Piscataway Manor," 2400 acres of which he sold to Charles Egerton, Sr. His home was "Calvert's Rest," on Calvert's Bay, which is still standing. He was a member of the House of Burgesses and of the Council; he was also Deputy Governor of the Province. In 1661/2 he married Elizabeth Stone (who survived him), eldest daughter of Governor William Stone (1603-1660) and Verlinda Cotton (d. 1675), daughter of Andrew and Joane Cotton of Bunbury, Cheshire, England, and a sister of the Rev. Dr. William Cotton of Northampton County, Va.

ISSUE:

i.   Charles, b. 1662; d. 1733; m. (1) 1690, Mary Howson, daughter and co-heir of Robert Howson (or Howison) of Stafford County, Va., where he (Charles Calvert) resided for a time; m. (2) Barbara (Kirke?), daughter of Martin and Mary Kirke, of St. Mary's County, who (Mary Kirke) in her will of 1734 mentions her daughter "Barbary (sic) Calvert." She survived Charles Calvert and married, secondly, Andrew Foy.

Issue by 1st m.:

1.   Sarah—untraced.
2.   Anne—untraced.

ii.   Elizabeth, b. 1644; d. 1684; m. Dec. 20, 1681, Captain James Neale, Lord of Woolaston Manor.

Issue:

1.   Mary Neale, b. 1683; d. 173—; m. (1) 1702, Charles Egerton, Jr. (d. 1703); m. (2) 1707, Jeremiah Adderton (d. 1713); m. (3) 1718, Joseph van Swearingen; m. (4) 1726, William Deacon.

iii.   William, b. 1666; d. ——; living, 1696, in St. Mary's County.

11. iv.   GEORGE, b. 1668, of whom later.

v.   Richard, b. 1670; d. u. Nov. 11, 1718. He was of age in 1691 (see W. R. C. No. 1, page 570, Land Office, Annapolis).

According to an unverified family record, he married, in Westmoreland County, Va., Sarah —————; this record also gives the date of his birth as 1669, and adds the following children. (The compiler cannot vouch for this line, however.)

Issue:

1. Robert, who emigrated to Texas (sic) and founded Calvert City.
2. John, m. Mary Calvert, dau. of Joseph and gr. dau. of Cornelius Calvert of Norfolk and Princess Anne Counties, Va.
3. Francis, m. Hannah Brent; s. p.

11. GEORGE CALVERT[6] (William,[5] Leonard,[4] George,[3] Leonard,[2] John[1]), b. 1668; d. after 1739; m. c. 1690, Elizabeth Doyne. (Two other wives have been mentioned, viz: Anne Notley and Hannah Neale). This George Calvert has been confused with the one of the same name (born Dec. 15, 1672) who studied for the priesthood at Liège in 1692, but, at his own request, was allowed to leave the College and did *not* become a priest, as commonly supposed. (See Jesuit Records at Georgetown University).*

ISSUE:

i. Charles, b. 1691.
12. ii. JOHN, b. c. 1692, of whom later.
iii. George, living (1761) in Prince William County, Va.
iv. James (?).
v. Elizabeth.
vi. William.
vii. Thomas (?).

12. JOHN CALVERT[7] (George,[6] William,[5] Leonard,[4] George,[3] Leonard,[2] John[1]), b. c. 1692, in Maryland; d. 1739, in Prince William County, Va. He was granted land (across the Potomac River from the family seat in Maryland) in Prince William County, Va., July 16, 1724 (See Deed Book D, pages 47-8 and 141-3, Manassas, Va.). He m.

* (Prov. Ct. Archives, 1683, p. 366; "Chronicles of Colonial Maryland," p. 53, note.)

c. 1711, Elizabeth Harrison (supposedly the daughter of Benjamin Harrison III, of Virginia.)

ISSUE:

13.   i. GEORGE, b. 1712; of whom later.
     ii. Thomas, b. 1714; m. 1734, Sarah Harrison.
    iii. Burr, m. Adah Fairfax.
    iv. Cecilius.
     v. William.
    vi. Obed (?).
   vii. Elizabeth.

13. GEORGE CALVERT, JR.[8] (John,[7] George,[6] William,[5] Leonard,[4] George,[3] Leonard,[2] John[1]), b. 1712; d. May 19, 1782, in Culpeper County, Va. (whither he had moved from Prince William County before the Revolutionary War). After the death of Frederick, sixth and last Lord Baltimore, in 1771, he was the next heir to the title, but he never put forth a claim and soon after cast in his lot with the revolting Colonies. He lived at "Deep Hole Farm," Prince William County, across the Potomac River (on which it was situated) from Maryland; he died at "The Horse Shoe," in Culpeper County. When Benedict Arnold invaded the Valley of Virginia in 1781 he was called to the colors and commissioned Captain of a Company of Militia in Culpeper County by Thomas Jefferson, then Governor of Virginia, on May 19, 1781, his original commission (signed by Jefferson) being in the possession of the writer of this article. He m. (1) c. 1740, Anne Crupper, a sister of Gilbert Crupper of Prince William County, Trooper in the French and Indian War; m. (2) 1779, Mary Deatherage (d. 1810), widow of Robert Deatherage (d. 1777) and daughter of Francis and Susannah (Dabney) Strother, of St. Mark's Parish, Culpeper County.

ISSUE, BY FIRST M.:

14.   i. JOHN, b. 1742, of whom later.
17.   ii. GEORGE, b. 1744, of whom afterward.
    iii. Jane, b. 1746; d. ——; m. (1) c. 1768, Captain John Maddox, R. N.; m. (2) John Settle; m. (3) ———— Grymes.

Issue by 1st m.:

1. Jane Maddox, b. 1770.
2. Mary Maddox, b. 1772; d. 1816; m. 1789, William Deatherage.
3. Sarah Maddox, b. 1774.

Issue by 2nd m.:

1. John Calvert Settle, m. 1806, Sarah Turner.

Issue:

 (1) Jane Settle, m. her cousin, George Thorne (q. v.).
iv. Lydia, b. 1748; m. Archibald Bigbee.
v. Sarah, b. 1749; m. ———— Rookard.
vi. Anne, b. 1751; d. 1822; m. 1766, Captain William Lindsay (d. 1792) of "Colchester," Prince William County, and "Laurel Hill," Culpeper County, Va.

ISSUE BY SECOND M.:

i. Mary, b. 1780; d. 1809; m. 1805, Nicholas Thorne.

Issue:

1. George Thorne, b. 1806; m. his cousin, Jane Settle (q.v.).
2. Mary Thorne, b. 1808.

14. JOHN CALVERT[9] (George,[8] John,[7] George,[6] William,[5] Leonard,[4] George,[3] Leonard,[2] John[1]), b. 1742; d. 1790. He lived both in Maryland and Virginia; he married in the former state and died in the latter. He was Captain in the Revolution among the Virginia Forces (like his father and brother). Washington, Culpeper (now Rappahannock) County, was laid out upon his land in 1796-7. (See Hening's "Statutes at Large," vol. 15, page 30). He m. (1), 1765, Sarah Bailey (who lived only a few years); m. (2) 1772, Hellen Bailey (sister of his first wife), who survived him. They were daughters of John Bailey (d. 1789) of "Hunting Ridge," Baltimore County, Md., and Helen Newsome (Nussum) (d. 1801); and granddaughters of George Bayley (d. 1754) of that county (whose seal shows the crest of the Bayleys of Northallerton, Yorkshire). The wife of this George Bayley was Sarah Maclane, daughter of Hector Maclane (d. 1722) of Baltimore County and granddaughter of Hector Maclane of St. Mary's County and his

wife, Sarah Morgan, daughter of Captain Thomas Morgan (d. 1697) of that county.

ISSUE BY FIRST M.:

15.   i. CECILIUS, b. Dec. 29, 1767, of whom later.
      ii. Henrietta, b. 1769; m. ———— Birch; s. p.

ISSUE BY SECOND M.:

      i. Sarah, b. 1774; d. s. p.; m. 1803, John Heaton.
      ii. Anne, b. 1776; d. s. p. 1848; m. 1799, Captain David J. Coxe.
21.   iii. Elizabeth, b. 1777, of whom later.
      iv. Hannah, b. 1778; d. 1861; m. 1793, John Jett.
      v. Delia, b. 1780; d. u. 1873.
      vi. Gettie, b. 1785; d. 1816; m. 1801, Gabriel Smither.

15. CECILIUS CALVERT[10] (John,[9] George,[8] John,[7] George,[6] William,[5] Leonard,[4] George,[3] Leonard,[2] John[1]), b. Dec. 29, 1767, in Baltimore County, Md.; d. in Missouri, Feb. 14, 1852. He was baptized at old St. Paul's Church, Baltimore, on Dec. 31, 1767 (see Register of St. Paul's Parish in the Maryland Historical Society). He moved to Virginia with his father and there, in Culpeper County, married, in 1797, his first cousin, Nancy Beck Calvert (1773-1835) (q. v.), daughter of George and Lydia Beck (Ralls) Calvert (q. v.). He moved with his family to Kentucky and later to Missouri, where he died.

ISSUE:

      i. John, b. April 29, 1799; d. u. March 15, 1846.
      ii. George, b. April 25, 1802; d. April 29, 1865; m. 1835, Willie Anne Woods.

Issue:

      1. John Strother, b. 1836; d. 1886.
      2. George Washington, b. 1838; d. 1913.
      3. Benjamin Franklin, b. 1840, of Willows, Calif.
      4. Sarah Anne, b. 1842; m. her cousin, Samuel Ralls Calvert (q. v.).
16.   iii. ZIBA, b. Aug. 31, 1804; of whom later.
      iv. Sarah Anne, b. July 24, 1810; m. James Wood.
      v. Elizabeth, b. June 6, 1812; d. 1850; m. Elijah Pepper.
      vi. Gabriel, b. Jan. 27, 1814; d. Nov. 3, 1898.

16. ZIBA CALVERT[11] (Cecilius,[10] John,[9] George,[8] John,[7] George,[6] William,[5] Leonard,[4] George,[3] Leonard,[2] John[1]),

b. Culpeper County, Va., Aug. 31, 1804; d. Warren Township, Missouri, Oct. 11, 1886; he lived in Bourbon County, Ky., when a child and later moved to Marion County, Mo., and m. Dec. 24, 1834, Mary Ferguson (1811-1875).

16a.   i.   JAMES MADISON, b. May 29, 1836; of whom later.
      ii.   Emily, b. Sept. 29, 1837.
    iii.   America Virginia, b. June 4, 1840.
    iv.   Samuel Ralls, b. Nov. 28, 1841; d. Sept. 24, 1882; m. Oct. 28, 1869, his cousin, Sarah Anne Calvert (1842-1899) (q. v.).

> Issue:
>
> 1.   Elizabeth, b. May 3, 1871.
> 2.   Albert, b. Aug. 31, 1873.
> 3.   Jacob, b. Jan. 12, 1877.
> 4.   Samuel, b. July 30, 1880; d. Feb. 14, 1890.

     v.   John Quincy, b. April 4, 1845; m. Jan. 7, 1877, his cousin, Elvira Calvert (q. v.).

> Issue:
>
> 1.   Bernard Carson.
> 2.   Mary Elizabeth, d. April 7, 1889.
> 3.   Charles Leonard.
> 4.   Sarah Virginia.
> 5.   Emily Catherine.
> 6.   Lillie May.
> 7.   Susan Gertrude.

    vi.   Mary Anne, b. Jan. 14, 1848; d. May 12, 1868; m. Dec. 19, 1866, James W. Sharp.

> Issue:
>
> 1.   Mary Anne Sharp, b. April 17, 1868; m. Aug. 28, 1888, Taylor Mason Donley.

   vii.   Sarah Elizabeth, b. Sept. 15, 1851; m. Nov. 4, 1885, William D. Head.

> Issue:
>
> 1.   Calvert Head, b. April 19, 1888.

  viii.   Ziba Milton; b. Jan. 10, 1857; unmarried.

16a. JAMES MADISON CALVERT[12] (Ziba,[11] Cecilius,[10] John,[9] George,[8] John,[7] George,[6] William,[5] Leonard,[4] George,[3] Leonard,[2] John[1]), b. May 29, 1836; m. (1) April 29, 1875, Mary Malisa Taylor (1850-1877); m. (2) April 11, 1880, Catherine Ann Taylor, a sister of his first wife. James Madison Calvert is a prominent farmer of Hunnewell, Missouri, and his family records have been of much assistance in the compilation of this sketch.

ISSUE, BY FIRST M.:

i. Jacob Tipton, b. March 27, 1877.
ii. Alonzo Pulliam, twin to Jacob Tipton, b. March 27, 1877.

ISSUE, BY SECOND M.:

i. Dau., b. Dec. 29, 1886; d. Dec. 31, 1886.
ii. Catherine Anne, b. Feb. 4, 1892; d. May 12, 1914.

17. GEORGE CALVERT[9] (George,[8] John,[7] George,[6] William,[5] Leonard,[4] George,[3] Leonard,[2] John[1]), second son of George and Anne (Crupper) Calvert of "Deep" Hole Farm," was b. Feb. 6, 1744; d. in Culpeper County, May 22, 1821. He was a Captain in the War of the Revolution and made his home in Culpeper County while his brother lived in Maryland. He m., Feb. 7, 1764, Lydia Beck Ralls.

ISSUE:

18. i. RALLS, b. Oct. 9, 1767, of whom later.
     ii. Margaret, b. 1770; m. 1794, John Adams.

Issue:

1. Mariah Adams, m. 1816, her cousin Nimrod Hambrick, Jr. (q. v.).
2. Elizabeth Adams, m. 1822, Lewis David Massie.

Issue:

(1) Margaret Elizabeth Massie, m. 1843, her cousin Oliver Hazard Perry Smith (q. v.).

Issue:

(a) Mary Elizabeth Frances Smith, b. April 30, 1845; d. March 18, 1913; m. 1869, David Steele.
(b) John Perry Smith, b. April 29, 1847; m. 1881, Frances Bell.
(c) Anna Melvina Smith, b. May 25, 1849; m. Jan. 16, 1875, John Hangar Rush, great-grandson of Dr. Benjamin Rush, Signer of the Declaration of Independence.
(d) Lewis Edward Smith, b. 1851; d. July 31, 1914; m. 1878, Clara Weir.
(e) Robert Issachar Smith, b. 1857; d. 1863.
(f) Virginia Emma Smith, b. June 5, 1855; d. Sept. 8, 1909; m. Dec. 8, 1886, Samuel McClure.
(g) William Bernard Smith, b. 1858; d. 1859.

(2) Mary Virginia Massie.

(3) John William Massie, m. Mary Cloud.

(4) Thomas Bernard Massie, m. Margaret Bragg.

20. iii. GEORGE, b. 1771, of whom afterward.

    iv. Anne ("Nancy") Beck, b. 1773; d. May 18, 1835; m. 1797, her cousin, Cecilius Calvert (q. v.).

    v. John, b. 1775; m. 1804, Anne Askin.

    vi. Lydia, b. 1777; m. 1794, George Wheeler.

    vii. Elizabeth, b. 1779; m. 1800, Charles Williams.

  viii. Catherine, b. March 25, 1781; d. Oct. 20, 1852; m. (1) 1801, Henry Green; m. (2) 1809, Jacob Mathews.

    ix. Hannah, b. 1783; m. 1805, Peter Link.

    x. Jane, b. 1785; d. Nov. 8, 1804; m. 1804, George Craver.

    xi. Sarah, b. 1786; d. 1856; m. 1803, John Kaylor (1784-1866), from whom descends Mrs. Vera L. Outwater, of Kansas City, Mo., whose valuable records have contributed towards this article.

    xii. Cecilius, b. 1789; U. S. Army, 1814, 16th Virginia Regiment of Militia.

  xiii. Mariah, b. 1791; m. (1) 1808, Jacob Myers; m. (2) Nimrod Hambrick. The son by the second marriage was Nimrod Hambrick, Jr., who married his cousin, Mariah Adams (q. v.).

18. RALLS CALVERT[10] (George,[9] George,[8] John,[7] George,[6] William,[5] Leonard,[4] George,[3] Leonard,[2] John[1]), b. Oct. 9, 1767, Culpeper County, Va.; d. June 29, 1815, in Culpeper County, where he lived all his life. His home was Washington, where he was Postmaster, and there he died. He m., Nov. 15, 1790, Mary Wade Strother, daughter of Captain John and Anne (Strother) Strother, granddaughter of John and Mary Willis (Wade) Strother of "Wadefield," and great-granddaughter of Francis and Susannah (Dabney) Strother of St. Mark's Parish, Culpeper County (whose daughter, Mary, widow of Robert Deatherage, it will be remembered, was the second wife of George Calvert of "Deep Hole Farm."

ISSUE:

i. Jeremiah Strother, b. Sept. 10, 1791; d. April 18, 1867; m. April 8, 1816, Priscilla Smither (1796-1888).

Issue:

1. Mary Anne, b. Jan. 16, 1817; m. Oct. 31, 1845, James C. Watkins, at Bolton, Ala.

2. Sarah Hunt, b. May 9, 1819; d. April 2, 1833.
3. Eliza Jane, b. Oct. 18, 1821; d. Dec. 15, 1821.
4. Katherine Kennerly, b. Jan. 21, 1823; m. Feb. 2, 1846, Colonel Thomas D. Johnston, at Seguin, Texas.
5. James Lockhart, b. Sept. 19, 1825; killed during Civil War; m. Frances Tabor.
6. Susan Sophia, b. Feb. 2, 1827; m. Feb. 2, 1847, Colonel John Coffee Hays ("The Texas Ranger"), at Seguin, Texas.
7. Samuel Ralls, b. July 21, 1831.
8. Elizabeth Priscilla, b. Dec. 7, 1832; m. April 6, 1853, John Twohis; s. p.
9. William Lancelot Strother, b. Jan. 21, 1835; killed during Civil War.
10. Martha Frances, b. June 26, 1837; m. Dev. 19, 1854, Alfred Shelby, of Kentucky.
11. Edward Pendleton, b. Aug. 15, 1840.

ii. Anne Strother, b. Aug. 15, 1793; d. Nov. 1, 1861; m. (1) 1811, Issachar Smith (1784-1819); m. (2) 1823, Henry Spiller (1791-1842).

Issue by 1st m.:

1. John Ralls Smith, b. Feb. 18, 1812; m. Feb. 16, 1837, Lucy Anne Allen.
2. Mary Catherine Smith, b. Dec. 30, 1813; m. Aug. 4, 1836, John Rudacill.
3. Oliver Hazard Perry Smith, b. March 10, 1815; d. Jan. 8, 1887; m. March 10, 1843, his cousin, Margaret Elizabeth Massie (q. v.).
4. Elizabeth Smith, b. March 4, 1818; m. Feb. 10, 1844, Enoch Brown.

19. iii. GEORGE, b. Oct. 20, 1795, of whom later.
iv. Lydia Beck.
v. Martha.
vi. Patsey.
vii. John Strother, Major Tenth Virginia Regiment, C. S. A.; father of the late Judge George Ralls Calvert of New Market, Va., who left many notes of the Calvert Family.
viii. Edward, m. Mary Frances Jenkins.
ix. Ralls.
x. Mary.
xi. Katharine Kennerly, m. ——— Hollingsworth.
xii. Lucy, d. 1848; m. 1844, James Leake Powers (1799-1889), whose first wife was her cousin, Martha Anne Nicklin (q. v.), daughter of Joseph and Elizabeth (Calvert) Nicklin.

19. GEORGE CALVERT[11] (Ralls,[10] George,[9] George,[8] John,[7]

George,[6] William,[5] Leonard,[4] George,[3] Leonard,[2] John[1]), b. Oct. 20, 1795; d. Sept. 23, 1871; m. May 11, 1819, Elizabeth Lovell Carr (1802-1874), daughter of Joseph and Delia (Strother) Carr.

ISSUE:

i. Olivia Jane, b. March 16, 1820; d. April 28, 1881; m. William Chamblin.

ii. Anna Maria, b. Dec. 2, 1821; d. Feb. 7, 1900; m. April 7, 1840, Dr. Samuel Keerl Jackson of Norfolk son of the Rev. Dr. Edward Jackson.

Issue:

1. Edward Calvert Jackson, b. 1841; Upperville, Va.
2. William Congreve Jackson, b. 1843; d. 1861.
3. Anna Maria Jackson, b. 1845; d. 1897; m. Robert J. Tucker of Bermuda and Virginia.
4. Henry Melville Jackson, b. July 28, 1849; d. May 4, 1900; Bishop Coadjutor of Alabama and a brilliant preacher. He m. (1) July 24, 1873, Rebecca Lloyd, daughter of John and Eliza Armistead (Selden) Lloyd; m. (2) April 21, 1880, Violet Lee Pace, daughter of James Baker and Elizabeth (Neale) Pace; m. (3) April 17, 1895, Caroline Toney Cochrane, daughter of Judge John and Caroline (Toney) Cochrane.
5. Churchill Calvert Jackson, b. 1850; d. 1897; m. Elizabeth Wilson.

Issue:

1. Anna Calvert Jackson, m. James Burr Warwick.
2. William Congreve Jackson, m. Marguerite Kemp of Baltimore.

6. Olive Caldwell Jackson, b. 1857; m. Francis Taliaferro Stribling; s. p.
7. Marshall Parks Jackson, b. 1860; d. 1907; m. Josephine Ross.
8. George Calvert Jackson, b. 1862; d. i.

iii. Amanda Carr, b. Nov. 18, 1823; d. u. Jan. 24, 1904.
iv. Joseph Carr, b. June 8, 1825; d. s. p. Aug. 18, 1892.
v. Robert Singleton, b. Sept. 13, 1829; d. May 23, 1830.
vi. Caldwell Carr, b. Jan. 28, 1831; d. Sept. 14, 1909; m. June 25, 1879, Mary Landon Armistead Rosser, daughter of Joseph Travis and Mary Walker (Armistead) Rosser.

Issue:

1. Mary Rosser, b. 1882.
2. Landon Ralls, b. May 26, 1884.
3. Elizabeth Lovell, b. 1886; d. i.

20. George Calvert[10] (George,[9] George,[8] John,[7] George,[6] William,[5] Leonard,[4] George,[3] Leonard,[2] John[1]), second son of George and Lydia Beck (Ralls) Calvert of Culpeper County, was b. 1771; d. ——; m. Oct. 19, 1809, Anne (Jennings) Norman.

ISSUE:

  i. Sarah Anne, m. ———— Thompson.
  ii. Benjamin, m. Amanda Hunniman.
  iii. Samuel Ralls.
  iv. George Edward, b. 1820; d. 1907; m. 1846, Mary Frances Hughes.

Issue:

    1. Thomas Hughes, d. s. p.
    2. Mary Virginia, m. William Hand (1826-1910).
    3. Cecil, m. ———— Wagner.
    4. Walter.
    5. John Ralls, m. Jane Portlow.
    6. Anne Frances, m. Charles H. Rosson.
    7. George (the eleventh of that name).
    8. Mathew James Preston Hughes, b. 1857; d. 1907; m. Anne B. Mosby.

Issue:

      (1) Bernard Yancey.

  v. Elizabeth, m. George Estes.
  vi. Jesse.
  vii. John Jett.

21. Elizabeth Calvert[10] (John,[9] George,[8] John,[7] George,[6] William,[5] Leonard,[4] George,[3] Leonard,[2] John[1]), third (and eventually eldest) daughter and co-heiress of John and Hellen (Bailey) Calvert of "Hunting Ridge," Baltimore County, Md., and "Poplar Grove," Culpeper County, Va., was b. Feb. 21, 1777, in Maryland; d. Dec. 15, 1833, in Virginia. She m., Jan. 7, 1802, in Culpeper County, Va., Dr. Joseph Nicklin (1776-1853), Surgeon in the War of 1812 and son of Joseph and Martha (Richards) Nicklin of Chester County, Pa., and Frederick County, Va. He was later a member of the House of Delegates and a well-known physician.

ISSUE:

22. i. John Bailey Nicklin I, b. Feb. 23, 1803, of whom later.
    ii. Joseph Marshall Nicklin, b. April 21, 1805; d. s. p. March

10, 1846; m. 1830, Mary Newton Lane, daughter of George Steptoe and Elizabeth Taliaferro (Stribling) Lane and first cousin to Harriet (Lane) Johnstone; also cousin to Lucy Ware (Webb) Hayes, wife of President Hayes. Joseph Marshall Nicklin had in his possession the parchment tree of the Calverts when his office and all its contents (including this tree) were destroyed by fire nearly a century ago.

iii. Levi Orme Connor Nicklin, b. Feb. 18, 1807; d. July 24, 1876; m. Dec. 18, 1832, Margaretta Shriver. Their son, Cecilius Calvert Nicklin (1838-1863) was killed in the Civil War.

iv. Martha Anne Nicklin, b. Dec. 18, 1809; d. March 25, 1843; m. May 27, 1837, James Leake Powers (1799-1889), who afterwards, surviving her, married her cousin, Lucy Calvert (q. v.). Her daughter, Miss Martha Anne Nicklin Powers, inherited many heirlooms and has furnished much assistance in the preparation of this article. She lives in the old home at Washington, Va.

v. Jacob Richards Nicklin, b. Aug. 20, 1811; d. July 11, 1887; Colonel, C. S. A.; m. (1) 1843 Susan Eastham; m. (2) Oct. 24, 1855, Susan Maria Hunter. Their daughter, Mrs. H. J. Beagen of Chester, Pa., has also assisted in the preparation of this sketch.

vi. William Henry Harrison Nicklin, b. June 13, 1813; d. Nov. 11, 1881; m. May 1, 1838, Mary Jane Nelson.

22. JOHN BAILEY NICKLIN I[11] (Elizabeth Calvert,[10] John,[9] George,[8] John,[7] George,[6] William,[5] Leonard,[4] George,[3] Leonard,[2] John[1]), b. Culpeper County, Va., Feb. 23, 1803; d. Franklin, Pa., Oct. 22, 1891; m. at "Locust Grove," Jefferson County, Va., March 23, 1830, Catharine Thornton Pendleton (1806-1874), only daughter of Benjamin Pendleton (1781-1853), and Elizabeth Strother (1784-1822), daughter of Benjamin Strother (1750-1807) of "Park Forrest," Jefferson County, Va. (He was a Midshipman in the Revolutionary Navy and later served in the Land Forces). Catharine Thornton (Pendleton) Nicklin was a great-grandniece of the distinguished Judge Edmund Pendleton (1721-1803).

ISSUE:

i. Benjamin Strother Nicklin, b. Oct. 8, 1831; d. Aug. 17, 1873; m. Oct. 25, 1853, Sarah White Hersey. He was Captain, U. S. A., 1861-65.

1904, the Countess Elsa von Moltke.

v.   Samuel Church Nicklin, b. Feb. 18, 1840; d. Sept. 29, 1911;
     m. Sept. 7, 1865, Harriet Utley.

23. vi. JOHN BAILEY NICKLIN II, b. Aug. 5, 1843, of whom later.

ii. Elizabeth Catherine Nicklin, b. Nov. 29, 1833; d. Sept. 10,
     1910; m. Jan. 9, 1851, Espy Connoly.

iii. Martha Virginia Nicklin, b. March 9, 1836; d. May 22, 1838.

iv. Mary Marshall Nicklin, b. Jan. 19, 1838; d. May 28, 1921;
     m. March 15, 1871, John Nelson Emery.

Issue:

1.   Joseph Emery, b. June 24, 1868; d. Aug. 11, 1868.
2.   Mary Virginia Emery, b. Nov. 1, 1869; m. Aug. 22, 1899,
     Paul Browne Patterson.
3.   Frederick Strother Emery, b. Aug. 6, 1874; m. Aug. 23,

vii. Lucy Crane, b. April 25, 1846; d. Oct. 2, 1846.

viii. Laura Pendleton Nicklin, b. Sept. 5, 1848; d. April 10, 1872;
      m. 1870, Dr. Charles B. Ansart.

ix.   William Fuller Nicklin, b. March 11, 1852; d. Feb. 18, 1858.

23. JOHN BAILEY NICKLIN II[12] (John Bailey Nicklin,[11] Elizabeth Calvert[10], John,[9] George,[8] John,[7] George,[6], William,[5]
Leonard,[4] George,[3] Leonard,[2] John[1]), b. Allegheny City,
Pa., August 5, 1843; d. Chattanooga, Tenn., May 6, 1919;
Private, Company "K," 100th Pennsylvania Regiment
("Roundheads"); Drum Major, 55th Pennsylvania Regiment, 1861-65. Settled in Chattanooga, Feb. 26, 1866, and
resided there until his death. Mayor of Chattanooga 1887-
89; President Board of Education, 1893; President Southern (Baseball) League 1901; 33rd Degree Scottish Rite
Mason; Grand Commander, K. T., etc.; m. Sept. 6, 1871,
at Chattanooga, Eliza Kaylor, eldest daughter of Daniel
Pringle Kaylor (1827-1898) of New York and Chattanooga, by his first wife, Sarah McBryde (1827-1873),
daughter of Henry and Mary (Whitfield) McBryde of Ireland and Canada.

ISSUE:

i.   Benjamin Patten Nicklin, Colonel, Infantry, U. S. A., Camp
     Benning, Ga.; b. Jan. 24, 1873; m. Manila, P. I., Oct. 31,
     1910, Margaret Anne Peele Hayes, daughter of James and
     Ida Helen (Soothoff) Hayes; s. p.

ii. Dwight Pendleton Nicklin, b. March 22, 1875; m. June 15,

1905, Daisy Hope Harrison, daughter of Major-General William Cole Harrison C. V. (great-great-grandson of Benjamin Harrison, Governor of Virginia and Signer of the Declaration of Independence) and Mary Jane Lattner; s. p.

iii. Samuel Strang ("Sammy Strang") Nicklin, b. Dec. 16, 1876; Captain, Infantry, World War; President Chattanooga Baseball Club, 1919-20-21.

iv. John Bailey Calvert Nicklin, b. Dec. 17, 1891; Lieutenant, World War; member: Maryland Historical, Ark and Dove, Colonial Wars, Sons of the American Revolution, Sons of Confederate Veterans, Military Order of Foreign Wars, American Clan Gregor and National Geographic Societies; American Legion, etc.; compiler of numerous historical and genealogical sketches.

NOTE—Obed Calvert (q. v.) is ancestor of the Hon. Jesse B. Calvert of Macomb, Ill. The line is as follows: Obed Calvert, b. c. 1720; Jesse Calvert, b. c. 1742, Maryland; d. Manassas, Va.; James, b. c. 1767; Jesse, b. Anne Arundel County, Md., 1793; d. Savannah, Mo., 1878; George, 1832-1890; Jesse B. Calvert, 1868——.

The compiler has examined (or had examined) the court records at La Plata, Leonardtown, Baltimore, Marlborough and Annapolis, Md.; Manassas, Culpeper, Fairfax, Orange and Stafford, Va. Besides the foregoing authorities, the family records of the compiler have furnished the chief material for this sketch, as well as those of other members of the family.

FATTI MASCHI PAROLE FEMINE

THE CALVERT FAMILY

JOHN BAILEY CALVERT NICKLIN

PART III

THE " MT. AIRY " LINE

24. BENEDICT (SWINGATE, otherwise) CALVERT[8] (Charles,[7] Benedict Leonard,[6] Charles,[5] Cecil,[4] George,[3] Leonard,[2] John[1]), was born (about 1724) several years before his father's marriage to Mary Jannsen. Charles Calvert, fifth Lord Baltimore, acknowledged the paternity of this natural

son and was very devoted to him. (Perhaps he realized, in some indefinable manner, that through him alone his line was to be perpetuated?). But he never revealed the secret of his mother's identity. (It is said that his mother was one of the daughters of King George II., and that therefore he did not dare divulge the secret or keep the boy in England.) However this may be, Benedict was sent to Maryland (in charge of Captain Vernon), where he was under the care of Dr. George Stewart of Annapolis. (Under date of August 31, 1728, Charles Lowe, cousin of the Calverts, wrote to Benedict Leonard Calvert, Jr., mentioning that this Charles, Lord Baltimore, had gone on a Scandinavian trip, having made a will before sailing in which he left 2000 pounds " to a Naturall Son by the name of Benedict Swingate." See this *Magazine* Volume III, page 323.). In 1744 Benedict Swingate or Calvert was appointed Collector of Customs at Patuxent and the next year he became a member of the Council. He made his home at " Mt. Airy " in Prince George's County, and there he died Jan. 9, 1788. He m., April 21, 1748, Elizabeth Calvert (q. v.), dau. of the Hon. Charles Calvert (Governor of Maryland 1720-7) and Rebecca Gerrard, his wife.

ISSUE:

i. Rebecca, b. Dec. 25, 1749; d. i.
ii. Eleanor, b. 1754; d. Sept. 28, 1811; m. (1) Feb. 3, 1774, Colonel John Parke Custis (1753-1781) (a son of Martha Washington by her first husband, Daniel Parke Custis); m. (2) 1783, Dr. David Stewart.

Issue, by 1st m.:

1. Elizabeth Parke Custis, b. Aug. 21, 1776; d. Jan. 1, 1832; m. March 20, 1796, Thomas Law, nephew of Lord Ellenborough and son of the Bishop of Carlisle.
2. Martha Parke Custis, b. Dec. 31, 1777; d. July 13, 1854; m. Jan. 6, 1795, Thomas Peter.
3. Eleanor Parke Custis, b. March 21, 1779; d. July 15, 1852; m., at " Mt. Vernon," Feb. 22, 1799, in the presence of George and Martha Washington and on the former's last birthday, Lawrence Lewis, nephew of General George Washington.

4. George Washington Parke Custis, b. April 20, 1781;
d. Oct. 10, 1857; he built the beautiful mansion, "Arlington," on the Potomac River near Washington City;
he m., 1805, Mary Lee Fitzhugh, dau. of Colonel William and Anne (Randolph) Fitzhugh of "Ravensworth."

Issue:

1. Mary Anne Randolph Custis, b. at "Arlington"
Oct. 1, 1808; d. at Lexington, Va., Nov. 5, 1873;
m. at "Arlington," June 30, 1831, Lieutenant Robert Edward Lee, U. S. A. (afterwards General,
C. S. A.).

iii. Charles, b. Oct. 3, 1756; d. u. 1777.

iv. Elizabeth, m. June 15, 1780, Dr. Charles Stewart (1750-1822).

v. Edward Henry, b. Nov. 7, 1766; d. July 12, 1846; m.
March 1, 1796, Elizabeth Biscoe (1780-1857); a quo Miss
Helen Chapman Calvert of Alexandria, Va.

25. vi. GEORGE, b. Feb. 2, 1768; of whom later.

vii. Philip, d. y.

viii. Leonard, d. y.

ix. Cecilius, d. y.

x. John, d. after 1788.
xi. William, d. after 1788. } Living at the date of their
xii. Ariana, d. after 1788. } father's death (1788).

xiii. Robert, d. y.

25. GEORGE CALVERT[9] (Benedict,[8] Charles,[7] Benedict Leonard,[6] Charles,[5] Cecil,[4] George,[3] Leonard,[2] John[1]), b. at
"Mt. Airy" Feb. 2, 1768; d. at "Riverdale" Jan. 28,
1838; m. June 11, 1799, Rosalie Eugenia Stier (1778-1821), dau. of Henri Joseph Stier, of Antwerp, and Maria
Louise Peeters, his wife.

ISSUE:

i. Caroline Maria, b. July 15, 1800; d. Nov. 25, 1842; m.
June 19, 1823, Thomas Willing Morris of Philadelphia.

ii. George Henry, b. Jan. 2, 1803; d. s. p., May 24, 1889; he
was a distinguished author; m. May 8, 1829, Elizabeth
Stewart (1802-1897), dau. of James and Rebecca (Sprigg)
Stewart.

iii. Marie Louise, b. 1804; d. 1809.

iv. Rosalie Eugenia, b. Oct. 19, 1806; d. May 6, 1845; m.
Nov. 11, 1830, Charles Henry Carter (1802-1892) (grand-

son of "Light Horse Harry" Lee and nephew of General Robert Edward Lee, C. S. A.), a quo Mildred (Carter), Viscountess Acheson, of London.

26. v. CHARLES BENEDICT, b. Aug. 23, 1808; of whom later.

    vi. Henry Joseph Albert, b. 1811; d. 1820.

    vii. Marie Louise, b. 1812; d. 1813.

    viii. Julia, b. Jan. 31, 1814; d. June 8, 1888; m. May 7, 1833, Dr. Richard Henry Stuart.

    ix. Amelia Isabella, b. 1817; d. 1820.

26. CHARLES BENEDICT CALVERT[10] (George,[9] Benedict,[8] Charles,[7] Benedict Leonard,[6] Charles,[5] Cecil,[4] George,[3] Leonard,[2] John[1]), b. at "Riverdale," Prince George's Co., Md., Aug. 23, 1808; d. there May 12, 1864; m. June 6, 1839, Charlotte Augusta Norris (d. Dec. 7, 1876), dau. of William and Sarah (Martin) Norris.

ISSUE:

    i. Ella, b. March 20, 1840; d. Feb. 17, 1902; m. Sept. 3, 1861, Duncan G. Campbell.

    ii. George Henry, b. Nov. 29, 1841; m. Dec. 26, 1872, Frances Seybolt.

27. iii. CHARLES BALTIMORE, b. Feb. 5, 1843; of whom later.

    iv. William Norris, b. Oct. 12, 1845; d. Sept. 7, 1889; m. March 12, 1888, Laura Hunt.

Issue:

      1. Rosalie Eugenia, m. Dr. W. W. Holland of Baltimore.

    v. Eugenia Stier, b. Dec. 19, 1846; d. u. Nov. 30, 1894.

    vi. Jules van Havre, b. Oct. 30, 1848; d. Aug. 4, 1849.

27. CHARLES BALTIMORE CALVERT[11] (Charles Benedict,[10] George,[9] Benedict,[8] Charles,[7] Benedict Leonard,[6] Charles,[5] Cecil,[4] George,[3] Leonard,[2] John[1]), b. at "Riverdale," Feb. 5, 1843; d. Aug. 31, 1906; member of the Maryland Legislature 1864-66-67; Trustee of the State Agricultural College, from which he graduated in 1863 with the degree of A. B.; m. June 14, 1866, Eleanor Mackubin, dau. of Dr. Richard Creagh and Hester Ann (Worthington) Mackubin of "Strawberry Hill," Anne Arundel County, Md.

ISSUE:

    i. Eleanor Gibson, m. June 8, 1892, W. Gibson Cary of Baltimore.

ii. Hester Virginia, m. Dr. Henry Walter Lilly of North Carolina.

iii. Charlotte Augusta, m. Thomas Henry Spence.

iv. Charles Benedict, b. Nov. 8, 1871; d. July 2, 1872.

v. Richard Creagh Mackubin, b. Dec. 31, 1872; m. Zoe Ammen Davis.

vi. George Henry, b. Oct. 2, 1874; m. Cornelia Russell Knight.

vii. Rosalie Eugenia Stier.

viii. Elizabeth Stewart, m. June 5, 1906, William Douglas Nelson Thomas.

ix. Charles Baltimore, b. Oct. 9, 1878.

THE " MYSTERIOUS LINE "

28. As much uncertainty surrounds the paternity of this Charles Calvert as does the maternity of his son-in-law, Benedict Swingate or Calvert of " Mt. Airy." The claim that he was a son of Charles Calvert, third Lord Baltimore, is unsupported entirely save by the bare assertion that he was " uncle of Lord Baltimore " (i. e., Charles Calvert, fifth Lord Baltimore). (There is not a little reason to believe that he was identical with the Captain Charles Calvert Lazenby of His Majesty's Footguards in 1718.) He came to Maryland and was appointed Governor in 1720. In 1722 Mrs. Margaret Lazenby died in Anne Arundel County; she was called " aunt to our present Governor," who was this Charles Calvert. Of course, there is nothing to indicate why Captain Lazenby should have been permitted to assume the name of Calvert unless he were of Calvert blood. (Perhaps he was a natural son of Charles Calvert, third Lord Baltimore, by a Miss Lazenby?). In the will of the Hon. Benedict Leonard Calvert, Jr. (1700-1732), son and namesake of the fourth Lord Baltimore, mention is made of his " God-daughter, Elizabeth, daughter of Charles Calvert, Commissary-General," but no mention is made of any relationship, which certainly would have been made if her father were his uncle, it seems! On the other hand, there is a possibility that Governor Charles Calvert might have been a posthumous son of the Hon. Philip Cal vert (1626-1682) (q. v.) and his second wife, Jane Sewall,

step-daughter of Charles Calvert, third Lord Baltimore. But again we are lacking in evidence to support this theory. As a final effort to place him correctly, it is somewhat reasonable to think that he may have been a son of George Calvert, Esq. (b. 1669) (q. v.), himself a son of the Hon. William Calvert and Elizabeth Stone, his wife. This Charles Calvert, Governor of Maryland from 1720 to 1727, is said to have been born in 1691. The student of Calvert history must decide for himself where to place him in the genealogy. So Governor Charles Calvert still remains one of the unsolved mysteries among the Calvert lineage. He was succeeded (1727) in the governorship by the Hon. Benedict Leonard Calvert, Jr. (1700-1732) (q. v.) and he then became a member of the Council and so remained until his death six years later. He m. Nov. 21, 1722, Rebecca Gerrard (d. 1735), dau. of John and Elizabeth Gerrard of Prince George's County, Md.

ISSUE:

i. Charles, b. Nov. 2, 1723; d. Jan. 15, 1724.
ii. Anne, b. 1726; living 1734; untraced. (She evidently died young.)
iii. Elizabeth, b. Feb. 24, 1730; d. July 7, 1798; m. April 21, 1748, Benedict Swingate, or Calvert (q. v.) of "Mt. Airy." (See this *Magazine*, Volume I, page 290.)

THE CALVERT FAMILY

John Bailey Calvert Nicklin

Addenda et Corrigenda

Part IV

DESCENT OF THE TITLE (ACTUAL AND " DE JURE.")

(See Chart Pedigree.)

Sir George Calvert, Knight, was created (by King James I.) Baron (i. e., Lord) Baltimore of Baltimore, County Longford, Ireland, in 1625; he died 15 April, 1632, and was succeeded (Governor the Honorable Leonard Calvert being his second son) by his eldest son, Cecil Calvert.

Cecil, second Lord Baltimore, b. 1605; d. 1675; m. 1627, Lady Anne Arundell and was succeeded by his only surviving son, Charles Calvert I.

Charles, third Lord Baltimore, b. 1637; d. 1715; married four times and was succeeded by his only surviving son (by his second wife, Mrs. Jane Sewall, née Lowe.), Benedict Leonard Calvert I.

Benedict Leonard, fourth Lord Baltimore, b. 1679; d. 1715; m. 1698, the Lady Charlotte Lee and was succeeded by his eldest son, Charles Calvert II.

Charles, fifth Lord Baltimore, b. 1699; d. 1751; m. 1730, Mary Jannsen and was succeeded by his only surviving son, Frederick Calvert.

Frederick, sixth and last Lord Baltimore, b. 1732; d. 1771; m. 1753, the Lady Diana Egerton and died without lawful issue, when the title (wrongfully) became " extinct" (1771). The heir, however, was George Calvert, Esq., of " Deep Hole Farm," Prince William County, and "The Horse Shoe," Culpeper County, Virginia, who was heir-male of Governor the Honorable Leonard Calvert (supra), as follows:

Leonard Calvert (d. 1647), second son of the first Lord Baltimore, was Governor of Maryland, 1634-1647; m. Anne Brent (1642) and left an only son,

William Calvert (d. 1682), Deputy Governor, etc.; m. Elizabeth Stone (dau. of Governor William Stone) and left as his heir (his other sons having died without issue male) his son,

George Calvert Esq., who m. Elizabeth Doyne and left as his heir his eldest son,

John Calvert Esq. (d. 1739), who m. Elizabeth Harrison of Virginia and left as his heir his eldest son,

George Calvert Esq. (d. 1782) (supra), of " Deep Hole Farm " and " The Horse Shoe," etc., de jure seventh Lord Baltimore, being the heir-male of Governor the Leonard Calvert (q. v.). At his death the claim descended to his elder son, by his first wife (Anne Crupper),

John Calvert Esq. (d. 1790), of " Hunting Ridge," Baltimore County, Md., de jure eighth Lord Baltimore. At his death the claim descended to his only son, by his first wife (Sarah Bailey),

Cecilius Calvert Esq. (d. 1852), de jure ninth Lord Baltimore; he married his first cousin, Anne Beck Calvert, dau. of his uncle, George Calvert Esq., Jr. (1744-1821), and left as his heir his eldest son (Ziba Calvert Esq., being the *third* son),

John Calvert Esq. (d. 1846), de jure tenth Lord Baltimore; he died unmarried and left as his heir, his brother,

George Calvert Esq. (d. 1865), de jure eleventh Lord Baltimore; he m. Willie Anne Woods and left as his heir his eldest son,

John Strother Calvert Esq. (d. 1886), de jure twelfth Lord Baltimore; he died unmarried and left as his heir his brother,

George Washington Calvert Esq. (d. 1913), de jure thirteenth Lord Baltimore; he died unmarried also and left as his heir his brother,

Benjamin Franklin Calvert Esq., of Willows, California, de jure fourteenth Lord Baltimore. As he has no issue, his heir is his first cousin, James Madison Calvert, of Hunnewell, Mo., eldest son of the late Ziba Calvert (q. v.) and grandson of Cecilius, de jure ninth Lord Baltimore. He is therefore heir-presumptive to the Barony, if restored.

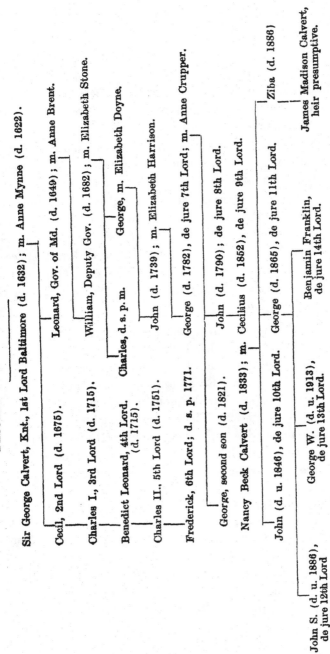

DESCENT OF THE TITLE (BALTIMORE).

Corrections

Two deeds recently sent me from Prince William County, Virginia, indicate that the wife of John Calvert (d. 1739), George[6], William[5], Leonard[4], George[3], Leonard[2], John[1], was Jane, and not Elizabeth, Harrison. The first deed speaks of "Burr Calvert alias Harrison, son of Jane Harrison . . . . of Westmoreland County," and the second (dated 1739), "between Thomas Calvert alias Harrison, and Sarah his wife, and John Carr . . . . lands in Prince William County left by Burr Harrison between George Calvert alias Harrison, Burr Calvert alias Harrison, and Thomas Calvert Harrison." This would also indicate that there were only *three* sons, instead of five or six, although, of course, there may have been more than tradition to supply the data of the other children. (See Deed Book D., pages .7-8, Manassas.) There may, however, have been more than one marriage between the Calverts and Harrisons in Virginia.

Page 52, line 4.   Read degree, not degrete.

Page 55, line 36.   Read Philipson, not Philipsin.

Page 57, line 20.   Read Oct., 13., 1731, not 1751.

Page 57, line 22.   Read Cecilius, not Cecelius.

Page 57, line 3.   Read Epsom, not Epson.

Page 58, line 22.   The matter beginning "Before his marriage" and ending "who lived at 'Mt. Airy,'" properly belongs to a footnote to follow after line 4, ending "riotous living," as it does not pertain to Frederick, Lord Baltimore, but to his father.

Page 58, line 32.   Read d. s. p. l., not d. s. p. l.

Page 58, line 33.   Read Epsom, not Epson.

Page 191.   The order of the children of the Hon. William Calvert was inverted for the first two, as Elizabeth was the eldest child, not Charles. Read, therefore: i. Elizabeth, b. 1662. ii. Charles, b. 1664; etc.

Page 191, line 32.   Read: iii. William, b. 1666; d. s. p. m., etc.

Page 192, line 21. Read: i: Charles (?), d. s. p. m., the interrogation point indicating the doubt as to his paternity as referred to on pages 317-318.

Page 195, line 23. The complete issue of George Calvert and Willie Anne (Woods) Calvert is as follows:

   i. John Strother, b. 1836; d. 1896, unmarried.
  ii. George Washington, b. 1838; d. 1913, unmarried.
 iii. William Wood, b. 1840; d. 1908, unmarried.
  iv. Sarah Anne, b. 1842; d. 1899; m. 1869, her cousin, Samuel Ralls
      Calvert (q. v.).
   v. Mary Elizabeth, b. 1844; d. s. p.
  vi. Ziba Jesse, b. 1846; d. 1903, unmarried.
 vii. Benjamin Franklin, b. Sept. 27, 1850; heir to the Barony of
      Baltimore.
viii. James Gabriel, b. 1852; d. s. p. m. 1885.
  ix. Susan Catherine, b. 1853; d. 1886.
   x. Elvira Jane, b. 1856; m. 1877, her cousin, John Quincy Calvert
      (q. v.).
  xi. Martha Virginia, b. 1858; d. 1879.
 xii. Edward Green, b. 1860; d. u.

Page 197, line 4. The Catherine Anne (b. Feb. 4, 1892; d. May 12, 1914) here mentioned as a daughter of James Madison Calvert and his second wife, Catherine Anne Taylor, is in error as this was the second wife herself. She was born Feb. 4, 1852, and died May 12, 1914, leaving no issue.

Page 199, line 12. Read: John Twohig, not Twohis.

Page 203, lines 1-2-3-4 belong after line 13 as wife of Frederick Strother Emery. Read: Frederick Strother Emery, b. Aug. 6, 1874; m. Aug. 23, 1904, the Countess Elsa von Moltke.

v. Samuel Church Nicklin, etc.

Page 203, line 15. Read: Lucy Crane Nicklin.

The first seventeen lines of page 203 were so mixed up that it is thought advisable to give them in their correct order, which is as follows:

  ii. Elizabeth Catherine Nicklin, b. Nov. 29, 1833; d. Sept. 10, 1910;
      m. Jan. 9, 1851, Espy Connoly.
 iii. Martha Virginia Nicklin, b. March 9, 1836; d. May 22, 1838.
  iv. Mary Marshall Nicklin, b. Jan. 19, 1838; d. May 28, 1921; m.
      March 15, 1866, John Nelson Emery.

1. Joseph Emery, b. June 24, 1868; d. Aug. 11, 1868.
2. Mary Virginia Emery, b. Nov. 1. 1869; m. Aug. 22, 1899, Paul Browne Patterson.
3. Frederick Strother Emery, b. Aug. 6, 1874; m. Aug. 23, 1904, Elsa, daughter of Count and Countess Max von Moltke.

 v. Samuel Church Nicklin, b. Feb. 18, 1840; d. Sept. 29, 1911; m. Sept. 7, 1865, Harriet Utley.

23. vi. John Bailey Nicklin II., b. Aug. 5, 1843; d. May 6, 1919; of whom later.

 vii. Lucy Crane Nicklin, b. April 25, 1846; d. Oct. 2, 1846.

 viii. Laura Pendleton Nicklin, b. Sept. 5, 1848; d. April 10, 1872; m. 1870, Dr. Charles B. Ansart; s. p.

 ix. William Fuller Nicklin, b. March 11, 1852; d. Feb. 18, 1858.

Page 203, line 37, add (to record of Colonel Benjamin Patten Nicklin, U. S. A.): Member of the Society of the Cincinnati in the State of Virginia.

Page 318, line 5. Read 1668, not 1669.

CHARLES CALVERT (1663-1733) AND SOME OF HIS DESCENDANTS.

By John Baily Calvert Nicklin.

Charles Calvert, eldest son of the Hon. William Calvert (1642-1682) (by his wife, Elizabeth Stone, daughter of Governor William Stone and his wife, Verlinda Cotton) and grandson of Governor Leonard Calvert (1606-1647), was born in 1663 and died in 1733. (Aug. 14, 1722, he gave his age as "59 years or thereabouts." Chancery Book No. 3, page 750, Annapolis. March 28, 1721, he gave his age as "57 years or thereabouts." Chancery Book No. 2, page 661. On page 706 of the same book, under date of Dec. 2, 1710, Robert Bowlin's testimony stated that "About 12 years ago was the full time of this deponent's being acquainted with Mr. Richard Calvert, he being then in Virginia along with his mother." Madam Elizabeth Calvert, widow of the Hon. William Calvert, evidently remained unmarried after the death of her husband. On Feb. 11, 1707, she brought suit against Philip Lynes. On Aug. 19, 1720, it was stated that " Richard Calvert died intestate at the house of William Young. Charles Calvert, his brother, was his heir-at-law." Chancery Book No. 3, page 868. March 8, 1721, Joshua Doyne, aged 32, and Jesse Doyne deposed, stating that " Richard Calvert died in the fall of 1718." Chancery Book No. 3, page 874). On Dec. 14, 1669, " William Calvert, Esq., his Lordship's nephew, took the oath of a Justice of this Court in pursuance of his Lordship's instructions bearing date the eighth and twentieth day of July last past." (Liber JJ., page 33, Land Office, Annapolis. On page 40 he is mentioned as " Colonel William Calvert, Justice.")

Charles Calvert, Esq., moved from Charles County, Md., to Stafford County, Va. (across the Potomac River) about 1690. " Liber Y No. 1, page 346, La Plata, Md., Jan. 13, 170½. Charles Calvert late of Charles County, otherwise called Charles Calvert of Stafford County, Va., Gentleman." Liber No. 2, page 37, Westmoreland County, Va. June 26, 1695, Charles Calvert witnessed a deed from Charles Ashton to Joshua Hudson. Sept., 16, 1688. " Charles Calvert, Esq., son and Heire of William Calvert, Esq., Deceased, and of Elizabeth ye widow and Relict of ye said William " and daughter of William Stone, deceased. Liber No. 14, page 35. Jan. 14, 1689. Charles Calvert, Esq., of St. Mary's County to Charles Egerton of said County, Merchant. April 5, 1690. Charles Calvert appeared before John Courts and John Addison, Justices of Charles County. In Stafford County, Va., 169¾ Charles Calvert married, as his first wife, Mary Howson (who died before 1699), daughter and co-heiress of Robert and Sarah Howson (the former being referred to as a " Merchant," which term was rather broadly used in the seventeenth century). Robert Howson came to Virginia about 1660. (Virginia Colonial Decisions, Thurston vs. Pratt. " Robert Howson was seized in fee of 450 acres of land—and died leaving issues 3 daughters: Anne, who married Rice Hooe; Mary who married Charles Calvert and Frances, who died unmarried. Northern

Neck Land Book No. 3, page 91, Richmond, Va. "Robert Howson of the County of Stafford. Whereas Charles Calvert alledges that he hath been for many years in possession of 418½ acres as marrying Mary ye daughter and co-heir of the aforesaid Robert Howson, by whom he hath issue two daughters, viz: Sarah Howson and Ann Calvert." April 3, 1705. Sarah Howson Calvert and Ann Calvert, their Escheat Deed for 218½ acres of land in Stafford. Ibid.). Late in life Charles Calvert, then a widower, returned to Maryland and died in St. Mary's County at the close of the year 1733. (His will was probated there on Dec. 31, 1733, and he cut his two daughters off with the proverbial shilling! They were, of course, provided for before their marriages.) (Liber W-Z., page 33, Stafford County, Va. "This note shall oblige me to deliver the two mulatto Children to Mrs. Hewitt to keep for my two Children, the mulatto Girl for Sarah Howson Calvert and the Mulatto Boy for Ann Calvert. As Witness my hand 14th October, 1699." Signed: Charles Calvert. Witnesses: Robert Alexander and John Allan. "October ye 16, 1699. Then Reced of Charles Calvert for the use of my two Granddaughters the within mentioned Mulattos. I say Reced by me." Signed: "Sarah Hewitt. Recorded 8th May, 1700." Mrs. Sarah Howson, widow of Robert Howson, married, secondly, Robert Hewitt who died in 1692.) Liber W-Z., page 277. Charles Calvert from the Proprietors of the Northern Neck 200 acres, April 4, 1703. For 980 pounds of tobacco Charles Calvert sells this land to William Fitzhugh, April 9, 1705. "At a Court held for Stafford County, June 14, 1705, Charles Calvert in person acknowledged this sale or assignment of land to Coll. William Fitzhugh—and is recorded by Nath. Pope, Cl. Cur." Charles Calvert married, secondly, in Maryland, Barbara Kirk, who survived him, by whom he had no issue. By his first marriage to Mary Howson he had two daughters:

I.   Sarah Howson Calvert, born about 1694.
II. Anne Calvert, born about 1696.

Of these daughters, Sarah Howson Calvert married (after

1717 and before 1726) Nathaniel Jones (1696-1754) (probably a descendant of Nathaniel Jones who died in Westmoreland County, Va., in 1662; wife Judith Jones. John Jones died in Westmoreland County in 1713, leaving two sons, Nathaniel and Charles, and three daughters, Elizabeth, Sarah and Anne Jones. The son Nathaniel was probably the husband of Sarah Howson Calvert.) This Nathaniel Jones died in Westmoreland County in 1754 and in his will mentioned his wife, Sarah Howson Jones; sons: John, David, Nathaniel, Charles and Calvert; daughters: Mary Peck, Sarah Franklin, and Frances Jones). The issue of Nathaniel Jones and his wife, Sarah Calvert, may therefore be set down as follows:

I. John Jones (died 1762), who married, Aug. 16, 1744, Eleanor Moss, daughter of John Moss (died 1746) and his wife, Margaret ———.
II. David Jones, who married, Feb. 18, 1763, Mary Boswell.
III. Nathaniel Jones, Jr.
IV. Charles Jones.
V. Calvert Jones (who was appointed "Overseer of the Highways" in Westmoreland County in 1757).
VI. Mary Jones, who married ——— Peck.
VII. Sarah Jones, who married ——— Franklin.
VIII. Frances Jones.

Of these, John Jones married, Aug. 16, 1744, Eleanor Moss and they had issue:

I. Charles Calvert Jones, born June 4, 1746.
II. Behethland Jones, born July 14, 1748; married, Feb. 14, 1770, John Peed and they had a daughter, Mildred Peed, who was born Sept. 22, 1772.
III. Nathaniel Jones, III., born Feb. 25, 1751.
IV. Sabra Jones, born Oct. 7, 1753; married, Feb. 8, 1778, William Crank.
V. Jane Jones, born March 16, 1762; married, June 3, 1782, Samuel Marshall.
VI. Eleanor Jones, who married, Dec. 27, 1774, Daniel Hamet.

Anne Calvert, the other daughter of Charles and Mary (Howson) Calvert, married, before 1714, Thomas Porter (who died Feb. 26, 1740) (Liber 5, page 253, Westmoreland County, Va. March 30, 1714. "Sarah Howson Calvert, Thomas Porter and Anne, his wife, which Sarah, Thomas and Anne are of the

County of Stafford, to John Pratt, 200 acres of land in West-moreland County, part of a patent granted to Robert Howson, April 15, 1667, whose heirs the said Sarah Howson Calvert and Anne Porter are "). In his will (recorded in Book M., Stafford County, page 285) Thomas Porter mentioned his sons: Calvert, Thomas, Benjamin, Nicholas, Joseph, Charles and John; daughters: Howson, and Anne; wife Anne; brother Samuel. (Sons, except Calvert, were under 18). The issue of Thomas and Anne (Calvert) Porter may therefor be set down as follows:

I. Anne Porter, born Oct. 13, 1717; died Sept. 22, 1727.

II. Henry Porter, "baptized ye 1 of May, 172¾." (Register of St. Paul's Parish).

III. Joseph Porter, born Aug. 7, 1726/7; married, Feb. 24, 1756, Jemima Smith of Overwharton Parish, Stafford County.

IV. Howson Porter, who married, Jan. 1, 1746, John Starke [1] and died April 11, 1755. (John Starke married, secondly, May 29, 1756, Hannah Eaves and they had a son, James Starke, born Feb. 7, 1757.) By his first wife, Howson Porter, he had issue:
1. Elizabeth Starke, born Aug. 16, 1749.
2. Sarah Starke, born Jan. 29, 1752.
3. William Starke, born Dec. 14, 1754.

V. Calvert Porter, who married, Sept. 21, 1749, Elizabeth Cash (He was a Revolutionary Soldier from Virginia.) They had issue:
1. Joseph Porter, Jr., born Oct. 21, 1750.
2. Calvert Porter, Jr., born March 1, 1752.
3. Thomas Porter, III, born Jan. 11, 1754.
4. Frances Porter, born Jan. 12, 1756.
5. Charity Porter, born Sept. 9, 1757.

VI. Anne Porter, born March 15, 1732.

VII. John Porter, born Aug. 4, 1734; died July 14, 1754; s. p.

VIII. Thomas Porter, Jr.

IX. Benjamin Porter.

X. Nicholas Porter.

XI. Charles Porter.

(Among the Revolutionary Soldiers from Virginia were: Calvert, Benjamin, Nicholas and Thomas Porter.)

In Stafford County, Va., at the close of the seventeenth century the names of Charles Calvert and his brother, George Calvert, and the latter's son, John Calvert, appear. In the

[1] Son of James and Elizabeth (Thornton) Starke.

Stafford County Order Book appears the following entry: " Oct. 8, 1690. George Calvert vs. John Tarkington " and on Nov. 10, 1692, another suit was filed by this George Calvert, " formerly of Charles County, Md." Charles Calvert's signature appeared under date of Oct. 14, 1699. On Dec. 9, 1703, the Stafford County Court ordered Mr. John Calvert paid one thousand pounds of tobacco for killing two wolves. When Prince William County was taken out of Stafford County, in 1730, John Calvert and his son, George Calvert, Jr., were thrown in the new county, where the former probably died; the latter later moved to and died in Culpeper County, Va., as George Calvert, Sr. His inventory was filed there May 12, 1782. Charles Calvert had previously returned to Maryland where he died three years after the formation of the new county. On Jan. 20, 1724, Thomas, Lord Fairfax, granted to George Calvert of Stafford County land on both sides of Powell's Creek (Then in Stafford, but later in Prince William County). On July 18, 1724, Thomas, Lord Fairfax, granted to Jacob Gibson and John Calvert (who was the son of George Calvert, Sr., and father of George Calvert, Jr.) of Stafford County " 306 acres situate and being located between the branches of Powell's Creek in the County of Stafford and the north Run of Quanticot Creek, paying yearly 1 shilling sterling for every 50 acres."

The name Behethland given to the daughter of John and Eleanor (Moss) Jones and granddaughter of Nathaniel and Sarah Howson (Calvert) Jones, indicates descent from Walter Jones who married Behethland Newton, daughter of Captain Thomas Newton (1678-1727) and his wife, Elizabeth Storke (1687-1759), daughter of Nehemiah Storke (died 1693) who married Behethland Gilson (1666-1693), daughter of Major Andrew Gilson of Stafford County, who married Behethland Dade, widow of Frances Dade (died 1663) and daughter of Captain Thomas Bernard of Warwick County, Va., whose wife Mary Bernard, was a daughter of Captain Robert Behethland who came to Virginia with Captain John Smith in 1607. (See the writer's article on Robert Behethland in the January issue of *The William & Mary Quarterly*). Nathaniel Jones, husband of Sarah Howson Calvert, was probably a descendant of the Nathaniel Jones who died in Westmoreland County in 1662; his widow, Judith Jones, married, secondly, John Whiston. He (Nathaniel Jones) was living in Westmoreland County as early as 1654 when Governor Richard Bennett granted to John Smith of Stanley Hundred 3,000 acres of Land in Westmoreland County adjoining the lands of Nicholas Lambson, Nathaniel Jones, Capt. Thomas Davis, John Williams, Stephen Norman, John Ewalton and Gervase Dodson, for the transportation of himself and nineteen other persons to the Colony of Virginia. ("John Smith" was an alias of Francis Dade, supra, first husband of Behethland Bernard) (1635-1720) (q. v.).

AUTHORITIES: Court records of Westmoreland, Stafford, and Prince William Counties, Virginia; Charles, St. Mary's and Prince George's Counties, Maryland; and the records of the Land Offices at Richmond and Annapolis. Also the Registers of St. Paul's and Overwharton Parishes, Virginia (Stafford and King George Counties). (Mrs. Ella Foy O'Gorman, of Washington, D. C., has very kindly assisted in the preparation of this little sketch). Compare, also, the writer's sketch of the Calvert Family in the *Maryland Historical Magazine* for the year 1921, especially pages 191 and 192.

DESCENDANTS OF FRANCIS CALVERT (1751-1823).

By JOHN BAILEY CALVERT NICKLIN.

Jacob Calvert (c. 1720-1772), son of John and Elizabeth (Harrison) Calvert, was born in Stafford Co., Va., and died in Prince William Co., Va. He evidently married Sarah Crupper (sister of Anne Crupper, the first wife of his brother, Capt. George Calvert of "Deep Hole Farm," Prince William Co.), since he brought suit against Richard Crupper (the father of Anne Calvert) to recover certain property. Order Book 1, page 314, Prince William Co. Jacob Calvert *vs.* Richard Crupper. Nov. 27, 1753. The case was "continued." Richard Crupper died in 1762 and his two sons-in-laws, George Calvert, Jr., and Jacob Calvert, were his executors, with William Bennett and John Reeves as securities, Feb. 22, 1762. Jacob Calvert died in 1772. His widow, Sarah Calvert, and his eldest son, Francis Calvert, were his executors, with William Farrow and George Calvert of Deep Hole Farm as securities, June 1, 1772. The will of Richard Crupper was presented by George Calvert, Jr., and Jacob Calvert, his executors on Feb. 22, 1762 and proved by the oaths of Thomas Machen, John Calvert and Nathaniel Overall. In 1736, April 22, Richard Crupper was mentioned as the administrator of the estate of William Maria Farthing, dec'd, so he may have married into the latter family. April 10, 1742, William Bayless, Richard Crupper and George Calvert were appraisers of the estate of Ludowick Jackson, dec'd, March 28, 1743. George Calvert, Burr Harrison and Thomas Dowell were appraisers of the estate of Thomas Wallis, dec'd. Aug. 13, 1740, Richard Crupper of Hamilton Parish, Prince William Co., sold to James Maxwell 180 acres which had been granted the said Crupper by the Proprietors Office of the Northern Neck, Feb. 28, 1728/9. Oct. 23, 1752, Richard Crupper was appointed "Surveyor of the Road in the room of Richard Kenner, Gent." June 25, 1753, "Marriage Articles between Richard Crupper and Anastasia, his wife, proved by the Oaths of James Triplet and Thomas Machen, two of the Subscribing Witnesses, and admitted to record." [She was Anastasia Wheeler, by birth, daughter of Richard Wheeler (1683-1734) of Maryland, and was married four times: firstly, to James Keen; secondly, in 1734, to Patrick Connelly; thirdly, in 1747, to Richard Johnson; and, fourthly, in 1753, to Richard Crupper, by whom she had no issue. After the death of her fourth husband she returned to Maryland where she died, in Charles Co., in 1764. She had moved to Virginia with her third husband and married there Richard Crupper, as before stated.] On March 25, 1754 Jacob Calvert was one of the appraisers of the estate of William Farrow, dec'd., and on Nov. 22, 1756, Richard Crupper was a member of the Grand Jury. On May 27, 1757, Richard Crupper, Jacob Calvert and George Calvert were members of a jury. On Feb. 22, 1762, George Calvert, Jacob Calvert, William Bennett and John Reeves gave bond for £500 for the administration of the estate of Richard Crupper, dec'd. On June 1, 1772, Sarah Calvert, Francis Calvert, William Farrow and George Calvert of "Deep Hole Farm" gave bond for £500 for the administration of the estate of Jacob Calvert, dec'd. (All of the foregoing data have been abstracted from the remaining Court Records of Prince William Co., Va., at Manassas.) Jacob and Sarah (Crupper) Calvert had at least five children.

Issue:

I. Francis (1751-1823), of whom later.

II. Mary, who married Lawrence Butler.

III. Jacob, who died in 1803; he married Prudence ———; s. p.

IV. Richard.

V. John, who died in 1812; he married Winifred Smith, daughter of Peter and Elizabeth Smith of Prince William Co. (They had at least three sons, viz.: George, Richard and Jacob Calvert.)

Francis Calvert (Jacob–John–George–William–Leonard–Sir George, Lord Baltimore), eldest son of Jacob and Sarah (Crupper) Calvert,[1] was born in Prince William Co., Va., in 1751

[1] See "The Calvert Family" in the *Maryland Historical Magazine* for 1921, Volume XVI.

and died in Kanawha Co., Va., July 11, 1823.[2] About 1788 he left his native county and soon thereafter settled in Bedford Co., Va., where, on Dec. 22, 1791, he was married to Elizabeth Witt (1772-1806), a daughter of Lewis and Anne (Mills) Witt of that county and granddaughter of William Witt. (Lewis Witt died in 1774 and his widow, Anne Mills Witt, died in 1816, both in Bedford Co., Va.) Francis Calvert married, secondly, Sept. 1, 1809, Elizabeth Rose, also in Bedford Co. (Both of the original marriage-bonds are still on file in the Court House at Bedford City, Va.).

Issue (by first marriage):

(6).   I. Robert, who was born Sept. 9, 1794; he married Feb. 26, 1816, Sarah Stretch.

    II. Mary, who was born Dec. 4, 1796; she married —— Hedley.

(1).   III. Mills Witt, who was born Feb. 3, 1799 and died Jan. 12, 1849; he married Kitty Slack.

(3).   IV. John Lewis, who was born April 28, 1803 and died April 30, 1863; he married Elizabeth Anne Slack, sister to his brother's wife.

    V. Nancy, who was born Feb. 26, 1805; she married —— Stone.

(1) Mills Witt Calvert, son of Francis and Elizabeth (Witt) Calvert, was born in Bedford Co., Va., Feb. 3, 1799, and died in Kanawha Co., Va., Jan. 12, 1849; he married, Sept. 19, 1826, Kittie Slack, sister to his brother's wife. She was born Oct. 23, 1805 and died July 27, 1879.

Issue:

(5).   I. Francis, who was born Aug. 15, 1827 and died Jan. 18, 1904; he married Eliza Oakes, who was born Sept. 8, 1824 and died April 23, 1904.

    II. John, who was born March 22, 1829 and died March 20, 1894; he married Nancy Hannigan, who was born Feb. 16, 1824 and died March 9, 1910.

    III. George, who was born March 26, 1831 and died July 19, 1851, unmarried.

    IV. Robert, who was born Dec. 17, 1883 and died July 8, 1834.

    V. Udocia Elizabeth, who was born April 1, 1835 and married, Oct. 8, 1853, Samuel Robinson.

(4).   VI. Cornelius, who was born Feb. 23, 1838 and died Oct. 25, 1892; he married twice: firstly, Drusilla Anne Oakes (sister to his brother's wife; she was born Aug. 25, 1831 and died June 6, 1884); secondly, in 1884, Dollie Dillard.

---

[2] He is said to have been a Revolutionary soldier from Virginia, but the tradition is unverified.

(2). VII. James Turner, who was born Feb. 6, 1840 and died June 18, 1905; he married Cynthia Frances Toney.

VIII. Caroline Octave, who was born May 4, 1842 and died Oct. 14, 1928; she married twice: firstly, Dec. 23, 1857, Josephus Patchell; and, secondly, Nov. 11, 1880, Archibald Dillard (brother to her sister-in-law, Dollie Dillard) (q. v.).

IX. William Tompkins, who was born Sept. 12, 1844 and died Dec. 26, 1871; he married, Sept. 4, 1868, Elizabeth Massey (who was born Sept. 23, 1847 and died Oct. 25, 1900).

X. Martha, who was born Nov. 14, 1846 and died July 1, 1894; she married, Dec. 22, 1865, Absolum Jordan Noble (who was born April 29, 1844 and died Sept. 15, 1925) (q. v.).

(2) James Turner Calvert, son of Mills Witt and Kittie (Slack) Calvert, was born Feb. 6, 1840 and died June 18, 1905; he married, March 24, 1867, Cynthia Frances Toney (who was born March 11, 1845 and died Feb. 8, 1914).

Issue:

I. Judith Caroline, who was born Sept. 25, 1867; she married, July 26, 1886, Robert Brabbin.

Issue:

1. Lorena Brabbin.
2. Thomas Brabbin.
3. Harold Brabbin.
4. Annie May Brabbin.
5. Robert Brabbin, Jr.
6. Alice Marie Brabbin.

II. William Joseph, who was born Nov. 13, 1869; he married twice: firstly, July 29, 1892, Kate Gray, s. p.; and, secondly, Lena Staton.

Issue (by second marriage):

1. Herman, who died young.
2. Carmen Corabelle.
3. James.
4. Carlton.
5. Francis.
6. Dorothy.

III. Catherine Elizabeth, who was born Nov. 21, 1871 and died Oct. 31, 1902; she married, Feb. 6, 1895, Hezekiah Halstead.

Issue:

1. Thomas Halstead.
2. Grace Halstead.
3. Faye Halstead.

IV. Annie May, who was born Feb. 19, 1874; she married, as his second wife, Absolum Jordan Noble (supra).

V. Martha Ellen, who was born June 12, 1876; she married, June 15, 1894, William Halstead, brother to her sister's husband.

Issue:

1. James Halstead, who died unmarried.
2. Nyde Halstead.
3. Frank Halstead.

4. Blanche Halstead.
5. Pansy Halstead.
6. Paul Halstead.
7. William Halstead, Jr.
8. Calvert Halstead.
9. Cameron Halstead.

VI. Mary Blanche, who was born Nov. 26, 1878; she married, Nov. 15, 1905, John Henry Campbell.
VII. John Francis, who was born Oct. 18, 1881; he married, June 3, 1903, Hattie Bullington.

Issue:

1. Clyde.
2. Frances.
3. Louise.
4. Turner.

VIII. Grace Adeline, who was born May 21, 1886; she married, April 20, 1910, Carry Rucker.

Issue:

1. Lois Lucile Rucker.
2. Cynthia Frances Rucker.
3. Calvert Rucker.
4. Grace Elizabeth Rucker.
5. Carl Lawrence Rucker.
6. Bryce Wilson Rucker.

(3). John Lewis Calvert, son of Francis and Elizabeth (Witt) Calvert, was born in Bedford Co., Va., April 28, 1803 and died in Kanawha Co., Va., April 30, 1863; he married, Aug. 30, 1825 Elizabeth Anne Slack (who survived him and married, secondly, Feb. 28, 1875, Henry Ashworth; s. p.). She was born Nov. 7, 1807, and died Nov. 12, 1882, and was a daughter of John and Nancy (Huddleston) Slack of Bedford and Kanawha Counties, and granddaughter of Abraham Slack and Abraham Huddleston of Bedford Co., Va. (Abraham Slack came to Virginia from Bucks Co., Pa., where he was a Revolutionary Soldier).

Issue:

I. Mary, who was born June 19, 1826 and died Dec. 9, 1915; she married, April 3, 1845, Enos Jarrett (who was born April 3, 1818 and died March 30, 1893).

Issue:

1. Elizabeth Anne Jarrett, who was born Feb. 9, 1846 and died July 17, 1885; she married, Oct. 26, 1865, George Rader.
2. Marietta Jarrett, who was born March 30, 1854 and died Oct. 22, 1928; she married, Aug. 28, 1875, Henry Burnett (who was born July 3, 1848 and died Oct. 11, 1928).

Issue:

(1). Enos Jarrett Burnett, who was born May 13, 1877; he married, Aug. 6, 1926, Lucile Crockett.

Issue:

(a). Robert Walker Burnett, who was born July 21, 1927.

3. Amanda Alice Jarrett, who was born Dec. 20, 1861; she married three times: firstly, June 30, 1881, George Wilcher; secondly, April 1, 1890, Lant M. Thomas; and, thirdly, Oct. 9, 1912, Jacob S. Fisher (s. p.).

Issue (by first marriage):

(1). George Robert Wilcher, who was born April 14, 1882 and died May 6, 1899.
(2). Elsie May Wilcher, who was born Sept. 4, 1884; she married twice: firstly, Graham Vickers; and, secondly, John C. Fauber; s. p.

Issue (by first marriage):

(a). Louise Vickers, who was born June 30, 1905.
(3). Charles Franklin Wilcher, who was born April 30, 1887; he married Elsie Jarrett.

Issue:

(a). George William Wilcher, who was born May 8, 1916.
(b). Alice Elizabeth Wilcher, who was born March 16, 1918.
(c). Mildred Pauline Wilcher, who was born Oct. 25, 1921.
(d). Charles Francis Wilcher, who was born Sept. 28, 1923.

Issue (by second marriage):

(1). Harry Enos Thomas, who was born Feb. 10, 1891; he married Effie Akers; s. p.

4. Sally Bell Jarrett, who was born July 4, 1868; she married Nov. 28, 1894, J. Frank Hudson; s. p.

II. Mills Lewis, who was born Oct. 23, 1828 and died June 27, 1893; he married, April 1, 1851, Mary Koontz (who was born Sept. 27, 1822 and died July 5, 1895); s. p.

III. Nancy, who was born Oct. 22, 1830 and died Nov. 4, 1900; she married, July 13, 1854, John Burke.

Issue:

1. Julius Brace Burke, who was born July 3, 1859 and died May 22, 1928; he married, Dec. 15, 1880, Chloe Pfost.
2. John Burke, Jr., who married Alice Good.
3. Thomas Burke.
4 Fanny Burke, who married Sherman Bullington.
5. Jennie Burke, who married —— Perry.
6. Nancy Burke, who married —— Willis.

IV. Jesse Witt, who was born Sept. 22, 1833 and died May 16, 1896; he married, July 29, 1858, Henrietta Cunningham (who died April 3, 1904).

Issue:

1. Mary Alice, who was born in 1859; she married, Nov. 25, 1881, Joseph M. Webb; s. p.
2. Virginia, who was born Nov 3, 1861.
3. John W, who was born in 1862; he married, Dec. 18, 1894, Bettie L. Kelly.

Issue:

(1). Ruby.
(2). Ira.
(3). Janice.

4. Henry Steptoe, who was born June 22, 1865; he married Addie Cox.
5. Elizabeth, who was born Sept. 4, 1868.
6. Catherine, who was born March 12, 1871.
7. Carrie.

V. Sally, who was born Jan. 2, 1837 and died Oct. 25, 1909; she married, June 14, 1854, Joseph Jubal Kuhn (who was born April 1, 1830 and died Sept. 11, 1879).

Issue:

1. Mary Elizabeth Kuhn, who was born June 8, 1855; she married, Sept. 14, 1876, Samuel Hudnell.

Issue:

(1). Maude V. Hudnell, who was born Nov. 29, 1879.
(2). Ethel M. Hudnell, who was born May 12, 1883; she married, April 23, 1902, Arthur E. Harmon.

Issue:

(a). Elizabeth Lucile Harmon, who was born April 10, 1903.
(3). Estelle C. Hudnell, who was born April 13, 1885; she married, April 14, 1904, D. Ray Moss.
(4). Stuart C. Hudnell, who was born Nov. 28, 1888; and died Nov. 17, 1912.
(5). Emmett D. Hudnell, who was born Feb. 10, 1893.
(6). Emory C. Hudnell, who was born Feb. 10, 1893, twin to Emory.
(7). Mabelle Burdette Hudnell, who was born Jan. 13, 1897.

2. Julia Anne Kuhn, who was born Jan. 30, 1857; she married, April 18, 1880, Charles Ralph Stafford (who was born July 13, 1856 and died Sept. 27, 1905).

Issue:

(1). William Joseph Stafford, who was born May 6, 1881.
(2). Alma Florence Stafford, who was born May 23, 1887; she married, July 3, 1906, Dr. Philip Barbour Pendleton (d. 1908).

Issue:

(a). Jane Stafford Pendleton, who was born July 8, 1907.
(b). Julia Louise Pendleton, who was born Jan. 3, 1909.
(3). Gertrude L. Stafford, who was born Aug. 1, 1891.
(4). John Francis Stafford, who was born Dec. 8, 1895; unmarried.

3. John Henry Kuhn, who was born Nov. 2, 1862; unmarried.
4. Virginia Kuhn, who died young.
5. James Albert Kuhn, who was born July 1, 1868; he married, May 17, 1894, Icie E. Lee.

Issue:

(1). Eva S. Kuhn, who was born June 10, 1895.
(2). Charles Joseph Kuhn, who was born July 7, 1899.
(3). Virginia Florence Kuhn, who was born July 22, 1901.
(4). James Lee Kuhn, who was born Dec. 31, 1903.

(5). Ira F. Kuhn, who was born Dec. 1, 1907.

(6). Claybourne Calvert Kuhn, who was born Jan. 29, 1911.

(7). Harold H. Kuhn, who was born Feb. 5, 1914.

(8). Irene Kuhn, who was born Aug. 29, 1920.

6. William Joseph Kuhn, who was born Feb. 10, 1871; unmarried.

7. Florence Calvert Kuhn, who was born Feb. 12, 1875; unmarried.

VI. Elizabeth Anne, who was born March 23, 1840 and died Sept. 1, 1845.

VII. Adaline, who was born May 14, 1843; she married, June 11, 1863, John Wesley Campbell (who was born Sept. 22, 1841 and died June 11, 1876), son of Henry Truxton Campbell (1816-1871) and his wife, Angeline Whitton, daughter of William Whitton of Bedford Co., Va., and his wife, Milly Witt, daughter of Lewis and Anne (Mills) Witt and sister to Elizabeth (Witt) Calvert (supra).

Issue:

1. Lavinia Ellen Campbell, who was born Feb. 29, 1864; she married, July 16, 1884, Thomas Howard Mohler.

Issue:

(1). Edith Mohler, who was born Sept. 11, 1886; she married, Feb. 15, 1911, Robert Cornell Sweet.

Issue:

(a). Robert Mohler Sweet, who was born Feb. 5, 1916.

2. James Albert Campbell, who was born April 30, 1866 and died, unmarried, March 20, 1884.

3. John Mills Campbell, who was born Feb. 13, 1868; he married, Dec. 21, 1892, Sadie Brown (who was born April 6, 1868 and died Oct. 16, 1908).

Issue:

(1). Lucy Myron Campbell, who was born Oct. 20, 1894; she married, Sept. 21, 1915, John Eggleton; s. p.

(2). Frank Elliott Campbell, who was born May 2, 1896 and died June 29, 1897.

(3). Howard Mohler Campbell, who was born Dec. 18, 1898; World War; unmarried.

4. Frank Allen Campbell, who was born Jan. 15, 1870 and died Aug. 27, 1887.

5. Emma Campbell, who was born Dec. 22, 1871; she married, June 2, 1891, George Crittendon Moore.

Issue:

(1). Adaline Moore, who was born Jan. 28, 1895; she married, June 30, 1920, Robert Hamilton Ledbetter.

Issue:

(a). Robert Pierre Leadbetter, who was born April 28, 1921.

(b). Myron Ledbetter.

(2). Rodney Campbell Moore, who was born May 24, 1898; World War; he married, Feb. 11, 1923, Gussie Faye Dailey.

Issue:

(a). Rodney Campbell Moore, Jr., who was born July 13, 1929.

6. Myron Grant Campbell, who was born Feb. 5, 1874; he married, Jan. 7, 1898, Virginia Tasker.

Issue:

(1). James Albert Campbell, who was born Oct. 10, 1898; World War; unmarried.
(2). Nelle Campbell, who was born Nov. 21, 1900.
(3). Addie Grace Campbell, who was born Sept. 14, 1904.

7. Lucy Campbell, who was born Feb. 15, 1876; she married, Sept. 19, 1906, Chastine Bickers.

Issue:

(1). Myron Campbell Bickers, who was born June 24, 1909.
(2). Adaline Calvert Bickers, who was born Feb. 23, 1914.
(3). Emma Lucille Bickers, who was born Dec. 13, 1916.

VIII. Katherine, who was born March 30, 1846 and died Aug. 22, 1918; she married, May 21, 1863, Charles Alexander Campbell (brother to her sister's husband).

Issue:

1. Lewis Campbell, who married Elizabeth Webster.
2. Charles Alexander Campbell, Jr., who was born Aug. 12, 1870; he married, Dec. 25, 1895, Julia Anne Webster, sister to his brother's wife.

Issue:

(1). Howard Eustace Campbell, who was born Sept. 28, 1906 and died in infancy.
(2). Everett Lester Campbell, who was born June 30, 1908.
(3). Gladys Marie Campbell, who was born Jan. 25, 1911.
(4). Sybil Lucile Campbell, who was born April 10, 1915.

3. John Campbell.
4. Mills Campbell.
5. Cora Campbell, who married Sherman Webster, brother to the wives of her brothers.

IX. John Allen, who was born Feb. 19, 1850 and died Jan. 28, 1922; he married, Nov. 2, 1871, Ruth J. Webb (who was born Sept. 16, 1847 and died Aug. 13, 1907); s. p.

(4). Cornelius Calvert, son of Mills Witt and Kittie (Slack) Calvert, was born Feb. 23, 1838 and died Oct. 25, 1892; he married twice: firstly, June 16, 1859, Drusilla Anne Oakes; and, secondly, Dollie Dillard.

Issue (by first marriage):

I. Ebenezer Oakes, who was born April 6, 1860 and died in 1906; he married, Nov. 10, 1882, Anne L. Bradshaw; s. p.
II. Mills Allen, who was born in 1862 and died in 1911; he married, March 3, 1891, Nena Cabell.

Issue:

1. Robert C., who was born April 11, 1892.
2. Francis.
3. R. Neal.
4. Evelyn.

III. James William, who was born Dec. 19, 1866, he married twice; firstly, Sept. 1, 1892, Iva C. Little; and, secondly, May 9, 1902, Isabel Bannister.

Issue (by first marriage):
1. Carlysle, who married Erma Andrews.
2. Chelyan, who married Charles E. Smith.

Issue:
(1). Calvert Ross Smith.
(2). Charles E. Smith, Jr.
(3). James Smith.
(4). Marshall Smith.
(5). Iva Smith.

Issue (by second marriage):
1. Mary Louise, who married Edward S. Brown.

Issue:
(1). Edward S. Brown, Jr.
2. William Lewis.
3. Margaret.
4. Sarah.
5. Robert Littlepage.
6. Russell Frazier.

IV. Ida May, who was born in 1861 and died in 1917; she married, July 29, 1887, Elbert Riverton Hoffman.

Issue:
1. Irene Hoffman, who married Earl Hood.

Issue:
(a). Drusilla Anne Hood.
2. Elbert Leslie Hoffman, who was born May 7, 1897; he married, Feb. 3, 1922, Elizabeth Smith.

Issue:
(1). Elbert Leslie Hoffman, Jr., who was born Feb. 27, 1923.
3. Arthur Hoffman, who married Mary Jones.

Issue (by second marriage):
I. George, who was born June 15, 1885; lives in Baltimore, Md.

(5). **Francis Calvert**, son of Mills Witt and Kittie (Slack) Calvert, was born Aug. 15, 1827 and died Jan. 18, 1904; he married, June 6, 1850, Eliza Oakes (sister to Drusilla Anne Oakes who married Cornelius Calvert) (supra).

Issue:
I. Katherine, who was born April 22, 1851 and died Sept. 26, 1884; she married, Oct. 28, 1869, William H. Knight.
II. Drusilla, who was born Jan. 31, 1854; she married, July 27, 1870, Mandeville J. Massey.
III. Fanny E., who was born Sept. 9, 1857; she married Aug. 18, 1892, Robert E. Hagan.
IV. Mills Witt, who was born March 11, 1859; he married, Nov. 2, 1894, Fanny May Hoffman.

Issue:

1. Helen Lavinia, who was born Aug. 28, 1898.
2. Catherine Alethia, who was born June 30, 1906.
3. Ralph Witt, who was born Aug. 28, 1908.

V. James Francis, who was born April 1, 1861 and died June 24, 1922; he married, Nov. 12, 1891, Lelia Fennemore.

VI. Alethia, who was born Nov. 15, 1863 and died Oct. 10, 1892; she married, May 19, 1886, John A. Jarrett.

(6). **Robert Calvert,** eldest son of Francis and Elizabeth (Witt) Calvert, was born in Bedford Co., Va., Sept. 9, 1794 and died in Ohio, Sept. 19, 1851; he and four of his sons (Mills, Ira, William and Jesse) were Dunkard Ministers. Robert Calvert married, Feb. 26, 1816, in Bedford County, Sarah Stretch (who was born Aug. 15, 1793), daughter of John and Susannah (Landis) Stretch of that county.

Issue:

I. John, who was born Jan. 30, 1817 and died Sept. 10, 1897; he married twice: .firstly, Elizabeth Miller; and, secondly, Elizabeth Sheeley.

Issue (by first marriage):

1. Eli.
2. Robert.

Issue (by second marriage):

1. Sarah.
2. Frank.
3. Margaret.
4. Thatcher.
5. Ira.

II. Mills, who was born Nov. 8, 1818; he married Susannah Garman.

Issue:

1. Noah, a Dunkard Minister.
2. Joseph,[3] a Dunkard Minister; he married Sarah Mahala Hixson (q. v.) (1857-1905).
3. Quinter, a Dunkard Minister.

III. Ira, who was born April 11, 1820; he married Rachel Jones.

Issue:

1. Mills.
2. John.
3. Frank.
4. Anne.
5. Elizabeth.
6. Rebecca.
7. Emma.

(7). IV. Francis, who was born June 5, 1823; he married twice: firstly, Rebecca Leedy; and, secondly, Sarah Giltner.

V. William, who was born Feb. 24, 1826; he married twice: firstly, Sarah Weaver; and, secondly, Louise Weaver.

---

[3] (1845-1917).

VI. Joseph, who was born Feb. 24, 1826 and died Sept. 2, 1827; twin to William.

VII. Moses, who was born March 14, 1828 and died Dec. 9, 1914; he married Sallie Haigh.

Issue:

1. Dennis, who died in infancy.
2. Hanna, who died in infancy.
3. Spencer.
4. May.
5. Newton.
6. Kate.
7. William.

VIII. Joel, who was born Aug. 31, 1830 and died Oct. 31, 1911; he married, March 26, 1866, Anne (Guthrie) Hixson,[4] daughter of James and Mahala (Hardy) Hixson.

Issue:

1. Luther Dewitt, who was born Feb. 22, 1867.
2. James Quinter (1871-1900).
3. Thomas Mills, who died young.
4. Annie May, who was born May 25, 1871.

IX. Jesse, who was born Oct. 16, 1832 and died Nov. 28, 1902; he married, June 15, 1858, Barbara Anglemyer (who was born Nov. 26, 1836 and died June 15, 1908).

Issue:

1. Alfred, who died in infancy.
2. Catherine, who died in infancy.
3. Ida May, who was born July 29, 1862; she married, Dec. 24, 1885, Henry Newton Baker.

Issue:

(1). Jessie Barbara Baker, who was born Nov. 7, 1886; she married, Feb. 14, 1908, Samuel A. Craig.

Issue:

(a). Calvert Craig, who was born April 6, 1909.
(b). Virginia Frances Craig, who was born Aug. 30, 1911.

4. Anna Isabella, who was born May 30, 1870; she married, in 1898, Charles A. Shorb.

Issue:

(1). Charles Calvert Shorb.
(2). Jesse Calvert Shorb.

5. Elmer, who died unmarried.
6. Myrtle Irene, who died young.

X. Susannah, who was born Dec. 2, 1835 and died Oct. 21, 1837.

XI. Elizabeth Jane, who was born Aug. 8, 1839 and died Sept. 1, 1895.

[4] She was born Jan. 4, 1837 and died Feb. 15, 1879; she married, firstly, March 13, 1856, Sebastian Burnett Hixson (who was born May 13, 1836 and died Oct. 26, 1859. Her mother Mahala (Hardy) Hixson was born July 10, 1805 and died Oct. 13, 1843. Sarah Mahala Hixson, daughter of Sebastian Burnett and Anne (Guthrie) Hixson, married, Jan. 10, 1878, Joseph Garman Calvert, son of Mills and Susannah (Garman) Calvert (q. v.). They had three sons: Merrill Quinter, Ellston Albon and Urville Orville Calvert.

(7). Francis Calvert, son of Robert and Sarah (Stretch) Calvert, was born June 5, 1823; he married twice: firstly, Rebecca Leedy; and, secondly, in 1863, Sarah Giltner.

Issue (by first marriage):

I. William.
II. Joan.
III. John, of Warsaw, Indiana.
IV. Elizabeth.
V. Sarah.

Issue (by second marriage):

I. Belle.
II. Nellie.
III. Georgiana.
IV. Grace.
V. Hogan Gaines.

NOTE: Francis Calvert, by his second wife, Elizabeth Rose, had several children. Of them little has been found by the Compiler. Following is a list of these children (none of whose descendants has it been possible to trace):

Issue:

I. Leah, who died young.
II. Jane.
III. Charles.
IV. Francis.
V. Elijah.
VI. Elizabeth.

ABSTRACTS OF ORIGINAL RECORDS.

Deed Book W., p. 351, Sept. 4, 1786, Prince William Co., Va. Joseph Butler for love and affection to his grandsons and granddaughters, Joseph Butler, Jacob Calvert Butler, Sarah Anne Butler and Mary Calvert Butler [5] sons and daughters of Lawrence Butler, dec'd., a negro slave named Jack, now in the possession of their mother, Mary Butler, to continue so " during her widowhood only." Witnesses: Frances Hays, Richard Calvert and Thomas Keys.

Will Book H., p. 50. Dated Sept. 27, 1788 and probated Jan. 8, 1793, will of Joseph Butler: wife Anne; sons James Carter Butler, Joseph Butler, William Butler, Charles Butler and deceased son Lawrence Butler's children, viz: Sarah Anne,

[5] Called " Molly " in this deed.

Jacob Calvert, Joseph, and Mary Calvert Butler; daughters Catherine Botts, Frances Barker, Anne Butler and Mary Carter; son-in-law David Carter.

Deed Book D., p. 151, May 26, 1739. George Calvert, Jr., of Hamilton Parish, County of Prince William, bargains and sells to John Gregg 306 acres on or near Powell's Creek, being one-half part of a tract of land granted to Jacob Gibson and John Calvert, deceased, father of the aforesaid George. George Calvert, Jr., lives on this land which was granted to Jacob Gibson and John Calvert by Deed from the Proprietors Office of the Northern Neck of Virginia, bearing date July 16, 1724, for which was paid one ear of Indian Corn. May 27, 1739. George Calvert, Jr., of Hamilton Parish, and Anne, his wife, for 3500 pounds of tobacco sell to John Gregg a certain tract of land. (Deed Book D., p. 143.)

Order Book 2, p. 188, March 24, 1755. A lease from John Tayloe, Esq., to Jacob Calvert," was farther proved by the oath of John Calvert, one of the witnesses thereto and admitted to Record." (Note: this John Calvert was evidently a son of George Calvert, Sr., uncle of George Calvert, Jr., and of Jacob Calvert, his brother.—Compiler.)

Ditto, p. 279, Aug. 26, 1755. Administration on the estate of Robert Crupper, dec'd., granted to John Bayles, Gent. Ordered that Nathaniel Overall, George Calvert, Francis Ash and Richard Grigsby, or any three of them, inventory and appraise the said estate.

Order Book 3, p. 255, Feb. 28, 1757. "Ordered that the Churchwardens of Dettingen Parish bind John Crupper, orphan of Robert Crupper, dec'd, to Jacob Calvert until he attain to lawful age, Elizabeth Crupper, mother of the said John, Consenting freely to same."

Ditto, p. 262, March 7, 1757. Proof of Public Claims presented by Gilbert Crupper, Humphry Calvert and John Calvert for their services for His Majesty. (Note: Humphry and John Calvert were the sons of George Calvert, Sr., beforementioned. He died in 1771 and on Dec. 2, 1771 his widow, Esther Calvert,

gave bond, with Obed Calvert, Thomas Stone, Foushee Tebbs
and Thomas Blackburn for £500 for the administration of his
estate.—Compiler.)

N. N. Book, L. O., Richmond, Va., p. 53.   July 16, 1724.
Thomas, Lord Fairfax, to George Calvert of Stafford County,
92 acres of land on both sides of the main run of Powell's Creek,
annual rental 1 shilling sterling for every 50 acres.   (Note:
this was probably George Calvert, Sr., uncle of George Calvert,
Jr., and Jacob Calvert, although it may have been still another
George, the father of John Calvert and the son of the Hon.
William Calvert of Maryland.—Compiler.)

Ditto, p. 45, July 18, 1724.   "Thomas, Lord Fairfax, to
Jacob Gibson and John Calvert of Stafford County, 306 acres
of land situate and being between the branches of Powell's Creek
in the county of Stafford and the north Run of Quanticot Creek,
paying annually 1 shilling sterling for every 50 acres" (Note:
Prince William County was formed from Stafford in 1730,
hence this land was later in the latter county, of course.—Compiler).

Ditto, p. 113. Feb. 26, 1730.   Thomas, Lord Fairfax, to
Richard Crupper of Stafford County, 122 acres of land situate
in the said county of Stafford. Book I., p. 205, March 3, 1772.
Thomas, Lord Fairfax, to Obed Calvert of Prince William
County a grant of land, near the land of George Calvert, containing 212 acres. Book E., p. 404, Jan. 18, 1741. To Thomas
Calvert 110 acres of land upon the branches of Powell's Creek
in Prince William County, adjoining the survey of John Justice. Book F., p. 99, April 2, 1743. To Richard Crupper of
Prince William County 69 acres on the north side of Occoquan
river, adjoining the land of one Singleton (Note: these lettered
books are in the Land Office at Richmond and deal with Prince
William County.—Compiler.)

Stafford Co., Dec. 9, 1703 (Order Book).   "To John Calvert
for 2 wolves head, 600 pounds of tobacco."   (This was, of
course, a bounty paid for killing wolves, at that time doubtlessly a continual menace to the early inhabitants of this
county.)

Ditto, Order Book 2, p. 242, March 11, 1691½. "Robert Crupper claims 1000 pounds of tobacco for his services." (This was probably the father of Richard Crupper who died in Prince William County in 1762—Compiler.)

Ditto, p. 310, Nov. 10, 1692. "George Calvert Complains against Patrick Hume in a plea of debt for that that is to say that he stands indebted to the Plaintiff the sum of 900 pounds of tobacco due for bill and one gallon of rum to be made into Punch wherefore the Pltf hath brought his action agst the said Patrick Hume and craves Judgement agst him for the said debt with costs of suite. Ordered that Hume pay with cost alias Execution."

Ditto, p. 315, Nov. 11, 1692. Robert Brent vs George Calvert. Suit for unpaid account. Calvert affirmed that he had made payment and the case was non-suited and Brent had to pay Calvert "50 pounds of tobacco with costs alias Execution." Brent appealed to the General Court at James City. "Captain George Brent became security with the said Robert Brent to prosecute his appeal and Mr. Richard Gibson with the said George Calvert to answer the said appeal." (Note: one can only speculate here that this George Calvert was the father of John Calvert who died in Prince William County before 1739 and that Richard Gibson was the father of Jacob Gibson who patented land with John Calvert in 1724 and for whom Jacob Calvert was doubtlessly named.—Compiler.)

"A List of Claims for horses, provisions and other necessarys—for public Service as valued in specie by the Justices of the Court of Prince William County," etc., included the names of several members of the Calvert Family, viz.:

John Calvert, Sr., for 1 beef (250 ℔)...............£4/ 3sh/4d
Humphrey Calvert for 2 days driving Cattle......... 2sh/8d
Sarah Calvert [6] for 1 beef (300 ℔).................£5/ 0 /0
Obed Calvert, Jr., for 1 beef (110 ℔)...............£1/16sh/8d
Obed Calvert for pasturage for 288 hd Cattle & 3 horses 11sh/9d
Jesse Calvert for 1 beef (110 ℔)...................£1/16sh/8d

Taken from the original from the Revolutionary War Records in the Department of Archives of the State Library in Richmond, Virginia.

[6] Widow of Jacob Calvert (d. 1772).

Minute Book, Feb. 28, 1774, Bedford Co., Va. " On the
motion of Ann Witt letters of Administration is Granted her
on the Estate of Lewis Witt, Dec'd. . . . who made Oath and
gave Bond with Security according to Law."

Order Book, May 24, 1779. " On the motion of Mrs. Ann
Witt (who has a son in the continental service) she is allowed
£30-0-0 for the support of her and her family (to be paid into
the hands of William Leftwich, Gent.) which is ordered to be
certified to the Treasurer of the State."

Marriage Bonds. " Know all Men by these presents that
we Francis Calvert and Roland Witt are held and firmly bound
unto Henry Lee, Esquire, Governor or Chief Magistrate of
the State of Virginia in the Sum of Fifty pounds to the which
payment well and truly to be made to the said Henry Lee or
to his Successors we bind ourselves and each of us, our, and
each of our Heirs, Executors, and Administrators jointly and
severally firmly by these presents sealed with our Seals and
dated this 20th day of December 1791.

The Condition of the above Obligation is such that whereas
there is a marriage shortly intended to be had and solemnized
between the above bound Francis Calvert and Elizabeth Witt,
now if there shall be no Lawfull Cause to obstruct the said
marriage then the above Obligation to be void else to remain
in full force."

Francis Calvert   L. S.
Rowland Witt [7]   L. S.

Ditto, Sept. 1, 1809. Francis and William Dickerson, bond
for $150.00 for the marriage of the said Francis Calvert and
Betsy Rose.

Ditto, Nov. 26, 1798. John Slack and Thomas Alexander,
bond for $150.00 for the marriage of the said John Slack and
Nancy Huddleston. Nov. 25, 1798. Consent of Mrs. Mary
Huddleston to the marriage of her daughter, the said Nancy
Huddleston, to the aforementioned John Slack. Witnesses:
Thomas Alexander and Sarah Huddleston. (NOTE: Thomas

---

[7] Brother of Elizabeth (Witt) Calvert (*supra*).

Alexander and Sarah Huddleston, witnesses to the marriage-bond, were later joined in matrimony, on May 26, 1800. Sarah and Nancy Huddleston were the daughter of Abraham Huddleston who died in Bedford County in 1785. His widow, Mary Huddleston nee Patterson, married, in November, 1798, Abraham Slack, father of John Slack who married, at the same time, her daughter, Nancy Huddleston! Abraham Slack, who was a Revolutionary Soldier in Bucks Co., Pa., and Abraham Huddleston migrated from Bucks Co., Pa., to Bedford Co., after the close of the War.—Compiler.)

Ditto, Nov. 7, 1798. Abraham Slack and Henry Lloyd, bond for $150.00 for the marriage of the said Abraham Slack and Mary Huddleston. (NOTE: this was the widower, Abraham Slack, who married the widowed Mary Huddleston nee Patterson, daughter of Joseph Patterson who died in Bedford Co., Va., in 1811 and in his will mentioned his daughter Mary Slack. Nancy Huddleston, wife of John Slack, died at Cabin Creek, Kanawha Co., Va., Sept. 25, 1862, aged 81 years, 11 months and 25 days. Her husband, John Slack, died in the same county in 1826, aged about 50 years. They were the parents of the wives of Mills Witt Calvert and his brother, John Lewis Calvert, before-mentioned.—Compiler.)

It may not be amiss to call attention to the fact that the family of this Jacob Calvert of Stafford and Prince William Counties, Virginia, represented a branch of the foremost family of the Colony of Maryland. The Calvert Family has long been extinct in the male line in Maryland, but from the branch which moved across the Potomac River and settled in Virginia has come innumerable descendants in both the male and female lines. The compiler wishes to say a word about the mythical Calvert Estate which exists in imagination only, in spite of the ridiculous notices which appear from time to time in the American newspapers. When Frederick, 6th and last Lord Baltimore, died in Naples in 1771 he left the Province of Maryland to his illegitimate son, Henry Harford, who never obtained control of the property. This Lord Baltimore, although married had no lawful issue, so he divided his estate, which was quite large, between his two lawful sisters (Louisa, the wife of John Browning, and Caroline, the wife of Sir Robert Eden) and five of his *illegitimate* children, viz: Henry Harford, Frances Mary Harford (his children by Hester Whelan), Sophia Hales and Elizabeth Hales (his children by Elizabeth Dawson), and Charlotte Hope (his child by Elizabeth Hope). Since this Lord Baltimore died in 1771 he could hardly have leased any Baltimore land to the B. & O. Railroad which did not exist until more than 50 years after his death! The compiler has made an exhaustive search of the records of Maryland and has no hesitation in saying that there was, there is and there never will be any Calvert Estate due to the descendants of the Calvert Family of Maryland! He has no expectation that his statement will be believed by those deluded persons who are still seeking after this mythical estate, nevertheless he makes this statement for what it may be worth to those who wish to know the truth. " Verbum sapientibus." *

Acknowledgements: The Compiler wishes to thank all those who in any way have helped him with his searches after data of the Calvert Family, especially Mrs. Thomas Howard Mohler of Saint Albans, W. Va., and Mrs. Ella Foy O'Gorman of

---

* The myth of the " Calvert Estate " has been kept alive largely through the instrumentality of some dishonest persons who have used the story as a bait whereby to secure contributions of cash from credulous descendants of the Calverts. Briefly the facts are as follows: Frederick, 6th lord Baltimore, in his effort to break the entail created by his father's will, devised the Province of Maryland to his natural son, Henry Harford. By the terms of her father's will, the Province was to revert to Louisa Browning, eldest sister of Frederick.

Proceedings in chancery were instituted in England, against the executors of Frederick's will, in order to assert the rights of Mrs. Browning, under the will of her father. Eventually the case came for a hearing before the High Court of Chancery; but in the meanwhile, the United States of America had declared themselves independent; and the Lord Chancellor declined to go on with the hearing on the ground that it would be only a waste of time, *as let the Province belong to which it would, he had no power to give the rightful owner possession.*

Between the years 1785 and 1790, the Agents for the American Loyalists

Washington, D. C. It was through the efforts of Mrs. O'Gorman, in her Calvert searches among the original surviving records of Prince William Co., Va., that discovery was made of the proper place of Francis Calvert (1751-1823) (q. v.) in the Calvert Pedigree. It is a matter of regret that in spite of all search in Washington, in Richmond and in Manassas, no record was found of the services of this Francis Calvert in the War of the American Revolution, although he was said to have served. But the pre-Revolutionary and Revolutionary records are largely missing from the Prince William County Court House now, owing to loss by fire and war and theft, while many of the records still preserved have been badly mutilated. It is also a matter of regret to the Compiler that one or two branches of the Calvert Family were not courteous or interested enough to answer his letters and send their personal data for inclusion. Had this been done, the foregoing sketch would have been a complete record of the descendants of Francis and Elizabeth (Witt) Calvert of Bedford Co., Va.

---

settled Harford's claim for the sum of £70,000, his estimate of loss having been £447,000.

The General Assembly of Maryland, by Act of October session 1780, "An Act to seize, confiscate and appropriate all British property within the State," settled the matter for all time, although as late as 1825 representatives of the Brownings continued to memorialize the Legislature for relief, but that body decided that the matter was closed.—[EDITOR].

SOME NOTES CONCERNING SIR GEORGE CALVERT (1579-1632), FIRST LORD BALTIMORE, AND HIS FAMILY FROM THE ENGLISH RECORDS.

By John Bailey Calvert Nicklin.

Entries from the Parish Register of St. Martin's-in-the-Fields, London.

Baptisms:

August 18, 1608. Mrs.[1] Dorothy Calvert.

November 18, 1609. Elizabeth[2] Calvert, daughter of Mr. George.

July 18, 1613. George Calvert.

December 5, 1615. Helen[3] Calvert.

March 8, 1617. Henry[4] Calvert.

January 31, 1618. John[5] Calvert.

Burials:

February 1, 1618. John [5] Calvert.

February 16, 1570. Henry [6] Calvert. (Probably a near relative of the Baltimore Family.)

[1] The modern "Miss."
[2] Elizabetha, fil. Mr. George, in the original.
[3] Helena in the original.
[4] Henric' Colvard in the original.
[5] Joh'nes in the original.
[6] Henricus Colvert in the original.

BAPTISMAL REGISTER No. 1, BEXLEY, KENT. DIOCESE OF CANTERBURY.

March 2, 1606. Cecill Calvert, sonne p.rmogenit [8] [1] of Mr. John [2] Cal't and M[ris] Anne Minne his wife. Ye godfathers were ye Earles of Cumberland [3] and Salsburie [4] whose substitutes were S[r] Oliffe and S[r] John Leighes; [5] ye godmother Lady Wooten, [6] substitute M[ris] Butler, [7] mother of M[ris] Cal't. (The ceremony was performed by William Luffe, Vicar, M. A. Oxon. From a letter to the compiler written by the Rev. Charles Moore, M. A., R. N., present Vicar of Bexley, sending a copy of the record.)

[1] Eldest.
[2] A strange error on the part of the parish clerk evidently, used instead of George.
[3] Henry Clifford (1591-1643), fifth Earl of Cumberland, was the only son of Francis (1559-1641), fourth Earl of Cumberland, the other godfather of Cecil Calvert.
[4] Robert Cecil (1563-1612), first Baron Cecil of Essendon, first Viscount Cranborne and first Earl of Salisbury. He was a son of William, Lord Burghley, Lord Treasurer to Queen Elizabeth. It was in honor of this Robert Cecil, Earl of Salisbury, that Cecil Calvert, afterwards the second Lord Baltimore, received his surname, the Earl having been the patron of the first Lord Baltimore. Frances Cecil (died Feb. 4, 1643/4), daughter of the first Earl of Salisbury, married, July 25, 1610, Henry Clifford (1591-1643), fifth Earl of Cumberland. Probably Frances Calvert, daughter of the first Lord Baltimore, was named in honor of Frances, Countess of Cumberland.
[5] Probably Sir Oliffe Leigh of Addington, who was born Nov. 24, 1559, and married Jane, daughter of Sir Thomas Browne (see Le Neve's *Knights*, p. 137). Sir John Leigh(es) was probably a brother or a near relative of Sir Oliffe.

⁶ Unless she were the wife of Sir Henry Wotten (1568-1639), author and diplomatist, who was knighted by King James I, I cannot place her. Sir Henry Wotten left London in 1604 and was for many years ambassador abroad.

⁷ Elizabeth, daughter of Sir Thomas Wroth (1519-1573) of Durance in Enfield, Middlesex, by his wife, Mary, daughter of Richard, Lord Chancellor Rich, temp. Henry VIII. Elizabeth Wroth, who died August 14, 1614, married twice: firstly, George Mynne (who died May 20, 1581); and, secondly, Nicholas Butler, Esq.

EXTRACT FROM THE PARISH REGISTER OF ST. DUNSTAN'S-IN-THE-WEST, FLEET STREET, LONDON, E. C., VOLUME 4.

"15 April 1632.¹ The Rt. hono^ble George Lord Baltimore was buried from the backside of the Bell." [(Believed to be Bell Inn or Tavern, a house and grounds belonging originally to the Knights Hospitaliers of St. John.) (Cf. Walter G. Bell, "Fleet Street in Seven Centuries," p. 248, Pittman, London, 1912; and T. C. Noble, "Memorials of Temple Bar," p. 109, Bateman, London, 1869.) The present site is Bell Yard, adjoining the Royal Courts of Justice. (From a letter written by the Rev. Dr. A. J. MacDonald, present rector of St. Dunstan's.)]

¹ This date shows that Lord Baltimore did *not* die on April 15, 1632, as has been heretofore believed, but probably a few days or a week before the 15th. It is strange that Mr. William Hand Browne in his "George and Cecilius Calvert," pp. 33-4, falls in error by stating that the church of St. Dunstan's-in-the-West, Fleet Street, London, was destroyed by fire.

EXTRACT FROM THE CHURCH WARDEN'S ACCOUNT BOOK OF ST. DUNSTAN'S-IN-THE-WEST FOR 1628/9-1644/5 UNDER "RECEIPTS FOR BURIALLS," PAGE 422.

"Aprill. It¹ — the XVth for the ground in the Chancell for ye Lord Baltimore.

It. for the Knell.²	11s, 4d
It. for the Peales.³	8s
It. towards the cloth.⁴	2s

¹ Item. "the XVth" refers, of course, to the day of the month, the 15th. Apparently the charge for the ground in the chancel was unknown when the entry was made, or it had not been paid.

² Tolling the bell for a long period before the funeral.

³ Joyful peal after the service (?).

⁴ Probably a pall over the coffin. A major part of this charge was paid. the full fee on the same folio ranges from 1/- to 3/4. (The last four notes are from the Rector of St. Dunstan's.)

EXTRACT FROM THE MARRIAGE REGISTER OF ST. PETER-UPON-CORNHILL, LONDON, E. C. 3.

November 22, 1604. Thursday. Mr. George Calvert of St. Martines in the field gentleman. And Mrs. Anne Mynne of Bexler in Hertfordshire, by license Cant. (The Register was signed by " Will'm Ashboold, parson.") ¹

¹ Bexler should be Bexley which is (now) in Kent. The license was issued from Canterbury and William Ashbold, then rector, evidently performed the ceremony as he signed the register. (Information from the Rev. J. A. Smith Bullock, present rector of St. Peter-upon-Cornhill).

CORRECTION.

MATERNAL ANCESTRY OF SIR GEORGE CALVERT.

By FRANCIS B. CULVER.

We feel that in view of the approaching end of Maryland's Tercentenary celebration, it is opportune to correct a false notion, on the part of several historians, concerning the maternal ancestory of Sir George Calvert.

In Foster's *Visitation of Yorkshire,* 1584-1612, *et seq.,* there appear two conflicting versions with respect to the name of the mother of Sir George Calvert (1579-1632). On page 500, *sub* " Calvert of Danby Wiske," the first Lord Baltimore is mentioned as a son of Leonard Calvert and his wife *Alice,* the daughter of " John Crosland of Crosland." On page 509 (*ibid.*), *sub* " Crosland of Helmsley," George Calvert is mentioned as a son of Leonard Calvert and wife *Grace,* a daughter of " Thomas Crosland of Crosland " by—(daughter) of—" Hawksworth of Hawksworth." Later writers have adopted the one or the other version as their fancy seems to have dictated. Let us eliminate first the incorrect pedigree.

Thomas Crosland (or, Crossland), of Crosland Hall in the parish of Almondbury, Yorkshire, died in the year 1587, on a journey to London, and was buried September 2, 1587. He married (1) Marina or Mariana Hawksworth, daughter of Walter Hawksworth of Hawksworth. She was buried at Almondbury in 1565. He married (2) Joanna ——, who died and was buried at Almondbury, July 11, 1575.

Thomas Crossland had issue, nine children as follows: By first wife, Thomas and Anne: By second wife, George, John, Michael, Luke, *Grace* (born Feb. 8, 1572/3) who "married Leonard Calvert of Kipling in Yorkshire," Lucy and Susannah (See *The Genealogist,* xii. 199-204).

From the aforegoing data, it is obvious that Grace Crossland, who was born in 1573, could not have been the mother of Sir George Calvert (1579-1632), yet could have been a second wife of Leonard Calvert, even though twenty years his junior and, thus, step-mother of Sir George Calvert.

Another pedigree is supplied by the clever and zealous Calvert family genealogist, Benedict Leonard Calvert (1700-1732), Oxford graduate, who drew up and wrote, with his own hand, a Calvert pedigree in which he mentions the mother of Sir George Calvert as " Alicia, daughter and *heiress* of John Crosland of Crosland " (*Maryland Historical Magazine* II. 369). This is the correct pedigree, because on no other grounds could the Calvert descendants have exercised the heraldic privilege of *quartering* the Calvert and Crossland arms. Further, an " heiress," in the heraldic sense, indicates a daughter of a family in which there are no sons. Where there are several such daughters, all have equal status and are styled " coheiresses."

GEORGE CALVERT (1700-1771) AND SOME OF HIS DESCENDANTS (1731-1931).

By John Bailey Calvert Nicklin.

George Calvert, son of George and Elizabeth (Doyne) Calvert (See *Maryland Historical Magazine,* volume 16, page 192), was born in Stafford County, Va., about 1700 and died in Prince William County, Va., in 1771; he was twice married: firstly (according to private records of the Harrison Family), about 1725, to Sytha Elizabeth Harrison (See Harrison note); and, secondly, in 1741, to Mrs. Esther Stone, widow of Francis Stone of Prince William County, who died in 1740. (As Prince William County was formed from Stafford County in 1730, there was no change of residence, but merely one of county lines.)

Issue (by first marriage):

I. George Calvert " the Younger," who died in 1802; he married ——— ———.

    Issue:

      1. George.
      2. John, who married Susannah ———.
      3. Cynthia, who married ——— Calvert, her cousin.
      4. Levi.
      5. Margaret(?), who married Hezekiah Fairfax (See Fairfax Note).

II. John, who died in 1788; he married Elizabeth ———.

    Issue:

      1. Enoch.
      2. John
      3. ———, who married her cousin, Francis Calvert.
      4. Chloe, who married John Jackson.
      5. Charlotte, who married John Davis.
      6. Elizabeth, who married John Redman.

(1) III. William (1732-1812), who married Hannah ———.

IV. Humphrey, who died in 1802; he married Catherine ———.

    Issue:

      1. Humphrey, who died in 1823.
      2. George.
      3 William.
      4. John, who died in 1815; he married Elizabeth ——— (d. 1829).

      Issue:

        (1) Elias.
        (2) Susannah.
        (3) Elizabeth.
        (4) Nancy.
        (5) Catherine.
        (6) Ada.
        (7) Jesse.
        (8) James.
        (9) Pressley.
        (10) Barrard (?Gerrard?).

(1) WILLIAM CALVERT, son of George Calvert, Sr., and his first wife, Sytha Elizabeth Harrison, was born in Prince William County, Va., Feb. 22, 1732, and died in Kentucky, Aug. 17, 1812; he married, about 1757, Hannah (?Harrison?), who died in Kentucky on Aug. 17, 1807.

Issue:

    I. Elisha, who was born about 1758 and died before June 22, 1784, when Basil Calvert was called "brother and heir-at-law of Elisha Calvert, deceased," a Revolutionary Soldier.

(8)   II. Basil (1760-1833), who married Nancy Triplett.

(15) III. John (1762-1824), who married twice: firstly, Mary McCurdy; and, secondly, Grace Appleby.

(1a) IV. Landon (1764-1809), who married Anne Wood Howison.

(19)   V. Gerrard (1765-1840), who married Rosanna McIlwaine.

    VI. William, who was born in 1768.

    (1a) LANDON CALVERT, son of William and Hannah Calvert, was born in Prince William County, Va., March 17, 1764, and died in Lewis County, Ky., Jan. 2, 1809; he married, Jan. 30, 1787, Anne Wood Howison (who was born June 8, 1766, and died Dec. 28, 1845), daughter of Stephen Howison (who died Feb. 1, 1815) and his wife, Mary Brooke (who died Oct. 14, 1808), daughter of Basil Brooke. (See Brooke note.)

Issue:

    I. John Wood, who was born Nov. 19, 1787, and died ———; he married twice: firstly, Oct. 13, 1822, Sarah McDaniel (who was born Sept. 19, 1802, and died July 2, 1839), daughter of John and Martha (Carrington) McDaniel and granddaughter of William and Nancy Carrington; and, secondly, Feb. 11, 1845, Nancy Davis.

(2)   II. William Howison (1790-1861), who married Lavinia Stratton.

    III. James, who was born Oct. 5, 1792, and died ———; he married, Jan. 3, 1839, Mary Friar (who died Aug. 8, 1842).

    Issue:

    1. Tilsman Stephen, who was born March 20, 1842.

    IV. Mary Anne, who was born Dec. 16, 1795, and died Aug. 19, 1829; she married, March 10, 1814, Samuel Foxworthy, son of William and Clarissa (Calvert) Foxworthy of Prince William County, Va. (See Foxworthy Note).

(5)   V. Nancy Brooke (1799-1873), who married John McDaniel, Jr.

    VI. Stephen, who was born Oct. 28, 1802.

(18) VII. Sally, who was born May 2, 1805; she married, Nov. 18, 1828, Craven Calvert.

(16) VIII. Dudley, who was born Oct. 27, 1808, and died April 22, 1881.

(2) WILLIAM HOWISON CALVERT, son of Landon and Anne Wood (Howison) Calvert, was born May 27, 1790, and died Jan. 2, 1861. He moved to Lewis County, Ky., with his father in 1800. Records of the War of 1812, War Department, Washington, D. C., show that he was a sergeant in Capt. Richard Seward's Company, 3rd (Page's) Regiment, Kentucky Mounted Volunteers, from Aug. 28, 1813, to Nov. 3, 1813. These records also show that his father-in-law, Col. Aaron Stratton, was a major in the same regiment. On Nov. 24, 1814, William Howison Calvert married Lavinia Stratton, a daughter of Col. Aaron Stratton (supra) and his wife, Lavinia ————. (Aaron Stratton was probably identical with the Aaron Stratton born Nov. 16, 1773, son of Johnathan and Abigail Stratton, nee Barnes, of Marlboro, Mass.) William Howison Calvert and his wife, Lavinia Stratton, settled at Helena, Ark., in 1826.

ISSUE:

(3)   I. Joel Stratton (1817-1860), who married Elizabeth Tulley.

  II. Mariah Anne, who was born April 28, 1818.

  III. John Wood, who was born April 7, 1820.

  IV. Fulton, who was born March 17, 1822.

(7a)   V. Lavinia Jane (1824-1905), who married Hansbury Dickerson Turner.

  VI. William Dudley, who was born April 16, 1829.

  VII. Amelia Sarah.

  VIII. Bedford N.

  IX. James Howison.

(3) JOEL STRATTON CALVERT, son of William Howison and Lavinia (Stratton) Calvert, was born March 3, 1817, and died Aug. 5, 1860; he married, March 8, 1842, Elizabeth Tulley (who was born Nov. 19, 1825, and died July, 1896), daughter of Berry and Lucrecia (Young) Tulley of Bedford County, Tenn.

ISSUE:

 I. William Howison, who was born April 1, 1843; d. y.

 II. Leonidas Johnson, who was born March 2, 1850; he married, Feb. 4, 1872, Priscilla Jane Nichols, daughter of Shadrach Anderson Nichols and his wife, Ellen Jane (McAhran) Jones.

III. Mary Rankin, who was born July 18, 1853; d. y.

IV. Lavinia Jane, who was born Jan. 17, 1856; d. y.

(4) V. Joel Stratton, who married Avarilla Nichols, Dec. 22, 1878.

VI. Mayberry Tulley, who was born March 7, 1860; d. y.

(4) JOEL STRATTON CALVERT, JR., son of Joel Stratton and Elizabeth (Tulley) Calvert, was born Feb. 5, 1857; he married, Dec. 22, 1878, Avarilla Nichols (who was born Feb. 1, 1858, and died Oct. 18, 1927), daughter of Shadrach Anderson Nichols and his wife, Ellen Jane (McAhron) Jones Nichols (supra).

ISSUE:

I. Clemency Benham, who was born Sept. 26, 1879; she married, April 14, 1907, John Edgar Harris of El Dorado, Ark.; s. p.

II. Ellen Jane, who was born Feb. 16, 1882; she married, Dec. 26, 1917, James Daniel O'Donnell, III, of Brooklyn, N. Y.

ISSUE:

1. James Daniel O'Donnell, IV., who was born May 5, 1919.
2. Beatrice Calvert O'Donnell, who was born Nov. 13, 1923.

III. Frederick Milton, who was born Oct. 20, 1883, and died Aug. 3, 1886.

IV. Preston Rucks, who was born July 13, 1886; he married, Dec. 5, 1915, Alma Webb; s. p.

V. Norma Leone, who was born Sept. 18, 1900; she married, March 18, 1921, Elmer Jay Brown.

ISSUE:

1. Avaellen Calvert Brown, who was born Dec. 28, 1921.
2. Elmer Jay Brown, Jr., who was born April 8, 1925.
3. Katherine Joel Brown, who was born March 12, 1927.

(5) NANCY BROOKE CALVERT, daughter of Landon and Anne Wood (Howison) Calvert, was born April 5, 1799, and died Sept. 15, 1873; she married, March 16, 1820, John McDaniel, Jr. (who was born Jan. 25, 1799, and died Oct. 31, 1869), son of John and Martha (Carrington) McDaniel (supra).

ISSUE:

I. Randolph McDaniel, who was born Nov. 30, 1820, and died Aug. 14, 1821.

II. James Howison McDaniel, who was born Feb. 10, 1822.

III. Antoinette McDaniel, who was born July 14, 1824, and died Nov. 29, 1843; she married James M. Halbert.

Issue:

1. Andrew Jackson Halbert.
2. James A. Halbert, who married, in 1869, C. L. Hannah.

Issue:

(1) Lee Halbert.
(2) J. J. Halbert.
(3) Bell Halbert.
(4) Blanche Halbert.

IV. Ambrose Dudley McDaniel, who was born Oct. 6, 1826, and died Sept. 6, 1888; he married Marie E. Osborne (who died Jan. 22, 1889).

Issue:

1. Martha Antoinette McDaniel, who was born Aug. 6, 1854, and died May 3, 1906; she married Dr. Allen G. Gray (who was born June 19, 1839, and died Dec. 11, 1895).

Issue:

(1) Pinkney Gray, who was born Oct. 15, 1874, and died Dec. 2, 1883.
(2) Molly Grey, who was born June 17, 1877; she married, Jan. 21, 1903, Joseph Moore Campbell.

Issue:

(a) Joseph Ernest Campbell, who was born Oct. 12, 1904.
(3) Allen Bertrand Gray, who was born Oct. 30, 1882; he married Lenice Halbert.
(4) Albert Ernest Gray, who was born Nov. 20, 1887; he married Ivy Hasley.

2. John McDaniel, who was born Dec. 2, 1855, and died in 1867.
3. Leonidas Osborn McDaniel, who was born Oct. 18, 1857; he married twice: firstly, Feb. 7, 1883, Ida B. Casteel *; and, secondly, Nov. 28, 1899, Callie Scott.

Issue (by first marriage):

(1) Eula Mae McDaniel, who was born June 5, 1886; she married Henry H. Carroll.

Issue:

(a) Snowden Pressley Carroll.
(2) Monie Lee McDaniel, who was born Jan. 16, 1889; she married Wiley Jones.
(3) Grover McDaniel, who died young.

* She was born Feb. 15, 1861, and died Oct. 6, 1898.

(4) Clara McDaniel, who died young.

(5) Luther Webb McDaniel, who was born March 16, 1893.

(6) Josephine McDaniel, who was born Feb. 26, 1895.

ISSUE (by second marriage):

(1) Mary Louise McDaniel, who was born Sept. 21, 1902.

(2) Ruth McDaniel, who was born Nov. 5, 1903.

(3) Leonidas Osborne McDaniel, Jr., who was born Jan. 18, 1906.

(4) Sidney Scott McDaniel, who was born July 21, 1908.

(5) Juanita McDaniel, who was born Aug. 29, 1918.

4. Sidney Thomas McDaniel, who was born June 1, 1859; he married twice: firstly, Louise Kirby (who was born May 5, 1864, and died Dec. 19, 1898); and, secondly, Lizzie Worrell (who was born Feb. 1, 1877).

ISSUE (by first marriage):

(1) Louis McDaniel, who was born July 3, 1890; he married, April 16, 1914, Montine Kirkpatrick.
ISSUE:

 (a) Montine McDaniel, who was born April 9, 1915.

 (b) Jennie Lou McDaniel, who was born Aug. 14, 1916, and died Dec. 2, 1916.

 (c) Laura Louise McDaniel, who was born Dec. 2, 1917.

 (d) Marjorie McDaniel, who was born March 7, 1920.

(2) Sidney Ambrose McDaniel who was born Aug. 14, 1891; he married, Oct. 2, 1909, Annie Mae Stewart.
ISSUE:

 (a) Sarah Evelyn McDaniel, who was born Oct. 2, 1910.

 ((b) Annie Louise McDaniel, who was born Jan. 20, 1915.

ISSUE (by second marriage):

(1) Carl McDaniel, who was born Dec. 19, 1901.

(2) Samuel McDaniel, who was born Jan. 9, 1903.

(3) Mildred McDaniel, who was born Nov. 9, 1909.

(4) Thomas McDaniel, who was born Jan. 9, 1915.

(5) Elizabeth McDaniel, who was born Oct. 9, 1916.

5. Ella Dudley McDaniel, who was born 1862 and died in 1876.

6. Sterling Price McDaniel, who was born Dec. 17, 1864; he married twice: firstly, Marjorie R. Lewis; and, secondly, Sarah Jane Evans.

ISSUE (by second marriage):

   (1) Charles Wellington McDaniel, who was born Sept.
10, 1886; he married, March 18, 1906, Emily Joe
Mitchell.

7. Ambrose Dudley McDaniel, Jr., who was born Nov. 22,
1869; he married, in 1892, Bessie Davis Lynch.

ISSUE:

   (1) Beatrecia McDaniel, who was born Jan. 8, 1893.
   (2) Finis Dudley McDaniel, who was born Jan. 4,
1896; he married, Sept. 12, 1926, Alta Calhoun.

8. Arthur Jackson McDaniel, who was born Jan. 10, 1875; he
married, March 15, 1907, Clyde Mae Conlan.

ISSUE:

   (1) Annie Mae McDaniel, who was born March 22, 1909.
   (2) Kathryn Elise McDaniel, who was born Sept. 2,
1910.

V. Martha Anne McDaniel, who was born Feb. 12, 1828; d. y.

(6) VI. John Landon McDaniel (1829-1902), who married Margaret
Eleanor Davis.

VII. William Howison McDaniel, who was born in 1834 and died
Oct. 21, 1904; he married Mollie Fondren (who was born
Aug. 11, 1842, and died Sept. 26, 1919).

ISSUE:

1. Willie McDaniel, who was born July 24, 1870, and died
Feb. 3, 1915; she married John W. Naylor.

2. Nannie Eleanor McDaniel, who was born June 21, 1877,
and died Sept. 21, 1919; she married Syd Benjamin
Trapp.

ISSUE:

   (1) Syd Benjamin Trapp, Jr., who was born June 2,
1897, and died April 6, 1921.
   (2) Mary Howison Trapp, who was born Aug. 4, 1906,
and died Jan. 11, 1910.

3. Ada McDaniel, who was born April 15, 1878, and died
April 17, 1910; she married Percy Harrison Barker.

ISSUE:

   (1) Percy Harrison Barker, Jr., who was born Dec. 26,
1904; he married, Jan. 27, 1925, Frances Mc-
Dougal.

(6) JOHN LANDON McDANIEL, son of John and Nancy
Brooke (Calvert) McDaniel, was born Sept. 29, 1829, and died

March 14, 1902; he married, March 15, 1851, Margaret Eleanor Davis, daughter of John and Lavicy (Tygart) Davis.

ISSUE:

I. William McDaniel, who was born April 24, 1852; he married, Oct. 9, 1873, Nancy Rebecca Bell (who was born March 5, 1855, and died Sept. 7, 1926), daughter of David and Sallie Bell.

ISSUE:

1. Kenneth Bell McDaniel, who was born Sept. 3, 1874, and died Sept. 7, 1889.

2. Mattie Bernice McDaniel, who was born Jan. 21, 1876; she married twice: firstly, April 12, 1895, Benjamin Davis; and, secondly, Sept. 15, 1916, William Bartie Parker.

ISSUE (by first marriage):

(1) Emmet Theodore Davis, who was born Oct. 23, 1896; he married, Dec. 23, 1917, June Petty.

ISSUE:

(a) June Marcette Davis, who was born March 3, 1924.

(2) David William Davis, who was born March 6, 1898, and died July 2, 1898.

ISSUE (by second marriage):

(1) Eunice Pearl Parker, who was born Oct. 29, 1881; she married three times: firstly, Feb. 15, 1896, Omar Steward Gibson (who died Feb. 5, 1899); secondly, Oct. 25, 1902, Paul J. Kibby; and, thirdly, July 1, 1922, Price Hill.

ISSUE (by first marriage):

(a) Eunice V. Gibson, who was born May 3, 1897; she married, Dec. 3, 1914, Porter Goodrich.

ISSUE:

Paul Franklin Goodrich, who was born Dec. 22, 1916.

Georgia Evelyn Goodrich, who was born Nov. 11, 1917.

Porter Jack Goodrich, who was born Jan. 23, 1925.

(2) Rubin Harold Parker, who was born March 4, 1883, and died Sept. 9, 1899.

        (3) Wirta Lee Parker, who was born Jan. 22, 1892; she married, May 6, 1914, Louis Bray Matsinger.

ISSUE:

          (a) Louis Bray Matsinger, Jr., who was born Jan. 5, 1916.

          (b) Mattie Lee Matsinger, who was born Feb. 8, 1918.

        (4) Cecil Herbert Parker, who was born Oct. 27, 1894.

(7)   II. Elizabeth McDaniel (1855-1927), who married Louis Rollwage, son of Frederick Rollwage and his wife, Mena Kuker of Hanover, Germany.

    III. Mary Frances McDaniel, who was born Sept. 17, 1857, and died June 1, 1861.

    IV. Katherine McDaniel, who was born Sept. 6, 1859; she married Benjamin Perkins.

ISSUE:

      1. Louis Rollwage Perkins, who was born Sept. 29, 1884; he married, July 27, 1915, Eloise Leake.

ISSUE:

        (1) Margaret Worthington Perkins, who was born Sept. 23, 1918.

        (2) Jane Day Perkins, who was born March 22, 1921.

      2. Margaret Elizabeth Perkins, who was born Oct. 24, 1892; she married, May 7, 1919, Stephen Frank French, D. O. S.

ISSUE:

        (1) Stephen Frank French, Jr., who was born May 7, 1920.

        (2) Robert Perkins French, who was born June 16, 1922.

        (3) Katherine Louise French, who was born March 8, 1924.

    V. Robert Jackson McDaniel, who was born June 11, 1862; d. y.

    VI. John Landon McDaniel, Jr., who was born March 22, 1865, and died 1879.

    VII. James Henry McDaniel, who was born Jan. 12, 1867; he married twice: firstly, Lela Eugenia Usery (who was born Dec. 18, 1879, and died Aug. 20, 1906); and, secondly, Nora Laura Shillings.

ISSUE (by first marriage):

      1. James Clyde McDaniel, who was born Jan. 28, 1898, and died Nov. 15, 1898.

2. Lela Laura McDaniel, who was born March 6, 1900.
3. Claud McDaniel, who was born July 22, 1902.

ISSUE (by second marriage):

1. Nena Mae McDaniel, who was born Feb. 28, 1908.
2. Mollie McDaniel, who was born Jan. 29, 1909, and died Jan. 10, 1919.
3. James Henry McDaniel, Jr., who was born Sept. 1, 1911.
4. Jessie Lee McDaniel, who was born Jan. 29, 1915.
5. Rodney Woodroe McDaniel, who was born Oct. 10, 1918, and died April 16, 1920.
6. Margaret Beatrice McDaniel, who was born March 15, 1921.

VIII. Nancy Brooke McDaniel, who was born Aug. 24, 1869, and died in 1908; she married William Hargraves.

ISSUE:

1. Edna Hargraves.
2. Gladys Hargraves.
3. Frederick Hargraves.
4. Lola Hargraves.
5. Katie Hargraves, who married Marcus Brown.

IX. Dudley Calvert McDaniel, who was born Aug. 24, 1869; he married Lula Thomas.

ISSUE:

1. Dudley Landon McDaniel, who was born Oct. 12, 1892; he married, Dec. 28, 1921, Laura E. Wadsworth.

   ISSUE:

   (1) Bernadine Jarvis McDaniel, who was born Nov. 29, 1923.

2. Hugh Ernest McDaniel, who was born Feb. 3, 1895; he married, April 13, 1913, Clyde Ione Long.

   ISSUE:

   (1) Willie Belle McDaniel, who was born Feb. 7, 1914.
   (2) Dudley Calvert McDaniel, who was born April 5, 1916.
   (3) Hugh Gilbert McDaniel, who was born April 23, 1918.
   (4) Thelma Ione McDaniel, who was born July 17, 1920.

X. Malissa McDaniel, who was born Sept. 14, 1871; she married, Feb. 4, 1890, John Iva Whittington (who was born Oct. 4, 1870, and died May 28, 1912).

ISSUE:

1. Emma Sue Whittington, who was born Nov. 11, 1891;
she married, Aug. 1, 1910, William Richard Fisher.

   ISSUE:

   (1) John Edward Fisher, who was born May 24, 1911.
   (2) Margaret Louise Fisher, who was born March 3,
   1913.
   (3) William Richard Fisher, Jr., who was born Sept.
   28, 1914.
   (4) Juanita Fisher, who was born Nov. 3, 1916.
   (5) Gladys Marie Fisher, who was born Aug. 20, 1918,
   and died Sept. 6, 1921.
   (6) Robert Whittington Fisher, who was born July 28,
   1920.
   (7) Emily Malissa Fisher, who was born Aug. 30, 1922.

2. Joe Clifford Whittington, who was born June 9, 1893;
he married, Dec. 22, 1912, Zelma Luvenia Royal.

   ISSUE:

   (1) Johnnie Luvenia Whittington, who was born Oct.
   8, 1914.
   (2) Clifford Harold Whittington, who was born May
   6, 1916.
   (3) Eloise Whittington, who was born Feb. 2, 1918.
   (4) Ralph Malden Whittington, who was born Feb. 14,
   1920.
   (5) Ernest Steward Whittington, who was born Sept.
   2, 1922.
   (6) Doris Virginia Whittington, who was born Aug.
   1, 1924.
   (7) Mary Luvinia Whittington, who was born Aug. 15,
   1926.

3. John Claud Whittington, who was born June 9, 1893, and
died in 1894.

4. Nora Louise Whittington, who was born Sept. 5, 1895;
she married, Nov. 4, 1914, Everett Anderson.

   ISSUE:

   (1) Mildred Anderson, who was born Aug. 1, 1915.
   (2) Stella Mae Anderson, who was born Oct. 20, 1916.
   (3) Gladys Anderson, who was born Dec. 20, 1918.
   (4) Clayborne Anderson, who was born Aug. 6, 1920.
   (5) Helen Anderson, who was born March 13, 1924.
   (6) Vernon Curtis Anderson, who was born Aug. 2,
   1925.

5. Erwin Whittington, who was born Aug. 12, 1897, and died in 1911.
6. Lela Maurice Whittington, who was born Sept. 10, 1899.
7. James Jones Whittington, who was born Nov. 11, 1901.
8. Mabel Whittington, who was born Nov. 27, 1903.
9. Ola Mae Whittington, who was born Sept. 9, 1905.
10. Thomas Henry Whittington, who was born Oct. 11, 1907.
11. Hubert Whittington, who was born Feb. 12, 1909, and died Jan. 6, 1924.
12. Margaret Malissa Whittington, who was born Dec. 3, 1911.

XI. Margaret Ella Nora McDaniel, who was born Sept. 25, 1874; she married, Feb. 27, 1900, Edward Bruce Smith.

ISSUE:

1. Jessie McDaniel Smith, who was born Dec. 16, 1901, and died in 1901.
2. Edward Bruce Smith, Jr., who was born April 18, 1902; he married, Aug. 28, 1928, Nancy Scott (who was born Sept. 30, 1905).
3. William Archibald Smith, who was born Sept. 2, 1905; he married, Oct. 28, 1926, Jenelle Eldridge.
4. Gene Vertriece Smith, who was born June 11, 1907.
5. John Landon Smith, who was born March, 1912, and died April, 1913.

XII. Lloyd Guy McDaniel, who was born May 27, 1878; he married, Dec. 23, 1899, Rachel Phillips.

ISSUE:

1. Gladys McDaniel, who was born Sept. 30, 1901.
2. Chester McDaniel, who was born Aug. 3, 1902; he married, June 2, 1927, Arline Sprott.
3. Lloyd Guy McDaniel, Jr., who was born Feb. 1, 1905.
4. Rachel Eugene McDaniel, who was born Aug. 27, 1906.
5. Mayme Evelyn McDaniel, who was born Nov. 5, 1908.
6. Marvin McDaniel, who was born Feb. 22, 1910.
7. Marcus T. McDaniel, who was born Aug. 4, 1914, and died Oct. 8, 1915.
8. Robert Landon McDaniel, who was born Feb. 3, 1916.

(7) ELIZABETH McDANIEL, daughter of John Landon and Margaret Eleanor (Davis) McDaniel, was born Dec. 14, 1855, and died Nov. 14, 1927; she married, Oct. 9, 1873, Louis Rollwage (who was born in Cincinnati, Ohio, April 24, 1851, and died April 11, 1905).

Issue:

I. Minnie Louisa Rollwage, who was born Aug. 26, 1874; she married twice: firstly, Nov. 9, 1898, Charles T. Harrison (who died Dec. 3, 1899); and, secondly, Dr. John Lemuel Jelks.

Issue (by second marriage):

1. John Lemuel Jelks, Jr., who was born Dec. 25, 1904; he married, Dec. 6, 1925, Marie Spicer.

Issue:

(1) John Lemuel Jelks, III., who was born Sept. 23, 1926.
(2) Joan Jelks, who was born Nov. 8, 1928.

2. Louis Rollwage Jelks, who was born Nov. 16, 1906; he married, May 5, 1929, Ruth Goddard (who was born Dec. 5, 1908).

II. Alice May Rollwage, who was born July 30, 1876; she married twice: firstly, Oct. 30, 1901, Chester McRae (who was born Dec. 23, 1873, and died Oct. 9, 1904); secondly, April 15, 1909, the Rev. Watson Mumford Fairley of Raeford, N. C.

III. Louis Frederick Rollwage, who was born June 24, 1878; he married, Aug. 16, 1905, Myrtle Mizell.

Issue:

1. Mizell Rollwage, who was born May 27, 1906.
2. John Edgar Rollwage, who was born Feb. 16, 1908.

IV. Anna Katherine Rollwage, who was born April 22, 1880; she married, Oct. 30, 1901, John William Alderson.

Issue:

1. Ada Louise Alderson, who was born Sept. 1, 1903; she married, Sept. 3, 1922, James Prentice DeRossitt.

Issue:

(1) James Prentice DeRossitt, Jr., who was born Dec. 27, 1923.
(2) Martha Anne DeRossitt, who was born Dec. 12, 1925.
(3) Ada Louise DeRossitt, who was born July 12, 1928.

2. John William Alderson, Jr., who was born Jan. 6, 1906.

V. Robert Allison Rollwage, who was born April 6, 1882, and died March 23, 1899.

VI. Margaret Alleyne Rollwage, who was born Nov. 20, 1894; she married, Sept. 5, 1914, Edwin Price Wright.

Issue:

1. Edwin Price Wright, Jr., who was born Dec. 13, 1916.
2. Robert Louis Wright, who was born April 3, 1918.

(7a) LAVINIA JANE CALVERT, daughter of William Howison and Lavinia (Stratton) Calvert, was born Sept. 6, 1824, and died ——, 1905; she married Hansbury Dickerson Turner.

ISSUE:

I. James Hansbury Turner.
II. Lawson Dickerson Turner.
III. William Sumpter Turner.
IV. Thmosa Landon Turner.
V. John Calvert Turner.
VI. George Bedford Turner, who was born in 1846; he married Henrietta Davis.

    ISSUE:

    1. Ruby Sidney Turner.
    2. Thomas Lindsay Turner.
    3. Sidney Surrey Turner.
    4. Shelby George Turner.
    5. Chester Lawson Turner, who was born in 1873; he married Virginia Evelyn Butler.

        ISSUE:

        (1) Virginia Lucile Turner.

(8) BASIL CALVERT, son of William and Hannah Calvert, was born about 1760 in Prince William County, Va., and died in 1833 in Mason County, Ky.; he married, about 1780, Nancy Triplett. (According to the List of Revolutionary Soldiers of Virginia there was a Basil Calvert in the Spottsylvania County Militia and as this is an unusual name, it is probable that the Basil Calvert of Prince William County was identical with the Basil Calvert of Spottsylvania, who was a Revolutionary Soldier.)

ISSUE:

(11)   I. Walter, who was born in 1781; he married Pamelia Calvert.
    II. Elizabeth, who married, March 24, 1808, John Foxworthy. (See Foxworthy Note.)
    III. Dilly, who married Charles Daugherty.
    IV. Nancy, who married Timothy Bray.
(12)   V. Mansfield, who was born in 1792; he married Anne Triplett.
(13)   VI. William C., who was born in 1794; he married Mary Calvert.
(14)   VII. Basil, who was born in 1796; he married Elizabeth Green.
(9)   VIII. Thomas, who married twice: firstly, Maria Stephenson; and, secondly, Eliza Hord.
    IX. Fannie, who married, May 20, 1802, Henry Feagan.

(9) THOMAS CALVERT, son of Basil and Nancy Calvert, was born Jan. 9, 1798, and died Sept. 25, 1874; he married twice: firstly, Dec. 9, 1819, Maria Stephenson, a daughter of John and Alcy Stephenson of Lewis County, Ky.; and, secondly, Elizabeth Hord (1814-1879). (Note: John Stephenson died in 1832; he was a son of Colonel Hugh Stephenson, who died in 1776, of the Continental Line, Revolutionary War, and his wife, Anne ———. Among the heirs of Col. Hugh Stephenson who were granted land by the State of Virginia for his services, under date of June 22, 1842, were: Mary, Julia, Thomas and Clifton Calvert. In one record they were mentioned as: Thomas and Mary Calvert, Clifton and Julia A. Calvert, which seems to mean two husbands and two wives. Compiler.)

ISSUE (by first marriage):

    I. Harriet, who died young.

    II. Helen, who was born in 1833; she married Alexander Hamilton Conner, Dec. 18, 1854.

(10)   III. Walter Stephenson (1822-1896), who married Louisa Maria Evans.

    IV. Thomas, who was born in 1830; he married Judith Robinson, Feb. 10, 1857.

    V. Louise Anne, who married Charles Pearce.

    VI. Susan, who married, in 1837, John Grant.

ISSUE (by second marriage):

    I. Delia, who married Orville Mitchell.

    II. Oscar, who was born in 1841 and died in 1897; he married Lida E. Dawson.

    III. Laura Baltimore, who was born in 1844; she married twice: firstly, William E. Moss; and, secondly, Dr. Shackleford, her brother-in-law.

    IV. Robert Anderson, who was born Jan. 18, 1849, and died Jan. 31, 1884. He married Clara Keyes.

    V. Mary Eliza, who was born in 1855; she married Dr. Shackleford.

    VI. Belle, who married, Nov. 25, 1873, Thomas Calvert.

    VII. Harriet, who married William McIlvaine.

    VIII. Jesse, who married Mrs. Carrie Early Duvall, Feb. 26, 1885.

    IX. Hamilton.

    X. Josephine, who married twice: firstly, Jacob Keller; and, secondly, Thomas Kelly.

(10) WALTER STEPHENSON CALVERT, son of Thomas and Maria (Stephenson) Calvert, was born Oct. 20, 1822, and died Jan. 22, 1896; he married, Sept. 9, 1847, Louisa Maria Evans (who was born Nov. 9, 1827, and died Aug. 24, 1901).

ISSUE:

    I. Elizabeth Gorsuch, who was born in 1849; she married Archibald Piper.
    II. Alexander Hord, who married Mrs. Kate Reed; s. p.
    III. Sarah Katherine, who married Charles Meng.
    IV. Helen Maria, who married Dr. Weaver.
    V. James Gorsuch.
    VI. Pearce Thomas, who married Fannie Reed.

(11) WALTER CALVERT, son of Basil and Nancy Calvert, was born in 1781 and died in ——; he married four times: firstly, —— Stevenson; secondly, Dec. 10, 1832, Pamela Calvert *; thirdly, Mahala Calvert; and fourthly, Harriet Brown.

ISSUE (by first marriage):

    I. Jane Reed, who was born in 1826.
    II. Charles, who married, June 6, 1855, Lucy White, daughter of Peyton White.

        ISSUE:

        1. Helen Toy, who married Robert Applegate.
    III. Clifton, who married, Dec. 22, 1847, Jane Leach.†

        ISSUE:

        1. Elizabeth, who married Robert Lovel.

ISSUE (by second marriage):

    I. Alcey, who was born July 20, 1836.
    II. Walter, who was born Oct. 11, 1841.

ISSUE (by fourth marriage):

    I. John.

(12) MANSFIELD CALVERT, son of Basil and Nancy Calvert, was born in 1790 and died April 8, 1872; he married, Aug. 22, 1815, Anne Triplett (who was born Dec. 25, 1794, and died Aug. 6, 1876).

---

* She was born April 19, 1801, and was a daughter of James and Alcey Calvert (q. v.).

† He married, March 14, 1845, Julia Anne Stephenson, so Jane Leach may have been the wife of another Clifton Calvert.

ISSUE:

    I. William, who was born Oct. 31, 1822, and died Jan. 22, 1896.

    II. Francis, who was born June 1, 1835, and died June 16, 1901.

    III. Mary, who was born in 1838; she married Andrew Jackson Calvert (q. v.).

    IV. Thomas J., who married Mary Evans.

(13) WILLIAM C. CALVERT, son of Basil and Nancy Calvert, was born in 1794 and died June 13, 1875; he married, Jan. 31, 1813, Mary Calvert (who was born in 1797 and died Nov. 20, 1856, a daughter of Mrs. Jane Calvert).‡

ISSUE:

    I. Mary Jane, who was born in 1826 and died April 8, 1845.

    II. James, who died Feb. 29, 1853; he married Mary Lloyd.

    III. William, who was born Oct. 28, 1829, and died March 14, 1898. He married, in 1859, Louisa White.

    IV. Sarah Anne, who was born in 1831 and died July 8, 1871; she married John C. Arthur (who died July 7, 1875).

    V. Maximillian Owens, who was born June 30, 1834 and died ———; he married, May 15, 1860, Margaret Poe (who died Dec. 15, 1896).

        ISSUE:

        1. Margaret Anne, who was born March 18, 1861; she married ——— Smith.

        2. William J., who was born Feb. 7, 1863; he married Jessie Swartz.

---

‡ William Calvert married, about 1792, Jane Calvert.

ISSUE:

    I. Allison, who was born in Charleston, S. C., 1794, and died in Mason Co., Ky., 1870; he married, in 1816, Catherine Bramel.

        ISSUE:

        1. William Thomas, who was born in 1828; he married Julia Anne Calvert, daughter of Archibald Calvert, who married, April 13, 1831, Caroline Clift.

        ISSUE:

        (1) Allen, who married Ella McDonald.

        2. Cebron.

        3. George Washington, who married, Oct. 23, 1854, Clarissa Foxworthy.

        4. Jasper, who married, in 1859, Osa Williamson.

        5. Harriett.

        6. Delilah.

    II. William F.

    III. Mary, who married her cousin, William C. Calvert (supra).

Issue:

    (1) Margaret.

    (2) Neva.

    (3. Eula, who married John Pollard.

    (4) Bernice, who married Manford Pickrell.

    (5) Clyde S., who married Rebecca Redmond.

    (6) Woods, who married —— Spencer.

3. Maxmillian C., who was born April 18, 1865; he married twice: firstly, Nov. 30, 1887, Elizabeth Peyton; and secondly, June 24, 1896, Elizabeth Calvert, daughter of the Rev. William H. Calvert.

4. Minnie Bell, who was born Nov. 30, 1867; she married George Caywood; s. p.

5. Lou Odie, who was born March 14, 1870; she married —— Royse.

6. Marguerite Elizabeth, who was born July 4, 1872, and died unmarried.

7. Thomas J., who was born April 4, 1874; he married Maude ——.

VI. Charles M., who married Mary Stiles.

(14) BASIL CALVERT, JR., son of Basil and Nancy Calvert, was born about 1796 and died in 1845; he married, Feb. 12, 1822, Elizabeth Green.

Issue:

    I. Harriett, who was born in 1825; she married, June 12, 1845, Stephen Chandler (who was born in 1820).

    II. Basil, who was born in 1830; he married, Jan. 20, 1851, Mary Aetna Wallingford.

    III. William, who was born in 1832 and died in 1888; he married twice: firstly, Eliza Heth; and secondly, Mary Bramel.

        Issue (by second marriage):

        1. William Southern.

        2. Alice, who married Abner Bramel.

    IV. Elizabeth, who was born in 1834; she married Enoch Berry.

    V. Alice, who was born in 1842; she married —— Owens.

    VI. Anne Eliza, who was born in 1844; she married W. F. Thomas.

    VII. Malinda, who married Stephen W. Parker.

    VIII. Nancy, who married Thomas Berry.

    IX. Andrew Jackson, who married his cousin, Mary Calvert, daughter of Mansfield Calvert (q. v.).

        Issue:

        1. Ida, who married Frank Strode (who died in 1929).

(15) JOHN CALVERT, son of William and Hannah Calvert,

was born about 1762 and died in 1824; he married twice: firstly, in 1792, Mary McCurdy; and, secondly, Grace Appleby.

Issue (by first marriage):

I. James Morris.
II. John Napoleon.
III. Jane McCool.
IV. Nancy Brewer.
V. Mary, who was born in 1793 and died in 1851; she married, in 1812, Isaac Alldred.

Issue:

1. John Calvert Alldred, who was born in 1813 and died in 1893; he married Elizabeth C. Bates.

Issue:

(1) Huldah Elizabeth Alldred.
(2) Permelia Louise Alldred.
(3) Mary Levonia Alldred.
(4) Martha William Alldred.
(5) Elizabeth Ellen Alldred.
(6) Eliza Massie Alldred.
(7) Edward Anne Alldred.
(8) William Henry Clay Alldred.
(9) Huldah Bates Alldred, who was born in 1841 and died in 1911; she married John Thomas Grimm.

Issue (by second marriage):

I. George Washington, who was born in 1816 and died 1876; he married, in 1840, Elizabeth M. Rogers.

Issue:

1. Mary Anne Americus, who was born in 1841 and died in 1879; she married, in 1857, George, George W. Hart.

Issue:

(1) Elizabeth Hart, who was born in 1860; she married, in 1880, D. R. Bass.
(2) James Sterling Hart, who was born in 1868; he married Claudie Goss.
(3) George Calvert Hart, who was born in 1870; he married, in 1894, Hattie Tucker.
(4) Annie Hart, who was born in 1872; she married in 1896, L. A. Clark.
(5) Margaret Hart, who was born in 1876; she married, in 1895, J. W. Clark.
(6) John N. Hart.
(7) Henry Hart.
(8) Sarah Hart.

2. John Napoleon, who was born in 1843; he married, in 1866, Margaret McCurdy.

ISSUE:

    (1) Edward.
    (2) Franklin.
    (3) Bracie Jane.
    (4) William D.
    (5) George N.
    (6) Mary M.
    (7) Elizabeth.

II. David Carol, who was born in 1818 and died in 1882; he married Mary Hart.

ISSUE:

1. David.
2. Sarah Anne, who was born in 1841 and died in 1896; she married Marion Taylor.

ISSUE:

    (1) Emma Taylor.
    (2) John William Taylor.
    (3) Vannie Taylor.
    (4) Lucius Taylor.
    (5) Maud Taylor.
    (6) Josie Taylor.
    (7) Florence Taylor.
    (8) Arzilla Taylor.

3. Amy, who was born in 1845 and died in 1910; she married John Duffey.

ISSUE:

    (1) Ida Duffey.
    (2) Alta Duffey.
    (3) Mary Duffey.
    (4) Grace Duffey.
    (5) Zelah Duffey, who married William Spencer.

        ISSUE:

        (a) Amy Spencer.
        (b) Elton Spencer.
        (c) Ethel Spencer.
        (d) Grace Spencer.

4. Henry, who was born in 1847 and died in 1878; he married Laura Tucker.

ISSUE:

    (1) Georgia.

(2) Norah.
(3) Margaret.
(4) James.
(5) John E., who married Lillie Patterson.

ISSUE:

    (a) Clarence.
    (b) Lola.
    (c) Zana.
    (d) Dena.
    (f) Nola.

(16) DUDLEY CALVERT, son of Landon and Anne Wood (Howison) Calvert, was born Oct. 27, 1808 and died April 26, 1881; he married three times: firstly, in 1834, Eliza Thomas, s. p.; secondly, in 1838, Phoebe Richards (who died without issue in 1839); thirdly, in 1841, Elizabeth Richards (who was born in 1822 and died Dec. 9, 1876), sister of his second wife and daughter of Caleb and Mary Jane (Kinnard) Richards.

ISSUE (by third marriage):

    I. Martha Anne, who married George Washington Cooper.
    II. Lewis Campbell, who married Mary Burris.
    III. Mary Jane, who married William Joseph Hendrickson.
    IV. William Howison, who married Olive J. Campbell.
    V. Daniel Richards, who was born in 1855 and died, unmarried, Dec. 4, 1876.
    VI. Harriet Amanda, who married twice: firstly, David Hull; and secondly, George A. Fitch.
(17)   VII. Landon Caleb, who married Sarah Amanda Cropper.

(17) LANDON CALEB CALVERT, son of Dudley and Elizabeth (Richards) Calvert, was born in Concord, Ky., July 7, 1861; he married, Nov. 27, 1884, Sarah Amanda Cropper, daughter of William Edward and Anne (Bales) Cropper. They live in El Dorado, Kansas.

ISSUE:

    I. Elmer Milton, who was born Nov. 9, 1885; he married twice: firstly, Jan. 25, 1918, Nellie May Blackwell (who was born May 1, 1894 and died June 18, 1927); secondly, Edith Markle.

    ISSUE (by first marriage):

        1. Anna Pearl, who was born April 24, 1919.
        2. Sarah May, who was born April 22, 1921.

II. Clarence, who died young.

III. Anna Belle, who was born, July 16, 1889.

IV. Mabel Esther, who was born Feb. 8, 1894; she married, Nov. 27, 1912, Seth F. Greeley (who was born April 2, 1894).

> ISSUE:
>
> 1. Barbara Lou Greeley, who was born Dec. 31, 1913.
> 2. Wilda Faye Greeley, who was born Feb. 15, 1917.
> 3. Raymond Edmond Greeley, who was born March 21, 1920.

(18) SALLY CALVERT, daughter of Landon and Anne Wood (Howison) Calvert, was born May 2, 1805 and died ——; she married, Nov. 18, 1828, her kinsman, Craven Calvert, son of James Calvert (1766-1823), who married, Feb. 7, 1797, Alcy Cheek; grandson of Jesse Calvert (1742-1802), who married Mollica Brown; and great-grandson of Obed Calvert, Sr. (1720-1806), of Prince William County, Va.

> ISSUE:
>
> I. Robert.
> II. Francis.
> III. James.
> IV. William.
> V. Anne Wood, who was born Sept. 25, 1829.

(19) GERRARD CALVERT, son of William and Hannah Calvert, was born in Prince William Co., Va., in 1765 and died in Kentucky in 1840; he married, March 18, 1798, Rosanna McIlvaine (1781-1850).

ISSUE:

(20)   I. William Baltimore, who married Hettie Rigdon.

II. Jane, who married William Calvert.

III. Page, who married Sallie Day.

> ISSUE:
>
> (1) Jesse, who married twice: firstly, —— Moore, and, secondly, —— Davis.
>
> ISSUE (by first marriage):
>
>> (a) William, who married Sallie Perkins.
>>
>> ISSUE:
>>
>>> (a1) Foster.
>>> (b1) Lou Ann, who married Samuel Vice.
>>> (c1) Fenton, who married John Shultz.
>>> (d1) Dame, who married John C. Emmons.

   (e1) William.
   (f1) Ella, who married James Riley.
   (g1) Laura, who married Samuel Rogers.
   (h1) Emma, who married ——— Sousley.

ISSUE (by second marriage):

   (a) Jesse.
   (b) George Watson.

(20) WILLIAM BALTIMORE CALVERT, son of Gerrard and Rosanna (McIlvaine) Calvert, was born in Mason Co., Ky., in 1799 and died in 1864; he married twice: firstly, Dec. 15, 1815, Hettie Rigdon; and, secondly, in 1856, Mrs. Elizabeth (Evans) Jackson (1817-1870), widow of Houston Jackson.

ISSUE (by first marriage):

(21)   I. James McIlvaine, who married Janet E. Razor.
   II. William.
   III. Vincent, who married twice: firstly, ——— ———; and secondly, in 1884, Elma Crawford.

    ISSUE:

     1. Hettie.
     2. Mary.
     3. James, who was a Captain, C. S. A.

   IV. Marion.
   V. William Burgess, who was born in 1832 and died in 1924; he married his step-sister, Louisa Jackson, daughter of Houston and Elizabeth (Evans) Jackson (supra).

    ISSUE:

     1. Corilla, who married William McKissick.
     2. William.
     3. Serelda, who married Albert Fizer.
     4. Curtis, who was born in 1870 and died in 1885.
     5. Carrie, who married twice: firstly, Edward Plummer; and, secondly, Alfred Bailey.
     6. Lula, who married Ira Jones.
     7. Oddie, who married Charles Jordan.
     8. Charles.
     9. Annie, who married John Carpenter.

   VI. Corilla, who married, in 1844, Samuel Humphrey.
   VII. Nancy, who married William Hardaman.
   VIII. Melissa, who died young.
   IX. Marshall.
   X. Sanford, who died in the War Between the States.
   XI. George.

Issue (by second marriage):

(22)   I. Isaac, who married four times.
         II. Melissa.
         III. Myra Frances.
         IV. John, who died young.

(21) JAMES MCILVAINE CALVERT, son of William Baltimore and Hettie (Rigdon) Calvert, was born Nov. 16, 1816 and died June 29, 1861; he married, Jan. 19, 1837, Janet E. Razor (who was born Jan. 17, 1819, and died April 30, 1908).

Issue:

I. Elizabeth, who was born in 1842 and died in 1909; she married, in 1857, James Nelson Padgett.
II. John Baltimore, who was born Nov. 14, 1857; he married, Sept. 3, 1902, Gertrude Goodrich.
     Issue:
         1. John Dewitt, who was born April 25, 1903.
III. George William, who was born in 1846 and died in 1925; he married three times: firstly, Margaret Thompson; secondly, Elizabeth Cogswell; and, thirdly, Sarah Rachel Caskey, daughter of Robert Franklin and Lucinda (Blair) Caskey.

(22) ISAAC CALVERT, son of William Baltimore and Elizabeth (Evans) Jackson Calvert, was married four times: firstly, to Sophia Mahala Wallingford; secondly, to Sarah Teager; thirdly, to Serelda Gibbs; and, fourthly, to Elizabeth McCarty.

Issue (by first marriage):

I. Laura, who was married twice: firstly, ——— Hurst; and secondly, Price Hinton.

Issue (by second marriage):

I. Marshall.

Issue (by third marriage):

I. Myrtle.
II. Benjamin.
III. Mabel.

Issue (by fourth marriage):

I. Rowena.
II. Frailey.
III. Dell Mary.
IV. Lutie.
V. Helen.
VI. Jasper.
VII. Leona.
VIII. Mattie.
IX. Eunice.
X. Charles.

GEORGE CALVERT (1700-1771) AND SOME OF HIS DESCENDANTS (1731-1931).

By JOHN BAILEY CALVERT NICKLIN.

FOXWORTHY NOTE.

WILLIAM FOXWORTHY, born in Prince William County, Va., was a Revolutionary Soldier; he married Clarissa Calvert, whose parentage does not appear.

ISSUE:

    I. William, who married Elizabeth Hester.

    II. John, who married Elizabeth Calvert (q. v.), evidently a cousin.

    III. Samuel, who married Mary Anne Calvert (q. v.), evidently a cousin.

    IV. Thomas, who married Nancy Evans.

    V. Sallie, who married Rodham Kenner.

    VI. Delila, who married Isaac Evans.

    VII. Charlotta, who married John Fleming.

    VIII. Alexander (nicknamed "Sandy.") who married Nancy Glascock.

WILLIAM FOXWORTHY, JR., son of William and Clarissa (Calvert) Foxworthy, married Elizabeth Hester.

ISSUE:

    I. James, who died young.
    II. Henry.
    III. Huldah.
    IV. Joseph.
    V. John.
    VI. Sarah Mary.

JOHN FOXWORTHY, son of William and Clarissa (Calvert) Foxworthy, married Elizabeth Calvert, daughter of Basil Calvert (q. v.). She was evidently a cousin on his mother's side.

ISSUE:

    I. Baldwin Clifton, who married Sarah Anne DeBell.
    II. Urith, who married William Walker.
    III. Mary Anne, who married S. Clark Colter.
    IV. Melva Jane, who married Reese Davis, as his second wife.
    V. William, who married twice: firstly, Alice Everett; and, secondly, Polly Goddard Power.
    VI. James, who died young.
    VII. John, who died young.
    VIII. Elizabeth, who married Reese Davis (q. v.), as his first wife.
    IX. Nancy, who married Matthew S. Tolle.
    X. Thomas, who died young.
    XI. Ferdinand, who died young.

SAMUEL FOXWORTHY, son of William and Clarissa (Calvert) Foxworthy, was born Oct. 4, 1788 and died June 9, 1875; he married, March 10, 1814, Mary Anne Calvert (q. v.); both of them were under age at the time.

ISSUE:

    I. Landon William, who was born Jan. 30, 1815, he married Sept. 12, 1849, Armilda Bassett.
    II. Alexander, who was born April 4, 1817, died Jan. 9, 1899; he married, Sarah Goddard.
    III. James Houston, who was born April 4, 1817, died July 9, 1909.
    IV. Belleville, who was born Aug. 25, 1820, died July 9, 1871.
    V. Felitha May, who was born March 3, 1823, died Nov. 29, 1868.
    VI. Thomas Dudley, who was born Nov. 30, 1825, died 1893.
    VII. Nancy, who was born April 1, 1828; she married, in 1850, John Watts.

THOMAS FOXWORTHY, son of William and Clarissa (Calvert) Foxworthy, married Nancy Evans.

Issue:
> I. Mary, who married Joseph Glascock.
> II. Joseph.
> III. Evaline, who married William Clary.
> IV. Squire Evans, who married Sarah Catherine Kelly.
> V. Elizabeth, who died young.
> VI. John, who married ———, daughter of Reason Becket.

DELILA FOXWORTHY, daughter of William and Clarissa (Calvert) Foxworthy, married twice: firstly, Isaac Evans; and secondly, Obed P. Nute.

Issue (by first marriage):
> I. Charlotte Evans.
> II. Alexander Evans, who married ——— Norwood.

Issue (by second marriage):
> I. Charles Nute, who married Malinda Glascock.
> II. William Nute, who died young.
> III. Louisa Nute, who married Newman Glascock, brother of Malinda Glascock (q. v.).
> IV. James Nute, who married Sarah Seybold.

CHARLOTTA FOXWORTHY, daughter of William and Clarissa (Calvert) Foxworthy, married John Fleming.

Issue:
> V I. William Fleming, died aet. 22.
> II. George Fleming, who died aet. 22.
> III. Clarissa Fleming.
> IV. Alexander Fleming.
> V. Stephen Fleming.

ALEXANDER FOXWORTHY, son of William and Clarissa (Calvert) Foxworthy, married Nancy Glascock.

Issue:
> I. Martha Anne.
> II. Kittie.
> III. Leroy.

SQUIRE EVANS FOXWORTHY, son of Thomas and Nancy (Evans) FOXWORTHY, was born Oct. 8, 1821 and died Jan. 27, 1895; he married Sarah Catherine Kelly (who was born Aug. 13, 1839 and died Sept. 19, 1910).

Issue:

I. Mary Eveline, who was born Nov. 4, 1863 and died Aug. 11, 1909; she married James Arlington Stanley.

Issue:

1. Edgar Rice Foxworthy Stanley.

II. Sarah Margaret, who was born Nov. 29, 1865; she married Henry Bascom Norwood.

III. James Edgar, who was born Feb. 11, 1868; he married Sarah Matilda Hendry.

Issue:

1. Julia Catherine.

2. Lois Matilda.

IV. Isaac Evans, who was born Dec. 8, 1869; he married Lena Rivers Alexander.

Issue:

1. Ralph Morris, who died in infancy.

2. Lynn Evans.

V. Bettie Franklin, who was born Nov. 13, 1871 and died July 30, 1878.

VI. Charles Maltby, who was born April 18, 1875 and died May 1, 1930; he married Anna Louise Lukins.

Issue:

1. Margaret Cumber.

2. Mary Louise.

VII. Boyd Clifton, who was born April 28, 1878; he married Mary Norwood Turner.

Issue:

1. Eloise Nute, who was born Aug. 5, 1905.

2. Clifton Norwood, who born June 29, 1916.

3. Robert Evans, who was born Sept. 4, 1922.

SALLIE FOXWORTHY, daughter of William and Clarissa (Calvert) Foxworthy, married Rodham Kenner.

Issue:

I. Leroy Kenner, who married Mary Bell.

II. Willis Kenner, who died young.

III. Francis Kenner.

IV. Samuel Kenner, who married Emeline Given.

ALEXANDER FOXWORTHY, son of Samuel and Mary Anne (Calvert) Foxworthy, married Sarah Goddard.

Issue:

I. Mary Anne Foxworthy, who was born in 1844 and died in 1924; she married Thomas Power.

ISSUE:

    1. Annie Laura Power.

    2. Clarence Lamoine Power.

II. Laura Foxworthy, who was born June 1, 1846; she married Michael Trimble Goddard.

ISSUE:

    1. Amy Goddard.

III. James Alexander Foxworthy, who was born March 19, 1848 and died Jan., 1871; he married, Dec. 25, 1869, Leila Josephine Browning, daughter of Lewis Dabney Browning and his third wife, Nancy Johnson.

ISSUE:

    1. Nannie Lewis Foxworthy, who was born Oct. 29, 1870; she married, Nov. 12, 1891, George William Davis (who was born March 9, 1872).

    ISSUE:

        (1) Emily Leila Davis, who was born March, 1895 and died March 31, 1895.

        (2) William Browning Davis, who was born Dec. 12, 1896; he married, Dec. 25, 1929, Elizabeth Karnes.

        (a) William Browning Davis, Jr., who was born May 15, 1931.

        (3) James Foxworthy Davis, who was born Nov. 24, 1898. and died May 9, 1931.

        (4) George Norwood Davis, who was born Feb. 23, 1903 and died March 4, 1903.

        (5) Helen Morrill Davis, who was born Jan. 5, 1905; she married, Dec. 31, 1926, F. Gerard Johns of Lexington, Ky.

        (6) Mary Bruce Davis, who was born July 6, 1908; she married, Aug. 31, 1930, Marion Sidney Wallace.

IV. Elizabeth Masterson Foxworthy, who was born in 1850 and died in 1927; she married Dr. Alvin Wallingford.

ISSUE:

    1. Alexander Mark Wallingford.

V. Alice Sarah Foxworthy, who was born in 1852 and died April 29, 1923.

VI. Jane Avis Foxworthy, who was born May 25, 1855 and died Aug. 11, 1882.

VII. Kittie O'Bannon Foxworthy, who was born in 1857; she married Joshua Bell Glascock.

ISSUE:

    1. Joshua Alexander Glascock, who married Alice Seybold.

        (a) Kittie Glascock.

    2. Alice Glascock.

VIII. Francis Goddard Foxworthy, who was born March 18, 1860; he married Ella Wallingford; s. p.

WILLIAM FOXWORTHY, who married Clarissa Calvert, on May 10, 1778, was a son of John and Sarah (Northcutt) Foxworthy of Overwharton Parish, Stafford County, Va. He was born April 1, 1753 and died June 17, 1837. His wife, Clarissa Calvert, was born May 19, 1758 and died in 1846.

FAIRFAX NOTE.

WILLIAM FAIRFAX, son of John and Mary (Scott) Fairfax, was born in Charles Co., Md., about 1720 and died in Prince William Co., Va., in 1793; he married twice: firstly, Benedicta Blancett; and, secondly, in 1762, Elizabeth Buckner. (His will was dated Oct. 4, 1793 and probated Dec. 2, 1793.)

ISSUE (by first marriage):

    I. Ada, who married Burr Calvert.
    II. Anne, who married William Warder.
    III. Johnathan, who died in 1787; he married Sarah Wright.
    IV. Benedicta.
    V. Hezekiah, who married twice: firstly, Anne Mills; and secondly, Margaret Calvert (q. v.).
    VI. William, who married twice: firstly, Anne King; and secondly, Letitia Adams.
    VII. Elizabeth, who married John Pell.
    VIII. Sarah.

ISSUE (by second marriage):

    I. John, who was born Dec. 10, 1763 and died Dec. 25, 1843; he married twice: firstly, 1792, Mary Byrne (1770-1802); and secondly, 1808, Mrs. Nancy (Loid) Franklin (1772-1850).
    II. Catherine, who married James Gainer.

JOHN FAIRFAX died in Charles Co., Md., in 1735, and in his will, probated Jan. 13, 1735/6, he mentioned his daughters: Catherine, Elizabeth, Mary and Anne; his son William (then under eighteen years of age) and his wife, Jean.[1] The witnesses were: William Warder and John Machilevra.

---

[1] Evidently a second wife and *NOT* the mother of his son William (c. 1720-1793).

HARRISON NOTE.

BURR HARRISON, I., the Immigrant to Virginia, was born in London, England, Dec. 28, 1636 and was baptized in St. Margaret's, Westminster, Jan. 3, 1636/7.[2] He came to Virginia before 1660 and settled in that part of Stafford County which later became Prince William County. Hening's *Statutes* states that "In 1670 Burr Harrison was chosen one of His Majesty's Honourable Justices of the Peace." He was also appointed by the Governor of Virginia to be one of the ambassadors to the Emperor of the Piscataways. In the Virginia Calendar of State Papers are many references to him and his offices. He seems to have died in 1706. According to family records he married Frances Burdette of Maryland and had several children. A grant of land in 1698 shows that he also married the widow of William Mansbridge who died in Stafford Co., in 1697. Burr Harrison, I., had

ISSUE:

    I. Cuthburt.
    II. Burdette.
    III. Burr, who died in 1722; he married Mrs. Lettice Smith, nee Green.
    IV. Thomas (1665-1746), who married Sythia Elizabeth Short, of Maryland.
    V. William, who died Dec. 1, 1745; he married Sarah Hawley who survived him and married, secondly, Thomas Lewis (d. 1749).
    VI. Frances Anne.
    VII. Sarah Burdette.
    VIII. Sybil, who married Thomas Whitledge.
    IX. Mary.

THOMAS HARRISON, son of Burr Harrison, I., and his wife Frances Burdette, was born Aug. 7, 1665 and died Aug. 13, 1746; he married Sythia Elizabeth Short. Thomas Harrison patented tracts of land in four counties. He and his brother William, had large grants. Later he and another brother, Burdette, received grants. Capt. Thomas Harrison, as he was

---

[2] He was son of Cuthbert Harrison (baptized at St. Margaret's, Westminster, Jan. 11, 1607), son of Cuthbert and Alexander Harrison.

known, John West and Simon Pearson patented land together. In 1706 they received a grant of 4,639 acres. His estate on the Chappawamsic River was named for this river. He was vestryman, crown justice, captain of the militia and a member of the House of Burgesses from 1741 until his death in 1746.

Northern Neck Land Book No. 2, page 305. Land Office, Richmond. Feb. 12. 1698. " William Mansbridge of Stafford County died in 1697 seized of 200 acres of land in Quanticott Creek in the said county, leaving no heirs but his wife, Mary, with whom Burr Harrison hath intermarried." Mansbridge's deed was dated March 4, 1695/6, being for the uppermost part of a Patent of Thomas Dayes for 500 acres, of which the said Mansbridge, Matt Martyn and Thomas Burton did purchase 200 acres March 4, 1695/6. (Deed Book 1738-1741, Prince William Co., Va., Feb. 20, 1738. Between Thomas Calvert alias Harrison and Sarah, his wife, of the said county, and John Carr. Sell to the said Carr 200 acres on the north side of Quanticott Creek, it being the land that Burr Harrison left between George Calvert alias Harrison, Burr Calvert alias Harrison, and Thomas Calvert alias Harrison.)[3]

In 1700 Burr Harrison had married " the widow of Edward Smith and as she is now dead " he asked to be appointed guardian to Smith's children. In 1702 there was a deed from Burr Harrison as guardian of William, Edward and Katherine Smith, children of Edward Smith and Lettice, his wife, and grandchildren of Anne Scarlett of Stafford County. (*Virginia Magazine of History & Biography,* vol. 23, p. 315.) (Whether this was Burr Harrison I, or his son, Burr Harrison II, does not appear, but it is probably the latter as it would seem improbable that Burr Harrison I, had three wives in so short a period of time.—*Compiler.*)

---

[3] One might wonder if these 200 acres were the same 200 acres of land, and if this was the same Burr Harrison, of the patent of Feb. 12, 1698!

BROOKE NOTE.

(Neale-Taney-Howison Connection.)

Richard Brooke, died Jan. 16, 1633/4; he married, in 1552, Elizabeth (who died May 20, 1599), daughter of John Twyne.

Thomas Brooke, son of the preceding, was born 1561 and died Sept. 14, 1612; he married, about 1590, Susan (who died Sept. 15, 1612), daughter of Sir Thomas Foster, Knight, and his wife, Susan, daughter of Thomas Foster, Esquire.

Robert Brooke, son of the preceding, was born June 3, 1602 and died July 20, 1655; he came to Maryland on June 30, 1650 and became Lord of De la Brooke Manor; he married, secondly, May 11, 1635, Mary (who died Nov. 29, 1663), daughter of Dr. Roger Mainwaring, Bishop of St. David's.

Roger Brooke, son of the preceding, was was born Sept. 30, 1637 and died April 8, 1700; he married, secondly, in 1676, Mary Wolseley, daughter of Walter Wolseley and granddaughter of Sir Thomas Wolseley of Staffordshire.

John Brooke, son of the preceding, was born in 1687 and died in 1735; he married, in 1709, Sarah (Wargent?).

Basil Brooke, son of the preceeding, was born about 1714 and died in 1757; he married, firstly, about 1735, Dorothy Taney, daughter of Michael Taney (who died in 1743) and his first wife, Mary Neale, daughter of Capt. James Neale, Jr.

ISSUE:

I. Basil, born about 1736.
II. Michael, born about 1738.
III. Mary, born about 1740 and died 1808; she married, about 1757, Stephen Howison (who died in 1815).

ISSUE:

1. John, who was born Aug. 25, 1758 and died young.
2. William, who died, without issue.
3. James, who was born March 27, 1765.
4. Anne Wood (1766-1845), who married Landon Calvert (q. v.).
5. Sarah Anne, who was born in 1768; she married Peter Trone.
6. Stephen, who was born in 1770 and died young.
7. Alexander, who was born in 1773.
8. Stephen Howison III, who was born in 1776.
9. Samuel, who was born in 1780.

10. Mary Anne, who was born in 1780 and married John Pott; s. p.

11. William (1782-1805); s. p.

12. Robert D., who was born Nov. 24, 1787.

Stephen Howison (d. 1815) was a son of John Howison, the Immigrant to Maryland and Virginia, and his wife, Anne Wood; grandson of James Howison (d. 1680) of Scotland and his wife, Alison Ramsey; and great-grandson of Alexander Howison (d. 1637) of Scotland.

The will of Michael Taney, who died in 1743 in Calvert County, Maryland, was dated June 2, 1743 and probated March 24, 1743. He mentioned his wife, Sarah Taney; his son, Michael Taney, and his daughter, Dorothy Brooke, and her husband, Basil Brooke. The will of William Wargent of Dorchester County, Maryland, dated May 26, 1709, was probated March 14, 1710 and mentioned his wife, Mary Wargent, and his daughter, *Sarah Brook.*

Capt. James Neale (1615-1684) married Anne (died 1698), daughter of Benjamin Gill (who died Nov. 22, 1655). James Neale, Jr., their son, died in 1727; he married twice: firstly, in 1681, Elizabeth Calvert, daughter of William and Elizabeth (Stone) Calvert; and, secondly, in 1687, Elizabeth (1666-1734), daughter of Capt. John Lord of Westmoreland County, Virginia. Capt. James Neale (1615-1684) was a son of Raphael Neale of London, England, who married Mrs. Jane Forman; he was a grandson of John Neale of Bedfordshire and Wollaston, Northamptonshire, who married Grace Butler, and a great-grandson of Thomas Neale of Velden, Bedfordshire, who married Godiva, daughter of Richard Throckmorton. Mary Neale, daughter of Capt. James Neale, Jr. (who died in 1727) and his second wife, Elizabeth Lord (1666-1734), married Michael Taney (who died in 1743) and their daughter, Dorothy Taney, married Basil Brooke (q. v.). Capt. James Neale (1615-1684) was Lord of Wollaston Manor, in Maryland. He was very prominent in the early days of the Colony. His daughter, Henrietta Maria Neale, who was a God-daughter of Her Majesty, Henrietta Maria of France, wife of Charles I,

King of England, married twice: firstly, Richard Bennett, Jr.; and, secondly, Colonel Philemon Lloyd, both prominent Marylanders of Colonial Days.

Landon Calvert (1764-1809) was a descendant of Gov. Leonard Calvert (1606-1647), Lord of Trinity, St. Gabriel's and St. Michael's Manors, and of Gov. William Stone (1603-1660), Lord of Poynton Manor. Anne Wood Howison (1764-1845), wife of Landon Calvert (supra), was a descendant of Robert Brook, Lord of De la Brooke Manor, and of James Neale, Lord of Wollaston Manor.

Michael Taney, the Immigrant, came to Maryland in 1660 and was High Sheriff of Calvert County from 1685 to 1689; he died in 1692. His first wife, Mary Taney, was living in 1685; he married, secondly, Jane Trueman, daughter of Henry Trueman. Michael Taney, son of the preceding, died in 1703; he married Dorothy Brooke,[4] daughter of Roger and Dorothy (Neale) Brooke and granddaughter of James and Anne (Gill) Neale. Michael Taney III, son of the preceding, died in 1743; he married his cousin, Mary Neale, daughter of James and Elizabeth (Lord) Neale (q. v.). In 1687 (Liber IX, page 476, Land Office, Annapolis, Md.) the account of Thomas Banks shows that Michael Taney was the "husband of Margaret Beckwith," daughter of George Beckwith, deceased. Just which Michael Taney this was does not appear. Liber Xa, page 3, shows that Michael Taney died on May 22, 1692. This was, of course, the Immigrant, and Margaret Beckwith must have been one of his wives or a wife of his son, Michael Taney, II.

MISCELLANEOUS RECORDS FROM ORIGINAL SOURCES.

Prince William County, Va.

Will Book C., page 107, March 23, 1737. George Calvert was a witness to the will of John Walker. George Colvert (sic), a witness to the "annex" to the same will, with the same witnesses as to the will itself.

---

[4] She was born in 1678 and died in 1730.

Ditto, page 162, Nov. 23, 1738. Esther *Stone* was a witness to the will of Joseph Buchanan.

Ditto, page 246, June 23, 1740. Esther Stone returned an inventory of her deceased husband's (Francis Stone) estate.

Ditto, page 302, April 27, 1741. An additional inventory of the estate of Francis Stone, deceased, returned by Esther *Colvert* (sic).

Ditto, page 401, March 28, 1743. George Colvert (sic), Burr Harrison and Thomas Dowell were appraisers of the estate of Thomas Wallis, deceased, whose widow was Mary Wallis.

Will Book I, page 65. "Washington, Nov. 15, 1804. Most honored parents." A letter from William Howison on his departure, making disposition of his property. "Mr. Trone is to pay Samuel Howison." He mentioned John Howison and Samuel Howison; his brother Robert and his sister, Mary Ann Howison; also his brother, Stephen. The letter was addressed: "Mr. Stephen Howison, Sr., P. Wm. County, Virginia," and was probated on Sept. 2, 1805, as his will.

Will Book G., page 7, July 6, 1778. The inventory of the estate of Reuben Calvert, dec'd, was returned, appraised by: Francis Cornwell, Charles Stewart and Francis Jackson. Ditto, page 31, Dec. 8, 1778. Reuben Calvert's estate account with Sarah Calvert. Paid William Calvert, £6/4/6.

John Dowell,   £5/0/0.

George Latham,   £0/6/0.

Will Book K, p. 356, Jan. 9, 1815; probated March 6, 1815. Will of John Calvert. Wife Elizabeth; sons: Elias, Jesse, James Pressly and Barrard (Gerrard?); daughters: Susanna, Elizabeth, Nancy, Catherine and Ada. Witnesses: Charles Purcell, Charles Goodwin and Peyton Calvert.

Deed Book R., page 302, Aug. 7, 1770. Bond. Archibald Bigby, George Calvert and Jacob Marshall in regard to the execution of the will of George Bigby, late of Prince William County, dec'd. Signed: Arch: Bigbie, Geo. Colvert, Jacob Marshall. (Compiler's note: Jacob Marshall married Sarah Butler, a daughter of William Butler.)

Order Book 1, page 105, May 28, 1753. "Ordered that George Calvert Overseer of the Road with his hands clear the Road to Quantico Church."

Ditto, page 118, May 30, 1753. "The Trustees of the Town of Dumfries acknowledged a Deed to George Calvert for a lot in the said Town and was admitted to record."

Ditto, page 313, Nov. 27, 1753. "Ordered the Church-wardens of Dettingen parish bind Samuel Dobbins to George Calvert the younger, he obliging himself to teach him the shoe-maker's trade."

Order Book, 2, page 117, June 25, 1754. The last will and Testament of Thomas Calvert als Harrison was presented in court by Sarah Calvert, the widow, and relict of the said de-ceased, and Thomas Calvert, the other exor named in the said will, refusing to take the burthen of the executorship and the said widow and relict refusing to abide by the said will, is ad-mitted to administration with the will annexed is granted the said Sarah, she having taken the oath of an administratrix and entered into and Executed bond according to law with Thomas Reeves and John Calvert for her faithful administration of the said Estate."

Order Book 3, page 19, Nov. 24, 1755. "To George Calvert (the) Younger, patroler, five pounds of tobacco."

Ditto, page 46, March 21, 1756. "George Calvert the Younger made oath to the amount of services done by for his Majesty. Ordered the same to be certified."

Ditto, page 244, Nov. 22, 1756. County Levy: To John Calvert, Patroler, fifty pounds of tobacco. To Obed Calvert, Patroler, the same.

Ditto, page 255, Feb. 28, 1757. "Ordered that the Church-wardens of Dettingen Parish bind John Crupper, orphan of Robert Crupper, dec'd., to Jacob Calvert until he attain to lawfull age, Elizabeth Crupper, mother of the said John, Con-senting freely to same."

Ditto, page 262, March 7, 1757. Proof of Public Claims:

Gilbert Crupper, Humphrey Calvert and John Calvert furnished same and were ordered paid.

Order Book 4, page 4, Oct. 12, 1761. Richard Sturman and wife, Charity, vs John Calvert and wife, Susannah.

Ditto, page 38, Oct. 12, 1761. William Calvert is appointed Constable in place of John Calvert and ordered to be sworne.

Ditto, page 41, Nov. 24, 1761. George Calvert the Younger is appointed Constable in place of Charles Davis and ordered to be sworne.

Ditto, page 443, April 5, 1763. Reuben Calvert was appointed constable in room and precincts of William Calvert.

Bond Book, 1753-1786, page 7, June 25, 1754. Sarah Calvert, John Colvert and Thomas Reeves, bond for £200, acknowledged April 25, 1754, for the administration of the estate of Thomas Calvert, dec'd.

Ditto, page 21, Aug. 23, 1756. Lucy Peake, William Peake, Edward Hunston, Richard Rixey and George Calvert, bond for £1,000, acknowledged Aug. 13, 1756, for the administration of the estate of John Peake, dec'd. (Compiler's note: it is a matter for conjecture if the wife of this George Calvert was not a Peake.)

Ditto, page 97, Dec. 2, 1771. Obed Calvert, Thomas Stone, Esther Calvert, Foushee Tebbs and Thomas Blackburn, bond for £500, for the administration of the estate of George Calvert, dec'd.

Bond Book, 1815-1826, page 113, Aug. 4, 1823. Constant Cornwell, Thomas Nelson, Jr., Charles Beach, bond for the administration of the estate of Humphrey Calvert, dec'd.

Ditto, page 122, Jan. 6, 1824. Nathan Haislip, James Foster and James Terrell, bond for the administration of the estate of Reuben Calvert, dec'd.

Will Book C., page 377, March 29, 1742. Jane Colvert (sic) was a witness to the will of Francis Wright.

Will Book H, page 400, Sept. 1, 1788. Inventory of John Calvert, dec'd, filed by William Alexander, Benjamin Materson, Scarlett Madden and James Gwatkins.

Ditto, page 508, Jan. 5, 1803. Estate of Jesse Calvert, dec'd, appraised by James Howison, Alexander Howison and Obed Calvert, Junr.

Ditto, page 524, April 2, 1802. The inventory of the estate of George Calvert, dec'd, was recorded by Stephen Howison, Peter Trone and Alexander Howison.

Deed Book M, page 1, Sept. 28, 1749. John Taylor, Gent., to George Calvert of Dettingen Parrish, 150 acres of land lying on the branches of Quantico and on the west side of the road to Quantico Mill. "The said George Calvert now dwelleth on the said land." Witnesses: Thomas Leys and Richard Kenner.

Will Book G, page 395, June 9, 1788. The inventory of the estate of John Calvert, dec'd, was returned by William Alexander, Benjamin Matteson, Scarlett Madden and James Gwatkins. Among his possessions were: 6 negroes, 9 horses, 2 clots, 16 head of cattle and hogs, 40 sheep, 4 beds and furniture, 4 sets of weaving gear, 1 loom, 2 cotton wheels, 5 linen wheels, carpenters and plantation tools, the house Bible, 12 books, 5 tea cups & saucers, 5 coffee cups and saucers, a cream pot, 2 teapots, 2 quart and snuff bottles, 18 pewter spoons, 3 pewter soup dishes, and other small articles. Valued at £599-5-0.

Will Book H, page 102, Aug. 21, 1788. A sale of the personal property of John Calvert. Among the buyers were: Elizabeth Calvert, John Calvert, Francis Calvert, Zelah Calvert and Thomas Calvert.

Order Book, 1753-1755, page 183. Court held, Nov. 27, 1754. " George Calvert acknowledges deed of gift to his son, George Calvert. Esther, the wife of the said George Calvert, being first privately examined and thereto consenting, acknowledges her right of dower in the land given and it was thereupon admitted to record." (At the same Court similar deeds of gift were recorded from the said George Calvert to his other sons, John Calvert, William Calvert and Humphrey Calvert.— Compiler.)

Book 2, page 397, Sept. 24, 1804. Cynthia Calvert of the County of Bedford and State of Virginia to her son, Alexander

Calvert of Bedford County, power of attorney "to call upon John Calvert of Prince William County, the administrator of my father, George Calvert, deceased, for a just and full settlement."

Deed Book, Sept. 5, 1796. William Calvert and Hannah, his wife, to Arrington Wycliffe. Sale of land, "part given the said William Calvert by his father, George Calvert, dec'd, in the year 1754 and is bounded as followeth: Beginning at a red oak the beginning tree of the aforesaid George Calvert, Dec'd, Patent, and running along the line of the said patent till it encloses 65 acres," etc.

Will Book, Nov. 21, 1808; probated May 1, 1815. Will of Stephen Howison. Sons: John, Samuel, Robert, James, Alexander and Stephen Howison; daughters: Anne Wood Calvert, Sarah Anne Trone and Mary Ann Howison.

Will Book H, page 82. Dated Oct. 4th and probated Dec. 2nd, 1793. Will of William Fairfax. Wife Elizabeth. Six daughters: Anne Warder, Benedicta Fairfax, Catherine Gainer, Elizabeth Pell, Eada Calvert and Sarah Fairfax. Sons: Hezekiah, William and John Fairfax. To son Hezekiah, 300 acres of land "whereon he now lives." To son William, 400 acres of land "whereon I now live, . . . to let his mother and single sisters live on the land as long as they remain single or unmarried." To son John, 250 acres of land " purchased of Mr. Rodham Blancett." Executors: sons Hezekiah and William. Witnesses: John Thorn and Cornelius Davis.

Order Book, Sept. 8, 1762. John Calvert the younger, having attended 7 days as witness for John Calvert at the suit of John Hedges, it is ordered that John Calvert pay the said John Calvert the younger 175 pounds of tobacco.

Order Book, May, 1768. John Calvert, Junr., is appointed Surveyor of the Road in place of John Lansdal.

DETTINGEN PARISH VESTRY BOOK.

1765, Nov. 25. To John Calvert for keeping a child 6 months.
1767, Dec. 4. To Jacob Calvert for building a vestry house at Occoquam.

1772, Nov. 7. To John Calvert for keeeping a poor child
                3 months.

1773, Nov. 27. To John Calvert for keeping Jean Gibson.

1782, Apr. 2. To Elijah Calvert per account.

1782, Apr. 2. To Sarah Dial per account.

1790, Oct. 15. To Sarah Calvert for keeping James Mc-
                Intosh.

1790, Oct. 15. To Humphrey Calvert for keeping a child
                12 months.

1795, June 4. To Humphrey Calvert per account.

1795, June 4. Ordered paid Humphrey Calvert and Burr
                Peyton amount of their accounts.

" At a Vestry held at Quanticot Vestry House, 19 Nov., 1750,
Ordered that a vestry house be built at the Most Convenient
Place by Burr Colbert's plantation for holding of vestreys for
the Parish of Dettingen and that the church wardens agree
with workmen to build the same to which order."

Vestry, 9 Dec., 1757.   To Sarah Harris alias Calvert for bury-
                ing Griffith Watkins.

1758, Dec. 11. To John Calvert one levy overcharged.

1758, Dec. 11. To George Calvert the younger one levy over-
                charged.

1760, Dec. 15. To Obed Calvert one levy overcharged.

1763, Jan. 17. To William Calvert 3 Parish Levys over-
                charged.

1763, Jan 17.   To George Calvert one Parish Levy over-
                charged.

1763, Nov. 28. To Jacob Calvert per account.

1764, Feb. 19. To John Calvert per account.

1764, Feb. 19. To Reuben Calvert per account.

Order Book, November, 1768. William Calvert appointed
Constable in the room of John Calvert. Ditto, George Calvert
the younger appointed Constable in room of Joseph Davis,
April, 1763. Reuben Calvert appointed Constable in the room
and precincts of William Calvert.

Fee Book, June, 1813. John Calvert ordered to rescind administration on the estate of Humphrey Calvert, dec'd. Ditto, Winifred Calvert, administratrix of the estate of John Calvert, dec'd. (In the Fee Book between 1815 and 1837 are to be found the names of: Vincent Calvert, Rhodam Calvert, Tazewell Calvert, William Calvert and Elias Calvert.)

Deed Book L, page 196, May 22, 1749. Between Francis Watts and Thomas Calvert alias Harrison for and during the lives of the said Thomas Calvert als Harrison, Sarah, his wife, and William, son of Thomas Calvert als Harrison.

Bond Book, March, 1813. Levi Calvert appointed ord. for John Calvert, administrator of George Calvert, dec'd, to settle his administration.

Deed Book D, page 47, Feb. 20, 1745. Between Thomas Calvert alias Harrison and Sarah, his wife, on the one part, and John Carr, on the other part, land left by Burr Harrison, dec'd,[5] between George Calvert alias Harrison, Burr Calvert alias Harrison, and Thomas Calvert alias Harrison.

Deed Book Q, page 623, July 5, 1768. Kincheloe to Calvert. Mentioned land sold to John Kincheloe, about 1736/7, by George Calvert, lying in Powell's Run.

Deed Book W, page 245, Sept. 6, 1785. Mention of George Calvert, deceased,[6] and two of his sons, viz.: George and Humphrey Calvert, in a deed between Calvert and Chick.

Rule Book, 1803-1806, March 8, 1806. Susanna Calvert, widow of Jesse Calvert, deceased, vs James, Vincent, Obed, Jesse, William, Priscilla Calvert (wife of John Leatherwood), Jane Calvert (wife of William Calvert), Anne Calvert (wife of Francis Davis), children of the said Jesse Calvert, deceased, and William Leatherwood.

Deed Book Y, page 418, Sept. 2, 1794. Between Charles Dial and Sarah, his wife, formerly Sarah Calvert, widow of

---

[5] Died between 1721 and 1730. His will was recorded in Will Book K, of Stafford County, Va., which covers the beforementioned dates. He is said to have died in 1722. Will Book K is still missing from Stafford Court House.

[6] Died in 1771.

Reuben Calvert, deceased, and Thomas Calvert, son and heir-at-law of the said Reuben Calvert, deceased, and Mary Embly Calvert, his wife, all of Prince William County, and Zachariah Allen, 100 acres of land formerly granted to Burdett Harrison by the Proprietors of the Northern Neck on March 2, 1730, and conveyed to Reuben Calvert by Peter Cornwalt and Sarah, his wife, by deed bearing date of Dec. 3, 1773.

Bond Book, Dec. 2, 1771. Estate of George Calvert, deceased. Executors: Obed Calvert, Thomas Stone and Esther Calvert. Securities: Foushee Tebbs and Thomas Blackburn.

Will Book K, page 494. Dated 494. Dated Nov. 20, 1798 and probated Dec. 6, 1802. Will of Richard Grey. Wife Mary; daughters: Ellender Nelson and Emly Calvert; sons: Benjamin, Samuel, Charles, William, Richard and James Gray.

In the application for pension of George Mills, a Revolutionary Soldier, of Prince William County, Va., dated Aug. 7, 1832 (at which time he was 76 years old, hence born about 1756), it was stated that he died May, 27, 1838 and that he married, on March 9, 1785, Mrs. Lydia Cooksey, nee Calvert, widow of Obed Cooksey. They lived " about three miles from the Town of Occoquam." The application of Spencer Calvert of Caldwell County, Ky., dated May 20, 1833, when he was " aged about 72 years " (hence born about 1760), stated that he served from Prince William County, Va., in the Third Virginia Regiment under Capt. Valentine Peyton and that he had a brother in the same regiment. In another place it was stated that Raleigh Calvert was a brother of this Spencer Calvert.

Hening's *Statutes of Virginia*, volume 7, page 24, March, 1756, Prince William County. Colonial Soldiers: Corporal Lewis Reno, Corporal William Farrow, and Trooper William Peake. " To George Calvert, Jr., for an express, 6 s. 8 d."

Warrant 3185, Elisha Colbert, private Continental Line for 3 years. A warrant to Bazil Colbert, brother and heir-at-law to Elisha Colbert, June 22, 1784. (Virginia Land Office.)

Fayette County, Ky., March 5, 1821; probated April, 1821.

Will of Levi Calvert. Wife Veny; granddaughter Nancy Moore; daughter-in-law, Catherine [7] Calvert (widow of deceased son, Peyton Calvert); "late daughter," Sally Moore; "late son, Jesse Calvert"; son George Calvert; daughters Eleanor Machifee (McAfee) and Polly Calvert.[8]

"A List of Claims of Prince William County for provisions taken for Public Service," allowed in 1783, includes the names of John Calvert, Sr., Humphrey Calvert, Sarah Calvert, Obed Calvert, Obed Calvert, Jr., and Jesse Calvert. (From a photostatic copy of the original in the Department of Archives of the State Library, Richmond, Virginia, said copy being in the possession of the compiler.)

Northern Neck Book A, page 43, Land Office, Richmond, Va. July 16, 1724. 92 acres of land granted to George Calvert in Stafford County, being on both sides of the Main Run of Powell's Creek; the lines joins George Enoe. On Dec. 28, 1722, a warrant was obtained for laying out this land which was surveyed by Capt. Thomas Hooper, deceased, late surveyor, under date of April 5, 1723. Ditto, page 45, July 18, 1724. To Jacob Gibson and John Calvert, 306 acres in Stafford County. On Dec. 28, 1722, they "obtained a warrant, from the office for laying out this land and having returned a survey under the hands of Capt. Thomas Hooper, Dec'd, late surveyor, dated April 6, 1723," etc. The land was situated between the Branches of Powell's Creek and the North Run of Quantico Creek in Stafford County,—to a small oak on a Ridge on the South East side of Neil Cobby's Branch.

Mason County, Kentucky. Will of James Calvert, dated June 6, 1823 and probated in July, 1823. Wife Alcey. Sons: Sanford, Craven, James, Redman, Charles, Madison and Jesse Calvert. Daughters: Permelia Calvert, Caroline Peed and Mary Calvert. Grandson Edward, son of Jesse and Nancy Calvert. Witnesses: William Berry and Walter Calvert. Administration granted to James Peed.

[7] Nee Neal (or O'Neal).
[8] Married ——— Cavanaugh.

Lewis County, Kentucky. Marriage Bonds. Sanford Calvert, Widower, and Mariah Wilson, Widow, Jan. 16, 1834. Dudley Calvert and Eliza Thomas, Sept. 20, 1834. Dudley Calvert and Phoebe Richards, April 18, 1838. Dudley Calvert and Elizabeth Richards, Sept. 29, 1841. Clifton Calvert and Jane Leach, Dec. 22, 1847. Craven Calvert and Sarah Calvert, Nov. 18, 1828.

Lewisburg, Ky. Baptist burying ground at the Baptist Church. Grave-stone inscriptions: Mansfield Calvert died April 8, 1872, in the 82nd year of his age. Nancy, wife of Mansfield Calvert. Born Dec. 25, 1794. Died Aug. 6, 1876. F. M. Calvert. Born June 1, 1835. Died June 16, 1901. Thomas J. Calvert. Born May 22, 1819. Died Oct. 26, 1876. Mary H., daughter of T. J. and M. F. Calvert. Born Feb. 23, 1867. Died Dec. 21, 1882. Mary F., wife of T. J. Calvert. Born Feb. 3, 1832. Died Feb. 22, 1882. Robert Anderson Calvert. Born Jan. 18, 1849. Died Jan. 21, 1884. William Calvert. Born March 24, 1832. Died March 8, 1888. William S. Calvert. Born Oct. 31, 1822. Died Jan. 22, 1896. Louise M., wife of William S. Calvert. Born Nov. 1, 1827. Died Aug. 24, 1901. Oscar M. Calvert. Born 1841. Died 1897. Fannie B., daughter of Oscar M., and Lida D. Calvert. Born Nov. 8, 1877. Died Dec. 20, 1879. Elizabeth Hord Calvert. Born 1818. Died 1879. Capt. Thomas Calvert. Born Jan. 9, 1798. Died Sept. 25, 1874. A. J. Calvert. Born 1834. Died 1903. Inscriptions from the Goddard, Fleming Co., Ky., burying ground. Burgess Calvert. Born 1832. Died 1924. Elizabeth Calvert. Born May, 1817. Died July 16, 1870. Curtis Calvert. Born March, 1870. Died Oct. 6, 1885.

Mason Co., Ky. Will of William Calvert, dated May 23, 1811, and probated Sept. 9, 1811. Sons Jarrard (Gerrard?) and William heirs. Other children referred to, but not named. Witnesses: John Rust, David Corman and Nathaniel Harland.

Marriages on Mason Co., Ky., Records.[9]

Henry Feagan and Fannie Calvert, May 20, 1802.

John Foxworthy and Betsy Calvert, March 24, 1808.

James Peed and Caroline Calvert, Sept. 2, 1819.

Robert Young and Nancy Calvert.

Archibald Calvert and Caroline Clift, April 12, 1831.

Harrison Calvert and Elizabeth Feagan, Feb. 14, 1828.

James Calvert and Amanda W. Clift, Oct. 31, 1833.

George Calvert and Eleanor Thompson, Oct. 19, 1832.

Basil Calvert and Elizabeth Green, Feb. 12, 1822.

Walter Calvert and Parmelia Calvert, Dec. 10, 1832.

Fielding G. Calvert and Emily King, March 28, 1833.

Stephen Chandler and Harriet Calvert, June 12, 1845.

Basil Calvert and Mary Etna Wallingford, Jan. 30, 1851.

Alexander H. Conner and Helen M. Calvert, Dec. 18, 1854.

Charles G. Calvert and Lucy Anne White, June 6, 1855.

Jasper N. Calvert and Osa Williamson, December, 1859.

William F. Calvert and Louisa White, 1859.

Maximillian O. Calvert and Margaret Poe, May 15, 1860.

Gerrard Calvert and Rosanna McIlvaine, March 18, 1798.

Burwell Calvert and Anne Jervice, Oct. 10, 1797.

Hedgeman Triplett and Catherine Calvert, Oct. 21, 1817.

William Calvert and Polly Calvert, Jan. 31, 1813.

Mansfield Calvert and Anne Triplett, Aug. 22, 1815.

Jesse Calvert and Harriett Davis, April 18, 1816.

Allison Calvert and Catherine Bramel, Feb. 8, 1816.

Vincent Calvert and Sally Pool, Jan. 10, 1808.

Thomas Calvert and Susan A. Bolenger, March 22, 1882.

Richard Carr and Amelia Calvert, Jan. 13, 1881.

Charles T. Calvert and Lizzie D. Kirk, Dec. 30, 1885.

A. H. Calvert and Lucy C. Reed, Dec. 8, 1886.

Jesse Calvert and Carrie Duvall, Feb. 26, 1885.

Maximillian Calvert and Lizzie Peyton, Nov. 30, 1887.

C. S. Calvert and Nannie Glascock, June 21, 1894.

[9] From Mrs. G. W. Davis, Flemingsburg, Ky.

R. L. Calvert and Stella Vice, Sept. 30, 1894.
Maximillian Calvert and Elizabeth Calvert, June 24, 1896.
Clarence Calvert and Millie Bramel, Feb., 1904.
James Tamer and Julia Anne Calvert, Aug. 5, 1829.
Thomas R. Calvert and Judith Anne Robinson, Feb. 10, 1857.
Thomas G. Calvert and Belle Calvert, Nov. 25, 1873.
Charles G. Calvert and Mary Angeline Calvert, April 27, 1870.
R. C. Calvert and Eva Hughes, Dec. 29, 1887.

Feb. 10, 1832. John Foxworthy and Walter Calvert, administrators of the estate of Zeal (sic) Calvert. Allison Calvert, Mansfield Calvert, John D. Burgess, William Calvert, John Foxworthy, Thomas Calvert, James Calvert, Jesse Calvert, Jarred (sic) Calvert and others mentioned as having bonds or notes held by deceased. Mason Co., Ky.

Mason Co., Ky. Basil Calvert's division of land and slaves. Estate of Zeal Calvert a. 15. 3. 24. Ann Eliza a. 32. 3. 05. Alice, Hopper Place, a. 18. 3. 30. Harriett, Andrew Jackson, Basil, Nancy, Elizabeth, Malinda and William Calvert, children of deceased. Abner Hord and Thomas Ensor were appointed to settle this estate. Thomas and Mansfield Calvert were the executors. " Settlement was sworne to by Stephen Chandler and Stephen W. Porker, 4th day of April, 1849." This estate was divided, as to land and slaves, on March 11, 1848. (This settlement seems to indicate that Zeal Calvert was a son of Basil and predeceased his father.—Compiler.)[10]

" William Calvert. 1811. Agreeable to an order of the Court of Mason Co., Ky., to us directed for the purpose of appraising the personal estate of Wm. Calvert, deceased, after being duly sworne," etc. " Sworne and subscribed to before a justice of the peace for Mason County. J. Brown." The appraisement of slaves amounted to $1640. There were bonds due as follows: by William Calvert, Gerrard Calvert, John Foxworthy, Zeal Calvert, Jesse Calvert, S. Triplett, Gerrard Calvert, Basil Calvert, John Bray, Henry Feagan, Walter

[10] A plat of the division of the land of Basil Calvert shows that 38.2.00 acres went to Andrew Jackson Calvert.

Calvert, Jane Calvert and others. Sept. 30, 1811. Lawson Dobyns, Elias Hord and Dominick Harrison were the appraisers. (These names of appraisers also appeared as: Lawson Dobyns, John Howison and Elias Hord previously—Compiler.)

Will Book N, page 219, Mason Co., Ky. Will of Basil Calvert, dated March 18, 1845, and probated May, 1845. Children: Anne Eliza, wife of W. F. Thomas; Malinda, Nancy, Harriett, Basil, William, Andrew Jackson, Elizabeth and Alice Calvert. Brothers Mansfield and Thomas Calvert, exors. Witnesses: Addison Dimmitt and C. T. Marshall. Mansfield and Thomas Calvert made bond for $6.000 with William Sedden and Walter Calvert as their securities.

The will of Jane Calvert was dated Sept. 11, 1840. She mentioned her grandson, Adolphus Calvert, son of her deceased son, William F. Calvert; her son Allison Calvert and her daughter Mary Calvert, wife of William C. Calvert. Witnesses: Peter Lashbrook and Robert Humphrey.

NELSON COUNTY, KENTUCKY. CENSUS OF 1850.

Page 608. Foxworthy,	James.	Aged 49.	Born	Va.
	F. (female),	52.	"	"
	S. (female),	20.	"	Ky.
	A. (male),	19.	"	"
	James,	16.	"	"
	M. (female),	14.	"	"
	C. (female),	12.	"	"
	L. (female),	8.	"	"
Page 611. Foxworthy,	James.	Aged 80.	Born	Va.
	L. (female),	75.	"	"
	B. (male),	45.	"	"
	N. (female),	43.	"	"
Page 747. Calvert,	Jefferson.	Aged 28.	Born	Ky.
	Fannie,	20.	"	"
	Meloy A. (female),	4.	"	"
	Elizabeth,	2.	"	"
	Mary E.,	5/12.	"	"

Family 537.	Calvert,	Richard,	Aged 56.	Born Ky.	
		Elizabeth,	58.	"	"
		Harrison,	26.	"	"
		Jordan,	22,	"	"
		Walton,	18,	"	"
		Melvinia,	20,	"	"
Family 538.	Calvert,	Garrett,	Aged 47.	Born Ky.	
		Diana,	33.	"	"
		Dudley,	16.	"	"
		Mary E.,	13.	"	"
		Ellen,	11.	"	"
		Reuben,	6.	"	"
		Permelia,	3.	"	"
	Hahn,	Samuel,	23.		
		Elizabeth M.,	21.		
Page 715.	Marshall,	T. K.	Aged 34.	Born Ky.	
		Mary F.,	22.	"	"
	Calvert,	Sarah E.,	4.	"	"
		R. K.[11]	87.	"	"
		Elizabeth,	77.	"	"

1820 Census. Page 68. Richard Calvert.
                        Thomas R. Calvert.[12]

            Page 76. Richard Calvert.
            Page 78. Thomas R. Calvert.

SPENCER COUNTY, KENTUCKY. CENSUS OF 1850.

Page 144.	Boyle,	James,	Aged 45.	Born Ky.	
		Mary,	40.	"	"
		Ellen,	18.	"	"
		Charles,	16.	"	"
		Elizabeth,	14.	"	"

[11] Evidently Richard Kirkland Calvert (Compiler).
[12] These two Thomas R. Calverts seem to have had almost identical records, so they were probably the same person. The first Richard Calvert was listed as 45 years of age and upwards, while the second Richard was listed as being between 26 and 45 years of age.

	Marian (male),	11.	"	"
	Andrew,	9.	"	"
	James,	4.	"	"
	Catherine,	1.	"	"
Calvert,	Sarah,	13.	"	"
	Mary C.,	11.	"	"

Page 149. Calvert, Isobel, Aged 19 Born Ky.
(In the family of Judith Crook.)

Page 191. Calvert, Richard, Aged 19. Born Ky.
(In the family of George Mason, a saddler.)

Page 191. Calvert, Robert A., Aged 21. Born Ky.
Susan M., 19. " Va.

FRANKLIN COUNTY, KENTUCKY. CENSUS OF 1850.

	Colbert,	Isaac,	Aged 68.	Born Va.
		Elizabeth,	50.	" "
		Samuel,	19.	" Ky.
	Colbert,	Cyrus, Aged 20, 23 or 28.		Born Ky.
		Susanna R.,	19.	" "

NOTE: The foregoing Census records have been furnished the Compiler by Mrs. Ella Foy O'Gorman of Washington, D. C. Acknowledgement is hereby made to her.

By request the Compiler states that all descendants of Gov. Leonard Calvert (1606-1647), through his great-grandson, George Calvert (1700-1771), are eligible to the following societies: Lords of Colonial Manors, Descendants of Colonial Governors, Colonial Wars, Colonial Dames, Sons and Daughters of the Pilgrims, Orders of Founders of America, etc. The description of the Calvert coat-of-arms is Quarterly, first and fourth, paley of six, or and sable, a bend counterchanged; second and third, quarterly, argent and gules, a cross flory counterchanged. Crest: out of a ducal coronet or, two pennons, the dexter of the first and the other sable, staves gules. Motto: Fatti maschi, Parole femine. (Deeds for men, words for women).

Acknowledgments.

The Compiler wishes to thank all those members of the Calvert Family who have, in any way, assisted him in gathering data of this distinguished family, and especially the following: Mrs. Ella Foy O'Gorman, of Washington, D. C.; Mrs. William Mumford Fairley, of Raeford, N. C.; Mrs. John W. Alderson, of Forrest City, Ark.; Mrs. G. W. Davis, of Flemingsburg, Ky., and Mrs. John E. Harris, of El Dorado, Ark. It is always a matter of regret that there are so often members of this family, as in all others, who have no interest in the history of their forebears and who, as a result, ignore letters written to them or refuse their co-operation. Had all members of the Calvert Family (whom he requested for family data) complied with the Compiler's request, this sketch would have been more complete. However, he sends this forth, to join his other sketches of the Calverts, as a pioneer, with the hope that all interested descendants will send in their correct lines to him and also assist him in correcting the data already published so that at some future date he may be able to publish a book on the Calvert Family of Maryland and Virginia, descendants of the first Lord Baltimore, Sir George Calvert (1579-1632), through his second son, the Honorable Leonard Calvert (1606-1647), first governor of the Colony of Maryland and brother of Cecil Calvert (better known by the Latinized form of his name, *Cecilius*), second Lord Baltimore and first Proprietor of the Maryland Colony, the eldest son and heir of the first Lord Baltimore. The address of the Compiler is: 516 Poplar Street, Chattanooga, Tennessee. He will be glad to hear from any descendants who are interested in the history of their family, but he is not at all interested in the so-called Calvert Estate, the myth that has lured some descendants hitherto.

Recent investigations of Mrs. Ella Foy O'Gorman show that there is *proof* of only three children of the Immigrant, Burr Harrison, viz: Thomas, William and Sybil, who married Thomas Whitledge. It is probable that Burr Harrison who married Mrs. Lettice Smith, was also a son, but of Cuthbert, Burdette, Frances Anne, Sarah Burdette and Mary, *there is no proof whatever!* Also there is no proof that the Immigrant married Frances Burdette. [J. B. C. N.]

CHEW FAMILY.

By Francis B. Culver.

Armorial Bearings.

CHEW (of England).—*Argent, a chevron sable, on a chief azure three leopard's faces or* ("Thomas Book," pages 252-253).[1]

CHEW (of "Cliveden," Pa.).—*Gules, a chevron or, on a chief of the second three leopard's faces proper (Zieber).*[2]

The origin of the Chew family arms is obscure. Likewise, we encounter a difficulty in attempting to establish positively the place of nativity of John Chew, ancestor of the Maryland family. Chew Hundred, embracing the parishes of Chew Magna and Chewstoke, and Chewton Hundred, embracing the parishes of Chewton-Mendip and Chew Keynsham, were located in Somersetshire, England. At Chew Magna is Chew Court, the manorial mansion, and a few miles farther south are the ruins of Chew Priory, established under royal charter granted in the fourteenth century by Edward III. Chief Justice Benjamin Chew (1722-1810) named his countryseat, built in 1761 at Germantown, Pennsylvania, "Cliveden" (Cleveden) and there is a Clevedon in County Somerset. All of which seems to support the family tradition to the effect that the American Chew ancestor of this family came from Somersetshire, England. A certain John Chewe, Vicar of Walden St. Paul's (Abbots Walden), Hertfordshire, was buried 10 October 1558. There were Chews also in Lancashire. The "Somerset evidences" are not conclusive, of course; but there is every reason to believe that the family name Chew is a surname of local origin (*i. e.,* de Chewe).

---

[1] From "a miscellaneous collection of arms," reported by the Heralds' College of London.

[2] From the impress of the seal ring of Dr. Samuel Chew (1693-1743) of "Maidstone," Md., and later of Pennsylvania.

1. JOHN[1] CHEW came to Virginia in the ship *Charity* in 1621 or 1622 and his wife Sarah came about a year later in the *Sea Flower*. Both were living at Hog Island, opposite Jamestown, in 1624 (Hotten's " Emigrants," page 237).

He was a merchant and was evidently a man of substance since he owned a house at Jamestown shortly after his arrival, as is shown by a grant in 1624 to " John Chew, merchant," of one rood, nine poles, near his dwelling house in James City (Va. Mag., I. 87). In 1636 he had grants for some 1200 acres " in the County of Charles River," later called York County, and had probably been living in that locality for some years previously (Va. Mag., V. 341-342).

He represented Hog Island in the Virginia House of Burgesses 1623-1624 and 1627, and was a member for York County 1642-1644 (Colonial Va. Register, pages 53, 54, 63). He was also one of the justices of York County in 1624 and 1652 (Va. Mag., I. 197). His first wife Sarah died before 1651, and in that year he executed a deed (recorded in York County) in view of his intended marriage with Mrs. Rachel Constable (Va. Mag., I. 197). His sons Samuel and Joseph Chew are mentioned in the York County records in 1657 and 1659 respectively, and it appears from the same records that in 1668 John Chew was dead and his son Samuel was living in Anne Arundel County, Maryland.

John Chew and Sarah his first wife had issue, with perhaps other children, as follows:

2. I. SAMUEL[2] CHEW, born *circa* 1630, died 15 March 1676/7 (*of whom later*).

II. Joseph[2] Chew, born 1637, died 12 February 1715/6; married 27 December 1669, Margaret (—) Mills, widow of Thomas Mills of Anne Arundel County, Maryland. The age of " Joseph Chew, Sr., of Anne Arundel County," is recorded, in 1713, as 76 years (*Chancery Records*, Annapolis, Liber PL., folio 19), and his nephew Samuel Chew recorded in the old Chew family Bible: " My onkel Joseph Chew died 12 February 1715/6, being . . . years of age." It has been assumed that Joseph Chew was the progenitor of the Larkin Chew family of Spotsylvania County, Virginia, through a hypothetical first marriage with a " Miss Larkin." In " The Thomas Book," by the Rev. Lawrence Buckley Thomas, D. D., pages 276-284, under the caption "Chew, of Virginia," this line is traced from Larkin Chew through several generations.

2. SAMUEL[2] CHEW (*John*[1]) was born about 1630 in Virginia, and died 15 March 1676/7 (old style) in Anne Arundel County, Maryland. He moved from Virginia to Maryland before 1659 and took up his abode in Anne Arundel County. He entered his rights, 16 July 1659, for transporting himself, Robert Crouch, Thomas Madders and Hannah Rogers, and received a warrant for 400 acres (Md. Land Office, Liber 4, folio 54).

He represented Anne Arundel County in the Maryland Assembly in 1661 (Md. Arch., I. 396), was High Sheriff of the county in 1663 (*ibid.*, III. 481), and was one of its justices in 1665 and 1668 (*ibid.*, III. 534; V. 30). He was commissioned, 23 July 1669, a member of the Council of Maryland and a justice of the Provincial Court (*ibid.*, V. 54), and retained his seat in the council until his death (Liber C. D., folio 427; Md. Arch., II. 254, 377, 433; XV. 23, 75, 109, *et seq.*). In 1675 he was Colonel of the militia of Anne Arundel County (Md. Arch., XV. 59) and in this capacity was ordered to raise forces for defence against the Indians (*ibid.*, 47). He was also a member of the Council of War which convened 20 July 1676. He died, according to his family record, on the 15th of March 1676/7 (old style), leaving, among other bequests, "his seale gold ring" to his brother Joseph Chew.

Col. Samuel Chew married, about 1658, Anne Ayres, only daughter and heiress of William Ayres of Nansemond County, Virginia, who came to Maryland with his family before June 1652. On the 5th of October 1653, "Mr. William Ayres" demands land for transporting himself, Sarah his wife (then deceased), Ann Ayres his daughter, and nine servants" before June 1652; and Martha his now wife, and Margaret Sammes, his servant, since June 1652 (Md. Land Office, Liber A. B. H., folio 348). On 6 June 1663, Samuel Chew assigns to Sarah Marsh any rights that remain upon record "due to my father-in-law William Ayres" (*ibid.*, Liber V, folios 338, 339), and there is upon record at Portsmouth, Va., a power of attorney from " Samuel Chew, Esq., of Herrington, Anne Arundel County, Maryland, and Anne his wife sole daughter and heiress of Mr. William Ayres late of Nansemond County, Virginia, deceased " (Va. Mag., I. 197).

Mrs. Anne Chew survived her husband and died 13 April 1695. She was a prominent member of the Society of Friends, and their monthly meetings were long held at her house on Herring Bay. Col. Samuel and Anne (Ayres) Chew had issue as follows:

3.   I. SAMUEL³ CHEW, born *circa* 1660, died 10 October 1718 (*of whom later*).

4.   II. JOSEPH³ CHEW, born *circa* 1662/5, died 1 February 1704/5 (*of whom later*).

     III. Nathaniel³ Chew, died after 20 February 1695/6. He inherited "Poppinjay," 500 acres, in Calvert County, Md.

5.   IV. WILLIAM³ CHEW, died 28 February 1709/10 (*of whom later*).

6.   V. BENJAMIN³ CHEW, born 12 April 1671, died 3 March 1699/1700 (*of whom later*).

     VI. John³ Chew, died 17 February 1696/7.

     VII. Caleb³ Chew, died 8 May 1698. He was in his nonage in 1695.

    VIII. Sarah³ Chew, died 1740; married Captain Edward Burgess.

     IX. Anne³ Chew, died 28 January 1699/1700.

3. SAMUEL³ CHEW (*Samuel², John¹*) was born, about 1660, in Maryland and died 10 October 1718 in Anne Arundel County. By the terms of his father's will he inherited the home plantation " Herrington," on Herring Bay, and 300 acres called " Chew's Right," on Poplar Ridge. In his will dated 16 July and proved 31 October 1718 (Annapolis, Liber 14, folio 669), he is styled " merchant." His " landed estate," in addition to the tracts mentioned above, comprised " Ayres " (600 acres) at Herring Bay; " Wells," " Wells Hills," " West Wells " and " Little Wells " which he and Nehemiah Birckhead bought of George Wells; also, 318 acres bought of James Heath, being parts of " Burrage," " Burrage Blossom " and " Burrage's End "; and a parcel of land which he bought of Nathaniel Rigbie.

He married (1), 14 April 1682, Anne ——, who died 8 April 1702, and had issue (*infra*). He married (2), 29 June

1704, Elizabeth (—) Coale, widow of William Coale. She died 27 February 1709/10, *sine prole*. By his first wife Anne, Samuel Chew had issue as follows:

7.   I. SAMUEL[4] CHEW, born 28 May 1683, died 31 October 1736 (*of whom later*).

      II. Ann[4] Chew, born 2 July 1685, died 24 January 1694/5.

8.   III. JOHN[4] CHEW, born 8 April 1687, died 1718 (*of whom later*).

      IV. Joseph[4] Chew, born 1 April 1689, died young.

      V. Benjamin[4] Chew, born 1 April 1689, died 18 April 1698.

9.   VI. NATHANIEL[4] CHEW, born 5 August 1692, died 30 January 1727/8 (*of whom later*).

10.   VII. JOSEPH[4] CHEW, born 28 April 1696, died February 1754 (*of whom later*).

4. JOSEPH[3] CHEW (*Samuel[2], John[1]*) was born about 1662/5 and died 1 February 1704/5 in Anne Arundel County, Maryland. By the terms of his father's will he inherited a tract of 450 acres of land called " Sanetley." In Joseph Chew's will, proved 7 June 1705, the testator mentions his " son-in-law " (*i. e.*, stepson) Samuel Battee. He married (1), 17 November 1685, Mary Smith. He married (2), *ante* 1690, Mrs. Elizabeth (Hanslap) Battee [8] who was born about 1670 and died in 1716. She was one of the daughters of Henry Hanslap (died 1698) of Anne Arundel County. The will of Mrs. Elizabeth Chew, widow, was dated 23 April and proved 27 May 1716 (Annapolis, Liber 14, folio 96). She mentions her sons Samuel Battee, Joseph Chew and Henry Chew, who inherit the residue of her estate; her grandsons Joseph and Henry Chew; her granddaughter Elizabeth Chew; and her sister Susannah Gassaway. Her " brother " (*i. e.*, brother-in-law) Thomas Gassaway was appointed executor of the will, which requests that the testatrix be buried in Herring Creek graveyard.

Joseph and Elizabeth (Hanslap) Chew had issue as follows:

11.   I. JOSEPH[4] CHEW, born 1689 (*of whom later*).

12.   II. HENRY[4] CHEW, born 1693 (*of whom later*).

---

[8] "The Thomas Book " and other authorities err in giving her maiden surname as " Gassaway."

5. WILLIAM³ CHEW (*Samuel², John¹*) died 28 February 1709/10 in Anne Arundel County, Maryland. By the terms of his father's will he inherited a lot of ground in the town of Herrington.

He married, 20 December 1690, Sydney Wynn, daughter of Thomas and Martha Wynn of Pennsylvania, and had issue as follows:

13. I. BENJAMIN⁴ CHEW, born about 1700, died 1762 (*of whom later*).

II. SYDNEY⁴ CHEW, married Charles Pierpont (died 1748).

6. BENJAMIN³ CHEW (*Samuel², John¹*) was born 13 February 1670/1 and died 3 March 1699/1700. He married, 8 December 1692, Elizabeth Benson (born 1677), daughter of John and Elizabeth (Smith) Benson of Calvert County, Maryland. She married (2), 24 September 1702, Richard Bond of Calvert County, and died in 1725.

Benjamin and Elizabeth (Benson) Chew had issue as follows:

14. I. SAMUEL⁴ CHEW, born 30 October 1693 and died 16 June 1743 (*of whom later*).

II. Elizabeth⁴ Chew, born 13 March 1694/5, died 9 February 1726/7; married 22 December 1710 Kensey Johns (1689-1729).

III. Ann⁴ Chew, born 14 October 1696.

IV. Mary⁴ Chew, born in December 1698.

7. SAMUEL⁴ CHEW (*Samuel³, Samuel², John¹*) was born 28 May 1683 and died 31 October 1736 in Anne Arundel County, Maryland. He was a merchant, engaged in commerce and registered his own sailing vessels. He left to his three surviving sons the tracts "Ayres," "Carter Bennett," "Chew's Fortune," "Upper Bennett" and "Abington Manor."

He married, 26 August 1703, Mary Harrison, daughter of Richard and Elizabeth (Smith) Harrison, who was born 10 October 1684 and died 24 August 1725; and by her had issue as follows:

15. I. SAMUEL⁵ CHEW, born *circa* 1704, died 15 January 1736/7 (*of whom later*).

II. Ann⁵ Chew, died 1777; married, 11 August 1724, Philip Thomas (1694-1762), son of Samuel and Mary Thomas.

    III. Elizabeth[5] Chew, born 18 October 1709, died 29 July 1719.

    IV. John[5] Chew, born 19 September 1711, died 21 March 1726/7.

    V. Mary[5] Chew, born 1714, died 10 August 1770; married John Hepbourne.

16. VI. RICHARD[5] CHEW, born May 1716, died 24 June 1769 (*of whom later*).

    VII. Francis[5] Chew, died 24 May 1720.

17. VIII. FRANCIS[5] CHEW, born 1721, died 11 November 1775 (*of whom later*).

    IX. Elizabeth[5] Chew, born 11 June 1725, died 25 June 1726.

8. JOHN[4] CHEW (*Samuel[3], Samuel[2], John[1]*) was born 8 April 1687 and died in 1718 in Anne Arundel County, Maryland. He is styled " merchant," in the records.

John Chew is spoken of as deceased in the will of his father Samuel Chew dated 16 July 1718. His widow however did not take up the administration of his estate until November of that year, when she as administratrix filed a bond, bearing date of November 4th, in the amount of £3000 sterling (*Test. Proc.,* Annapolis, Liber 23, folio 257).

He married, in 1708, Elizabeth Harrison, who was a daughter of Richard and Elizabeth (Smith) Harrison, and a sister of Mary Harrison, the wife of John Chew's brother Samuel Chew. Mrs. Elizabeth Chew survived her husband and married, in 1722, Elihu Hall (*Friends* Records).

John and Elizabeth (Harrison) Chew had issue as follows:

18.   I. SAMUEL[5] CHEW, born *circa* 1709, died 1749 (*of whom later*).

    II. Anne[5] Chew, born *circa* 1711, married 17 August 1727 Joseph Hopkins (1706-1784), a Quaker, and moved to Harford County, Maryland.

    III. Sarah[5] Chew, married, 5 October 1732, Charles Worthington (1701-1774) of Harford County, Md.

    IV. Mary[5] Chew, died 1779; married, 11 October 1736, Peregrine Ward (1709-1759) of Cecil County, Md. This marriage was performed in Baltimore County, but is recorded in the register of St. Stephen's Parish, Cecil County. The marriage was evidently an elopement, since the bride's family were Quakers. The officiating clergyman was the Rev. Stephen Wilkinson, rector of Spesutia Church, St. George's Parish, Baltimore (now Harford) County.

9. NATHANIEL[4] CHEW (*Samuel[3], Samuel[2], John[1]*) was born 5 August 1692 and died 30 January 1727/8 in Anne Arundel

County, Maryland. In his will dated 12 January and proved 21 February 1728 he mentions his brother Samuel Chew, Sr., and Samuel Chew of " Maidstone."

He married Mary —— (died 24 August 1728), and had issue as follows:

    I. Nathaniel⁶ Chew.
   II. Joseph⁵ Chew.
  III. Ann⁵ Chew.

10. JOSEPH⁴ CHEW (*Samuel³, Samuel², John¹*) was born 28 April 1696 and died February 1754. He married Sarah —— and had issue as follows:

    I. Thomas⁵ Chew.
   II. Elizabeth⁵ Chew.
  III. Susannah⁵ Chew.

11. JOSEPH⁴ CHEW (*Joseph³, Samuel², John¹*) was born, about 1689, in Maryland and died, after 1756, in Virginia. By the terms of his father's will, proved 7 June 1705 in Anne Arundel County, Maryland, he inherited (subject to an entail) the tracts of land called " Yarrow " (500 acres) and " Yarrow Head " (500 acres), lying on the north side of the Potomac River in Prince George's County; " Sanetley " (450 acres), and " Chew's Meadows " on the west side of the Patuxent (*Rent Rolls,* Calvert and Prince George's counties). After his second marriage, and before 1756, he moved to Virginia and lived at Alexandria.

He married (1), 23 January 1710, Mary Ford and (2) Mrs. Mercy (——) Mauduit, who survived him and died, about 1775, in Virginia. By his first wife, Joseph Chew had issue as follows:

19.   I. JOSEPH⁵ CHEW (*of whom later*).
    II. John⁵ Chew, born 1713 in Anne Arundel County, Maryland. He married, moved to Virginia, and had issue as follows:
        (a) John⁶ Chew, of Loudoun County, Va.
        (b) Roger⁶ Chew, of Alexandria, Va.
   III. Henry⁵ Chew.
   IV. Samuel⁵ Chew.
   V. Elizabeth⁵ Chew, married Richard Weightman.

12. HENRY⁴ CHEW (*Joseph³, Samuel², John¹*) was born in 1693, and moved to Calvert County, Maryland. By the terms of his father's will he inherited (subject to entail) the tracts of land called "The Perches" and "Arches Meadows" in Calvert County, Maryland. He was ancestor of the Harford County Chews.

He married Elizabeth —— and had issue as follows:

    I. Henry⁵ Chew, moved to Calvert County.
20. II. JOSEPH⁵ CHEW, born 24 August 1719 (*of whom later*).

13. BENJAMIN⁴ CHEW (*William³, Samuel², John¹*) was born about 1700 and died in 1762. He moved to Cecil County, Maryland, before 1737; was appointed a Justice of the Peace, took the oath of office and served from 1743 to 1762 (Md. Com. Book, pages 60-148). He was disowned by the Nottingham Friends Meeting in October 1755. His will was dated June 1761 and proved 4 January 1763.

He married, in January 1726/7, Sarah Bond (died 1769) and had issue as follows:

21.   I. BENJAMIN⁵ CHEW (*of whom later*).
    II. Sarah⁵ Chew.
    III. Phinehas⁵ Chew, living in 1768.
    IV. Mary⁵ Chew, married, 29 July 1765, Thomas Elliott of Cecil County, Md.
    V. Ann⁵ Chew, married, 27 November 1768, Isaac Van Bibber of Cecil County, Md.
    VI. Henrietta⁵ Chew, married (1), in 1772, Samuel C. Davey; married (2), in 1783, John James.

14. SAMUEL⁴ CHEW (*Benjamin³, Samuel², John¹*) was born 30 October 1693 and died 16 June 1743. He was styled Samuel Chew "of Maidstone," a tract of land lying on the west side of Herring Creek Bay near Annapolis, Md., and was also known as Dr. Samuel Chew. He moved before 1740 to Dover, Delaware, and was appointed in 1741 Chief Justice of "the three lower counties"—Newcastle, Sussex and Kent—then belonging to Pennsylvania (Keith's "Provincial Councillors of Pennsylvania," page 325).

He married (1), 22 October 1715, Mary Galloway (1697-

1734), daughter of Samuel and Anne (Webb) Galloway, and had issue as follows:

  I. Sarah⁵ Chew, born 23 July 1716, died February 1717.
  II. Ann⁵ Chew, born 4 January 1719, died 2 October 1723.
  III. Elizabeth⁵ Chew, born 25 November 1720; married in 1749 Edward Tilghman (born 1713).
22. IV. BENJAMIN⁵ CHEW, born 29 November 1722, died 20 January 1810 (*of whom later*).
  V. Ann⁵ Chew, born 13 April 1725; married *circa* 1745 Samuel Galloway (died 1785).
  VI. Mary⁵ Chew, born 27 June 1727, died 28 May 1728.
  VII. Samuel⁵ Chew, born 29 April 1728, died 29 June 1729.
  VIII. Samuel⁵ Chew, born 3 August 1730, died 3 November 1730.
  IX. Henrietta⁵ Chew, born 17 March 1732, died June 1732.

He married (2), 29 September 1736, Mrs. Mary (Paca) Galloway, daughter of Aquila Paca, and had issue as follows:

  X. Samuel⁵ Chew, born 24 August 1737, died 25 May 1809; married Anna Maria Frisby, daughter of Peregrine Frisby, and died at Chestertown, Md., *sine prole*. He was a Judge of the Supreme Court for the three lower counties of Delaware, and Judge of Oyer and Terminer in 1773.
  XI. Mary⁵ Chew, born 6 September 1739, died 1 May 1740.
  XII. John⁵ Chew, born 21 March 1740, died 15 December 1807 at Chestertown, Md., unmarried.

15. SAMUEL⁵ CHEW (*Samuel⁴, Samuel³, Samuel², John¹*) was born about 1704 and died 15 January 1736/7 in Anne Arundel County, Maryland. He was styled Samuel Chew, "gentleman," in the records. In his will dated 13 January and proved 3 March 1736/7 at Annapolis, Md., he mentions "my kinsman Benjamin Chew of Cecil County."

He married, about 1727, Henrietta Maria Lloyd (daughter of Philemon Lloyd), who married (2), in 1740, Daniel Dulany, Sr. (1686-1753) and died 10 December 1765; by whom he had issue as follows:

23. I. SAMUEL⁶ CHEW, died in 1786 (*of whom later*).
  II. Henrietta Maria⁶ Chew, born in 1731 and died 17 May 1762; married, 18 February 1748, Edward Dorsey (died 1760).
  III. Philemon Llyod⁶ Chew, died 17 March 1770 *sine prole*.
  IV. Bennett⁶ Chew, married, in January 1763, Anna Maria Tilgh-

man (daughter of Edward). He died in Baltimore, having had issue Edward Chew, who died *sine prole.*

V. Margaret⁶ Chew, married, 13 October 1751, John Beale Bordley (1727-1804).

VI. Ann Mary⁶ Chew, died 15 January 1774; maried, 26 May 1763, William Paca (1740-1799), a signer of the Declaration of Independence, from Maryland, and later a Governor of the State.

16. RICHARD⁵ CHEW (*Samuel⁴, Samuel³, Samuel², John¹*) was born 16 May 1716 and died 24 June 1769 at Herring Bay, Anne Arundel County, Maryland.

He married, 5 January 1749/50, Mrs. Sarah (Lock) Chew (1721-1791), widow of his cousin Samuel Chew (died 1749), and daughter of William Lock (1679-1732).

Richard and Sarah (Lock) Chew had issue as follows:

    I. Mary⁶ Chew, born 27 December 1750, died 23 November 1793; married (1), 10 February 1767, Alexander Hamilton Smith, married (2) —— Lyles.

24. II. RICHARD⁶ CHEW, born 10 April 1753, died 6 June 1801 (*of whom later*).

    III. Samuel⁶ Chew, born 9 December 1755, died 1 February 1785, unmarried.

    IV. Lock⁶ Chew, born 14 November 1757, died 9 December 1793, *sine prole.*

    V. Francis⁶ Chew, born 10 July 1760.

    VI. Sarah Lock⁶ Chew, born 20 November 1761; married 1789 Nathan Lane.

25. VII. PHILEMON LLOYD⁶ CHEW, born 23 July 1765 (*of whom later*).

17. FRANCIS⁵ CHEW (*Samuel⁴, Samuel³, Samuel², John¹*) was born in 1721 and died 11 November 1775.

He married, 26 February 1749/50, Mary Lingan (died 1764) and had issue as follows:

    I. Samuel⁶ Chew, born 29 January 1755.

    II. Ann⁶ Chew, born 15 May 1759.

    III. Richard⁶ Chew, born 19 October 1761.

18. SAMUEL⁵ CHEW (*John⁴, Samuel³, Samuel², John¹*) was born about 1709, and died in 1749 in London. He married Sarah Lock (1721-1791), daughter of William and Sarah (Harrison) Lock. She married again, 5 January 1749/50, Richard Chew (1716-1769), a cousin of her first husband.

Samuel and Sarah (Lock) Chew had issue as follows:

26.   I. SAMUEL⁶ CHEW, born 1737, died 20 February 1790 (*of whom later*).

     II. John Lane⁶ Chew, married, in 1787, Mary Wilson and had John⁷ Chew, captain, U. S. N.

27. III. WILLIAM⁶ CHEW, born 1746, died 9 April 1801 (*of whom later*).

    IV. Elizabeth⁶ Chew, married (1) —— Smith; married (2) —— Sprigg.

19. JOSEPH⁵ CHEW (*Joseph⁴, Joseph³, Samuel², John ¹*) married . . . and had issue as follows:

    I. Nathaniel⁶ Chew, born 1748, died 22 December 1827 at West River, Anne Arundel County, *sine prole*.

28. II. JOHN⁶ CHEW, died *circa* 1815 (*of whom later*.)

20. JOSEPH⁵ CHEW (*Henry⁴, Joseph³, Samuel², John¹*) was born 24 August 1719 and died 22 January 1753. He moved to that portion of Baltimore County which is now Harford County, Maryland.

He married, in 1745, Sarah Sheredine, who was born 18 December 1726, died 7 January 1784; and had issue as follows:

    I. Elizabeth⁶ Chew, born 18 July 1747, died 25 September 1806; married, 24 November 1768, John Hopkins.

   II. Susan⁶ Chew, born 25 December 1749, died 15 December 1784; married, in 1780, Joseph Miller (born 1745), of Harford County, Md.

29. III. THOMAS SHEREDINE⁶ CHEW, born 8 June 1752 (*of whom later*).

21. BENJAMIN⁵ CHEW (*Benjamin⁴, William³, Samuel², John¹*) married 1 May 1750 Cassandra Johns, daughter of Richard and Ann Johns of Baltimore County, and had issue as follows:

30. I. NATHANIEL⁶ CHEW (*of whom later*).

22. BENJAMIN⁵ CHEW (*Samuel⁴, Benjamin³, Samuel², John¹*) was born 29 November 1722 at " Maidstone," Anne Arundel County, Maryland, and died 20 January 1810 at Philadelphia, Pennsylvania. He studied law at Philadelphia, went abroad in 1741 and entered the Middle Temple, Inns of Court, London. He returned to America after his father's death, was admitted to the bar in 1746 and began practice at Dover, Delaware (formerly under the jurisdiction of Pennsylvania). He moved to Philadelphia about 1754; and built his country seat, " Cliveden," on the Germantown road, in 1761.

He was a Commissioner of Boundaries for the three lower counties of Delaware in 1751; Speaker of the House from the same district in 1753-1758; Attorney General of Pennsylvania and member of the Provincial Council 1754-1769; Register General of Wills 1765-1776; Chief Justice of the Supreme Court of Pennsylvania 1774-1776; Judge and President of the High Court of Errors and Appeals 1791-1806 (Pa. Archives: Pa. Hist. Society Publications: Keith's " Provincial Councillors of Pennsylvania ").

He married (1), 13 June 1747, Mary Galloway (died 1755), daughter of John and Mary (Thomas) Galloway, and had issue as follows:

  I. Mary[6] Chew, born 10 March 1748, died 22 August 1794; married, 18 May 1768, Alexander Wilcocks (1741-1801).
 II. Anna Maria[6] Chew, born 27 November 1749, died in November 1812, unmarried.
III. Elizabeth[6] Chew, born 10 November 1751; married, 26 May 1774, Edward Tilghman (1750-1815).
 IV. Sarah[6] Chew, born 15 November 1753; married, 23 October 1786, John Galloway (of Samuel).
  V. Henrietta[6] Chew, born in September 1755, died 1756.

He married (2), 12 September 1757, Elizabeth Oswald (1732-1819), daughter James Oswald, and had issue:

31.   VI. BENJAMIN[6] CHEW, born 30 September 1758, died 30 April 1844 (of whom later).
 VII. Margaret[6] Chew, born 16 December 1760, died 29 May 1824; married 18 May 1787 Col. John Eager Howard (1752-1827).
VIII. Joseph[6] Chew, born 9 March 1763, died in September 1764.
 IX. Juliana[6] Chew, born 8 April 1765; married, 1 April 1793, Philip Nicklin.
  X. Henrietta[6] Chew, born 15 September 1767, died 8 March 1848, unmarried.
 XI. Sophia[6] Chew, born 13 November 1769; married, in 1796, Henry Philips (1767-1800) of Philadelphia.
XII. Maria[6] Chew, born 22 December 1771, died 27 March 1840, unmarried.

XIII. Harriet[6] Chew, born 22 October 1775, died 8 April 1861; married, 17 July 1800, Charles Carroll of "Homewood," Md.

XIV. Catherine[6] Chew, born 3 May 1779, died 28 May 1831, unmarried.

23. SAMUEL[6] CHEW (*Samuel[5], Samuel[4], Samuel[3], Samuel[2], John[1]*) was born in Anne Arundel County, Maryland, and died in 1786. He was styled Samuel Chew "of Herring Bay." By the terms of his father's will he inherited the tract called " Ayres " and other parcels of land. In 1785 he purchased from the heirs of William Brent, of Virginia, " Kent Fort Manor " on Kent Island, Maryland, which he left to his wife Elizabeth Chew for life, with remainder to his son Samuel Lloyd Chew. In 1787 the Manor, which contained 2005 acres, was divided and the southern moiety deeded by Samuel Lloyd Chew to his mother. In 1787-1789, the property was mortgaged to Charles Carroll of Carrolton, but the mortgage seems to have been paid off later (*Md. Hist. Mag.,* VI. 254; Deed Records of Queen Anne's County, 27 June 1797). Samuel Chew also owned " Chew's Farm," a manorial estate in the southern part of Washington County, Maryland.

Samuel Chew married, about 1750/5, Elizabeth Crowley (1729-1807), who was born in Maryland and died at Sodus Point, Wayne County, New York. According to the records of St. James Parish, Herring Creek, Anne Arundel County, Maryland, they had issue as follows:

I. Samuel Lloyd[7] Chew, born 6 September 1756, died in 1796; married, 1 July 1777, Dorothy Harrison, who was born 17 February 1758, of Richard and Rachel Harrison, and died 6 November 1791. Issue:

a. Samuel A.[8] Chew.

b. Bennett[8] Chew.

c. Henrietta Maria[8] Chew, married Henry C. Schnebly of Washington County, Md.

d. Elizabeth[8] Chew, married (1) William Deery; married (2) Eli Beatty of Washington County, Md.

II. Henrietta Maria[7] Chew, born 21 March 1759, died 21 April 1847; married, 5 September 1775, Benjamin Galloway (1754-1831), and moved to Washington County, Md.

III. Elizabeth[7] Chew, born in 1765, died 4 June 1854; married, 11 December 1781, Peregrine Fitzhugh (1759-1810). Both died at Sodus Point, Wayne County, New York.

24. RICHARD[6] CHEW (*Richard[5], Samuel[4], Samuel[3], Samuel[2], John[1]*) was born 10 April 1753 and died 6 June 1801. He was a Captain and afterward a Major in the Maryland Line (*Md. Arch.*, XII. 323).

He married (1), 4 February 1773, Margaret Mackall (1754-1779), daughter of James John Mackall, and had issue as follows:

    I. Richard[7] Chew, born 4 October 1773, died 20 June 1831; married, 20 December 1804, Elizabeth Hollyday (of Leonard).

    II. Mary Mackall[7] Chew, born 17 September 1776; married, in 1815, John Brengman of Kentucky.

He married (2), 2 May 1780, Frances Holland (died 26 September 1799), daughter of Thomas Holland of Calvert County, Md., and had issue as follows:

    III. Thomas Holland[7] Chew, born 27 October 1781, died 16 March 1840; married (1) Elizabeth Smith (d. 1825); married (2) Mary Davis (d. 1829).

    IV. William Holland[7] Chew, born 7 August 1784, died 11 September 1799.

    V. Sarah[7] Chew, born 16 March 1787, died 28 December 1790.

    VI. Philemon[7] Chew, born 20 February 1789, died 30 September 1850; married, 21 February 1813, Ann Maria Bowie Brookes (1789-1862).

    VII. Sarah Lock[7] Chew, born 28 April 1791, died young.

    VIII. Frances[7] Chew, born 19 April 1793.

    IX. Bettie Holland[7] Chew, born 19 September 1795, died 19 September 1797.

    X. Samuel Lock[7] Chew, born 29 July 1797, died 12 February 1798.

    XI. Bettie Holland[7] Chew, born 15 May 1799, died 18 October 1800.

25. PHILEMON LLOYD[6] CHEW (*Richard[5], Samuel[4], Samuel[3], Samuel[2], John[1]*) was born 23 July 1765. He married, 28 October 1790, Ann Bowie (1767-1827), daughter of William Bowie of Prince George's County, Md., and had issue:

    I. Margaret Bowie[7] Chew, born 17 September 1791; married, 14 May 1816 (*lic.*), Richard Ireland Jones.

    II. Eliza[7] Chew, born 14 January 1793.

    III. William Bowie[7] Chew, born 27 September 1794.

    IV. Richard[7] Chew, born 6 February 1796.

    V. Robert Bowie[7] Chew, born 21 February 1797.

    VI. Samuel[7] Chew, born 18 September 1798.

VII. Walter Bowie[7] Chew, born 29 November 1799.
VIII. Henry Mortimer[7] Chew, born 17 March 1801; married, 15 January 1833, Eliza Ann Haw.
IX. John[7] Chew, born 14 August 1802, died 23 August 1802.
X. Sarah Maria[7] Chew, born 9 December 1803.
XI. Ann Maria[7] Chew, born 19 October 1806.

26. SAMUEL[6] CHEW (*Samuel[5], John[4], Samuel[3], Samuel[2], John[1]*) was born in 1737 and died 20 February 1790. He was styled Samuel Chew " of Wells." He was a delegate to the Maryland Conventions of 1774-1775 and a member of the Association of Freemen of Maryland (Scharf's " History of Maryland," II. 184; *Md. Arch.*).

He married (1), 3 February 1763, Sarah Weems (died 1763), daughter of James Weems, and had issue as follows:

I. Samuel[7] Chew, born 1763, died about 1820. He moved to Kentucky in 1805; was married twice.

He married (2) Priscilla Claggett, daughter of the Rev. Samuel and Mrs. Elizabeth (Gantt) Claggett, and had issue as follows:

II. John Hamilton[7] Chew, born 14 September 1771, died 22 March 1830; married (a cousin) Priscilla Elizabeth Claggett (d. 1843), daughter of the Rt. Rev. Thomas John Claggett of Maryland, first P. E. Bishop in the United States, and had issue.
III. Thomas John[7] Chew, died 1797; married, 14 November 1793, Margaret C. Johns, *sine prole*. She married later, Colonel Washington Bowie.

27. WILLIAM[6] CHEW (*Samuel[5], John[4], Samuel[3], Samuel[2], John[1]*) was born in 1746 and died 9 September 1801. He married, in 1768, Elizabeth Reynolds (died 1801), daughter of Thomas Reynolds, and had issue as follows:

I. Sarah[7] Chew, born 11 July 1770, died 10 September 1843; married (1) in 1787 Allen Bowie, (2) Frisby Freeland, (3) Beverly R. Grayson.
II. Elizabeth[7] Chew, born 26 April 1772, died in June 1828; married —— Moseby, of Kentucky.
III. Francis Holland[7] Chew, born 12 December 1774, died 24 August 1834; married —— Calvit, of Mississippi.

    IV. Mary[7] Chew, born 4 June 1776, died 1 May 1821; married Thomas Reynolds, of Mississippi.

    V. William Lock[7] Chew, born 10 April 1778, died 17 July 1858; married, 22 October 1805, Rebecca Freeland (1785-1840).

    VI. Ann Reynolds[7] Chew, born 19 July 1780; married ―― Craig, of Kentucky.

28. JOHN[6] CHEW (*Joseph[5], Joseph[4], Joseph[3], Samuel[2], John[1]*) died about 1815 in Prince George's County, Maryland. He married . . . and had issue as follows:

    I. Robert[7] Chew, born 1777, died in 1837; married Tabitha Wilson and had issue.

    II. Nathaniel[7] Chew, born 1785, died in 1845; married, in 1814, Martha Bird and had issue.

    III. Walter[7] Chew, married Mrs. ―― (Jones) Cobb and had issue.

    IV. John[7] Chew, died unmarried.

    V. Ann[7] Chew.

    VI. Elizabeth[7] Chew.

    VII. Artridge[7] Chew.

    VIII. Agnes[7] Chew, married Hanson Clark, of Montgomery County, Maryland.

29. THOMAS SHEREDINE[6] CHEW (*Joseph[5], Henry[4], Joseph[3], Samuel[2], John[1]*) was born 8 June 1752 and died 15 February 1821. He married about 1790 Elizabeth Morgan, born 1 November 1772, daughter of William and Cassandra Morgan, and had issue as follows:

    I. William Morgan[7] Chew, born 14 July 1791; married, 12 February 1814, Anne Webster Richardson and had issue.

    II. Thomas[7] Chew, graduated M. D. in Baltimore; moved to Mississippi and died unmarried.

    III. Sarah[7] Chew, born 1 December 1792, died 13 November 1821; married, 11 April 1809, Samuel Worthington (died 1853).

    IV. Cassandra Morgan[7] Chew, born 12 November 1796, died 20 August 1844 unmarried.

    V. Edward Morgan[7] Chew, died 16 May 1878; married (1) Margaret Hopkins and (2) Caroline F. Hall, *sine prole*.

    VI. Eliza[7] Chew, married John W. Hopkins, son of Samuel and Rachel Hopkins, and had issue.

    VII. Margaret[7] Chew, died in 1865; married, in 1837, Isaac Wilson and had issue.

30. NATHANIEL[6] CHEW (*Benjamin[5], Benjamin[4], William[3], Samuel[2], John[1]*) was born, after 1750, and died 22 May 1827, in Maryland. He was a midshipman in the Continental Navy, Revolutionary War, and became a Captain. He lived in Cecil County, Maryland.

He married, 24 November 1793, Margaret Rodgers, daughter of Colonel John Rodgers, and had issue as follows:

I. John[7] Chew.
II. Benjamin Franklin[7] Chew.
III. Washington Pinkney[7] Chew, died 7 April 1850; married, 4 January 1831, Mary Hall (died 1838). He married (2), 10 Nov. 1840, Mary C. Boyd.
IV. Emeline R.[7] Chew.
V. Henrietta Mary[7] Chew, married, 18 November 1841, Dr. John J. Boyd of Harford County, Md.
VI. Elizabeth Ann[7] Chew.

31. BENJAMIN[6] CHEW (*Benjamin[5], Samuel[4], Benjamin[3], Samuel[2], John[1]*) was born 30 September 1758 and died 30 April 1844. He was admitted to the bar of Philadelphia, Pa., in 1786.

He married, 11 December 1788, Katherine Banning (1770-1855) and had issue as follows:

I. Samuel[7] Chew, born 8 December 1789, died 21 March 1795.
II. Eliza[7] Chew, born 4 May 1791, died 21 March 1795.
III. Benjamin[7] Chew, born 5 December 1793, died 17 August 1864; married, 11 July 1816, Margaret Elizabeth Tilghman (died 1817).
IV. Samuel[7] Chew, born 19 June 1795, died 21 August 1841. Admitted to the bar of Philadelphia 1816. Died unmarried.
V. John[7] Chew, born 23 January 1797, died in August 1815. Midshipman, U. S. N. Lost at sea.
VI. Eliza Margaretta[7] Chew, born 19 November 1798, died 11 February 1874; married, 25 July 1822, James Murray Mason.
VII. Henry Banning[7] Chew, born 11 December 1800, died 12 December 1866; married (1), 14 May 1822, Harriet Ridgely (1802-1835); married (2), 20 March 1839, Elizabeth Ann Ralston of Philadelphia (*sine prole*).
VIII. William White[7] Chew, born 12 April 1803, died 12 November 1851. Sec'y. of American Legation to Russia.
IX. Ann Sophia Penn[7] Chew, born 18 March 1805, died 9 May 1892, unmarried.
X. Joseph Turner[7] Chew, born 12 December 1806, died in 1835.
XI. Anthony Banning[7] Chew, born 24 January 1809, died in February 1854.

XII. Catherine Maria[7] Chew, born 12 May 1811, buried 26 October 1811.

XIII. Oswald[7] Chew, born 23 May 1813, died 8 June 1824. Drowned while bathing in the Schuylkill River.

NOTE.—The compiler is indebted to Messrs. Louis H. Dielman and F. Sidney Hayward for the use of their valuable and extensive gleanings, from the files of old newspapers, in the matter of marriage and death notices.

FAMILIES OF CHURCHILL, CROKER, FOX, COPLE-STONE, BONVILE, ELLICOTT, ETC., OF DEVON-SHIRE, ENGLAND, AND SOME OF THEIR DESCENDANTS IN AMERICA:

THE ELLICOTTS OF BUCKS COUNTY, PENNSYLVANIA, AND MARYLAND, EVANS OF BUFFALO, N. Y., CHAMPLINE OF WHEELING, CURTIS OF MOUNDSVILLE, FISHER AND FOX OF PHILADELPHIA.

Compiled by WILLIAM M. ELLICOTT.

Gitto de Lion, a noble of Normandy, living A. D. 1055, had issue two sons, Richard de Lion, Lord of Montalban, and Wandril de Lion, Lord of Courcil, from whom is descended the family of Churchill.

He married Isabel de Tuya, and by her had Roger de Courcil and Rowland (ancestor of the Courcils of Picton).

" Roger de Courcil, being of those who accompanied William, Duke of Normandy, in his invasion of this realm, A. D. 1066, had, in reward of his services, divers lands in Somersetshire, Dorsetshire and Devonshire (as appears by Domesday Book), among which was the Lordship of Churchill, in the County of Somerset, the place of his abode and from which he took his surname, being written in the old records Curichil, Cheuchill, Chirchil, etc."

He married Gertrude, daughter of Sir Guy de Torbay, and by her had—John de Chirchil, who married Joan de Kilrington, and by her had Sir Bartholomew de Chirchil who held the castle of Bristol for King Stephen.

He married Agnes, daughter of Sir Ralph FitzRalph, Lord of Tiverton, Devon, and had Pagan de Cherchill, who also left a son—Roger de Cherchill, living in the time of Edward I. His Son was Elias de Cherchelle. He married Dorothy, daughter of the ancient family of the Columbers, and by her had three sons; viz:

(1) John Churchill, married Joan Dwaney, leaving Margaret, and Agnes married to Thomas Gifford upon whom the Lordship of Churchill and other lands devolved.

(2) Giles Churchill, who held the lordship of Yealmpton and Lineham, Co., Devon, and had one daughter Agnes Churchill, who married Sir John Croker (of Crokeren Hele) and carried these estates to his family.

(3) William Churchill, from whom the family of the Dukes of Marlborough spring through eight generations to Sir Winston Churchill, born 1620.

(Taken from *Collins Peerage,* edition of 1810.)

The family of Croker, or Crocker, was one of the most ancient in Devonshire, being undoubtedly one of the old Saxon families. Prince, in his Worthies of Devon remarks, " There is a tradition in this county of three eminent families, that they were settled here before the Conquest, according to the old saw often used in discourse,—

" Crockers, Crewys and Coplestone,
When the Conquerer came, were at home."

He also says that in his time, the heir of this family, Courtnay Croker of Lineham, who died 1740, had told him, " that, when travelling in Saxony, he met some gentlemen of his name, and that they gave the same coat of arms as he doth, a plain argument that originally they came out of that country " This, however, is a trifle naif, in view of the fact that the first recorded ancestor, William Croker, dwelt at Crokeren Hele in 1308 and this place-name, together with Crokeren Tor on Dartmore and Crokeren well near Crediton, would seem to carry them back to the period of the drift of the Saxons into Devonshire as early as the 7th, or 8th century, long before there were any arms in use anywhere in Europe.

However, we find that, after three hundred and forty years, the male line of Churchill of Lineham became extinct and that Sir John Croker, of Hele, married the heiress, Agnes, daughter

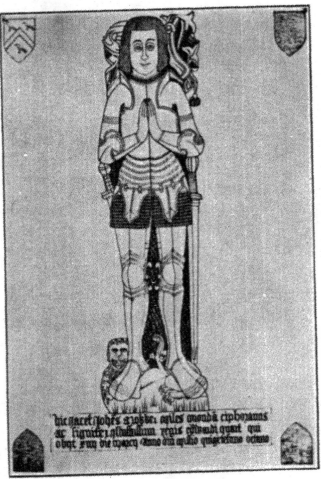

BRASS IN YEALMPTON CHURCH NEAR LINEHAM. EFFIGY OF
SIR JOHN CROKER (CROKKER), DIED 1508.

MANOR HOUSE OF THE LINEHAM ESTATE NEAR PLYMOUTH, DEVONSHIRE, BUILT BY COURTNAY CROKER, ESQ'R, EARLY IN THE NINTH [...]

of Giles Churchill, and thereafter resided at Lineham, a place of nearly three thousand acres which is occupied now by the descendants of James Bulteel, of Flete, who married, Mary, the heiress of Courtnay Croker Esq'r in the first half of the 18th century. It is occupied today by Mrs. W. E. P. Bastard and her daughters, the Misses Bulteel, the twenty-sixth generation of the blood living on the place, descended also from the Earls Grey.

The present house of which we show a photograph, is designed in the Georgian style, having been built by Courtnay Croker, but it stands on the cellar and foundations of an earlier house in the Tudor style, while there are dependencies which are clearly in the style of Queen Ann.

Among the attractions of Lineham are: several hundred acres of well stocked game preserves, three miles of trout fishing in the Yealm river, a lesser trout stream, hunting with the Dartmoor Hounds which are kept at Ivy Bridge, with the Modbury Harriers and with the Otter Hounds.

To return to William Croker of Crokern Hele (OE for Hold or Stronghold): his son, William, of Hele, tempus Edward III, had a son, Sir John Croker who married Agnes Churchill. Their son, Sir John Croker of Lineham, c. 1396, married the heiress of Corim, who brought him the estate of Hamerdon.

Their son, Sir John Croker, of Lineham and Hemerdon, married the heiress of Dawnay. He distinguished himself for his bravery at the battle of Agincourt under King Henry V. Their son was Sir John Croker of Lineham, and Yealmpton died May 8th, 1508, married to Elizabeth, daughter of Robert Yeo, of Heaton Sackville. The illustration here shown is taken from the *Brass* which is in the church at Yealmpton and was formerly attached to his tomb, since destroyed. He was cupbearer and standard bearer to Edward IV, and accompanied him into France and was honored by King Louis XI.

Prince, in his Worthies of Devonshire, says: " As to Sir John Croker, what brought him first into favor at Court, whether courage and skill at arms, or readyness of address, or what else, I do not find, but he became so gracious with king Edward IV, that he was admitted a sworn servant in the honourable office of Cupbearer, who, "in remuneratione servitii" gave him a cup d'or, having in the centre a rose p. p. r. for the crest unto his coat armour, and, moreover bestowed upon him the honour of knighthood. The crest was further augmented in 1475, by Louis XI, of France, with three fleurs de lys."

"The tomb of Sir John Croker, with his effigy in brass, is in the parish church of Yealmpton—a few miles from Plymouth—with the following inscription: "Hic Jacet Johannes Crokker, miles, quondam Ciphoramis ac Signifer illustrissime regis, Edwardi Quarti, qui obit Maii Viii, anno Domini, Millissimo quinquigessimo octavo.""

In 1497 he went to the defense of the city of Exeter against Perkin Warbeck, the imposter, represented to be the son of Edward IV, murdered in the Tower by order of Richard, Duke of Gloucester some years before.

Then came Sir John Croker of Lineham, son of the above and Elizabeth Yeo. He was the High Sheriff of the County, tempus, Henry VIII, and married to Elizabeth, daughter of Sir Lewis Pollard of Roborrow, Devon; whose son was John Croker, married to Elizabeth Strode, daughter of Richard Strode of Newnham, Devon; whose son, John Croker of Lineham, married Agnes, daughter and co-heiress of John Servington, of Tavistock.

Their eldest son, Hugh Croker of Lineham, *circa* 1580, married Agnes, daughter and co-heiress of John Bonvile, of Ivy Bridge, descended from Sir Nicholas Bonvile, of Wiscombe, Devonshire, and his son Sir William, who by his wife Joan, had issued Nicholas, who married Matilda, daughter and co-heir of Sir Thomas Pine, of Shute; of the same family as Sir Adrian du Pin, one of the knights of the Round Table of king Arthur's foundation, of the year of our Lord, 520,—says Prince; a persistent tradition in Devonshire.

Shute is a great estate near Axminster, about which there is much romance. It has given many knights to the crusades and to the wars of England. The gateway, with three towers and of two stories, and the ancient manor house, are in the Tudor style, while the house occupied by the de la Pole family, who now own it, is a large one farther within the park, in the Georgian style. The Bonviles settled at Wiscombe, reign Henry III and paid a rent of 22 Shillings to the Abbots of St. Michels in Normandy. Sir William Bonvile of Shute married Alice . . . and had issue John Bonvile married to Elizabeth, daughter of John Fitz Roger, whose son William Bonvile of Chewton (born at Shute) was knighted before 1447 while with the army in France. He was sheriff of Devon, 1443 and Seneschal of Aquitaine, 1442, 1448. He was summoned to Parliament as Willelmo Bonville, Domine Bonville de Chewton.

King Henry VI, was taken prisoner at the battle of Northampton, 1460, and was put in the custody of Lord Bonvile; but at the second battle of St. Albans, 1461, the Lancastrians were victorious and he was taken and beheaded. His son and grandson had been killed at the battle of Wakefield, and his great grand-daughter, Cicely, became his heiress. She married Sir Thomas Grey, created Marques of Dorset, whose mother was Elizabeth Woodville, whose first husband, Sir John Grey, was killed at St. Albans and she afterwards became the queen of Edward IV. However, William, Lord Bonvile, had by Elizabeth Kirkby, a natural son, John Bonvile, on whom he had settled the estate of Ivy Bridge near Yealmpton; whose name, after four generations, expired in a daughter and heiress, married to Hugh Croker of Lineham. (Prince's *Worthies of Devon*).

The descent from Hugh Croker and Agnes Bonvile is as follows:

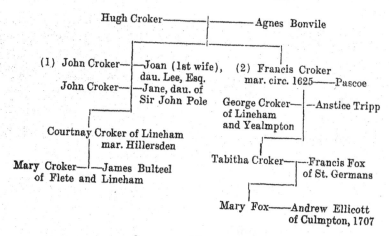

STRODE—FORTESCUE.

John Strode, of Strode, by his wife, Jane, daughter of Burleigh, of Clenacomb, had issue, Richard who married Margaret, daughter of Henry Fortescue, of Wood, and it was their descendant who married John Croker, son of Sir John Croker, tempus Henry VIII.

This family and the Earls of Fortescue are descended from Sir John Fortescue, Captain of Meaux, a famous soldier under king Henry V; and from Sir Richard le Forte, who, after the battle of Hastings, was called Fort Escu, because in the battle, he had defended the Conqueror with his *strong shield*.

POLLARD—COPLESTONE.

Walter Pollard of Horwood lived in the time of Henry III and after several generations, to John Pollard who married Eleanor, daughter of John Coplestone of Coplestone—whose son Robert had a son Lewis, 1465-1540, whose daughter Elizabeth married Sir John Croker of Lineham. Of the Coplestones Prince says, " When this family first grew into eminence I do not find. It was eclipsed as most of the Saxon families were, a long while by the interposition of the Norman Conqueror." They appear in the reign of King Edward II in which William de Coplestone and Richard Coplestone are set down as witnesses to a deed. Which Richard had issue Adam, who had issue John, who, by his wife, daughter of John Graas, of Ting Graas, had issue, John Coplestone, of Coplestone, who by Elizabeth his wife, had a daughter, Eleanor, married to John Pollard, Esq'r of Horwood. " They were wont to be styled Coplestone, the " White Spur." This office was made by creation of the King, the ceremony whereof was thus: What gentleman the king was pleased to bestow this honor upon, he was wont to put about his neck a silver collar of SSSS—and to confer upon him a pair of silver spurs. Whereupon, in the west part of the kingdom, they were called the White Spurs, by which they were distinguished from knights, who were wont to wear guilt spurs, the title being hereditary and belonging to the heir male of the family.

Fox of St. Germans.

Burke, in his History of the Commoners states, that " the numerous families of Fox at present residing in the west of England sprang from one common ancestor, a Francis Fox, who married, in 1646, Dorothy Kekewich. Tradition represents him to have come from Wiltshire, from the parish of Farley, or that of Pitton, somewhere in 1645, during the commotions of the Civil War, and he is stated to have been descended from the same family as the celebrated Sir Stephen Fox, ancestor of the Earls of Ilchester and Lords Holland. Dorothy Kekewich was of a noted family of Exeter, whose house at Catchfrench near Liskeard, became their residence on first settling in Cornwall." At the present moment, the head of the family is Sir Trehawke Kekewich, Baronet and in Exeter Cathedral there is a monument to General Robert George Kekewich, Defender of Kimberly and leader of the Devon troops in the Boer War. The family seat is at Peamore, four miles from Exeter.

The son of Francis Fox and Dorothy Kekewich was Francis Fox (2) who married Tabitha Croker, daughter of George Croker of Lineham, Esq'r. and whose daughter was Mary Fox who married Andrew Ellicott of Culmpton, 1707. The family of Fox have been distinguished for their scientific and humanitarian activities. Some of them shared in the sufferings of Friends, who were persecuted over a considerable period. One member of the family, Mr. Joseph Fox, surgeon, of Plymouth, in 1778, having a third interest in two vessels at the time war broke out between France and England, disapproved strongly of his partners determination to arm them as privateers to prey on French commerce. Nor would he sell his interest to his partners. As privateers the ships were very successful and Mr. Fox, having exacted his share, made a protracted search for all the French owners who had suffered through the activities of the vessels, and paid each one his share of the losses, so far as they could be ascertained.

Another member of the family of Fox discovered kaolin in Cornwall, the basis of a flourishing industry in the manufacture of porcelain. Robert Were Fox, on the occasion of a visit to his cousins in the United States in 1794, was introduced to President Washington by Andrew Ellicott, and was appointed United States Consul at Falmouth, Cornwall, which office was held after him by his son and grandson.

Mr. Barclay Fox of Grove Hill and Penjerricks, Falmouth Cornwall, is the present head of the family. His landed estate is a very considerable one. The Estate of Penjerricks, many years ago, was developed as an arboretum and on it one finds rare specimens of shrubs and trees from Tasmania, New Zealand, the United States, and other places. Huge tree ferns are placed together with Sequoia Gigantia, the "big trees" of California, and the Rhodadendrons of half a dozen climes are shown in company with our native variety of the Appalachian mountains.

ELLICOTT OF DEVONSHIRE AND MARYLAND.

The difficulties surrounding an examination into the origins of this name are so great that it is unlikely that much light will ever be shed upon it beyond the early part of the seventeenth century when the record of the American Ellicotts begins.

The Right Reverend Charles John Ellicott, late Bishop of Gloucester and Bristol, Chairman of the Committee for the Revision of the New Testament, whose Gothic monument may be seen in Gloucester Cathedral; and of whom it is said that out of four hundred meetings of the committee, he attended three hundred and ninety-eight,—is authority for the statement that the Ellicotts were a clan in south west England and that there is a church back of Dartmore where may be found numbers of mediaeval brasses of the name, possibly at Bratton-Clovelly. The name is a biblical one in origin, being derived from Elias, the prophet, a very popular saint in the middle ages when the adoption of surnames became common. The ending, -cott, is nothing more than a "diminutive," as is the -ot in Eliot, found in French and English. The two names are interchangeable, and one finds the son or daughter of an Ellicott given as Elliott, or vice versa, in church records of marriages or baptisms.

Thomas Elyat of Exeter, in the sixteenth century, left a house with a beautiful mullioned front running through three stories to the Church, and a Bishop of Exeter, when he built a library at the Palace, removed it bodily and attached it to his new building.

Elyat is, of course, one of the many modifications of the original name of Elicot or Eliot, as found in the Harlean MSS.

The Earls of St. Germans (Cornwall) are Eliots, and some of their monuments may be seen at the chapel of the great house.

This family flourished, says Burke, for several generations in Devonshire before its removal to Cornwall. John Eliot an ancestor, married Joan, daughter of John Bonvile of Shute.

Sir John Eliot of Port Eliot, in Cornwall, M. P. and knight, committed to the Tower for "undutiful speeches"—and afterward because he was one of the managers of the impeachment of the Duke of Buckingham,—is singled out by John Foster, the constitutional historian, as "the most illustrious confessor of the cause of liberty of the time of Charles I." He died a prisoner in the Tower of London. From him the Barons and Earls of St. Germans are descended.

The secretary of the Devon and Cornwall Record Society writes that the church records at Culmpton of the seventeenth century, having been destroyed, it is, so far, impossible to link the Ellicotts of that place with the Exeter family which rose to a position of prominence about 1590, when Henrie Ellacott and his son, George, were successively Governors of the Merchants Venturers Guild and Sheriffs of the city, though they had investments in Culmpton and the period would seem to indicate it.

Their arms are given in the Herald's Visitation of 1620: Lozengy, Or and Azure, a Bordure Gules, while to the Ellicotts of Culmpton has been tscribed, by the author of the Families of Fox, Ellicott and Evans, by Mr. Charles W. Evans of Buffalo, N. Y., the same shield, except that Sable takes the place of Azure. The crest of the Culmpton family, is given as an oak tree, with the motto: Sto Super Vias Antiquas. This may have been an earlier arms, locally used, and those confirmed to the Ellacotts of Exon in 1620, with a " difference," replacing sable with azure, just as the spelling of the name is slightly changed by the use of an *a* to take the place of *i* in the correct manner. This spelling, however, was not recognized by the Herald.

Thus we begin with the research of Dr. R. Hingston Fox, of London, made in 1911. He finds the Ellicotts in the valleys of the Exe, the Clist and the Culm in the sixteenth and seventeenth centuries under various spellings, and in the Culm valley they were generally engaged in the manufacture of cloth and allied industries.

The will of John Ellicot of Culmpton was probated in 1677 and lists considerable property in houses, goods and money. Robert Ellicot, the brother, was a merchant and was born about the year 1615. They were both sons of an earlier Robert. He was one of the earliest Friends and showed great zeal for his faith and the protection and encouragement of his fellows in his religion at a time when this entailed severe and repeated persecutions.

The Friends had rediscovered " passive resistance " and, wherever they were at this period, the jails swarmed with them.

Under Charles II, Robert Ellicot spent several months in prison until he was released under the king's proclamation.

He opened his house for worship regularly during the hottest persecution under the Conventicle Act, and for marriages, of which there were several certificates dated at his house. He suffered the distraint of his goods for his steadfast adherence to liberty of worship, besides further imprisonment under the later acts of Parliament. The "Sufferings of Friends" give numerous instances of persistant opposition to the abuses, judicial and otherwise, of a time to which we look back with something less than pride.

The harshness of the law of those days is indicated by the fact that there were on the statutes at least one hundred minor offences for which a child, a woman or a man might be executed; and the maimings, the filthy prisons with their barbarous administration were a by word among those who were cognizant of their abuse. The Westminster Review in an article in 1869 has to say: "Without derogating from the high stand maintained by other bodies of Discenters, we think there is not one among them who will not yield the palm to the ' persistant Quakers' as the foremost champions of civil and religious liberty." Robert Ellicot survived his wife Mary nearly fifty years and died in 1712 at 97 years of age. He leaves his house in Culmpton to his daughter and her husband, Thomas Lake, during their lives and afterward to his son Andrew, who had taken up the cloth making industry. Andrew's name is found among those of Friends imprisoned in Exeter goal, in 1683. He married, in 1677 Elizabeth Hodge, of Zealmanacord parish. It was his eldest son Andrew who married Mary Fox, daughter of Francis Fox (2) of St. Germans, whose mother was Tabitha Croker, daughter of George Croker Esq'r of Lineham and Plymouth. This Andrew Ellicott emigrated to Bucks County, Penna., in 1730 in company with his son Andrew who became the progenitor of the Ellicotts of Bucks County, Penna., and of Maryland. He married Ann Bye, daughter of Nathaniel Bye of Buckingham, of an influential family of landowners, but the succeeding generation had a hard struggle since they were orphaned when their father died in 1741. Their mother married George Wall, an Englishman, by whom she had a son, George Wall, Jr., who attained to position as a man of scientific knowledge, a member of the American Philosophical Society and "Colonel-Lieutenant" of Bucks County. He was interested with the Ellicotts in the foundation of Ellicotts Mills in Maryland.

Andrew Ellicott and Ann Bye had five sons, Joseph, Andrew, Nathaniel, Thomas and John. In recompense to a benefactor, Samuel Armitage, who seems to have stood in the place of guardian in their early youth, they persuaded him to build a mill (they had all been trained in mechanical occupations which gave them a mastery over mechanical problems and an outlet for their undoubted genius in this department of knowledge). Mr. Armitage afterward acknowledged his indebtedness, saying that the "Ellicott boys" had made him comfortable for life.

Joseph Ellicott, the eldest, born 1732, married Judith, daughter of Samuel Bleaker and Sarah, his wife. In 1766, he sailed from Philadelphia in the ship "Hibernia" to visit England and to receive his greatgrandfather's estate in Culmpton, which amounted to the substantial sum of 1500 pounds Sterling. He visited his relatives, the Foxes in Plymouth and in St. Germans and found them "both agreeable and learned."

In July 1757, he sailed by the "Charming Rachel" for Philadelphia, requiring fifty two days for the voyage. He was High Sheriff of Bucks County, Penna., in 1768-9. He rose to eminence in the arts and sciences, particularly in the art of clock making and mechanical pursuits, and was the companion of Rittenhouse and Franklin. His musical clock is still famous. It has four faces, records the movement of the celestial bodies, the hours, minutes and seconds, and the years, for one century. It also plays twenty-nine tunes of pre-Revolutionary times.

His descendants are numerous and the most famous of the American Ellicotts was his eldest son, Andrew, of West Point

Military Academy, variously known as the Astronomer and the Surveyor. In the Philadelphia Directory and Register of 1794, he is listed as the Geographer General of the United States. He had two other sons, Joseph and Benjamin, who established the Holland Land Company whose holdings bounded on lakes Erie and Ontario, and the Niagara River and covered what are now eight counties of the state of New York. Their headquarters were at Batavia where there are interesting relics, and both Joseph and Benjamin became rich men; but being bachelors, their wealth descended to the children of Andrew, the Astronomer, and other relatives.

Andrew led an exceedingly active and useful life. He was Major of the Elkridge Company. He surveyed parts of the boundaries of several of the original states, including that between Canada and the United States near the Niagara river, and the southern boundary of New York. He and David Rittenhouse continued the Mason and Dixon line, from a point near Cumberland, Md., west, to the south-west corner of Pennsylvania, and then ran the west line north to Lake Erie. He surveyed the boundaries of the District of Columbia, assisting Major Pierre l'Enfant by running lines for his plan of the city of Washington, and later, on the recommendation of President Washington, replaced l'Enfant in planning the city. He has left as a memorial to his work, a Journal covering the four years from 1796 to 1800, when he was engaged in the survey of the boundary between the Spanish and American possessions, now the northern boundary of Florida; an intensely interesting story of how the Spanish king, in spite of the new treaty, gave secret instructions to his representatives to frustrate the running of the boundary line, and how his patience, prudence and good will triumphed and averted hostilities with the Indians who were secretly set upon the small party in the swamps and rivers along the route. He died at the end of his service as the first professor of mathematics at the West Point Military Academy, in 1828.

Andrew and Ann Bye Ellicott had a son, Andrew, who married (1) Elizabeth Brown and by her had eight children, the eldest being Jonathan, born 1756.

He married (2) Esther Brown, a cousin of Elizabeth, and had by her six children, among them Thomas, born 1777, father of William M. Ellicott of Montrose, Md.

Jonathan married Sarah 'Harvey, whose daughter Letitia married Thomas R. Fisher of Philadelphia in 1829, whose ancestor left numerous descendants and had large grants of land from the Penns. From this marriage are descended the Fisher connection of Wakefield, the Carpenters of Germantown and the Foxs of Wakefield and Foxburg, Pennsylvania.

Ellicott's Mills (now Ellicott City) was founded in 1772 by Andrew and John Ellicott, sons of Andrew and Ann (Bye) Elicott. They studied their problem thoroughly and had found a convenient and adequate water power adjacent to a rich farming country where they were to be the first to introduce wheat growing, the Maryland planters having confined themselves almost exclusively to tobacco raising for shipment to Europe. They effected an arrangement with Charles Carroll of Carrollton by which he was to plant a large acreage in wheat and they were to build a road from the mills to his estate at Doughoregan Manor. Flour was also shipped from Elkridge Landing and merchandise brought from England on the return voyage.

During the period of the Revolution the Ellicotts barely sustained themselves, but with peace in 1783, prosperity was resumed and, what with improvements in the mills, wharves in Baltimore with extensive warehouses and a wider market, the fortunes of the family were established. Joseph, Andrew and John Ellicott transacted business as Ellicott and Company, and Ellicotts Mills took on the appearance of a business and social community. The Ellicott graveyard and the old Meeting House stand on a precipitate hill near the Washington road overlooking the gorge of the Patapsco, reminding one of Devonshire scenery, and in the graveyard are to be seen the graves of the founders and numerous others of the family. They intermarried with the well known Tyson family and were associated with them in business.

The Ellicotts had also iron mills and Thomas Ellicott, the son of Andrew Ellicott, was president of the Union Bank of Baltimore. John H. B. Latrobe the famous engineer and architect of the United States capitol, was one of his directors.

In his Life of Mr. Latrobe, the late John E. Semmes quotes him as follows: " By far the most remarkable person here was the late Thomas Ellicott, a man of rare qualities, of extraordinary intelligence, and as fit to command an army as to determine questions of bank policy. His physique was remarkable. He must have been six feet four inches; a great, thin, broad-shouldered person with a massive square brow, shadowing deep sunk eyes that lit up a face whose complection was a pale, unhealthy one, with a stern determination. A heavy jaw and tightly compressed lips made firmness and iron will the characteristics of his countenance.

" His stride was corresponding to his height; and strangers turned as he passed to look at the commanding person of Thomas Ellicott.

" Eleven men were on the Board, but it was Mr. Ellicott's will that swayed their actions. He was born in 1777 and died in 1859.

" There were few men that the late Roger B. Taney had more regard for than Mr. Ellicott."

However, prior to 1837, a combination was formed against Thomas Ellicott, and fortune turned against the Ellicotts of this line.

Thomas Ellicott married Mary Miller, daughter of William and Ann Emlin Miller of Avondale, Chester County, Pennsylvania. The Avondale grant from William Penn had been one of 12,000 acres. Mary Miller inherited large farms and a house in the Dutch Colonial style built in 1731, where the family subsequently resided. Their son, William Miller Ellicott, born in 1807, married Sarah Cresson Poultney of Baltimore, daughter of Thomas and Ann Poultney. In our day when cultural matters have, to some extent, been obscured by material expansion, the following note set in the back of a heavy gold watch of the period, made by J. Tobias of Liverpool, is interesting: " My father gave me this watch as a reward for translating the New Testament from Greek and writing it out in English; which I did, beginning the same 1st. mo. 30th 1821 and ending it 9th mo. 9th 1822. This manuscript is among my father's papers at Avondale, Chester Co., Penna. (dated) 5/5/1829. W. M. Ellicott."

The manuscript, too, is carefully preserved, together with a card given him by his loving instructors, the Sulpician Fathers at St. Mary's Seminary, for diligent study and good deportment. He had sufficient command of the Greek language at the age of fourteen years to undertake this translation!

Of the eight daughters of Thomas Ellicott, Elizabeth married James S. Pike, of Calais, Maine, in 1855. He was the Washington Correspondent of the New York Tribune, was given a position in the South in reconstruction days, which he resigned to write a denunciatory book about the abuses in the south. He had been made U. S. Minister to Holland by President Lincoln.

William M. Ellicott and Sarah Poultney Ellicott, of Montrose, Baltimore, Co., Md., had issue, Thomas, William, Lindley, David, Lewis and Mary. Thomas married Caroline Allen and had issue: Thomas, Francis A., Susan, Sarah P., William, Rachel and Nancy P.

The second son, William M. Ellicott, Jr., married in Philadelphia 1860, Nancy Morris Ellis, daughter of Charles and Mary Luke (Morris) Ellis, who was grand-daughter of Captain Samuel Morris of Revolutionary fame.

The Murrays of Rockburn and Eubank, Howard County, Md., are descended from this family, also, through the marriage of Anthony Morris with his second wife Elizabeth Hudson in 1752. Dr. Thomas Morris Murray, born at Rockburn 1851, married 1900, Eleanor Vinton Clark. They reside at their place, Gwyn Careg, at Pomfret, Conn., and at Boston, Mass. The Chestons of West River, Maryland, are also descended from Anthony Morris. Samuel Morris, son of Anthony Morris by his first wife Sarah Powel, was born at Philadelphia 1734; died 1812. He was descended from Anthony Morris (2), of London, the immigrant, whose family became active in the affairs of the colony of Pennsylvania, sometimes in opposition to the Penns, and which produced several members of the Provincial Assembly and two colonial mayors of Philadelphia, and were otherwise distinguished. At the beginning of the Revolution he was appointed Captain of the First Troop, Philadelphia Light Horse, the famous " City Troop " of our time, and commanded it throughout the war, being present at the battles of Princeton, Brandywine, Monmouth and German-town. During the terrible winter of 1777 at Valley Forge they were present and serving as Life Guards to General Washington. In the memorial chapel at that historic place there is a memorial to him with his likeness, after St. Memin, carved in the oak of the choir stalls. The site of the camp is shown near the headquarters of General Washington. Morris was a member of the Committee of Safety, the Council of Safety, the Provincial Assembly, the General Assembly, the Committee of Grievances and the Navy Board. He was also Governor of the " State in Schuylkill " or Fish House Club, the oldest social club in the country; and Master of the Gloucester Fox Hounds, now the Rose Tree Hunt, each for periods of forty-five years. It is interesting to note that his descendant, Major Effingham B. Morris, Jr., who distinguished himself at the capture of Mont Fauçon in the Great War by the American forces, is the present commander of the City Troop.

The Morris House at 225 So. Eighth Street in Philadelphia is one of the few remaining houses of the Revolutionary period still in use by the same family and in its original condition and appearance. It is owned by Effingham B. Morris and is ocupied by his son, Major Effingham B. Morris, Jr., as his winter residence.

Samuel Morris married in St. Peter's Church, Philadelphia,

SAMUEL MORRIS OF PHILADELPHIA, DIED 1812.
AFTER ST. MEMIN.

1755, Rebecca Wistar, daughter of Caspar Wistar and sister of the Revolutionary surgeon, who figured notably at the battle of Germantown and for whom the flowering vine, Wistaria, is named.

One of his sons was Luke Morris, who married Ann Pancoast, whose daughter Mary Luke Morris married Charles Ellis of Philadelphia, the well known philanthropist, born 1800 and died 1874.

Charles Ellis was descended from Thomas Ellis, Gentleman of Merionethshire, Wales, who emigrated from Pembrokeshire to Philadelphia in 1680, after suffering persecution, indignities and imprisonment for conscience sake. He became Registrar General of the colony and a member of the committee of three who were appointed to govern it under William Penn. He was a man of wealth and made investments in property in Philadelphia and elsewhere in Pennsylvania.

Nancy Morris Ellis daughter of Charles Ellis (great grandson of Thomas Ellis) and Mary Luke Ellis, married William M. Ellicott, Jr., of Baltimore in 1860. Their children were, Charles Ellis Ellicott and William M. Ellicott, of Baltimore, and Mary M. E. Hess, Edith Ellicott Powers and Lydia E. Morris, of Philadelphia. Their descendants are numerous. The family occupied the homestead of the Ellis family in the Muncy Valley, Pennsylvania, near the west branch of the Susquehanna river, which was built about 1810, destroyed by the Iroquois Indians and rebuilt in 1812. William Ellis, father of Charles Ellis, married Mercy Cox, of Deer Creek, Md., whose mother was of the influential Goldhawk family having large estates near London. On the occasion of the incursion of the Iroquois, William Ellis rode many miles along the Susquehannah, in the direct path of its advance, to warn the inhabitants and to bring the women and children to the frontier fort at Muncy where he cared for them during this foray which caused such havoc in the new settlements.

Charles E. Ellicott of Baltimore and his wife, Madelene Le Moyne Ellicott have two son. C. Ellis Ellicott, Jr., who married

Anne, daughter of the Right Rev. John Gardner Murray, late Bishop of Maryland, and Dr. Valcoulon Le M. Ellicott, who married Mary, daughter of Clarendon I. T. Gould, a member of a well known Canadian family, residing in Baltimore. His brother William M. Ellicott (3rd) married; first Elizabeth Tabor King, daughter of Francis T. King, the philanthropist and financier; and, second, Anna Goldthwaite Campbell, daughter of Duncan G. Campbell, who was son of Mr. Justice John A. Campbell, of the U. S. Supreme Court, her mother being Ella Calvert, of Riversdale, descended from the Lords Baltimore of Woodcote, Surrey, England, Proprietors of the Palatinate of Maryland.

Other descendants of Thomas Ellicott and Mary Miller Ellicott of Avondale, Pa., and of their son William Miller Ellicott, of Montrose, Baltimore County, Md., are: the family of the late Mrs. Arthur Steuart, Mrs. Francis A. White, Mrs. C. Prevost Boyce, Colonel and Mrs. Walter Sturgill, U. S. A.; William H. Ellicott, the family of C. Lewis Ellicott and Lily Thompson Ellicott, his wife, and the late Major William M. Roberts, U. S. Army, whose widow and heir is Ella Prendergast Roberts, of Baltimore Co., Md.

NOTE: All the facts about the descendants of Andrew Ellicott and Ann Bye of Bucks county, Pennsylvania, may be found in the book of Mr. Charles W. Evans, Buffalo, N. Y., entitled, *The Biographical and Historical Account of the Families of Fox, Ellicott, Evans and Others.*

Other References: Prince's *Worthies of Devonshire;* Risdon; Vivian; Burke's *History of the Commoners;* Burke's *Peerage;* Joseph Foster, *Descendants of Francis Fox of St. Germans.* (Head, Hole & Co., London, 1872, Pub.); Collin's *Peerage,* edition of 1810; *Bank of Maryland Conspiracy,* by Thomas Ellicott, 1839; *Ancestry of Rosalie Morris Johnson,* by R. Winder Johnson (Ferris & Leach); *Andrew Ellicott, His Life and Letters,* C. van C. Mathews (The Grafton Press, New York.)

THE COHENS OF MARYLAND [1]

Aaron Baroway

The Cohen family of Baltimore has long been prominent in the annals of Maryland. Its records, which are in an admirable condition, comprise much more than lists of dates of births, deaths, and marriages. They contain, on the one hand, much which is of interest for the past of American Jewry and, on the other hand, data of value to students of Maryland history. They offer Jacob I. Cohen's noble Memorial [2] to the session of 1823-24 of the General Assembly of Maryland and Col. Mendes I. Cohen's account of the bombardment of Fort McHenry.[3] The family records narrate more than the arrival in Baltimore during the first decade of the nineteenth century of a widowed Jewess and her seven young children and the usual family events connected with them. These records inform us that

---

[180] On December 2, 1856, Jefferson Davis sent him Lecompte's address, as "Lecompton, Kansas Territory" and Pearce at once wrote him, receiving a reply promptly, which he sent Davis, who acknowledged it on January 4, before he had shown it to the President.

[1] Numerous members of the Cohen family have assisted in the preparation of this article. Miss Eleanor S. Cohen (57) furnished a great part of the materials utilized, and facilitated access to other sources. A large part of the information embodied in it was gathered by Professor David S. Blondheim, who made a preliminary draft of the family tree and assisted the writer in other respects as well. Professor Blondheim received valuable aid from the late Jacob I. Cohen (65), Miss Bertha Cohen (64), Mrs. Isaac Coale, Jr. (73), Mrs. Augusta MacMannus (26), Mr. Alan M. Cohen (74), Lieutenant Barney L. Meeden (52), Mr. Louis H. Dielman, Professors Alexander Marx and Jacob H. Hollander, Mrs. Julius Wolf, and Dr. Harry Friedenwald, among others.

[2] See Jacob I. Cohen (6), p. 366.

[3] See Mendes I. Cohen (10), p. 371.

these children and their descendants lived in accordance with the noblest traditions of their ancestors and that they became defenders of their city, financiers of large means and uncompromising integrity, leaders in the medical, legal and engineering professions, public servants of recognized importance, lovers of the arts, and leaders in Baltimore's society. Because the family records are becoming scattered—some have already been deposited in two distinct libraries [4]—the task of digesting their contents will become more and more difficult, and it is fitting, at a time when they are still well preserved and accessible, to present them to students of the history of Maryland.

1. MEYER COHEN.[5]

Born about 1700(?). Issue: Joshua Cohen (2).

The Cohen family is descended from Meyer Cohen, who lived in Oberdorf, near Nördlingen, in the district called the Riess, not far from Ansbach, Bavaria, in the early part of the eighteenth century. From the date of birth of his son, Joshua, we may assume that Meyer Cohen was born about 1700. He is known to family tradition as the Holy Rabbi. Benjamin I. Cohen (53) explained in a MS. note in the possession of Miss Eleanor S. Cohen (57), that he was given this title because of his great learning. According to family tradition, his Hebrew name with his Hebrew title was *Ha-Kadosh Rabbi Meïr*. In English " the Holy " is the equivalent of the Hebrew *Ha-Kadosh*. If the traditional explanation of the reason for the title is correct, it represents an exceptional use of the term, which is generally applied to Jews who gave up their lives for their faith. Neither family tradition nor available information about Oberdorf illuminates this obscurity.[6]

---

[4] The Cohen-Etting Papers are now in the library of the Jewish Theological Seminary of America, New York. A number of the papers of Mendes Cohen (60) are in the possession of the Maryland Historical Society.

[5] Each member of the family by birth has been given a number. The numbers precede the names in the genealogical table and in the subtitles, and follow the names in the body of the article.

[6] Ludwig Müller, *Aus fünf Jahrhunderten, Beiträge z. Gesch. d. jüd. Gemeinden im Riess* (Augsburg, 1900) (*Sonderabdruck aus d. Zeitschrift d. hist. Ver. f. Schwaben u. Neuburg*, 1899 u. 1900), records, p. 139, that

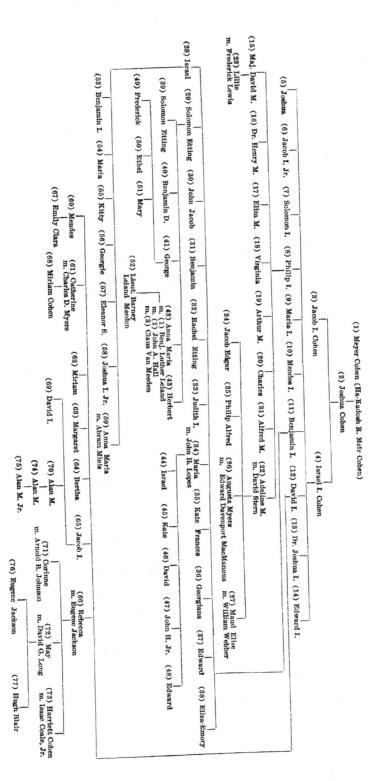

2. Joshua Cohen.

Born 1720. Died February 7, 1771. Son of Meyer Cohen. Married Peslah, the daughter of Jacob, who was born in 1723, and died August 26, 1797. Lived and lies buried at Oberdorf. Issue: Jacob I. Cohen (3) and Israel I. Cohen (4).

3. Jacob I. Cohen.[7]

Born January 2, 1744, at Oberdorf. Died October 9, 1823, at Philadelphia, Pa. Son of Joshua and Peslah Cohen. Married (1) in 1782 Elizabeth [Esther or Hester] Whitlock Mordecai (see *infra,* p. 361), who was born in 1744, and died August 22, 1804, at Richmond, Va., and (2) Rachel Jacobs, who died November 1, 1821, at Philadelphia, Pa. No issue.

Jacob I. Cohen immigrated to this country from his native land in 1773. For a short time he resided in Lancaster, Pa. From that city he removed to Charleston, S. C.[8] Shortly after his arrival in Charleston, Jacob I. Cohen enlisted in Captain Lushington's Company, which was part of the Charleston Regiment of Militia. He participated in the defense of Charleston, and was a member of the expedition to Beaufort in February 1779. That he was a member of Lushington's Company,[9] and

about 1723 there was a "Rabbinats-Substitut" in Oberdorf and, p. 180, that there were twenty-six Jewish families in Oberdorf in the same year. Was Meyer Cohen this "Rabbinats-Substitut" or vice-rabbi?

[7] According to family tradition, the *I.* which appears in the names of many members of the Cohen family, *e. g.,* Jacob I. Cohen (3) and Benjamin I. Cohen (53), was not an initial letter of a name. The letter *I.* was perhaps used to distinguish these Cohens from the many other descendants of Aaron with similar given names.

[8] Herbert T. Ezekiel and Gaston Lichtenstein, *History of the Jews of Richmond* (Richmond, 1917), p. 17. Undated excerpts from *Jewish Record,* Richmond, in possession of Mrs. Augusta MacMannus (26).

[9] Barnett A. Elzas, *The Jews of South Carolina* (Philadelphia, 1905), pp. 83-107, who apparently did not know of the existence of Captain Lushington's letters (see note 10), wrote, p. 84, that "we have no record of Jacob I. Cohen as a member of Lushington's Company." Now that Ezekiel and Lichtenstein, *op. cit.,* is available, Mr. Elzas should have no difficulty in identifying Isaiah Isaacs, the partner of Jacob I. Cohen in war as well as business.

was on the Beaufort expedition is determined beyond doubt by two letters from Lushington [10] in the possession of Miss Bertha Cohen (64) as well as by a statement [11] by Jacob I. Cohen committed to writing by his nephew, Dr. Joshua I. Cohen (13). [12] Prior to the end of the Revolution, [13] Jacob I. Cohen re-

---

[10] Leon Hühner, "Some Additional Notes of the History of the Jews of South Carolina," *Publications of the American Jewish Historical Society*, Vol. XIX (1910), p. 155:

"So. Carolina   April 6, 1779

"This certifies that Jacob I. Cohen enrol'd himself in my Company on his arrival from the Northward here, and has been with me a volunteer on ye Expedition to Beaufort and has in every respect conducted himself as a good soldier and man of courage.

Sig.   R. Lushington,
Captain of ye Chas Town Regt."

Ibid., p. 156:
"3d Compy.   Charlestown, South Carolina—January 11, 1779

"This certifies that Mr. Jacob I. Cohen is enrolled in the Company of the Charleston Regiment of Militia (called the *Free Citizens*) under my command.

Sig.   R. Lushington.
No. 1"

[11] *Ibid.*, p. 155, *et seq.* The first sheet of the statement bears the inscription: "This account given me by my uncle Mr. Jacob I. Cohen (above) from memory in his 87th year. June 7, 1822. Balto." Reference to Jacob I. Cohen's membership in Lushington's company is also made in Leon Hühner, "Jews of South Carolina from the Earliest Settlement to the End of the American Revolution," *Pub. Amer. Jew. Hist. Soc.*, Vol. XII (1904), p. 50; Max J. Kohler, "Incidents Illustrative of American Jewish Patriotism," *Pub. Amer. Jew. Hist. Soc.*, Vol. IV (1896), p. 96, quoting Dr. Isaac Leeser's article, *Occident*, Philadelphia, Vol. XVI (1858), p. 142; Ezekiel and Lichtenstein, *op. cit.*, p. 343 (note 23), quoting *Richmond Inquirer*, October 17, 1823, which, in turn, had copied from a recent issue of the *Philadelphia Daily Advertiser*.

[12] Our Jacob I. Cohen is not to be confused with one Jacob Cohen who raised a company of cavalry in Cumberland County, Virginia, during the Revolutionary War, and with another Jacob Cohen who appears as a prisoner on the prison ship *Torbay* in the Charleston harbor. Cf. Leon Hühner, "Jews of Virginia from the Earliest Times to the Close of the Eighteenth Century," *Pub. Amer. Jew. Hist. Soc.*, Vol. XX (1911), p. 96, *et seq.*; Ezekiel and Lichtenstein, *op. cit.*, p. 17; Elzas, *op. cit.*, pp. 83-107.

[13] From Ezekiel and Lichtenstein, *op. cit.*, p. 15, we may infer that he arrived in Richmond between May, 1780, and December 10, 1781.

moved to Richmond, Va., where he became associated in business with Isaiah Isaacs, who also had been a member of Lushington's company. Their partnership was very successful. Reference to them is found in a number of old records.[14] The dissolution agreement entered into by Cohen and Isaacs "was written in Hebrew script, and deposited with the other records."[15]

In 1782 Jacob I. Cohen married Elizabeth Whitlock Mordecai, widow of Moses Mordecai, who died in 1781. Elizabeth Whitlock had been born a Christian in England, and had embraced Judaism prior to her marriage to Moses Mordecai, by whom she had three sons. Upon her conversion to Judaism she adopted the Jewish name of Esther, sometimes written Hester. Because of her many good deeds she was beloved by the entire community.[16] She died August 22, 1804, and was buried at Richmond.[17]

During his residence in Richmond, Jacob I. Cohen was prominent in civic as well as in financial affairs. He is mentioned in official records as having served as a grandjuryman on November 11, 1793.[18] In 1794, he, John Marshall, and others were trustees of the Masonic Hall.[19] In January, 1795, he was elected a member of the Common Hall (City Council) to succeed Col. Bushrod Washington.[20] He was foreman of the grandjury in May, 1804.[21] By a provision in his will, the

[14] Ezekiel and Lichtenstein, *op. cit.*, p. 15.

[15] *Ibid.*, pp. 15 and 16.

[16] *Ibid.*, p. 18. Caroline Myers Cohen (37), *Records of the Myers, Hays and Mordecai Families*, printed privately (Washington, about 1913), pp. 25 and 26.

[17] Ezekiel and Lichtenstein, *op. cit.*, p. 18, quote tomb-stone inscription.

[18] *Ibid.*, p. 77.

[19] *Ibid.*, p. 19.

[20] *Ibid.*, p. 64, with the following quotation from the Hall record: "'It appearing that Mr. (Colonel) Bushrod Washington has moved out of the city . . . . the Hall proceeded to supply the vacancy . . . . a majority of votes was found in favor of Mr. Jacob I. Cohen, who appeared and qualified to his seat. . . .' Col. Washington was a nephew of General George Washington, who was then president."

[21] *Ibid.*, p. 80.

City of Richmond was to receive the proceeds from the sale of certain of his negroes who, after his death, might not want their freedom, and to distribute yearly in bread among the poor on the Fourth of July the income from the proceeds.[22] He was one of the trustees to whom Isaiah Isaacs deeded the Franklin Street (Richmond) Cemetery.[23]

Jacob I. Cohen lived in Philadelphia from about 1806 to the time of his death.[24] Presumably during this period, he married Rachel Jacobs, a daughter of Israel Jacobs, of Philadelphia. The esteem in which he was held by his fellow-Jews of Philadelphia is well attested by their election of him as *parnass* (president) of the Mickvéh Israel Congregation for the year 1810-1811 and their desire to have him serve as *parnass* in 1820-1821. He declined the last election.[25] He died October 9, 1823, in Philadelphia.[26]

4. ISRAEL I. COHEN.

Born April 8, 1751, at Oberdorf. Died July 29, 1803, at Richmond. Son of Joshua and Peslah Cohen. Married on December 21, 1787, Judith Solomon, who was born in 1766, and died April 5, 1837, at Baltimore. Issue: Joshua Cohen [the elder] (5), Jacob I. Cohen, Jr. (6), Solomon I. Cohen (7), Philip I. Cohen (8), Maria I. Cohen (9), Mendes I. Cohen (10), Benjamin I. Cohen (11), David I. Cohen (12), Joshua I. Cohen [the younger] (13), and Edward I. Cohen (14).

The exact date of Israel I. Cohen's immigration to this country is not known. It is certain that he was living in Virginia as early as 1784, for a court record shows that he and Joseph Darmstadt were naturalized on the 6th of December, 1784, at a court held for Henrico County.[27]

[22] *Ibid.*, pp. 331 and 332.
[23] *Ibid.*, p. 281.
[24] *Ibid.*, p. 19 and p. 343.
[25] Henry Samuel Morais, *Jews of Philadelphia* (Philadelphia, 1894), pp. 45 and 61.
[26] Ezekiel and Lichtenstein, *op. cit.*, pp. 330-335, with his will *in extenso*.
[27] *Ibid.*, p. 29.

Although information about Israel I. Cohen's communal life is not very abundant, there is ample evidence that he was a public-spirited citizen. He was one of eight citizens of Richmond who, on March 26, 1795, volunteered to serve as constables for three months and without remuneration for the purpose of preserving peace and order.[28]   Moreover, his name appears several times in the records of the Court of Hustings. On March 14, 1796,[29] he was a juryman.   The record for April 10, 1798, shows that one Solomon Raphael was ordered to deliver up a detained apprentice girl "to her master and Judith Cohen, wife of the said Israel I. Cohen."[30]   He was a signer of a petition to the President and the Directors of the Bank of the United States for the establishment of a branch in Richmond, and was a subscriber for shares in the Academy of Arts and Sciences of the United States of America, established in Richmond in 1786.[31]   He was also a trustee of the Franklin Street Cemetery.

While in Europe in 1787, Israel I. Cohen married in Bristol, England, on December 21, Judith Solomon, of that city. He returned with her to Richmond on September 21 (or 27), 1787.[32]   He died intestate[33] July 29, 1803, in Richmond, and was buried there in the Franklin Street Cemetery.[34]

Israel I. Cohen was also known as Asher Abraham (Cohen). To explain this situation, Benjamin I. Cohen (53) wrote:

"The reason why my Father is called Asher and my Great-grandfather Asher Abraham when they were really named Israel is this: My Great-grandfather fell sick unto death and in accordance with the custom in such cases a meeting of the con-

---

[28] *Ibid.*, p. 64.
[29] *Ibid.*, p. 77.
[30] *Ibid.*, p. 78.
[31] Samuel Oppenheim, "Jews and Masonry in the United States before 1810," *Pub. Amer. Jew. Hist. Soc.*, Vol. XIX (1910), p. 66.
[32] The dates of marriage and return to Richmond are given here as they are found in family records.
[33] Ezekiel and Lichtenstein, *op. cit.*, p. 80.
[34] *Ibid.*, p. 29, with copy of tomb-stone inscription.

gregation (*minyon*) was called in the *schule* [synagogue] and his name was changed to Asher Abraham. The family still knew him as Israel and my father was named after him. It was however thought advisable to call him as it is written in making the Hebrew record."

In 1808 Judith Cohen, Israel I. Cohen's widow, moved to Baltimore with seven children: Jacob I., Jr. (6), Philip I. (8), Maria I. (9), Mendes I. (10), Benjamin I. (11), David I. (12), and Joshua I. (13). "In this city the children received such educational advantages as the town afforded." [35] Judith Cohen died in Baltimore on April 5, 1837, and was buried in the family cemetery on West Saratoga Street, Baltimore.

5. Joshua Cohen.

Born June 28, 1788. Died September 12, 1788. Eldest son and child of Israel I. and Judith Cohen.

6. Jacob I. Cohen, Jr.

Born September 30, 1789, at Richmond. Died April 6, 1869, at Baltimore. Second son and child of Israel I. and Judith Cohen. Unmarried.

After their arrival in Baltimore, Jacob I. Cohen, Jr., and his brothers engaged in business. At first they were agents in the lottery and exchange system. [36] Their widely-known banking business was conducted under the name of Jacob I. Cohen, Jr. and Brothers. Their operations were extensive, and their reputation for successful and upright dealings gave their firm high standing. In 1831 they opened a banking house on Baltimore street East of Calvert street. In 1836 they erected a banking house on the Northeast corner of Baltimore and Calvert streets. It was of their firm that *The Sun* wrote: [37]

[35] " Mr. Mendes Cohen on ' the Cohen Collection of Egyptian Antiquities ' and Its Collector, Colonel Mendes I. Cohen," *Johns Hopkins University Circulars*, Vol. IV, no. 35 (Dec., 1884), p. 22.

[36] *Baltimore American*, April 9, 1869, p. 4.

[37] *The Sun*, Baltimore, May 17, 1837.

" The Messrs Cohen's of this city have not suspended specie payments. They say that they are abundantly able to redeem all their bills, and will do so. It must be a matter of felicitation to all good men, to find one Banking House avowing its ability to meet its obligations, and at the same time proving the truth of its avowal by its practice: The Banks of the North unite in swearing that they are safe and sound, possess abundance of means to pay with, but will not pay? Who will not either doubt their ability, or the truth of their avowals? One or the other must be doubted, there is no escaping it."

Jacob I. Cohen's name is frequently mentioned in connection with progressive enterprises of his time. He was actively interested in the Philadelphia, Wilmington and Baltimore Railroad Co. in its early days, and was a vice-president and director of that company for many years. He was a director of the Baltimore and Ohio Railroad Co. and president of the Baltimore Fire Insurance Co.[38]

It was largely due to the untiring energy of Jacob I. Cohen, Jr., that the Maryland Legislature finally confirmed the constitutional amendment whereby it became possible for Jews to hold office in Maryland. The Legislature had declined for many years to remove the disability, although they were urged without interruption by the more liberal-minded citizens of the state and the country to do so. Maryland was at that time the only state in the Union to debar Jews from holding state and municipal offices. From 1816 to 1826 Jacob I. Cohen, Jr., led the movement to relieve his fellow-Jews of their disqualification. He prepared the petitions and amendments which were presented at every session, and he maintained the fight until 1826, when his and his co-workers' efforts finally met with success.[39]

The plane on which he conducted these political activities

[38] *Baltimore American*, April 9, 1869, p. 4; *Jewish Encyclopedia*, IV, p. 144, *s. v. Cohen;* Ezekiel and Lichtenstein, *op. cit.*, p. 30.

[39] *Jewish Encyclopedia*, VIII, p. 360-361, art. *Maryland*. Isidor Blum, *The Jews of Baltimore: A Historical Sketch* in *Jews of Baltimore* (Baltimore, 1910), p. 7.

may be judged from a memorial which he prepared for presentation to the session of 1823-24 of the General Assembly of Maryland. This document, aptly characterized by Professor Hollander as "marked by singular loftiness of sentiment and dignity of tone," [40] is preserved among papers relating to the "Jew Bill" presented to the Maryland Historical Society by the late Mendes Cohen (60). It is as follows:

"To the Honorable the GENERAL ASSEMBLY OF MARYLAND.
"The Memorial of the subscribers, Citizens thereof,
"RESPECTFULLY REPRESENTS:

"Your Memorialists are of that class of the Citizens of Maryland, long subjected to the pressure of political disqualifications, by the operation of a religious test in the Constitution of the State; and they approach your Honorable Body with this their prayer, that an Act passed the 29th of January 1823 'to extend to all the citizens of Maryland the same civil rights and religious privileges that are enjoyed under the Constitution of the United States,' may be confirmed at the present session, becoming thereby part of the Constitution.

"Your Memorialists, feeling it incumbent on them at this stage of the proceeding, address themselves on the subject, to your Honorable body, in the honest confidence, which the American is educated to entertain in his fellow citizens, and in the legislative guardians of his rights. It is not their wish, to obtain from your honorable body, a grant of exclusive privilege; because such a privilege would be hostile, not only to the principles of our institutions, but to the express provisions of that charter which we have all alike, sworn to support: but it is equal rights which they petition; their voice is not raised in favor, but in opposition, to exclusive privilege; they ask an equality of rights with their fellow citizens. If the disqualifications under which they labor, were imposed as the penalty of law for civil delinquencies, for habits of social intemperance, or a disregard of the obligations of religion, they would blush to murmur; but it is, as they humbly apprehend, the

[40] *Jewish Encyclopedia*, VIII, p. 361b.

retribution for a too honest perseverance in conscientious faith, unmindful of political disqualifications, of social inconvenience, and of individual contumely: and this same manly and virtuous constancy, which, exerted in the cause of their Country, would entitle them to be honored as patriots, exposes them to proscription, when exercised in the service of the acknowledged God. They firmly flatter themselves, and have at length some reason to believe, that your enlightened Councils will suffer no longer, those strange anomalies to endure—that the period has arrived at last, when conscience and reason, the peculiar gifts of an Omnipotent benevolence, will be respected, and persecutions be abandoned to the Inquisitor and the Bigot. Are their doctrines immoral? They are the foundation of the general faith. Are they dangerous? It is no part of them to work conversions. Are they new? Ancient as the revelation of the Almighty truth. Your memorialists, with all humility, are at a loss to understand what there is so peculiarly exceptionable in these their tenets, as to have induced a solitary, but persevering departure, from the sublime system of our American political jurisprudence: why even at this moment, when the whole American pulse throbs with indignation, at the civil and religious proscriptions, renewed and asserted in the old world, the good people of Maryland alone, should find it necessary or expedient, to continue for a moment, the disqualification of any class of their fellow Citizens. Your Memorialists beg leave to remind your Honorable Body, that the honors of office in our happy Republic, are not assumed, but conferred; not usurped by guilty ambition, but bestowed directly or indirectly, by popular confidence; that to disqualify any class of your citizens, is for the people to disqualify themselves: can it be necessary, can it be wise or politic at this day, for the people to disqualify themselves on the score of opinion only, from consulting merit in the selection of their public servants?

"Your Memorialists do not here propose, a voluminous discussion of the great principles involved in the question, which they desire to bring before you; because it is one, as they apprehend, at this day, almost universally understood. It is the same which has agitated like a tempest, the human family from its earliest existence; has armed the hands of men in wide and desolating wars; has stained nations and families with intestine crime; trampled the charities of life; and driven societies from their natural homes, to seek an asylum more hospitable, on the billows of the deep or amid the recesses of the desert: a question which, as it mainly contributed to populate this our common Country, was here first and fully understood: and one, the liberal and happy results of whose true nature, our own Maryland, though too long misled upon the subject, evinced at the last session of her Legislature, and as your Memorialists trust, will again prove to the world on the present occasion, are deeply felt and thoroughly appreciated.

"America, instructed in the school of adversity and oppression, and warned by the calamities of nations, has attained the haven of political happiness, by the guide of political wisdom. Moderate in her might, she has never sought to find in power, the foundation of new rights, but metes out to the weak the same measure with the strong. It was reserved for her to discover, that true policy consists in Justice, which, whilst it secures the confidence and devotion of her own Sons, entitles her to the reciprocity of the stranger. Above all, America has been the first to respect opinion and the human mind, that mysterious and sacred relation of sublunary Man to Celestial Wisdom; nor has thought to controul the measureless elasticity of that principle, which created for exclusive allegiance to the Omnipotent alone, is beyond the reach of temporal restraints. America has wisely relinquished it to the insidious policy of regal governments, to make an instrument of religion: she has forever sundered the spiritual from the temporal concerns of men, and convinced mankind that disqualifications and persecution are only fruitful of disunion and hate;—toleration and equal rights, of good will and peace on earth.

"Your Memorialists humbly apprehend that a peculiar and most important crisis hath occurred in the political world, and in the history of man; and if in the eastern hemisphere, his struggles for civil and religious liberty, hitherto ineffectual, have been smothered in their birth, it is now particularly important that, successful throughout the west, no speck should endure upon the purity of that code, sublime in its nature, as in its origin, it is confessedly divine.

"As fellow citizens of Maryland, as Brethren of the same human family; for the honor of the State, for the great interests of humanity; your Memorialists humbly pray at your hands, that the Bill before you may be confirmed."

That there was no unwillingness to elect Jews to office was seen soon after the adoption of the amendment. In October, 1826, Jacob I. Cohen, Jr., and Solomon Etting were elected to membership in the First Branch of the City Council. Cohen represented the sixth ward. He was re-elected a number of times, and for some years (1845-51) he was president of his branch of the Council. He was elected to the First Branch from the eleventh ward in 1849 without distinction of party.[41] His work in the City Council was distinguished for his insistence upon economy and for his practice of holding public officers to strict accountability.

He participated actively in many undertakings. He was one of the founders of Baltimore's public school system. For the first nine years of its existence (1830-38) he was secretary and secretary-treasurer of the Board of Public School Commissioners.[42] He was one of the Commissioners of Finance of the City of Baltimore [43] and a member of the Ancient and Honorable Mechanical Company of Baltimore.[44] He called to order the immense "war meeting" in Monument Square, May 23, 1846, held for the purpose of passing, in the name of the citizens of Baltimore, resolutions referring to the Mexican War.[45]

Jacob I. Cohen, Jr., died April 6, 1869, and was buried in the family cemetery on West Saratoga street.

[41] Baltimore American, April 9, 1869, p. 4; Jewish Encyclopedia, IV, p. 44, s. v. Cohen; Ezekiel and Lichtenstein, op. cit., p. 30.

[42] Jewish Encyclopedia, IV, p. 144, s. v. Cohen; Blum, op. cit., p. 5.

[43] Blum, op. cit., p. 5.

[44] Jewish Encyclopedia, IV, p. 144, s. v. Cohen.

[45] J. Thomas Scharf, Chronicles of Baltimore (Baltimore, 1874), p. 516.

7. Solomon I. Cohen

Born 1791. Third son and child of Israel I. and Judith Cohen. He did not move to Baltimore. It seems that he continued to live in Richmond.[46]

8. Philip I. Cohen.

Born April 17, 1793,[47] at Richmond. Died September 30, 1852, at Norfolk. Fourth son and child of Israel I. and Judith Cohen. Married January 25, 1826, Augusta Myers, who was born December 28, 1797, at Norfolk, Va., and died April 26, 1876, at New York. Issue: David M. Cohen (15), Henry M. Cohen (16), Eliza M. Cohen (17), Virginia Cohen (18), Arthur M. Cohen (19), Charles Cohen (20), Alfred M. Cohen (21) and Adeline M. Stern (22).

When Philip I. Cohen was about eighteen years of age, the War of 1812 broke out. In 1814, he became a private in Captain Nicholson's Company of Baltimore Fencibles, and participated in the defense of Fort McHenry.[48] Later he moved to Norfolk, Va., where, on January 25, 1826, he married Augusta Myers, daughter of Moses Myers. At the time of his death in 1852, he was postmaster of Norfolk.[49] He is buried in the family cemetery in Baltimore. His wife, who survived him by twenty-five years, is also buried there.

9. Maria I. Cohen.

Born September 30, 1794, at Richmond. Died January 23, 1834, at Baltimore. Only daughter and fifth child of Israel I. and Judith Cohen. Unmarried. Buried in family cemetery at Baltimore. Also known as Miriam.

[46] Ezekiel and Lichtenstein, *op. cit.*, p. 87, note that on May 27, 1817, Solomon I. Cohen and Moses N. Cardoza were made administrators of the estate of Abraham N. Cardoza. Was this Solomon I. Cohen our No. 7?

[47] This date of birth is that found on Philip I. Cohen's tomb-stone. Family records give the Hebrew date of birth as Nisan, 26, 5553, which corresponds to April 8, 1793.

[48] William H. Marine, *British Invasion of Maryland, 1812-1815* (Baltimore, 1913), p. 249.

[49] Ezekiel and Lichtenstein, *op. cit.*, p. 30.

10. Col. Mendes I. Cohen.

Born May 25, 1796, at Richmond. Died May 7, 1879, at Baltimore. Fifth son and sixth child of Israel I. and Judith Cohen. Unmarried.

Mendes I. Cohen was eighteen years of age when, in 1814, he joined the Twenty-Seventh Regiment because he was under the impression that that regiment would be sent to defend Washington. Discovering that he was mistaken, he left the regiment, and joined Captain Nicholson's Fencibles, and was in Fort McHenry during the bombardment.[50] Many years later he narrated to Benjamin I. Cohen (53) his experiences in connection with the battle. Benjamin I. Cohen's record of them reads:

" Reminiscences of the Bombardment of Fort McHenry 'The Star Fort' in Sept., 1814. Narrated by Col. M. I. Cohen.

" Capt. Nicholson being a Judge of the Balto. Co. Ct. could not accept a command under the U. S. Govt. he was not therefore made a Captain without a commission & his Company, known as Nicholson's Artillery Fencibles, consisted entirely of volunteers. They never enlisted individually but offered their services to the Govt. in a body. They were accepted & stationed in the Star Fort, (now Ft. McHenry). On account of the peculiar nature of their service they drew no rations, but were paid in money by the Govt. each man furnishing his own provisions. In this Co. were Jacob I. Cohen, Jr., Mendes I. Cohen, Philip I. Cohen, George Williams, Cumberland Williams & Nathaniel Williams. Every morning at about 6 o'clock, a small covered cart left the N. W. cor. of Howard & Market Sts. for the fort with food sent by the families for the members of this Co. The Cohens had a large stone jug around which was tightly sewn a cover of carpet, this was filled with coffee each morning & sent by the cart, always arriving there

---

[50] *The Baltimorean,* May 20, 1876; Marine, *op. cit.,* p. 249; *The Sun,* Baltimore, May 8, 1879.

good & hot.   In the Fort were several Houses, in one of which were quartered two Companies of militia, in another Major Armistead, in another Nicholson's Artillery & there were also a small number of regular troops in the Fort.   Some time previous to the Bombardment J. I. Cohen, Jr. procured special permission to visit Philadelphia for the purpose of nursing a dying relative, he had been a member of the Co. from its inception; but this circumstance prevented his participation in the defense at the time of the attack of the Star Ft.

" The Bombardment was on Tuesday.   A few days previously the British had evacuated Washington, the Americans had posted videttes [bidettes] along the shores of the Bay & they reported that on coming out of the mouth of the Potomac, the British Fleet had gone down the bay & it was supposed has [sic] passed out at the Capes.   This movement turned out to be a feint & after proceeding a short distance down, the Fleet turned & came up to Baltimore.   On the Saturday afternoon before the attack the fake Information was rec'd [sic], that the British Fleet had gone down the Bay & the Artillery Co. & the two Co.'s of militia determined to march [sic] up to the City. They were however unable to agree who should command the entire body on the march up & therefore Capt. Nicholson's Artillery came up alone and the two Militia Co's. remained at the Fort.   During Saturday night information was received that the British were nearing the City & the non-commissioned officers went around to the houses of the different members of the Co. telling them to meet at once at the Cor. of Howard & Market Sts. & to proceed to the Fort with all possible speed. Col. Cohen then a youth of 18 shared a room with his Brother Philip in the House now No. 142 W. Balto. St.   Worn out by the events of the day he slept soundly & his Brother was awakened & went to the Fort leaving him still asleep.

" At daylight he awoke & missing Philip enquired where he was.   On being told he dressed as quickly as possible & snatching a hasty breakfast he walked walked [sic] down to the Fort. On reaching Federal Hill where there were then no Houses he saw the whole British Fleet off North Point.

"This was Sunday morning the attack took place of [sic] Tuesday. During the firing of Bombs &c. at the Flag in the center of the Fort which afforded a fair mark for the enemy's gunners, in order to protect our men they were ordered to march outside of the Star Fort & stand under the walls where they were safe from shot & shell. While there a shell struck the powder magazine where there were many barrels of this explosive. It was Col. Cohen's duty to go there & get out the cartridges.

"When the shell struck it was deemed necessary to roll out the barrels of powder as the magazine was not bomb-proof. They were rolled under the walls among the men & Col. Cohen recollects sitting on one which had no head [sic]; but was merely covered by a piece of woolen stuff. While in this interesting position Mr. Williams [sic] serving man brought down a large basket of provisions which were divided among the members of the Command & eagerly eaten by them.

"Philip I. Cohen was standing by the side of Lieutenant Clagett when the latter was killed & Col. Cohen was next to Sergeant Clemm when he was struck down & assisted to place him upon a litter.

"During the firing Col. Cohen could see the ship upon which was Francis S. Key distinguishable by its flag of truce. After the British retired Mr. Key landed at the Fort & produced a copy of the 'Star Spangled Banner' which was copied first by one of the men then by another, and they all amused themselves trying to find a tune for it.

"Col. Cohen's recollections of the night attack & many other incidents of that eventful period are quite vivid & afford a refreshing example of patriotism to the descendents of those who so gallantly defended the old 'Star Fort.'

"Balto. 10/2 1878.   BENJN. I. COHEN."

"This period of peril and excitements seems to have put an end to attendance in school, and shortly thereafter he [Mendes I. Cohen] became engaged in business. Somewhat later he

joined his brothers of the banking firm of J. I. Cohen, Jr., &
Brothers, and conducted at New York the branch of the house
in that city." [51] He retired from business in 1829, and made
an extensive foreign tour. While in London he was frequently
the guest of N. M. Rothschild, and accompanied the latter on
a trip to Paris. He was in Rome during the pontificate of
Gregory XVI., to whom he was presented. He studied the art
treasures and antiquities of Rome while in that city, and visited
all the points of historic interest in Italy, Sicily and Greece.
While in Constantinople he was the guest of the captain of the
United States sloop of war *John Adams*. Later a vessel in
which he was travelling was wrecked off the coast of Asia
Minor, and he almost lost his life and his trunks and papers.
With horses and Mohammedan escort he travelled along the
coast of Asia Minor and over its mountains. While sailing for
Cyprus, he was almost wrecked again. He went to Syria,
where he was a guest in the camp of Ibrahim Pasha when the
latter attacked St. Jean D'Acre, and it was Mendes I. Cohen
who gave to the English consul at Alexandria the first information which he received about the attack. Mendes I. Cohen was
the first person to bear the American flag up the Nile after the
ratification of the treaty with Turkey. This flag, which was
made out of the shirts and the handkerchiefs of the sailors on
the boat, is still preserved by Miss Bertha Cohen(64). He went
to Damascus and Aleppo, and visited Palestine. Then he proceeded to Russia. These travels occupied about six years.[52]
He made other visits to Europe, on one of which he attended
the coronation of Queen Victoria in 1837.

The above-mentioned trip on the Nile lasted four and a half
months. Travelling in his own boat, he ascended as far as the
Second Cataract. While making this trip, he " lost no opportunity to acquire objects of antiquarian value, when such were

---

[51] "Mr. Mendes Cohen on 'the Cohen Collection,'" *J. H. U. Cir.*, *loc.
cit.*, p. 22.

[52] *The Baltimorean, op. cit.* Another and somewhat different account of
this tour is given in " Mr. Mendes Cohen on 'the Cohen Collection,'" *J. H.
U. Cir., op. cit.*, p. 22.

obtainable from first hands, or from sources which left no doubt as to their authenticity." [53] These articles, which formed the basis of the "Cohen Collection of Egyptian Antiquities," were procured at Thebes, Memphis and other points. To these he added objects which he purchased at the sale of Consul-General Salt's great collection in London in 1835.[53] The entire collection, which consisted of 689 objects, has been described as the first of its kind brought to this country.[54] It was sold in 1884 by Mendes I. Cohen's nephews, at a nominal price, to the Johns Hopkins University, where it is known as the "Cohen Collection of Egyptian Antiquities." [55]

Mendes I. Cohen's collection of coins and medals is said to have been the second finest in the world. The catalogue [56] issued for the sale of this collection lists 2329 different items representing coins and medals of many countries and periods. It is said to have been worth twenty thousand dollars.[57]

In 1836 Governor Veazey appointed Mendes I. Cohen one of his aides. A letter announcing the appointment stated that it was made in recognition of his services during the War of 1812, and conferred upon him the commission of Colonel.[58] Thereafter he was known, and all records likewise refer to him, as Colonel Mendes I. Cohen.

[53] "Mr. Mendes Cohen on 'the Cohen Collection,'" *J. H. U. Cir.*, *op. cit.*, p. 22.

[54] *Pub. Amer. Jew. Hist. Soc.*, xxviii (1922), p. 251, referring to Caroline R. Williams, "The Place of the New York Historical Society in the Growth of American Interest in Egyptology," *New York Historical Society Quarterly Bulletin*, April, 1920, pp. 5 and 6.

[55] "Mr. Mendes Cohen on 'the Cohen Collection,'" *J. H. U. Cir.*, *op. cit.*, p. 22, gives a partial catalogue of the collection.

[56] Catalogue of a very Celebrated and Valuable Collection of Gold, Silver and Copper Coins and Medals, The Property of Col. M. I. Cohen, of Baltimore, to be Sold at Auction by Messrs. Bangs, Merwin and Co., 656 Broadway, New York, Monday, Tuesday, Wednesday, Thursday and Friday, the 25th, 26th, 27th, 28th and 29th October, 1875, Commencing at 3 o'clock P. M., Catalogued by Edward Cogan (New York, 1875).

[57] *The Baltimorean*, *op. cit.* The unusually fine collection of stamps which is supposed to have belonged to a member of the Cohen family may have been collected by Mendes I. Cohen. Neither the collection nor data concerning it have been found.

[58] *The Sun*, Baltimore, May 8, 1879.

Col. Cohen was a member of the Maryland Historical Society; vice-president of the Hebrew Benevolent Society; director of the Fireman's Insurance Co., and Baltimore and Ohio Railroad Co. At a meeting held October 6, 1858, at which Col. Cohen presided, plans for the Hebrew Hospital of Baltimore were made.[59] He was a member of the Maryland Legislature in 1847-48.

Col. Cohen died May 7, 1879, and was buried in the family cemetery in Baltimore.

THE COHENS OF MARYLAND.

Aaron Baroway.

---

11. Benjamin I. Cohen.

Born September 17, 1797, at Richmond. Died September 20, 1845, at Baltimore. Sixth son and seventh child of Israel I. and Judith Cohen. Married December 15, 1819, Kitty Etting, who was born November 25, 1799, and died April 26, 1837. Issue: Israel Cohen (28), Solomon Etting Cohen (29), John Jacob Cohen (30), Benjamin Cohen (31), Rachel Etting Cohen (32), Judith I. Cohen (33), Maria Lopez (34), Kate Frances Cohen (35), Georgiana Cohen (36), Edward Cohen (37), and Eliza Emory Cohen (38).

Benjamin I. Cohen was one of the foremost bankers in Baltimore. A member of the banking firm of Jacob I. Cohen, Jr., and Brothers, he was one of the seven persons who, on February 26, 1838, formed the (first) Baltimore Stock Board,[60] which

[60] Isaac F. Nicholson, *Baltimore Stock Exchange, Historical Sketch* (Baltimore, n. d. [1898]), p. 6.

existed, apparently, only for a few months. At the organization meeting he was selected as a member of the Standing Committee. It seems that he was active in the affairs of the second Stock Board, which was organized six years later, and which became the present Stock Exchange. On November 16, 1844, he was elected vice-president of the Board,[61] and on February 5, 1845, he was made president. After his death, the first to occur among its members, the Board met on September 22, 1845, and adopted the following resolution: [62]

"*Resolved,* That as testimonial of respect for their late President, Benjamin I. Cohen, the business of the Board be suspended for this day; and that the members of the Board, collectively and individually, beg leave to offer to the family of Mr. Cohen their regret and sympathy for the afflicting bereavement they have sustained."

Activities connected with the "Jew Bill" bring to light the esteem in which Benjamin I. Cohen was held by his fellow-citizens. Governor Worthington, while illustrating to the General Assembly of 1823-24 the injustice which the Jewish citizens of Maryland were suffering, left us the following record: [63]

"The strongest case applicable to the subject, is one at present existing, and may thus be related:—Early in the spring of the existing year, 1823, a number of spirited young men formed a volunteer corps of riflemen, known by the name of the 'Marion Corps;' without any previous knowledge on his part, of even the existence of this company, they unanimously determined, and did elect Benj. I. Cohen their captain—a commission was received from Governor Stevens, but not qualified to of course, in consequence of the existence of the *test* law; the corps were made acquainted with this fact, and a resignation on his part of the command by the captain-elect—at a

[61] Israel Cohen, *Sketch of the Formation and Progress of the Baltimore Stock Board* (Baltimore, 1865), pp. 9 and 10.
[62] *Baltimore American,* Baltimore, Sept. 23, 1845.
[63] W. G. D. Worthington, *Speech on the Maryland Test Act, 1824,* Baltimore, 1824, p. 19.

meeting of the corps, *called for the purpose,* it was unanimously determined *that no captain should be elected* until the fate of the bill at present before the legislature, should be decided, and the corps is, at this time, commanded by the first lieutenant. This was the corps to which was presented *the flag,* by Governor Stevens, on behalf of Mr. Cohen, as a testimony of his gratitude for their highly distinguished marks of esteem."

Evidently Benjamin I. Cohen was active in creating sentiment for the passage of the " Jew Bill." It was he who wrote on December 16, 1818, to E. S. Thomas, a member of a committee of the House of Delegates, to urge him to introduce a bill " to extend to persons of the Jewish Religion the same civil privileges that are allowed to other religious sects."

In addition to his captaincy in the Marion Corps, Benjamin I. Cohen was at one time a lieutenant in the Columbia Volunteers, which were attached to the Fifth Regiment of Maryland Militia. The latter commission resulted from appointment by Charles Ridgely, of Hampton.[64]

Benjamin I. Cohen married, on December 15, 1819, Kitty Etting, then twenty years of age, the fourth daughter of Solomon and Rachel Etting.

In 1828 he erected a handsome residence at the southwest corner of Charles and Saratoga streets. His gardens and hot-houses extended to Cathedral street, the present site of the Rennert Hotel. Benjamin I. Cohen, it is said, was the first citizen of Baltimore to introduce gas in his residence. Mr. and Mrs. Benjamin I. Cohen played a prominent part in the social life of Baltimore. For the descendants of Baltimoreans of their day, the account of a fancy dress ball given by Mr. and Mrs. Benjamin I. Cohen makes interesting reading indeed.[65]

Benjamin I. Cohen was a man of many interests and accomplishments. He is reputed to have been a charming violinist, and a botanist and horticulturist. Scharf notes that he was the chairman of a meeting held on November 13, 1832, for the

[64] *Ibid.,* p. 19.
[65] *Maryland Historical Magazine,* XIV (1919), pp. 348-358.

purpose of organizing a horticultural society.[66] From 1825 to 1845 he was an officer of the German Society of Maryland, probably the oldest benevolent organization in Maryland.[67]

Both Benjamin I. and Kitty Cohen are buried in the family cemetery on West Saratoga street.

12. DAVID I. COHEN.

Born April 30, 1800, at Richmond. Died July 4, 1847, at Baltimore. Seventh son and eighth child of Israel I. and Judith Cohen. Married Harriett (Rahmah) Cohen, who was born November 9, 1801, and died July 27, 1889. Issue: Mendes Cohen (60), Catherine Myers (61), Miriam Cohen (62), Margaret Cohen (63), Bertha Cohen (64), Jacob I. Cohen (65), and Rebecca Jackson (66).

David I. Cohen was a member of the banking firm of Jacob I. Cohen, Jr., and Brothers. He was also one of the seven persons who, on January 29, 1844, founded the (second) Baltimore Stock Board, which became the Baltimore Stock Exchange.[68] He was a member of the Committee on Rules and Regulation at the organization meeting.[69] It is interesting to note in connection with the rules and regulation formulated by David I. Cohen's committee that one rule specified that " the fine for non-attendance at the calling of the roll shall be 25 cents, unless . . . absent on religious attendance, their office being closed for the day," [70] a provision adopted out of regard for the Cohen family whose Sabbath and holidays did not coincide with those of the other members. At the semi-annual election of the Board held August 12, 1845, David I. Cohen was elected vice-president.

David I. Cohen married Harriett Cohen, of Swansea, Wales. Husband and wife are buried in the family cemetery on West Saratoga street.

[66] Scharf, op. cit., p. 465.
[67] The Sun, Baltimore, Feb. 26, 1911.
[68] Nicholson, op. cit., p. 11.
[69] Ibid., p. 12.
[70] Ibid., pp. 15 and 16.

13. Dr. Joshua I. Cohen.

Born August 30, 1801, at Richmond. Died November 4, 1870, at Baltimore. Eighth son and ninth child of Israel I. and Judith Cohen. Unmarried.

Joshua I. Cohen was a distinguished figure. Graduating as a physician from the University of Maryland in 1823, he became one of the earliest aurists in this country; indeed, he may have been the first. He was treasurer of the Medical and Chirurgical Faculty of Maryland from 1839-56 and its president from 1857 to '58, professor of geology and mineralogy in the academic department of the University of Maryland, a member of the American Philosophical Society,[71] a charter member of the Maryland Historical Society,[72] and a member of the Anacreontic Society.[73] He was a founder and vice-president of the Hebrew Hospital.[74] He published a monograph entitled "Post-Mortem Appearances in a Case of Deafness"[75] and a catalogue of his collection of autographs and currency of colonial times.[76] He collected a large and valuable library of Hebrew books, which were catalogued some years ago by Dr. Cyrus Adler.[77] This library was presented in 1915 by Miss Bertha Cohen (64) and her nieces Mrs. A. B. Johnson (71), Mrs. D. Grigsby Long (72) and Mrs. Isaac Coale (73) to the library of Dropsie College, Philadelphia. Joshua I. Cohen was a lover of music, and is mentioned as an amateur player.[78]

[71] *Jewish Encyclopedia*, IV, p. 145; *s. v. Cohen*.

[72] *Md. Hist. Mag.*, XIV (1919), p. 14.

[73] "Diary of Robert Gilmor," *Md. Hist. Mag.*, XVII (1922), p. 244.

[74] *Jewish Exponent*, Philadelphia, July 4, 1890. The clipping which is the source of this information was lent by Professor Hollander to Professor Blondheim.

[75] Friedenwald, Dr. Harry, "Early History of Ophthalmology and Otology in Baltimore," *Johns Hopkins Hospital Bulletin*, Aug.-Sept., 1897.

[76] *Jewish Exponent*, Philadelphia, July 4, 1890, *op. cit.*

[77] Cyrus Adler, *Catalogue of a Hebrew Library, being the collection, with a few additions, of the late Joshua I. Cohen, M. D., of Baltimore, now in the Possession of Mrs. Harriett Cohen* (12), privately printed, Baltimore, 1887.

[78] "Diary of Robert Gilmor," *op. cit.*, p. 244.

He also participated in the work which resulted in the removal of Jewish disabilities in Maryland. His fairness of mind during the struggle is well illustrated by the letter [79] which he wrote (February 2, 1819) to Mordecai M. Noah. In this letter he refuted Noah's statement in the *National Advocate* that the defeat of a recent " Jew Bill " had resulted from opposition to it on the part of the Catholics of Maryland. It was at Dr. Cohen's suggestion that John P. Kennedy and others inaugurated the legislation leading to the removal in 1847 of the discrimination against the Jews in the laws of evidence, and that, later, the Maryland Constitutional Conventions of 1850 and 1867 were asked to eliminate the test act entirely.[80]

Dr. Cohen was buried in the family cemetery at Baltimore.

14. EDWARD I. COHEN.

Born November 19, 1802, at Richmond. Died July 23, 1803, at Richmond. Ninth son and tenth child of Israel I. and Judith Cohen.

15. MAJ. DAVID MYERS COHEN.

Born December 7, 1826, at Norfolk. Died May 28, 1891, at New York. Eldest child of Philip I. and Augusta Cohen. Married December 5, 1875, in New York, Matilda Stern, who was born April 3, 1845, at Duesseldorf, Germany, and died February 3, 1910. Issue: Lillie Lewis (23).

David M. Cohen was a major in the United States Marine Corps.

16. DR. HENRY M. COHEN.

Born April 17, 1828, at Norfolk. Died October 6, 1888, at New York. Second son and child of Philip I. and Augusta Cohen. Unmarried.

Henry M. Cohen was a physician of ability. He retired from active practice a number of years prior to his death. He was one of the committee of natives of Virginia who were in-

---

[79] A copy of the letter is in the possession of Miss Eleanor S. Cohen (57).
[80] *Jewish Encyclopedia*, VIII, p. 361, art. *Maryland*.

vited to take part on July 2, 1858, in the procession accompanying the removal of the remains of President Monroe from New York to Richmond. On January 1, 1876, he was made Superintending, Recording and Testamentary Certificate Clerk in the Surrogate's Office in New York.

17. ELIZA M. COHEN.

Born September 13, 1829, at Norfolk. Died March 28, 1904, at New York. Eldest daughter and third child of Philip I. and Augusta Cohen. Unmarried.

18. VIRGINIA COHEN.

Born April 22, 1831, at Norfolk. Died June 23, 1834, at Baltimore. Second daughter and fourth child of Philip I. and Augusta Cohen. Buried in family cemetery, Baltimore.

19. ARTHUR M. COHEN.

Born May 13, 1833, at Baltimore. Died January 3, 1885. Third son and fifth child of Philip I. and Augusta Cohen. Unmarried.

Arthur M. Cohen lived for many years in Montreal, Canada, where he was an officer of the Bank of Montreal. Only after his death it became known to his family that he had become a British subject.

20. CHARLES COHEN.

Born February 24, 1835, at Baltimore. Died August 18, 1836. Fourth son and sixth child of Philip I. and Augusta Cohen. Buried in the family cemetery at Baltimore.

21. ALFRED M. COHEN.

Born January 14, 1837, at Baltimore. Died September 20, 1858, at Mobile, Ala. Fifth son and seventh child of Philip I. and Augusta Cohen. Unmarried. Buried at Mobile, Ala.

22. ADELINE M. STERN.

Born May 25, 1839, at Norfolk. Died March 28, 1889. Third daughter and eighth child of Philip I. and Augusta

Cohen. Married January 10, 1872, David Stern of New York [brother of Matilda Stern, who married Major David M. Cohen (15)], who was born September 30, 1842, at Duesseldorf, Germany. Issue: Jacob Edgar Stern (24), Philip Alfred Stern (25), August M. MacMannus (25), and Maud Elise Webber (27).

23. Lillie Lewis.

Born June 23, 1879, at New York. Only child of David M. and Matilda Cohen. Married February 1, 1910, Frederick Lewis, who was born January 1, 1879, at Vienna. No issue.

24. Jacob Edgar Stern.

Born November 4, 1872. Eldest child of Adeline M. and David Stern. Married December 11, 1907, at Waterbury, Conn., Lilabell Damon, who was born December 25, 1876, at Meriden, Conn. No issue.

25. Philip Alfred Stern.

Born May 11, 1874. Died December 29, 1898. Second son and child of Adeline M. and David Stern. Unmarried. He was a civil engineer, a graduate of the City College of New York.

26. Augusta Myers MacMannus.

Born February 27, 1877. Elder daughter and third child of Adeline M. and David Stern. Married October 16, 1901, in New York, Edward Davenport MacMannus, who was born September 20, 1865, at New York, and died March 19, 1917, at New York. No issue.

27. Maud Elise Webber.

Born February 25, 1880. Younger daughter and fourth child of Adeline M. and David Stern. Married June 3, 1903, in New York, William Webber, who was born April 29, 1880, in New York. No issue.

28. ISRAEL COHEN.

Born September 12, 1820. Died June 3, 1875. Eldest child of Benjamin I. and Kitty Cohen. Married October 3, 1850, Cecilia Eliza Levy, who was born October 3, 1830, at Charleston, S. C., and died November 14, 1916, at Baltimore, Md. Issue: Benjamin I. Cohen (53), Maria Cohen (54), Kitty Cohen (55), Georgie Cohen (56), Eleanor Septima Cohen (57), Joshua I. Cohen, Jr. (58), and Anna Maria Minis (59).

A bachelor of arts of the University of Maryland, from which he was graduated with many honors and prizes, Israel, or " Iz," as he was known to his friends, Cohen entered the banking house of his father, with whom he was associated for many years under the firm name of Benjamin I. Cohen and Son. After his father's death, he continued the business under his own name.

The records of the (second) Stock Board, of which Israel Cohen was also a founder, contain many references to his activity in its affairs. He was appointed May 23, 1864, a member of the committee to which was entrusted the property at 45 E. Fayette street which had recently been bought by the Board. At a dinner given June 22, 1865, in its new headquarters at the above-mentioned address, Israel Cohen read a sketch entitled " The Formation and Progress of the Board." The Board liked the sketch so well that it ordered the sketch printed. It is a chronological table of events, with comments, occasionally humorous. In 1866, he was elected president of the Society of Members of the Baltimore Stock Board for Mutual Relief, a beneficial society.[80a]

Israel Cohen first proposed the erection of the Academy of Music. The idea resulted from an incident which occurred at a performance at the Concordia, to which Israel Cohen and his wife had gone in the company of the French consul and his wife. In the midst of the performance there was a cry of " fire." Mrs. Cohen remarked that " it's a shame there should be no place in Baltimore " like the Academy of Music in Phila-

[80a] Nicholson, *op. cit.*, pp. 11, 41, 42, 44, 46 and 47.

delphia "where a woman can sit in safety and listen to
music." [81] He acted as secretary of the meeting held March
22, 1873, for the purpose of founding the Academy of Music.[82]
He raised most of the money for the theatre. His statement
that it would be his monument was borne out by the fact that
his death took place five months after the theater was completed.[83]

Israel Cohen married Cecilia Eliza Levy, second daughter
and third child of David C. and Anna Maria Levy, in Philadelphia, October 3, 1850. The Levys had formerly resided in
Charleston, S. C., where Cecilia was born. A friend paid this
tribute to her:

" . . . An invalid for almost a quarter of a century, she bore
her suffering and infirmity with patience, resignation and for-
titude; she did not succumb, but steadfastly pursued her activities and interests of mind, of heart and of hand. Her wide
reading kept her clear and cultured mind awake and elastic and
her conversation brilliant and fascinating. Her interests in all
humanity, but especially in her suffering Jewish brethren, were
unflagging even to the last hours of consciousness . . .

" . . . Her classic features, the thin nose, the beauteous lips,
the soulful eyes, the silver hair brought to mind the well-known
picture of Whistler's mother, save that the latter had less of
beauty and charm. . . ." [84]

Of Israel Cohen it is said that he would sacrifice every personal consideration in the pursuit of the happiness of others.
He was ready in counsel and gentle and tender in judgment.
His heart responded to the suffering and his hand to the
needy.

Israel and Cecilia E. Cohen are buried in the Saratoga street
cemetery.

---

[81] "Cohen-Etting Papers" in the Library of the Jewish Theological
Seminary of America, New York.

[82] Scharf, op. cit., p. 677.

[83] "Cohen-Etting Papers," op. cit.

[84] Harry Friedenwald, "Cecilia E. Cohen," *Jewish Comment*, Baltimore,
November 24, 1916, p. 156.

29. SOLOMON ETTING COHEN.

Born February 16, 1822. Died December 17, 1878, at Philadelphia. Second son and child of Benjamin I. and Kitty Cohen. Married August 30, 1842, Anna Maria Denny, who was born November 25, 18—. Issue: Solomon Etting Cohen (39), Benjamin D. Cohen (40), George Cohen (41), Anna Maria Van Meeden (42), and Herbert Cohen (43).

30. JOHN JACOB COHEN.

Born February 9, 1823. Died May 10, 1825. Third son and child of Benjamin I. and Kitty Cohen.

31. BENJAMIN COHEN.

Born November 4, 1824. Died December 9, 1824. Fourth son and child of Benjamin I. and Kitty Cohen.

32. RACHEL ETTING COHEN.

Born October 14, 1825. Died September 28, 1913. Eldest daughter and fifth child of Benjamin I. and Kitty Cohen. Unmarried.

Rachel Etting Cohen was well-known in musical circles in Baltimore. She was one of the founders of the Oratorio Society and the Philharmonic Society. She was a close friend of Louis Moreau Gottschalk and Theodor Hablemann and other famous musicians of her day. She was ever ready to assist young musicians. She was esteemed as an accompanist.[85]

It is related of her that, when she was about eight years old, on one occasion when Ole Bull, who was visiting her father, dropped his handkerchief while playing, she picked it up, and begged him to permit her to keep it. Her request was granted. The following day she cut the kerchief in " four divides," and gave one piece to each of her three young musical friends. The next time Ole Bull returned, he heard of her act, and gave her

---

[85] E. S. C., " Rachel Etting Cohen," *Jewish Comment*, Baltimore, October 30, 1913.

a handkerchief marked " O. B." This handkerchief has been deposited with the Maryland Historical Society.

Rachel Etting Cohen was buried in the family cemetery.

33. JUDITH I. COHEN.

Born November 20, 1827. Died August 25, 1829. Second daughter and sixth child of Benjamin I. and Kitty Cohen.

34. MARIA LOPEZ.

Born August 18, 1830. Died September 14, 1905. Third daughter and seventh child of Benjamin I. and Kitty Cohen. Married October 4, 1854, John Hinton Lopez (eldest child of David and Catherine Lopez), who was born February 8, 1833, at Charleston, S. C., and died May 23, 1884 at Charleston, S. C. Issue: Israel Lopez (44), Kate Lopez (45), David Lopez (46), John Hinton Lopez, Jr. (47), and Edward Lopez (48).

35. KATE FRANCES COHEN.

Born February 25, 1832. Died May 18, 1890. Fourth daughter and eighth child of Benjamin I. and Kitty Cohen. Unmarried. Buried in the family cemetery, Baltimore.

36. GEORGIANA COHEN.

Born February 1, 1834. Died December 19, 1905. Fifth daughter and ninth child of Benjamin I. and Kitty Cohen. Unmarried. Buried in the family cemetery, Baltimore.

37. EDWARD COHEN.

Born November 15, 1835. Died January 18, 1888, at Richmond. Fifth son and tenth child of Benjamin I. and Kitty Cohen. Married December 6, 1865, Caroline Myers, who was born December 5, 1844. No issue.

At sixteen years of age, Edward Cohen entered the commission house of Samuel Etting, his maternal uncle. Later he became associated with the brokerage house of his brother Israel Cohen.[86] On February 21, 1860, he was elected Fourth Sergeant of Company F of the Maryland Guard Battalion, which was organized to aid civil officers in the enforcement of law during unrest in the city.[87] On June 11, 1860, he was chosen First Sergeant of Company G of the same organization.[88] When the Civil War broke out, in spite of the fact that he had begun business on his own account in Baltimore, he left this city to cast in his lot with the Confederacy.[89] Ill health prevented him at first from joining the Confederate Army. For a while he was engaged in government work in South Carolina and in the Medical Purveyor's office in Richmond. Later he became a lieutenant in the Third Battalion of Virginia Infantry in General Joseph E. Johnston's army. He served in the field from 1864 to 1865.[90] At the end of the war he found himself penniless, but immediately began business in Richmond as a stockbroker.[91] In March, 1867, he was instrumental in establishing the Merchants and Mechanics Savings Bank, of which he became cashier.[92] He held this position for many years. Later he became president of the City Bank of Richmond, which position he held until the time of his death.[93]

The following tribute, dated on the day following the death of Edward Cohen, eloquently expresses the esteem in which he was held in Richmond.

" Richmond, Va., Jan'y 19th, 1888.

" On the assembly of the Stock Board today the death of

Mr. Edward Cohen,

was announced, whereupon the following resolutions were adopted, and the Board adjourned until Saturday the 21st, and the Secretary was instructed to have these proceedings printed

---

[86] Ezekiel and Lichtenstein, *op. cit.*, pp. 202-203.
[87] Maryland Guard Battalion, 1860-1861, *Md. Hist. Mag.*, VI (1911), p. 119.
[88] *Ibid.*, p. 121.
[89] Ezekiel and Lichtenstein, *op. cit.*, pp. 202-203.
[90] *Ibid.*, p. 188.   [92] *Ibid.*, p. 197.
[91] *Ibid.*, pp. 202-203.   [93] *Ibid.*, p. 203.

so as to notify all corresponents of the death of Mr. Cohen, and explain the absence of the usual reports:

"We record with sincere and profound sorrow the death of Mr. Edward Cohen. He was a just, upright man, and thoroughbred gentleman; unflinchingly faithful to his trusts, ready to do and endure whatever his conceptions of duty required of him: vigilant, prudent, sagacious, earnest, and unsparing of his energies of mind and body in protecting and advancing the interests of those who looked to him. His daily life and his sacrifices and services as a private man, as a public-spirited citizen, to his friends, to his community, to our State, and to the South have made him a good name and a memory that will be honorably and affectionately cherished."

At the time of his marriage in December, 1865, to Caroline Myers, only daughter and second child of Samuel Hays and Eliza Kenyon Myers, Edward Cohen was almost unknown in Richmond. In the course of a few years, he became one of its most prominent citizens. He was a man of real public spirit, but was extremely modest. When the Westmoreland Club was organized in 1877, against his protest he was made its president. He was deeply interested in the work of the Fire Department of Richmond, and was always active in its work.[94]

Edward Cohen was actively engaged in matters of Jewish interest. He was secretary of the Beth Shalome Congregation for many years, and even for a longer period was a member of its Board. His name is frequently mentioned in the congregational records.[95] It was through his work that the reservation in the old Franklin Street Cemetery was covered with heavy masonry.[96] He was president of the Hillel Lodge, Number 91, Kesher Shel Barzel, in 1877.

His wife is still living, and resides at present in Washington. She is the author of "Records of the Myers, Hays and Mordecai Families."[97]

[94] *Ibid.*, p. 203.
[95] *Ibid.*, pp. 58 and 251.
[96] *Ibid.*, p. 203.
[97] See foot note 16.

38. Eliza Emory Cohen.

Born April 18, 1837. Died May 7, 1837. Sixth daughter and eleventh child of Benjamin I. and Kitty Cohen.

39. Solomon Etting Cohen.

Born June 26, 1843. Died August 8, 1847, at Harper's Ferry, W. Va. Eldest child of Solomon Etting and Anna Maria Cohen.

40. Benjamin Denny Cohen.

Born September 13, 1845, at Philadelphia. Died July 23, 1847. Second son and child of Solomon Etting and Anna Maria Cohen.

41. George Cohen.

Born November 14, 1847, at Harper's Ferry, W. Va. Third son and child of Solomon Etting and Anna Maria Cohen. Issue: Frederick Cohen (49), Ethen Coen (50), and Mary Coen (51). Recent efforts to locate George Cohen and his children have proved futile. No exact information about them is to be obtained. George Cohen, it seems, is dead.

42. Anna Maria Van Meeden.

Born July 27, 1849, at Philadelphia. Died October 3, 1914. Only daughter and fourth child of Solomon Etting and Anna Maria Cohen. Married (1) March 1876, Benjamin Luther Leland, who was born September, 1846, and died January, 1880; divorced about 1879. Married (2) about 1884 John A. Hall; divorced about 1890. Married (3) March 12, 1898, Claus Van Meeden, who was born October 15, 1851, and died November 3, 1914. Issue (by Benjamin Luther Leland): Barney Leland Meeden (52).

43. Herbert Cohen.

Born March 9, 1851, at Chester, Pa. Died February 7, 1852, at Philadelphia, Pa. Fourth son and fifth child of Solomon Etting and Anna Maria Cohen.

44. ISRAEL LOPEZ.

Born August 1, 1855. Died November 25, 1858. Eldest child of Maria and John Hinton Lopez.

45. KATE LOPEZ.

Born February 2, 1858. Died December 20, 1858. Only daughter and second child of Maria and John Hinton Lopez.

46. DAVID LOPEZ.

Born November 1860. Died 1872. Second son and third child of Maria and John Hinton Lopez.

47. JOHN HINTON LOPEZ, JR.

Born May 20, 1863. Died November 27, 1881, at Versailles, France. Third son and fourth child of Maria and John Hinton Lopez. Unmarried. Buried at Suresnes, France.

48. EDWARD LOPEZ.

Born June 13, 1871. Fourth son and fifth child of Maria and John Hinton Lopez.

49. FREDERICK COHEN.

Son of George Cohen (41). Probably dead. Had three children. Definite information about him, his children and his sisters (50 and 51) unavailable.

50 AND 51. ETHEL AND MARY COEN.

Daughters of George Cohen (41). Probably dead. Changed name to Coen. Both married.

52. LIEUT. BARNEY LELAND MEEDEN.

Born November 17, 1878. Son of Anna Maria and Benjamin Luther Leland. Married Meta Clara. Assumed step-father's name, Meeden. Lieutenant, United States Quartermaster Corps, Fort Wm. McKinley, Rizal, Philippine Islands.

53. BENJAMIN I. COHEN.

Born February 21, 1852. Died August 10, 1910, at Victoria, British Columbia. Eldest child of Israel and Cecilia Cohen. Married May 19, 1881, at Portland, Oregon, Sally Ella Harper, who died May 15, 1920, at Portland, Oregon.

Benjamin I. Cohen was graduated from the Baltimore Law School, was admitted to the Bar of Maryland, and practised law in Baltimore for a time. In 1879 he went to Portland, Oregon, where he practised law and in 1880 entered the employ of Corbitt and Macleay, wholesale grocers and importers, having charge of their insurance department for about five years. Later he practised law again until the Portland Trust Company, of which he was an organizer, was founded on April 22, 1887. He became president of the Portland Trust Company, and held this positon until his death. For a time he acted as statistician and secretary of the Board of Trade.[98]

He married on May 19, 1881, in Portland, Sally Ella Harper, fourth daughter and seventh child of Charles and Eliza Buckles Harper of Shepherdstown, W. Va., a granddaughter of Robert Goodloe Harper, of Harper's Ferry, W. Va. Mrs. Cohen became a Jewess five years before her marriage. Benjamin I. Cohen provided in his will that, after his wife's death, ten thousand dollars should be given by his estate to the Good Samaritan Hospital of Portland for establishing a room to be known as the Sally Ella Harper Cohen Room.

Benjamin I. Cohen was buried in the family cemetery in Baltimore. In September, 1920, Miss Eleanor S. Cohen gave to the Neighborhood House of Portland a memorial to him. A tablet on which his name is inscribed was erected there.

54. MARIA COHEN.

Born April 25, 1853. Died October 19, 1853. Eldest daughter and second child of Israel and Cecilia Cohen. Buried in family cemetery, Baltimore.

---

[98] *The Morning Oregonian*, Portland, Aug. 11, 1910.

55. KITTY COHEN.

Born July 19, 1854. Died January 19, 1856. Second daughter and third child of Israel and Cecilia Cohen. Buried in family cemetery, Baltimore.

56. GEORGIE COHEN.

Born November 14, 1856. Died May 27, 1871. Third daughter and fourth child of Israel and Cecilia Cohen. Buried in family cemetery, Baltimore.

57. ELEANOR SEPTIMA COHEN.

Born February 17, 1858. Fourth daughter and fifth child of Israel and Cecilia Cohen. Unmarried.

58. JOSHUA I. COHEN, JR.

Born June 25, 1860. Died November 17, 1885, at Los Angeles, Cal. Second son and sixth child of Israel and Cecilia Cohen. Unmarried. Buried at Los Angeles; memorial stone in family cemetery, Baltimore.

59. ANNA MARIA MINIS.

Born April 11, 1863. Died May 24, 1891, at Savannah, Ga. Fifth daughter and seventh child of Israel and Cecilia Cohen. Married October 8, 1890, Abram Minis, son of Abraham and Lavinia Florence Minis of Savannah, Ga. Buried in Laurel Grove, Savannah; memorial stone in family cemetery, Baltimore.

60. MENDES COHEN.

Born May 4, 1831. Died August 13, 1915. Eldest child of David I. and Harriett Cohen. Married Justina Nathan, who was born November 10, 1839, and died August 25, 1918. Issue: Emily Clara Cohen (67).

Mendes Cohen was educated in private schools.[99] At an early age, a liking for engineering became evident,[100] and he

[99] *Mendes Cohen* in *Jews of Baltimore* (Baltimore, 1910), p. 149.
[100] *Encyclopedia Americana*, VII, p. 216, art. *Cohen, Mendes.*

" entered the locomotive shops of Ross Winans with a view to preparation for the profession of Civil Engineer." [101] He became an apprentice machinist in the Winans establishment.[102] Because the men working in the Winans plant and the workers in the nearby Baltimore and Ohio organization met constantly, young Mendes Cohen had unusually advantageous opportunities " for acquiring facts and observing details." [103] That he made the most of these opportunities is indicated by the important positions of trust which he held in engineering and railroad work for many years thereafter. In 1851, when twenty years of age, he became assistant to the Engineer of the Baltimore and Ohio Railroad, and was assigned to work on the Broad Tree Tunnel.[104] Later two tasks of the motive power department —that of studying the adaptation of wood-burning locomotives for burning coal [105] and that of handling traffic on the ten per cent. temporary grade over Kenwood Tunnel—were entrusted to him.[106] In later life he considered himself quite fortunate in having worked with John Elger, who was the mechanical assistant to Jonathan Knight, the chief engineer of the Baltimore and Ohio Railroad.

Mendes Cohen was assistant superintendent of the Hudson River Railroad (1855-1861); [107] superintendent and president of the Ohio and Mississippi Railroad (1861-1863); [108] superintendent of the Reading and Columbia Railroad (1864-1866); [109] comptroller and assistant to the president of the

---

[101] Mendes Cohen, [Presidential] *Address at the Annual Convention at Hygeia Hotel, Fortress Monroe, Va.,* June 8, 1892, *Proceedings of American Society of Civil Engineers,* XXVI (1892), June, p. 535, *et seq.*

[102] Cyrus Adler, " Necrology: Mendes Cohen," *Pub. Amer. Jew. Hist. Soc.,* XXV (1917), pp. 145-147.

[103] Mendes Cohen, *Address, lóc. cit.*

[104] Adler, *Necrology, op. cit.,* p. 146.

[105] *Report on Coke and Coal used with Passenger Trains, on the Baltimore and Ohio Rail Road:* by Mendes Cohen, Baltimore, August 29, 1854.

[106] Adler, *Necrology, op. cit.,* p. 146.

[107] *Ibid.; Mendes Cohen in Jews of Baltimore, op. cit.,* p. 149; *Encyclopedia Americana, op. cit.,* VII, p. 216.

[108] Adler, *Necrology, op. cit.,* p. 146; *Encyclopedia Americana, op. cit.,* VII, p. 216.

[109] *Mendes Cohen in Jews of Baltimore, op. cit.,* p. 149.

Lehigh Coal and Navigation Co. (1868-1871); [110] and president of the Pittsburgh and Connellsville Railroad (1873-1875).[111] The standard of ethics which he maintained in all of his work is illustrated by his resignation from the presidency of one railroad when figures which he had furnished were altered when presented to the stockholders of the company.[112]

Mendes Cohen was a prominent figure among the civil engineers of this country. His *confrères* honored him in 1891 by electing him president of the American Society of Civil Engineers. His presidential address [113] at the convention at Fortress Monroe, Va., June 8, 1892, contains his record of the early engineering history of the Baltimore and Ohio Railroad from 1827 to the opening of the road to Wheeling, W. Va., in 1853. At various times he served on federal and municipal commissions. He acted as chairman of the Sewerage Commission of Baltimore (1893-1900); [114] as engineer to the municipal commission on car-fenders (1894); [115] and as a member of the board appointed in 1894 by President Cleveland to lay out the construction route of the Chesapeake and Delaware Canal.[116]

Mendes Cohen was for many years an active and honored member of the Maryland Historical Society. He acted as its corresponding secretary from 1882 to 1904 and as its president from 1904 to 1913. As a member and chairman of its library committee he rendered many valuable services.[117] It was through his initiative that the Society came into possession in 1887 of the Calvert Papers.[118] He arranged the deposit of

---

[110] Adler, *Necrology, op. cit.,* p. 146; *Mendes Cohen* in *Jews of Baltimore, op. cit.,* p. 149.

[111] *Mendes Cohen* in *Jews of Baltimore, op. cit.,* p. 149.

[112] Adler, *Necrology, op. cit.,* p. 146.

[113] Cf. note 101.

[114] *Mendes Cohen* in *Jews of Baltimore, op. cit.,* p. 149.

[115] Mendes Cohen, *Report on Car-Fenders Suitable for Use on Street Railways,* Baltimore, 1894.

[116] *Mendes Cohen* in *Jews of Baltimore, op. cit.,* p. 149.

[117] Henry Stockbridge, "Memorial of Mendes Cohen," *Md. Hist. Mag.,* X (1915), pp. 387-389.

[118] "Dedication of the H. Irvine Keyser Memorial Building," *Md. Hist. Mag.,* XV (1919), p. 20.

the Carroll Papers with the Society by Harriett Cohen (12), who had received them from Dr. Joshua Cohen (13), who had collected them from members of the Carroll family. He also arranged for the purchase by the Society for the State of Maryland of the replica of the Great Seal of Maryland found by Professor Jacob H. Hollander in the possession of a dealer in London.[119] When Mendes Cohen retired from the presidency of the Society in 1913, the Society ordered his portrait done in oils and hung in the Gallery of the Society.[120]

Mendes Cohen was one of the founders of the American Jewish Historical Society. He was a vice-president of that society from 1897 to 1902.

Mendes Cohen was interested in art, music, and intellectual pursuits. He was for many years a member of the Art Commission of Baltimore and a trustee of the Peabody Institute of the City of Baltimore.

Mendes and Justina Cohen were buried in the Saratoga Street Cemetery.

61. Catherine Myers.

Born October 3, 1833. Died August 18, 1888. Eldest daughter and second child of David I. and Harriett Cohen. Married Charles D. Myers of London, England, who was born June 12, 1843, and died May 29, 1884. Issue: Miriam Cohen Myers (68). Buried in family cemetery, Baltimore.

62. Miriam Cohen.

Born September 5, 1835. Died March 3, 1894. Second daughter and third child of David I. and Harriett Cohen. Unmarried. Buried in family cemetery, Baltimore.

63. Margaret Cohen.

Born February 20, 1837. Died August 3, 1902. Third daughter and fourth child of David I. and Harriett Cohen. Unmarried. Buried in family cemetery, Baltimore.

[119] *Md. Hist. Mag.*, x (1915), pp. 189-191.
[120] *Md. Hist. Mag.*, viii (1913), pp. 97 and 387.

64. BERTHA COHEN.

Born April 12, 1838. Fourth daughter and fifth child of David I. and Harriett Cohen. Unmarried.

65. JACOB I. COHEN.

Born November 6, 1841. Died January 22, 1920. Second son and sixth child of David I. and Harriett Cohen. Married Ellen Mordecai (daughter of Moses C. and Isabel Mordecai, of Charleston, S. C.), who was born June 25, 1837, and died August 13, 1915. Issue: David I. Cohen (69) and Alan M. Cohen (70). Both Jacob I. and Ellen Cohen are buried in the family cemetery.

Jacob I. Cohen was a well-known lawyer in Baltimore. He is said to have been the best examiner of titles in Baltimore. When asked how he managed to attain his proficiency in spite of the poor condition of his eyesight, he replied that, as he knew where to look for the important items in records, he was able to avoid much unnecessary labor. He was also a member of the Maryland Guard Battalion, 1860-1861.[121]

66. REBECCA JACKSON.

Born September 25, 1844. Died June 13, 1899. Fifth daughter and seventh child of David I. and Harriett Cohen. Married Eugene J. Jackson, who was born April 9, 1833, and died December 13, 1883. Issue: Corinne Johnson (71), May Long (72) and Harriett Cohen Coale (73). Eugene J. Jackson was a son of John D. and Louisa Solomon Jackson. The latter was a granddaughter of Haym Solomon.[122] Both Rebecca and Eugene J. Jackson are buried in the Saratoga Street cemetery.

---

[121] *Md. Hist. Mag.*, VI (1911), p. 128.

[122] *Pub. Amer. Jew. Hist. Soc.*, II (1894), p. 6: Joshua Cohen (13) wrote to Jared Sparks a letter dated October 29, 1865, containing the following sentence: "The matter [of Haym Solomon's services to Robert Morris] was brought up to my mind recently by the marriage of a greatgrandson of Mr. Solomon to a niece of mine, one of the young ladies of our household."

67. EMILY CLARA COHEN.

Born August 3, 1866. Died September 18, 1903. Only child of Mendes and Justina Cohen. Unmarried. Buried in family cemetery, Baltimore.

68. MIRIAM COHEN MYERS.

Born December 28, 1873. Died September 3, 1900. Only child of Catherine and Charles D. Myers. Unmarried. Buried in family cemetery, Baltimore.

69. DAVID I. COHEN.

Born September 14, 1870. Died June 20, 1871. Elder son and child of Jacob I. and Ellen Cohen. Buried in family cemetery, Baltimore.

70. ALAN MORDECAI COHEN.

Born January 21, 1872. Died September 6, 1913. Younger son and child of Jacob I. and Ellen Cohen. Married Emily Johnson of Ithaca, N. Y. Issue: Alan M. Cohen (74). Buried in family cemetery, Baltimore.

71. CORINNE JOHNSON.

Born February 13, 1866. Eldest daughter and child of Rebecca and Eugene J. Jackson. Married November 25, 1908, Arnold Burgess Johnson, of Massachusetts, who died February 2, 1915.

72. MAY LONG.

Born May 4, 1867. Second daughter and child of Rebecca and Eugene J. Jackson. Married July 16, 1907, David Grigsby Long, of Virginia. Issue: Eugene Jackson Long (76) and Hugh Blair Long (77).

73. HARRIETT COHEN COALE.

Born March 12, 1872. Third daughter and child of Rebecca and Eugene J. Jackson. Married November 16, 1898, Isaac Coale, Jr., who was born June 2, 1861.

74.　Alan M. Cohen.

Born February 2, 1895.　Only child of Alan M. and Emily Cohen.　Married January 2, 1920, Elizabeth Doris Buda, who was born January 1, 1898.　Issue: Alan M. Cohen, Jr. (75).

75.　Alan M. Cohen, Jr.

Born August 17, 1920.　Only child of Alan M. and Elizabeth Doris Cohen.

76.　Eugene Jackson Long.

Born June 29, 1908.　Elder son and child of May and David G. Long.

77.　Hugh Blair Long.

Born September 27, 1910.　Younger son and child of May and David G. Long.

CROMWELL FAMILY.

A Possible Cromwell Clue

FRANCIS B. CULVER

Authorities disagree with respect to the origin of the Cromwell family of Maryland. The favorite hypothesis traces this family back to Sir Oliver Cromwell of Hichen Brook, Knight, an uncle of Oliver Cromwell, the Lord Protector of England. Sir Oliver had a son, Henry Cromwell [1] who, it is claimed, came to Virginia in 1620, returned to England, where he married, and had issue: William, John, Richard, and Edith Cromwell, the immigrants to Maryland.

There is *no evidence* to support this claim, neither is there evidence tending to substantiate a claim that the Maryland Cromwells were related in any degree, immediately or remote, to the family of the illustrious Oliver whose ancestral surname was originally Williams. It is fair to state, however, that Thomas Cromwell (1680-1723) of Maryland, a son of William Cromwell, the immigrant, gave the name Oliver to one of his sons.

There were other Cromwell families in England, as acceptable as any of the Hichen Brook line, albeit less renowned, among which we may, perhaps, discover the progenitor of the Cromwells of Maryland. A certain family bearing this surname resided in Wiltshire during the seventeenth century, and

[1] The baptismal name of Henry is "conspicuous for its absence," among the earlier Maryland Cromwells.

it possesses a special interest in the present instance by reason of the duplication of certain baptismal names, peculiar to the English family, in the Maryland family of Cromwell.

The latter settled in the Province prior to 1670. At least, two members of this family, William and John Cromwell, were in Maryland before that year, it is certain. The other two members, Richard and Edith Cromwell, arrived a few years later, perhaps. At any rate, the earliest mention of them in the provincial records is of a later date. We know that William, John, and Richard were brothers, and Edith was their sister.

The name of Cromwell, however, occurs quite early in the Maryland records. One Gershom Cromwell, planter, immigrated to the Province in 1653, accompanied by his wife Ann, and his daughter Rebecca Cromwell, and six years later patented a tract of land containing 300 acres, called "Cromwell." This tract is described as " lying on the east side of Chesapeake Bay, beginning at a marked oak standing upon a point called Cromwell's Point, near the mouth of a creek called Harris Creek . . . running to a creek called Island Creek, on the west side of said creek, running south and by west into Choptank Bay," etc. (Talbot County Rent Rolls: Annapolis, Warrant Book IV. 49, 239, 363). Gershom Cromwell was a witness under the will of Thomas Hawkins, dated 2 Oct. 1656 (Annapolis, Testamentary Proceedings III. 278). We know nothing further concerning Gershom Cromwell or his descendants.

In Virginia also, the name of Cromwell occurs very early. A certain John Abercrumway [Abercrombie], of York County, Virginia, in his will dated 4 April 1646, mentions " my countryman William Crumwell " [Va. County Records (by Crozier) VI. 15], and a Mary Crumwell appears to have been transported into Virginia by John Nicholls, Northampton County, in 1655 (Greer's "Early Virginia Immigrants," page 84).

We shall notice first, the four Cromwells mentioned above, in the order named, and then direct our attention to the Wiltshire family already mentioned as showing the same baptismal names as the Maryland Cromwells.

WILLIAM CROMWELL OF MARYLAND

WILLIAM CROMWELL arrived in Maryland in 1667, according to his own statement. He appears first in Calvert County, but soon removed to Ann Arundel County, taking up land on the south side of the Patapsco River, on the west side of Curtis Creek. He possessed lands also in old Baltimore County, where he resided, being known as William Cromwell " of Baltimore County." According to the records, on 8 Oct. 1679, " came William Cromwell of Baltimore County, and proved his right to 50 acres of land for transporting himself into this Province to inhabit twelve years since." A land warrant was issued to him the same day (Annapolis, Warrant Book WC. No. 2, 11.)

It appears, however, that on 4 June 1670, one Henry Hosier [2] of Calvert County, merchant, proved his rights to 1050 acres of land " for transporting into this Province to inhabit," twenty-one persons, among whom were William and John Cromwell (Annapolis, L. O. XII. 554). Again, on 11 March 1671, a certain Benoni Eaton claimed rights to land for transporting into the Province eleven " servants," among whom was one Will: Cromwell (*ibid.* XVI. 439). Benoni Eaton assigned his rights to George Robotham of Calvert County (*ibid.*).

Benoni Eaton was a ship captain, a member of the English house of Benoni Eaton and Company (Annapolis, Provincial Court Records, MM. 602), and styles himself in his will, dated 1 June 1675 and proved 31 May 1677, " Benoni Eaton of St. Mary Magdalen, Bermondsey " (Va. Mag. XIV. 88). In 1679, Deborah Eaton of " Rederith " near London, widow, relict and executrix of Benoni Eaton, late of London, " mariner," is mentioned (Annapolis, *Liber* WRC-No. 1; 146, 155). I am not aware that any relationship between this Benoni Eaton and the Eatons of New England has been suggested. Savage mentions a Nathaniel Eaton (b. 1609), of Cambridge, Mass., who fled to Virginia, but returned to New England. He was a brother of Hon. Theophilus Eaton of New Haven, Conn., and had a son named Benoni Eaton, a Cambridge, Mass., man, who married Rebecca ——, and died in 1690, according to Savage.

On 16 Dec. 1670, George Yate of Ann Arundel County, Md., Deputy Surveyor, for a valuable consideration, etc., assigned to John Cromwell and William Cromwell, both of Calvert County, planters, all his right, title, and interest to and in a certain warrant to the extent of 300 acres of land, the same being part of a warrant for 615 acres granted to the said George Yate on

[2] Henry Hosier was a witness under the will of Sampson Waring of Calvert County, in 1663. He removed to the Eastern Shore of Maryland, and was a "Commissioner" for Kent County in 1675, and a member of the Maryland General Assembly from Kent, between 1678 and 1686, the year of his death.

12 Dec. 1670. The aforesaid tract of 300 acres was patented by the Cromwells on 1 July 1671, under the name of the "Cromwells' Adventure." It was situated on the south side of the Patapsco, on the west side of Curtis Creek, in Ann Arundel County, being held of the Manor of Ann Arundel (Annapolis, Certificates and Patents XVI. 151: XIII. 80).

On 9 Oct. 1679, William Ball of Baltimore County, who "proved his right to 50 acres of land for transporting himself into this Province to inhabit seventeen years since," assigned his warrant to William Cromwell, by virtue of which the land was granted to the latter under the name of "Hunting Quarter," lying in old Baltimore County, on the south side of Patapsco River, and west of Curtis Creek, "to be held of the Manor of Baltimore." On 20 February 1679 (o. s.), George Holland of Ann Arundel County, for a valuable consideration, assigned to William Cromwell of Baltimore County, 34 acres out of a warrant for 760 acres. These two tracts of land, purchased and acquired by William Cromwell, together with the 50 acres granted him on 8 Oct. 1679, on account of his own transportation, were combined to make up a larger tract of 134 acres, to which was given the name of "Hunting Quarter" (Annapolis, Certs. and Pats. XX. 319: Warrants WC. No. 2; 11, 48).

In 1677, William Cromwell purchased "Mascall's Hope" (100 acres) from John Boring; "David's Fancy" (100 acres) from Rowland Thornburgh in 1680, and part of "South Canton" (84 acres) from Richard Cromwell, et al., in 1682 (Balto. County Deeds IR-PP. 17, 50; IR-MM. 193). On 12 January 1681/2, "Philip's Fancy" (61 acres) was granted to William Cromwell and surveyed to him 1 April 1682 (Balto. County Rent Rolls: Certifs. and Pats. XXI. 499). The latter tract was sold on 26 Dec. 1700, by William Cromwell, Jr., Gent., son of William Cromwell, Gent., the original grantee (Balto. County Deeds HW-No. 2. 69).

The name of William Cromwell occurs in the Annapolis "Testamentary Proceedings" of 1679, to wit: On 12 March 1678/9, George Parker of Calvert County, prayed a citation against William Cromwell and Nicholas Ruxton, both of Baltimore County, "to render a true account of ye goods of Robert Wilson, late of the same county, deceased, which said citation was issued under ye seal, immediately for them to appear, 3 June 1679." Again, on 26 Sept. 1679, " came William Cromwell of Baltimore County, and shewed the Judge here that

Richard Mascall, of ye same county, deceased intestate, and prayed that administration be unto the said Cromwell given." William Davis and William Ball were appointed to appraise the estate, and Thomas Long and William Ball were Cromwell's sureties (*Lib.* x. 365: xi. 89, 198, 212, 315).

There appears to have been some sort of relationship or close friendship between the aforesaid William Ball,[3] on the one hand, and William Cromwell and his wife Elizabeth (Trahearne) Cromwell, on the other. The former was a witness under Cromwell's will, probated in 1684, and one of the appraisers of his estate. Ball died in 1685, and in his will dated 10 April 1684, bequeathed personal property to Elizabeth Cromwell, widow of William, and realty in entail to her son William Cromwell, Jr. Richard Cromwell was a witness under the will of William Ball (Balto. County Wills i. 65). The Annapolis "Testamentary Proceedings" show that in 1685, Elizabeth Cromwell had become the wife of one George Ashman.

William Cromwell died in 1684. His will was dated 19 June 1680, and filed with the Court on 1 May 1684. He refers to "my executrix, by her maiden name Elizabeth Trahearne, now my dearest and loving wife," to whom he bequeaths a life interest in "Cromwell's Adventure," his dwelling plantation, with 100 acres adjoining called "Mascall's Hope." To his son William, a minor, he devises "Mascall's Hope" when he shall become "of age," and the dwelling plantation after his wife's decease. To his son Thomas, he devises the land on the west side of Curtis Creek called "Hunting Quarter," 134 acres. He mentions *his brother John Cromwell* in the body of the will, and in a codicil appoints *his brother Richard Cromwell* one of the "overseers" with John Willmot. The witnesses under the will were William Ball, Thomas Clark, and Elizth. (Edith?) "Geste" (Gist).

William Cromwell married Elizabeth Trahearne; perhaps, a second wife and, possibly, herself a widow. She married, *circa* 1685, George Ashman (d. 1699). On 6 Aug. 1706, the "additional account" of Thomas Cromwell, administrator of Elizabeth Ashman, deceased, who was executrix of George Ashman, was filed (Balto. County Admin. Accts., ii. 245). William Cromwell had issue:

---

[3] William Ball, who died in 1685, refers in his will to his wife Mary, who had, probably, predeceased him. Is it possible that she was the Mary Crumwell who was transported to Virginia in 1655?

i. William, b. 1678: d. 1735: m. Mary Woolgist (b. 1674), daughter of Arthur Woolgist, of Whorekill Town, Delaware Bay, by his wife Margaret Johnson, daughter of Aaron Johnson of New Castle, Delaware.

ii. Thomas, b. 168-; d. 1723: a Quaker: m. 1705, in West River Meeting (Ann Arundel County), Jemima Morgan, daughter of Thomas Morgan, and widow of James Murray.

iii. Philip, mentioned in the will of George Ashman (d. 1699).

iv. (?) Joshua, (according to certain authorities).

JOHN CROMWELL OF MARYLAND

JOHN CROMWELL was living in Calvert County in 1670, with his brother William, as we learn from the following certificate for land, issued by George Yate, the Deputy Surveyor: " Know all men by these presents that I, George Yate of the County of Ann Arundell, for a valuable consideration, etc., have granted, bargained and sold, etc., unto John Cromwell and William Cromwell of Calvert County, planters, all my right, title, etc., in a warrant for 300 acres of land, part of a warrant for 615 acres. Dated 16 Dec. 1670.

" By virtue of a warrant granted unto George Yate of the County of Ann Arundell, Gent., for 615 acres of land, bearing date the 12 Dec. 1670, 300 acres thereof being assigned by the aforesaid Yate unto John Cromwell and William Cromwell, both of Calvert County; These are therefore in humble manner to certifie that I, George Yate, Deputy Surveyor under Jerome White, Esq., Surveyor General, have laid out for the aforesaid Cromwells a parcell of land lying on the south side of Patapsco River, and on the north side of Curteus (Curtis) Creek in Ann Arundell County, called the " Cromwells' Adventure ": Beginning at a bounded white oake standing in a fork of a branch of Curteous (Curtis) Creek, and running by the land of John Browne called " South Canton," west southwest 160 perches to a bounded red oake, then north northwest 320 perches to a bounded red oake, then east northeast to a bounded white oake of Richard Mascall's land, then south southeast to the first bound Tree, containing and now laid out for 300 acres of land more or less, To be held of the Mannor of Ann Arundell. (Signed) George Yate, D. S. (Annapolis, Certifs. XVI. 151). The " Cromwells' Adventure " was patented 1st July 1671.

In 1714, Joshua and William Cromwell made an equal division of this tract between themselves and, in 1725, Joshua Cromwell mortgaged his holdings (150 acres) to Benjamin Tasker (Balto. County Deeds TR-A. 329: IS-H. 181).

In one of the Baltimore County Rent Rolls the following entry appears: "'Cromwell's Adventure,' 300 acres, surveyed 10 [*sic!*] Dec. 1670, to John and William Cromwell on the south side of Patapsco and north side of Curtis Creek (None of the Cromwells claims it)."

That John and William Cromwell were brothers is further corroborated in the testimony of one John Mash, given in March 1727: "John Mash of Baltimore County, aged about 60 years, swears that about 50 years ago [1677] he saw a bounded tree and that he was told by his master, *John Cromwell, and William Cromwell his master's brother,* and John Broad, that the said bounded tree was the beginning line of Mascall's Hope" (Balto. County Court Proc. HWS-No. 3, 6).

John Cromwell died, probably, before 1714, intestate. There appears to be neither record of his marriage nor name of his wife, but according to the late Wilson M. Cary, a careful genealogist, John Cromwell had issue:

i. Joshua,[3a] of Baltimore County, "son and heir": d. after 1748: m. Frances Ingram(?)

RICHARD CROMWELL OF MARYLAND

RICHARD CROMWELL is mentioned as the brother of William Cromwell in the codicil to the latter's will, *circa* 1684, and was appointed, by the testator, one of the " overseers " in connection with the management of the estate (Balto. County Wills I. 72). He is referred to as " my brother," *i. e.*, brother-in-law, in the will of Christopher Gist (d. 1691), who had married Edith Cromwell.

The first record of the name of Richard Cromwell in Maryland appears a few years subsequent to the earliest mention of his brothers, William and John Cromwell. This may be accounted for by the supposition that Richard was a younger brother, or that he arrived in the Province later, or both. It is certain that he was of adult age in 1682, when he and Christopher Gist (*circa* 1655-1691), acquired from Robert Clarkson, 245 acres of land called " South Canton," lying on the south side of Patapsco River. In 1686/7, there was assigned to Richard Cromwell, out of a warrant granted to Thomas Lightfoot, a parcel of land called " Cromwell's Addition " (160 acres), adjoining " South Canton."

[3a] According to some, a son of William Cromwell (d. 1684).

Richard Cromwell was a witness under the will of his brother-in-law Christopher Gist, 17 February, 1690/1, and he appears as administrator of one William Cole's estate in 1691 (Balto. County Court Proc. F-No. 1, 94). In 1694/5, Richard Guest (Gist), "son of Richard [*sic!*] and Edith Guest, late of Baltimore County, deceased, comes in to Court and consents to live with his uncle, Mr. Richard Cromwell," until he arrives at the age of twenty years (*ibid.* G-No. 1, 379).

Under the Act passed 9 June 1692, establishing the Church of England in the Province of Maryland, Richard Cromwell was appointed one of the six original vestrymen of Old St. Paul's Parish, in Baltimore County, as the following record shows:

September Court 1693 :—" Wee the Vestrie men for Potapsco Hundred met together att the house of major John Thomas [resolved] that att Pettete's Old Feild was the most convenient Place for to Erect a Church, and also appointed John Gay to be Clerke of the Vestrie, Mr. Watkings, Absent. And att another meeting the Last Saturday in August att Master Demondedie's [Dimondidier's] did confirme the Aforementioned proceedings, Mr. Watkings also Absent." (Signed)

George Ashman	Nicholas Corban
John Ferry	Richard Sampson
Francis Watkings	Richard Cromwell.[4]

At the March Court of Baltimore County, 1694/5, Thomas Lightfoot son of John and Ann Lightfoot, deceased, comes into Court and agrees to serve " Mr. Richard Cromwell " until twenty one years of age, provided that the said Cromwell take the estate of the said Thomas Lightfoot into his own hands, rendering an account of the same. So ordered (*ibid.* G-No. 1, 384).

Richard Cromwell appears in the list of Baltimore County " Taxables " of 1694, residing on the south side of Patapsco Hundred, with the following " taxables " on his place: namely, Wm. Barber, Jno. Eaglestone, Jno. Robinson, Edw. Russell, and two slaves (*ibid.* G-No. 1, 275). In 1696, he was one of the three Commissioners appointed on behalf of Baltimore County in connection with the matter of establishing the new boundary line between Baltimore and Ann Arundel Counties

[4] Balto. County Court Proc. G-No. 1, 126.

(Balto. County Land Records IS-IK. 86). He was one of his Majesty's Justices in 1696, and was an incumbent of the same office in 1701 (Md. Arch. xx. 466: Annapolis, Prov. Court Proc. TL-No. 2, 322).

On 27 April 1699, Richard Cromwell, Gent., for love and affection, etc., gives personal property to John and Jonas Williams, sons of Jonathan Williams, and on 1 May 1699, he is a witness to a "deed of gift" from Elizabeth Gibson to her son Thomas Gibson (Balto. County Deeds, TR-RA. 343, 347). He was a trustee under the will of James Murray of Patapsco Neck (Md. Hist. Mag. II. 246), and on 30 Sept. 1707, administered upon the estate of Thomas Edmonds, at which date he "affirms" to the account filed (Balto. County Admin. Accts. II. 144). This affirmation does not, necessarily, prove that he was a Quaker, but may, perhaps, indicate that he had conscientious scruples regarding the taking of an oath.

Besides his land holdings already mentioned, there was surveyed to Richard Cromwell, in 1695, a tract of 200 acres called "Cromwell's Range" in Baltimore County, on the north side of the Patapsco, located on "Hunting Ridge." In 1699, Nicholas Fitzsimmons conveyed to Richard Cromwell 300 acres of land called "Cordwainer's Hall"; and in 1705, Richard Gist of Baltimore County, "Carpenter," conveyed to Richard Cromwell of Baltimore County, Gent., the land called "Gist's Rest" (Balto. County Rent Rolls: Land Records).

In addition to the above mentioned lands, Richard Cromwell in 1707 "was possessed" of the following tracts:—"Utopia" (214 acres), surveyed 1670 to Robert Willson for 1320 acres; "Long Point" (250 acres) surveyed 1682 to David Jones; "Welcome" (100 acres) surveyed 1684 to Charles Gorsuch; "Maiden's Dairy" (248 acres) surveyed 1695 to Thomas Hooker (Balto. County Rent Rolls), and "Content" (150 acres) surveyed 1682 to George Saughier, in Ann Arundel County (A. A. Co. Rent Rolls).

The will of Richard Cromwell is dated 17 Aug. 1717, and was proved 23 Sept. 1717. The original is still on file in the office of the Register of Wills, at Baltimore, Md. He leaves personal property to his "cousin," i. e. nephew, Joshua Cromwell, to Margaret Rattenbury (his granddaughter) and, in the event of her death, to Hannah Rattenbury (sister of Margaret): also, legacies to his "mother-in-law, Besson," and to Edith Gist, daughter of his "cousin" (nephew) Richard Gist by Zipporah Murray, his wife: he bequeaths £30 and a ring to his "cousin" (nephew) Richard Gist, a ring to his "brother-in-law" James Phillips, and a ring to his "cousin" (nephew) Colonel Thomas Cromwell: he leaves £10 to Isaac Laroque,[5] and wearing apparel to Nicholas Besson. To his eldest son Richard (*non compos mentis*) he gives one shilling, with provision for his proper maintenance: to his wife Elizabeth, and "youngest son" John, he leaves the entire estate to enjoy, equally; but if the wife shall marry, she is to receive her "third portion," and in the event of his son John's death, all is to go to Edith Gist, who is to care for the son Richard Cromwell aforesaid. His wife Elizabeth, and "youngest" son John, were appointed executors. The witnesses under the will were William Cromwell, James Jackson, and Jabez Murray (Balto. County Wills I. 144).

The Inventory of the estate, amounting to £1512.13.5¾, was filed 13 Nov. 1717, and was approved by Thomas and Joshua Cromwell (nephews) as "next of Kin" (Balto. Inventories v. 299). On 8 June 1719, the account of "Elizabeth and John Cromwell, executors of Richard Cromwell, late of Baltimore County, deceased," was rendered, wherein they charge themselves with the estate heretofore exhibited in the Prerogative Court, amounting in "currency" to £1512.13.5¾, and also with sterling money in England due the estate £389.8.4 or, in "currency" £519.4.5, and with tobacco made on the plantation amounting, in "currency," to £169.19.8. Payments are credited as having been made to John Rattenbury, Margaret Rattenbury (on account of legacy left to her), to Nicholas Besson (on account of legacy to Margaret Besson), to Richard Gist and his daughter, to Joshua Cromwell and to Isaac Laroque (Balto. Co. Admin. Accts. I. 158). Elizabeth Cromwell makes "affirmation" to the correctness of the aforesaid account, which may indicate that she was a Quaker, or at least had scruples concerning the taking of an oath.

There is a probability that Richard Cromwell married more than once, for he refers in his will to a "brother-in-law" James Phillips. As he also refers to his "mother-in-law Besson" (*i. e.* Margaret Besson, wife of Thomas Besson, and daughter of George Saughier, through whom the tract of land, in Ann Arundel County, called "Content," evidently fell to Richard Cromwell), it is apparent that his last wife, Elizabeth, who sur-

[5] Formerly a "servant" of Richard Cromwell (Balto. Co. Court Proc. HWS-No. 4, 243).

vived him, was a daughter of Thomas Besson. She was, doubtless, much younger than her husband.

Richard Cromwell had issue:

i.   Richard, *non compos*, unmarried.
ii. John, d. 5 Aug. 1733: m. Hannah Rattenbury, daughter of Dr. John
     Rattenbury, of Baltimore County, Md.

EDITH CROMWELL OF MARYLAND

Edith Cromwell was born, probably, about 1660, and was,
therefore, quite young when her brothers, William and John
Cromwell, settled in Maryland. She married (1) about 1682,
Christopher Gist (1655-1691): (2) about 1692, Joseph Williams (1660-1693): (3) about 1693, John Beecher.

On 14 June 1682, Christopher Gist, with Edith his wife, and
Richard Cromwell, deed to William Cromwell part of " South
Canton " (Balto. County Deeds IR-MM. 193).

In March 1692/3, Edith Williams of Baltimore County,
widow, deeds to her son Richard Gist (Balto. County Court
Proc. F-No. 1, 360).

In March 1694/5, Richard Guest (Gist), son of Christopher
and Edith Guest, late of Baltimore County, comes into Court
and consents to live with his uncle " Mr. Richard Cromwell,"
until 20 years of age (*ibid*. G-No. 1, 379). He was, probably,
apprenticed to learn the carpenter's trade, in accordance with a
custom of Colonial times (Balto. Land Records IR-P.P., 192).

The will of Edith Beecher [*née* Gist], of Patapsco River,
Baltimore County, was dated 23 May 1694 (date of filing in
Court is unrecorded). She left her son Richard Gist to the care
of her brother Richard Cromwell and Thomas Staley, " to be
put to school," etc. (Baldwin's Md. Calendar of Wills IV. 240:
Balto. County Court Proc. G-No. 1, 543). Mrs. Edith (Cromwell) Beecher died about 1694/5.

On 27 Aug. 1708, was filed the second additional account, by
Benjamin Williams of Ann Arundel County (administrator of
Joseph Williams, of Baltimore County, deceased), of the
" effects unadministered by Edith Williams otherwise Beecher,"
wherein reference is made to Richard Cromwell's guardianship
of young Gist, son of said Edith (Balto. County Admin. Accts.
II. 122).

Edith Cromwell, by her first husband, Christopher Gist, had
issue:

i. Richard *Gist*, b. 1683: d. 22 Aug. 1741: m. Zipporah Murray. He was styled "Captain Richard Gist," and was 54 years old in 1737 (Ann Arundel Court Records).

We are now sufficiently acquainted with the facts relating to the early history of the Cromwells of Maryland to enable us to consider the Wiltshire Cromwell family, wherein a strikingly similar group of baptismal names will be noticed.

JOHN CROMWELL OF WILTSHIRE, ENGLAND

The will of JOHN CROMWELL, of Malmesbury, Wilts, is dated 23 Dec. 1639. He desires to be buried in the churchyard of St. Paul's, in the borough of Malmesbury, and then proceeds to make the following bequests: " To my wife Edith, part of the house I dwell in nexte the Forestreete; viz., the halle, entry, shoppe and Buttermey w'th. Rooms over same, with the garden access to the Backside and to the well for Water, so long as shee the said Edith keep herself in my name, if shee shall not outlive the lease from the Burgess and Burrow of Malmesbury.

" To said Edith also four of the best kine, the best Bedd and furniture, the great Kettle and middle post, all the pewter she brought when I was married to her, all the wood in the Back- arde, 100 of cheese and 2 quarters of malte, two flitches of Bacon, and the best fatted Pigg, the Table Board in the Halle w'th. frame, 2 Barrells, and use of the Presse in the Halle and all her apparell, lumes, woolen and all my household linen.

" To my sonne Phillipp, 40 shillings to be payd him att his returne into England: To John Crumwell, son of said Phillip Crumwell, £5, and my will is that my wife Edith shall have use of said five pounds to breede and bring up the said John Crum- well untill he is fitt to be placed Apprentice: To Edith, daugh- ter of said Phillipp Crumwell, 20 shillings.

" To my sonne Richard, the rest. My sonne Richard to keep the 6 kine, till 25th March nexte. (Signed, with mark) John Crumwell.

The " overseers " named in the will were Robert Arche, gent., and Thomas Burgess, yeoman: the witnesses were Roger Jarrett, Thos Burgess, William Smith. The will was proved at " Chipperton " [Chippenham], where the rectory of Great Somerford is located, on 19 February 1639/1640. The inven- tory of the estate, dated 20 January 1639/40, was exhibited, on the same day the will was filed, by the aforesaid " overseers " and amounted to £204.16.4 (Archdeaconry of Wilts, filed Wills, 1639, old No. 53).

In the Malmesbury Abbey Church Registers, the originals of which I have had copied, is the following entry under the "Burials": "Buryed ye 27th of December [1639] John Crumwell of this Towne, one of ye Chiefe Burgesses."

The expression "Chief Burgess" is probably the same as the strictly local term of "capital burgess." It refers to the holders of land granted by King Athelstan (died 940 A. D.), to the men of Malmesbury. There are twenty-four capital Burgesses, and they hold a larger section or allotment of land than the ordinary Commoners. There is a field in Great Somerford, Wilts, that is still called "Cromwell's Leaze."

John Cromwell [6] of Malmesbury, Wilts, died *circa* 25 Dec. 1639: m. Edith [6] ——, and had issue:

i. William [6] (perhaps), bpt. 20 Oct. 1605, at Great Somerford, Wilts (no further record).

ii. Philip,[6] b. 1610, or 1612, at Malmesbury, Wilts: d. 30 March 1693, at Salem, Massachusetts: m. (1) Margaret —— (d. July 1634, at Malmesbury, Wilts): m. (2) 22 Jany. 1634/5, at Malmesbury, Eleanor Cooper: m. (3) Dorothy —— (1607-1673), in Massachusetts: m. (4) Mary —— (1611-1683), in Massachusetts: m. (5) Margaret —— (*vide infra*).

iii. Richard,[6] married Elizabeth ——, sister of Margaret Baynam (d. 10 Dec. 1642, at Malmesbury). He had a daughter, Mary, bpt. 23 Jany. 1641/2, at Malmesbury. There is no later record of him in the Malmesbury records.

iv. Thomas,[6] b. *circa* 1617(?), at Malmesbury, Wilts: d. 17 March 1686, at Salem, Massachusetts: m. *circa* 1640, Anne ——, at Malmesbury (*vide infra*).

PHILIP CROMWELL OF WILTSHIRE, ENGLAND, AND SALEM, MASS.

PHILIP CROMWELL, son of John Cromwell (d. 1639) of Wiltshire, was born *circa* 1610-1612, at Malmesbury, Wilts. His age is given as "about 50 years" in 1664, "about 74 years" in 1686 (Essex Institute Hist. Coll. VIII. 26: New England H. and G. Register VI. 249), and his gravestone gives his death as occurring 30th March 1693, at the age of 83 years.

He was evidently in New England at the date of his father, John Cromwell's will, 23 Dec. 1639. He had a wife Eleanor (*née* Cooper), whom he had abandoned in England, with her infant son John Cromwell. Both mother and child were domiciled at the home of her father-in-law at Malmesbury.

Philip Cromwell was bequeathed only 40 shillings by his father, "to be payd him att his returne into England." It is

---

[6] The reader will notice the recurrence of each of these names among the earliest generations of the Maryland Cromwells.

probable that he had left England *circa* 1639 on account of a certain marital indiscretion.[7] He was, it appears, a "gay blade," and was married five times. On 3rd of 12th month, 1643, Richard Cromwell and others were presented by the Salem, Mass., Grand Jury for living absent from their wives, and according to the Salem Court Records, on 5 Sept. 1647, Richard Cromwell is mentioned as "living from his wife 7 or 8 years, and not sending her any relief for self or child he left with her." It was ordered that "he be engaged to go over to England to his wife, with liberty to returne if he see cause, etc., before December" (Essex Institute Hist. Coll. xxxix. 367).

Philip Cromwell's occupation is given as wheelwright, and also as butcher or "slaughterer," in Salem. He lived on the south side of Essex Street, between Derby Square and Central Street. In 1664, Philip Cromwell, butcher, conveyed to Major William Hathorne and Mr. Walter Price, feoffees in trust for his wife Dorothy Cromwell, widow of Allen Kenniston (or Kynaston), his house and "slater houses," etc. He was a "freeman" in 1665, and Selectman 1671-1675. He died at Salem, Mass., 30 March 1693, aged 83 years, according to his gravestone, and his estate fell to his only surviving child, John Cromwell.

Philip Cromwell married (1) *circa* 1633, Margaret ——, who died and was buried at Malmesbury, Wilts, 15 July 1634: m. (2) on 22 January 1634/5 Eleanor Cooper, at Malmesbury. She died, probably, in England: m. (3) Dorothy ——, widow of Allen Kenniston (Kynaston). She died at Salem, Mass., 27 Sept. 1673, aged 67 years (gravestone): m. (4) on 19 Nov. 1674, Mary ——, widow of Robert Lemon. She died at Salem, 16 Nov. 1683, aged 72 years: m. (5) Margaret ——, widow of John Beckett, who survived him.

His will, filed 4 April 1693 [*Liber* iii. 105] mentions his wife Margaret, a brother Thomas Cromwell, and a son John Cromwell. Philip Cromwell had issue:

By 1st wife, Margaret:

i. John, bpt. 11 July 1634: buried 31 July 1634, at Malmesbury.

By 2nd wife, Eleanor Cooper:

ii. John,[8] bpt. 26 June 1635, at Malmesbury, Wilts: d. at Salem, Mass.,

---

[7] "Anne Bunch ye base borne Daughter of Ideth Bunch & ye reputed father is Richard Crumwell was baptized the XXVIII Februarie 1638/9" (Malmesbury Abbey Register).

[8] Savage incorrectly credits this child to Philip Cromwell's wife, Dorothy Cromwell.

30 Sept. 1700, aged "near 65 years" (gravestone): married, at Salem, Mass., Hannah, daughter of Jacob Barney, Sr., who survived her husband.

[There was a John Cromwell, with wife Milicent (d. 25 May 1656, at Malmesbury)].

iii. Edith, bpt. 9 July 1637: buried 27 May 1642, at Malmesbury.

THOMAS CROMWELL OF WILTSHIRE, ENGLAND, AND SALEM, MASS.

Thomas Cromwell, son of John Cromwell (d. 1639) of Wiltshire, was born *circa* 1617, at Malmesbury, Wilts. His age is given as 43 years in 1660 (New England H. and G. Register vi. 249). He died 17 March 1686 at Salem, Mass.

" Thomas Cromwell came over later than his elder brother Philip, and in company of his nephew John, whose estates his daughters inherited: *Viz.*, (I) Ann, who m. (1) Benjamin Ager: m. (2) in 1672, David Phippen: (II) Jane, who married 1665/6, Jonathan Pickering. Thomas Cromwell is called a tailor, in the deed records " (Essex Institute Hist. Coll. xxxix. 367, *et seq*). He witnesses a will at Salem, Mass., in 1654, and Thomas and Ann Cromwell are witnesses in 1655 (New England H. and G. Register vi. 249).

Thomas Cromwell married *circa* 1640, Ann ——, and had the following children, all baptized at Malmesbury, Wilts:

i. Edith, bpt. 8 Jany. 1643/4: d. 2 February 1643/4, at Malmesbury.
ii. Thomas, bpt. 16 Sept. 1645, at Malmesbury: d. 16 March 1663, at Salem, Mass.
iii. Agnes, bpt. 18 March 1646/7, at Malmesbury.
iv. Jane, bpt. 4 July 1649, at Malmesbury: m. 1665/6, at Salem, Mass., Jonathan Pickering.
v. A daughter (? Ann), bpt. 18 July 1651: (?) married (1) Benj. Ager: (2) David Phippen.

CONCLUSION

From the foregoing, one may readily see the striking duplication in the baptismal names occurring in these two families—the Cromwells of Maryland and the Crumwells of Wiltshire. These names are William, John, Richard, Edith, Thomas, and Philip. It is true that the majority of these names occur also in the immediate family connection of Oliver Cromwell, the Lord Protector of England. In fact, some of these names are in more or less common usage and are not peculiar to any one family, but the name of Edith is sufficiently rare to make its recurrence, along with the other identical baptismal names, a matter of some importance. When we consider, moreover, that John Crumwell of Malmesbury, in Wiltshire, left sons who had settled in Massachusetts a few years prior to the arrival of the Cromwells in Maryland, and if we may assume that Captain Benoni Eaton, who transported in his ship William Cromwell to Maryland some time prior to 1671, was a relative of the Eatons of Massachusetts, we may have an appreciable collection of circumstantial evidence on which to ground a hypothesis. On the other hand, the claim of the Oliver Cromwell relationship, when critically examined, vanishes into a thing of mist and vapor.

From the foregoing genealogical sketches, it will be observed that two of the recorded sons of old John Cromwell of Malmesbury may be eliminated as possible progenitors of the Maryland Cromwells. We have yet to account for a third known son of John Cromwell, of Wiltshire, Richard Cromwell, whose wife was Elizabeth, and who had a daughter Mary, baptized at Malmesbury Abbey 23 January 1641/2. We next find mention of him in an entry on the register a few months later, in a reference to the burial of "Margaret Baynam, the sister of Richard Crumwell's wife, 10 Dec. 1642." After this date all trace of Richard Cromwell appears to be lost. It may be noted, in this connection, that there exists a seeming tradition which claims a Richard Cromwell, of the Lord Protector's family, as the ancestor of the Maryland Cromwells.

There was, perhaps, a fourth son of John Cromwell, of Wiltshire, William Cromwell, baptized at Great Somerford, Wilts, 20 Oct. 1605. Beyond this reference, however, there appears to be no further mention of him in the local records. We may, therefore, conjecture the possibility of either Richard or William Cromwell, sons of John Cromwell of Malmesbury (d. 1639), being the parent of the four Cromwells who settled in Maryland in the latter half of the 17th century.[9]

I have had copies made from the Cromwell entries in the Malmesbury Abbey Church Register (1626-1670), and in the Bishop's Transcripts, at Salisbury, of the Registers of Great Somerford, Wilts (original records destroyed by fire prior to 1707). The entries are given hereunder.

---

[9] A John Cromwell of Malmesbury, whose wife Milicent died 23 May 1656, is not accounted for. He may have been a son of John Cromwell (d. 1639), but this is merely conjecture. A John Cromwell died at Great Somerford, Wilts, in Dec. 1669.

CROMWELL ENTRIES IN MALMESBURY ABBEY CHURCH
REGISTERS:

1634:   Baptized the 11th of July John Crumwell ye son of
        Phillip and Margaratt Crumwell.
        Buried the 15th of July Margarett Crumwell the wife
        of Phillippe Crumwell
        Buried the last of July John Crumwell the son of
        Phillip and Margaret Crumwell.
        Married the same 22d day of January in the morn-
        inge about nyne of the clock Phillip Crumwell and
        Elnor Cooper.

1635:   Baptized XXVIth of June John Crumwell sonne of
        Philipp and Eleanor Crumwell.

1637:   Baptized the 9th July 1637 Idith Crumwell the
        daughter of Philip and Eleanor Crumwell.

1639:   Buryed the 27th of December John Crumwell of this
        Towne, one of ye Chiefe Burgesses.

1641/2:   Baptized the XXIIII of Januarie Mary the daughter
        of Richard and Elizabeth Crumwell.

1642:   Buryed Edith Crumwell the dr. of Ellinor Crumwell
        the 27th of May 1642.
        Buryed the Xth of December 1642 Martha Baynam
        the sister of Richard Crumwell's wife

1643/4:   Baptized the VIIIth of Januarie 1643 Edith Crum-
        well daughter of Thomas and Anne Crumwell
        Buryed the second of Februarie Edith Crumwell ye
        dr. of Thomas & Anne Crumwell of this Towne.

1645:   Baptized the 16th of September Thomas the sonne of
        Thomas and Anne Cromwell of this Towne

1646/7:   Baptized 18th Martii Agnis the dr. of Thomas &
        Agnis [sic!] Crumwell of this Towne

1649:   Baptized the 4th Julye 1649 Jane Crumwell the
        daughter of Thomas and Anne Crumwell

1651:   Baptized the 18 July 1651 . . . the dr. of Thomas
        and Anne Crumwell.

1656:   Milicent the wife of John Crumwell of Malmesbury
        deceased May 23 & was buried May 25 1656.

CROMWELL EXTRACTS FROM REGISTERS OF GREAT SOMERFORD,
WILTS, (*taken from the Bishop's Transcripts, at Salisbury
Registrar's Office*)

1605 :   Baptized William son of John Cromwell 20 Oct. 1605

1619 :   Baptized Mary daughter of Richard Cromwell 4 May
           1619

1620 :   Baptized Mary daughter of Richard Cromwell I Jany
           1620/1
           Buried Richard son of Richard Cromwell 24 June
           1620.

1669 :   Buried John Cromwell 10 Dec. 1669

1700 :   Richard Freeth & Ann Cromwell married 24 June
           1700.

CROMWELL FAMILY.

CORRECTION.

In the December, 1918, issue of the *Maryland Historical
Magazine* (Vol. XIII, p. 397), a clause in the will of John Cromwell of Wiltshire, was inadvertently omitted. It follows certain
bequests to his wife, Edith Cromwell, and reads thus:

" To my sonne Thomas, the Halle w'the the chamber over
wherein Ellinor the wife of Phillipp Cromwell my sonne now
dwelleth and also the lofte over the noste and 2 best kine next
to those given my wife, one halfe hundred of cheese and 4
bushells of malte and one halfe householde stuffe not already
given."

On page 399, lines 4 and 7, *Richard Cromwell* should be,
Philip Cromwell.

FRANCIS B. CULVER.

THE ANCESTRY OF REV. HATCH DENT.

FRANCIS B. CULVER.

The Rev. Ethan Allen, D. D., in his *Clergy in Maryland of the Protestant Episcopal Church*, page 17, gives the following brief biography of Hatch Dent:

" A native of Trinity, Charles County—had been an officer in the U. S. Army—brought up in the Church—was ordained by Bishop Seabury in 1785, and became Rector of Trinity, Charles County, his native parish, and in 1797, in connection with it, of William and Mary, Charles County, for a year. He had a private school which in 1796 grew into the Charlotte Hall School, of which along with his parish, he was the first principal: was five times a member of the Standing Committee. He died 1800, aetat.—."

Ridgely's *Historic Graves of Maryland*, page 41, mentions the Dent memorial at Charlotte Hall, consisting of a flat tombstone which was transferred from the glebe of Trinity Parish on July 30th, 1883, and which bears the following inscription: " Rev. Hatch Dent, son of Hatch and grandson of John Dent of Yorkshire, England, one of the early settlers of the Province of Maryland, was born May 1757 [1751] and died December 30th, 1799. An honored officer in the Army of the Revolution of 1776, and an Eminent Teacher and Minister of the Church. Ordained by Bishop Seabury in 1785."

The tombstone record to the contrary, notwithstanding, Rev. Hatch Dent was not a grandson of the settler, John Dent. The parents of Hatch Dent were Hatch Dent (born 1707 in St. Mary's County; died after 1783 in Charles County) and his wife Ann (Poston) Dent.

Hatch Dent, the father, deposed in 1768 that he was 61 years old, and that *his* father was John Dent. In 1779, he gave his age as 72 years (Charles Co., Md. *Land Books* No.

60, folio 410; No. 67, folio 473). He married about 1728 and had several children of whom the Rev. Hatch Dent (born May 20th, 1751) appears to have been the youngest (see *Trinity Parish Register, Charles County, Md.*).

Hatch Dent, Sr., was the son of John Dent, but not the settler of that name who died in 1712, in St. Mary's County. The proof of this is established by an original Certificate on file in the Land Commissioner's Office, Annapolis, Md., marked "Charles County 310," and bearing date August 19th, 1720:

"By virtue of a Warrant of Resurvey, etc., bearing date the 13th of March last, granted unto John Dent of Charles County, to resurvey a tract of land called

Cumberton,	originally on	17 May 1668	granted unto	Francis Pope;	200 acres
Reading,	"	" 10 June 1671	"	" Abraham Rhodes:	300 "
Evan's Addition,	"	" 10 June 1671	"	" Edward Evans;	100 "
Barnaby,	"	" 29 July 1674	"	" John Dent,	
			the father of the aforesaid John Dent;	60 "

reducing ye said several tracts into one entire tract and adding thereunto such contiguous lands as should be vacant to any or every of the aforesaid tracts. These are to certify that I have resurveyed and laid out for and in the name of the aforesaid John Dent ye several tracts or parcels of land aforementioned, with the addition of 509 acres, and reduced all into one entire tract called "Dent's Inheritance," etc., containing and laid out for 1169 acres to be held of Calverton Manor."

Then follows a petition recorded fourteen years later, to wit: "The petition of John Dent, of Charles County, humbly sheweth that his father John Dent, in his lifetime had resurveyed for him a certain tract of land called "Dent's Inheritance," containing 1169 acres, whereof 509 acres was found to be vacant land added, for which the said John Dent made good rights, etc. . . . but before his Lordship's grant to him given did issue, he the said John died," etc. (11 June 1734).

This last named John Dent, the petitioner of "1734," was the son of John Dent the grantee under the warrant of Resurvey of 1720, who unfortunately died before the certificate was issued. That the petitioner, John Dent, aforesaid, was the brother of Hatch Dent, Sr., is proved by a Deed of Gift from said John Dent, bearing date March 10th, 1732/3, " in consideration of the natural love and brotherly affection," etc., conveying to said Hatch Dent a tract of 144 acres of land in Charles County, being part of " Dent's Inheritance " (*Charles County Land Records.*, Lib. M, No. 2, folio 322).

The brothers, John and Hatch Dent, Sr., were sons of John Dent (born 1674 in St. Mary's County; died about 1732 in Charles County) by Mary Hatch (died 1725), who was probably the first wife of the last mentioned John Dent (see Annapolis, *Testa. Proc.*, XXIX, 268; *Inventories* XI, 356).

John Dent (1674-1732) was the son of the immigrant, John Dent of Yorkshire, England (born about 1645: died 1712 in St. Mary's County) by his wife Mary Shercliff (born 1647: living in 1712), daughter of John Shercliff (died 1663) of St. Mary's County, who married Anne Spinke, sister to Henry Spinke.

John Dent, the immigrant, came to Maryland about 1663. He acquired considerable estates under the will of John Harrison, of Charles County, which was executed in 1690 and proved in 1708, and owned other estates, besides. He was styled " Captain " and " Gentleman." He was Justice of St. Mary's County 1679, 1680, 1685; of the quorum 1694; captain of Chaptico Hundred 1689; captain of the Foot 1694; and a Vestryman of King and Queen Parish in 1696 (*Md. Arch.*, XV, 256, 326; XVII, 379; XX, 138; XIII, 241; XX, 106; XXIII, 18).

Rev. Hatch Dent (1751-1799). Therefore, was the son of Hatch Dent (1707-*post* 1783) and Ann Poston; grandson of John Dent (1674-1732) and Mary Hatch (d. 1725); great grandson of Capt. John Dent (1645-1712) and Mary Shercliff (1647-*post* 1712).

Rev. Hatch Dent married in 1778 Judith Poston (1758-

1814). His brothers and sisters were: John Dent (b. 1729); Mary Dent (b. 1732); Catharine Dent (b. 1734); Ann Dent (b. 1737); Lydia Dent (b. 1739); Esther Dent (b. 1742); Rhoda Dent (b. 1744); Capt. Hezekiah Dent (b. 1747).

SOME FRIENDS OF "YE FRIENDS IN YE MINISTRY"

By Emerson B. Roberts

George Fox came to Maryland in 1672 to visit among the Friends on both sides of the Bay. While at the head of Third Haven, he was at the home of John Edmonson, wealthy planter and merchant, and one of the earliest Quaker settlers on the eastern shore. Out of his Talbot visit came the first Meeting in Maryland, organized likely in the home of Wenlock Christison. From this came Betty's Cove Meeting with its Meeting House on Miles River, which continued until at " our joint Quarterly Meeting for both shores, held at ye home of Ralph Fishbourne ye 27th day of ye First Month 1683, the Meeting decided upon this greater house, it being unanimously agreed that Betty's Cove Meeting be removed to Ye Great Meeting House." Third Haven Meeting House—" sixty foote long, forty four foote wide . . . framed with good white oak . . . ye roof double raftered . . . and studded . . . well braced " stands today, not only the oldest Meeting House in America, but an enduring monument to those who framed it. Many families who worship there today bear the names of those at the first meeting, the 24th of the 8th month, 1684. It is of some of those first Quaker families in Talbot that we write.

I. THE DIXONS

The Dixons were identified with Talbot County before 1681, the year " Dixon's Lott " was surveyed for William Dixon. Throughout the centuries they have preserved Quaker ideals; they are connected by marriage with other Quaker families of Talbot—Bartlett, Kemp, Stevens and others, yet prominent in Maryland affairs, and with Christison, Harwood, Ball, Marsh, Taylor, Sharp and Gary—Quaker families whose names now survive only in the records, but whose blood is preserved through the descendants of daughters.

Like several of the other Quaker families the Dixons were first in Calvert, then Patuxent, and probably for some time in the area later to become Dorchester before they came to Talbot.

Robert Dixon is recorded as present by proxy at a General Assembly at St. Mary's, Monday, 5th of September, 1642, " to consult and advise on matters involving the Safety of the Colony (*Archives of Maryland*, I, 162). In August of the same year, he with others, was assessed 30 pounds of tobacco by the Assembly. In a tax statement of the same year he is called "Robert Dixon of St. Mary's County."

Robert Dixon and Elizabeth Dixon "of The Cliffs," Calvert County, appear in the records of that county in June 1675 as witnesses to the will of Richard Evans "of the Cliffs." This Robert Dixon made his will May 1, 1688, though it was not probated until May 21, 1695 (Land Office, Wills, Liber 7, 51). In it he mentions three sons, none of whom is of age. John and Joseph on becoming of age, are to inherit "Huttson's Clifts," and Robert at the age of twenty-one is to have "one hundred acres on the eastern shore in the possession of John Edmondson," the prominent Quaker planter and merchant in lower Talbot. There can be little doubt that these acres were in upper Dorchester or in lower Talbot, near the Choptank River, the region in which are to be found the Edmondsons, as well as other families closely related by blood and religious ties to the Dixons. Likely the tract was a part of that Dorchester survey for Robert Dixon, patented to him May 4, 1664, as "John's Garden." It is adjacent to "Cold Spring," surveyed April 16, 1664, for Robert Harwood, another early Talbot Quaker with whom the Dixons had close ties. Robert Dixon's daughters, whom he also mentions in his will, were Elizabeth, Mary, Sarah and Rosamond. All of them appear to have been under sixteen in 1688. His wife was Elizabeth, but the name of her father is not known.

It seems likely, though documentary evidence cannot be produced, that the first Robert Dixon of St. Mary's and Calvert, possessing as he did land in Dorchester and in Talbot, is the brother of that William Dixon, first of the name in the Talbot records.

For William Dixon [1] the Talbot land records show two surveys: "Dixon's Lott," 100 acres, surveyed May 26, 1681, and "Cumwhitton," 200 acres, surveyed January 4, 1684. In the Calvert Papers (Talbot Rent Roll) the latter is recorded to William *Dickinson*, but there can be no doubt that this is William Dixon, for the original papers are yet in the possession of the family.

---

[1] See Burke, *Landed Gentry* (1939), Dixon of Cumwhitton, County Cumberland.

In 1686 in Talbot, William Dixon was a witness to a deed by John Bayley.

In Talbot land records there is another land transaction by William Dixon, planter. In 1691 he sold to John Edmondson, merchant, one half part of a tract called "Brandford," containing 1008 acres, on the west side of Delaware River and north side of Western Branch, between the Millcheck and the land of William Wilson called "Cambridge." This land had been purchased by William Dixon in 1683 'from William Rigeway. William Dixon and John Edmondson sold 600 acres called "Improvement" (presumedly the other half) on Duck Creek to John Howell of England for £40. This land must be in Delaware or in Maryland near the Delaware line.

William Dixon's home was on Miles River, the tracts being "Fausley" and "Ye Ending of Controversie," the site of "The Villa" erected in the 1870's by Mr. Richard France of Baltimore. Dixon is also to be remembered as the first in Talbot to provide freedom for his slaves—long before the consciences of other Quakers prompted them to do so.

By his wife, Elizabeth, whom he married June 4, 1680, as her third husband, and of whom more subsequently will be said, William Dixon had a son, William, born 14th of the 12th month, 1682, baptised 7th of the 4th month, 1701, who died young (Third Haven records). William Dixon's will, dated May 16, 1708, is recorded in Talbot (Liber EM 1, f. 251). In it he refers to his nephew, Isaac Dixon, as "my own brother's son," but unfortunately does not name the brother, leaving us only the inference that Isaac was son or grandson of that Robert Dixon who possessed the 100 acres on the eastern shore and who left his son Robert in charge of John Edmondson. To this nephew, Isaac, William Dixon left land on the Miles and Chester Rivers which has become the nucleus of the estate that continues in the possession of the Dixons. The tracts are "Bennett's Hill," "Dixon's Outlet" and "Ashby Asteemee." In his will he mentions his sister's son, Joseph Ash, and his sister's daughter, whom he calls Elizabeth Watt of Bramton. Also he mentions his son-in-law (step-son) Peter Harwood, who is to heir "Cumwhitton." Of interest is the fact that he left 50 acres, along with some personal effects, to two old Negroes, Mingo and Mimkine. While the will of William Dixon appears to be a sufficient document, nevertheless a bill was passed by the House, October 28, 1710, confirming the last will and testament of William Dixon (Proprietary Papers I, 1701-1733).

Isaac Dixon,[2] planter, and Elizabeth Harwood, daughter of Peter and Elizabeth Harwood, were married in 1710, their intention being declared in the Monthly Meeting, 28th of the 12th month, 1709, and again on the 30th of the 1st month, 1710, when she was called "Elizabeth Harwood, the younger" (MSS. Third Haven Meeting II, 35 and 36).

Isaac and Elizabeth increased the landed property of the Dixons. At Isaac's death, March 22, 1736, he held land in both Talbot and Queen Anne's. In Talbot, besides "Bennett's Hill" and "Dixon's Outlet," he held the Wenlock Christison and Robert Harwood tract, "Ye Ending of Controversie." His will (Talbot Co., HB 2, 206 and Annapolis, Wills, Liber 21, f. 742 and Accounts, Liber 16, f. 282 and Liber 18, f. 83) records his children:

1. Christopher Dixon, who was born 1722, died unmarried, 1741

2. Isaac Dixon, who was born June 24, 1724, died 1777, married 1747, Mary ———, by whom he had issue presently to be mentioned.

3. John Dixon, who was born 10th of the 8th month 1726, died 1790, married 1757, Elizabeth Kemp, daughter of John Kemp and his wife, Magdaline Stevens, and had three sons, Isaac, John and James, and two daughters, Sarah who married a Wilson, and Elizabeth who married twice, both times "outside the good order," first, August 16, 1791, Edmund Carville, Sr., of Annapolis, and second, William Bryan, Sr., of Talbot and Queen Anne's. The marriage of Elizabeth Dixon to Edmund Carville appears in both the Quaker records of Third Haven and in the Anne Arundel County Court. The Carvilles were Churchmen. The minutes of Third Haven Monthly Meeting for the sixth, seventh, eighth and tenth months. 1793 record the "going out in marriage of Elizabeth Carville, late Dixon, daughter of John Dixon," and show the granting of a certificate of removal for her

---

[2] Born 1696, says Burke, *Landed Gentry* (1939).

directed to Indian Spring Monthly Meeting. The record in the Anne Arundel Court reveals the date, August 16, 1791 (Hall of Records, Anne Arundel Marriages).[3]

Edmund and Elizabeth Carville had a family of sons and daughters. The eldest child, a daughter, Sarah, born September 27, 1792, married James Lowe Bryan. Edmund Carville died in the summer of 1812 at his home plantation "Crafford" (or Crayford) on Kent Island. His widow married William Bryan, Sr., of Talbot and Queen Anne's, but by him she had no children. The first wife of William Bryan was Catherine Lowe, daughter of Captain James Lowe and great-granddaughter of John Lowe, of Grafton Manor, and his wife Mary Bartlett, Quakeress.

In 1776 John Dixon was residing in the Mill Hundred of Talbot County. He died intestate in 1790. The inventory of his estate, dated December 17, 1790 (Talbot Co., Liber JGA, f. 260), names his children.

4. Elizabeth Dixon, who married, 4th day of the 10th month, 1735, Joseph Atkinson. Her witnesses were her brothers, Christopher and Isaac (Third Haven Records).

We return to Isaac Dixon, 1724-1777. He married, 1747, Mary ———. Perhaps it was the fact that he was married by a priest (Third Haven Records I, 99) that caused him to be left one shilling by his grandfather, Peter Harwood, in 1756. Isaac Dixon, true to the traditions of the family, added to his acres. With the property that had come to him, he passed to his heirs "Ashby," 800 acres, and "Cottingham," 900 acres, both of which are in Talbot and adjacent to the earlier Dixon estates. Isaac Dixon's will, 1777 (Talbot Co., JB 3, f. 23), records his children:

1. William Dixon, born March 6, 1748, died 1812, married, 1770, Anne Parish, of whom presently.

---

[3] In passing let it be noted that Dr. Gaius M. Brumbaugh, who has done so much to preserve Maryland records, has made an easily excusable error in transcribing this particular record. In *Maryland Records* he has the name as Edmund Carroll, rather than Edmund Carvoll. Examination of the original, however, (Hall of Records) leaves no doubt. It is not surprising that others, less skilled than Dr. Brumbaugh, in transcribing other Carvoll or Carville records, have made the same error—doubtless due to the almost indistinguishable difference in the two names in script, and to the fact that the eye expects to see "Carroll" in Maryland records in almost every county, while Carvoll is relatively rare.

2. Robert Dixon, born 1757, married Ann Berry, daughter of James Berry, and had a son, James. In his will, November 13, 1781 (Talbot Co., JB 3, f. 65) he says he is of Third Haven Monthly Meeting, and, after mention of his wife and son, leaves some inheritance to his sisters, Elizabeth and Rachel, " provided neither of them accomplish their marriage outside the good order."

3. Ann, born 1752, married ———— Atkinson.

4. Elizabeth, born 1754.

5. Mary, born 1759.

6. Rachel.

William Dixon, 1748-1812, married 1770, Anne Parish of West River, Anne Arundel County. The marriage was by a priest and for it Anne was disowned on the 30th of the 8th month, 1770. (Third Haven Records, Vol. 4, p. 106, and Vol. 5, p. 222.) Of this marriage there was one son, Robert Dixon, known as " Robert Dixon of Moreland," and six daughters, Rachel Watts, Mary Fairbanks, Rebecca Ruse, Susan, Ann and Elizabeth, who died unmarried in 1826. In her will (Talbot Co., JP 8, f. 312) she refers to her nephew Isaac Dixon, her niece Sarah, and to her sister, Rebecca Ruse.

From Robert Dixon of Moreland is descended Mr. James Dixon, the present representative of the Dixon family in Talbot through the line on the accompanying chart. This Robert Dixon married at Bayside, July 2, 1802, Elizabeth Fairbanks, daughter of James Fairbanks and his wife, Elizabeth Troth.

II. GARY

John Gary came to the province as an early immigrant, but whether he resided first at Patuxent or in Dorchester is uncertain. Whether he was a brother or otherwise related to Stephen Gary, another worthy and prominent Quaker immigrant of 1662 to Dorchester is not certain, but probable. However, John Gary's wife was Judith, and she seems to have come with him into Maryland. There were two children, John Gary, Jr. and Elizabeth, who was born in 1633. The date of death of the elder John Gary does not appear, but his widow, Judith, had remarried before March 6, 1650, Dr. Peter Sharpe, eminent Quaker physician of his day (*Archives*, X, 139).

DIXON OF TALBOT

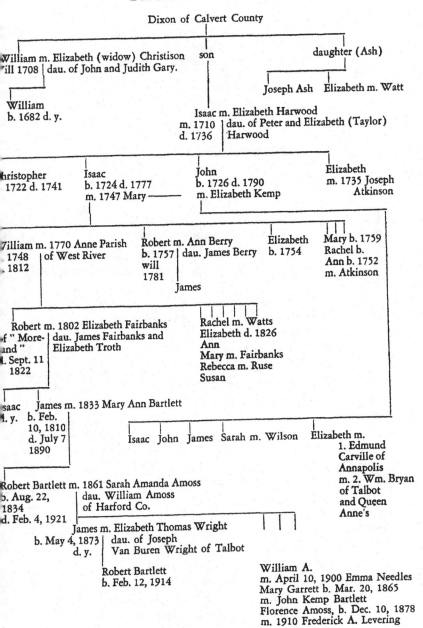

Dixon of Calvert County

William m. Elizabeth (widow) Christison
ill 1708 | dau. of John and Judith Gary.

son

daughter (Ash)

Joseph Ash   Elizabeth m. Watt

William
b. 1682 d. y.

Isaac m. Elizabeth Harwood
m. 1710 | dau. of Peter and Elizabeth (Taylor)
d. 1736 | Harwood

hristopher
1722 d. 1741

Isaac
b. 1724 d. 1777
m. 1747 Mary —

John
b. 1726 d. 1790
m. Elizabeth Kemp

Elizabeth
m. 1735 Joseph
Atkinson

Villiam m. 1770 Anne Parish
1748 | of West River
, 1812

Robert m. Ann Berry
b. 1757 | dau. James Berry
will
1781

James

Elizabeth
b. 1754

Mary b. 1759
Rachel b.
Ann b. 1752
m. Atkinson

Robert m. 1802 Elizabeth Fairbanks
f " More- | dau. James Fairbanks and
and " | Elizabeth Troth
. Sept. 11
1822

Rachel m. Watts
Elizabeth d. 1826
Ann
Mary m. Fairbanks
Rebecca m. Ruse
Susan

saac
. y.

James m. 1833 Mary Ann Bartlett
b. Feb.
10, 1810
d. July 7
1890

Isaac   John   James   Sarah m. Wilson

Elizabeth m.
1. Edmund
Carville of
Annapolis
m. 2. Wm. Bryan
of Talbot
and Queen
Anne's

Robert Bartlett m. 1861 Sarah Amanda Amoss
b. Aug. 22, | dau. William Amoss
1834 | of Harford Co.
d. Feb. 4, 1921

James m. Elizabeth Thomas Wright
b. May 4, 1873 | dau. of Joseph
d. y. | Van Buren Wright of Talbot

Robert Bartlett
b. Feb. 12, 1914

William A.
m. April 10, 1900 Emma Needles
Mary Garrett b. Mar. 20, 1865
m. John Kemp Bartlett
Florence Amoss, b. Dec. 10, 1878
m. 1910 Frederick A. Levering

Of John Gary, Jr., there is the statement of George Fox in his
Journal—

We went this week [in 1672] to a General Meeting from which we
went about eighteen miles further to John Gary's, where we had a very
precious Meeting, praised be the Lord God forever. . . . On the second
of the twelfth month [1673] we had a glorious Meeting at Pattexon
and after it went to John Gary's again, where we waited for a boat to
carry us to the Monthly Meeting at the Cliffs, to which we went, and
living Meeting it was, praised be the Lord: This was on the 6th of the
12th month.

His Dorchester survey, " Cedar Point," 200 acres, was made on
December 10, 1662, and that for 600 acres as " Gary's Chance,"
February 2, 1664.

John Gary, Jr., died in 1681 in Calvert County. In his will
(Annapolis, Liber 2, f. 156) he refers to his wife Alice; his
mother Judith, then the widow Sharpe; his sister, Elizabeth
Sharpe, and her daughter, Sarah; his sister, Elizabeth Dixon and
her Harwood children; and to Stephen Gary, the relationship not
being stated.

Elizabeth Gary is important in a study of Talbot Quaker families and their descendants, for, as Argotta to the French Kings,
she is to Talbot Quakers, " the mother of them all." She was
born in 1633 and died in 1696 in Talbot. She married three
times, first Robert Harwood, after what has been described as the
strangest courtship on record (*Archives* X, 499) ; second, the distinguished Wenlock Christison; and third, William Dixon. By
her first marriage she had three sons, John, Peter and Samuel
Harwood. By her second husband, Wenlock Christison, she had
one daughter, Harney. After the death of Wenlock, Elizabeth
remained a widow about a year, marrying April 8, 1680, William
Dixon, the first Dixon of the Talbot records. The minute in the
Third Haven Record runs thus: " 1680, eighth day of the fourth
month, called June, at the home of Elizabeth Christison. . . . " By
this marriage there was one son, William, who died young.

The widow Dixon did not survive her third husband. Her will
is dated October 30, 1696, and was proven April 16, 1697 (Annapolis, Liber 7, f. 264). In the document she states that she is
the wife of William Dixon, whom she leaves as her executor and
legatee. She speaks of her eldest son John Harwood, and of her
son Peter Harwood. She speaks of Harney as her " eldest

daughter." It is not apparent, however, that there were younger daughters. Neither the Talbot testamentary records nor the Third Haven register reflect such. In her will she clearly identifies herself by the mention of a tract of 800 acres, "Emergency," located in The Fenwick Colony in New Jersey, purchased by her brother, John Gary. This tract she left to her son, John Harwood.

III. HARWOOD

Robert Harwood appears first in the land records of Anne Arundel County where the survey of 100 acres, "Woolman," is recorded November 26, 1651. Then in September, 1657, Robert Harwood of Patuxent was paid 0100 for going with a message up to Captain Fuller from the Court (*Archives*, I, 365). By 1662 he was on the eastern shore. On April 16, 1664, appears the Dorchester survey, "Cold Spring," 200 acres, for Robert Harwood. Perhaps he was the son of John Harwood whom we find in 1638 in St. Mary's Hundred (*Archives*, I, 29), or perhaps the son of that Peter Harwood brought into Virginia in 1641 by Ambrose Bennett of Isle of Wight County (Greer, *Virginia Immigrants*), or himself that Robert Harwood, aged 17, immigrant to Virginia, 1635 in the ship Safety (Hotten, *Original Lists*, p. 120). These possibilities present an interesting study.

George Fox, on his visit to Maryland, abode at least one night at the home of Robert Harwood. In his *Journal* is this record:

But on the day following we traveled hard: and though we had some trouble in the Boggs in our way, we rode about Fifty Miles: and got safe that night, but very weary to a Friend's house, one Robert Harwood, at Miles River in Mary-land; This was the 18th of the 7th month [1672].

Robert Harwood died in 1675. His will (Annapolis, Book 2, f. 354) was probated May 27, 1675. In it he mentions his wife and children, but only one son, Peter, is called by name. The family was as follows:

1. John Harwood
2. Peter Harwood, born 1668, died 1756, married July 20, 1690, Elizabeth Taylor, daughter of Thomas Taylor. (For the ancestry of Elizabeth see *Maryland Historical Magazine*, XXXIII, p. 280 ff., "Captain Phillip Taylor and Some of His Descendants " by the present writer.)

3. Samuel Harwood, who married in 1710 Elizabeth Troth, daughter of William Troth of "Troth's Fortune."

Peter Harwood, 1668-1756, and his wife, Elizabeth, appear in a land record of Kent County (L. R. No. 8, f. 258) 1719-26, in which they make over to Christopher Hall a certain tract. This record states that Peter and Elizabeth Harwood acquired this tract by the will of William Dixon, late of Talbot County. The witnesses to this instrument are Isaac Dixon and Peter Sharpe, the grandson of old Doctor Peter Sharpe, through William, his son.

Peter Harwood died in 1756, his widow surviving. The *Maryland Gazette* for October 7, 1756, contains a notice of his death: "Talbot County, September 27, 1756. Yesterday died here, after a lingering indisposition of two or three years, Mr. Peter Harwood, in his ninety-fourth year. He was born and lived all his time in this county" (*Maryland Historical Magazine*, XVIII, p. 151). His will is recorded in Easton and in Annapolis (Liber BT 2, f. 78). The children were:

1. Elizabeth Harwood, who married, in 1710, Isaac Dixon, of whom we have treated.

2. Robert Harwood, born 1709, married Mary ———, and had issue, one son, James, born 1737, and four daughters, Ann, born 1731; Mary, born 1733; Elizabeth, born 1735; and Rachel, born 1739. Robert Harwood of Talbot County was named in the Assessment Bill of 1760 granting £60,000 for the security and safety of the Province, as one of the Commissioners for Talbot. The bill did not pass so Robert Harwood presumedly had no official service on this account (*Archives*, LVI, p. 288).

3. Peter Harwood, Jr., married Susannah Steward (born Susannah Kemp), September 7, 1744. The will of Susannah, 1751, is recorded (Annapolis, Wills, DD 7, f. 89).

IV. CHRISTISON

Much has been written of Wenlock Christison. There is no thought to repeat here. Most of the printed sources are readily available.[4] The briefest summary of his public life will suffice.

[4] Harrison, *Wenlock Christison and the Early Friends of Talbot*; Bishop, *New England Judged* (London, 1661, 1667 and 1700); Norris, *The Early Friends of*

In 1660 he was in prison in Boston, charged with being a Quaker. Previously he had been at Salem, later at Plymouth. Stripes on his naked body laid on with deliberation, robbed of his waistcoat, his Bible taken for fees, imprisonment, suffering, his friend William Leddra condemned and " hung upon a Tree at Boston for being such a one as is called a Quaker." At Hampton, now within the borders of New Hampshire, he was sheltered by Eliakin Wardel, a Friend, " contrary to law," and Eliakin was arrested and fined. In June, 1664, Wenlock came to Boston from Salem to meet two women apostles and Friends, Mary Thompson and Alice Gary, recently come from Virginia where they had received persecution and indignity. Again in 1665 Wenlock Christison was apprehended on the old charge. Wenlock, with the two women, was banished from the province, " stripped to the waist, and made fast to a cart, and whipped through Boston, Roxbury and Dedham." Wenlock had ten stripes in each town, and his companions six apiece. A period of respite in Rhode Island followed, but at last impelled by what motive, we know not, the three came again to Boston, under some protection of one of the King's Commissioners. Again there was collision with authority, and trial and sentence that Alice, Mary and Wenlock be whipped out of the jurisdiction. Shortly after, all embarked— Wenlock for Barbados, and the two women for the Bermudas, never to return to New England. Uncertain years follow, but in 1670 Wenlock Christison and Alice Gary are in Maryland.

Dr. Peter Sharpe, " chirurgeon," of the Cliffs, Calvert County, and Judith his wife, transferred to Wenlock Christison, August 1, 1670, " in consideration of true affection and brotherly love which we have and bear unto our well beloved brother Wenlock Christison in Talbot County, and also for other divers good causes and consideration we at this present especially moving . . ." one hundred and fifty acres of land, known by the name " Ending of Controversie " (Land Records of Talbot County, No. 1, f. 120). In 1672 the benevolent and wealthy old Doctor remembered Christison in his will, and with him, significantly, Alice Gary, as follows:

Maryland (1862); Forman, " Wenlock Christison's Plantation, ' the Ending of Controversie ' " in *Maryland Historical Magazine*, XXXIV, p. 223; Tilghman, *History of Talbot County*, and various histories of Maryland.

I give to ye Friends in ye Ministry, namely: Alice Gary, William Cole and Sarah Marsh, if then in being; . . . Wenlock Christison, and his wife . . . in money or goods, at the choice of my executors, forty shilling worth apiece; also, for a perpetual standing, a horse, for the use of Friend in ye Ministry . . .

Another Friend, Henry Willocks, on the twentieth of the first month, 1670/1 made over a man-servant to him for no materia consideration. In October, 1677, there is record of a purchase by Wenlock Christison from John Davis of part of the tract of lanc called " Ashby," and there is no consideration mentioned in the deed. So Wenlock Christison prospered.

The first Quaker meeting recorded in Talbot was at Wenlock Christison's the twenty-fourth of the first month, 1676.

Wenlock Christison was twice married. In the New England record of him, there is no mention of wife or children. In 1672 Dr. Peter Sharpe in his will refers to a wife. In Births and Burials, Third Haven Records, page 2, is recorded " Elizabeth Christison, daughter of Wenlock and Mary Christison, born 5th month, 13th day, 1673." May Wenlock have married Mary Thompson, his co-sufferer? We do not know. Nor of her death do we know, but the Third Haven Record contains this:

Att our Men's Meeting at Wenlock Christison's the fourteenth day of the 5th month, 1676, Wenlock Christison declared in the meeting that if the world or any particular person should speak Evilly of the Truth, or Reproach friends for his proceedings in taking his wife, that then he will give further satisfaction and clere the Truth and Friends by giving forth a paper to condemn his hasty and forward proceedings in that matter, and said that were the thing to do again, he would not proceed so hasty, nor without the consent of friends.

This refers to his marriage to the widow Harwood, who was born Elizabeth Gary. The censure, doubtless, was for non-conformity in not securing " The consent of friends " in advance of the event. There seems no other inference to draw; there is no other mention of the matter in the records.

Christison had three daughters—Mary and Elizabeth by his first wife, and Harney by his second wife. The eldest daughter, Mary, married John Dine, who once resided upon St. Michael's River, but later removed to Kent Island. In 1684 she sold her portion of the estate she had from her father to Isaac Dixon. Tilghman has suggested that Elizabeth married Peter Harwood, but the

eferences in this paper show that this is not likely. Rather it
seems she married first, Murtaugh Harney of Miles River, and
had by him a daughter whose name is not preserved, but who
was a beneficiary under the will of Matthew Smith, brewer of
Philadelphia. Secondly she married about 1699 Thomas Hopkins.
With her second husband she administered on the estate of the
first (Annapolis, Account XIX-1/2, f. 109).

The will of Matthew Smith, brewer of Philadelphia, late of
Maryland, is dated May 29, 1705 (Philadelphia City Hall, Wills,
Book B, p. 433). It is confirmatory of the relationships previously outlined. He says that he was formerly of Maryland. He
leaves a bequest of a plantation on Kent Island to the daughter
of Murtaugh and Elizabeth Harney, and the inference is that
Murtaugh Harney is not living for he provides that Friend
Thomas Hopkins shall look after the estate for her until she is
of age or is given in marriage. That she was quite young may be
further inferred from the fact that in the original will he left a
blank for her name, which evidently at the time he did not know
and intended to supply later. Then he leaves a substantial bequest
of real estate in Bohemia Manor to " Friend Thomas Hopkins
and his children by his wife, the daughter of Wenlock Christison." Because of its interest, the author of this article has deposited a photostatic copy of the original of the will of Matthew
Smith with the Maryland Historical Society.

William Dixon informs the meeting yt his Daughter-in-law [step-
daughter] is stole away and married by a priest in ye night, contrary to
his and his wife's minds; that he has opposed ye same, and refused to
pay her portion, for which he is cited to appear before ye Commissary
General, and now he desires to know whether ye meeting would stand by
him, if he should sue ye priest yt so married her. Ye meeting assents and
promises to stand by him in it, he taking ye meeting's advise from time
to time in his proceedings therein. (Third Haven Records.)

Whether this refers to the marriage of Mary or Elizabeth is
not clear. John Dine, we surmise, was not a Quaker; Murtaugh
Harney possibly was, but the marriage may not have been in
accordance with the rules of the Society; Thomas Hopkins was a
Quaker, and the same remark applies; Harney was, at the time,
an infant of tender years.

In 1674 we find Wenlock Christison a petitioner to the Assembly of Maryland in the matter of oaths and affirmations (Ridgely,

Annapolis, p. 60). In 1676, he was elected to the House of Burgesses from Talbot, and in this capacity he served his county and his province, presumedly until his death. Christison died early in the year 1679, for we find that the Half Yearly Men's Meeting, held at John Pitt's on the eastern shore in Talbot, eighth month, 1679, action was taken relative to securing Elizabeth Christison for what legacies were given to John Stacy, his old servant of many years, by Wenlock Christison, " he now being set free" (MSS. Records, Maryland Friends). The will (Annapolis, Wills, Liber 2, f. 89) is dated February 25, 1678, and probated May 20, 1679. In it he mentions his wife, Elizabeth, daughters Mary and Elizabeth, and an unborn child. He mentions his sons-in-law (step-sons), Samuel, Peter, and John Harwood, a daughter-in-law, Elizabeth Harwood, and his brother-in-law, William Sharpe.

In the records of Third Haven, 23rd of the 5th month, 1680, there is inventory of the personal property of Wenlock Christison. His old home, now in ruins, has been given some of the recognition it deserves in the recent article by Dr. Forman in this *Magazine*. Christison deserves a niche in any Hall of Fame.

V. SHARPE

Dr. Peter Sharpe, " Chirurgeon " of Calvert County, was an eminent Quaker. He resided in Calvert though he held patents in Dorchester and in Talbot.

"Sharpe's Island," important as the stepping stone by which the first settlers of Dorchester, principally Quakers, came there from Calvert, 1657 and thereafter, has all but vanished. It took its name from the old doctor, its first patentee. Col. Tilghman, the historian of Talbot County, studied its narrowing confines, and assures us that a century ago it comprised seven hundred acres; in 1848 it was found by survey to contain 438 acres, and a few decades later than that it was so popular as a cool, breeze-swept resort that a hotel of real proportions was built upon it, but by 1900 not a trace of the hotel remained, the island then being reduced to 90 acres. In 1910 its diminishing territory embraced only 50 acres, and today, if one crosses that way, when a westerly breeze combines with a high tide, one will see the seas washing completely over the tiny fragments that remain. And Sharpe's

Island, when it was surveyed for the picturesque old doctor, was a handsome estate of more than a thousand acres. It is easy to see with the mind's eye its inviting shores as one looked eastward from the cliffs of Patuxent. Also the map of the Chesapeake, made by Captain John Smith, becomes more real when we think of Sharpe's Island as it was in the first decade of the 17th century.

We do not know that Dr. Sharpe ever resided on his island; indeed, it seems more likely that he resided over the cliffs of Calvert County, which are immediately opposite on the western shore and in plain view, simply numbering his acres on the island with those patented to him in Dorchester and in Talbot, as parts of his outlying possessions. In Dorchester, his patent is for "Sharpe's Point," 200 acres, surveyed December 29, 1662; in Talbot, "Chestnut Hill," 1000 acres, surveyed July 1, 1665; while in Calvert, the rent rolls of Lord Baltimore reveal only "Sharpe's Outlet," 200 acres, surveyed February 26, 1664. In the Dorchester rent rolls, the next items to the Sharpe patent are a patent to John Edmondson and one to John Gary, bearing further testimony to the early migrations of these families from Calvert, across the bay, by the way of Sharpe's Island, to Dorchester and the eastern shore.

Dr. Sharpe married Judith, the widow of John Gary, and had by her son, William, a daughter Mary and possibly, a second daughter Elizabeth. William Sharpe, who married, 1673, Elizabeth Thomas, daughter of Thomas Thomas, was the father of Peter Sharpe whom we have found in Kent County records in land transactions with the Dixons. Mary Sharpe married, before February 9, 1690, William Stevens, son of William Stevens of Dorset County (*Maryland Historical Magazine*, X, 284).

Dr. Peter Sharpe died in 1672, and his will bears testimony to several of the family relationships of early Calvert and Talbot Quaker families (Annapolis, Wills, Liber 1, f. 494). He mentions Robert and Elizabeth Harwood and their children, and Friend in the Ministry, Wenlock Christison and his wife, William Cole, Sarah Marsh, John Burnett and Daniel Gould. He also mentions Alice the wife of John Gary. Nicholas Oliver he calls "cousin."

GARY, SHARPE, HARWOOD AND CHRISTISON

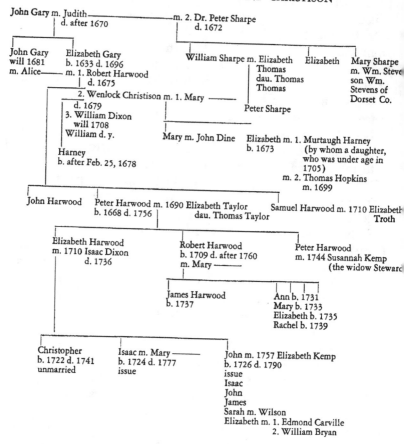

John Gary m. Judith —————————— m. 2. Dr. Peter Sharpe
　　　　d. after 1670　　　　　　　　　　d. 1672

John Gary　　Elizabeth Gary　　　　William Sharpe m. Elizabeth　Elizabeth　Mary Sharpe
will 1681　　b. 1633 d. 1696　　　　　　　　　　　Thomas　　　　　　　m. Wm. Steve
m. Alice——　m. 1. Robert Harwood　　　　　　　　dau. Thomas　　　　　son Wm.
　　　　　　　d. 1675　　　　　　　　　　　　　　Thomas　　　　　　　Stevens of
　　　　　2. Wenlock Christison m. 1. Mary ————　　　　　　　　　　Dorset Co.
　　　　　　d. 1679　　　　　　　　　　　　　Peter Sharpe
　　　　　3. William Dixon
　　　　　　will 1708
　　　　　William d. y.　　　　　Mary m. John Dine　　Elizabeth m. 1. Murtaugh Harney
　　　　　　　　　　　　　　　　　　　　　　b. 1673　　　　(by whom a daughter,
　　　　　Harney　　　　　　　　　　　　　　　　　　　　who was under age in
　　　　　b. after Feb. 25, 1678　　　　　　　　　　　　　1705)
　　　　　　　　　　　　　　　　　　　　　　　　　m. 2. Thomas Hopkins
　　　　　　　　　　　　　　　　　　　　　　　　　m. 1699

John Harwood　　Peter Harwood m. 1690 Elizabeth Taylor　Samuel Harwood m. 1710 Elizabeth
　　　　　　　　b. 1668 d. 1756　　　dau. Thomas Taylor　　　　　　　　　　　　　Troth

Elizabeth Harwood　　　　Robert Harwood　　　Peter Harwood
m. 1710 Isaac Dixon　　　b. 1709 d. after 1760　m. 1744 Susannah Kemp
d. 1736　　　　　　　　　m. Mary ————　　　　　（the widow Steward

　　　　　　　　James Harwood　　　Ann b. 1731
　　　　　　　　b. 1737　　　　　　Mary b. 1733
　　　　　　　　　　　　　　　　　Elizabeth b. 1735
　　　　　　　　　　　　　　　　　Rachel b. 1739

Christopher　　Isaac m. Mary ————　John m. 1757 Elizabeth Kemp
b. 1722 d. 1741　b. 1724 d. 1777　　b. 1726 d. 1790
unmarried　　　issue　　　　　　　issue
　　　　　　　　　　　　　　　　Isaac
　　　　　　　　　　　　　　　　John
　　　　　　　　　　　　　　　　James
　　　　　　　　　　　　　　　　Sarah m. Wilson
　　　　　　　　　　　　　　　　Elizabeth m. 1. Edmond Carville
　　　　　　　　　　　　　　　　　　　　　　2. William Bryan

IDENTITY OF EDWARD DORSEY I.

A New Approach to an Old Problem.

By CAROLINE KEMPER BULKLEY.

(Copyright 1938, by Caroline Kemper Bulkley.)

I.

THE PROBLEM STATED.

The origin and English ancestry of Edward Dorsey continue to be a problem to genealogist and historian. A man who was the progenitor of a large and widespread clan, allied to the most important families in Maryland's early history, remains to his descendants a shadowy figure without a background. Tradition and much fallacy printed as fact have been accepted without investigation.

My first researches in the matter, following in the footsteps of others, proved to my mind that all given theories of origin were untenable. I studied English histories and heraldries, finding them all available in American libraries.[1] J. Watney's *Account of St. Osyth's Priory, Essex* (1871), Achille DeVille's *Chateau d'Arques* (Rouen, 1839), and Rev. J. N. Worsfold's *History of Haddlesey* (1894), were imported from England.

Since actual records of Edward Dorsey are lacking in England and America, my re-study approached the problem from the angle of names associated with the immigrant in this country. If the English residence of any one of his near neighbors who were landholders can be traced, there is still a chance of further light on the origin of Edward Dorsey.

No more fanciful nonsense was ever written about Shakespeare's second-best bed than that which has been woven around imagined connections of Edward Dorsey, the colonist. When my extensive reading had formed a background and standard

[1] The Library of Congress, Newberry Library, Chicago; the public libraries of St. Louis, St. Paul and Cincinnati, six university libraries and several historical society collections in America.

of judgment, recent research in Virginia archives and in the new Hall of Records at Annapolis, produced many documents of which photostats and certified copies furnish exact testimony. Comparing and correlating these with former results confirmed some conclusions and refuted others.

From the British Museum and the Society of Genealogists in London we learn that no general survey of the Darcie name or its variants has ever been made. The Irish branch has a set of charts which utterly ignores any British branches. A wide search in the Prerogative Court of Canterbury has provided wills in abundance, not elsewhere collected, which together with those printed in an early volume of the *Transactions*[2] of the Essex Archaeological Society, by its industrious secretary, Mr. H. W. King, furnish a very complete file of wills. A similar search for wills recorded in small London Courts was made by Mr. C. L. Ewen, and by myself in Annapolis.

Lists of immigrants rarely mention an actual home location, but if such a fact is given for one person of a group it may be a clue to another's "home town" or neighborhood. Headrights are a mixed blessing as to identification but, taken in connection with others, are often helpful. Seals are mainly wafers; few carry an impression and when they do, it is seldom heraldic.

This study of Dorsey is therefore based on the group with which he came or settled, and the reason for his coming is assumed to be a matter of trade which, at that time, was as basic in a man's life as kinship. These assumptions are not weakened by finding that little investigation has been made of the names selected from among his neighbors. It is none the less important historically to know that a certain group clung together in locating themselves in two places in Virginia and in the flight to Maryland, where they continued to be neighbors.

An exclusively religious motive for immigration is not found

---

[2] This file was found by Dr. Arthur Adams, librarian of Trinity College, in Yale University Library.

Seal from original will of Joshua Dorsey[2] 1687. In Hall of Records at Annapolis. Beneath is the witness signature of Edward Dorsey[1] from a Tr'd deed in the records of Lower Norfolk County at Portsmouth, Virginia.

in Colonial history, except in Massachusetts. Modern historians accept "merchandizing" as the basic reason for American colonization. This is no new thesis and the aggrandizement of "freedom to worship God" long ago received a rather caustic commentary in William Robert Scott's *Joint Stock Companies* (p. 14).[3]

Patents for superfluities ["luxuries" in our day] were censured by the House of Commons, such as gold and silver thread, playing cards, keeping of unlawful games . . .

Into the last category fell "Footeball," for which a "Tommy" Dorsey and a Bennett were gaoled at Uxbridge.

The playing card grant was the most obnoxious. It was a grant to Edmund Darcie, who had been given power from the Privy Council to search shops for cards that did not bear his seal. This Edmund was a merchant of Tangier, where he died; his heir was Captain Henry Darcie of London, and the witch-hunting justice, Brian Darcie, was Edmund's brother.

Such search-warrants were much abused; merchants in foreign trade who rather assumed the place of small ambassadors, not supported by the state, would not stand for such a law. The encouragement for the use of private capital and energy in foreign trade was explained in part by Sir Edwin Sandys when he advocated the establishment of the Virginia Company:

What else shall become of gentlemen's younger sons, who cannot live by arms when there are no wars, and learning preferments are common to all and mean? So that nothing remains for them save only *merchandise* . . . unless they turn serving men which is a poor inheritance.[4]

The introduction of the photostat is making history over; for documents read as wholes often tell, or lead to, a different story; further, the camera can not err. A long and broad perspective is essential to clear judgment of a great man. Of an unimportant one, we get no perspective unless we find him in a

---

[3] State Papers, Dom. Elizabeth, CCLXXIX, 93 *Calendar*, 1601-1603, p. 46.
[4] House of Lords *Journals*, 1604, I, p. 334.

group. This is very apparent in studying land grant locations
in Virginia and the seating of those who went up into Maryland to escape old Governor Berkeley's persecutions, to which
later reference will be made.

II.

THE SEVEN EDWARDS.

Authorities for pedigrees quoted here are heraldic charts,
local histories, and wills in the Public Record Office, London;
also Chancellor, Jacob, Dugdale and J. W. Clay. The wonderful chart of D'Arcy antiquarians of Ireland has been consulted
in the editions of 1905, and 1920, extended to 1935, by Rev.
E. P. P. C. Thompson of London. These charts date back to
Regnvald (Rognvald), father of Rollo the Dane. On the basis
of them Canon d'Arcy and the Primate of Ireland, the Lord
Archbishop of Armagh, are members of the "Falaise Committee," founded to preserve the memory of William the Conqueror. This is the only French society known to me that is
similar to our own organizations.

1.   Thomas D'Arcy of Hornby, in his will of 1605, named a
son Edward, who seems to fit the facts about an "absentee
landlord," mentioned in Clay's *Extinct and Dormant Peer-
ages* and Poulson's history of Holderness, county York.
The record is of a petition from inhabitants of Freer-Stain-
forth "tenants of one Edward Darcy Esquyer who offered
to sell us but houldeth yt at so unreasonable a price as wee
are never able to pay and for that we are in choyce to purchase yt ourselves or to cheuse our landlord." No other
record of this Darcy has ever been found.

Thomas of Hornby confuses the issue by having had
three wives, two of whom were named Elizabeth, the other
"Collubia." His second eldest and his youngest son were
named Thomas, and two others bore the name of Edward,
if we accept what has been printed in various books. His
first wife, Elizabeth Conyers, had one son 'Mr. Conyers
Darcy' as recorded by several writers, yet on her tomb-
stone is inscribed "which Elizabeth had by the said Thomas

two sonnes and one daughter." One might reasonably assume that the wife's maiden name was given to the first son and the second eldest was "Thomas the Elder" of York, whose will (1653) shows that he also indulged in three wives. He had a son Richard, whose mother was Susan Foord (Foard); a Foard family were in Dorchester County, Maryland, with Richard Preston, in whose will Richard Darcy is mentioned as a kinsman. A Richard Darcy was a headright of Cornwallis and Mr. Secretary Lewger. A seal used by a Dorchester County Darcy in 1749 does *not* connect him with any specific branch of the family. Thomas Darcy of York had a son Edward by his third wife, but no birth date is to be found. It seems improbable, to say the least, that the last child of an old man dying in 1653 could have been born early enough to identify him as our immigrant.

2.   Sir Arthur d'Arcy, Lord Lieutenant of the Tower and Captain of the Isle of Jersey, died in 1561. He was sent into the North to pacify the rebellion of Aske, for participation in which his own father had been beheaded. Sir Arthur had a son who became Sir Edward of Dartford in Kent, 1584-1612.

3.   Sir Edward Darcy of Kent had a grandson Edward, 1610-1669, who was quite notorious. He could not have been the father of the man who came to America before 1642. This Edward left no male heirs, although records of him are numerous; notably in Public Record Office documents.

4.   The twelve children of Conyers d'Arcy (see *supra*) are listed by Poulson, Dugdale and Clay, but not by Jacob. An Edward is given as born 1619/20, "died same year." This presented a possibility in case the death record were a mistake, but a search of Hornby records by the Rev. Mr. Beamish showed no record of such a babe.

5.   Thomas of York (will 1653) had one son named Edward by his third wife Jane, but he is far outside the possible dates.

6.   Burke's Irish Gentry, no longer considered an authority, gives to Nicholas of Platten (Corbettstown branch of the family) a son Edward, but the date is far too early for any connection whatsoever.

7.   " Edward Darcie aged 13 in 1632 licensed to go to Bergen with his master " is recorded in Fothergill's Exchequer records.

It must be emphasized that the line of Edward in Kent ran out in heiresses, as did the whole English clan finally. The widow Blower of the Kentish branch turns up in Chancery suits, as second wife to Sir Edward of Dartford (see no. 3), a fact nowhere else chronicled.[5] The College of Arms can produce records of Lady Elizabeth Barnes as administratrix of the estate of her father, Edward Darcy (1610-1669), but denies having any references to an emigrant of that name. In Essex the witch-hunting Brian D'Arcy is prominent in the story as a high Justice, and we have seen that his brother Edmund of London and Tangier comes to light in the playing card monopoly business.

But pursuing elusive Edwards, only the seventh, a boy of thirteen in the year 1632, appears as the possible immigrant. Whether he evolves into the Virginia-Maryland citizen or not, and whether his parentage and original home are ever known, he is the most intriguing of the seven. The possibilities are tangled with almost invisible clues which may be found in American records and which might mean everything or nothing.

It is unfortunate that John Camden Hotten decided arbitrarily what names to copy in *Persons of Quality* bound for the American Colonies, but Gerald Fothergill's publication of those omitted is a great help. He explains that it was easier to get a license to go abroad—that is, to the Low Countries—than to go to America direct. Many are licensed to go beyond seas, to cross to European ports, or to travel, who *may have* eventually reached our shores. Fothergill's lists contain many Virginia

---

[5] Similarly, just one record has been found of the second marriage of Dame Mary d'Arcy to an Offley.

family names, but I have used a transcript, together with a reprint of the names in Hotten, to make clearer the names from the Exchequer Records of the King's Remembrancer, No. 16.

"Edward Darcie—lycensed April 18th 1632, aged thirteen, to go with his master Richard Gips to Berghen." [6]

This Richard Gips (Gibbs) [7] made two other journeys with "2 servants," but Edward Darcie is not again mentioned. It is probable that Gibbs was of the family known to have been Copyholder tenant of Peet Hall at West Mersea, on the island between Colne and Blackwater Rivers. Peet Hall stood on the mainland connected by a Stroude (causeway) with the island and opposite was St. Osyth of the Essex Darcies. The estate was owned by Viscountess Savage, the persecuted recusant heiress of the last male of that line, Thomas, Lord D'arcie of Chiche-St. Osyth.

In histories of the Netherlands there are six Bergens described, with variable spelling, but among commercial towns is one Bergen "aproom" (for Op Zoom) which is used more than any other except the historic Flushing. This Bergen was on the river Zoom, a tributary of the Scheldt, twenty-seven miles from the river mouth, near to Middleborough and Zerrick Zeas.

The phrase "master" in the sailing list quoted, does not necessarily imply that the child Darcie was either servant, apprentice or page, since the precise designation would have been used, if known. Many wills bequeathed young sons to powerful kinsmen or close friends, to be in their care as "friends and servants." They were entitled to everything that could be done for their "advancement"—though education

---

[6] Fothergill's publication of the lists began in the *Genealogist*, Vol. 23, and this entry is found on page 125 of that issue. Publication continued until Vol. 26, when it stopped abruptly, without explanation.

[7] The only Richard Gips (Gyps) found in Annapolis records is a witness to the will of John Thurmer in Calvert County— a Bennett connection. A Howard-Wyatt boundary in Anne Arundel County speaks of "Nathaniel Gibbs' line," and slight references are found to a Nicholas Gibbs. A Lawrence will of 1684 names an Edward Gibbs as a brother-in-law, giving his mother's name as Mary Garner or Gardiner.

was much less important than "a place in the world" or "preferment." Going out into the world at thirteen, it should not surprise us that such a boy never learned to write, and among the early American colonists that was neither odd nor discreditable.

Having no date for an historical picture of Edward Dorsey of the 17th century, he is probably described fairly well in this picture of the youth of that period given by Quennell in a recent *History of Every Day Things.*

An eight-year-old wore for the winter a baize gown faced with fur; for high days he had a suit of ash colored satin, doublet, hose and stockings matching, as well as his silk garters, and Roses—doubtless rosettes. Add an embroidered girdle and a cloak of the same color trimmed with squirrel fur, and we have before our eyes a charming figure, further adorned with a taffeta pickadel, which was a large stiff collar fashionable in England at the time of James I. As an economic fact we are told that a typical boy wore out five pairs of shoes " in the yeare."

With the handicaps of the first colonists, no such gay little man could have landed in Virginia, nor can we confirm any mental picture of his founding a family almost in a wilderness. We must leave him setting forth one April day with his " master " toward the ripe culture of Holland. That he is the identical Edward Dorsey who later journeyed across a wide ocean to Virginia, we can not assert, but at all events he is the only one of the seven Edwards who can be fitted into the known chronology.

III.

THE SOJOURN IN VIRGINIA:

On the Western Branch of Elizabeth River.

The failure of direct references to establish the exact date of Edward Darcie's arrival in Virginia makes it imperative to consider the records of his known friends and neighbors. Morgan P. Robinson, the Secretary of the Virginia Historical

Society and State Archivist, has published exhaustive studies of the formation of counties, in which changes of name may be followed in chart form. Confusion of names is thus lessened and it is easier to follow the lines of the small area we are studying on the maps in Mrs. Nugent's wonderful work on early grants (*Cavaliers and Pioneers*).

For the present let us consider only the eight miles of Elizabeth River, with its Western Branch coming in north of Portsmouth and its Eastern Branch south of Norfolk. Any map shows clearly the Western Branch and the James River; between the two was one of the numerous creeks called Broad,[8] and on this were located Matthew Howard and his wife Ann. In Nugent there is no further mention of Howard but Robert Taylor figures five times as a headright. According to printed records Taylor was on the Broad Creek a year before Matthew Howard, although Taylor's western boundary as recorded February 8, 1637, was Matthew Howard. In May, 1638, Howard's grant on the Western Branch of Elizabeth River is bounded north by the Broad Creek.

Below Howard and Taylor (from west to east) were seated Edward Lloyd, Richard Owen, and Cornelius Lloyd. Most illuminating is the fact that (1) Browne, (2) Fleetwood and (3) Wright were just below Cornelius Lloyd; to these three men Cornelius Lloyd assigned Edward Dorsey's name in three distinct grants. The assignment to Browne is quoted by Nimmo, those to Browne and Fleetwood are given in Greer, but we can scarcely consider these as primary. Wright also used his name, and Parrott, living near Bennett, used the names of several persons whose headrights are mentioned with Dorsey's in assignments.

The date at which a headright was presented in court with a demand for land, is apparently of little account, but what does

[8] There were many creeks called Broad everywhere. On the north side of Western Branch, maps show three creeks and local historians say the name here should indicate that it was the broad creek of the three—*i. e.* the middle one, which is not more than three miles from the junction of the Western Branch with Elizabeth River proper.

matter is that headright names were generally those of close neighbors or of persons who had arrived together. Whatever the reason for this—it might be due to restricted means of communication—the fact is of real value in group study.

There are four assignments in which twenty-two names appear and the question is—who assigned them? Cornelius Lloyd? All the names are those of near neighbors and Lloyd demanded and received 8000 acres. If he brought *at one time* such a large number of headrights, the Land Office records should show the grant. It does not; therefore the grant is not in Mrs. Nugent's book. But it is found in the *Minutes of Lower Norfolk County Court*, under date of 15th December, 1642.

Because of the contiguity of these lands and people, it seems a reasonable inference that the majority were newcomers at about that date. The records of this locality [9] for some ten years, when it was Lower Norfolk County (organized in 1637), were read for me three times and I have myself read them in the Virginia Historical Magazine, from a transcript made years ago by Judge John H. Porter, Commissioner in Chancery. In 1897 the *New England Historical and Genealogical Register,* Vol. 47) published Lea's "Headrights of Lower Norfolk County," in three sections, with many fine notes. These two printed lists preserve the *sixty numbered names* of Cornelius Lloyd's grant of 1642.[10]

When I first knew the record at Portsmouth, the latter part of Edward Dorsey's name was still legible—no. 16. Now three holes, shown in a tracing made at that time, have grown larger and nothing beyond no. 21 is visible at all. I owe to Mr. C. F. McIntosh, Mr. F. W. Sydnor of the State Library, and to Mrs. Bessie H. Ball, formerly of the clerk's office, the minute transcriptions which attest the fact that Cornelius Lloyd used Edward Dorsey's headright as early as December 15, 1642. But for these early copies this bit of essential evidence would be completely lost.

[9] Prior to this date "burned when Bacon 'fired' Jamestown."—James City County records.

[10] The actual grant of 8,000 acres he transferred to Captain John Sidney.

Internal evidence from the four assignments, the combination of grants and the use of the same names interchangeably, lead me to believe that Edward Dorsey was already in that locality, and with people whom he knew, before 1642. The known fact that Matthew Howard had with him " two persons unnamed " suggests the tantalizing possibility that one could have been Edward Dorsey. The date of the grants, 1637-1638, would make the boy of thirteen in the year 1632 about seventeen or eighteen at that time. He could legally hold land at the age of sixteen, but evidently he did not. Cornelius Lloyd's use of his name as a headright in 1642, when Edward Dorsey was twenty-three makes the suggestion rather doubtful, but not impossible.

Many of the associated names of neighbors appear in the passenger list of the *Globe* (see Hotten), but not Dorsey's, so that it is more than probable that he was even then with the persons to whom he and his family clung in all their wanderings for three generations—the Howards and the Owings (Owens). We have documentary proof that the Owens antedated 1637. True, this Richard Owen had no children, but he himself went to the second Howard-Dorsey settlement in Maryland.

It is at first confusing to find the name of William Julian as a landholder on both the Western and the Eastern branch of Elizabeth River. We are now considering only the Western branch, and Julian's first dividend was on the South side of James River toward Jordain's Journey, next to Taylor and Parker. Thus we have the group on the Western Branch composed of:

Julian, Taylor, Edward Lloyd,[11] Cornelius Lloyd, and Owen;
Ewen, Parker, Bennett, Mauldin, Brice;
Wright, Brown, Fleetwood, Parrott (next to Bennett);
     Darcie as a headright only.

[11] Edward Lloyd's history is well known; he married (1) Alice Crouch, (2) Frances Watkins, (3) Grace Parker. Mauldin was the son of Grace Parker Lloyd. Owen we find as a witness of the will of John Watkins at the Chapel of Ease.

On the Eastern Branch of Elizabeth River.

William Julian, " antient planter," is shown by recorded grants to have acquired six hundred acres " on the South side of Eastern Branch of Elizabeth River containing three necks, one neck being on the Southward turning of said river." He sold two necks to Robert Taylor. On the back of this deed is the record of Taylor's sale of two hundred acres to Edward Dorsey.[12]

Thus emerges the actual title quoted by Mr. McIntosh.

The land lies on Ferry Point, once offered to the United States for a capital-site, and sometimes called Washington Point. Here is Edward Darcie's land, so close to the site of the Chapel of Ease that today it is spoken of as " ten minutes away," across the blue waters of the Eastern Branch.

Lower Norfolk County records, beginning in 1637, afford not only the first documentary proof of Darcie's location in America but evidence concerning a number of the neighbors and friends associated with him here and later in Maryland. Thomas Tod was one of these, a justice and vestryman of Elizabeth River Parish. Tod's first grant in 1637 was close to Julian's, Taylor's and Darcie's holdings, being defined as " On the South side of the Eastern branch of Elizabeth River about six miles from the mouth of *said branch.*" This is measuring from the almost rectangular confluence of the Eastern and Southern branches opposite Portsmouth. Elizabeth River in itself is very short, encircling Lambert's Point (known as the " glebeland ") and entering James Bay. Six miles from the mouth of " said branch " is therefore a well defined location. Nowhere else could there have been necks on the *south* side.

Thomas Tod had a second grant in 1638, " between Captain Thomas Willoughby and Captain Adam Thorogood " up to the back creek called Little Creek, including " a fresh water pond and an Indian field." On Thorowgood land is a house built in 1636, now being advertised for sale as " the oldest brick house

---

[12] Taylor's deed from Julian is in Lower Norfolk County records, Book B, page 127.

in America." On his land too stood an old church, its graveyard now lying under the waters of Lynnhaven River. Forrest says that a tall man, wading up to his chin, may feel the stones and decipher the inscriptions with his toes. The baptismal font and a pewter alms basin are still in use in the famous Old Donation church nearby.

Mr. R. D. Whichard has studied out the sites of four historic churches in this neighborhood and has presented me with the magnificent port map and a large city map of Norfolk. On the port map he has drawn an outline of what Julian's six hundred acres would cover; it closely approximates Thomas Tod's location "six miles from the mouth."

We meet the name of Edward Darcie in two other Norfolk County Court documents. One is a deed from John Browne [13] to Darcie for cattle bought in 1642, hardly remarkable except that it raises the question of why Dorsey was said to be "transported" by Cornelius Lloyd, or at least his name used as a headright,—which rather implies coming at the charge of Lloyd—if he had means to buy land and plenish himself with cattle. The third document, in which he appears as a witness only, is a quit-claim title to Virginia land, executed by Thomas Tod [14] in favor of James Sallard, Abraham Parrott and Alexander Hall. It is dated October 1649, on the eve of departing for Maryland. The Julian-Taylor-Dorsey deed is naturally the most important.

The date of the Lloyd grant of 1642 and the 1649 deeds of Tod and Brown prove that Edward Darcie was a resident of Elizabeth River Parish for seven years or more. If he is the boy aged thirteen in 1632, he was born in 1619, and it is quite possible that he might have come over in 1636, or even 1635, because a residence long enough to prove stability and intention to remain, was considered a prerequisite for colonists demanding headright land.

Thomas Tod was twenty-three at the time of his first grant

[13] Lower Norfolk County records, Book A, part III, page 36.
[14] Lower Norfolk County records, Book B, page 134.

in 1637—therefore born in 1614, as was Cornelius Lloyd according to his recorded age in 1642. These associations with men of about the same age are the only hints in Virginia of Dorsey's age. They indicate that he must have been born in the first quarter of the century, and not after 1625 as has been often asserted.[15]

Much feeling has been aroused over the title of "boatwright," used by and given to Dorsey. If we read historians on the motives for English colonization in America, we shall find that even the most conservative stress the production of naval stores as a strong incentive. Dutch supplies of this kind had been cut off from England and nowhere could more abundant materials be found for ship building and fitting than on the Norfolk peninsula.[16]

Dorsey's land lies on the point at the foot of what is now Chestnut Street and on it stand the ruins of the old Marine Hospital. Thomas Tod's land was near by: he was a justice and a church warden. His title in various documents is "Shipwright," and the records of Norfolk County Court show that he won a suit (September 10, 1642) against Colonel Francis Trafford[17] for "work done upon a vessell belonging to said Trafford."

What more likely than that Edward Dorsey was in business with or for his near neighbor, who seems to have been a successful man of affairs in his day?

Across the river at Portsmouth, the United States shipyards proudly boast that they stand on the very site of the oldest colonial shipbuilding in America. The whole locality has a background of marine history, even though, like Dorsey himself, no early records remain to tell the whole story.

Virginia knew no more of Edward Dorsey after his migra-

[15] The McIntosh list from records of affidavits does not include Dorsey.
[16] Mr. W. F. Craven, in articles now running in the *William and Mary Quarterly*, says that England's need of naval stores was one of the paramount reasons for colonizing. Mr. Craven, formerly of New York University, is now at the College of William and Mary.
[17] Trafford is a family name in the pedigree of Viscountess Savage.

tion to Maryland, but his land was never sold—at least there is no record of sale—and any who remembered him wondered what his fate had been. This doubt survives to the present day and the whole object of this study is to try and uncover traces of his life.

Thus on the Eastern branch of Elizabeth River, we have the following more or less allied group:

> Darcie holding land next to Wollman and Tod; Wyatt, Claiborne and Edward Owen on land bought from Julian; opposite, surrounding the Chapel of Ease, Norwood, Watkins, Gaither *et al.*, all of whom moved to Maryland.

IV.

THE CHAPEL-OF-EASE.

The Chapel-of-Ease was built after 1638, ten miles south of the Parish Church of Elizabeth River; "twoward town," though the settlement was not then named Norfolk. Its boundaries extended from Tanner's Creek to the north side of the Eastern branch of Elizabeth River. The Parish of Elizabeth River was certainly established before any other south side county organization, though later it was divided along a line closely following the present Princess Anne boundary, and Lynnhaven Parish was set up.

The earliest settlers of Jamestown Island in 1607 were followed two years later by those who made the old Indian village of Kicoughtan into Hampton, the oldest settled spot of English speaking people still extant. To this town Benjamin Syms left money for the first free school in America (1634) and twenty-five years later Eaton carried further this public benefit. To this day there is a Syms-Eaton school in Hampton, its origin antedating by a year the ubiquitous Boston Latin School.

From Hampton the county name crossed the river James to Willoughby's Point and what are now Norfolk and Princess Anne descend from Elizabeth City County, with an interval of about ten years as Lower Norfolk.

St. Paul's Church in Norfolk City stands on the site of the

Chapel-of-Ease or Conventic'le (so written by an English clergyman of to-day). When Mr. Conway W. Sams ran out the chain of title to this church site, for the Altar Guild's *History of St. Paul's,* the first link of the Willoughby grant was described as on the north side of the Elizabeth River. John Watkins bought the land that became the site of St. Paul's and sold it to John Norwood. For our purpose we could easily rest on these two sales alone, but we have further evidence. John Norwood, being sheriff, was called into court to account for his stewardship of the "glebeland" on Lambert's Point. He was expected to lease it so that the income might support a minister, if and when they had one. The implied indictment of Norwood's business sense was completely quashed, and the vestry finally had to dispose of the land because it was too poor to farm. Many records exist regarding this squabble and the land is fully identified on Mr. Sams's map as Lambert's Point.

This John Norwood was akin to Governor Bennett and a neighbor of Dorsey at this time and later in Maryland, where the two were land partners. He was also sheriff in Maryland. His successor in Virginia was Richard Conquest. He it was who posted on the Chapel-of-Ease the summons to the "seditious sectuaries" to appear before the Court of October, 1649, to defend themselves for non-attendance at their parish Church.

Here we land in the midst of the red-hot controversy between old Governor Berkeley and the handful of Virginia Puritans; a controversy both political and religous that raged for about ten years. Before 1642 Richard Bennett,[18] Hugh Brent, the Carters and Lawsons, living near Nansemond, had removed to the Indian country (Chickacoon), because of Berkeley's persecutions. The most conspicuous victim of the Puritan-baiting was Elder Durand, who is recorded as having a grant of 600 acres on the Rappahannock River, 4 November 1642—to which document is appended a later note: " This is voyd said Durand being a banished man and soe incapable of holding any land in this colony."

[18] The Virginia Historical Commission has placed a marker at the Bennett location.

Major R. S. Thomas relates the story in Volumes IV and V of the *Virginia Magazine*. Sheriff Conquest, on May 6, 1648, heard William Durand preach to the people, " as he had done for three months." Conquest ordered the people to return home, which they would not do. He then attempted to arrest Durand, calling on Edward and Cornelius Lloyd to assist him, but they in fact released the preacher. Some months later Durand's property was attached to pay the costs " while he was the King's prisoner." His " servant " Thomas Marsh became security for him, and later, when Durand had left the country, Marsh paid the charges—which have been incorrectly reported as taxes, thus reflecting on the Elder's honesty.

Intolerant old Governor Berkeley went out of his way to harry this small band of non-conformists at the very time the Parliament of England, under the growing influence of Cromwell's power, had prohibited the use of the Book of Common Prayer. No swift news in those days, so that the so-called Puritans had to give bond to appear in court to defend themselves against charges of a misdemeanor which was none!

That the group we are considering, which followed Edward Lloyd into Maryland, were all Puritans is by no means proven. The arguments for this view of them have been mainly taken from a thesis of the late J. H. Latané, prepared years ago and evidently the work of a young student, probably for his first doctorate. Major Thomas and others among recent investigators deny that this party, taking its departure from the neighborhood of the Chapel-of-Ease, was all Puritan or that religious persecution was the main factor in their unrest and desire for change.

The general statement made by J. W. Warfield that the migrants to Maryland came from the neighborhood of Sewall's Point [19] has been the cause of some confusion. It is quite true, but the disappearance of the shore line, under the Naval Base, and of the parish church that stood there, lead to misunder-

[19] Curiously enough, this name remains as given to one of the biggest of piers, described in the latest Port circular and map.

standing. That was not the church of Edward Dorsey, Thomas Tod, Richard Wollman, John Norwood or John Watkins. Norfolk antiquarians are sure of the approximate location of Sewall's Point, and its parish church, but that location does not relate to the Conventic'le or Chapel-of-Ease, ten miles southward.

Below the Naval Base extends the Army Supply Base, on the North side of Lafayette River—this being the modern name for Tanner's Creek, because a creek can not benefit by legislation for rivers and harbors. On the Port Map radius lines, one mile apart, show Tanner's Creek to be within five miles of Norfolk centre, and Sewall's Point is in the eight miles radius. This verifies Warfield's estimate of the "neighborhood of Sewall's Point; it is about three miles square."

It is certain that land grants, court records, and incidental references prove that the group—whether Puritan or Church of England in religious sympathies—removed from the neighborhood that now lies about St. Paul's Church. This historic building was the only one standing after the town was destroyed by Lord Dunmore on New Year's Day, 1776. It is a landmark in itself of Revolutionary times; its site that of the Chapel-of-Ease built more than a century earlier.

V.

The Hegira and First Settlement In Maryland.

We have no details of the manner of exodus, and few dates to fix the time when the group we are following left Virginia or arrived in Maryland. Several students of the period have written on this obscure bit of religious and secular history, among them Dr. Ethan Allen, for years Historiographer of the Diocese of Maryland. In his history of Saint Anne's Parish, he says: "In 1649 . . . a company of emigrants from Virginia settled in the neighborhood and on the very ground in part, of what is now the city of Annapolis."

Dr. Allen accounted this company Puritans, but we now

know that not all were of this persuasion. He remarks also that they had sprung up in Virginia within six years and their preachers had been sent from Massachusetts on application from Mr. William Durand. Referring to Governor Berkeley's severity against the Puritans, Dr. Allen says the early laws were made " tho' there were as yet none there."

It has been said that Lord Baltimore's Governor for Maryland, Captain William Stone, invited these Virginians to come into Maryland. Their first settlement was at Greenberry Point, then called Town Neck. Eight persons took out patents—William Pell, George Saughier (Sapher) Robert Rockhould, William Penny, Christopher Oatley, Oliver Sprye, John Lordkin and Richard Bennett (Kilty's *Land Holder's Assistant*). The whole tract eventually passed to Richard Bennett alone and Town Neck, through many changes of title and ownership, finally became Greenberry Point, as it is today.

It is of record that warrants of survey (not patents) were issued to Elder Durand, Edward Lloyd and Samuel Withers. Though no subsequent records of patents granted are in the Land Office it does not discredit the fact, long known, that Edward Lloyd had the power to lay out and grant land to these persons. Many landholders of later years refer to surveys of 1650 and 1651, on which they based legal sale or purchase, although no such originals are on file.

All settlers of Maryland were required " to have taken an oath of fidelity to us & our heirs . . . to defend against all powers whatsoever," and it has been inferred that, because no patents are recorded for these Virginians, they refused that oath. That may be, since the pledge was binding on their descendants likewise, but a modified oath permitted the Puritans of Town Neck to send representatives to the House of Burgesses in 1651, which must have been about a year after they came.

This group of Bennett, Durand, Edward Lloyd and Samuel Withers, the avowed Puritans, is definitely placed on the north side of the Severn near Greenberry Point, almost opposite the Naval Academy. It is this settlement that is always referred

to as " *The* Providence of Maryland " in the documents of
Edward Lloyd.

The much larger group in and around present-day Annapolis,
includes names well-known to us from study of Virginia locations; especially Dorsey, Wyatt, Tod, Howard, and Norwood.
So far as may be inferred from vague personal allusions, most
of the group were Church of England, forming within a few
years the Parish of St. Anne's.

Crossing the Severn to the south side, we run into Spa Creek,
which was Tod's Creek in 1651, and Tod's Harbour covered
what is called the Annapolis Peninsula, extending to one hundred acres within present limits of Annapolis. Thomas Tod
brought from Virginia a tendency to spread himself wherever
he lived and usually left legal records of his transactions. His
confirmation of title to some Virginia land at the October Court
of 1649 and his appearance in Maryland, seeking land warrants, at the Spring Court of 1650, are the guiding dates for
the group hegira. In fact he seems to have been resettled in
Maryland within a month after leaving Virginia.

Thomas Tod's bounds were " the bayside on the east from
Tod's Creek up to Deep Cove "—this being " Dorsey's Creek,"
lately rechristened St. John's College Creek. Thus we have
Tod and Dorsey across the creek from each other, as the two of
them had faced Norwood and Watkins across the Elizabeth
River at the site of the Chapel-of-Ease. This same Norwood is
here a next neighbor to Dorsey and Wyatt.

To complete the group picture of transplanted Virginians,
we have Proctor's Landing, just below Tod's holdings, and
Richard Acton just above him, with a Hall in the same neighborhood. Above Dorsey, Norwood and Wyatt, were Marsh,
Howard and Hammond, in an apparently continuous " bloc,"
and Warfield and Gates to the west of them. These families
became closely interlocked by the intermarriages of the second
generation.

For lack of complete evidence, we can not read his title clear
to Edward Dorsey's ownership of this property, but it is in-
disputable that he did possess it. The record in the Land

Office (Liber II, [Margin Liber G G] (98)) reads: "(125) Edward Dorsey assigns to George Yate 400 acres: Warrant XI November M. D. C. L. (1650); to Edward Dorsey for 200 acres of land the which he assigned away as followeth: as also 200 acres more part of a warrant for 400 acres granted John Norwood and Edward Dorsey dated xxiiij February M D C L i (1651); said Dorsey of County of Ann[sic] Arundell, Boatwright, consideration already received, all my right, title, interest, claim and demand of an—in a warrant for 200 acres of land bearing date sixteen hundred and fifty [so written out] and also to 200 acres more being the one half of a warrant for 400 acres, the one half belonging to Capt. Norwood bearing date one thousand six hundred fifty one unto George Yate, etc."

The date of this assignment, duly signed and sealed, is April 23, 1667 and the witness is John Howard, eldest son of the Virginia Matthew and Ann Howard. A year later (August 24, 1668) there is a deed filed from Yate to Dorsey for sixty-eight acres of the above "Dorsey" tract. In the same year one James Connoway assigned back the "right for 1000 acres" to George Yate, who transfers sixty acres to "Darsy." George Yate was deputy surveyor and the sixty acres "called Dorsey" are described as "beginning at a bounded pine upon a point" and running up the Severn to "a Coave called Freeman's up said cove to the line of the land of Capt. John Norwood," etc.

All these transactions of 1667 and 1668, together with the fact that Edward Lloyd's grants, assignments, or whatever they were called, are not on record anywhere, raise many questions. It is contended that the Edward Dorsey who signed the records of 1667-1668 may have been the son Edward. This is highly improbable, since Edward Dorsey the younger could not have had land in his own right from warrants cited of 1650 and 1651, nor did *he* ever name himself as "boatwright" in the documents known to bear his signature.

Those who deny that the record quoted was signed by Edward Dorsey, Senior, argue from the story many times repeated that he was drowned in 1659. No evidence has ever been produced to prove this: there *is* an authentic record of an Edward Dorsey who was drowned, but who the person was, or whether the name may be mistakenly recorded cannot be determined.

It is clear that the signer of the 1667-1668 deeds was the father Edward Dorsey, and as further testimony that he was alive after 1659 is a document assigning land—the Bush-Manning tract—bought by "my father Edward Dorsey from Thomas Marsh in 1661." This same land is later confirmed to Manning in a warrant and power of attorney to Sheriff Stockett from Colonel Edward Dorsey, the son, giving these facts.

At all events the property "called Dorsey" remained in the family after 1668 and until Margaret Larkin, the second wife of Colonel Edward Dorsey, and *her* second husband, John Israel, sold it to William Bladen in 1706. It figures in Bladen's long rent roll and the title passed to the United States (from Reese and wife) in 1867, under the name of "Strawberry Hill Farm" or Dorsey Enlarged, meaning that the tract comprised sixty-seven acres.

The site of the original Naval Academy was bought by the Army in 1808 and used as Fort Severn until 1848, when it was transferred to the Navy. The section including Bluff Point or Cemetery Point, which was a part of the Dorsey tract, is only nineteen years younger than Tod's Harbor as the site of the Naval Academy. This is common knowledge in Annapolis, now proved by existing documents, but hitherto generally ignored by writers.

It is perhaps inevitable that historic towns should drop old names as they grow, but it is perplexing and annoying to the student of old times. Bloomsbury Square in Annapolis is an instance. The name was formerly given to a tract west of St. John's College, which is now a region of mean houses. In its heyday it belonged to Colonel Edward Dorsey, presumably bought from Thomas Tod, but the deeds in proof of it were lost in a fire.

The Committee for the Restoration of Colonial Annapolis has prepared a map of the old sites and on this, Bloomsbury Square abuts at the southwest on the small circle where St.

Anne's Episcopal Church stands. The "town house" of Colonel Edward Dorsey is marked by a symbol signifying "not now in existence." The Daughters of the American Revolution marked with a bronze tablet a house called the Dorsey-Marchand-England house, at 211 Prince George Street. Mr. England has restored its lovely garden, which I greatly enjoyed on his invitation. The place is a private apartment house, not open to the public. Whatever its old relation to the Dorsey property, it seems too far from the known holdings of the family to be accepted as Colonel Dorsey's first town-house.

Mr. Trader, the Chief Clerk of the Land Office, has given deep and careful study to the documents in his charge and he concludes that what he marks as the Dorsey-Nicholson-Carpenter House, in which the first Maryland Assembly was held, is the first town residence of the Dorsey family. This conclusion is partly based on the knowledge that 211 Prince George's street is not the house where Governor Nicholson lived and held Assembly, which house is no longer standing. Another argument lies in the fact that the high-tempered, bachelor Governor lived in a tavern, specifically stated to have been a large house built for Colonel Edward Dorsey, and kept by Hester Gross, a widow Warman, whose menfolk had been prominent in official circles. She might well have been a tenant of Colonel Dorsey's house, since the families had always been near neighbors. She was of Catlyn ancestry from the settlement at Elizabeth River in Virginia.

An interesting sidelight comes from the fact that Governor Nicholson and Edward Dorsey II helped to establish King William's School, now St. John's College. The site of the latter is just across the way from the "house built for Colonel Dorsey"—that is, Hester's tavern.

The following summary of the first Maryland locations for the group under consideration is based upon the original patents or records for each family and is therefore proof beyond question.

Between Town Neck and Annapolis proper, *south* side of Severn, *north* side of Dorsey's Creek:

Dorsey and Norwood in partnership opposite Tod; Howard, Hammond, Wyatt, Warfield and Gates; then a tendency to move southwesterly below Tod, Acton and Hall to the vicinity now called South River.[20]

VI.

SEALS.

Under the efficient direction of Dr. James A. Robertson, the large collection of original wills in the Maryland Hall of Records at Annapolis is being repaired and catalogued by the most modern methods. I have been able to examine a good many myself. The Dorsey wills up to 1762 number about forty, and of the seals attached to them only five bear impressions. By photostats and expert identification all that can be learned from them has come to light.

1. Caleb Dorsey (will dated 1742). The arms on this seal were identified for me by Mr. Stafford F. Potter as those of Gough. A decade later, in the will of Caleb's wife, a daughter Sophia is found as the wife of Thomas Gough. The seal is illustrated in *Anne Arundell Gentry*, by H. W. Newman (page 108); and in *Founders of Ridgely, Dorsey and Greenberry Families* (page 36), by Dr. Henry Ridgely Evans.

2. Madame Henrietta Maria Dorsey (will proved 1762). She was the daughter-in-law of Caleb and wife of Captain Edward Dorsey, who is called the attorney or counsellor. Madame Dorsey is described as " too weak " to make or sign her will and it was done for her by Stephen Bordley, " her clergyman." Governor Paca was a witness, " the brother-in-law of the testatrix."

This seal bears the intaglio head of a long-nosed, curly-bearded, bewigged gentleman, utterly impossible as an heraldic

[20] In this region Col. Edward Dorsey in 1664 sold to his brothers, John and Joshua, Hockley, which remained in possession of the heirs of Hon. John Dorsey. From the shore of South River and above it, the second generation of the above families settled.

After a resurvey of this region it was called *Providence*, Amos Garrett's resurvey, not to be confused with " *The* Providence of Maryland."

personage.   Nor is it the impression from a ring given by
Queen Henrietta Maria to the first baby called by her name.
The child so honored was the daughter of Captain James Neale,
a contemporary of George Calvert, and it was of course handed
down in some line in Virginia; but it furnishes no clue whatever to Dorsey origins.

3.   Edward Dorsey, third (who signs himself Junr), son of
Colonel Edward, had a seal ring bequeathed to him by his
father, but its fate is unknown.   His will (1753), has had the
most minute scrutiny and has been photostated by every known
method.   It has caused much controversy and the latest printed
statement calls it a " mutilated, indecipherable " wax seal.
This is true but, coupled with the statement is the idea that it
would show Dorsey arms, if it could be deciphered.   After
much study I can not fully agree with this opinion.

Another observer has said it " shows no evidence of ever
having received an impression," which is a very questionable
conclusion.   I give my own reading of the blurred fragments,
although *no other* person sees the same things, because it may
tend to quiet the controversy.   *a.* The curved shadow of a round
helmet at the upper back; two highlights as of a neckpiece front,
facing left in profile: *b.* Two very rigid sections of an esquire's
mantling, plainer than anything else.   All edges are broken off.
If there was originally a bordure this might happen the more
easily.   Thus the charge would appear *couped* (of which we
have but one example, Attelounde) and may be described as
two chevrons, or chevronels.   If there was a bordure, this is
the Tyrrell shield, *not couped.*   Tyrrell does enter into the
question of the Essex Darcies, but in very ancient times.[21]   The
final fact brought out by a dozen different lightings is that the
more this seal is enlarged, the less it reveals.

4.   The autograph and seal of Colonel Edward Dorsey, as
used in his lifetime affords several examples, although his will
(1705) is not at Annapolis.   Dr. Evans says the seal is too

[21] Chancellor's *Sepulchral Monuments of Essex* has articles under both
names.

blurred to be deciphered. The seal used on documents still extant is not heraldic, and few can read its rebus form. The rebus was the current fashion abroad, and appears many times in J. Watney's *St. Osyth,* for the Abbot John Vintnor. These carvings may have been a part of old Essex memories. This seal is to be found on bonds of 1676 and indubitably spells Edward Darcie. The several blazons frequently referred to as Dorsey arms have never been authenticated, although use of them is widespread.

5. Joshua Dorsey (will 1687). Here again we have symbolism, not heraldry. Its symbolism, however, is so sharply limited to this one place and example, and it is so unlike any other, that it provokes much thought. Of course E. D. are not the initials of Joshua, nor does it seem likely that they are those of his brother Edward, when the latter uses the rebus many times within a decade (1676-1687). It might be the rebus of Joshua's father. Officials of the Virginia State Library and Mrs. Bessie H. Ball of the Norfolk County Clerk's Office, agree that old time clerks made an effort to copy a man's mark as exactly as possible, when transcribing documents; frequently with curious results.

The signature of Joshua's father on the Tod deed in Virginia is so like the lettering on the ring that it is easy to think that the ring originally belonged to Edward Darcie, the immigrant. The form and shape of the letters is like those in use long befor his time. Other factors in the design of the ring are not to be lightly dismissed by calling them " a tree and a coil of rope," or " a root " to the tree. The arms of the d'Arcies or Darcies of Essex, going back to the Tolleshunt branch and to Henry, Lord Mayor of London, have always been the earliest form, as quoted by Mr. R. F. d'Arcy and as delineated in Foster's *Feudal Coats of Arms* and Chancellor's *Sepulchral Monuments of Essex.* Here can be found, from several ancient tombs, the three cinquefoils alone or on shields by themselves. The crest for all these branches is described and illustrated in the Jack edition, 1905, of Fairbairn's *Crests* (1834). It is a demi-virgin clothed in "purpure," bearing in her right hand a branch of three cinquefoils [22] exactly like that on the ring except that there it is slipt—*i. e.*, cut with no root. The double carrick knot, a sailor's knot, might be the Wake badge from a monk's girdle. John Sibsie of Virginia is said to have had a partner in London, an attorney, named Richard Wake, who traveled about the world somewhat, and this old Yorkshire family had descendants in Kent known to have owned property held, at another time, by Darcies. This is the sole authentic clue pointing our immigrant to an English family.

By persistent following of such threads of evidence, we may some day find the real man.

VI.

Conclusion.

Those who have strong feeling aroused by the title of "Boat-wright," attached to Edward Dorsey's name, should realize how essential it was to an Englishman of his day to be an acknowledged member of a Guild. Indeed, to this day it is regarded as an honor.

In early colonial times, artisans were few and hard to find, and not every man who assumed the protection of a guild could have been an artisan. We have still much to learn on this question. For example, Francis Mauldon, carpenter, making incendiary speeches against Lord Baltimore at the time of the Puritan uprising, did not represent "the lower classes," as Dr. C. M. Andrews asserts. Mauldon was the son of Grace Parker (proven by her will, 1697) and his stepfather Parker was a member of the "Hamburgh Company." [23] His second stepfather, Edward Lloyd, Grace Parker's third husband, was the leader of the Virginia-Maryland Puritans.

[22] No other woman, virgin, or mermaid, carries anything like this branch. The Lincolnshire d'Arcy's bust of a woman crowned with roses is distinctly different.

[23] There was a firm called John Hanbury and Company about 1650, but this Parker, or his father, was a grantee of the Virginia Company in 1609, "an old sea captain of Elizabeth's time" and Commander of Anne Arundel County.

Force of circumstances may have made Edward Dorsey a boatwright. He lived in an age when problems of transportation were concentrated on watercraft and were quite as vital as those of stage coaches and railroads, motor vehicles and airplanes, to later days. Probably he was not a mere "artisan," but being obliged to join some guild in order to be a citizen, he could have selected no other occupation of greater public usefulness in the new land to which he migrated.

Later in his life, he is called a Planter and in a legal document signed by his son Edward, he is given the title of Gentleman.

It can be proved likewise that he was not a Puritan. The group in Maryland that formed a part of St. Anne's Parish, were of the same faith that they had been in Virginia, when they were clustered about the Chapel-of-Ease. The assertion has been made that they became Quakers at a later time, but no proof is offered; in fact chronologically it could not have happened.

If Edward Dorsey's descendants would keep in mind the events in England during his lifetime, we could construct a better story from contexts about this Maryland group. Such novels as Margaret Irwin's, especially *The Stranger Prince,* are a valuable aid to such understanding. Known facts are few and contexts sadly needed, but only on facts can a solid superstructure be built out of whatever may be discoverable in the future.

Edward Dorsey's life was assuredly " a wand'ring to find home." Three times he tried his mettle against the unbroken wilderness. What he was or did is to be measured by the conditions he had to fight, not the least of which was the constant dread of Indians. Around the Maryland settlement lay unbroken forests where wild beasts were perhaps less frightful than wild men.

If one stands on the tract " called Dorsey "—Strawberry Hill Farm—from its lovely bluff one looks over the blue waters of Dorsey's Creek, the Severn River and Chesapeake Bay and may recall that by the will of Gates, his children were enjoined to allow the Dorseys the privileges of "the woods and the Spring." This stands as law to the present day; none may be shut off from the only fresh water, nor from the only road available to reach the outside world.

Driving on around the base of the point on Ramsey Road and up to the first terrace in the cemetery, it is easy to picture what a scene of peace and beauty spread before the eyes of that Edward Dorsey who once stood here. Even the eleven sea-planes resting on the placid waters below are no discordant note.

Going on to the second terrace one finds the Post-Graduate School and Hospital of the Naval Academy and the golf course; one returns by another bridge over the sparkling waters of Dorsey's Creek to St. Anne's Church and its cemetery in the Annapolis of today, which again recall times long gone.

It is more difficult to travel forward from those wilderness days to the bustling present, but one reflects with satisfaction that there could be no more beautiful fruition than this modern institution devoted to youth, courage and advancement—yet not unmindful of the past.

PRISCILLA OF THE DORSEYS: A CENTURY-OLD MYSTERY

By FRANCIS B. CULVER

Family traditions are often untrustworthy, as the experienced genealogist knows. The writer recalls a glaring example of the truth of this state-ment in the case of a young man who desired to join an hereditary patriotic society in the right of a Revolutionary War ancestor. According to his family tradition, that ancestor was said to have been a " General in the Army, who served seven years and was wounded five times." Investigation revealed the actual facts of the case were as follows: The ancestor was drafted, at the age of sixteen years, in the county militia; later, he served

; a wagonmaster for less than a year when he caught the smallpox, was
ivalided to his home and never returned to the service. His name does
ot appear on the extant military rolls, but it is recorded in the files of the
ension Office at Washington, where the facts are given in detail. How
iis utterly false family-tradition started, no one appears to know. It may
ave been merely a hoax on the part of someone unknown.

Another instance of false tradition bears upon a problem of a genealo-
ical sort. Among the files of an old newspaper known as the *Common-
ealth,* published at Frankfort, Franklin County, Ky., in the issue dated
Sept. 1839, an obituary notice appears, which reads as follows: [1]

> "Another patriot of the American Revolution gone. Colonel
> Robert Wilmot departed this life at his residence in Bourbon county,
> Ky., on the 20th of August last, at the advanced age of 82 years.
>
> "When but 18 years of age he was commissioned by the Legis-
> lature of Maryland (his native State) a Lieutenant of Artillery, in
> which capacity he immediately joined the Revolutionary army and
> continued in active service until the close of the war; during which
> time his patriotism and valor were signally displayed in the battles
> of Monmouth, Ver Planck's Point, Gates' Defeat and Stony Point.
> When 24 years of age he was united in marriage to *Miss Priscilla
> Dorsey, daughter of the Hon. Caleb Dorsey of Maryland*; [2] and in
> the year 1786 came with his family to Kentucky and settled on a large
> and fertile tract of land in Bourbon county, which he occupied until
> his decease, and upon which he reared a family of four sons and five
> daughters," etc., etc.

This obituary was signed with the initials R. W. S. [Robert Wilmot
Scott, a grandson and namesake of the deceased].

The Wilmots were a well known and highly respected family of Baltimore County, connected by intermarriage with the Cromwells, Merrymans,
Talbots, Towsons, Owings, Gittings, Bowens, and other prominent old
families of that county. [3]

"Colonel" Robert Wilmot was born in Baltimore County, Md., on 25
Dec. 1757. He married, by license dated 8 Oct. 1781, one Priscilla
Dorsey, whose father most certainly was *not* "the Hon. Caleb Dorsey"
as stated in the obituary notice cited above. For, anyone who knows the
history of "Hampton," that fine old estate near Baltimore, is cognizant of
the fact that Priscilla Dorsey, youngest of the ten children of the Hon.
Caleb Dorsey, Jr., "of Belmont" (by his wife Priscilla Hill), married on
17 Oct. 1782, at Old St. Paul's Church, Baltimore, Charles Ridgely
Carnan, [4] son of John and Achsah (Ridgely) Carnan, and grandson of

---

[1] See *Register of the Ky. State Historical Society*, Vol. 27 (Jan. 1929) p. 446.
[2] The italics are the writer's.
[3] See *Md. Hist. Magazine*, V, 333.
[4] Conformable to a provision in the will of his childless uncle, Captain Charles
Ridgely, dated 7 Apl. 1786, young Carnan adopted the name "Charles Carnan
Ridgely" and was also styled "of Hampton."

Charles and Prudence Carnan, of Reading, in Berkshire, England. The chart which follows may serve to explain the lineage:

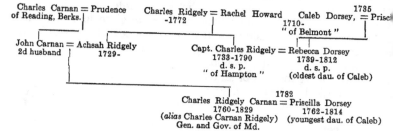

Now, Priscilla Dorsey, the "war bride" of Lieut. Robert Wilmot of Baltimore County, was married 9 October, 1781; or just one year before the marriage of Priscilla Dorsey (daughter of Caleb), to Charles Ridgely Carnan (afterward known as Charles Carnan Ridgely). It is impossible that these two Priscillas were one and the same person, due to the fact that Priscilla Wilmot signed as a witness to the will of Capt. Charles Ridgely (d. 1790), dated 7 Apl. 1786 (Balto. Will Book No. 4, folios 450 *et seq.*) and, further, that the Captain's widow, Mrs. Rebecca Ridgely (née Dorsey), in her will dated 22 Apl. 1811 and proved 3 Oct. 1812, bequeathed to her namesake "Rebecca Wilmot, daughter of Robert and Priscilla Wilmot [of Kentucky] the sum of two hundred pounds current money of Maryland" (Baltimore Will Book No. 9, folio 265). The Wilmot home in Bourbon County, Ky., was situated near the railroad which runs between Paris and Lexington, about ten miles northeast of the latter place.

According to Maryland and Kentucky sources, Robert and Priscilla (Dorsey) Wilmot had issue as follows:

1. William, b. 2 Apl. 1783; d. 1834, unmarried.
2. Rebecca, b. 3 June 1785; married Joel B. Scott of Franklin Co., Ky., and had issue.
3. Charles, b. 25 Nov. 1786; died in infancy.
4. Charles, b. 27 Apl. 1788. No record.
5. Robert, b. 5 Jan. 1791; married Miss Mansfield and had issue.
6. Polly, b. 3 Nov. 1792; married Philemon Price and removed to Illinois.
7. Sarah, b. 13 Aug. 1794; married (1)—Flint, (2)—Chenowith, (3)—Samuel Hitt.
8. Priscilla, b. 20 Mch. 1798; married Richard Keene of Scott Co., Ky., and had issue.
9. Nancy, b. 17 Aug. 1799; married Daniel Stephens and removed to Indiana.
10. John, b. 26 May 1802; died young.
11. John Fletcher, b. 13 Jan. 1806; married Harriet ———.

There were several "Priscillas" in the Dorsey family of Maryland, which has been a prolific one, especially in the counties of Anne Arundel, Baltimore and Howard. The Dorsey's spread themselves through town, hamlet and countryside, and it has been said that even "the woods were full of them." Can anyone solve the problem of the parentage of Mrs. Priscilla (Dorsey) Wilmot?

THE DORSEY (DOSSEY) FAMILY OF CALVERT COUNTY

By NANNIE BALL NIMMO

In the year 1660 Richard Preston, of "Preston's Cliffs" in Calvert County, brought into the province, Ralph Dosey and John Smith. To Ralph Dosey, on the 25th of July, 1663, he assigned his rights for the transportation,[1] whereupon Ralph *Dasey* demanded 100 acres of land by right of the said assignment. Ralph Dosse is found in Talbot County in 1669.[2]

In 1668 Captain James Connaway proved his rights for bringing James Dorsey and others into the province,[3] and on the 12th of October 1674 John Dossey of Dorchester County, demanded land for service performed in this province.[4]

The above named Ralph, James, John, were named in the will of Richard Preston of Calvert County, made in 1669. In event of the death of his son James, kinsmen James and John Dorsey to possess a patent of land for 600 acres, kinsman Ralph Dossey, land on Little Choptank River. The name is spelt both Dorsey and Dossey in the will.[5]

Ralph and John Dossey settled on the Eastern Shore of Maryland, and left descendants. The late Mrs. Hester Dorsey Richardson, noted genealogist, was descended from John Dossey of Dorchester County.

James Dorsey established himself on a 200 acre tract of land called "Bennett's Desire" on the east side of the Patuxent River, near Hunting Creek, Plum Point being on the other side of the Ridge.[6]

This land adjoined the land of Francis Billingsley, a Quaker, and it is thought that James Dorsey too was a Quaker, as was his son James.[7]

The will of John Gill, witnessed by James Dossey, was probated in 1687. To Elizabeth, daughter of John Johnson, was bequeathed personalty; the residue of the estate was given to Martha Morris, the daughter of Martha Dossey, who was named as executrix.[8]

Nathaniel Cranford and his wife Martha Cranford were administrators of that will in 1687.[9] Martha Cranford must have been at least 18 years

---

[1] Patent Book, 5, 535. Land Office, Annapolis.
[2] *Archives of Maryland*, 54, 451. Land Office, Annapolis.
[3] Patent Book, 11, 337. Land Office, Annapolis.
[4] Patent Book, 18, 116. Land Office, Annapolis.
[5] Baldwin, *Calendar of Maryland Wills*, I, 50.
[6] Calvert County Rent Rolls, Calvert Paper 882, Maryland Historical Society.
[7] Wills, v. 25, 48. Hall of Records, Annapolis.
[8] Baldwin, *Calendar* I, 50.
[9] Administration Accounts, V. 9, 89, Hall of Records.

of age at this time, probably born about 1669. It is assumed that Martha Dossey was the wife of James Dossey, but there must have been another wife, possibly a Rebecca, mother of some, if not all, of his children.

James Dorsey is named in the list of Inhabitants of Calvert County in 1684,[10] and witnessed the will of Thomas Jessops.[11] In 1711 James Dossey witnessed the will of George Pascall.[12]

James Dorsey and his wife were living in 1723, when on the 22 of May, their son John Dossey made his will, leaving to his mother ¼ of his estate, the remainder was bequeathed to his father, sister Rebecca Talbot and his brothers. His brother James was made executor. Personalty was left to Elizabeth Stallings.[13]

While neither will nor administration account has been found for James Dorsey, the names of his children are known, viz.; James, Timothy, Richard, John, William, Philip and Rebecca Talbot.

James Dorsey, Jr. as eldest son was heir to the homestead on "Bennett's Desire," "where now lives Young Dorsey Hance," not in the original house, that having burned down. The place seems now known as "Bunker Hill."

James, Jr., made his will in 1758, naming his wife Mary, and his eleven children, viz; James, Mary, Rebecca, John, Sarah, Philip, Daniel, Francis, Benjamin, Joseph.[14]

Mary became the wife of John Davis Scarfe, Rebecca the wife of James Crawford, Sarah wife of John Standford.[15]

James, Jr.'s lands, were "Garden," "Robinson's Rest," "Deer Quarter," "Bennett's Desire."

His sons Philip and Daniel were taxed by the vestry of All Saints Parish as bachelors in 1761.[16] In 1770 his son John, gave his age as 40 years, his daughter Rebecca as 34 years, while that same year, his son Philip claims to have been born in 1736.[17]

Timothy Dossey, of James, Sr. died intestate in 1732. His Inventory[18] names (his brothers), James and William, as next of kin (his brothers) Richard and Philip as administrators. The account shows that Richard, Philip and Timothy had been in partnership; their shares of the business were divided.[19]

Philip Dossey of James, Sr. born in 1705,[20] was a member of Christ Church Parish. He married 1st, Ann Allen, named in the will of Charles

---

[10] Henry J. Berkley, "First Century of the County of Calvert," MS, Md. Hist. Soc.
[11] *Baldwin, Calendar*, 1, 134.
[12] *Baldwin*, 3, 195.
[13] *Baldwin*, 5, 153.
[14] Will Book 31, 402, Hall of Records.
[15] Administration Accounts, 49, 340, Hall of Records.
[16] All Saint's Parish, Calvert County, Vestry Proc. Copy, Md. Hist. Soc.
[17] Chancery Record, W. K. no. 1, 251, 292, Hall of Records.
[18] Inventories, 17, 63, Hall of Records.
[19] Accounts, 11, 644, Hall of Records.
[20] Chancery Record, W. K. no. 1, 257.

Allen of Calvert County. In 1733,[21] Philip Dossey and his wife, Ann, sign as next of kin, in the Inventory of Charles Allen in 1734.[22]

The children of Philip and Ann are recorded in the Christ Church Parish Register, namely, James, born 8 Sept. 1735, Elizabeth born 26 of July, 1738, Ann born April, 1741, Rebecca born March 5th 1742.[23]

In his will Philip names them as "my 4 children."

There is no record of the death of Ann, but the parish record shows that Philip, son of Philip and Martha, was born the 11 of August, 1759.[24]

In 1750 Philip Dossey and Joseph Skinner were appointed as inspectors for Plum Point and Shinting Creek.[25] Philip does not seem to have lived on the home place, his lands were a resurvey on several tracts, "Tawney's Addition," "Young's Nest," "Young's Pasture."[26]

He made his will in Calvert County, December 6, 1774, leaving to his wife Martha, a horse and half of his estate during life, at her death to be divided among his children. To son Philip he leaves 2 negroes and a horse, to be divided among his 4 children, should Philip die. His son James is named as executor, son Philip is left in his care.[27]

John Dossey and Francis Dossey, sons of James Dossey, Jr., sign as next of kin in his inventory.[28]

His wife Martha was still living on the 7 of March, 1775, when, with James Dossey, she administered on the estate of her husband, Philip Dossey.[29]

James Dossey, son of Philip, came into possession of "Young's Forrest," and "Tawney's Addition."[30]

Philip Dossey, Jr. was but 14 years of age when his father died, and seems to have inherited no land, being the youngest child and by a 2nd wife. When 19 years of age he signed the oath of Fidelity, and is found on the Returns of William Harris, March 2, 1778, for Calvert County.[31]

In 1782 he is still unmarried,[32] paying taxes on 2 slaves and 2 horses, possibly the 1 horse inherited from his mother, for his father had left to him 1 horse and to his mother 1 horse. This would indicate that his mother was dead. He married before 1784 or about that time, and in 1786 had a wife, one child and 4 slaves.[33] His wife was Barbara Broome, by whom he had William Henry Dossey (Doctor) m. Judith Brasure Skinner in 1811, Ann Dossey m. Henry Carr, Dorcas Dossey m. David Simmons,

[21] *Baldwin Calendar*, 7, 116.
[22] Inventories, 1734, Hall of Records.
[23] Christ Church Register, Calvert County, Copy, Md. Hist. Soc.
[24] Christ Church Register, p. 57.
[25] Maryland State Papers, No. 1, Black Book, No. 1, 677, Hall of Records.
[26] Debt Books, Calvert County, Land Office.
[27] Magruder's Maryland Colonial Abstracts, II, 21.
[28] Magruder's Maryland Colonial Abstracts, II, 21.
[29] Testamentary Proceedings, 46, 205, Hall of Records.
[30] Debt Book, Calvert County, Land Office.
[31] Margaret R. Hodges, "Unpublished Revolutionary Records of Maryland," vol. 6, 12: also Rev. Records, Hall of Records.
[32] 1782 Tax List, Calvert County, Land Office.
[33] 1786 Tax List, Calvert County, Maryland Historical Society.

Walter P. Dossey, born 1795 d. 1833, m. Dec. 22, 1818, Ann Sedwick Ireland, born 1788, died 1834.

Rebecca Dossey died unmarried in 1810.[34]

Philip Dossey, Jr. died in 1818. He retained the name Dossey.

Walter P. Dorsey, b. 1795, and his wife Ann Sedwick Ireland, had issue:

Dr. Richard Dorsey.

Philip Henry Dorsey, b. Calvert Co., 1827; d. St. Mary's Co. 1899, m. Ann Letitia Bryant in 1865. She was b. 1836, d. 1895.

Susan M. Dorsey.

Alethea Dorsey married Young Parran Dawkins; issue, Judge Walter Parran Dawkins.

Ann Dorsey m. Joseph Griffith.

Walter W. Dorsey m. Julian Marie Sedwick.

Philip Henry Dorsey b. 1827 and his wife Letitia Bryant had issue:

Walter B. Dorsey m. Elizabeth Maddox Turner.

Nannie R. Dorsey m. James J. Stone of St. Mary's County, issue Luke Dorsey Stone.

Philip H. Dorsey.

Ellen Alethea Dorsey m. Frank Tilton Gibson.

Richard Luke Dorsey, deceased.

Amy R. Dorsey unmarried.

The name Dossey is no longer heard, the descendants use the name Dorsey, and so it was spelt in the Parish Registers.

---

[34] Philip Dossey Bible Records in possession of Mrs. Frank Tilton Gibson, Takoma Park, Md.

THE DUNN FAMILY OF KENT COUNTY.

CHRISTOPHER JOHNSTON.

1. ROBERT DUNN,[1] the ancestor of this family, came to Maryland in 1649 and settled on Kent Island, which at that time was in Kent County. 22 March 1649/50, Robert Dunn of the Isle of Kent assigns to William Body of the same place, his right to 100 acres of land due for his transport into the Province anº 1649 (Kent Co., Lib. A, fol. 2). He was one of the representatives for Kent County in the Maryland Assembly in 1663 (*Md. Archives,* i, 460), and in 1669 (ib. ii, 157), and was a Justice for the County 1664-1669 (*Md. Archives,* iii, 512; v, 37). On the 5th of April 1652 he swore allegiance to the Commonwealth of England (*Old Kent,* p. 60), and he held the office of Clerk of the County before 1669 (ib. 220). He was commissioned High Sheriff 1 May 1673 and held office until his death, Thomas Marsh, his successor, being commissioned 15 June 1676 (Lib. C. D., fol. 87, 111. 149). Robert Dunn's wife was named Joan, and in 1665 she joined her husband in a deed. 29 Sept. 1665, Robert Dunn of the Isle of Kent and Joan his wife convey to William Granger of the same place, one half of a tract of 200 acres formerly granted to William Porter on Parson's Creek, Vaughan's Bay (Kent Co., Lib. A, fol. 160). The Kent County register of burials shows that Robert Dunn died 12 May 1676, and in Testamentary Proceedings (viii, 71) is the following entry:—18 May 1676, Joane Dunn of Kent County exhibited the will of Robert Dunn, late of Kent County deceased, and craved a commission to prove the same. The will, however, does not appear upon record and is probably lost. 10 April 1677, was filed the inventory of Robert Dunn late of Kent County, deceased (Inv. and Acc'ts, iv, 48); and 26 July 1679, Joane Workman, executrix of the said Robert Dunn, rendered her account of the said deceased's estate (ibid. vi, 210). In the interval she had become the wife of Anthony Workman of

Kent Co., and she was living in 1692, but probably died not
very long after. 27 January 1691/2, Anthony Workman
and Joan his wife convey to John Oulson, planter, Cooper's
Quarter, 50 acres, on Kent Island (Kent Co., Lib. B., fol.
317). Anthony Workman died in September or October
1708, and names in his will his wife Susanna, so that he
married again after the death of Joan. The dates of birth
and death of Robert Dunn's children are taken from the
Kent County register. By Joan his wife he had issue:—

  i. William Dunn,[2] d. an infant and was buried 19 May 1656.
  ii. Susanna Dunn, b. 21 July 1656.
  iii. Joan Dunn, b. 5 March 1660.
  iv. Rebecca Dunn, b. 26 July 1663.
  v. Alice Dunn, d. 9 August 1678.
2. vi. Robert Dunn, b. 1674; d. 1729.

2. ROBERT DUNN [2] (*Robert* [1]) of Kent County was born in
1674, and died in 1729. The date of his birth is derived
from a deposition wherein "Mr. Robert Dunn Sen[r]." gives
his age as 52 years in 1726 (Kent Co., Lib. J.S. no. 10,
fol. 40); while the date of his death is furnished by the
date of probate of his will. His parentage is proved by a
deed recorded at Chestertown. 24 March 1695/6, Robert
Dunn of Kent Co., Gent., and Mary his wife convey to
Anthony Workman of said County, Gent., two tracts on
Kent Island, viz:—one tract called North East Thicket,
200 acres, formerly taken up by John Russell, and from
him descended to William Coursey, and by him assigned
to Robert Dunn *father to the now vender,* as by patent,
dated 6 August 1650, may appear; the other tract being
100 acres, formerly taken up by Henry Ashley and coming
by several assignments to Robert Dunn as by patent, dated
6 August 1650, may appear &c. (Kent Co., Lib. M., fol.
35). Robert Dunn was elected Vestryman of St. Paul's
Parish, Kent Co., 5 April 1703, 29 March 1712, 30 March
1719 &c. (Vestry Book). In 1720 his two sons Robert
and William Dunn occupied pew no. 28 in St. Paul's
Church (ibid.). The will of Robert Dunn of Kent
County, dated 30 Dec. 1710, was proved 28 Nov. 1729
(Annapolis, Lib. 19, fol. 877). It mentions testator's
wife Mary; his sons Robert and William; his daughters
Jane and Mary Dunn; and his brother James Harris.
Robert Dunn was twice married. His first wife was Mary
daughter of William Harris, and sister of James Harris,

whom he calls his " brother " in his will just quoted. She was buried, according to the St. Paul's register, 15 Dec. 1709. The second wife of Robert Dunn, also named Mary, survived him for nearly nine years. As "Mary Dunn of Kent County " she made her will 19 March, 1737, and it was proved 1 August 1738. She mentions her daughter Elizabeth, wife of Philip Davis; her grand-children Charles Ringgold, Hannah Blakiston, and Mary Blakiston (executrix); and her friend Vincent Hatcheson Senior. She was the widow of Robert Park (or Peark), who died in 1708, and they had two daughters, viz—a) Elizabeth Park (d. 1760), mar. 1°, 1705, Charles Ringgold, 2°, 1723, Philip Davis (d. 1749), b) Anne Park, mar. William Blakiston (d. 1737). It is quite evident that Mrs. Mary Park had no issue by Robert Dunn, her second husband.

Robert Dunn and Mary (Harris) his first wife had issue :—

3. i. Robert Dunn,³ b. 1693; d. 1745.
4. ii. William Dunn, buried May 1728.
iii. James Dunn, bapt. 28 May 1699; d. young.
iv. Jane Dunn, bapt. 1 March 1701.
v. Mary Dunn.
NOTE. Dates of baptism and burial from register of St. Paul's, Kent Co.

3. ROBERT DUNN ³ (*Robert,*² *Robert* ¹) of Kent County, was born in 1693 and died in 1745. In a deposition, made in 1732, he gives his age as 39 years, and refers to "my father Robert Dunn" (Kent Co., Lib. J.S. no. 16, fol. 254). He represented his County in the Assembly 1722-1724, and in 1724 is styled "Captain" probably holding that rank in the county militia (MS. House Journals). From 1735 to 1745 he was one of the Justices and Commissioners for Kent County (Commission Book). He married Ann daughter of Michael Miller of Kent Co. (b. 1675; d. 1738) and Martha (d. 1746)) his wife. Ann Miller was born 4 February 1698 (St. Paul's register), and is mentioned in her father's will, dated 17 January, proved 10 February, 1738 (Kent Co., Lib. 2, fol. 85), as " my daughter Ann wife of Robert Dunn," her husband Robert Dunn being appointed one of the executors. Mrs. Ann Dunn may have died between this date (1738) and 1744, since her mother Mrs. Martha Miller in her will, dated 27 Nov. 1744, proved 5 April 1746 (Kent Co., Lib.

3, fol. 3), does not mention her daughter Ann, but only her "grand daughter Rebecca Wickes" who was Ann's daughter. Robert Dunn died in 1745 intestate. 14 March 1745, From Kent Co. Robert Dunn his administration bond by Joseph Wickes and James Dunn his administrators in £3000 stg., dated 22 Feb'y 1745—Sureties Wm. Hynson and Wm. Wilmer (Test. Proc. xxxi, 627). Some six years later the final account was rendered by the administrators. 23 July 1751, Account of Joseph Wickes and James Dunn of Kent Co., administrators of Robert Dunn late of said County deceased. Payments:—To Prideaux Blakiston who intermarried with Martha widow of William Dunn, for her share of Robert and Michael Dunn's portions who died in their minority (being children of said William Dunn), and William son of said William Dunn deceased. Representatives are the accountant Joseph, in right of his wife Rebecca daughter of deceased, the accountant James son of deceased, and Darius, Hezekiah, and Martha Dunn children of deceased. The dates of birth given below are from St. Paul's register.

Robert Dunn and Ann (Miller) his wife had issue:—

5.   i. James Dunn⁴ b. 10 June 1728.
      ii. Darius Dunn, b. 4 January 1731.
      iii. Hezekiah Dunn, b. 16 May 1734.
      iv. Rebecca Dunn, b. June 1726; mar., before 1744, Joseph Wickes
          (b. 1719; d. 1785).
      v. Martha Dunn.

4.   WILLIAM DUNN³ (Robert,² Robert¹) was buried, according to St. Paul's register, in May 1728. He married Martha daughter of Michael Miller and sister of his brother Robert's wife. She was born 16 Sept. 1701, and married her second husband, Prideaux Blakiston, 27 July 1729 (St. Paul's). Her father, Michael Miller in his will, dated 17 Jan'y, proved 10 Feb'y, 1738 (Kent Co., ii, 85), leaves land to his grandsons William and Michael Dunn, and £10 to his "daughter Martha now wife of Prideaux Blakiston." Her mother also, whose will, dated 27 Nov. 1744, was proved 5 April 1746 (Kent. Co., iii, 3), leaves a bequest to "my daughter Martha wife of Prideaux Blakiston."

The will of William Dunn of Kent Co. is dated 21 Feb'y 1728/9 and was proved 14 June 1729 (Annapolis, xix, 739). To his wife Martha, testator leaves all his personal estate; my three children to the care of their grandfather Robert Dunn, and their uncle Robert Dunn; my wife and my father Robert Dunn executors. There would seem to be a discrepancy here. According to the parish register, William is said to have been buried in May 1728; while the will is dated 21 February 1729 (New Style) and was proved 14 June following. It would seem, therefore, that William Dunn was buried in May 1729 and not in 1728. William Dunn and Martha (Miller) his wife had issue:—

    i. Robert Dunn,[4] b. 11 Feb'y 1722; d. a minor.
   ii. William Dunn, b. 4 Oct. 1725.
  iii. Michael Dunn, b. 19 Feb'y 1727; d. a minor.

5.   James Dunn [4] (*Robert,*[3] *Robert,*[2] *Robert* [1]) was born 10 June 1728, and was twice married. The names of his two wives, and the dates of birth of his children, as here given, are taken from St. Paul's Parish register.
James Dunn and Martha Ann his first wife had issue:—

    i. James Dunn,[5] b. 9 May 1751.

By his second wife Elizabeth, James Dunn had issue:—

    i. Ann Dunn, b. 15 May 1754.
   ii. Elizabeth Dunn, b. 9 May 1756.
  iii. Hezekiah Dunn, b. 7 Oct. 1757.
  iv. Robert Dunn, b. 28 Nov. 1759.
   v. Rebecca Dunn, b. 15 Sept. 1761.
  vi. James Dunn, b. 17 January 1764.
 vii. Michael Dunn, b. 3 January 1766.
viii. Darius Dunn, b. 5 August 1767.
  ix. Curtis Dunn, b. 23 Nov. 1769.

EGERTON FAMILY

By Francis B. Culver

. CHARLES[1] EGERTON, whose will was dated 27 Jan. 1669 and proved 15 June 1669 in Lower Norfolk County (now recorded at Portsmouth), Virginia, was, according to tradition, the father of Charles Egerton, founder of the Egerton family of Maryland (*Virginia Magazine*, XXXI, 348). The senior Egerton is mentioned in the Virginia records as follows:

1662 June 14—Inventory of the estate of Captain Francis Emperor, taken this date, lists among certain " bills " the name of " Charles Egerton, 340 pounds of tobacco " (*Lower Norfolk Antiquary*, IV, 84).

1664 June 14—" Charles Egerton, 200 acres in Lynnhaven Parish in the Lower County of New Norfolk: 150 acres at a small creek on the west side of John Holmes' house, running up the creek south-southwest, etc.; 50 acres being three small hummocks joined together by small ostums [?] upon Hog Island in little creek in Lynnhaven. Granted to Samuel Mayson 18th Feb. 1653, by him sold to Thomas Bridge who sold to Egerton. (*Cavaliers and Pioneers*, by Nell Marian Nugent, I, 518).

1667 Nov. 20—" Charles Egerton in the County of Lower Norfolk in Virginia . . . give . . . unto Anne Bennett's two sons, George and Edward, my plantation which I live upon . . . cows between the boys and their sister Elizabeth . . . so that their mother, when she cometh into the County again, may . . . have a living out of the land and stock . . . if Thomas Bennett will come out of the Bay and live with them, he may. I will not hinder nor molest him." (Norfolk County Clerk's Office, Book E, 32; *Virginia Magazine*, XXXI, 347.)

NOTE: Mrs. Ann Bennett was a daughter of Henry Snaile. She married Thomas Bennett of Lower Norfolk County, Va., and St. Mary's County, Md. Her daughter Mary Bennett married (1) Thomas Ewell, (2) Maximilian Boush, (3) Rev. Jonathan Saunders (died *ante* 1700), rector of Lynn Haven Parish in 1695, whose daughter Mary Saunders (died 1762) married in 1719 Cornelius Calvert.

1669 April 27—The will of Charles Egerton, proved 15 June 1669, mentions Anne Snayle " which now goeth by the name Anne Bennett, to her four children, that is to say: George,

Edward, Elizabeth and Mary—my lands when they come of age (Norfolk County, Va., Clerk's Office, Book E, 51; *Virginia Magazine*, XXXI, 347). The Inventory of Estate, 11 May 167 includes one Bible valued at 30 lbs tobacco, five printed boo. (at 10 lbs. each) valued at 50 lbs. tobacco (*Lower Norfo. County Antiquary*, I, 106).

POST MORTEM NOTE: 1688—Whereas one Charles Egerto. Desct., Late of this County . . . gave and bequeathed unto the fou children of Anne Benitt: George, Edward, Elizabeth and Mary or such of them as shall live to come to age, all his Land to bee equal. Divided . . . and whereas George and Edward . . . died in the Minority, Soe that Elizabeth and Mary beinge the onely Survivin Children of the said Anne Benett and being of Competent and Lawf age and being both married, Elizabeth the Elder to Henry Collins an Mary the younger to Thomas Ewell, Doe . . . make . . . Division an Partition . . . Sixty acres . . . old Fields and Seared ground . . portion of Elizabeth . . . all woodlands . . . remaining part . . . on hundred and four acres is the Shair part and proportion of Mary th younger Daughter now wife of Thomas Ewell . . . ye forth yeare o the Reigne of our Sovereign Lord King James ye Second . . ."
Signed: Henry Collins (seal), Elizabeth Collins (seal), Thoma Ewell (seal), Mary Ewell (seal). (Norfolk Co., Lib. 5, fol. 74.)

2. CHARLES[2] EGERTON, of Lower Norfolk County, Virginia and o St. Mary's County Maryland, died in St. Mary's County in 1699

1675 June 16—Charles Egerton was on a jury to inquire into an accusation of witchcraft against one Joan Jenkins (*Lower Norfolk Co., Va., Antiquary*, VII, 50).

1683 Feb. 1—Deed to Charles Egerton of Lower Norfolk County, Va., from William Thomas and Susan his wife, of Lankford Bay, Kent County, Md., for 19,000 pounds of tobacco in cask, "all that plantation and tract of land called Punckney Marsh, in St. Michael's Hundred in St. Mary's County, between the land of Richard Atwood and Hugh Manning, 200 acres." (Signed) William Thomas, and witnessed by George Parker and Robert Carvile. Acknowledged, 2 Dec. 1684 (Provincial Court Records, Annapolis, Liber W. R. C. no. 1, folios 312 et seq.).

1685 Oct. 3—At a Court held at St. Mary's City, Randolph Brandt, *Charles Egerton* and ten others were on the jury in the case of one Rebecca Fowler of Calvert County, Md., accused of witchcraft (Judgment Records of Provincial Court of Maryland, Liber T. G. (2) 1682-1702; *Maryland Historical Magazine*, XXXI, 283, 284).

1687—" One Raymond, a Papist priest, did publicly in Court declare that he intended the house of *Mr. Charles Egerton*, the house of Captain Robert Jordan and the house of Henry Usdick to meet at, there celebrate the Mass and other rites of their church " (*William and Mary Quarterly*, I°, I, 47).

1689 Jan. 14—Deed from Charles Calvert of St. Mary's County, gent., son and heir of William Calvert, Esq., deceased, to Charles Egerton of St. Mary's County, Merchant, conveys for the sum of 30000 lbs. of tobacco 2400 acres of land. " Whereas, Ye Rt. Hon. Cecilius Calvert, late Lord Proprietary, etc., of Maryland, by Letters Patent dated 11 Feb. 1662, did grant unto the said William Calvert, deceased, a tract of land on the east side of Piscataway River and on the south side of Piscataway Creek, beginning at a marked oak ye bound tree of Randolph Henson [Hanson?] and running [etc.], then laid out for 3000 acres; and, Whereas further, ye said William Calvert upon marriage of his daughter Elizabeth with James Neale of Charles County, gent., did give unto the said James Neale and his wife, or one of them, 600 acres part of the aforesaid 3000 acres, which 3000 acres are situated in Charles County and are a part of ye land that was reserved for ye Indians in 1668 " . . . (Annapolis, Land Records, Charles County Deed Book (abstract), Lib. R. No. 1, 1690-92, fol. 134).

NOTE: " Piscataway " was patented to the Hon. William Calvert, given to his daughter Elizabeth and her husband James Neale who, in turn, gave it (or possibly part of it) to their daughter Mary the wife of Charles[3] Egerton, which said Mary after Egerton's death married Jeremiah Adderton. Mary and Charles[3] Egerton sold it on 15 Jan. 1703 to James Heath and his heirs (Annapolis, Liber P. C., folio 659).

1694 Dec. 12—Charles Egerton filed in Lower Norfolk County Court House a Power of Attorney for his son Arthur, wherein the former and his wife Anne referred to themselves as formerly of Elizabeth River, Virginia, late of St. Mary's County, Maryland.

1699—. The will of Charles Egerton, of St. Mary's County, dated Mch. 11 and proved April 11, 1699, devised to his wife Anne, for life, " Pountney's Marsh," elsewhere written " Punckney Marsh," and named her executrix and residuary legatee of his personal estate. He devised to his son George the plantation aforesaid, after his wife's death and also a right in land bought from Charles Calvert which was purchased from Robert Large;

To his son Charles, land on Potomac River, called "Piney Neck"; * To his other four sons John, Thomas, Randolph and James Egerton jointly, 2400 acres in the freshes of Potomac River, on the north side of the river, generally called "Piscataway," they to make an equal division of the said 2400 acres into four parts. "As for what other lands I have within the capes in Virginia or Maryland, the same to be sold and disposed of by my executors." To his daughter Mary, he bequeathed 20000 lbs. of tobacco, "provided my executors like her marriage choice; otherwise, one shilling." None of his sons was to leave their mother until 25 years of age. To the Rev. Father John Hall, 1000 lbs. of tobacco more, on the anniversary of the testator's death. The guardians for his minor children were appointed: namely, Mr. John Hall, Mr. Thomas Groning, Mr. John Sermot and Mr. William Herbert. The executors named, were his sons Charles and John Egerton (St. Mary's County Wills, Liber P. C. no. 1, folios 123 *et seq.*; *Maryland Calendar of Wills*, II, 174).

The Rent Rolls of Prince George County (1696-1723) show that "Piscataway" was in the possession of "Richard Calvert, John Egerton, Thomas Egerton, Randall Egerton and —— Egerton, each 600 acres."

Charles[2] Egerton married Anne Porter, widow of John Godfrey. After Egerton's death, she became the wife of —— Boucher and died in 1712. The will of Anne Boucher of St. Michael's Hundred, St. Mary's County, Md., dated Jan. 20 and proved Feb. 7, 1712, bequeathed personal property to her sons Thomas, Randolph, James and George Egerton (executor and residuary legatee) and her daughter Mary Underwood (*Maryland Calendar of Wills*, III, 236). The surviving children of Charles and Anne Egerton were as follows:

3.   I. CHARLES[3] EGERTON, oldest son, died *circa* 1705 (of whom presently).

II. John[3] Egerton

III. George[3] Egerton

IV. Thomas[3] Egerton

V. Randolph[3] Egerton

VI. James[3] Egerton

In 1699, Charles[2] Egerton devised to his sons John, Thomas, Randolph and James, 2400 acres of the Piscataway Tract. On 10 Nov. 1715, Thomas, Randolph and James Egerton of St. Mary's County, conveyed to Thomas Edelen of Prince George's County, Md., the said 2400 acres. On 31 July 1717, "James Egerton of the Province of Maryland, married Miriam Tatum, maiden of Norfolk County, Va., daughter of Elizabeth Tatum." The marriage bond was witnessed by Rand. Egerton and Moses Kidwood (*Lower Norfolk County Antiquary*, III, 41).

VII. Mary[3] Egerton, married —— Underwood.

* "Piney Neck" seems to be a geographical place-name and not a patented tract name (see Thomas' *Chronicles of Colonial Maryland*, p. 349).

3. CHARLES[3] EGERTON, eldest son of Charles[2] Egerton, was born before 1677 and died *circa* 1705 at "Piney Neck" in St. Mary's County, Maryland. In 1702, he married Mary Neale, born in 1682, daughter of Capt. James Neale (1650/5-1727) who married in 1681 Elizabeth Calvert (died 1684), daughter of Hon. (Col.) William Calvert (1643-1683) by his wife Elizabeth Stone. The last named was the daughter of Gov. William Stone (1604-1660) and his wife Verlinda Cotton? (died 1675).

In 1702, James Neale of Wollaston Manor, Charles County, Maryland (son of James and Anne (Gill) Neale), born about 1650 in Europe, conveyed to Mary his daughter by his first wife (Elizabeth Calvert) all the lands received with Elizabeth Calvert as her marriage portion, showing that Mary was her mother's only child. On 10 April 1702, James Neale of Charles County, Md., gent., and Elizabeth his wife conveyed to Charles Egerton, gent. of St. Mary's County, "who hath lately married Mary, daughter of the said James Neale," 600 acres part of a tract of 3000 acres, formerly in Charles County, but now in Prince George's County, Md., patented to William Calvert, Esq., and the aforesaid 600 acres thereof given in marriage with his daughter Elizabeth (Calvert) to the said James Neale (Pr. Geo. Co., Liber A, 449).

Charles Egerton died intestate. On 5 Mch. 1705, the Administration Bond on the estate of Charles Egerton, late of St. Mary's County, deceased, was given by his widow Mary Egerton, as administratrix. James Neale of Charles County and Charles Beckwith of St. Mary's County were her sureties in the sum of £400 sterling (Annapolis, Test. Proc., Lib. 19-c, 40).

Mrs. Mary (Neale) Egerton married (2) Jeremiah Adderton (died 1713); (3) Joseph Van Sweringen (died 1721) and (4) William Deacon. On 17 May 1708 was filed the account of Jeremiah Adderton (d. 1713) and Mary his wife, adm'x of Charles Egerton of St. Mary's County (Annapolis, Inv. and Accts., Liber 28, fol. 221); and on 30 Dec. 1710 a further Account was filed by the same couple (*ibid.*, Lib. 32-B, fol. 11).

Between 1713 and 9 Sept. 1715, the widow married her third husband, Joseph Van Sweringen (d. 1721), and about 1722/23 she married her fourth, William Deacon. On 8 Mch. 1721, as Mary Van Sweringen of St. Mary's County, widow, she deposed her age as 39 years.

By her first husband, Charles Egerton, Mary Neale had issue as follows:

  4. I. JAMES[4] EGERTON, born *circa* 1703; died 1768 (of whom presently).
    II. Charles[4] Egerton, died *circa* 1738.

4. JAMES[4] EGERTON was born *circa* 1703 and died in 1768, in St. Mary's County, Maryland. The will of James Egerton of St. Mary's County was dated 16 Jan. 1765 and proved 26 July 1768 (St. Mary's County Will Book T. A. no. 1, folio 559; Annapolis, W. B. 36, 531). He bequeathed to his son, Charles Calvert[5] Egerton, three negro slaves together with the three negroes mentioned in a deed of gift to the said son, "when he arrives at 18 years of age." Also, to his said son Charles Calvert[5] Egerton he devised his dwelling plantation at "Piney Neck," formerly the property of Charles[2] Egerton (died 1699) who devised it to his eldest son Charles[3] Egerton. The latter died in 1705, intestate, and the estate was inherited by his eldest son James, mentioned above. In addition to the "Piney Neck" estate, which James's will stipulated should not be disposed of until his son arrived at 21 years of age, Charles Calvert Egerton was devised one other tract called "Bluestone Neck," and was made residuary legatee. The will also mentions: "My grandson Michael Jenifer, son of Michael Jenifer and Mary Ann his wife; my grandson Parker Jenifer and my granddaughter Dorkey Jenifer; to my son-in-law Michael Jenifer, a young cow and calf, in full of his deceased wife Mary Ann's part of my estate."

  The testator's friend, Richard Swan Edwards, was to have the care of Charles Calvert Egerton's estate until the latter attained the age of 18 years, but Edwards refused to serve. The will was witnessed by John Tennison, Samuel Cottrell and Charles Loe (Lowe?). No wife is mentioned in the will.

  James[4] Egerton had issue as follows:

  5. I. CHARLES CALVERT[5] EGERTON, born *circa* 1748; died 1778 (of whom presently):
    II. Mary Ann Egerton, died *ante* 1765; married Michael Jenifer.

5. CHARLES CALVERT[5] EGERTON was born *circa* 1748 and died in 1778 in St. Mary's County, Maryland. The will of Charles Calvert Egerton of St. Mary's County was dated 19 Sept. 1777 and proved 5 May 1778 (St. Mary's County Will Book, J. J. no. 1, folios 58 *et seq.*).

  The testator named his wife Mary as his executrix and gave her his lands during her widowhood. He mentioned his five children in order as follows: James (eldest), Calvert, Ann. Sarah, and Bennett Egerton. The will was witnessed by Bennett Biscoe, Solomon Jones and James Biscoe.

Charles Calvert Egerton married (Mary Bennett?) and had issue as follows:

6.   I. JAMES⁶ EGERTON, born *circa* 1770 (of whom presently).
     II. Calvert⁶ Egerton, died 14 May 1833 aged 59 years, *sine prole*.
     III. Ann⁶ Egerton.
     IV. Sarah⁶ Egerton.
7.   V. BENNETT⁶ EGERTON (of whom presently).

JAMES⁶ EGERTON (*Charles Calvert⁵*, etc.), of Chaptico, St. Mary's County, Maryland, was born about 1770. In 1799, he purchased from Henry Neale 250 acres of " Bashford Manor." On 17 Feb. 1807 a deed from James Eden of St. Mary's to James Egerton, for the sum of $2300.00 current money, conveys 277 acres, part of " Bashford Manor," lying on Chaptico Bay between the lands of said James Egerton and Edward and John Maddox, known commonly as the " Indian Fields."

James Egerton married (1) 1792 Matilda Bond of Benedict, St. Mary's County, Maryland (daughter of " Col. Richard Bond and Susanna Key ") and had issue as follows:

     I. Susanna Key⁷ Egerton, born 1794; married (1) 14 Feb. 1811 Edward Wilder (1770-1828), of Charles County, Md., and had issue; married (2) ——— Kent. She removed from Maryland to Kentucky about 1830.
8.   II. CHARLES CALVERT⁷ EGERTON, born 26 Feb. 1797; died 27 May 1862 (of whom presently).
     III. Richard⁷ Egerton, born 1798.

James Egerton married (2) in 1805 Eliza Chesley and had issue as follows:

9.   IV. ROBERT CHESLEY⁷ EGERTON (of whom presently).
     V. Elizabeth⁷ Egerton, married Thomas Swann of Louisville, Ky.

7. BENNETT⁶ EGERTON (*Charles Calvert⁵*, etc.) Married (1) Ada DuBois and had issue as follows

10.   I. JOHN B.⁷ EGERTON (of whom presently).
11.   II. CHARLES CALVERT⁷ EGERTON (of whom presently).
12.   III. DuBOIS⁷ EGERTON (of whom presently).

8. CHARLES CALVERT⁷ EGERTON (*James⁶, Charles Calvert⁵*, etc.) was born 26 Feb. 1797 in St. Mary's County, Maryland and died 27 May 1862 in Baltimore, Md. He is buried in Green Mount Cemetery, as likewise is his second wife, Rebecca Callis, born 3 Dec. 1803, died 7 April 1888, sister of his first wife.

Charles Calvert Egerton married (1) Susan Callis (1801-1822) and had issue as follows:

     I. James Henry⁸ Egerton, married ——— Wolff and had issue, one son.
     II. Rebecca Ann⁸ Egerton, married (1) William Lawrence. Issue: William, Rev. Edward, Willard and Ida Lawrence.

Charles Calvert Egerton married (2) Rebecca Callis (18(
1888) and had issue as follows:

13. III. PHILIP ALEXANDER[8] EGERTON (of whom presently).
IV. Mary Annette[8] Egerton, married Wesley Wilson, son of John Fletc
Wilson of Portland Manor, Anne Arundel County, Md., and h
issue: Lelia, died aged five years.
V. Rosetta[8] Egerton, married William P. Whiting of Hampton, Va., a
had issue: William Kennon, married Kate Viers; Florence Beve
married Wills Lee of Hampton, Va.; Wesley Wilson, d. unm.; M
Mallory, married Fred. Webster; Rosetta, married Samuel Parran.
14. VI. CHARLES CALVERT[8] EGERTON (of whom presently).
VII. Clara[8] Egerton, married Robert Dibley of N. Y. Issue: Eliza, Jul
Clara, Isabel, Robert.
VIII. Julia[8] Egerton, married Robert D. Semmes. Issue: Clara, married Jo
D. Bird.
15. IX. WILLIAM A.[8] EGERTON (of whom presently).
X. Eleanora B.[8] Egerton, died unmarried.
16. XI. SAMUEL EDWIN[8] EGERTON, born 18 Nov. 1839; died 17 Aug. 18
(of whom presently).
XII. Virginia[8] Egerton, died in infancy.

9. ROBERT CHESLEY[7] EGERTON (*James[6], Charles Calvert[5]*, etc.)
of Petersburg, Va., died 1852; married 1830 Clarinda Smit
(died 1869) and had issue as follows:

I. Laura[8] Egerton, born 1831; died in infancy.
II. Robert Laurence[8] Egerton, born in 1833; married in 1880 Jennie Buckl
of Louisville, Ky.
III. Janet Smith[8] Egerton, born in 1835.
IV. May Elizabeth[8] Egerton, born in 1838; died in 1859.
V. William Bridgewater[8] Egerton, born in 1840.
VI. Susan Melville[8] Egerton, born in 1842; married (1) in 1861 Cap
Robert Freeman, (2) Dr. D. W. Hand of St. Paul, Minn.
VII. Louisa Clarinda[8] Egerton, born in 1845; married in 1869 Wm. Evele
Cameron of Petersburg, Va., who later became Governor of Virginia
VIII. James Chesley[8] Egerton, born in 1847; married in 1869 Virginia An
Lefler and removed to Minneapolis. Issue: Walter Chesley Egerto
and Maude Cameron Egerton.
IX. Robert Oscar[8] Egerton, born in 1851; married Bessie Stuart Hall o
Petersburg, Va.

10. JOHN B.[7] EGERTON (*Bennett[6], Charles Calvert[5]*, etc.) married
twice. He married (1) ——— Higgenbotham, who died *sine*
prole. He married (2) ——— Fowler, and had issue as follows:

I. John B.[8] Egerton.
II. Maud[8] Egerton.
III. a daughter.
IV. a daughter.
V. a daughter.

11. CHARLES CALVERT[7] EGERTON (*Bennett[6], Charles Calvert[5]*, etc.)
was born in 1816 and died in 1893. He was in command of
Maryland Troops at Harper's Ferry at the time of John Brown's
raid, 16 Oct. 1859. Gen. Charles C. Egerton commanded the
Second Light Brigade, from Baltimore, in the M. V. I. He

married Elizabeth Hall of Howard County, Md., and had issue as follows:

    I. Minnie[8] Egerton, married J. T. Ringgold.
    II. Mary[8] Egerton, married M. E. Reid.
    III. Sophia[8] Egerton.
    IV. Virginia[8] Egerton.

. DuBois[7] Egerton (*Bennett[6]*, *Charles Calvert[5]*, etc.) married Ada McCrea and had issue as follows:

    I. John B.[8] Egerton, removed to Long Island, N. Y.
    II. Mary DuBois[8] Egerton, married Professor Thayer of Boston.

. Philip Alexander[8] Egerton (*Charles Calvert[7]*, *James[6]*, *Charles Calvert[5]*, etc.), married Margaret Schley Saunderson. Removed to New York City. Issue as follows:

    I. Edgar[9] Egerton.
    II. Ella[9] Egerton.
    III. Henry[9] Egerton.
    IV. Frank[9] Egerton.
    V. Minnie[9] Egerton.

4. Charles Calvert[8] Egerton (*Charles Calvert,[7]* *James,[6]* *Charles Calvert[5]*, etc.), married Virginia Turner and had issue as follows:

    I. Charles Carroll[9] Egerton.
    II. Emma[9] Egerton.
    III. Lulie[9] Egerton.
    IV. Virginia[9] Egerton.
    V. Maud[9] Egerton.

5. William A.[8] Egerton (*Charles Calvert[7]*, *James[6]*, *Charles Calvert[5]*, etc.), married Ellen Wilson of New York and had issue as follows:

    I. Bayard[9] Egerton, married Mamie Sauerberg.
    II. Nellie[9] Egerton, married (1) Richard Lee Fearn; (2) Admiral Plunkett, U. S. N.
    III. Bessie[9] Egerton, married Fred. Hutchinson.

6. Samuel Edwin[8] Egerton (*Charles Calvert[7]*, *James[6]*, *Charles Calvert[5]*, etc.) was born 18 Nov. 1839 at Chaptico, Md., and died 17 Aug. 1895 at Baltimore, to which city he removed at the age of 18 years. His wife, Elizabeth Duvall Wilson, was born on 18 Aug. 1849 at Wakefield, Westmoreland County, Va., spent most of her young life at Portland Manor, Anne Arundel County, Md., the home of her grandfather, and died 3 Sept. 1905 at Baltimore. Both are buried in Green Mount Cemetery.

Samuel Edwin Egerton married 20 Nov. 1866, at St. James Church, Anne Arundel County, Elizabeth Duvall Wilson and had issue as follows:

I. Samuel E.[9] Egerton, born 7 Dec. 1867; died in 1868. Buried in Gr
Mount Cemetery.

II. John Fletcher[9] Egerton, born 6 Jan. 1869; died 25 Feb. 1925 at Man
P. I.; married Susan Yeatman of Norfolk, Va., *sine prole.*

17. III. STUART[9] EGERTON, born 21 Nov. 1870 (of whom presently).

18. IV. SAMUEL EDWIN[9] EGERTON, born 6 Aug. 1872 (of whom presently)

V. Kennon Whiting[9] Egerton, born 4 April 1874; died 27 Nov. 19
married Agnes Moore of Danville, Va., *sine prole.*

VI. Elizabeth[9] Wilson[9] Egerton, born 25 April 1876; died 21 June 18
Buried in Green Mount Cemetery.

VII. Florence Beverly[9] Egerton, born 9 Jan. 1878; married Brig. Gen. Wal
Driscoll Smith, U. S. A. Issue.

VIII. Martha Rankin[9] Egerton, born 9 Jan. 1880; married Admiral Ernest
King, U. S. N., born 23 Nov. 1878 at Lorain, Ohio.

IX. Helen Duvall[9] Egerton, born 15 Jan. 1881; died 12 Dec. 1881. Bur
in Green Mount Cemetery.

X. Ethel Wilson[9] Egerton, born 30 Aug. 1882; died 26 Nov. 1884. Bur
in Green Mount Cemetery.

17. STUART[9] EGERTON (*Samuel Edwin*[8], *Charles Calvert*[7], *Jame
Charles Calvert*[5], etc.) was born 21 Nov. 1870, at Baltimor
Maryland. Stuart Egerton married 21 Oct. 1896 Martha N
White, born 4 Sept. 1873, daughter of Gen. James McKenr
White (1842-1925) and had issue as follows:

19. I. STUART WILSON[10] EGERTON, born 15 Aug. 1897 (of whom presently

20. II. JAMES McKENNY WHITE[10] EGERTON, born 12 July 1905 (of who
presently).

18. SAMUEL EDWIN[9] EGERTON (*Samuel Edwin*[8], *Charles Calvert*
James[6], *Charles Calvert*[5], etc.) was born 6 Aug. 1872, at Balt
more, Maryland.

Samuel Edwin Egerton married 7 April 1896 Bessie Appleto
Tyler (died 1 Dec. 1937), daughter of George Tyler, and ha
issue as follows:

I. a son, died in infancy.

II. a son, died in infancy.

III. a son, died in infancy.

IV. Elizabeth[10] Egerton, married William Conklin.

V. Samuel James[10] Egerton, died 10 July 1936, unmarried.

VI. John Wilson[10] Egerton, married 13 April 1936 Martha Jane Broderick
daughter of Bartlett C. Broderick.

19. STUART WILSON[10] EGERTON (*Stuart*[9], *Samuel Edwin*[8], *Charle
Calvert*[7], *James*[6], *Charles Calvert*[5], etc.) was born 15 Aug. 189
and is a practising physician of Baltimore, Md. He received hi
A. B. degree in 1918 and his M. D. degree in 1923, at the John
Hopkins University. He was Lieutenant in the 67th Field Ar
tillery in 1918. He married 25 Sept. 1923 Katherine Bailey Lalor
born 3 Dec. 1901, dau. of Wm. B. Lalor of Phila., Pa., and ha
issue as follows:

I. Katherine Bailey[11] Egerton, born 12 Sept. 1925.

II. Martha Stuart[11] Egerton, born 23 June 1927.

0. JAMES McKENNY WHITE[10] EGERTON (*Stuart*[9], *Samuel Edwin*[8], *Charles Calvert*[7], *James*[6], *Charles Calvert*[5], etc.) was born 12 July 1905 and is a practising attorney-at-law of Baltimore, Md. He received his A. B. degree at Princeton University in 1927 and was graduated from the Harvard Law School in 1930. He married 5 May 1931 Carolyn Howell Griswold, born 5 Dec. 1908, dau. of Benjamin Howell Griswold, Jr., and grand dau. of Alexander Brown of Baltimore, and had issue as follows:

    I. McKenny White[11] Egerton, Jr., born 28 March 1932.
    II. Benjamin Griswold[11] Egerton, born 23 Jan. 1935.
    III. Stuart[11] Egerton, 3rd, born 23 Aug. 1938.

EGERTON—CALVERT

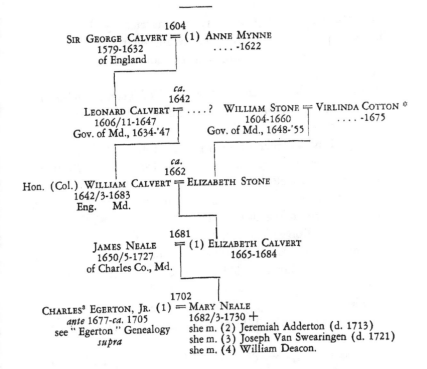

* Verlinda Cotton is usually given as the maiden name of the wife of Gov. William Stone of Maryland. Mr. J. B. Calvert Nicklin, however, believes that he has evidence to prove that she was Verlinda Graves, a daughter of Capt. Thomas Graves of Virginia, and a sister to Ann the wife of Rev. William Cotton and to the wife of Capt. William Roper. Cotton (d. 1646) in his will called Stone and Roper his brothers-in-law.

SOME OLD BIBLE RECORDS OF THE EMORY FAMILY OF MARYLAND.

FRANCIS B. CULVER

The following extracts are taken from an old Oxford Bible (1728), in the possession of Mrs. J. Woodley Richardson, of Harford County, Maryland.

Thomas Lane Emory, Senior, was born in the year 1751 and died 2 May 1828, aged 77 years.

Thomas Lane Emory, Jr., was born in the year 1789 and died in the year 1835, aged 46 years.

Thomas Lane Emory, Junior, was married by the R^t Revd Bishop Kemp to Eliza Harwood Grant on the thirteenth of June in the year of our Lord one thousand eight hundred and fifteen.

Eliza Lindenberger Emory, first child of Thomas and Eliza, was born on Friday the 15th of November 1816 at twenty minutes after three o'clock A. M.

George Lindenberger [Emory], second child of Thomas and Eliza, was born on Thursday the 7th of December 1820 at ten minutes after 12 o'clock P. M.

Isabella Rebecca [Emory], second daughter of Thomas and Eliza, was born on Wednesday the 22^d of March 1822 at fifteen minutes after twelve o'clock P. M.

Thomas Lane [Emory], second son of Thomas and Eliza, was born on Friday the 25th of November 1825 at 4 o'clock P. M.

Daniel Grant [Emory], third son of Thomas and Eliza, was born on Thursday the 14th of February 1828 at ¼ before 5 o'clock P. M.

Thomas Lane Emory died on 2^d May 1828, aged 77 years.

Mary [Emory], sixth child and third daughter of Thomas and Eliza, was born 24th October 1831, about 12 o'clock A. M.

Thomas Lane Emory died on 5th February, at 5 o'clock in the evening, in the 46th year of his age.

Eliza Harwood Emory, widow of Thomas L. Emory died on Tuesday 15th of June 1852, at 2 o'clock A. M. in the 57th year of her age.

Daniel Grant [Emory], third son of Thomas and Eliza was married at Glencoe, Baltimore County, on 2nd of October 1855, by Rev. Dr William E. Wyatt, to Emma Rosalie, daughter of William J. Ward.

Emma Rosalie, their first child was born 27 July 1856, and died 18 February 1858.

Lillian Grant, their second child was born 20 October 1858.

Emma Rosalie, wife of Daniel Grant, died 24 October 1858.

Thomas Lane, second son of Thomas L. and Eliza H. Emory, died 28th of October, 1863, in New Orleans, La.

Eliza Lindenberger Emory, eldest child of Thomas L. and Eliza H. Emory, died 22 November 1863.

John Sanderson Price was married by Rev. Charles C. Grafton at St. Paul's Church, Baltimore, 13 Oct. 1859, to Mary, third daughter of Thomas L. and Eliza Harwood Emory.

Ezekiel Forman was married 24 January 1756 to Augustene Marsh.

Capt. John Emory, Jun., died 11th of January 1761, aged six[ty] and three years, and was buried 14th of same month— the text of his funeral sermon was taken out of the 112th Psalm, 7th verse.

Daniel Grant died 29th of June 1816, in the 83rd year of his age.

GENEALOGICAL NOTES ON THE EMORY FAMILY OF MARYLAND.

December, 1927.

The ancestors of the present Emory and Amory families of America were the same and for many generations prior to 1700 were residents and land owners in the adjoining counties of Somerset and Devon and Gloucester in England. Early local records also indicate a branch of the family in Essex about 1634.

The present name of Emory-Amory was, so far as can be determined, originally Amauri, in France, about the 12th century, and during a period of about three hundred years the spelling of the name was changed to D'Amorie, Amorie, D'Amory and about 1600 became Amory and Emory.

Regardless of the several variations in spelling by certain

generations of the family, which was characteristic of that period, the pronunciation of the name as Em-ory has remained the same since the very earliest times. In this connection it is interesting to note the following extract from a letter dated May 15, 1731, Bristol, England, to Thomas C. Amory of Boston, from a cousin, a Mrs. Julia O'Connor: "I have some papers in my hand wch cou'd give you light wch is your right in the county Kerry whither I am bound soon from this place (Bristol) where I have been about a fortnight and have been making inquiry of some of yr relations, the *Emorys,* for so they write their name, about yr estate in Somersetshire and they tell me it is in very good condition . . . . " Page 106-107 (The Descendants of Hugh Amory, 1605-1805, by Gertrude E. Meredith, London, 1901).

Among the early English ancestors of the family were Robert de Amory, Lord of Bucknell 1257, Giles D'Amorie (later Amorie and Amory about 1550), Giles and Thomas Amory 1579, John Amory 1606, Thomas 1667, and John Emory who died in Somersetshire in 1657. At this time local records also show that members of apparently the same family were living in Essex and possibly a branch under the name of Emery in Kent.

The fact that the different members of the family of Somerset, Gloucester and Essex were of the same stock and closely related is indicated in the similarity of their arms with crests in two instances being the same.

According to the English records and authorities as listed hereon, the following arms were granted:

(1) Giles D'Amorie (Amory), 1592; Arms: Barry nebuly of six argent and gules, over all upon a bend sable three bezants or. Crest: out of a mural coronet or, a talbots azure eared or. (College of Arms; Robson's British Herald, 1830; Royal Crest Book, MacLaren, London 1883.)

(2) Emory als Amory—Amery, Essex 1634; Arms: Barry nebuly of six argent and gules, in chief three annulets gules. Crest: out of a mural coronet a demi-horse, or maned or collared gu, studded or. Motto: "Fedelis et Suavis" (College

of Arms; The Visitation of Essex 1634, Harleian Society, Vol. 13; Edmondson's Complete Heraldry, London 1870; Royal Crest Book, London 1883).

(3) Amory-Emory, Somerset; Arms: Barry nebuly of six argent and gu, a bent az. Crest: out of a mural coronet or, a talbots head az eared of the first. (College of Arms, London; Burke, Descendants of Hugh Amory by Meredith, London 1901.)

(4) Emory of Somersetshire, died 1657; Arms: Barry of six, gu or, in chief three cinquefoils or. Crest: A demi-unicorn rampant and erased, gu, hoofed and armed or crined sa. (Descendants of Hugh Amory by Meredith 1901; Elvens Book of Crests; College of Arms, London; Royal Crest Book.)

Family arms—Amory—Amorye—Amorie—in window of St. Peter's Church or Cathedral in Exon. Devon., Vol. I (Carew's Scroll of Arms, 1588).

The two American branches of the family were first represented in this country by the emigration of Arthur Emory to the province of Maryland in 1665, direct ancestor of the Maryland Emorys and by Thomas Amory, ancestor of the Boston Amorys, who settled first about 1690 in South Carolina, a few years later moving to Boston, Mass.

Arthur Emory arrived in the province of Maryland from Somersetshire, England, in 1660, with his wife, Mary and two children. He received from Lord Baltimore, in 1667, several direct formal grants of land on the Choptank, Wye and Chester Rivers, in Talbot and Queen Anne's Counties (Liber 12, p. 61, Anno. 1668; Date of grant June 30, 1668). He married his second wife, Ann Smith, prior to 1671, a daughter of Robert Smith. He married the third time, Catherine Vanderfort, a daughter of Michel Paul Vanderfort, whose family emigrated from Dermont, Flanders, and was granted large estates about 1640 on the site of the present city of Brooklyn, New York.

Arthur Emory died in 1699 and by his second wife left two sons, Arthur, Jr. and John, by his third wife, Catherine, he left two sons, William and a second Arthur, and also a daughter, Ann. Catherine afterwards married Edmund Prior, and died, according to her will, in 1749. (Wills, deeds, grants, etc., Land office records in Annapolis, Liber X, folio 391 and copies Talbot County wills in Ann Arundel County Courthouse, Liber H, folio 269.)

Arthur Emory Jr., born 1666, was one of the earliest members of the first county court of Queen Anne's, 1708. He had a pew in Wye church and was a vestryman in St. Paul's parish in 1704. He died September 22, 1747, and lies buried at Ingleside, originally known as " Emory's Fortune," which was one of the earliest colonial estates of the Emory family. It is located near the present village of Queenstown, his tombstone shows that he had two wives, Anne died Nov. 10, 1721, and Jockline (Jacqueline) Littilen. His will (Arthur 1747) probated November 25th, 1747, shows he left the following sons and daughters: John Jr., Arthur III, Thomas, Gideon and James and also four daughters.

Thomas Emory was the father of Thomas Lane Emory of Baltimore and the " Woodridge " Emory branch, now of Baltimore County, are descendants of Gideon Emory. Gideon married Mary Marsh, daughter of Thomas Marsh 1716. He died 1784 leaving sons, Wm. Wilson, Gideon Jr., John and James.

Francois *Guidon* (Gideon), Cambrai, France, Sous Lieutenant au 46 Reg. de Ligne, buried Ashburton Churchyard, Devon, French prisoner of war, 1815, age 22. Page 185, Devon Notes & Queries, Vol. 2, 1903.

Thomas Lane Emory of " Warrington " was the ancestor of the Richard Emory family of Baltimore county, represented at this time by Emory Warfield, Henry M. and S. Davies, sons of the late Henry M. Warfield and his wife Anna Emory, also Mary and Isabel Emory, sisters of Daniel Grant Emory, who married a daughter of Alexander Fulton and left a son, Thomas Emory and a daughter, Letlia.

Arthur 2nd, brother of Arthur, 1747, married Ann ———— and left the following sons: William, Edward and *Giles*.

John Emory Senior, son of Arthur 1st, 1699, was Lord Baltimore's Deputy Surveyor and Receiver of Quit Rents in 1726 and in 1750-60 was one of the surveyors who represented Maryland in the survey of the boundary line between Maryland and Pennsylvania on the Chesapeake and Delaware Peninsula, which was afterwards prolonged by Messrs. Mason and Dixon in the famous Mason and Dixon line. He was a pew holder in Wye church in 1723. He received through his elder brother, Arthur, 1747, by deed of gift from his father in 1683, " Bachelor's Chance." The other Emory colonial estates at this time were " Ingleside," " Warrington," " Coursey on Wye," " Saint Paul " and " Brampton."

John Emory married Ann ———. He died in 1763 and his will probated December 23, 1763, shows he left the following sons: Charles The Elder, John, Thomas, James, William and Charles The Younger, and daughters, Elizabeth and Ann.

John Emory of " Brampton " later " Poplar Grove," son of John Emory surveyor 1763, was born about 1710. He married Margaret Marsh, a sister of Mary and Sarah, wives of Gideon Emory 1st and John Emory Jr., 1765, and daughter of Thomas Marsh, 1712, who was a direct descendant of Augustine Hermann, the famous Bohemian noblemen, Lord of Bohemia Manor, in Cecil County, Maryland. He died intestate about 1740, leaving his widow, Margaret (who later married David Register) and two sons, John and Thomas and a daughter Sarah (married Thomas Falcomer).

John Emory married Juliana Hawkins (first wife) December 14, 1758 (St. Luke's Parish Church, Church Hill, Maryland), and about this time added to his own his step-father's name " Register " to distinguish him from several other John Emorys of his day.

The grandsons of Arthur Junior, 1747, and his brother John, 1763, were represented in the Revolutionary War as officers by the following: Gideon Emory, 2nd Lieut. 5th Maryland Regt., Dec. 10, 1776; Richard Emory, Captain 5th Maryland Regt., Dec. 10, 1776, Brevet Major Oct. 4, 1777, Thomas Lane

Emory, 1st. Lieut., 4th Eastern Shore Bn., 1776, later Captain 5th Maryland Regt., John Register Emory, 1st Lieut. in James O'Bryon's Company, 20th Bn., Maryland Militia, date of commission Jan. 3, 1776, he saw active service against Lord Dunmore and later took part in the battle of Long Island (Maryland Muster Rolls in the Revolution, 1775-83, Vol. 18, Archives of Maryland; McSherry's History of Maryland, 1850; Historical Register of Officers of the Continental Army, by Francis B. Heitman, 1914).

John Register Emory was a member of the Queen Anne's County Board of Justices of the Peace, in 1777. He inherited from his father "Poplar Grove" in Queen Anne's County, originally known as "Brampton." In addition to "Brampton" the estate was at that time made up of "Conquest," "Corsica" and "Cintra" (Cintra, a town in Portugal, which up to about 1640 had been a dependency of Spain), the total consisting of approximately two thousand acres, covering all of that section known as Spaniards Neck at the junction of the Corsica and Chester rivers. "Poplar Grove" is one of the very few colonial estates in America which has been continuously owned by the same family and inherited from generation to generation up to the present time. It is the only one now remaining in possession of the Emorys in Maryland. The original section of the brick manor house was built about 1700 according to tradition and the formal terraced gardens of boxwood on the rear lawn are known to be the oldest gardens in this country.

Robert Emory, a son of John Register Emory by his first wife, married Frances Thomas, daughter of Tristram and Ann Thomas of Wye Neck. Their son was John Emory, later the noted bishop of the M. E. Church, founder of Emory University in Georgia, etc. Bishop Emory's son, Robert 2nd, was for many years president of Dickinson College. With the exception of Bishop Emory the Emorys from the earliest times have been associated with the history of the Anglican and afterwards the Protestant Episcopal Church. John Register Emory's second wife was Ann Costin, to whom he was married Nov. 2,

1765. He died in 1790, his wife died June 4, 1802. They left the following children: John Emory, born Dec. 22, 1766; Margaret Emory, born Aug. 11, 1768; Ann Emory, born Sept. 25, 1770; Richard, born Feb. 4, 1773; Elizabeth, born May 17, 1777; William, born 1780, and Thomas, born March 24, 1782. Thomas Emory, later known as General Thomas Emory, inherited " Poplar Grove " from his father. He married June 13, 1805, Anna Maria Hemsley, born March 5, 1787, daughter of William Hemsley of " Cloverfields," who served in the Continental Congress 1782-3, was colonel of a battalion from the county which stamped out a Tory insurrection and later was active in collecting supplies for the Continental Army. His mother was Anna Maria Tilghman, daughter of Richard Tilghman of " The Hermitage " and Anna Maria Lloyd of " Wye."

General Thomas Emory was a member of the Maryland House of Delegates, the State Senate and Executive Council of the governor under the old Constitution. He was an officer in the war of 1812, serving as a major in the 9th Cavalry District and took active part in the defence of Queenstown against the attack of the British. He was also first president of the Eastern Shore Railroad and one of the Commissioners to negotiate an internal loan for the state of Maryland, visiting England for that purpose in 1838.

Among other Emorys who served as officers in the war of 1812 were John M. G. Emory, Captain Smith's Co., 4th Maryland Regt., and John Emory, Captain in the 38th Regt. (British Invasion of Maryland 1812-15 by Wm. M. Marine 1913).

General Thomas Emory and Anna Maria Hemsley had the following children:

Ann, born March 24, 1806, married Dr. Wm. H. Thomas of Easton.

Sarah Hemsley, born Jan. 17, 1808, married Wm. Cooke Tilghman.

Thomas Alexander, born March 9, 1809, married the daughter of General Winder.

William Hemsley, born Sept. 9, 1811, married Matilda W.
    Bache.
Henrietta Earle, born Jan. 30, 1814, married Rev. David
    Kerr of " Foxley Hall " (which was originally the colonial
    estate of Charles Emory, now owned by Col. Oswald Tilgh-
    man).
Robert Junior, born 1815, died unmarried.
John Register, 2nd, born 1818, married Alice Gray Bourke-
    Burke.
Albert Troup, born August 9, 1821, married Sarah Winder.
Frederick, born Sept. 9, 1829.
Blanchard, born Nov. 22, 1831, married Mary Bourke, sister
    of Alice.
Augusta Forman, born October 3, 1824.

General Wm. Hemsley Emory, a graduate of West Point, was
commissioned a second Lieut. in the U. S. Army 1831, and later
promoted to Major General in 1865. He had extensive active
service in the Mexican and Civil Wars and was decorated for
gallantry in the battles of San Pasqual 1846, and San Gabriel
1747. His wife, Matilda Bache, was a great granddaughter of
Benjamin Franklin and granddaughter of Alexander Dallas,
Secretary of War and also of the Treasury 1814-1818. General
Emory died Dec. 1, 1887, leaving the following children: Campbell Dallas, Thomas, George and William Hemsley 2nd, and
daughters Sarah and Victoria. Campbell Dallas graduated from
West Point in 1856 and as Lieut. Col. of the U. S. was decorated in front of Petersburg, Virginia. His wife was Clara
Tilton, daughter of Col. Tilton. He died March 11, 1878.
William Hemsley 2nd was born Dec. 17, 1846. He graduated
from the Naval Academy in 1866 and on Nov. 5, 1906, he was
promoted to Rear Admiral, U. S. Navy. Admiral Emory had a
distinguished career and was in command of the cutter " Bear "
during the famous Greely Relief Expedition in Alaska and for
several years was Naval Attache at the American Embassy in
London. Admiral Emory married Blanche Willis. He died

July 14, 1917, and left his widow and a son, Wm. Hemsley 3rd, and daughters Matilda Hemsley and Blanche Willis.

Thomas Alexander, who married Miss Winder, died leaving a son, Levin Winder Emory, a daughter Marianna, who married Judge John M. Robinson, Chief Justice of the Md. Court of Appeals. Judge Robinson died leaving a son Ralph Robinson of Baltimore and daughters Alice and Marianna, the latter married Admiral Fullam, U. S. N. Levin Winder Emory died some years ago and lies buried at " Waverly."

John Register 2nd, inherited " Poplar Grove " from his father, General Thomas Emory. He married Alice Grey Bourke, a daughter of Edward Grey Bourke and Mary Bordely Cox. Edward Grey Bourke, born 1804, was a son of Wm. Young Bourke and Eliza Grey, of Delaware. Her brother Andrew married Miss Rogers, daughter of the famous Commander Rogers of the U. S. Navy. Col. John Register Emory 2nd, of " Poplar Grove," was commissioned a 2nd Lieut., 6th Inf., U. S. Army, and saw active service during the Seminole War in Florida (Historical Register, U. S. Army, 1903). He resigned from the service several years prior to the Civil War in order to take over the active management of the large estate left to him by his father. He was one of the largest land and slave owners of his time in Maryland, he died March 29, 1880, and lies buried in the family graveyard at " Poplar Grove." He left the following children: Edward Bourke, who inherited " Poplar Grove." He married Henrietta Tilghman, daughter of Lloyd Tilghman and died leaving his widow and sons, Lloyd Tilghman and Edward Bourke and a daughter Henrietta.

John Register Emory 3rd, born in 1850, married Anna Gibson, daughter of Woolman Gibson, of " Woodlawn," and a sister of the late U. S. Senator Charles H. Gibson, Col. W. H. Gibson and Capt. S. H. Gibson, U. S. Marine Corps. Among the ancestors of Woolman Gibson were Jonathan and Woolman Gibson of John, officers of the 4th Eastern Shore Bn., of the Continental Army. John Register Emory 3rd died January 1925 and with his wife Anna lies buried in the cemetery at

Centreville. Their children are Major John Register Emory 4th, U. S. Army (resigned 1921), born June 16, 1883, and Major Woolman Gibson Emory, U. S. Marine Corps, born July 19, 1885.

Anna Hemsley, married Senator Wm. Turpin of "Locust Hill," Queen Anne's County, Maryland. She died in 1885 leaving the following children: Commander Walter S. Turpin, U. S. Navy, who died in 1915, John Register Emory Turpin, William Turpin, Alice Turpin, Anna Turpin and Isabel Turpin.

Alice Grey married Harry Wilmer, who died leaving his widow and sons, Dr. Harry Bond Wilmer, Peregrin, Van Bibber and a daughter Phoebe.

Blanchard, born Nov. 22, 1831, married Mary Bourke. He died leaving the following sons: Frederick, who was for many years director of the Consular Service of the State Department in Washington, Edmund, Blanchard Jr., of "Bloomfield," Tilghman, and daughters Isabelle and Mary.

Blanchard Emory, Jr., married Mary Kerr, daughter of the Rev. David Kerr of "Foxley Hall," they left the following children: Edward B. of Blanchard, Allan and Blanchard 3rd.

Frederick, mentioned above, was the Emory genealogist and the author of the early history of the Emory family, he married and died leaving no children.

Isabelle and Mary married brothers, George and Tilghman Davidson.

FAMILY OF WILLIAM FARIS (1728-1804)

THE ANNAPOLIS SILVERSMITH [1]

By LOCKWOOD BARR

Having been reared in Philadelphia where he served an apprenticeship as a watch and clockmaker and silversmith, William Faris sometime before 1757 settled in Annapolis and worked at his trade until his death August 5, 1804.

William Faris on March 29, 1761, married Priscilla Woodward, the daughter of Abraham Woodward and Priscilla Ruley, of Anne Arundel County. Their children, all born in Annapolis, were:

1. A son unnamed	b. Jan. 3, 1762	d. ———————		infant
2. William	b. Dec. 5, 1762	d. ———————	m. Kesiah Hoskins
3. Charles	b. Sep. 29, 1764	d. Sep. 1, 1800	bachelor
4. Rebecca (I)	b. Nov. 29, 1765	d. Oct. 14, 1768	infant
5. Hyram	b. Jan. 18, 1769	d. Aug. 30, 1800	bachelor
6. St. John	b. Dec. 27, 1770	d. July 27, 1796	bachelor
7. Ann	b. May 9, 1773	d. Mch. 17, 1860	m. Capt. Wm. Pitt
8. Abigail	b. Mch. 10, 1775	d. ———————	m. Capt. Arch. Kerr
9. Rebecca (II)	b. Dec. 11, 1778	d. Aug. 19, 1800	not married

William Faris died intestate in 1804. His mantle was inherited by his principal apprentice, William McParlin,[2] who took over the business and conducted it until his death in 1850. McParlin purchased the Faris home at 25-27 West Street. This property Faris had taken over from the estate of Philip Syng, the Annapolis silversmith who resided there until his death in 1738.

William McParlin married Cassandra Hillary Beall Woodward, a niece of Mrs. Faris who made her home with the McParlins until her death on March 14, 1817, aged seventy-eight years.

The relations of William Faris to his offspring, his critical attitude towards his sons with whom he constantly quarreled, his adoration of his daughters, particularly Ann, and the reaction of these children to their parent, shed light upon this strange and fascinating man from an angle not to be gained from other sources. We know what his children did and a little of what they

---

[1] See *Maryland Historical Magazine*, Vol. XXXVI, No. 4 (Dec. 1941), pp. 420-439, for a brief biography of William Faris by Lockwood Barr, whose wife, Berenice Owens, is a descendant through Ann Faris and Capt. William Pitt.

[2] A brief biography of William McParlin appears in *Maryland Silversmiths* by J. Hall Pleasants and Howard Sill (Baltimore, 1930), pp. 60-61.

said: That is in his Diary.[3] He carefully recorded their faults and virtues.

William Faris, Jr. (2), was born in Annapolis on December 5, 1762. The date and place of his death have not been found. Like his brothers, he served his apprenticeship at clockmaking under his father; and like his brothers, he quarreled with his father and left home.

There is no positive evidence that he was in the Army during the Revolution, but he was old enough to have served a short period at the close of the War. The first definite reference to him was in 1790 when he was twenty-eight years old. He was then in Norfolk, Virginia. That reference is in the poem, " The Will of William Faris," by Charlotte Hesselius.

> . . . My Buckels and Cane to my son William I give
> And no more, because he's got substance to live,
> His road I took care in his youth to instruct him
> Tho' I say it myself, a princess might trust him.
> The dog grew ungrateful, set up for himself,
> And at Norfolk, they say, he has plenty of pelf.
> Since he's gone away it will be best for his brothers. . . . [4]

The records at Norfolk do not make any reference to William Jr. nor to his activities in that place, but presumably he was following his trade. The following entries in the Diary of William Faris tell their own story of his wanderings.

1793. Jan. 7. This evening a Capt. Sinnett come heare and told me he saw my son William in the Havannahs and that he was well and was doing very well, that he had altered a grate deal for the better about 2 mos. ago.

1793. May 1. Received a letter from my son William dated Havannah, March 24th.

1797. Jan. 8. In the Evening I saw Capt. Farling at Mr. Randals who told me he saw my son William at Jackomel in the Island of [illegible. There is a seaport named Jackmel in Haiti].

1800. Nov. 3. Received a letter from my son Wm. in Edenton, North Carolinya, Directed to Mr. Wm. Pitt.

1801. Feb. 11. this Afternoon a young man by the name of Nathl.

[3] " Extracts from Diary of William Faris," appeared in the *Maryland Historical Magazine*, Vol. XXVIII, No. 3 (Sept. 1933), pp. 197-244. The original Diary is in possession of Sumner A. Parker of Baltimore, a direct descendant.
[4] Printed in Pleasants and Sill, *Maryland Silversmiths, 1715-1830* (Baltimore, 1930).

Smith called heare to let me know that he was just from Edenton, North Carolina, that he was Acquainted with my son William, thay Boarded in the same house together, and he tells me that my son has been in Edenton upwards of two years past & that he has 40 or 50 Watches in his Window.

After 1801, Faris lost contact with his son William, as there are no further references to him in the Diary.

In the October, 1799, term of court at Edenton, William Faris witnessed a will that was probated. On December 11, 1803, there was recorded in the Court House there the marriage bond of a William Faris and Kesiah (Hoskins) O'Neill, a widow. In 1786 Kesiah Hoskins had married Peter O'Neill, whose will was probated in Chowan County, North Carolina, May 19, 1803. It mentions his wife Kesiah, his daughters Katherine and Elender, and sons Charles and Tully. No record of these children has been discovered. The date of birth of Kesiah cannot be found. Search has failed to discover even the date and place of her death. At the time of his marriage William, Jr., was forty-one years old. No reference to children by this marriage of Kesiah and William has been discovered. No silver made by William Faris Jr. has been found and no clocks have been attributed to him. Apparently he was primarily a watchmaker and jeweler.

Charles Faris (3) was born September 29, 1764. He died a bachelor on September 1, 1800, aged thirty-six years. Charles served his apprenticeship in his father's shop.

He became one of the leading silversmiths of Maryland during his brief career and his silver is the work of a master craftsman and artist. In the Metropolitan Museum of Art in New York there is an exquisite silver service by him, consisting of a tall graceful coffee pot, a creamer and a sugar bowl. His touchmark was C^s Faris. In the *Maryland Gazette,* May 26, 1796, appeared this advertisement:

Charles Faris
Clock and Watchmaker
Annapolis

Has received an assortment of gold and silver warranted watches, gold, gilt and steel watch chaines, and Seals, plated Castors, Candlesticks and Salts, with many other articles in his line, which he will sell Low for Cash.

Charles Faris and his father were quarreling continually, and n the Diary there are many references to their disagreements. Evidently he worked in his father's shop until 1793 when there s an entry in the Diary to the effect that Charles had opened his own shop. He continued to live in the family home, however, until 1797 when he departed because of a squabble.

1797. June 4. Sunday. since last Wednesday Charles has left off Breakfasting here—he comes to Dinner & when he comes mumbles out something like, how do you do papa, in a manner that appears to me that he would Rather not speak at all, today at Diner Charles took it into his Head to get up in a pet without Eating his Diner, when he came in he never spoke a word to me—nor I to him—

1797. Sep. 10. Charles Faris came heare this morning & asked me how I did, I Reply'd to him and asked him if he spoke to his Brother and had made up with him, he said he was willing to make up with Hyram if so he would speak to him, I said not till then, he said no, I told him he ought and that I expected that he would, for to my certain knowledge he was very much in the Rong and that he had Use Hyram very Ill and that if he did not speake to him, that I would never speake to him more. Hah! says he, I am not the first son you have turned out of Doors and that I had never done anything for him—and it appears to me from his present and former Conduct to me for 12 months Past that he has been Wanting to Quarrel with me. He took up his hat and went off.

1797. Sep. 24. I told Mrs. Faris to tell *her son* Charles that if he did not comply with my Request that he should not have the Washing done here any longer.

In 1800 fever swept Annapolis and Baltimore and by summer it was an epidemic. William Faris nearly died himself and lost three of his children—Rebececa on Aug. 19th, Hyram on Aug. 30th and Charles on Sept. 1st. These entries from the Diary tell part of that tragedy.

1800. Aug. 24. I am very Unwell—am afraid Charles is going to be sick.

1800. Aug. 28. Charles is very weak and low this afternoon he got up and walked 3 or 4 steps to a chair and fainted.

1800. Aug. 31. Poor Charles is much worse to Day, so much so that the Doctrs has no hopes of his Recovery but while thare is life thare is hopes.

1800. Sept. 1. About 2 o'clock this morning my son Charles Faris died of Yellow Fever in 36 year of his age.

Hyram Faris (5) was born January 18, 1769. He died a bachelor on August 30, 1800, aged thirty-one. Like his brothers, he grew up in his father's shop and became a skilled workman.

In the *Maryland Gazette*, issue of September 12, 1793, there appeared the announcement of Hyram Faris who styled himself watch- and clock-maker, Church Street, Annapolis, informing the public that he had opened a shop next door below Mr. Nicholas Brewer and directly opposite the General Court Office, where he carried on the above business in all its branches and likewise carried on silversmith and jewelry business. No silver bearing his mark, however, has been found.

In the book of shop designs of William Faris, now in the possession of the Maryland Historical Society, there is a beautiful design for a painted tall clock face on which is inscribed "Hyram Faris." These shop designs are reproduced in *Maryland Silversmiths*. Hyram was quite a painter, and there is a miniature on ivory of Capt. St. John Faris, the sea captain, which is attributed to Hyram.

In her poem, "The Will of William Faris," Charlotte Hesselius has this to say about Hyram:

> . . . all the tools in my shop to said Hyam I give
> And, if he minds work, he'll make out to live.
> My coat, which I turned, is a very good brown
> And may serve many years to parade in the town.
> 'Twill be good as ever if he takes my advice,
> And the buttons of silver will make it look nice,
> The place in the back which is greased by my club
> Would come out if he'd take good care to rub
> It with soap and with brush or good spirits of wine
> Which will freshen the cloth and make it look fine.
> The coat he must wear with my corduroy breeches
> When Abbey has given them a few odd little stitches.
> And Ab' will be kind, I know, to her brother,
> Because he's the favorite of me and his mother.
> A pair of silk hose I had when a boy
> Intend shall be his: 'twill give him much joy.
> To own these said hose he has begged for so often
> But they ne'er shall be his till I'm safe in my coffin.

Most of what is known of Hyram is disclosed in the entries in the Diary, some of which are quoted:

1793. Dec. 21. Hyram sett off *to walk to Baltimore* this morning at 10 oclock to see his Brother St. John and to Endeavour to Stop him from going the Voyage to Amsterdam on acc't of the Algereans.

1793. Dec. 24. Hyram expects to sail to Morrocco and intends wrighting to me from the Capes. He laughs about the Algereens. [Where he went or what he did on this voyage is not recorded.]

1794. Sep. 16. Lieutenant Davidson brought Hyram's substitute [in the militia] and I paid him 35 Dollar.

1795. Nov. 23. this afternoon Hyram show'd me a letter wrought by Governor Stone Recommending him to the President—requesting he would appoint Hyram an office in the Mareen Service.

1795. Nov. 29. Hyram apply'd to Mr. George Dent & he has given him a Letter of Recommendation to the Secretary of War for a Lieutenants Commission in the Mareen Service.

1799. Mch. 20. After Braekfast Hyram went down to Charles' Shop.

1799. Apr. 2. this afternoon Hyram's moved his Chest away from my House to where I don't know.

1799. Apr. 4. this morning Hyram came heare to bid the family fare Well, he's going to Baltimore. He bid his mother & sisters farewell, he came to me, I asked him if he was going to leave he answered yes, I then told him he might go where he pleased, I had nothing to say to him, he went off.

1799. Apr. 5. I am informed that Hyram went off for Baltimore, in some Boat to Day, he has not been near since yesterday morning.

1800. May 11. Hyram came Home from Baltimore in the Packett.

1800. June 6. Between 8 & 9 oclock my Ungrateful Son Hyram left me to go to Baltimore and I never Expect to see him More.

1800. Aug. 28. Nancy Received a letter from her Brother Hyram dated the 26th, he says that he shall go on Board in 4 or 5 Hours the Ship Commerce—Capt. Tompson[?] to Amsterdam. [Apparently he did not go on that journey—note the next entry.]

1800. Aug. 30. Hyram died of yellow fever.

St. John Faris (6) was born on December 27, 1773. He took to the sea as a lad, and at the early age of twenty-one was an officer on sailing vessels in the trans-Atlantic trade out of Baltimore. He died a tragic death at sea on July 27, 1796, aged twenty-three years, on his vessel the *Hebe* of Baltimore, of which he was captain. Yellow fever broke out on his boat and most of the crew and passengers were ill and many died. Capt Faris was a bachelor.

Capt. Faris was the favorite son of the " Old Man " who was always bursting with pride at the accomplishments of his seafaring son. His arrivals and departures were faithfully chronicled in the Diary.

1793. May 5. A letter from my son Saint. He is well. He left Liverpool the 7th March and arrived at Baltimore the 2nd of May (nearly two months). He sent his Mother Yarn and Mrs. Stevens's Silk he carried to be Died.

1793. Dec. 3. Tuesday morning got up Earley & went down to the point to see my son St. Braekfast'd with him where he boards and after braekfast went to see Capt. Francis DeCross in a large 3 Decked ship called the Gift of God of Bordux—but last from St. Domino.

1794. July 22. This morning about 8 o'clock Saint sett off for Baltimore in the Stage in Company with Mr. Angel the printer—to take the Snow Commerce as Captain. [James Angell was one of the proprietors of the *Maryland Journal* of Baltimore.]

1794. Oct. 22. Capt. St. John Faris sett off—to go to St .Michels on the Eastern Shore to take Charge of his new ship.

1794. Nov. 8. in the evening I receiv'd a letter from my son Capt. Faris, his ship is called the Hebe.

1795. Jan. 1. Capt. St. John Faris came home from Baltimore his ship at anker in the Bay. Bound to Croney in Spain, then to St. Jubes, from there to Lisbon, then to Petersburgh in Russia.

1795. Nov. 20. A letter from Capt. Faris, he arrived in Baltimore yesterday, had a passage of 60 Days from Hamburg to Fell's Point.

1796. Jan. 21. about 10 o'clock Capt. St. John Faris went on board in Capt. Thomas's Boat and by 11 o'clock was under way bound to Amsterdam.

And here William Faris records in his Diary real tragedy.

1796. Aug. 19. Arrived at New York the Ship Atalanta Capt. Holbrook's Log Book, Aug. 5th, saw a ship haveing a Signal of Disress, we hoisted out our yawl and Went on Bord, she proved to be the Hebe of Baltimore, which sailed from Amsterdam May 7th under the Command of St. John Faris with 23 passengers bound to Baltimore. When they had been a few weeks at sea a number of them were attacked with a contageous Destemper of which Capt. Died in a few days. at the time we boarded her there was 7 dead, the first and second mate and many of the passengers confined to their berths and only 3 hands left capable of working the Vessel. They had lost by sickness upwards of 100 persons.

1796. Wednesday Aug. 24. in the Tuesday paper I see a further acct. of my Poor Son [St. John], it's from the Same Vessel, Capt. Rich'd Holbrook who says Capt. Faris was taken sick the 20th of July and Died on the 27th.

Ann Faris (7) was born on May 9, 1773, in Annapolis. She died on March 17, 1860, aged 67 years, in Baltimore. Ann married Capt. William Pitt, a prosperous and successful ship-owner and operator of a line of pilot vessels. Capt. Pitt was born on January 14, 1768, and ided on December 29, 1848, aged 80 years.

le was the son of Capt. John Pitt of Baltimore, also ship-owner
nd sea captain.

Here are two entries from the Diary about "Nancy," as her
ather called her:

796. June 19. this morning Mr. Pitt Brackfasted with us and after
Brackfast he asked mine and Mrs. Faris's consent for our Daughter Nancy,
either of us had any objection to him therefore I suppose it will not be
ong before they are married.

796. Thursday July 7. this Evening Wm. Pitt was married to my
Daughter Nancy by Parson Higgenbottom. Present Mrs. Thomas, Mrs.
Stevens, Mrs. Golder & Miss Ackmead, Mr. Whitcroft, Mr. McMyers &
Capt. Gardner.

Capt. William Pitt was a widower, having first married Hannah Williams on January 29, 1795. She died a bride and was
buried September 27, 1795. To Capt. Pitt and Ann Faris were
born nine or more children, as follows:

1.	Priscilla Ann	b. Mar. 13, 1797	d. July 17, 1798
2.	Rebecca Maria	b. June 7, 1798	d. Jan. 1, 1834
3.	Hannah Williams	b. Jan. 16, 1800	d. July 23, 1837
4.	William Faris	b. Dec. 11, 1801	d. Oct. 18, 1821
5.	John Charles	b. Aug. 2, 1803	d. June 16, 1876
6.	Joseph Henry	b. July 12, 1805	d. Sept. 3, 1822
7.	Charles Faris	b. Feb. 7, 1808	d. Apr. 8, 1887
8.	Priscilla Eliza	b. Dec. 8, 1809	
9.	Eliza	b. July 4, 1812	d. July 13, 1802

A portrait of Rebecca Maria Pitt, credited to Eichholtz, is owned
by Mrs. Charles T. Maxwell, Sioux City, Iowa, a descendant; and a
companion portrait of John George Chappell, her husband, is
owned by Miss Sallie L. Chappell, a descendant, of Washington,
D. C. A portrait of Mrs. Ann Faris Pitt with her infant daughter,
Hannah Williams, is owned by Miss Marion McP. Abrahams, of
Baltimore, a descendant through Hannah Williams Pitt.

Charlotte Hesselius gives us this thumb-nail sketch of Ann:

> . . . To Nancy, the darling of me and my wife,
> I give and bequeath the spinnet for life
> Once I thought she would play with the help of a master
> But, it grieves me to say, she learned not a bit faster,
> Harry Woodcock I trusted to teach her to play,
> But I soon found 'twas money and time thrown away;
> So she did what was right, made me save all my pelf,
> And picked out a tune here and there by herself.

Through Ann Faris and Capt. William Pitt there have bee[n] many descendants. A record has been compiled of several of th[e] families which stem from Ann, and their offspring down to th[e] present generation. A copy of this record has been filed with th[e] Maryland Historical Society.

Rebecca Maria Pitt on July 17, 1817, married John Georg[e] Chappell of Baltimore. They had a number of children, amon[g] them being William Pitt Chappell, the grandfather of Berenic[e] Owens, of Pelham Manor, New York, wife of the author.

Priscilla Eliza Pitt, upon the death of her sister, Rebecca Maria[,] married her brother-in-law, Chappell, and they had a number o[f] children.

Hannah Williams Pitt on February 17, 1820, married Frederic[k] Littig, who subsequently added Shaffer to his name. They ha[d] eight or more children. Upon her death in 1837, Frederick Litti[g] Shaffer married Catherine Ann Smythe, daughter of Capt. James Smythe, of St. Mary's, Georgia, and they had eight or more children. Capt. Smythe was the great-great-grandfather of Berenice Owens.

Of William Faris Pitt, John Charles Pitt and Joseph Henry Pitt there is no record of descendants. Charles Faris Pitt married Catherine Chappell, sister of John George Chappell. Their descendants include Miss Sophie Pitt and the late Faris C. Pitt, of Baltimore.

Abigail Faris (8) was born on March 10, 1775, in Annapolis. The date of her death has not been found, but it was before 1836 since she is not mentioned in the will of her husband written in that year. On January 21, 1802, at the age of twenty-seven years, she married Capt. Archibald Kerr, of Baltimore, a sea captain and ship-owner, who before his marriage had spent much of his time on business in Annapolis where he was a frequenter of the tavern of Faris. The marriage is recorded by William Faris in his Diary as follows:

1802. Jan. 21st. Thursday, in the Evening my Daughter Abigail was married to Capt. Archd Kerr by Mr. Ralph Higgenbotham, present Mr. Stevens & wife, Miss Ranken, Mrs. Brice, Mrs. Randel, Nancy & Polly Harwood, the 2 Miss Owens, Mr. Thos. Harwood & 3 Gentlemen from Baltimore, Capt. Philip Grabell, Mr. Ruben Ettings, Ludwell Taylor.

The Diary records that on November 16, 1803, there was born " a fine Boy & that thay are all well and harty."

304. April 11. Abee & nurse a[nd] littel Allexr. & Charrity went off the Packet to Baltimore. [This child was christened Archibald but lled Alexander in his infancy].

The children of Abigail Faris and Archibald Kerr compiled om his will, the Diary and other sources were:

1. Archibald, Jr.   b. Nov. 16 1803   d. before 1836
2. Charrity (?)   m. William Patterson
3. Georgiana   m. Henry Donnell Hunter
4. Isabella   m. William H. Steuart
5. Washington   b.   d. 1832

The grandchildren were Archibald Kerr, son of Archibald, Jr.; George and Henry, sons of William Patterson. Capt Kerr's will s dated November 21, 1836, and filed May 6, 1839.

The Baltimore City Directories for 1802 and 1803 list Capt. Archibald Kerr, Mariner, on Alisann, now Aliceanna, Street, Fells Point. In 1807 and 1808, he was at 47 Fells Street, where in 1810 he operated a rope store. In later directories he was at various addresses in Fells Point.

FRISBY FAMILY.*

By Francis B. Culver.

1. JAMES[1] FRISBY, the founder of the Maryland family, was in Virginia as early as 1654. He died in Cecil County, Maryland, in 1674. The records of Lower Norfolk County, Virginia, show that on 2 August 1654, "Edward Lloyd of Severne in the Province of Maryland, gent.," conveyed to "James Frisby of Virginia, planter," 600 acres of land on Elizabeth River, originally granted to Jonathan Langworthy, etc. (Lower Norfolk Wills and Deeds, Liber C, folio 189). In 1655/6, Frisby is styled "Merchant," and also "Mr.," in the records. At a

---

* The compiler is indebted to Dr. J. Hall Pleasants, of Baltimore, for the use of the latter's extensive collection of Frisby family data.—F. B. C.

Court held 15 April 1664, upon petition of James Frisby, Merchant, a certificate was granted him for 1150 acres of land, for transporting into the Virginia Colony himself, his wife and four children, and seventeen other individuals, including four negro servants. It is impossible to determine from this Certificate or Warrant, how many years previously these persons were brought into the Colony, or whether they came in one group or at separate intervals of time. It is possible that James Frisby arrived in Virginia by way of one of the British West Indian dependencies.

He removed to the present Cecil County, Maryland, where as early as 1663 he had acquired a tract of land called "Burle's Journey" and, on 22 May 1665, patented 350 acres on Sassafras River in Cecil (then a part of Baltimore County), granted him by the Lord Baltimore for transporting himself, his wife Mary and five children, James, William, Thomas, Mary and Jonas Frisby (Md. Patents, VIII. 130). He was appointed a Commissioner of Kent (Island?) on 4 June 1665 (Md. Arch. III. 529). The will of James Frisby of Sassafras River was dated 22 December 1673 and proved 12 October 1674 (Liber II. 11).

James Frisby and Mary his wife had issue as follows:

2.   I. JAMES[2] FRISBY, born 1651; died in 1704 (*of whom later*).
3. II. WILLIAM[2] FRISBY, born *ante* 1664; died in December, 1713 (*of whom later*).
   III. Thomas[2] Frisby, died 1685, *sine prole*.
   IV. Mary[2] Frisby.
   V. Jonas[2] Frisby, died, *sine prole?*

2. JAMES[2] FRISBY (*James[1]*) was born in England(?) in 1651 and died in Cecil County, Maryland, in 1704. There is on record in Lower Norfolk County, Virginia, a deed dated 5 January 1682, from James Frisby [2nd] of Cecil County, Maryland, to Thomas Hodges of Elizabeth River, said county, conveying 600 acres of land (granted originally to Jonathan Langworthy) which, by various transfers became the property of one John Watkins and of "Edward Lloyd who married ye widow of said Watkins . . . ye land was sold unto my father James Frisby, late deceased, by deed ye 2 August 1654 and afterward, by a ferme deed under ye hand and seale of John Watkins ye son and heir of ye said John Watkins ye land was confirmed unto my said father James Frisby, deceased, bearing date ye 15 September 1658 and recorded in the records of Lower Norfolk County ye 16 September and now descended by right of inheritance unto me ye said James Frisby as heir to my said father James Frisby, deceased." [Signed] James Frisby and Sarah Frisby. On record with this deed and entered 10 November 1683, is a power of attorney from James Frisby (obviously the father), of date 21 September 1674, which reads as follows: " James Frisby of Sassafras River, in Maryland, to my loving friend Captain John Hatton of Lower Norfolk County in Virginia, to convey to Thomas Hodges of Nansemond in Virginia (the aforesaid) 600 acres in Elizabeth River " (Lower Norfolk Deeds, Liber 4, folio 154). Hence, the deed of 1682, executed by James Frisby (2nd) and his wife Sarah, was a confirmatory deed to the land which his father, by power of attorney, had authorised John Hatton to convey in 1674. James Frisby is mentioned in 1692 as a " brother " or a " relative by marriage," of Captain Peregrine Brown, an English shipmaster (Md. Arch., VIII. 331-337; xiii. 318, 319). He was appointed a Commissioner of the Peace for Cecil County, 6 June 1676 (Md. Arch. XV. 77); Commissioner and Justice of Cecil County, 13 December 1680 (*ibid.*, XV. 326); of the " Quorum," 8 October 1681 (*ibid.*, XVII. 43); member of the Maryland Assembly, 1676, 1678, 1681/2; member of the Council, 1691-1703 (*ibid.*, VIII. 283, 284, *et seq.*); styled " Captain," 1683/4.

The will of James Frisby of Cecil County, Maryland, was dated 10 September 1702 and proved 19 June 1704 (Liber III. 268). He devised to his sons Thomas and William certain lands—the dwelling plantation (to Thomas) and land thereunto contained in five patents (to Thomas and William), *viz't.*, " Burle's Journey," " Frisby's Addition," " Frisby's Wild

Chase," " Frisby's Point," " Baltimore Fields "; to son James, " White Marsh," " Hardgrove's Choice," " Frisby's Prime Choice," " Frisby's Farm," " Frisby's Forest," part of " Broad Oak " (300 acres on the south side of Sassafras River); to son Peregrine, personalty (no land); mentions daughter Sarah Robinson and son-in-law Thomas Robinson; sons Peregrine and William to remain in England to be educated, and to be looked after by a Justice in England who shall be selected by Thomas and James Frisby.

James Frisby married, about 1675, Sarah Read (perhaps, a sister of the wife of William Southby of Talbot County [1]) and had issue as follows:

    I. James[3] Frisby, born 18 June 1676; died in infancy.
    II. Mary[3] Frisby, born 14 February 1678/9; died unmarried.
    III. Sarah[3] Frisby, born 28 March 1680; died 1719/31; married (1), on 6 July 1697, Thomas Robinson and (2), on 24 February 1708, Stephen Knight (d. 1745).
4.   IV. THOMAS[3] FRISBY, born 15 February 1681; died *circa* 1715/16 (*of whom later*).
5.   V. JAMES[3] FRISBY, born 3 August 1684; died 18 December 1719 (*of whom later*).
6.   VI. PEREGRINE[3] FRISBY, born 25 July 1688; died in 1738 (*of whom later*).
    VII. Mary[3] Frisby, born 2 July 1690; died *ante* 1704, unmarried.
    VIII. Jacob[3] Frisby, born 19 October 1693; died *ante* 1704?
    IX. Frances[3] Frisby, born 15 May 1696; died *ante* 1704?
    X. Francis[3] Frisby, baptized 7 July 1697.
7.   XI. WILLIAM[3] FRISBY, born 22 August 1699; died in 1724 (*of whom later*).

3. WILLIAM[2] FRISBY (*James[1]*) was born in England(?) before 1664, died in Kent County, Maryland, in December, 1713 and was buried in St. Paul's parish 17 December 1713. He was named second in the list of his father's five children for whose transportation the father received land in Maryland in 1665. He patented in 1687 " Swan Island " (18 acres) in Kent County (Md. Patents, Liber 22, folio 256; Liber I. R.-I. L., No. C, folio

[1] On 22 July 1678, William Southebee gave a power of Attorney to his " trusty friend and brother-in-law, James Frisby " (Cecil County Deeds, Liber I. 108-110).

301). The Kent County Rent Roll for 1707 shows him then possessed of " Hinchingham " (700 acres) and " Swan Island " (18 acres). The later Kent Rent Roll (1720-1725), which may, however, refer to his son William, shows that " William Frisby " then possessed 422 acres of " Great Oak Manor " (1550 acres), resurveyed in 1673 for John Vanheck on the south side of Worton Creek; 700 acres of " Hinchingham " (2200 acres) surveyed in 1669 for Thomas Hynson on the east side of Chesapeake Bay, near Swan Island; " Swan Island " (18 acres) on Tavern Creek, surveyed 4 August 1686 for William Frisby. The following tracts in Cecil County, possessed by " William Frisby " (as shown by the Cecil Rent Roll), may refer to his son William, viz[t]: " Clement Hill," surveyed 3 August 1658 for Clement Michaelson on the north side of Sassafras River; " Frisby's Purchase " (50 acres), surveyed by James Frisby on the north side of Sassafras. It is to be noticed that in William Frisby's will dated in 1713,[2] he names the following tracts: To son William, 400 acres " Frisby's Purchase " and " Bay Neck " (part of " Swan Point ") on the north side of Farley Creek; to son James, " The Island " (100 acres), between Swan and Tavern creeks, " Swan Island " (18 acres), " Frisby's Conveniency " (300 acres); to son Stephen, " Swan Point " (400 acres) and dwelling plantation, " Cornelius' Hills " (150 acres) and " Frisby's Purchase," on the north side of Sassafras River in Cecil County (Md. Calendar of Wills, IV. 6). William Frisby was a Commissioner and Justice of Kent County, Maryland, 1685-'88, 1694-'98 (Md. Arch., XVII. 378; VIII. 23; XX. 131; XXIII. 403); Presiding Justice, 1686-'88, 1697 (Md. Arch., V. 460; VIII. 23; XXIII. 128); Major of Kent County Militia, 1694 (ibid., XX. 131); Member of the Maryland Assembly, 1694-'96, 1704-1710 (ibid., XIX. 30, 417, 556; XXVI. 31, 475, 545; XXVII. 30, 499).

[2] The administration bond was filed in April, 1714 by Ann Frisby, ext'x., with St. Leger Codd and Michael Miller as sureties (Annapolis, Test. Proc., XXII. 327).

William Frisby married (1), *circa* 1684, Mary [née Carpenter ?] who died in May, 1699 and had issue as follows:

8. I. WILLIAM³ FRISBY, born *circa* 1684; died in 1738 (*of whom later*).
    II. James³ Frisby, born 3 September 1685; died in September, 1721. He was born at Sassafras River, " in the house formerly belonging to Mr. Simon Carpenter " (d. 1676).
    III. Richard³ Frisby, died in August, 1703.
    IV. Thomas³ Frisby, died in May, 1711.
    V. Stephen³ Frisby, died in January, 1712.

William Frisby married (2) Rachel —, who died in September, 1703, *sine prole*. He married (3) Ann —, who died *post* 1721, and had issue as follows:

VI. Stephen³ Frisby, born *circa* 1712; died in November, 1714.
VII. Anne³ Frisby, born in 1713/14; died *post* 1775; married 1737/40 Peregrine⁴ Frisby (*Peregrine³, James², James¹*) of Cecil and Kent counties, Maryland.

4. THOMAS³ FRISBY (*James², James¹*) was born 15 February 1681 and died about 1715/16 in Cecil County, Maryland. He married (1), *circa* 1702/3, Frances Wells (died 1713), daughter of George and Blanche (Gouldsmith) Wells of Baltimore County, Maryland. He married (2) Augustina Herman (died 1724/7), daughter of Casparus Augustine Herman of Cecil County [she married (2), in 1719, Roger Larramore (died 1721); and (3), in 1723, Henry Rippin].

Thomas Frisby, by his first wife Frances Wells, had issue as follows:

I. Thomas⁴ Frisby, born 21 January 1703/4; died *ante* 1734, *sine prole*.
II. Mary⁴ Frisby, born 28 September 1705; died *sine prole*.
III. Mary⁴ Frisby, born in March, 1709; married, 14 August 1729, Thomas Henderson of Anne Arundel County, Maryland.
IV. James⁴ Frisby, born in April, 1711; died *ante* 1734, *sine prole*.
9. V. PEREGRINE⁴ FRISBY, born in April, 1711; died *circa* 1747 (*of whom later*).
VI. Sarah⁴ Frisby, born *circa* 1713; died *ante* 1757; married (1), *post* 1735, Thomas Holland (1700-1742) of Calvert County, Maryland; married (2) Robert Freeland (died 1757) of Calvert County.

5. JAMES³ FRISBY (*James², James¹*) was born 3 August 1684 and died 18 December 1719, in Cecil County, Maryland.

He was at first named William, but was baptized " James " on 13 June 1688 (Family Records). He was a member of the Maryland General Assembly, 1715-1719 and was styled " James Frisby of Cecil County, gentleman," in the records. His will was dated 14 November and proved 30 December 1719, leaving his entire estate to his wife Ariana (Liber XVI. 4).

Captain James Frisby married, 9 February 1713/14, Ariana Vanderheyden (1690-1741), daughter of Matthias and Anna Margaretta (Herman) Vanderheyden of Cecil County, Maryland [She married (2), in 1723, Thomas Bordley (died 1726) of Annapolis, Md.; she married (3), in 1728, Edmund Jennings (died 1756) of Annapolis and, later, of Yorkshire, England].

James and Ariana (Vanderheyden) Frisby had issue as follows:

    I. Sarah[4] Frisby, born 7 December 1714; married, 9 September 1730, John Brice (1706-1766) of Annapolis.

    II. Ariana Margaret[4] Frisby, born 8 September 1717; married William Harris (died 1748) of Kent County.

    III. Francina Augustina[4] Frisby, born 16 August 1719; died in 1766; married (1), on 25 September 1735, Dr. William Stevenson (died 1739) of Annapolis; married (2), on 3 May 1742, Daniel Cheston of Kent County, Maryland.

6. PEREGRINE[3] FRISBY (*James*[2], *James*[1]) was born 25 July 1688 and died in 1738. He deposed his age as 42 years in 1731 (Liber I. R., no. 2, folio 607). This deposition is incorrectly attributed to " Benjamin " Frisby in the Md. Hist. Magagine, XXIII. 147. He was a member of the Maryland General Assembly from Cecil County in 1713/14. On 15 December 1718, James and Peregrine Frisby of Cecil County, gentleman, with Ariana and Elizabeth their wives, respectively, conveyed to William Frisby of said county, gentleman, in consideration of a partition due unto the said William Frisby, all the several tracts of land mentioned in five conveyances from Thomas Frisby to James and Peregrine Frisby, bearing date 19 June 1714, viz[t]—the remaining part of " Burle's Journey," the remaining part of " Frisby's Wild Chase," " Frisby's Addition," " Frisby's

Point" and "Baltimore Field," lying on the north side of Sassafras River (Cecil County Deeds, Liber 3, folio 364).

Peregrine Frisby married Elizabeth Sewell (died 1751/2), daughter of Major Nicholas and Susanna (Burgess) Sewell, and had issue as follows:

10. I. PEREGRINE[4] FRISBY, born 15 March 1713/14; died (will 1744/74), *of whom later.*

II. Nicholas[4] Frisby, died in infancy.

III. Susanna[4] Frisby, born 19 June 1718; married, *circa* 1738, Richard Tilghman (1705-1766).

IV. James[4] Frisby, died in infancy.

11. V. JAMES[4] FRISBY, born 30 August 1722; died in 1755 (*of whom later*).

VI. Sarah[4] Frisby, born 3 September 1727; married Philemon Charles Blake (died 1761).

VII. Ann[4] Frisby, born 3 September 1727; died in March, 1793; married (1) John Rousby (1728-1751); married (2), in 1752, William Fitzhugh (1721-1798) of Virginia and Maryland.

VIII. Elizabeth[4] Frisby, born 25 February 1729/30; married James Lloyd (1717-1768).

7. WILLIAM[3] FRISBY (*James[2], James[1]*) was born 22 August 1699 and died in Cecil County in 1724. His will was dated 20 January 1722/3 (See Annapolis, Chancery Proc., I. R. no. 4, folios 222, 226, 229).

William Frisby married, *circa* 1720, Mary Sewell, daughter of Major Nicholas and Susanna (Burgess) Sewell [she married (2), in 1725, Dominic Carroll of Cecil County; married (3), *ante* 1737, John Baldwin (died 1752) of Cecil County]. William and Mary (Sewell) Frisby had issue as follows:

I. Ncholas[4] Frisby, born in 1721; died in 1728.

II. Mary[4] Frisby, born 10 December 1723; died in 1736.

8. WILLIAM[3] FRISBY (*William[2], James[1]*) was born *circa* 1684 and died (intestate) in Kent County, Maryland, in 1738. He received, under the will of his father in 1713, four hundred acres, "Frisby's Purchase" and part of "Swan Point," on the north side of Farley Creek. The hereunder mentioned tracts were to go to his brother Stephen and, in the event of Stephen's death, *sine prole*, were to pass to William aforesaid and James Frisby.

As Stephen (the second of this name) died an infant in 1744, the lands were vested in William and James as follows: " Swan Point " and dwelling plantation (400 acres), " Cornelius' Hills," *alias* " Cornelius Town " (150 acres), and " Frisby's Purchase," on the north side of Sassafras River in Cecil County. James, the brother, also died, in 1721, leaving most of his estate to his brother William. Under his father's will, James received " The Island " (100 acres), " Swan Island " (18 acres), " Frisby's Conveniency " (300 acres), part of " Hinchingham." In 1738, just before his death, the Debt Book shows that William Frisby owned the following lands in Kent: Part of " Hinchingham " (400 acres), " Swan Island " (18 acres), part of " Great Oak Manor " (422 acres) and one lot in Chestertown. William Frisby died (intestate) early in 1738 and, as " Major " William Frisby, his estate was administered upon, 28 April 1738, by his widow Jane, with Augustine Thompson of Queen Anne's County and Thomas Smith (Smythe) of Kent, as sureties in the amount of £4000 (Test. Proc., XXX. 409, 458). The inventory was signed by Ann Frisby and Thomas Smythe as " Kin " (Inv., xxiii. 294). Jane Frisby survived her husband about twenty-four years and did not remarry. She died probably in 1762 and her will names three sons, William, James and Richard, and a daughter Mary Granger. William Frisby held various civil and military offices. He was a Commissioner and Justice of Kent, 1726-1733 and of the quorum in 1732 (Md. Commission Book); Sheriff of Kent in 1715 (Hanson's " Old Kent," page 356).

William Frisby married, *circa* 1710, Jane Thompson (died 1762), daughter of Colonel John and Judith (Herman) Thompson, and had issue as follows:

> I. Richard[4] Frisby, bapt. 5 May 1711; died young.
> II. Mary[4] Frisby, born 1713; died 1768/76; married (1), in 1734, Thomas Smythe (c. 1710-1741); married (2), *ante* 1744, William Granger (died 1752).
> 12. III. WILLIAM[4] FRISBY, born 1715/22; died in 1779 (*of whom later*).
> IV. Anne[4] Frisby, born 1721; died 21 April 1756; married Thomas Marsh.

13. V. JAMES[4] FRISBY, born 1725; died in 1807 (*of whom later*).
14. VI. RICHARD[4] FRISBY, born *circa* 1726/30; died in 1790 (*of whom later*).

9. PEREGRINE[4] FRISBY (*Thomas[3], James[2], James[1]*) was born in April, 1711 and died in Baltimore County, Maryland, *circa* 1747. The estate of Captain Peregrine Frisby of Baltimore County was administered upon, 25 March 1747, by the widow Mary Frisby (Annapolis, Test. Proc. XXXII. 95). The inventories of the estates of Peregrine and Mary Frisby, both deceased, were filed on 24 May 1749 by Mary Henderson, adm'x. (Baltimore Inventories, Liber II. folios 229, 276).

Peregrine Frisby married, 26 January 1738, Mary Holland (1721-1749), daughter of Francis and Susanna (Utie) Holland of Baltimore County, and had issue as follows:

  I. Frances[5] Frisby, born 4 August 1741; and died *ante* 1776; married, *circa*, Greenberry Dorsey (1730-1798).
  II. Sarah[5] Frisby, born 24 July 1744.
15. III. THOMAS PEREGRINE[5] FRISBY, born 15 September 1746; died in 1781 (*of whom later*).

10. PEREGRINE[4] FRISBY (*Peregrine[3], James[2], James[1]*) was born 15 March 1713/14 and died (will 1744/74).

Peregrine Frisby married, 1737/40, Anne Frisby (1713-*post* 1775), daughter of William[2] Frisby (d. 1713) and his third wife Ann (—) Frisby, and had issue as follows:

  I. Anna Maria[5] Frisby, born 2 March 1740; married Samuel Chew (1737-1809).
  II. Peregrine[5] Frisby, born *ante* 1744; died *ante* 1775, *sine prole*.

11. JAMES[4] FRISBY (*Peregrine[3], James[2], James[1]*) was born 30 August 1722 and died in 1775. His will, dated 22 January 1775 and proved 16th February following, in Cecil County, mentions his wife Sarah; his sister Elizabeth Lloyd; his nephews Frisby Lloyd, Charles Blake and Nicholas Lloyd; his aunt Anne Douglas; and Thomas Noxon, son of Benjamin Noxon late of Newcastle County, deceased; Samuel Chew of Kent County, Delaware, and his wife Anne "my niece," *et al.*

James Frisby married Sarah Noxon (died *post* 1780),

daughter of Thomas Noxon (died 1743) of Newcastle County, Delaware, and had issue as follows:

    I. Peregrine Noxon[6] Frisby, born 21 February 1758; died *ante* 1775?

12. WILLIAM[4] FRISBY (*William*[3], *William*[2], *James*[1]) was born 1715/22 and died in Kent County, Maryland, in 1779. He was Captain in the Kent County Militia in 1776 (Md. Arch., XI. 246, 423, 470), and Major in the 13th Battalion of Kent Militia in 1778 (MSS. Md. Muster Rolls).

William Frisby married (1), *circa* 1742/3, Mary Young (1723/6-*post* 1764), daughter of Joseph and Mary (Kelley) Young, and had issue as follows:

    I. William[5] Frisby, born 3 January 1744; died *ante* 1770; married Cordelia ——.
    II. Mary[5] Frisby, born 27 December 1746; died *sine prole.*
    III. Jane[5] Frisby, born 12 December 1748.
    IV. Anne[5] Frisby, born 3 July 1751.
    V. Joseph[5] Frisby, born *circa* 1751; died 1790/1800.
    VI. Martha[5] Frisby, born 19 August 1754; married(?) William Gleaves.
    VII. James[5] Frisby, born in 1755; died *post* 1779.
    VIII. Milcah[5] Frisby, born *circa* 1760; married —— Hollis.

William Frisby married (2), *post* 1764, Elizabeth (—) Gleaves (died *c.* 1799) and had issue as follows:

    IX. Elizabeth[5] Frisby, died *ante* 1779.
16.   X. JAMES[5] FRISBY, died *ante* 1816 (*of whom later*).

13. JAMES[4] FRISBY (*William*[3], *William*[2], *James*[1]) was born in 1725 and died in 1807. On 26 August 1788, he deposed his age as "about 62 years" (Annapolis, Chancery Proc., XVI. 520). As his father died intestate in 1738, he inherited none of the latter's lands, all of which passed to his elder brother William, as heir at law. On 16 July 1747, William and his wife Mary conveyed, "for love and affection," to his brother James "Frisby's Convenience" (200 acres), part of a larger tract called "Hinchingham," purchased in 1698 by their father from William Hambleton (Kent County Deeds, Liber J. S., no. 26, folios 38, 177). On 4 November 1756, James Frisby purchased from Ann, widow of Charles Scott of Kent County, 300 acres of "Stepney Heath Manor" (*ibid.*, J. S., no. 28, folio 242), etc. He owned the following tracts [Kent County Debt Book (1769) and Tax List (1783)]:

Tracts	1769	1783
Part of "Hinchingham" (gift from brother William)	200 acres	150 acres
Part of "Hinchingham" (son John's)	50 "	.... "
"Sewell's Manor" (belonged to James of Cecil Co.)	1000 "	(in Delaware)
Part of "Stepney Heath Manor" (from Ann, widow Scott)	300 "	450 acres
Part of "Stepney Heath Manor" (from James Smith of John)	1 "	.... "
"Holy Land" (from James Smith)	130 "	107 "
"Gresham's College" (held for son John)	366 "	.... "
"New Key" (Land Commission 1757)	200 "	168 "
A lot in Chestertown, Kent County	.... "	.... "
"Fairlee"	.... "	480 "
"Swamp Resurveyed"	.... "	483 "
Total	2247 "	1838 "

James Frisby was a Commissioner and Justice of Kent in 1763, 1768-1774 (Md. Commission Book, MSS.).

James Frisby married (1), in 1746/50, Sarah Gresham (born 14 July 1730), daughter of John Gresham of "Gresham's College," Kent County, and his wife Hannah Hynson, daughter of Colonel Nathaniel Hynson, and had issue as follows:

17.   I. John[5] Frisby, born *ante* 1752; died *ante* 1800 (*of whom later*).

James Frisby married (2), in 1752/60, Rebecca Ringgold (*c.* 1727-*ante* 1767), daughter of Thomas Ringgold of Eastern Neck, Kent County, and his wife Rebecca Wilmer, daughter of Simon and Rebecca (Tilghman) Wilmer, and had issue as follows:

   II. James[5] Frisby, born in 1753/6; died *circa* 1 February 1797, *sine prole*.
  III. William[5] Frisby, born in 1761/2; died *circa* 1790 in Kent County; married, *ante* 1787, Elizabeth Hanson, *sine prole*. [she m. (2) in 1792 Dr. Edward Worrell (1753-1804)].

IV. Rebecca[5] Frisby, born *ante* 1763; died *ante* 1785, under 16 years of age.

V. Anna Maria[5] Frisby, born 1763/4; died *circa* 1814; married, *ante* 1786, John Rowles (d. 1802) of Kent.

James Frisby married (3), *ante* 1769, Margaret Moore (died *ante* 1777) daughter of James Moore of Kent County, and had issue as follows:

VI. Sarah[5] Frisby, born *circa* 1770; died *ante* 1807.

VII. Margaret[5] Frisby, born 1770/5; died 1807/14; married, 1790/6, Dr. Morgan Brown (1769-1841) of Kent.

James Frisby married (4), *circa* 1777, Ann Wilmer (d. 1785?), daughter of William and Rose (Blackiston) Wilmer, and had issue as follows:

18. VIII. RICHARD[5] FRISBY, born 25 October 1777; died 24 March 1845 (*of whom later*).

IX. Mary[5] Frisby, born 3 March 1779; married in 1804 Dr. Joseph Nicholson Gordon (1775-1849).

X. Peregrine[5] Frisby?, born 1779/85; died young.

XI. Rebecca[5] Frisby, born 12 January 1785; died 22 July 1827; married, 20 May 1806, the Rev. Simon Wilmer (1779-1840). She was buried at Swedesboro, N. J.

14. RICHARD[4] FRISBY (*William*[3], *William*[2], *James*[1]) was born *circa* 1726/30; died in January, 1790. He owned a plantation, located upon a part of a large tract of 1000 acres called "Coney Warren," and also smaller tracts at the head of Worton Creek. He was a Commissioner of Kent County 1762-1774 (Md. Commission Book); a Justice in 1774 (Md. Arch. XVI. 273); Vestryman of Chester Parish 1767-1770. His will, dated 12 January 1790 and proved 25th March following, names his wife Martha, his brother James Frisby and brother-in-law Thomas Jarvis James; his son Richard, Jr., to be brought up as a doctor. His widow married John Kennard of Kent County, Maryland.

Richard Frisby married Martha James, daughter of Jarvis and Sarah (Moore) James and had issue as follows:

19. I. RICHARD JAMES[5] FRISBY, born in 1789 (*of whom later*).

15. Thomas Peregrine[5] Frisby (*Peregrine[4]*, *Thomas[3]*, *James[2]*, *James[1]*) was born 15 September 1746 and died in Harford County, Maryland, in 1781. The will of Thomas Peregrine Frisby, of Harford County, dated 23 February and proved 23 April 1781, devised to his son William Holland Frisby " Black Island " and part of " Collett's Points," part of " Frisby's Convenience " and part of " Planters Delight." The said lands lie together on the Bay Shore, being parts of the old Wells tracts. His will further prescribed how the division line between the lands of his son William H. Frisby and those of his son Thomas P. Frisby was to run. He devised to his son Thomas Peregrine Frisby all his lands on the Bay side, except those previously given to his son William H. Frisby, *vizt*—parts of " Coheirs Lot," " Collett's Points " and " Frisby's Convenience." To his son John Frisby he devised the lands he bought of Amos Card " and lives on," being parts of " Middleborough " and " Smith's Folly Resurveyed." These lands lie south of Swan Creek, near Boothby Hill. He appointed his wife Mary Frisby as guardian to his children until they should become of age, with a proviso, if she should die before that time, the testator's relative, Francis Holland, should be their guardian (Wills Liber A. J., no. 2, folio 304). On 29 May 1782, Mary Frisby the widow, with Francis Holland and Greenberry Dorsey, gave bond for the administration of the estate; the inventory was taken in September following. On 14 April 1792, " Mary Loney, late Mary Frisby, came and made oath," etc. (Inv. Liber G. B., no. 1, folio 155).

Thomas Peregrine Frisby married Mary —— (1750-1819), later the wife of William Loney (1752-1807), and had issue as follows:

I. William Holland[6] Frisby, died *circa* 1810/11, *sine prole.*
II. Thomas Peregrine[6] Frisby, died in December, 1813; married, 29 August 1811, Mrs. Susanna (——) Mahan, *sine prole?* [Note: One Thomas Frisby died in Harford County, Md., in 1826 and W. R. Brooke was the administrator].
III. John[6] Frisby, died in 1802.
IV. Harriet[6] Frisby, born in 1774.

16. James[5] Frisby (*William[4]*, *William[3]*, *William[2]*, *James[1]*) died *circa* 1816. His estate was administered upon, 12 March 1816, by John Stoops and Rebecca Frisby.

James Frisby married, *ante* 1800, Rebecca Stoops and had issued as follows:

    I. William[6] Frisby, born *post* 1811.
    II. Elizabeth[6] Frisby, born *circa* 1810; died 14 March 1862; married John B. H. Anderson (1809-1863).
    III. Susan R.[6] Frisby, born 1810/16; married, 28 December 1852, Dr Alexander M. Anderson (1816-1859).

17. John[5] Frisby (*James[4]*, *William[3]*, *William[2]*, *James[1]*) was born *ante* 1752 and died *ante* 1800.

John Frisby married ——— ——— and had issue as follows:

20.   I. William[6] Frisby, born 1775/8; died 1811/16 (*of whom later*).
    II. Sarah[6] Frisby.
    III. John[6] Frisby [Perhaps, the John Frisby of Sussex County, Delaware, who died in 1816, leaving wife Betsy and issue].
    IV. Jane[6] Frisby [Perhaps, the Jane Henrietta Frisby, born 15 January 1795, who married in 1812 the Rev. Lemuel Wilmer (1795-1869)].

18. Richard[5] Frisby (*James[4]*, *William[3]*, *William[2]*, *James[1]*) was born 25 October 1777 at " Violet Farm " (near St. Paul's Church), Kent County, and died 24 March 1845. About 1811, he made his principal residence in Baltimore County. On 30 August 1814, Sir Peter Parker landed a party of men at Mr. Frisby's estate, in Kent County, who burned the buildings and their contents, with a loss of not less than $8,490. At that time Mr. Frisby was actively engaged on the Committee of Vigilance and Safety, in preparation for the defense of Baltimore. He died at his residence, " Oxford," in Baltimore County.

Richard Frisby married (1), 17 June 1806, Sarah Barroll (born 1769), doubtless a daughter of the Rev. William and Ann (Williamson) Barroll, but had no issue.

Richard Frisby married (2), 13 August 1811, at " Oxford " near Baltimore, Elizabeth Brown (1787-1854), daughter of James and Elizabeth (Stansbury) Brown of Baltimore County.

[Mrs. Elizabeth B. Frisby married (2) James Edwards]. Richard and Elizabeth (Brown) Frisby had issue as follows:

    I. Ruth Elizabeth Edwards[6] Frisby, born 31 July 1812; married, 26 August 1834, the Rev. Alfred Holmead, of Washington, D. C.

    II. James Edwards[6] Frisby, born 22 December 1813; died 6 January 1838; married, 12 March 1834, Eleanor Merryman (1813-1838), daughter of Nicholas and Nancy Merryman, and had one daughter Elizabeth Edwards[7] Frisby.

    III. Ann Maria Wilmer Chew[6] Frisby, born 2 November 1815.

    IV. Mary Rebecca Brown[6] Frisby, born 28 August 1817; died 24 November 1819.

    V. Richard William Henry[6] Frisby, born 20 May 1819; died 31 July 1820.

    VI. Mary Rebecca Brown[6] Frisby, born 14 October 1820.

    VII. William Richard[6] Frisby, born 21 June 1823; died 24 December 1823.

    VIII. John Jacob[6] Frisby, born 9 December 1825.

19. RICHARD JAMES[5] FRISBY (*Richard[4]*, *William[3]*, *William[2]*, *James[1]*) was born in 1789.

He married, *circa* 1815, Mary Ann Buchanan (1798-1874), daughter of James and Anne (Groome) Buchanan of Kent County, and had issue as follows:

21.   I. WILLIAM GROOME[6] FRISBY (*of whom later*).
22.   II. RICHARD J.[6] FRISBY (*of whom later*).
    III. Ann Elizabeth[6] Frisby, married, 22 December 1840, Sylvester Sanner of St. Mary's County, Md.
    IV. Mary Ann[6] Frisby.

20. WILLIAM[6] FRISBY (*John[5]*, *James[4]*, *William[3]*, *William[2]*, *James[1]*) was born 1775/8 and died 1811/16. He married twice. His first wife was Frances Wilmer. His second wife was Elizabeth Wilmer (sister of Frances) by whom he had no issue.

William Frisby married (1) Frances Wilmer (died *ante* 1813), daughter of John Lambert and Elizabeth (Carmichael) Wilmer, and had issue as follows:

    I. Richard W.[7] Frisby.

    II. (Margaret) Elizabeth[7] Frisby, born 9 March 1807; died 9 July 1852; married, 29 June 1824, Samuel E. Briscoe.

21. WILLIAM GROOME[6] FRISBY (*Richard James[5]*, *Richard[4]*,

William[3], *William*[2], *James*[1]) married, 8 February 1849, Mary Matilda Fisher, daughter of D[r]. Jacob and Mary Ann (Ringgold) Fisher, and had issue as follows:

    I. Mary[7] Frisby.
    II. William Groome[7] Frisby, died young.
    III. Charles Jacob[7] Frisby, buried 28 December 1874 (Green Mount Cemetery, Baltimore).
    IV. Matilda[7] Frisby.
    V. William Groome[7] Frisby.

22. RICHARD J.[6] FRISBY (*Richard James*[5], *Richard*[4], *William*[3], *William*[2], *James*[1]) married, (lic.) 20 January 1853, Catherine Humphries and had issue as follows:

    I. Richard J.[7] Frisby.
    II. Emily C.[7] Frisby.

The European Ancestors of Barbara Fritchie, born Hauer

CHARLES C. HOWER

THREE PRINCIPAL GROUPS of Hauer immigrants seemed to have come to America in pre-Revolutionary times, one in 1737,[1] another one in 1751,[2] and a third, the group to which Barbara Fritchie, born Hauer, belongs. While working up his own family history (the second of these groups) over the past thirty years the author of this article found the tradition in a number of places that we were related to Barbara Fritchie. This interest in the Hauer group to which Barbara belongs stemmed largely from desire to prove or disprove this supposed relationship. Though it now seems that the tradition is not true, there is nevertheless enough interest in Barbara, both among bearers of the Hauer/Hower name and the general public, to warrant publication of data about her father's family in Europe which has recently come to light.

It is widely known that the Bible of John Nicholas (Johan Nicklaus) Hauer, father of Barbara Fritchie, is on display in the Fritchie house in Frederick, Maryland; also that on the inside of the front cover he wrote the facts about his place and date of birth and the date of his migration to America. The place names in the difficult old German script have been variously read. For one who possesses some knowledge of the German language and German geography the correction of the regional names is easy. "Nassaur", as it sometimes appears, is Nassau; "Farbucken" is Saarbrücken; "Lithingen" is Lothringen, better known to Americans as Lorraine. The village name is more difficult, and its identification is the nub of this

---

[1] Ralph Beaver Strassburger and William John Hinke. *Pennsylvania German Pioneers* (1934: Repr. Baltimore, Genealogical Pub. Co., 1966). Vol. L, pp. 194, 195, 197. Ship, *William*, John Carter, Master, from Rotterdam Oct. 31, 1737. This group of Hauers are said to have come from Baden, but the name of the village is unknown. They may be related to the Hauer immigrants of 1751. *The Descendants of Hans Miehll Hauer, 1720-1970* by Mrs. Jane Hower Auker, of Mifflintown, Pennsylvania is a study of the descendants of the 1737 immigrants.

[2] *Ibid.*, Vol. 1, p. 464. Ship, *Brothers*, Capt. William Muir, from Rotterdam, September 16, 1751. This group of Hauer immigrants came from Blankenloch, near Karlsruhe, Germany. The writer has a good list of this family group from the records in Blankenloch. They are now well located in Lancaster County, Pennsylvania and the present Lebanon County, Pennsylvania. In collaboration with Mrs. Agnes Hower Wells of Huntsville, Ohio, the writer plans to publish this group this year.

468

ticle. Ignoring this problem for the present, the passage, in English translation
th the regional names corrected, reads as follows:[3] "This Bible belongs to me,
icholas Hauer, born in Germany in Dildendorf situated in district Nassau, Saar-
ücken in German Lothringen, born anno Domini 1733 on the 6th of August. Left
y native land the 18th of May, 1754, arrived here and lived in Bentztown, Fred-
ick, Maryland from the 8th of October."[4]

The name of the village has been variously reported as Dildendorf, Dillendorf,
nd Dellendorf. In the course of his search for the village the writer contacted Dr.
ritz Braun of Kaiserslautern, West Germany, and asked his advice in identifying
nd locating the village. Dr. Braun replied[5] that there was no Dildendorf or Dillen-
orf which fitted the rest of the geographical description and reasoned that the
illage in question was actually *Diedendorf: Ich glaube nämlich dass es sich im Falle
es Nickolaus Hauer um Diedendorf bei Finstingen in Lothringen handelt.*[6] Dieden-
orf is on the Saar in Lorraine between Strasbourg and Saarbrücken, or more pre-
isely, between Saar-Union to the north and Fénétrange to the south. Fénétrange is
he French form for Dr. Braun's Finstingen.

There, unfortunately, the matter rested for twenty-seven years. Two or three
ttempts to check it by correspondence failed. In January, 1969, a faculty colleague
f the writer, Prof. B. Pierre Lebeau, a native of France, visited his brother Prof.
ean Lebeau of the University of Strasbourg. As an act of friendship, having made
rrangements in advance by telephone with the local pastor, *Mlle.* Klein, they drove
o Diedendorf on January 10.

They found there the old birth records in a volume entitled *Geschicht der Alten
Reformisten Kirche, 1699-1789.*[7] The existing record book would seem to be a
copy of the original since the records for the whole ninety-year span are in the same
hand. There is evidence, however, of care and accuracy. No marriage or burial
records were found. However, both the Lebeau brothers and the pastor were pressed
for time, and it may be possible that a careful search would reveal more records.
The pastor said that although Hauers live in that area now, they are newcomers
and are not descended from the eighteenth century Hauers. Although it is a matter
for regret that more was not found, even the discovery of the birth records was a
piece of luck: many such records were lost or destroyed in World War II.

On receiving the book, the Lebeaus looked first for the birth record of Nicholas
Hauer and immediately found it; the date of birth, 6 August 1733, agreed exactly
with the one in the Bible at Frederick. Having thus proved that this was indeed the

---

[3] Translation by Mr. Devilo Colgate Brish of Frederick, Maryland.
[4] For information on this Bible and the present condition of the writing therein see Dorothy Mackay
Quynn and William Rogers Quynn, "Barbara Frietschie", *Md. Hist. Mag.* (1942), XXXVII, Appendix
II, "The Barbara Frietschie Bibles", pp. 401-403.
[5] Letter Dr. Fritz Braun to Charles C. Hower, Oct. 19, 1952.
[6] Translated freely: "I believe, that is to say, that in the case of Nicholas Hauer we are dealing with
Diedendorf near Finstingen in Lothringen."
[7] English translation: *History of the Old Reformed Church, 1699-1789.*

right place and right set of records, they proceeded to scan the entire volume a
excerpted thirty-two Hauer births spanning the years 1706-1766. The paren
names are given with each entry, but there seem to be no baptismal records w
names of their sponsors. The mothers' names are listed sometimes with the femin
ending -in, sometimes without. Apparently a mother's name is found sometimes in
French form, sometimes in a German form, e.g. Ourz-Würz. These birth recor
were brought back to America as a single list in chronological order. The writer h
arranged them by families as well as he could. Abbreviations and spellings in t
original have been carefully retained. The list follows:

PETER HAUER and CATHARINA BURGUT
or BURGERIN
1. Jacob Richard Hauer, 1 Jan. 1706
2. Marc. Quirin. Hauer, 9 Feb. 1710

JOH. ADAM HAUER and MARGARETHA MANGEOT
or MANGOT
1. Joh. Jacob Hauer, 7 Aug. 1718
2. Joh. Jacob Hauer, 25 Feb. 1727
3. Anna Catharina Hauer, 27 Feb. 1735
4. Maria Magdalena Hauer, 20 Aug. 1737
5. Anna Margaretha Hauer, 20 Aug. 1737

OTTO HAUER and CATHARINA GUTH or GUTHIN
1. Dorothea Maria Hauer, 13 June 1728
2. Anna Christina Hauer, 20 Nov 1729
3. Joh. Felix Daniel Hauer, 20 July 1731
4. Joh. Nicklaus Hauer, 6 Aug. 1733 (the father of Barbara Fritchie)
5. Anna Catharina Hauer, 16 Sept. 1737
6. Joh. Elias Hauer, 12 Feb. 1741
7. Anna Susanna Hauer, 1 May 1744
8. Johann Christian Hauer, 3 Apr. 1746
9. Daniel Hauer, 24 March 1748
10. Joh. Jacob Hauer, 16 May 1751

JACOB HAUER and MARIA MAGDALENA SCHEURERIN
1. Elias Heinrich Hauer, 21 May 1738
2. Maria Margretha Hauer, 15 Jan. 1741
3. Elias Hauer, 25 July 1744

JOH. ADAM HAUER, JUN. and ELIZABETHA KOCH
or KOCHIN
1. Johannes Hauer, 11 March 1743
2. Stephan Hauer, 1 Jan. 1745
3. Jeremias Hauer, 15 June 1747
4. Joh. Adam Hauer, 6 Sept. 1749

5. Joh. Jacob Hauer, 6 March 1751
6. Paulus Hauer, 27 March 1756

JOH. ADAM HAUER and SUSANNA OURZ
(the same Adam as the above?)

7. Maria Sophia Hauer, 29 June 1760
8. Maria Hauer, 17 July 1762
9. Johann Ludwig Hauer, 6 Apr. 1766

JEREMIAS HAUER and MAGDALENA WURZ or OURZ

1. Joh. Adam Hauer, 19 Dec. 1754
2. Maria Magdalena Hauer, 26 Jan. 1761
3. Maria Sophia Hauer, 20 June 1762

It thus appears that Nicholas Hauer was one of ten children born to Otto and Catharina (Guth) Hauer. An interesting point here is that the Christian name Otto does not seem to be found elsewhere in this or any other known Hauer group, in Germany or America. This seems somewhat remarkable.

Now that we have unquestioned identification of Nicholas Hauer's birthplace and a complete, authentic list of his brothers and sisters, the question arises, "How many members of this family besides Nicholas migrated, and what became of them in America?" Two only, Nicholas and Daniel, are definitely proved to have migrated. It is quite probable that Jacob, the youngest, also did. Although this is somewhat outside the author's field of competence, he will attempt a listing of Nicholas' family and very brief accounts of Daniel's and Jacob's descendants.

It seems strange that a family as well-known and as intrinsically interesting as that of Nicholas Hauer has, apparently, never been well researched and published. Even Nicholas' wife is not well identified, and there seems not to be complete agreement on the list of their children. For the children's names the writer is dependent primarily upon two lists. One was supplied by Miss Eleanor Abbott of Frederick and by Mr. Devilo Colgate Brish, also of Frederick; their versions are identical, probably the same in origin. The other is published by Dorothy Mackay Quynn and William Rogers Quynn in the *Maryland Historical Magazine* and is the product of their own research in original sources.[8] The writer acknowledges deep indebtedness to this article. The Abbott list omits Jacob whose birthdate is known and not open to question. The Quynn list omits John Lewis whose exact birthdate in Frederick is given in the Abbott list. They also omit Maria Elizabeth, the third child, apparently taking her as the Mary who married George Adams. This daughter, according to the Abbott list, married Jacob Steiner. Furthermore, the usage of the times was to employ the middle name rather than the first. This daughter was probably known as Elizabeth, not Mary.

But before listing the children we must consider the problem of the mother's

[8] Quynn, "Barbara Frietschie," Appendix III, p. 404.

Barbara Fritchie. *Maryland Historical Society.*

identity. The only thing certain is that her name was Catherine. The Abbott tradition is that she was Catherine Zeiler, or Zealer. The Quynns believe that the name was more probably Ziegler, and they make a very plausible case.[9] The writer can add this: in the records of the Evangelical Reformed Church at Frederick there appears an entry[10] to the effect that the "Widow Hauer", aged ninety-one, was buried 24 July 1834. Someone has pencilled in "Barbara Fritchie's mother." This would place her birth about 1743. If this identification is correct, she was only about thirteen

---

[9] On this whole problem see Quynn, "Barbara Frietschie." pp. 403–404.
[10] William J. Hinke, trans. "Records of the Evangelical Reformed Church of Frederick, Maryland", 1941, at the Historical Society of the Evangelical and Reformed Church. Lancaster, Pa., p. 338.

rs old when Nicholas Hauer migrated in 1754, and it would thus appear that
ir marriage took place in America. This identification, however, seems question-
le. The Quynns state[11] that they had found no trace of her for many years before
cholas' death and that she was not listed among his heirs. This too may be a small
int in favor of the name Ziegler. The sponsor at Barbara's baptism in Lancaster
is Mrs. Barbara Gamber, or Gampert, and Gambers and Zieglers are found in
ise association in Cumberland Co., Pa., in the early 1800's.[12]
Problems concerning the date and place of Nicholas Hauer's death are also
mplex. Miss Abbott told the writer only that he died in Kentucky while visiting
s daughter Mary, Mrs. William Adams. The Quynns, citing the records of the
eformed Church in Frederick,[13] say that the date was 11 Dec. 1799; family tra-
tion names Madison Co., Ky. as the place. This version also calls Mary Hauer's
isband George Adams instead of William Adams. George Adams has not been
entified with certainty in Madison Co., Ky., and there is no trace of Nicholas
auer there.

We come at last to the children of Nicholas Hauer noting again that available
sts do not agree wholly. The writer has the birth and baptismal dates and the
imes of sponsors for the first four children from the records of First Reformed
hurch, Lancaster, Pa., and will include them. The list:

1. Catherine Hauer; b. 16 Oct. 1760 at Lancaster; bpt. 16 Nov. 1760, sponsors
   Christ and Catherine Leib; she m. Major Peter Mantz, an aide-de-camp to
   Washington.
2. Jacob Hauer; b. 12 March 1762 at Lancaster; bpt. 4 Apr. 1762; sponsor Jacob
   Glatz; Jacob's name does not appear on the Abbott-Brish list, and nothing
   seems to be known about him; perhaps he died young.
3. Maria Elizabeth Hauer; b. 16 Mar. 1765 at Lancaster; bpt. 24 Mar. 1765;
   sponsors Justice (Justus?) Trepert and wife Dorothy; she m. Jacob Steiner.
4. Barbara Hauer; b. 3 Dec. 1766 at Lancaster; bpt. 14 Dec. 1766; sponsor Mrs.
   Barbara Gamber, or Gampert; she m. Casper Fritchie.
5. Daniel Hauer; b. 11 Nov. 1768 at Frederick, Md.; m. Margaret Mantz.
6. John Lewis Hauer; b. 25 Nov. 1770 at Frederick; no further information; his
   name does not appear on the Quynns' list.
7. Margaret Hauer; b. 1771 at Frederick; m. John Stover.
8. Henry Hauer; m. Catherine Keplinger.

---

[11] Quynn, "Barbara Frietschie," p. 404.
[12] William J. Hinke, "Records of Ziegler's Church, Mifflin Twsp., Cumberland Co., Pa., 1797-
840", p. 25, Historical Society of the Evangelical and Reformed Church, Lancaster, Pa. Among the
onfirmands at Zion Church on June 1, 1823, were Peter Gamber, Mary Ann Ziegler and Joseph Hower.
hese Howers would seem to be from the 1751 immigrant group. This Zion Church is probably Zion
utheran Church at Newville, Pa. which later absorbed Ziegler's Church, as stated by the pastor at
lewville in conversation with the author in October 1971.
[13] Quynn, "Barbara Frietschie," p. 404, fn. 9.

9. Mary Hauer; m. William Adams (Abbott) or George Adams (Quynn); went
   Kentucky and her father Nicholas is said to have died while visiting her the
10. George Hauer; b. March, 1775 (Quynn).

In connection with the above list it is interesting to note that three of the fo
Hauer children born at Lancaster were given the Christian name of the sponsor
baptism. This might conceivably indicate relationship, and Nicholas did have
sister Catherine. However, the names Jacob and Catherine are extremely comm
and the point should not be pressed. The name Barbara does not appear at all
the entire Diedendorf list. The writer's co-worker Agnes Hower Wells has recen
made the ingenious suggestion that Mrs. Dorothy Trepert, sponsor at the baptis
of Maria Elizabeth, might have been the eldest child of Otto and Catheri
Dorothea Maria, b. 13 June 1728. Chief objection to this would seem to be the c
tom, noted previously, of using the middle name rather than the first name.

We turn now to Nicholas Hauer's brother Daniel. If information on Nichol
family seemed sparse, this is much more the case with Daniel. At least his identi
is now unquestioned, and we have the exact places and dates of birth and deat
Before the discovery of the Diedendorf list the source for his date and place
birth was the diary of one Jacob Englebrecht. The Quynns refer to it in their article
but there is a much fuller reference to it in an earlier issue of the *Maryland Historic
Magazine*.[15] This item reads as follows: "Jacob Englebrecht says in his diary f
July 6, 1827 that Daniel Hauer told him that he—Hauer was born in Lothring
[sic], Germany, March 24, 1748, left London for America August 24, 1769—Bar
De Kalb being a passenger on the same ship—arrived in Philadelphia Januar
1770. He came to Frederick about the year 1771. He died August 18, 1831." T
exciting thing here is that again, as in the case of Nicholas, the birth date recorde
on this side of the Atlantic agrees perfectly with the one found at Diedendorf.

Supplementing this statement a little is a letter[16] by Daniel J. Hauer of Perr
Maine, a great-great grandson of Daniel Hauer. In this letter he traces his descer
from Daniel and says that Daniel was born "in Dildendorf on the Rhine in Germa
Loraine", was educated at Wittenberg being a schoolmate of Baron De Kalb, lande
at Philadelphia in 1769, joined his brother Nicholas and that both of them moved t
Frederick, Maryland. He explains that Daniel's name does not appear on the shi
lists because he visited London and Southampton en route instead of sailing direct
from Rotterdam. He concludes with the statement that he had a complete record o
the descendants of these two brothers with dates and that they could only be relate

---

[14] Ibid., p. 229.
[15] *Maryland Historical Magazine*, Vol. 10, No. 1, p. 81 under "Notes". Item contributed by Agne
Hower Wells.
[16] Letter, 1914, Daniel J. Hauer to Lloyd C. Hower of Siegfried, Pa., historian of the second Howe
group mentioned in the opening paragraph, in response to a reunion notice. Photostat of this one page
undated, in possession of the writer through the courtesy of Jane Hower Auker, present historian of tha
oup.

other Hauers through ancestors in Lorraine. He also noted that the male lines
m Nicholas and Daniel were nearly extinct. Most unfortunately, Daniel J. Hauer's
ords were later burned and seem lost to posterity.

There are obvious errors here. Daniel's birthplace was Diedendorf, not Dilden-
rf, and was on the Saar, not the Rhine; he cannot have joined Nicholas in Lan-
ster in 1769 since Nicholas went from there to Frederick between 1766 and 1768.
the other hand there is at least one item of great interest here and in the Engle-
echt diary, the linking of Daniel Hauer with Baron De Kalb. This would seem to
impossible, or at least highly improbable, since the Baron was some 27 years
der than Daniel and it would seem that their stations in life were so different that
eir ways would be unlikely to cross. There is no record either, in biographies avail-
le to the writer, of a trip to America by the Baron in 1769 or 1770. He did come
a secret agent of the French government in 1762 and again in 1777 with LaFayette.
Still one hesitates to write off so specific a story completely, and there are certain
her aspects of the history of these Hauer families which have led the writer to
onder if they may have been, in their European origins "a cut above" the Hauers
om Baden. Would a man wholly devoid of learning have named a son Marcus
uirinius, as Peter Hauer of Diedendorf did in 1710? Another interesting complica-
on is the ambivalence of this family with regard to denominational affiliation. The
urches attended by them at Diedendorf, Lancaster, and Frederick were all
eformed. Yet Wittenberg is the citadel of Lutheranism, and the Rev. Daniel J.
Hauer, D.D., a grandson of Daniel Hauer, was a prominent Lutheran clergyman;
urthermore he named his son Luther Melanchthon Hauer, nothing could be more
utheran. It would be most interesting to know just what political and religious up-
eavals brought these Hauers to Diedendorf and what their economic and social
tatus was. Before soaring too far, however, on such flights of fancy we should
erhaps recall that in Frederick, Nicholas was a hatter and Daniel a drygoods
merchant.

There is little information about Daniel Hauer's family. The Quynns remark[17]
that the 1790 census shows him with a large family, and indeed it does: 6 white males
ver 16; 2 free white males under 16; 8 free white females; no slaves. The Quynns
ay too[18] that his wife's name was Catherine and that several apparent leads to
Catherine, wife of Nicholas, turned out to be to Catherine, wife of Daniel. Nothing
else seems to be known about her. Could the "Widow Hauer," buried in 1834, have
been this Catherine instead of Nicholas' wife? Daniel himself died, as has been
noted, 18 August 1831.[19]

Of all these children (though some of the young persons counted in the census
may not have been Daniel's children) the only one known to the writer is George.

---

[17] Quynn, "Barbara Frietschie," p. 403.
[18] ibid, Appendix III, p. 403.
[19] Englebrecht Diary and stone in Mt. Olivet Cemetery, Frederick, Md., the inscription of which
opied by the author in 1947. Also, Jacob Mehrling Holdcraft, *Names in Stone*, Ann Arbor, Mich., 1966,
. 545.

He married Catherine Shellman[20] in Frederick, Maryland, 9 October 18[ ]
Their son was the Rev. Daniel Jacob Hauer already referred to. He was bor[n]
Frederick on 3 March 1806, died 26 November 1901, and is buried at Hanc[ ]
Pennsylvania. He married Henrietta Warner who was born in Baltimore in [ ]
Their son was Luther Melanchthon Hauer born in Loudoun Co., Virginia, 15 [ ]
1831, and he married Anna Norris, a native of Baltimore, born 11 Feb. 1835[ ]
their 8 children we shall list here only the two whose letters have helped so great[ly]
this compilation. Their daughter Henrietta was born in Baltimore on 25 June [ ]
and married Charles William Harvey on 4 Nov. 1880. A number of Harvey desc[end]
ants live in Indianapolis, Indiana. Mrs. Harvey's brother, Daniel J. Hauer, was b[orn]
in Baltimore on 26 May 1871 and married Abbie Clark. In 1913 he was livin[g]
Perry, Maine; was a civil engineer, editor, and author. He had a son Daniel J. Ha[uer]
Jr. and a daughter, Edith May, who were living in 1969.

It seems rather likely that Joh. Jacob Hauer, born on 16 May 1751, also migra[ted]
In 1951 the writer exchanged letters with Mrs. Ella Gerlaugh Howett of Ely[ria]
Ohio. Mrs. Howett was a D.A.R. member by descent from one Jacob Hower w[ho]
according to her statement was born in Germany, migrated to Frederick Cou[nty]
Maryland and served in the Revolution under John Collars. Regarding Jac[ob's]
grave she stated: "We found the grave [Jacob Hower] in cemetery out in countr[y]
Frederick Co., Md."[22] No one now living seems to know the location of the gra[ve]
and it is not listed in Holdcraft's Names in Stone.[23] Dr. John P. Dern has kin[dly]
examined the proof of the 3300-name supplement to Names in Stone now in pro[cess]
of publication and reports that this grave is not listed there either. If it could [be]
found, with names still legible, this Jacob's identity might be either proved or [dis]
proved. This Jacob had a son, John Hower, 1784-1854, who lived near Clear Spri[ng]
Maryland, and migrated in 1833 to Alpha, Greene County, Ohio, where he [is]
buried. His descendant, Mr. Lawrence D. Hower of Fairborn, Ohio, who died ab[out]
a year ago, accumulated a great deal of information on this family.[24] There is rea[lly]
no evidence that this Jacob belongs to the Diedendorf group except the stateme[nt]
that he was born in Germany and migrated to Frederick County, Maryland. A[ ]
in favor of this identification is the apparent absence of other Hauer groups fr[om]
Frederick County in early times. The absence of this Jacob from the 1790 cens[us]
records seems strange.

---

[20] Letter, Henrietta Hauer Harvey of Indianapolis, Ind., sister of Daniel J. Hauer of Perry, M[aine]
dated 16 July 1914.

[21] War of 1812 Bounty Land Records at National Archives, Washington, D. C. B. L. Wt. 83,4[ ]
Catherine states she was a widow living in Frederick on 18 June 1856 and that George, her husband d[ ]
22 Oct. 1848.

[22] Letter, Mrs. Ella Gerlaugh Howett to Charles C. Hower, dated 12 Apr. 1951.

[23] Jacob Mehrling Holdcraft. Names in Stone. p. 545.

[24] For information on this Jacob Hower and his descendants, see Portraits and Biographical Albu[m]
Greene and Clark Counties, Ohio. Chapman Brothers, 1880. pp. 553-554.

Finally, the writer has heard the story from two Hower-descended persons that their ancestor was a Rev. Christian Hower; that he was a Lutheran minister in Revolutionary times; that he was a brother to Barbara Fritchie's father; and that he was the youngest of five brothers, he being born in America, the others in Germany. It is now well demonstrated that the ancestor of these persons was indeed a Rev. Christian Hower. However, he was a Methodist, not a Lutheran, minister and was born at Stumpstown (Fredericksburg), now Lebanon County, Pennsylvania, 6 May 1791.[25] He died at Burbank, Wayne County, Ohio, 21 Nov. 1868. He is almost without doubt a member of the group descended from the 1751 immigrants from Blankenloch.

Although there were five brothers at Diedendorf (the first Daniel probably died) and one was named Christian, nothing else about this story seems to fit. Still it seems risky to dismiss categorically a story that is so specific in its details and a relationship which has been so firmly believed. Thus although the author has had qualms about rejecting belief in this relationship, he has found no evidence whatever to support it, and the negative opinions of Dr. Fritz Braun and Daniel J. Hauer should be rather conclusive.

---

[25] See lengthy obituary in *The Western Christian Advocate*, Jan. 27, 1869, p. 31. This is a Methodist Church publication. Though they print "Stempstown" instead of Stumpstown, there seems to be no doubt that this man was born at Stumpstown (now Fredericksburg). There is good evidence that he was a brother of a Hower woman well known to have been born there. Item courtesy of Agnes Hower Wells.

THOMAS GERARD AND HIS
SONS-IN-LAW

By Edwin W. Beitzell

MARYLAND historians have given scant attention to one of the most important political figures and largest landholders in the province durng the period 1637-1673. He was Dr. Thomas Gerard, Gentleman, born about 1605, at New Hall, Lancashire, England, son of Sir Thomas Gerard. The Gerards were an ancient and distinguished Roman Catholic family of Lancashire. John Gerard, brother of Sir Thomas, was a Jesuit priest and was tortured in the Tower during one of the religious upheavals in England. He later founded a college at Liège. Frances, a daughter of Sir Thomas, became a nun at Gravelines in Flanders. The family history has been traced back to the time of the General Survey of the Kingdom in 1078.[1]

The first of the Gerards to arrive in Maryland were Richard and his sister Anne, the widow Cox. Anne later married Thomas Greene, the second governor of Maryland. They arrived with the first colonists who came on the *Ark* and the *Dove* in 1634. Richard return to England in 1635 and became famous in the service of the King. Thomas Gerard, brother of Richard and Anne, arrived in Maryland in 1637 and was chosen as a burgess from St. Mary's Hundred on February 19, 1638.[2] In England he had married Susannah, the daughter of Abel and Judith Snow. They had five children at the time of moving to Maryland and claimed 2,000 acres of land for transporting them into the Province.[3] Five more children were born to Thomas and Susannah after they were established in the Province.

---

[1] William Playfair, *British Family Antiquity* (London, 1811), VI. Horace Edwin Hayden, *Virginia Genealogies* (Washington, D. C., 1931), p. 490. Edwin W. Beitzell, "The Gerard and Cheseldine Families," MS in possession of the author, copy in Maryland Historical Society.

[2] *Archives of Maryland*, I, 29.

[3] The children were Susannah, Justinian, Frances, Temperance, and Elizabeth. Louis Dow Sisco, "Land Notes, 1634-1655," *Maryland Historical Magazine*, VIII (1913), 262. *Archives of Maryland*, XLIX, Letter of Transmittal, xxvi.

On March 16, 1639, Cecilius, second Lord Baltimore, erected
t. Clement's Hundred and appointed Thomas Gerard as "Con-
ervator of our Peace" within the Hundred.[4] Probably the first
ame conservation law in the Province was contained in this curi-
us document, which provided that severe penalties were to be
ssessed against "all persons whatsoever that Shall unlawfully
respass upon any our game of Deer, Turkies Herons or other wild
owl or Shall destroy them their nests or eggs, either upon our
and or waters. . . ."[4] On November 3, 1639, the St. Clement's
Manor grant was made to Gerard. This grant made him one of
he largest land holders in Maryland, as has been noted by Dr.
J. Hall Pleasants.[5] With subsequent additional grants of land,
he Manor included the whole neck of land extending from the
head of St. Clement's Bay over to the Wicomico River, totaling
some 11,400 acres of land. Also included in the grant were the
Heron Islands of St. Clement's, St. Katherine's and St. Cecilia's,
afterwards called St. Margaret's.[6] The grant provided for the
establishment of a Court Baron and a Court Leet and the records
of St. Clement's Manor are the only ones of this unusual type of
court proceedings known to be in existence in Maryland.[7]

In addition to the practice of medicine in both Maryland and
Virginia, Gerard was active in provincial affairs from the time of
his arrival. His selection as burgess from St. Mary's in 1638 has
been noted. On July 19, 1641, he was chosen burgess from St.
Clement's Hundred.[8] Sometimes between these dates he removed
his residence to Longworth's Point (now known as Colton's and
also Kopel's Point), a high bluff on St. Clement's Manor overlooking St. Clement's Island and commanding a sweeping and
beautiful view of the Potomac River, St. Clement's Bay and the
Virginia shore. Because of his duties at St. Mary's City, he retained a town house, Porke Hall, at the city.[9] It appears likely
that the manor house at Longworth Point was erected about 1644,
for on November 1, 1643, Gerard made an agreement with Cornelius Canedy, a brickmaker, whereby Canedy undertook to make

[4] *Archives of Maryland*, III, 89.
[5] *Ibid.*, LVII, Introduction, xlii.
[6] *Ibid.*, LI, 506.
[7] *Ibid.*, LIII, 627, and Introduction "Maryland Manorial Courts" by J. Hall
Pleasants, lxi-lxv.
[8] *Ibid.*, I, 105.
[9] *Ibid.*, IV, 143; XLI, 265, 533, 544.

brick for Gerard for a period of three years.[10] This house wa
destroyed by Richard Ingle during the Ingle Rebellion.[11] Th
second house was destroyed by the British on June 13, 1781
during the Revolutionary War, and one of Gerard's descendants
Herbert Blackistone, was carried off as a prisoner of war.[12]

An incident that occurred on the morning of March 23, 1641
has been recorded in nearly every Maryland history while hi
many worthwhile contributions to the growth of the infant prov
ince and his achievements in many fields have been forgotten. A
complaint by the Protestants against Gerard was read before the
Assembly

... for taking away the Key of the Chappel and carrying away the Books
out of the Chappel and such proceedings desired against him for it as to
Justice appertaineth [.]

Mr Gerard being charged to make answer the house upon hearing of
the Prosecutors and his defence found that Mr Gerard was Guilty of a
misdemeanor and that he should bring the Books and Key taken away
to the place where he had them and relinquish all title to them or the
house and should pay for a fine 500l [pounds] tobacco towds the maintenance of the first minister as should arrive [.] [13]

It is generally believed that the chapel mentioned is one Gerard
erected on St. Clement's Manor, although the petition of the
Protestants was presented by David Wickliff of St. George's Hundred which might indicate that the chapel in question was located
in St. Mary's City or St. George's Hundred. In any event, Gerard,
despite his prominence in the Province, was dealt with promptly
and severely for his interference with Protestant worship. Although there has been much speculation as to the reasons for
Gerard's closing the Protestant Chapel, no theory has been substantiated. Thomas Gerard was a Roman Catholic, but his wife
and children were Protestants. It is a matter of record that
Gerard erected a chapel on St. Clement's Manor for his family,
friends, and servants. John Walter Thomas has written that this
chapel was located on St. Paul's Creek, a little below the present
All Saints' Protestant Episcopal Church and was the third Protestant church to be erected in Maryland.[14]

---

[10] *Ibid.*, X, 214; XLI, 52.
[11] Bernard C. Steiner, *Maryland During the English Civil Wars, Part II*, Johns
Hopkins University Studies XXV (Baltimore, 1907), 54.
[12] *Archives of Maryland*, XLV, 295.
[13] *Ibid.*, I, 119.
[14] *Chronicles of Colonial Maryland* (Cumberland, 1913), p. 198.

All Saints Church is located on Tomakokin Creek, now commonly called Cobrum Creek, approximately eight miles from Longworth Point, the original home of Gerard on St. Clement's Manor. The writer has been puzzled for some years as to why Gerard should have located the chapel, erected for his family, friends, and servants, eight miles from his manor house, in what was then the forest or backwoods, approximately ¾ of a mile from a boat landing. A review of the early Maryland maps at the Library of Congress answered this question. The Gerard chapel was not located near the present All Saints Church nor on St. Paul's Creek, for the only St. Paul's Creek was due to a mapmaker's error. St. Patrick's Creek is located about one mile from Longworth Point, the Gerard home, and this name is mentioned in the sale of 220 acres of land in 1666 by Gerard to Edward Connery.[15] The earliest Maryland map that shows the creeks in question is dated 1794 and gives the name St. Paul's Creek in error for St. Patrick's Creek.[16] This error was repeated on subsequent maps until 1840.[17] The error was repeated again on maps dated 1841 and 1852 but was finally corrected in 1865.[18] It appears correctly as St. Patrick's Creek on subsequent maps. It is apparent from this that the Gerard chapel was erected at the head of a branch of St. Patrick's Creek, in King and Queen Parish, about a mile from the Gerard home, which was convenient by land or water to the whole community living on this neck of land. On December 16, 1696, the Provincial Council ordered that

" the Vestry of King and Queen parish in St Maries County make inquiry of Capt Gerard Slye [grandson of Thomas Gerard] concerning one hundred acres of land, Said to be given to the Church by Mr Thomas Gerrard Senr. . . .[19]

Slye attempted to deny this gift but was unsuccessful. In 1750 the vestry of King and Queen Parish was authorized to sell the glebe land given by Gerard and to purchase a glebe nearer the center of the parish.[20] The Maryland Assembly, on June 1, 1750,

[15] *Archives of Maryland*, LVII, 283.
[16] Library of Congress, Maps Division, *Map of Maryland, 1794 Issued by U. S. Constitution Sesquicentennial Commission.*
[17] *Ibid., Map of Maryland 1840 by John H. Alexander.*
[18] *Ibid., Map of Maryland 1865 by S. J. Martenet.*
[19] *Archives of Maryland*, XX, 584.
[20] Historical Records Survey, Works Project Administration, *Inventory of Diocese of Washington Archives. The Protestant Episcopal Church* (Baltimore, 1940), I, 232.

in view of a petition that " the Parish Church therein is so situate
that the said Petitioners cannot, without riding a great Distanc
attend the service of God there " authorized the purchase of on
acre of land near *Tomachokin* Run for a *Chapel of Ease*.[21] It
evident from this that the Gerard chapel was not located o
Tomakokin Creek, the present site of All Saints Church, but wa
located away from the center of the parish, namely down nea
the tip of St. Clement's Manor and undoubtedly on St. Patrick'
Creek. Also it would appear that the Gerard chapel was standin
in 1750 and continued to be the Parish Church for some year
Eventually it disappeared and its location was forgotten. Bu
history has a way of repeating itself for in 1895 an Episcopa
Mission House was opened at Colton's (Longworth's) Point.[22] I
1900 the parochial chapel of St. Agnes was erected near Palmer'
on St. Patrick's Creek, undoubtedly near the location of the ol
Gerard Chapel.[23]

Considerable difficulty with the Indians on St. Clement's Mano
was experienced by the colonists, particularly in the stealing o
cattle and corn, which caused Lord Baltimore on October 29
1642, to grant a commission to Gerard to take whatever action
(including " the killing any of them if it shalbe necessary ") tha
might be required to put an end to the trouble.[24]

On November 17, 1643, Lord Baltimore appointed Thomas
Gerard as a member of the Provincial Council for " his diligen
endeavors for the advancem[t] & prosperity " of the colony.[25] Othe
appointments and commissions followed, such as one to look after
his Lordship's property and another to advise concerning Indian
problems and the like.[25] Gerard continued as a member of the
Council until the time of Fendall's Rebellion in 1659 and also
served as a Judge of the Provincial Court during this period.

It is apparent that Gerard, as a member of Lord Baltimore's
government, suffered damage at the hands of Richard Ingle during
Ingle's Rebellion in the year 1644-1646 because after the difficulties he obtained through court action part of Ingle's loot in settlement of his claim. Gerard was then sued by Thomas Cornwaleys

[21] *Archives of Maryland*, XLVI, 476-477.
[22] *St. Mary's Beacon*, Leonardtown, Oct. 4, 1895.
[23] *Inventory of Diocese of Washington Archives, op. cit.*, I, 233.
[24] *Archives of Maryland*, III, 119.
[25] *Ibid.*, III, 138, 140, 145, 150, 159, 163, 293.

who claimed that he had prior right to recover from Ingle.[26] This dispute dragged through the courts for several years.

Thomas Gerard, as is borne out by the *Archives of Maryland* not only was active in the practice of medicine, as a member of the Council, and a judge of the Provincial Court, but he was also an able farmer, a manufacturer of liquors, particularly peach brandy, and a breeder of fine cattle. Apparently he was also an excellent sailor for many of his trips between Longworth Point and St. Mary's City were made by boat, although the type of boat is not mentioned, in the *Archives*. He might also be described as one of the first realtors in Maryland for in the proceedings of the Provincial Court one finds records of the sale or transfer of many parcels of land.[27] Owing to his many activities he was involved probably in more court actions than any other man of his time. Perhaps this is the reason that he provided in his will that

if itt shall hereafter happen att anytime that any ambiguity doubt question or controversie do grow or rise concerning the true meaning and intent of this my will and testament I will therefore that my executor and executrix choose each of them a judicious person and according to their verdict let the doubt and dispute be ended without comenceing a suite att law.[28]

During the Puritan uprising (1654-1656) Gerard was appointed one of Governor Stone's captains. He took part in the battle at Herring Creek where he was captured with the rest of Stone's force. Although quarter had been promised, four of the men were executed by the Puritans and Gerard narrowly escaped with his life.[29] After the difficulties with the Puritans had been resolved, Gerard returned to his duties as a member of the Council under the governorship of Josias Fendall.

One of the men executed by the Puritans was William Eltonhead, a member of the Council and a close associate of Gerard. There are indications that Eltonhead married Jane, the daughter of Thomas Gerard, but conclusive evidence is so far lacking. Mrs. Jane Eltonhead, the wife of William, is a fascinating character and her life, if the whole story could be pieced together, would be a highly colorful one. Jane (nèe Gerard?), as it appears from the record, married first Thomas Smith (Smyth) who was cap-

[26] *Ibid.*, X, 218.
[27] *Ibid.*, XLI, 143, 188; XLIX, 573-582, 586-587; LVII, Introduction xlii, xliii, 220-226, 330-333, and *passim*.
[28] Wills, Vol. I, f. 567, Hall of Records, Annapolis.
[29] David Ridgely, *Annals of Annapolis* (1841), pp. 51-53.

tured by Governor Leonard Calvert after the reduction of Kent Island and hanged as a pirate for his part in leading the attack on the fleet of Captain Thomas Cornwaleys.[30] She was left a widow with two daughters, Gertrude and Jane.[31] Soon afterwards she married Captain Philip Taylor, who was an associate of her former husband and indicted with him, but who was lucky enough to avoid hanging. Apparently he died a natural death prior to 1649 and left two children, Sarah and Thomas.[32] Sometime after this, Jane married William Eltonhead of his Lordship's Council and became sister-in-law of Cuthbert Fenwick, who had valiantly fought her two previous husbands as Lieutenant of Captain Cornwaleys in the good pinace called the St. Margarett ". . . in the harbour of great wighcocomico in the Bay of Chesapeack on the tenth day of may in the yeare of our Lord one thousand six hundred thirty and five."[33] As we know, Jane soon lost her third husband, on March 28, 1655, after the battle at Herring Creek. There seems to have been no issue from this marriage as Jane testified that William Eltonhead

left all his Lands, with all his other goods & Chattles to her disposing, for the good of her, & her Children, & desired her to allow unto Robert ffenwick and Richard ffenwick [nephews] some part of the Lands, according to her discretion. . . .[34]

It is interesting to note that Culthbert Fenwick's will[35] was witnessed by Elizabeth Gerard, a daughter of Thomas Gerard and that both the Gerard and Eltonhead families were from Lancashire. It is difficult to piece together these ancient records, particularly so in the case of Jane Eltonhead who is often confused with her sister-in-law, Jane Eltonhead Fenwick.

On October 5, 1658, Thomas Gerard was the central figure in another religious controversy for on that date the Attorney General of the Province preferred charges against Father Francis Fitzherbert, S. J., that

. . . he hath Rebelliously and mutinously sayd tht if Thomas Gerard Esqr

---

[30] *Archives of Maryland*, I, 16-19, 466; IV, 23, 527; LVII, Introduction xliv, 249; Emerson B. Roberts, "Captain Philip Taylor and Some of His Descendants," *Maryland Historical Magazine*, XXXIII (1938), 282.
[31] *Archives of Maryland*, IV, 507; LVII, 249.
[32] *Ibid.*, IV, 23, 507, 527.
[33] *Ibid.*, IV, 23. See also *ibid.*, IV, 527; X, 496; XLI, 178, 261, 263.
[34] *Ibid.*, XLI, 178; see also, XLIX, 206.
[35] *Ibid.*, XLI, 263.

f the Councell) did not come & bring his Wife & Children to his
hurch, he would come & force them to his Church, Contrary to a knowne
ct of Assembly in this Prouince [.] [36]

[In his testimony,] Thomas Gerard Esq[r] sayth uppon oath, That hauing
onference wth M[r] ffitzherbert as they were walking in the woods, & in
s owne Orchard, Touching the bringing his children to the Roman
atholique Church, Hee gave m[r] ffitzherbert reasons, why it was not safe
or himselfe & this Depon[t], And the s[d] m[r] ffitzherbert told this Depon[t]
hat hee would compell and force them & likewise he sayd, th[t] hee would
xcommunicate him, ffor hee would make him know th[t] hee had to doe
[th] the bringing up of his Children, and his Estate.[37]

Gerard's testimony that it was not safe for him or Father Fitzherbert if the children were brought to the Catholic Church is
nexplicable. Whether this religious difficulty carried any weight
n Gerard's decision to break with Lord Baltimore in 1659
(Fendall's Rebellion) is problematical. The chances are that it
did not because the Court adjourned before the case was completed, and it was not finally settled until 1662 when Father
Fitzherbert was acquitted.[38]

On the same day that Gerard's religious difficulties with Father
Fitzherbert were aired, Richard Smith, the Attorney General also
made some very serious charges against Gerard before the Council.[39] He was accused of violating the secrecy of the Council, of
saying that Governor Fendall was a tool of the people of Anne
Arundel and was not above helping himself to the Provincial
revenues, that Capt. Stone, Job Chandler, and Dr. Luke Barber
were secretly playing into the hands of Richard Bennett, Lord
Baltimore's opponent, that the whole Council was a bunch of
rogues and he would not sit with them. Finally he was accused of
drunkenness. Gerard asked for and was granted time to answer
the charges against him, but the Attorney General let the suit
drop. This caused Gerard to write a letter of complaint to Lord
Baltimore who ordered the Council to give him satisfaction.[40] It
is of interest to note that in connection with the charge of drunkenness, Henry Coursey testified that

he was on board of Covills ship with M[r] Gerrard that the said Gerrard
had drunke something extraordinary but was not so much in drinke but
he could gett out of a Carts way & further saith not [.] [41]

---

[36] *Ibid.*, XLI, 144.
[37] *Ibid.*, XLI, 145.
[38] *Ibid.*, XLI, 566.

[39] *Ibid.*, III, 354.
[40] *Ibid.*, III, 384.
[41] *Ibid.*, III, 357.

Whether the other charges against Gerard were true or not
unknown as the Council did not pursue the matter. Probably ther
was a good deal of truth in the charges since they had been ove
heard at the home of his son-in-law, Robert Slye, at Bushwood.

In view of the long, trusted, and friendly relationship betwee
Gerard and Lord Baltimore, extending over a period of more tha
20 years, it is difficult to understand how Gerard could hav
thrown in with Fendall when the show-down came in 1659. Cer
tainly he had no love for the Puritans of Anne Arundel (wh
sided with Fendall), after his experience at Herring Creek i
1655 when several of his close associates and friends wer
executed and he himself narrowly escaped the same fate. Keepin,
this fact in mind it is easy to understand the statements attribute
to him in the charges before the Council. In the absence of an
of his personal papers (which the writer is still endeavoring t
locate) perhaps the best conjecture has been made by F. E. Sparks
in his book *Causes of the Maryland Revolution of 1689*, wherei
he states

The real causes of the disturbance that now arose [Fendall's Rebellion
are scarcely explained by Maryland historians. Governor Fendall i
charged with being the chief cause of the Rebellion. It is true tha
Fendall tried to keep in favor with the party of resistance [the Anne
Arundel Party] and that he was intimately connected with Gerard whose
party was destined to triumph in 1689; but it was really the question of
taxation that caused the so-called Fendall's Rebellion. It is sometimes
said it was a Puritan movement, and so it was in one sense; but Gerard
who seemed to be the real leader, was a Catholic who had been and was
then a member of the Council. In 1647 an act was passed by the Assembly
granting the Proprietor a duty of ten shillings on every hogshead of
tobacco exported from the province. This act, by the admission of the
Proprietor, was the cause of complaints.[42]

Actually, Lord Baltimore had written Fendall a letter concerning
the possibility of an Act for a duty of two shillings on every hogshead of tobacco exported to any port in Great Britain or Ireland
and of ten shillings exported to any other port.[43] Fendall, in
order to promote the rebellion, advised the Assembly and the
people that Lord Baltimore had ordered that if this Act was not
passed, then he, Fendall was to put into execution the Act for
Customs of 1646 (which had never been in force) for the pay-

[42] Johns Hopkins University Studies XIV (Baltimore, 1896), 501.
[43] *Archives of Maryland*, I, 420.

ent of ten shillings per hogshead on all tobacco exported out of
e Province. In reality also, Lord Baltimore had written Fendall
ask the Assembly to repeal the Act for Customs of 1646 and
rovide instead a straight duty of 2 shillings per hogshead of
obacco, which fact as Lord Baltimore later wrote, " he wickedly
oncealed from the people." [44] It is significant that Gerard in
is petition for a pardon, after the Rebellion, used the following
vords ". . . vpon mature deliberacon [being] Sensible that through
gnorance something hath been done by him whilst this Province
vas without Government," which indicate that he may have been
aken in by Fendall.[45] At the same time it would appear that the
Assembly also was deceived because the Speaker delivered a paper
o Fendall which read

Whereas the howse hath had certaine information that the Lord Proprietary
aath sent to the Secretary a Warrant and demand annexed to it to repeale
he Act of Ten shillings p hogshed. The Howse doe therefore desire and
request the said warrant and demand be exhibited to the publick viewe of
this Assembly forthwith.[46]

There is no record that such a paper was produced, and since Lord
Baltimore had directed the letter to Fendall, he must have concealed it.

Another event occurred in 1659 which may have influenced
Gerard in his decision to break with Lord Baltimore. He had, in
the right of his wife, laid claim to 1,000 acres of land (Snow
Hill) which had been granted in 1640 to Abel Snow, his brother-
in-law, who was now deceased. The land was repossessed by
Lord Baltimore under the Act for Deserted Plantations and had
been granted by him in 1652 to Richard Willan and James
Lindsey. Apparently there had been litigation for sometime.
Finally Philip Calvert, Secretary of the Province, appealed the
case to Lord Baltimore who ruled against Gerard and in his own
favor.[47] It should be remembered also that only a few years had
elapsed since the time of the Ingle Rebellion and the Puritan
Uprising and that the government of the Province was far from
secure. Under such conditions there was a great temptation for
any strong man to take the Government into his own hands rather
than again risk the loss of all his possessions.

It seems fairly evident that Gerard faced such a dilemma, with

[44] *Ibid.*, I, 421.
[45] *Ibid.*, XLI, 429.
[46] *Ibid.*, I, 383.
[47] *Ibid.*, XLI, 265, 373.

at least some fancied justification for his action. After he ha
reached a decision, it is evident that Gerard maneuvered to hav
the Assembly and the Council meet at a location where he woul
have a better opportunity to dominate the meetings. The idea
location was at St. Clement's Manor, which was far removed from
the usual meeting place, St. Mary's City, and where Gerard woul
be sure of the attendance of all his friends and adherents. Th
first and second meetings were held at the Gerard home at Long
worth Point on February 28, 1659.[48] All subsequent meeting
including the final meeting were held in the home of Robert Sly
(Gerard's son-in-law) at Bushwood on St. Clement's Manor.[49]
During a period of two weeks a struggle went on beween th
upper and lower houses of the Assembly. The lower hous
claimed themselves to be a lawful Assembly without dependenc
on any power in the Province and the highest Court of Judicature
There was considerable maneuvering back and forth between th
two houses. Finally Fendall on March 13, 1659, came out in th
open, taking the position that the burgesses (by the intent of th
King in Lord Baltimore's patent) could make and enact laws b
themselves and publish them in the name of the Proprietor. He
contended such laws would be in full force, provided they wer
agreeable to reason and not repugnant to the laws of England
The Secretary, Philip Calvert, brother of the Proprietor, of th
upper house declared that it was not in the power of the burgesses
by themselves without assent of the Lord Proprietary or the
Governor to enact any laws. Calvert then proceeded to poll the
upper house or Council. In addition to Fendall and Calvert only
four members were present: Gerard and Col. Nathaniel Utie supported Fendall; Baker Brooke and John Price supported Calvert
The following day Fendall expressed himself as being willing to
sit with the lower house as Governor on their terms. Calvert and
Baker Brooke " departed the howse (after leave asked) and given
in these words or to this effect (vizt) you may if you please, wee
shall not force you to goe or stay, uttered by the Governor [.] "[50]
The Rebellion was on.

The Rebellion collapsed after May, 1660, when Charles II
returned to the throne of England and the Proprietor was restored to favor at the Court. Lord Baltimore, in a furious letter
dated August 24, 1660, instructed his brother Philip Calvert, then

[48] *Ibid.*, I, 382.   [49] *Ibid.*, I, 383-391.   [50] *Ibid.*, I, 391.

Governor, to deal harshly with Gerard, Fendall, Hatch, Slye, and others who took a leading part in the revolt. They could be sentenced to death, be banished from the Province and suffer the loss of all their property.[51] Gerard's manor lands and other property were seized, and he was banished. He retired temporarily to his lands near the Machodoc River in Westmoreland County, Virginia, a 3,500 acre holding, known as Gerard's Preserve.[52] In a few months, however, he applied to the Maryland Council for a pardon which was promptly granted. He was restored to citizenship in the Province but forbidden to hold office or to have a voice in elections. His lands and other property were restored to him.[53] It is significant that while Fendall was required to pay a fine of 50 pounds Sterling, Gerard was required to pay 100 pounds Sterling and 5,000 pounds of tobacco, and, in addition, required to post 10,000 pounds of tobacco as collateral for his good behavior.

After the restoration of his estates Gerard returned to live in Maryland, where he continued his practice as a physician, looked after his lands, and completed more sales of property. His large family consisted of three sons and seven daughters. Perhaps this is why St. Clement's Manor was often referred to as Bedlam Neck. He had many friends on both sides of the Potomac River, and several of his daughters married Virginians. In addition to enjoying the favorite provincial drink of "burnt brandy," Gerard was not averse to cards and dice. One incident in the latter game resulted in a law suit which is recorded in the *Archives of Maryland*.[54] In 1666, after the death of his wife, Susannah, to whom he was very devoted, Gerard moved to his lands at Machodoc, in Westmoreland County, Virginia.[55] A fine old two-story brick house, set between two outside chimneys still stands there. The original widely overhung eaves of the hipped roof have been changed in recent years. The home is now owned by Mrs. Margaret A. Roberts. John Gerard, the only grandson is credited with having erected this house about 1685.[56] It was here that

---

[51] *Ibid.*, III, 396.
[52] L. D. Gardner, " The Garrett Family of Louisa County, Va.," *William and Mary Quarterly*, Series 2, XII, 13. Mrs. Nell Marion Nugent, *Cavaliers and Pioneers* (Richmond, 1934), pp. 198, 324, 424, 532.
[53] *Archives of Maryland*, III, 406-407.
[54] *Ibid.*, XLI, 585.
[55] *Ibid.*, LVII, Introduction, xlii.
[56] *Virginia, A Guide to the Old Dominion* (New York, 1940), p. 557.

Thomas Gerard together with Henry Corbin, John Lee, and Isaac Allerton, "that never-to-be-forgotten quartette of Bon-Vivants," entered into a contract in 1670, later recorded, to build a "Banquetting House" at or near the head of Cherive's (now Jackson's) Creek, where their estates joined. It was agreed that each party to the contract should "yearly, according to his due course, make an honorable treatment fit to entertain the undertakers thereof." [57] Bishop Meade cited this as an example of "riotous living." [58] After settling at Machodoc, Gerard married Rose Tucker, a widow with two children: Rose who married [————] Blackistone and Sarah who married William Fitzhugh. [59] Gerard died here in 1673, but in compliance with a request contained in his will, his body was taken to Longworth Point, his old home in Maryland, and buried there in the private burial grounds by the side of his first wife, Susannah. [60] This private cemetery still existed until a few years ago when one of the late owners of the land threw the tombstones over the bank into the Potomac River and leveled the plot. Not satisfied with this act of desecration, it has been reported that a guest at the hotel there at that time was permitted to open one of the graves and remove a skull. In a terrific storm in the summer of 1933 the hotel was wrecked and much ground washed away so that now there is no evidence whatsoever of the original Gerard home or burial grounds.

Although Gerard made elaborate provisions in his will for any children that might be born of his second marriage there was no issue. The children of his marriage to Susannah Snow were as follows: [61]

    1. Justinian, married Sarah ————, widow of Wilkes Maunders [62]
    2. Thomas, married Susannah Curtis [63]

---

[57] "Extracts from County Records," *Virginia Magazine of History and Biography*, VIII (1901), 171-172.

[58] *Old Churches, Ministers and Families of Virginia* (Philadelphia, 1857), II, 146.

[59] "Letters of William Fitzhugh," *Virginia Magazine*, I (1894), 269. L. G. Tyler, "Washington and His Neighbors," *William and Mary Quarterly*, Series 1, IV (1896), 35, 41.

[60] Tyler, *ibid.*, 82-84.

[61] Beitzell, "The Gerard and Cheseldine Families."

[62] Tyler, *op. cit.*, 36. W. F. Cregar and Christopher Johnson, "Index to Chancery Depositions, 1668-1789," *Maryland Historical Magazine*, XXIII (1928), 312, 319.

[63] *Ibid.*

3. Susannah, married (1) Robert Slye [64]
                          (2) John Coode [65]

4. Anne, married (1) Walter Broadhurst [66]
                      (2) Henry Brett [66]
                      (3) John Washington [66]

5. Frances, married (1) Col. Thos. Speake [67]
                          (2) Col. Valentine Peyton [67]
                          (3) Capt. John Appleton [67]
                          (4) Col. John Washington [67]
                          (5) Wm. Hardwick [67]

6. Temperance, married (1) Daniel Hutt [68]
                              (2) John Crabbe [68]

7. Elizabeth, married (1) Nehemiah Blackistone [69]
                          (2) Ralph Rymer [69]
                          (3) Joshua Guibert [69]

8. Jane or Janette married ————

9. John, married Elizabeth ———— [70]

10. Mary, married Kenelm Cheseldine [71]

None of Gerard's three sons long survived him. John died first, prior to 1678, leaving a son John and daughter Rebecca, who married Charles Calvert (Governor of Maryland, 1720-1727) in 1722.[72] The second John had no sons and his only child, Elizabeth, married Benedict Calvert in 1748.[73] Since his uncles died

---

[64] *Archives of Maryland*, XLIX, 576. "Notes and Queries," *Virginia Magazine*, III (1895), 322.

[65] *Archives of Maryland*, XX, xiv; XXIII, 443.

[66] Tyler, *op. cit.*, 35, 76. "Historical and Genealogical Notes," *William and Mary Quarterly*, Series 1, XVII (1908), 226. L. G. Tyler, "The Good Name and Fame of the Washingtons," *Tyler's Quarterly Magazine*, IV (1922-1923), 322. "Historical and Genealogical Notes," *ibid.*, IX (1927-1928), 70.

[67] Tyler, "Washington and His Neighbors," *op. cit.*, 36. "The Hardwick Family," *William and Mary Quarterly*, Series 2, III (1923), 99. "Sturman Family Notes," *ibid.*, XVII (1913), 11.

[68] Tyler, "Washington and His Neighbors," *op. cit.*, 36. "Virginia Gleanings in England," *Virginia Magazine*, XX (1912), 294.

[69] *Archives of Maryland*, XXII, viii, LI, xlvi. J. W. Thomas, *Chronicles of Colonial Maryland* (Baltimore, 1900), p. 13.

[70] Tyler, "Washington and His Neighbors," *op. cit.*, 36. "Notes to Council Journals," *Virginia Magazine*, XXXIII (1925), 300.

[71] Thomas Gerard in his will, probated October 19, 1673, left his daughter Mary, "White's Neck," "Mattapany," "St. Katherine's Island," "Westwood Lodge" (100 acres), and "Broad Neck." In the will of her husband, Kenelm Cheseldyne, dated December 6, 1708 (on file in the Hall of Records, Annapolis), he left the same tracts of lands to their son, Kenelm II, and daughter, Mary.

[72] "Historical and Genealogical Notes," *William and Mary Quarterly*, Series 1, V (1897), 142. Gardner, "Garrett Family," *op. cit.*, 13.

[73] Tyler, "Washington and His Neighbors," *op. cit.*, 35-36, 80, 87. "Historical and Genealogical Notes," *William and Mary Quarterly*, Series 1, V (1896), 68-69.

without issue, the Gerard family name became extinct at his deat
However, others of the Gerard name, probably of the same fami
in England, survived and it is likely that they descended fro
William Gerard, who obtained a grant of 125 acres of land
Westmoreland County on January 31, 1716.[74] The family nam
continues in England and the present holder of the title is Baro
Frederick John Gerard, M. C., of Lancashire. Thomas Gerard, Jr
was given Basford Manor and Westwood Manor by his fathe
He sold Basford Manor to Gov. Thomas Notley in 1677 and upo
his death in 1686, since he died without issue, Westwood Mano
passed to his brother, Justinian. Justinian was left St. Clement'
Manor (those portions not already settled on his sisters) by hi
father. He died without issue in 1688 and left everything to hi
widow, who later married Michael Curtis. They sold both West
wood and St. Clement's Manor to Charles Carroll on May 18
1711.[75]

Two of Gerard's daughters married Col. John Washington, th
great grandfather of George Washington, although he had n
issue by either of them.[76] The first was Anne Gerard who marrie
him in 1669. After her death, Colonel Washington married he
sister, Francis, on May 10, 1676. She survived Colonel Wash
ington and then married for the fifth time. A great granddaughte
of this fifth marriage, Anne Aylett, married in 1743 Augustine
Washington, a brother of George Washington. It is interesting
to note that Col. John Washington came from Lancashire, England, as did the Gerards. Possibly the families knew each othe
there.

Temperance Gerard married Daniel Hutt of Virginia. Hutt
was originally a New England sailing master and was convicted
in 1659 of illegally trading with the Indians in Maryland and
his bark, the *Mayflower*, was confiscated through action of the
Provincial Court. Although not an inhabitant of the Province at
this time, he was present at the sessions at St. Clement's Manor
and Bushwood which preceded Fendall's Rebellion. Subsequently
he was master of vessels engaged in the Barbados trade and made

[74] " Notes to Council Journals," *op. cit.*, 300.
[75] D. M. Owings, " Private Manors: An Edited List," *Maryland Historical
Magazine*, XXXIII (1938), 311, 319.
[76] Tyler, " Washington and His Neighbors," *op. cit.*, 35. " Historical and
Genealogical Notes," *William and Mary Quarterly*, Series 1, XVII (1908), 226.
R. M. Hughes, " Some Notes on Material Relating to William and Mary College,"
ibid., Series 2, III (1923), 99. Tyler, " Good Name and Fame," *op. cit.*, 322.

is home in Virginia.[77]   After the death of Hutt, Temperance married John Crabbe, a prosperous Virginia merchant.[78]

Walter Broadhurst who was the first husband of Anne Gerard first appears in the Maryland records in 1642 and was closely associated with Thomas Gerard from this time until he moved to Westmoreland County, Virginia, in 1657.   He appears to have been an adherent of Capt. Edward Hill, following the Ingle Rebellion.   Their son, Walter, returned to England where he married and had a family; he there died in 1707.   Henry Brett the second husband of Anne, whom she married in 1665 or 1667, was a Virginian.   He died prior to 1669.   There was no issue. As previously mentioned Anne's third husband was Col. John Washington of Virginia.[79]

The first and fifth husbands of Frances Gerard, Col. Thomas Speake and William Hardwick (Hardidge), were closely associated with Walter Broadhurst and Thomas Gerard, father of Frances. Both Speake and Hardwick are first mentioned in Maryland records in 1642 [80] when they were sent with an expedition of soldiers to Kent Island. Subsequently Hardwick, Broadhurst, and Gerard testified against Richard Ingle and a warrant was issued to Hardwick to arrest Ingle for high treason. They testified to Ingle's traitorious utterances when his ship lay anchored at St. Clement's Island, just off Longworth's Point.[81] Gerard was amply repaid by Ingle later when he burned Gerard's home. Undoubtedly Hardwick and Broadhurst were subjected to like treatment. It was noted that Broadhurst, like Gerard, became involved with Cornwaleys in the effort to recover property after the affairs in the Province had quieted down. After Colonel Speake's death, Frances married Col. Valentine Peyton, a Virginian, and moved there.[82] After Colonel Peyton's death, she married Capt. John Appleton, another Virginian, who died in 1676, whereupon she married Col. John Washington. Upon the death of Colonel Washington, she married William Hardwick, who had moved

[77] *Archives of Maryland*, XLI, 287, 302, 344, 410.
[78] Tyler, "Washington and His Neighbors," *op. cit.*, 36.   "Westmoreland County Records," *William and Mary Quarterly*, Series 1, XV (1906), 191.
[79] *Archives of Maryland*, II, 234, 324. Tyler, "Washington and His Neighbors," *op. cit.*, 35.
[80] *Archives of Maryland*, III, 119-122.
[81] *Ibid.*, II, 234, 237; IV, 231-233.
[82] Tyler, "Washington and His Neighbors," *op. cit.*, 36.

to Nomini in Virginia in 1650. Hardwick was described b[y] Nathaniel Pope, formerly of Maryland but then of Virginia a[s] "a well-beloved friend." [83]

There are indications that Janette or Jane Gerard, anoth[er] daughter of Thomas Gerard, married William Eltonhead, wh[o] was shot after being captured during the Puritan uprising, a[l]though there is much confusion on this score. Some writers hav[e] indicated that she married Richard Eltonhead and others tha[t] she was the first wife of Cuthbert Fenwick, famous in early Mary[-] land history, who subsequently married Jane Eltonhead, the siste[r] of William Eltonhead. There were so many Janes and so man[y] marriages that it will probably take another 300 years to com[-] pletely unscramble them.

Robert Slye married Susannah Gerard who was the eldest o[f] the Gerard girls.[84] She was given Bushwood Manor by her fathe[r] at the time of her marriage. Bushwood Manor subsequentl[y] descended to her son Gerard and grandson George, who willed i[t] to his nephew, Col. Edmund Plowden.[85] Robert Slye, althoug[h] he was the son-in-law of Thomas Gerard, accepted a position on the Puritan Council and as a Commissioner of the Province in 1654-1655.[86] This action within the family gives some idea o[f] the turmoil in the Province during this period. As previousl[y] noted the Assembly met at Slye's home preceding Fendall's Rebel[-] lion, and there is no doubt that he played an important role in this uprising also. Although Slye died considerably before the Rebellion of 1689, the family penchant for rebellion was to be carried on, this time strongly and successfully. According to Sparks' theory it was a continuation or revival of the so-called Fendall Rebellion of 1659. After the death of Robert Slye, Susan[-] nah married John Coode who organized and led the successful rebellion of 1689.[87] His chief lieutenants were two other Gerard sons-in-law, Kenelm Cheseldine and Nehemiah Blackistone. Kenelm Cheseldine married Mary, the youngest daughter of Thomas Gerard. Her dowry included St. Katherine's Island, Whites Neck, Broad Neck, Westwood Lodge (100 acres), and

[83] *Archives of Maryland*, X, 39, 122.
[84] *Ibid.*, XLIX, 575.
[85] Helen W. Ridgely, "*Historic Graves of Maryland* (New York, 1908), p. 30. *Archives of Maryland*, LIII, lxv.
[86] *Archives of Maryland*, III, 315; X, 412.
[87] *Ibid.*, XX, xiv; XXIII, 443.

Mattapany. The latter tract of land should not be confused with Mattapany-Sewell on the Patuxent River.[88] Nehemiah Blackistone married Elizabeth Gerard, whose dowry included St. Clement's Island, Longworth Point (the original Gerard home on St. Clement's Manor), and Dares Neck. She subsequently married Ralph Rymer and Joshua Guibert, both of Maryland.[89]

The history of the Protestant Rebellion of 1689 and the activities of Coode, Cheseldine, and Blackistone are too well known to be repeated here. The details may be reviewed in the *Archives of Maryland* of this period. The success of this rebellion put an end to religious freedom in Maryland for almost eighty years. It was not until the American Revolution that Maryland again became the " Free State." Strangely enough, within a comparatively few years after the Rebellion, the Coode, Cheseldine, and Slye families were brought into the Roman Catholic Church. This was the work largely of a great missionary priest of early Maryland history, Father William Hunter of the Society of Jesus.[90] George Slye built the first Sacred Heart Church at Bushwood, which is mentioned in his will dated in 1773.[91] He is buried there as are many of the Cheseldine family. Many of the Coode family also are buried in the Sacred Heart cemetery and at old St. Inigoes in the lower part of the County. Most of the Coode descendants are now living in Nashville, Tennessee. Many of the Cheseldine descendants are still living at White's Neck and in nearby Washington. This is true also of the Blackistone descendants. In recent years the beautiful old Blackistone home at River Springs has been restored and one of the family now owns Upper Brambly, which adjoins Bushwood. The original name was Bromley, named by Thomas Gerard after one of the Gerard family manors in England.

---

[88] See Note 71.
[89] Christopher Johnson, " Blackistone Family," *Maryland Historical Magazine*, II (1907), 57, 58, 177. See also Note 69.
[90] *Archives of Maryland*, XXIII, 448, 463. Ridgely, *op. cit.*, p. 30.
[91] St. Mary's County Will Records, Court House, Leonardtown.

Gerard's Daughters

JOHN WALTON

AS THE TURBULENT Lord of St. Clement's Manor in St. Mary's County and as a *bon vivant* in Westmoreland, Dr. Thomas Gerard has been remembered on both sides of the Potomac. He was, as many historians and genealogists know, the father of some remarkable daughters—the number and names of whom it is the purpose of this investigation to determine—who surely enjoyed some notoriety during their lifetime. One can assume this without being so ungracious as to rely on James Thomas Flexner's aspersion that John Washington, great-grandfather of the Father of our Country, married (after the death of his first wife, Anne Pope) two sisters in succession[1] "who had been accused before him, when he sat as justice of the peace, one with keeping a bawdy house and the other with being the governor's whore." [2] The daughters of Dr. Thomas Gerard must have been renowned for the number and standing of the husbands that they, individually and collectively, attracted.

It is not, however, the number and names of their husbands that is our primary concern here; we are going to try to settle the questions about who Gerard's daughters were. Beitzell, an authority on St. Mary's County families, has listed six, and possibly seven, daughters and three sons: [3]

---

[1] It is generally believed that John Washington married two of Gerard's daughters.

[2] James Thomas Flexner, *George Washington: The Forge of Experience* (1772-1775) (Boston, Mass.: Little, Brown and Company, 1965), p. 10.

Flexner may have obtained his information from an inaccurate reading of the Westmoreland County records. [See John Frederick Dorman, *Westmoreland County Deeds, Patents*, etc., 1665-1677, Part 1 (Washington, D.C., 1973).] These records contain a number of depositions with respect to statements made by one Richard Cole, who allegedly made vicious and slanderous remarks about many prominent people of good repute. The reference to Mrs. Brett (Anne _____ Broadhurst, Brett, Washington) keeping a bawdy house is in a deposition given by Robert Edwards and Mary Edwards, August 27, 1668, and sworn before Justinian Gerard. It was recorded October 28, 1668, pp. 25-25a. The reference to Frances Gerard Speke, Peyton, Appleton, Washington, Hardwick, as the Governor's whore is apparently taken from a deposition taken by James Colestram on September 12, 1668 and sworn to before Nicholas Spencer. It was recorded on October 28, 1668, pp. 25a-26. There is no indication here that Mrs. Brett and Mrs. Appelton were ever called before John Washington. As a matter of fact it is obvious from reading these depositions that Richard Cole's slander of a number of people, including the Governors of Virginia and Maryland, was recognized as the raving of an intoxicated and unbalanced man. See, for example, Robert Slye's deposition, pp. 18-18a.

[3] Edwin W. Beitzell, "Thomas Gerard and His Sons-in-Law," *Chronicles of St. Mary's*, vol. 10, nos. 10, 11 (October and November, 1962), pp. 300-312. See this article as originally published in the *Md. Hist. Mag.* Vol. 46 (Sept., 1951), pp. 189-206.

Justinian Gerard, married Sarah, widow of Wilkes Maunders.

Thomas Gerard, married Susannah Curtis.

Susannah Gerard, married first, Robert Slye, and, secondly, John Coode—a prominent leader in "Orange Revolution" in 1689,[4] and a shadowy figure in John Barth's *The Sot-Weed Factor.*

4. Anne Gerard, married, first, Walter Broadhurst, secondly, Henry Brett, and, thirdly, John Washington.

5. Frances Gerard, married, first, Thomas Speke, secondly Valentine Peyton, thirdly, John Appleton, fourthly, John Washington, and fifthly, William Hardwick.

6. Temperance Gerard, married, first, Daniel Hutt, secondly, John Crabbe, and thirdly, Benjamin Bianchflower.[5]

7. Elizabeth Gerard, married, first Nehemiah Blackiston, secondly, Ralph Rymer, and thirdly, Joshua Guibert.

8. Jane Gerard (possibly), married, first, Thomas Smyth, secondly, Philip Taylor, and thirdly, William Eltonhead.

9. John Gerard, married Elizabeth _____.

10. Mary Gerard, married Kenelm Cheseldine.

To the seven daughters named above—Susannah, Anne, Frances, Temperance, Elizabeth, Jane, and Mary—Alice Parran, chronicler of Maryland families, has added an eighth. She is Judith, wife successively of John Goldsmith and Richard Clouds.[6] Robert Slye, Jr., son of Robert and Susannah Gerard Slye, married Priscilla Goldsmith, daughter of John and Judith Goldsmith, according to Parran; Judith Goldsmith was a daughter of Dr. Thomas Gerard. From the will of Robert Slye, Jr. it appears likely that he did marry Priscilla Goldsmith. Named in the will are his wife, Priscilla, and the following children: John Slye, Judith Slye, Susannah Slye, and Sarah Slye.[7] But we have no evidence that Judith Goldsmith was a daughter of Dr. Thomas Gerard.

As will be shown later at the time of his death Dr. Thomas Gerard had only five living daughters. The evidence is conclusive that these five daughters were Susannah, Frances, Temperance, Elizabeth, and Mary. Since Judith and Anne were living at this time they cannot be included. The argument against Jane is both from silence and from chronology. We shall try now to settle the question about whom can be regarded as Gerard's daughters and thereby determine who can claim that they are his descendants.

Dr. Thomas Gerard, member of an ancient and great Lancashire County Catholic

[4] For an account of Coode's activities in the Revolution of 1689 see Michael G. Kammer, "The Causes of the Maryland Revolution of 1689," *Md. Hist. Mag.,* Vol. 55 (Sept., 1960), pp. 321 ff.
[5] The third marriage is not mentioned by Beitzell. See Westmoreland County, Virginia, Order Book, 1690-98, pp. 159a, 160.
[6] Alice Parran, *Register of Maryland's Heraldic Families,* Series II, Baltimore, Maryland, 1938, pp. 201-208; 154-155; 271. For Judith Goldsmith's marriage to Richard Clouds, see *Administrative Accounts,* 4-H, Folio, 96, Hall of Records, Annapolis, Maryland.
[7] Wills, Liber 16, folio 74, 180, Hall of Records.

family, was born in 1608-1609, probably in Newhall. In 1629 he married Susa
Snow, daughter of John and Judith (some say Edryth) Snow of Staffordshire, a
sister of Abel, Justinian, and Marmaduke Snow who were associated with I
Baltimore in the Maryland enterprise. Abel Snow held the manor of Snow I
Apparently, Dr. Thomas Gerard was a distant cousin of the Richard Gerard
came to Maryland in 1633 and returned to England in 1635. Richard was probab
descendant of Sir Thomas Gerard, the great Elizabethan. As far as is known
Thomas Gerard came to Maryland, first, in 1638;[8] after a return trip or two, bro
his family over in 1650.[9] On September 19 of that year he demanded 2000 acre
land for transporting himself, his wife, and five children into the province as we
Mr. Austin Hall (or Hull) and eight manservants and four woman servants.
children were Justinian, Susan, Frances, Temperance, and Elizabeth.[10]

Of all Baltimore's manorial Lords, Dr. Thomas Gerard probably governed
demesne in the most traditionally baronial style. At St. Clement's he held m
orial court—the Court Leet and the Court Baron[11]—he took advantage of prow
bial prerogatives of his position for the enjoyment of the good things of this wor
and he continued to acquire land. To the 3500 acres that lay across the Poton
in Westmoreland County he retreated after his unexplained participation
Josias Fendall's rebellion in 1660. There he married his second wife, a yow
widow by the name of Rose Tucker (by whom he had no children), and there
died in 1673. His body was brought back to St. Clements to lie by that of his f
wife, Susanna.[12]

A footnote to the history of Virginia records that Dr. Thomas Gerard, together w
Henry Corbin, John Lee, and Isaac Allerton, erected a "Banquetting House";[13] ma
years later an unusually strait-laced Bishop of Virginia cited the events that occur
in this house as an example of "riotous living" in the seventeenth century.[14]

The will of Dr. Thomas Gerard provides us with scant information about
children. Dated February 1, 1672, and proved October 19, 1673,[15] it refers to the th
sons and five daughters that will "survive" their father. The eldest son, Justinian, i
youngest son, John, and a daughter, Mary, then under twenty-one years of age a

---

[8] See Gust Skordas, ed., *The Early Settlers of Maryland. An Index to Names of Immigrants Comp
from Records of Land Patents, 1633-1680, in the Hall of Records, Annapolis, Maryland* (Baltimore, 196
p. 180.

[9] This sketch of Dr. Thomas Gerard's origin is taken from David Spalding's, C.F.X., "Thomas Gera
of Maryland and Virginia: Old World Roots," *Chronicles of St. Mary's*, vol. 7, (July, 1959), pp. 2–8; a
from the papers of Walter Weston Folger, a surety of the Baronial order of Magna Charta.

[10] *Md. Hist. Mag.*, VIII (1913), p. 262.

[11] For a description of these courts see James Walter Thomas, *Chronicles of Colonial Maryla*
(Baltimore, 1920), pp. 128-135.

[12] For this resumé of Dr. Thomas Gerard in America, I am indebted to David Spalding, C.F.
"Thomas Gerard: The Study of a Lord of the Manor and the Advantages of Manor Holding in Ea
Maryland," United States Catholic Historical Society *Historical Records and Studies*, XLIV (1956).

[13] Beitzell, "Thomas Gerard."

[14] Bishop William Meade, *Old Churches, Ministers and Families of Virginia* (Philadelphia, 1857),
p. 146.

[15] *William and Mary Quarterly*, series 1, IV, pp. 82–85.

ned. Very few other members of the household were mentioned; they were
-in-law Blaxstones (Blackistone), grandson, Peyton Gerard, deceased wife,
sanna, and wife, Rose.

The evidence shows clearly that the five daughters that would survive were
sannah, Frances, Temperance, Elizabeth, and Mary. First, there is no doubt that he
d daughters with those names; the first four he transported in 1650, and the fifth is
ntioned in his will as being under twenty-one years of age and, therefore, born after
50. It is also reasonably well substantiated that these five daughters did survive their
her. Therefore, if he did have other daughters, they would have predeceased him.
e know that Judith Goldsmith lived long after his death; that Anne Broadhurst
rett, Washington) is supposed to have died in 1675; and that the dates in the life of
ne Smyth (Taylor, Eltonhead) make it most unlikely that she was his daughter,
hough she predeceased him.

As for the daughters we know he had, Susannah, who married, first Robert Slye,
d, secondly, John Coode, was living in 1679.[16] She was in the courts, probably at
e instigation of her second husband, to ask for a separation of her interest—one
oiety—in the Bushwood estate from that of her eldest son (Gerard Slye) by her first
sband. Frances married John Washington, her fourth husband, supposedly in 1676
d lived to marry a fifth husband, William Hardwick.[17] Temperance was married to
aniel Hutt in 1669; five years later he died and Temperance married John Crabbe;[18]
d she lived to marry a third husband, Benjamin Blanchflower.[19] Elizabeth married
ehemiah Blackistone who died in 1693; she later married in succession Ralph
ymer and Joshua Guibert; and she died in St. Mary's County in 1716.[20] Mary, who
arried Kenelm Cheseldine, was mentioned in her father's will as one who would
rvive him. Thus, the five known daughters of Dr. Thomas Gerard were the ones
e referred to in his will. As for Jane, Judith, and Anne, there seems to be reasonably
nclusive evidence that they were not his daughters. They were, however, involved
the same social milieu as Gerard's daughters, and there are many intriguing and
ggestive family relationships that indicate the intricately interwoven society along
e lower Potomac. Therefore, in presenting the evidence against the likelihood that
ey, too, were Gerard's daughters, we shall include personal and family information
at will illumine here and there the realities of colonial life.

Jane is the only one of the three who predeceased Dr. Thomas Gerard and is,

---

[16] See Provincial Court Records, Liber M-M, folios, 403, 412, 419, 420 (1674); Provincial Court
udgments, Liber I, folio 122 (Fifth year of the Dominion of Charles, Lord Baltimore, 1679), Hall of
tecords, Annapolis. Also see William H. Browne, et. al., eds. *Archives of Maryland* (Baltimore,
883——), LXV, pp. 409-506.

[17] Beitzell, "Thomas Gerard"; see also, "The Hardwick Family," *William and Mary Quarterly*, series 2,
II (1923), p. 99.

[18] "Westmoreland County Records," *William and Mary Quarterly*, series 1, XV (1906), pp. 190-191.

[19] Westmoreland, County *Order Book, 1690-1698*, pp. 159a, 160.

[20] Beitzell, "Thomas Gerard"; Christopher Johnson, "Blackistone Family," *Md. Hist. Mag.*, II (1937),
p. 57, 58, 177; George Harrison Sanford King, *Addenda and Conigenda, Marriages of Richmond County,
Virginia, 1668-1853*. For her will see *Maryland Calendar of Wills*, V, p. 69.

therefore, not excluded by the logic of the evidence so far from the possibility of being one of his daughters.[21] According to Beitzell[22] she married, first, Thomas Smyth who was captured by Governor Leonard Calvert after the reduction of Kent Island in and hanged as a pirate, leaving his widow with two small daughters, Gertrude Jane.[23] Later she married Captain Philip Taylor, who died prior to 1649 and left children, Sarah and Thomas.[24] He may have died a natural death. In any event, married a third husband—Beitzell indicates that it was William Eltonhead, who taken prisoner after the Battle of the Severn and shot; but in her will, proved Febru 28, 1659, Jane mentioned a legacy to her son Thomas Taylor to be paid after the d of Edward Eltonhead had been paid.[25] No evidence has been found that Jane w Gerard. Moreover, it is not likely that a woman who had two husbands and children before 1649 was a legitimate daughter of a man who was born in 1609 married in 1629.

Judith lived long after 1673. Her husband, John Goldsmith, was one of menservants transported by Dr. Thomas Gerard in 1650; and, when he died in 1 he owned at least three estates. In his will he named the following children: Thom Notley Goldsmith, John Gerard Goldsmith, William Goldsmith, Judith (wife William Nisinger), Notley Goldsmith (a daughter), Priscilla Goldsmith, Marga Goldsmith, Sarah Goldsmith, and Elizabeth, wife of Thomas Jordan. He mentioned Thomas Love, a son-in-law. The wives of the others referred to as so in-law—William Nisinger and Thomas Jordan—are named, but no wife is nam for Thomas Love. She may have been a deceased daughter of John Goldsmith. Thomas Love may have been a step-son.[26] That he named a son John Gerard is evidence of any family relationship. John Gerard may have been the god father. John Goldsmith, who was obviously a man on the way up, may have selected names of prominent men for his sons; Thomas Notley, for example, probably related, was a prominent man, also.

There are more striking similarities between the Gerard names and those children of Thomas and Elizabeth Goldsmith Jordan; and there are other unexplain suggestions of a family connection. Thomas Jordan was a freeholder at St. Clemen in 1672,[27] and he may have lived there for sometime prior to that. His will sign October 15, 1716, mentioned the following children: Justinian Jordan, Gerard Jorda Thomas Jordan, Samuel Jordan, and Theodore Jordan.[28] Justinian Jordan marri

---

[21]Archives of Maryland, XLI, p. 178; XLIX, p. 206. See, also, her will Maryland Calendar of Wills, 12.

[22] Beitzell, "Thomas Gerard," p. 303.

[23] Archives of Maryland, I, pp. 16-19, 466; IV, pp. 23, 507, 527.

[24] Ibid.

[26] See Charles Frances Stein, A History of Calvert County (Baltimore, 1960), pp. 20-23 for a rat romantic account of the Eltonhead family.

[26] Will, P.C. 1, folio 44, Hall of Records, Annapolis.

[27] Maryland Archives, LXIII, p. 635. There seem to have been several different Jordan families in Marys and Westmoreland Counties.

[28] P.C. 1, folio 202, Hall of Records.

ary, a daughter of John Coode (whether by Susannah Gerard, his first wife, or by lizabeth his second wife, is unclear); and he and some of his descendants became rominent in the political life of St. Mary's County.[29]

It is doubtful that Mary Coode Jordan was a daughter of Susannah Gerard, but the vidence from John Coode's will is ambiguous. In that will of 1708, he mentioned his ife, Elizabeth and the following children: John Coode, William Coode, Richard Coode, Mary Coode, Ann Coode, and Winingfritt (Winifred) Coode.[30] He willed his ife the plantation on which he then lived with its livestock for her support during her atural life and for the support of the children she had by him until they reached the ge of sixteen if they remained with her that long. After her death that plantation was o be divided between Mary and Ann Coode. Also the "produce" of three negroes to e divided, after his wife's death, among his son, Richard Coode and the three laughters, Mary, Ann, and Winningfrit (Winifred). This will indicates that all the children except John and William were the children of his second wife.

Fourteen years later Richard Coode, Justinian Jordan and wife, Mary, Ann _____, and Winningfrit (Winifred) Coode went into court to recover a legacy of slaves and their increase left them by their father in care of his wife, Elizabeth, who had later married William Hook.[31] This action indicates that Elizabeth may have been a step mother of Richard, Mary, Ann, and Winifred Coode.

For reasons unknown, Elizabeth Jordan, daughter of John and Judith Goldsmith, wife of Thomas, and mother of Justinian Jordan, was indirectly a residuary legatee and executrix of the estate of Justinian Gerard. The latter married Sarah, widow of Wilkes Maunders, and to her left his whole estate including a large part of St. Clements manor, lands in Westmoreland County, Virginia, a house and land at Newhall, Lancashire, England, and all his personal property.[32] Sarah then married Michael Curtis, whom she predeceased and to whom she left much of the property she inherited from her second husband, Justinian Gerard (St. Clements Manor had been sold in 1711 to Charles Carroll.)[33] Michael Curtis died in 1716 and left one of the most remarkable wills in colonial Maryland, particularly with respect to the number of legatees, the generous provisions for his slaves, and the enumeration of small legacies.[34] As mentioned above, Elizabeth Jordan was one of the three residuary legatees and executor—the other two where Philip Briscoe, Sr. and Samuel Williamson, Chief Justice of the St. Mary Court—and to her he bequeathed several young slaves to be reared until the age of twenty-one and then, if the law permitted, to be set free, his "large Bible," and several other legacies. As a residuary legatee she received two hundred pounds.[35]

[29] See, for example, *Maryland Archives*, XXXIX, pp. 381-383; XXXVI, pp. 286-287.
[30] Wills, Liber 12, folios 341-2, Hall of Records.
[31] Chancery, Liber 3, Folio 975-76-77, Hall of Records.
[32] P.C. 1, folio 68, Hall of Records.
[33] "Interrogationes," folio 122, Hall of Records.
[34] P.C. 1., folio 211, Hall of Records. See John Walton, "The Will of Michael Curtis," *National Genealogical Society Quarterly*, vol. 52 (1970), pp. 108-116.
[35] Amount not mentioned in the will—see "Interrogationes."

The reason Elizabeth Jordan was named one of the three residuary legatees and executors of the estate of Michael Curtis is not known. She may have been a relative his deceased wife, of her second husband, Justinian Gerard, or of Michael Curtis himself. Or she may have been named because she was a neighbor and friend which she certainly was—whom he wanted to take care of his young slaves until they were old enough for manumission. But, whatever the reason, it was not because Judith Goldsmith, her mother, was a daughter of Dr. Thomas Gerard.

We still have Ann to account for. There is no documentary evidence that she was a daughter of Dr. Thomas Gerard. Apparently the fact that she named one of her sons by Walter Broadhurst, Sr., her first husband, Gerard Broadhurst, led Lyon G. Tyler to assume that she was.[36] Tyler may have been aware of other circumstantial evidence for this possibility, for example, the fact that Walter Broadhurst, Sr., Ann's first husband, wrote in his will, which was probated, February 12, 1658/59:

> As long as my wife continues a widow she shall have all my land for use and the whole stock until my said sons come of age. And if she marry I hereby constitute Mr. Thomas Gerard, Mr. Nathanial Pope, and Mr. Robert Slye overseers of my children.[37]

We have no evidence as to what Ann's maiden name was, but we do have what appears to be incontrovertible evidence that she was not a daughter of Dr. Thomas Gerard. We shall follow that evidence to this conclusion.

On January 10, 1650/51, Walter Broadhurst received a certificate for two hundred acres of land for importing himself, Ann his wife, Elizabeth Broadhurst, and Susan Broadhurst. (We know Elizabeth was a daughter and probably Susan, also.)[38] There is a record that he transported himself into the province of Maryland in 1638.[39] This information indicates that he came to Maryland, first, where he married and had two children and then moved across the Potomac into Northumberland County, Virginia, although it is possible that he returned to England before going to Virginia. If by 1650 he was married and had two children by his wife, Ann, then she must have been born not later than about 1628. Dr. Thomas Gerard was supposedly married about that time or, perhaps, a year later. Even though it is possible that she was his daughter, it is unlikely, since the chronology must be forced, and Dr. Thomas Gerard transported his family to Maryland in 1650 by which time Ann had two children by a husband who had come to Maryland in 1638.

Walter Broadhurst, Sr., died between January 26, 1658/59 and February 12, 1658/59, the dates respectively of the signing and probation of his will. His wife

---

[36] See Charles Arthur Hoppin, "The Good Name and Fame of the Washingtons," *Tyler's Quarterly Magazine*, IV (1922-1923), p. 322, and Lyon G. Tyler, "Washington and His Neighbors," *William and Mary Quarterly*, series 1, IV (1896), pp. 35, 76. It is to Mr. Hoppin's credit that he always recorded this supposition with a question mark: "Anne (Gerard?) Brodhurst."

[37] Westmoreland County (Virginia) Will Book, no. 1 (1653-59), p. 121. I am indebted to Mr. Thomas Martin of Ashland, Virginia, for his research in the Westmoreland and Northumberland County records.

[38] Fleet_____, Abstracts of Northumberland County Records, no. 1, p. 47.

[39] *Md. Hist. Mag.*, V, p. 373.

:rited his lands and a tavern at Nomini in Westmoreland County, which she
bably owned when she married John Washington in 1669.[40] However, before she
rried John Washington, she married, secondly, Henry Brett, sometime between
tember 6, 1665 and September 27, 1667.[41] Henry Brett died circa 1668/69, and by
tember 28, 1670, Ann had married John Washington.[42] Since John Washington
s later to marry an undoubted, thrice married and thrice bereaved, daughter of Dr.
omas Gerard, Frances Gerard, Speke, Peyton, Appleton (she was to mary the fifth
e), and since the ecclesiastical laws of the Church in Virginia forbade that a man
uld marry his deceased wife's sister[43] Hoppin has justified Tyler's supposition that
n and Francis were sisters as follows:

.. it is my belief that John Washington's second wife, Ann, and third wife, Frances were
aalf-sisters born of the two wives of Dr. Thomas Gerard.[44]

t since we know that Dr. Thomas Gerard had no children by his second wife, this
planation does not hold. Moreover, we do not know that half-sisters did not count;
hough with the precedent established in the Church of England for a broad
erpretation of ecclesiastical law as it applies to matrimony, and with the Anglican
tue of compromise, such an interpretation may have been valid. The problem is that
ere seems to be no possibility for half-sisters in the Gerard family.

The final evidence is that John Washington's will, written September 21, 1675,
entions "my loving wife, Mrs. Ann Washington." [45] Thus, Ann was living when Dr.
10mas Gerard wrote his will and mentioned the five daughters that would survive
m. It is true she did not survive him for many years, for on May 10, 1676, a
'oynture" was announced between John Washington and Mrs. Frances Appleton,
lict of John Appleton.[46] Hoppin calculates the date of Ann's death between
ptember 21, 1675 and February, 1675/76.[47]

The evidence that Ann Broadhurst, Brett, Washington was not a daughter of Dr.
10mas Gerard seems to be consistent. The estimated date of her birth, the
clesiastical law forbidding a man to marry his deceased wife's sister, and the
proximate date of her death would all require considerable forcing to fit them into
e known facts about Gerard's daughter. There is a bare possibility that her father
ought that Ann would die before he did; therefore the restriction in the will to the
ve daughters who would "survive" him. But in the light of the other evidence this
ference seems extremely tenuous.

---

[40] See Hoppin, "The Good Name and Fame of Washingtons," p. 325.

[41] *Ibid.*, p. 330.

[42] Westmoreland County Records, 1665-1677, folio 99. After a list of large debts left by Henry Brett,
rs. Ann Brett, als [sic] Washington is mentioned.

[43] The Reverend George J. Cleaveland, Registrar of the Diocese, Diocese of Virginia, Richmond, has
nt me the List of Prohibited Degrees of Matrimony, which include the prohibition against marrying a
an's deceased wife's sister. This List was made law by canon 99 in 1603 in the Church of England. The
eneral Assembly of Virginia required the clergy in Virginia to obey the canon and ecclesiastical laws of
ngland by acts passed in 1619, 1623, 1632, and 1661. See Hening, *Statutes at Large.*

[44] Hoppin, "The Good Name and Fame of Washingtons," p. 340.

[45] *Ibid.*, p. 340.

[46] *Northumberland County Records*, 1665-1677, folio 274.

[47] Hoppin, "The Good Name and Fame of Washingtons," p. 339.

GIST FAMILY OF BALTIMORE COUNTY.

Christopher Johnston.

---

1. CHRISTOPHER GIST,[1] the ancestor of this family, came to
Maryland and settled in Baltimore County before 1682,
though the precise date of his arrival is unknown. 7 March
1682, Robert Clarkson, of Anne Arundel County, conveys to
Christopher Gist of Patapsco River, Baltimore County,
planter, and Richard Cromwell of the same place a tract of
245 acres, called South Canton, in Baltimore County
(Balto. Co., I. R. no. A. M., 179-181). And, 14 Jan. 1682,
Christopher Gist and Edith his wife and Richard Cromwell
convey to William Cromwell, all the parties being "of Patapsco River, in the Province of Maryland," 84 acres, part
of South Canton. Richard Cromwell appoints "my brother
Christopher Gist" his attorney to acknowledge the deed
(*ibid.* fol. 193-195). 6 March 1682/3, "Christopher Gist"
was a member of the Grand Jury for Baltimore County
(Court Record), and he was commissioned, 4 Sept. 1689,
one of the Justices of the County (Archives, xiii, 243).
5 June 1683, Thomas and Ann Lightfoot, orphans of John
and Elizabeth Lightfoot, are apprenticed to "Christopher
Guest" (Court Record). Thomas Lightfoot died before
1688, but had married in the meantime and left a widow
Rebecca (Larkin) who gave bond, 7 August 1688, to
"Christopher Guest" of Baltimore County, planter, for the
conveyance of 320 acres formerly called Utopia, but now
called Rebecca's Delight (Balto. Co., R. M. no. H. S., 279-
281). The will of "Christopher Guest" of Baltimore
County, dated 17 February 1690/1, was proved 10 March
following (Balto. Co., R. M. no. H. S., 331). He leaves his
estate equally between "my dearly beloved wife and childe."
His wife is to be executrix. To John Robinson is left
a two year old heifer. To "my brother Richard Cromwell's child," a two year old heifer. £5 to "my mother
Guest if she be living." Christopher Gist's wife was Edith
Cromwell, sister of William, John, and Richard Cromwell,
and she was thrice married. Her second husband, Joseph

Williams, died in 1692, and his will, dated 24 September, was proved 3 November of that year (Annapolis, vi, 20 back). His wife Edith is appointed executrix, and four children are named, but of course they were by a former wife. Her third husband was John Beecher, but their wedded life was of brief duration, as she died in 1694. The will of Edith Williams of Patapsco River, Baltimore County, is dated 23 May 1694, but no date of probate is given. Her brother Richard Cromwell and Mr. Thomas Staley are requested to take "into their custody and tutelage my son Richard Gist, who I request may be put to school and there kept till he can wright and cast accompt fitting for Merchants Business." The same persons are requested to receive and take care of testatrix's estate, and deliver it to her son Richard Gist at 21 years of age (Balto. Co., R. M. no. H. S., 510). Although the date of probate is wanting, the following entry will give a close approximation. 16 June 1694, came John Beecher who married Edith the relict and executrix of Joseph Williams, late of Baltimore County deceased, and craved time to account &c. (Test. Proc. xv, 88). It is then apparent that the testatrix died in 1694 between 23 May and 16 June, but it is rather remarkable that, though married to John Beecher, she styles herself "Edith Williams" in her will. Christopher Gist[1] and Edith (Cromwell) his wife had an only child:—

2. i. CAPT. RICHARD GIST[2] b. 1684; d. 28 Aug. 1741; m. Zipporah Murray.

2. CAPT. RICHARD GIST[2] (*Christopher*[1]) was born in 1684, and died 28 August 1741. "Mr. Richard Gist" was 48 years old in 1732 (Chancery, I. R. no. 2, 60), and 49 in 1733 (Balto. Co., H. W. S. no. 3, 172), while "Capt. Richard Gist" was 54 years old in 1737 (A. A. Co., I. B. no. 1, 101). The date of his death is entered in the register of St. Thomas' Church, Baltimore County. 3 Nov. 1692, Edith Williams of Baltimore County, widow, gives to her son Richard Gist, a negro to be delivered to him at 16 years of age (Court Record) and, 21 Feb'y 1693/4, Thomas Hammond of Baltimore County, Gent., and Rebecca his wife late relict of Thomas Lightfoot of said County, Gent., deceased, convey to Richard Gist, son and heir of Christopher Gist, late of said County, Gent., deceased, the tract

Utopia, now called Rebecca's Delight (Balto. Co., R. M., no. H. S., 417). This was the tract for the conveyance of which, Rebecca widow of Thomas Lightfoot gave bond 7 August 1688 (see above). The will of Richard Cromwell, uncle of Richard Gist, is dated 12 August 1717, and was proved 23 September following (Balto., Lib. 1, fol. 144). Among other provisions he leaves two negroes to Edith daughter of Richard Gist, and bequeaths £30 and a gold ring to "my cosen (*i.e.*, nephew) Richard Gist." Capt. Gist was commissioned 2 March 1727 one of the Justices and Commissioners of Baltimore County and was reappointed continuously until his death. From 1 February 1735, he was Presiding Justice (Commission Book). The act for laying out and erecting Baltimore Town which passed the House 30 July, and was signed by Gov. Calvert 8 August, 1729, appointed Capt. Gist one of the seven Commissioners for carrying out its provisions, and he represented his County in the Provincial Assembly the last two years of his life 1740-1741 (House Journals). He is styled "Captain" in a deposition made in 1737 (see above) and in the House Journal in 1741, and doubtless held a commission as Captain in the County militia. Richard Gist married, 7 December, 1704, (*Friends' Records*), Zipporah Murray, daughter of James Murray (d. 1704) of Baltimore County and Jemima his wife, daughter of Capt. Thomas Morgan (d. 1698). 6 July 1711, Josephus Murray of Baltimore County, planter, conveys to his "sister Zipporah Gist" a tract of 100 acres in Baltimore County, called "Brother's Good Will" (Balto. Co., T. R., no. A, 141). Josephus Murray was one of the sons of James Murray and is named in his father's will. Mrs. Zipporah Gist survived her husband, and was living 25 April 1760 when she resigned her dower in some lands conveyed by her sons Christopher and Nathaniel Gist (Balto. Co., B. no. H., 149). Capt. Richard Gist gives, 5 Sept. 1728, to his "son Christopher Gist," 350 acres in Baltimore County (I. S. no. I., 196); to his "son Nathaniel Gist" he gives, 6 March 1731, the tract Gist's Search, 284 acres, in Baltimore County (I. S. no. L, 201); and to his "son Thomas Gist" he gives The Addition, 216 Acres, in Baltimore County (H. W. S. no. I. A., 189). There appears to be no deed of gift to his son William, but there cannot be the slightest doubt that William was the son of Capt. Richard, and he doubtless received from his father an equal share with his brothers. Edith Gist, Richard's daughter, is named in the will of her great uncle, Richard Cromwell cited above, while another daughter is known through a deed of her brother. 26 March 1742, Christopher Gist of Baltimore County, merchant, and Sarah his wife, convey to his sister Jemima Seabrooke and William Seabrooke her husband, tract Pleasant Green, 100 acres, in Baltimore County (Balto. Co., T. B. no. A, 132).

Capt. Richard Gist [2] and Zipporah (Murray) his wife had issue:—

3.   i.   CAPT. CHRISTOPHER GIST,[3] m. Sarah Howard; d. 1759.
4.   ii.   NATHANIEL GIST, m. Mary Howard.
5.   iii.   WILLIAM GIST, b. 1711; d. 19 Nov. 1794; m. Violetta Howard.
6.   iv.   THOMAS GIST, b. 1713; d. 1788; m. Susan Cockey.
       v.   EDITH GIST.
       vi.   JEMIMA GIST, m. William Seabrooke.

3.   CAPT. CHRISTOPHER GIST [3] (*Richard,*[2] *Christopher*[1]) was at first a merchant in Baltimore Town but, failing in business, he made an assignment to the firm of Cromwell and Stanbury, 6 June 1745 (Balto. Co., T. B. no. D, 202). In a later deed, dated 24 Sept. 1750, he styles himself "Christopher Gist late of Baltimore County, in the Province of Maryland, but now in the Colony of Virginia," and conveys to Tobias Stansbury, "Gist's Limepits" in Baltimore County, formerly surveyed and granted to Richard Gist, father of said Christopher, and where said Chistopher formerly lived (Balto. Co., T. R. no. D., 94). He settled on the Yadkin, explored Ohio and part of Kentucky for the Ohio Company in 1750, and was the guide and companion of Washington on his journey to Lake Erie in 1753. With his sons Nathaniel and Thomas, he took part, as guide and scout, in Braddock's expedition, and was present on the fatal field of battle, where that officers troops were cut to pieces. 1 October 1755, Christopher Gist was commissioned Lieutenant in the Virginia forces (*Va. Mag.,* i, 285), and in 1756 he was captain (*ibid.,* ii, 44) of a Company of Scouts which he raised for service on the frontier. The same year he went to the Carolinas to enlist Cherokee Indians for the English service, and for a time he served as Indian Agent. He died in the summer of 1759 of smallpox, in South Carolina or Georgia. His

Journals, edited by Wm. A. Darlington, were published at Pittsburgh in 1893. Christopher Gist married Sarah, daughter of Joshua Howard of Baltimore County, whose will dated 3 July, and proved 4 Sept., 1738 (Balto. i, 296) names his sons Francis, Cornelius, and Edward Howard, and his daughters Sarah, Mary, and Violetta Gist, and Elizabeth Wells. It is interesting to note that these ladies were the aunts of the distinguished Revolutionary worthy, Col. John Eager Howard, who was the son of their brother Cornelius.

Christopher Gist [3] and Sarah (Howard) his wife had issue:—

    i. RICHARD GIST,[4] b. 2 Sept. 1729; killed at battle of King's Mountain, 1780; said to have descendants in South Carolina.

    ii. VIOLETTA GIST, b. 4 July 1731; m. William Cromwell.

7. iii. COL. NATHANIEL GIST, b. 15 Oct. 1733; d. early in following century.

    iv. THOMAS GIST, settled in Kentucky; d. about 1786.

    v. NANCY GIST, d. unmarried in Kentucky.

4. NATHANIEL GIST [3] (*Richard,*[2] *Christopher* [1]) married Mary daughter of Joshua Howard and sister to the wives of his brothers Christopher and William. They had issue as recorded in St. Paul's register:—

    i. ZIPPORAH GIST,[4] b. 24 December 1732.

    ii. CHRISTOPHER GIST, b. 21 September 1734.

5. WILILAM GIST [3] (*Richard,*[2] *Christopher* [1]) was born in 1711, according to a deposition made in 1767, wherein he gives his age as 56 years (Chancery, D. D. no. 2, 179). He died 19 Nov. 1794, and the date is recorded in the register of St. Thomas's Parish, Baltimore County, where his marriage and the births of his children are also recorded. He married, 22 October 1737, Violetta, daughter of Joshua Howard, named in her father's will as " my daughter Violetta Gist '" (see above). Moveover, Cornelius Howard (son of Joshua) of Baltimore County, planter, conveys, 7 August 1771, to his " sister Violetta Gist and William Gist her husband," Lot 502 in Baltimore Town (Balto. Co., A. L. no. C, 650). She was therefore an aunt of Col. John Eager Howard of Revolutionary fame. William Gist [3] and Violetta (Howard) his wife had issue:—

8.   i. Maj. Joseph Gist,' *b.* 30 Sept. 1738; m. Elizabeth Elder.
     ii. William Gist, b. 23 Sept. 1742.
     iii. Anne Gist, b. 25 Nov. 1747; m. 18 Nov. 1766, James Calhoun, First Mayor of Baltimore.

Twins:
9.   iv. Thomas Gist, b. 19 May 1750; d. 1808; m. Ruth Bond.
     v. Elizabeth Gist, b. 19 May 1750; d. 16 Feb'y 1794; m. 26 Nov. 1775, Ramsay McGee.
     vi. John Gist, b. 26 July 1752; d. unmarried 1782.
     vii. Violetta Gist, b. 13 March 1755.
     viii. Ellen Gist, b. 26 Sept. 1757.
     Note. Sarah Gist, whose marriage to Andrew McClure, 28 May 1772, is recorded in St. Thomas' register, was probably also a daughter of William Gist.

6. Thomas Gist [3] (*Richard,*[2] *Christopher* [1]) was born in 1713, according to a deposition made in 1767, wherein he gives his age as 54 years (Chancery, D. D. no. 2, 179). His will, dated 19 February 1787, was proved 9 April 1788 (Balto., iv, 297). He was a member of the Baltimore County Committee in 1776 (Md. Arch., xi, 363). He married, 2 July 1735 (St. Paul's) Susan daughter of John Cockey of Baltimore County. She was born 2 Nov. 1714 and died in 1803. Her will, dated 7 March 1799, was proved 12 February 1803 (Balto., vii, 152). Thomas Gist [3] and Susan (Cockey) his wife had issue:—

   i. Elizabeth Gist,[4] b. 14 Feb'y 1736/7.
   ii. John Gist, b. 22 Nov. 1738.
   iii. Col. Thomas Gist, b. 30 March 1741; d. 22 Nov. 1813; commissioned, 4 Feb'y 1777, Colonel in Balto. Co. Militia (*Md. Archives*, xvi, 114.)
10.   iv. Gen. Mordecai Gist, b. 22 Feb'y 1742/3.
   v. Maj. Joshua Gist, commissioned, 4 Feb'y 1777, 1st Major in Balto. Co. Militia (*Md. Archives*, xvi, 114.)
   vi. David Gist, commissioned, 30 Aug. 1777, Second Lieutenant in Balto. Co. Militia (*Md. Archives*, xvi, 350.)
   vii. Rachel Gist.

7. Col. Nathaniel Gist [4] (*Christopher,*[3] *Richard,*[2] *Christopher* [1]) was born 15 October 1733, and was present, with his father and his brother Thomas, at Braddock's defeat on the Monongahela, in 1755. He later served with distinction in the Revolution. He was commissioned, 11 January 1777, Colonel of the Additional Continental Regiment; was taken prisoner at Charleston, 12 May 1780; and was retired 1 January 1781 (Heitman's *Register*). He settled in Kentucky where he built his homestead "Canewood," and died early in the nineteenth century, at an advanced age. Col. Gist married Judith Cary Bell, daughter of David and

Judith (Cary) Bell, and grandniece of Archibald Cary, mover of the Bill of Rights in the Virginia House of Burgesses. They had issue:—

   i. HENRY CARY GIST.[5]
   ii. THOMAS CECIL GIST.
   iii. SARAH HOWARD GIST, m. Hon. Jesse Bledsoe, U. S. Senator from Ky.
   iv. JUDITH CARY GIST, m. Dr. Joseph Boswell, of Lexington, Ky.
   v. ANNE CARY GIST, m. Nathaniel Hart, a brother of Mrs. Henry Clay.
   vi. ELIZA VIOLET GIST, m. Francs P. Blair. Their sons were Hon. Montgomery Blair, Postmaster General, and Gen. Francis P. Blair, Jr.
   vii. MARIA CECIL GIST, first wife of Benjamin Gratz of Lexington, Ky.

8. MAJ. JOSEPH GIST [4] (*William,*[3] *Richard,*[2] *Christopher*[1]) was born 30 Sept. 1738 (St. Thomas'). He was commissioned, 25 May 1776, quartermaster of Soldiers' Delight Battalion, militia of Baltimore County (Md. Arch., xi, 443); First Lieutenant 6 June 1776 (ibid. 467); and Major, 10 Sept. 1779 (ibid. xvi, 368). He married, 30 August 1759, Elizabeth daughter of John (d. 1762) and Jemima Elder, and his issue as recorded in St. Thomas's register:—

11. i. JOHN ELDER GIST,[5] b. 1 Jan'y 1761; m. 13 Nov. 1783, Frances Trippe (St. Paul's).
   ii. CECIL GIST, b. 12 Nov. 1762.
   iii. JOSEPH GIST, b. 12 Aug. 1764; d. 15 Dec. 1786 (St. Paul's).
   iv. JEMIMA GIST, b. 4 May 1766.
   v. JOSHUA HOWARD GIST, b. 3 Feb'y 1768.
12. vi. CORNELIUS HOWARD GIST, b. 25 Jan'y 1770.
Twins:
   vii. WILLIAM GIST, b. 6 June 1772; d. 13 Oct. 1773.
   viii. VIOLETTA GIST, b. 6 June 1772.
   ix. ELIZABETH GIST, b. 21 March 1774.
   x. JAMES GIST, b. 20 Feb'y 1776.
   xi. OWEN GIST, b. 9 Jan'y 1778.

9. THOMAS GIST [4] (*William,*[3] *Richard,*[2] *Christopher*[1]) was born 19 May 1750 and, dying intestate in 1808, his estate was administered by his widow Ruth and his son Thomas. The inventory was filed 5 Oct. 1808. Thomas Gist [4] married Ruth daughter of John Bond and had issue (with perhaps others):—

   i. THOMAS GIST.[5]
   ii. RUTH GIST, a minor in 1811.
   iii. WILLIAM GIST, a minor in 1811.

10. GEN. MORDECAI GIST [4] (*Thomas,*[3] *Richard,*[2] *Christopher* [1])
was born in Baltimore County, Md., 22 February 1742/3
(St. Paul's), and died in Charleston, S. C., 2 August 1792.
In 1774, he was a member of the Baltimore Independent
Cadets (Maga., iv, 373), but he soon occupied a more
responsible position. In January 1776 he was made Major of Smallwood's First Maryland Battalion, and commanded it at the battle of Long Island in August 1776,
in the absence of its Colonel and Lieutenant-Colonel who
were attending a court martial in New York. In 1777
he was promoted to Colonel, and was made Brigadier-
General, 9 July 1779. He was present at the surrender
of Cornwallis at Yorktown, and after the war settled near
Charleston, S. C. He married, first, Cecil Carnan (b.
1742, d. 21 July 1770), of Baltimore County, daughter of
Charles and Prudence Carnan of London, England, but
she died shortly after marriage. Gen. Gist married, secondly, 23 January 1778, Mary Sterrett, daughter of James
and Mary Sterrett, of Baltimore, and, thirdly, in 1783,
Mary (b. 2 June 1749) widow of Capt. Benj. Cattell (b.
July 1749, d. 1782) of South Carolina, and daughter of
George McCall of Philadelphia, Penna. By his first wife,
Gen. Gist had no issue. By his second wife he had a
son:—

   i. INDEPENDENCE GIST,[5] b. 8 Jan'y 1779; d. 16 Sept. 1821.

   By his third wife he had:—

   ii. SUSANNA GIST, b. 12 Nov. 1784; d. 23 July 1785.
   iii. STATES GIST, b. 1787; d. 1 Feb'y 1822.

11. JOHN ELDER GIST [5] (*Joseph,*[4] *William,*[3] *Richard* [2]) was
born 1 Jan'y 1761. He married 13 Nov. 1783, Frances
Trippe. St. Paul's register records his marriage, and the
births of two children, both of whom died young:—

   i. ELIZABETH GIST,[6] b. 17 Oct. 1784; d. 25 Oct. 1784.
   ii. JOHN GIST, b. 14 Dec. 1785; d. 14 Aug. 1786.

12. CORNELIUS HOWARD GIST [5] (*Joseph,*[4] *William,*[3] *Richard*[2])
was born 25 Jan'y 1770. He was Sheriff of Baltimore
in 1797, and subsequently removed to Brooke County, Virginia, where he died in 1830. He married Clara Rei-
necker. In his will (proved 26 Oct. 1830) and recorded

in Baltimore (Lib. 13, fol. 474) he names the following children (order of birth uncertain):

i. CORNELIUS HOWARD GIST.[6]
ii. WILLIAM GIST.
iii. GEORGE REINCKER GIST.
iv. JOSHUA GIST.
v. JOSEPH GIST.
vi. LOUISIANA GIST.
vii. PAMELA GIST, m. Conrad Fite.
viii. EMELINE GIST, m. Rev. Joseph Boyle, D. D.

INDEX